INSTITUTES

OF THE

CHRISTIAN RELIGION

BY

JOHN CALVIN

TRANSLATED FROM THE LATIN AND COLLATED WITH THE AUTHOR'S LAST EDITION IN FRENCH BY

JOHN ALLEN

SEVENTH AMERICAN EDITION, REVISED AND CORRECTED

WITH

AN INTRODUCTION ON THE LITERARY HISTORY OF THE INSTITUTES BY

BENJAMIN B. WARFIELD, D.D., LL.D.

AND

AN ACCOUNT OF THE AMERICAN EDITIONS

BY

THOMAS C. PEARS, Jr., L.H.D.

IN TWO VOLUMES

VOL. II.

✠

PHILADELPHIA

PRESBYTERIAN BOARD OF CHRISTIAN EDUCATION

INSTITUTES
OF THE
CHRISTIAN RELIGION

BY

JOHN CALVIN

TRANSLATED BY

JOHN ALLEN

Nom tamen omnino potuit mors invida totum
Tollere Calvinum terris; æterna manebunt
Ingenii monumenta tui: et livoris iniqui
Languida paulatim cum flamma resederit, omnes
Religio qua pura nitet se fundet in oras
Fama tui. BUCHANAN

INSTITUTES
OF THE
CHRISTIAN RELIGION

Book III, Chapter XIV

The Commencement and Continual Progress of Justification

FOR the further elucidation of this subject, let us examine what kind of righteousness can be found in men during the whole course of their lives. Let us divide them into four classes. For either they are destitute of the knowledge of God, and immerged in idolatry; or, having been initiated by the sacraments, they lead impure lives, denying God in their actions, while they confess him with their lips, and belong to Christ only in name; or they are hypocrites, concealing the iniquity of their hearts with vain disguises; or, being regenerated by the Spirit of God, they devote themselves to true holiness. In the first of these classes, judged of according to their natural characters, from the crown of the head to the sole of the foot there will not be found a single spark of goodness; unless we mean to charge the Scripture with falsehood in these representations which it gives of all the sons of Adam—that "the heart is deceitful above all things, and desperately wicked;" (*w*) that "every imagination of man's heart is evil from his youth;" (*x*) that "the thoughts of man are van-

(*w*) Jer. xvii. 9. (*x*) Gen. vi. 5; viii. 21.

ity; that there is no fear of God before his eyes;" (*y*) that "there is none that understandeth, none that seeketh after God;" (*z*) in a word, "that he is flesh," (*a*) a term expressive of all those works which are enumerated by Paul—"adultery, fornication, uncleanness, lasciviousness, idolatry, witchcraft, hatred, variance, emulations, wrath, strife, seditions, heresies, envyings, murders," (*b*) and every impurity and abomination that can be conceived. This is the dignity, in the confidence of which they must glory. But if any among them discover that integrity in their conduct which among men has some appearance of sanctity, yet, since we know that God regards not external splendour, we must penetrate to the secret springs of these actions, if we wish them to avail any thing to justification. We must narrowly examine, I say, from what disposition of heart these works proceed. Though a most extensive field of observation is now before us, yet, since the subject may be despatched in very few words, I shall be as compendious as possible.

II. In the first place, I do not deny, that whatever excellences appear in unbelievers, they are the gifts of God. I am not so at variance with the common opinion of mankind, as to contend that there is no difference between the justice, moderation, and equity of Titus or Trajan, and the rage, intemperance, and cruelty of Caligula, or Nero, or Domitian; between the obscenities of Tiberius and the continence of Vespasian; and, not to dwell on particular virtues or vices, between the observance and the contempt of moral obligation and positive laws. For so great is the difference between just and unjust, that it is visible even in the lifeless image of it. For what order will be left in the world, if these opposites be confounded together? Such a distinction as this, therefore, between virtuous and vicious actions, has not only been engraven by the Lord in the heart of every man, but has also been frequently confirmed by his providential dispensations. We see how he confers many blessings of the present life on those who practise virtue among men. Not that this external resemblance of virtue merits the least favour from him; but he is pleased to discover his great esteem of true righteousness, by not permitting

(*y*) Psalm xciv. 11; xxxvi. 1.
(*z*) Psalm xiv. 1—3. Rom. iii. 11.
(*a*) Gen. vi. 3.
(*b*) Gal. v. 19, &c.

that which is external and hypocritical to remain without a temporal reward. Whence it follows, as we have just acknowledged, that these virtues, whatever they may be, or rather images of virtues, are the gifts of God; since there is nothing in any respect laudable which does not proceed from him.

III. Nevertheless the observation of Augustine is strictly true—that all who are strangers to the religion of the one true God, however they may be esteemed worthy of admiration for their reputed virtue, not only merit no reward, but are rather deserving of punishment, because they contaminate the pure gifts of God with the pollution of their own hearts. For though they are instruments used by God for the preservation of human society, by the exercise of justice, continence, friendship, temperance, fortitude, and prudence, yet they perform these good works of God very improperly; being restrained from the commission of evil, not by a sincere attachment to true virtue, but either by mere ambition, or by self-love, or by some other irregular disposition. These actions, therefore, being corrupted in their very source by the impurity of their hearts, are no more entitled to be classed among virtues, than those vices which commonly deceive mankind by their affinity and similitude to virtues. Besides, when we remember that the end of what is right is always to serve God, whatever is directed to any other end, can have no claim to that appellation. Therefore, since they regard not the end prescribed by Divine wisdom, though an act performed by them be externally and apparently good, yet, being directed to a wrong end, it becomes sin. He concludes, therefore, that all the Fabricii, Scipios, and Catos, in all their celebrated actions, were guilty of sin, inasmuch as, being destitute of the light of faith, they did not direct those actions to that end to which they ought to have directed them; that consequently they had no genuine righteousness; because moral duties are estimated not by external actions, but by the ends for which such actions are designed.

IV. Besides, if there be any truth in the assertion of John, that "he that hath not the Son of God, hath not life;" (*c*) they who have no interest in Christ, whatever be their characters, their ac-

(*c*) 1 John v. 12.

tions, or their endeavours, are constantly advancing, through the whole course of their lives, towards destruction and the sentence of eternal death. On this argument is founded the following observation of Augustine: "Our religion discriminates between the righteous and the unrighteous, not by the law of works, but by that of faith, without which works apparently good are perverted into sins." Wherefore the same writer, in another place, strikingly compares the exertions of such men to a deviation in a race from the prescribed course. For the more vigorously any one runs out of the way, he recedes so much the further from the goal, and becomes so much the more unfortunate. Wherefore he contends, that it is better to halt in the way, than to run out of the way. Finally, it is evident that they are evil trees, since without a participation of Christ there is no sanctification. They may produce fruits fair and beautiful to the eye, and even sweet to the taste, but never any that are good. Hence we clearly perceive that all the thoughts, meditations, and actions of man antecedent to a reconciliation to God by faith, are accursed, and not only of no avail to justification, but certainly deserving of condemnation. But why do we dispute concerning it as a dubious point, when it is already proved by the testimony of the apostle, that "without faith it is impossible to please God?" (*d*)

V. But the proof will be still clearer, if the grace of God be directly opposed to the natural condition of man. The Scripture invariably proclaims, that God finds nothing in men which can incite him to bless them, but that he prevents them by his gratuitous goodness. For what can a dead man do to recover life? But when God illuminates us with the knowledge of himself, he is said to raise us from death, and to make us new creatures. (*e*) For under this character we find the Divine goodness towards us frequently celebrated, especially by the apostle. "God," says he, "who is rich in mercy, for his great love wherewith he loved us, even when we were dead in sins, hath quickened us together with Christ," &c. (*f*) In another place, when, under the type of Abraham, he treats of the general calling of believers, he says, It is "God, who quickeneth the dead, and calleth those things which be

(*d*) Heb. xi. 6. (*e*) John v. 25. (*f*) Eph. ii. 4, 5.

not as though they were." (*g*) If we are nothing, what can we do? Wherefore God forcibly represses this presumption, in the Book of Job, in the following words: "Who hath prevented me, that I should repay him? Whatsoever is under the whole heaven is mine." (*h*) Paul, explaining this passage, concludes from it, that we ought not to suppose we bring any thing to the Lord but ignominious indigence and emptiness. (*i*) Wherefore, in the passage cited above, in order to prove that we attain to the hope of salvation, not by works, but solely by the grace of God, he alleges, that "we are his workmanship, created in Christ Jesus unto good works, which God hath before ordained that we should walk in them." (*k*) As though he would say, Who of us can boast that he has influenced God by his righteousness, since our first power to do well proceeds from regeneration? For, according to the constitution of our nature, oil might be extracted from a stone sooner than we could perform a good work. It is wonderful, indeed, that man, condemned to such ignominy, dares to pretend to have any thing left. Let us confess, therefore, with that eminent servant of the Lord, that "God hath saved us, and called us with a holy calling, not according to our works, but according to his own purpose and grace;" (*l*) and that "the kindness and love of God our Saviour towards man appeared," because "not by works of righteousness which we have done, but according to his mercy he saved us; that being justified by his grace, we should be made heirs of eternal life." (*m*) By this confession we divest man of all righteousness, even to the smallest particle, till through mere mercy he has been regenerated to the hope of eternal life; for if a righteousness of works contributed any thing to our justification, we are not truly said to be "justified by grace." The apostle, when he asserted justification to be by grace, had certainly not forgotten his argument in another place, that "if it be of works, then it is no more grace." (*n*) And what else does our Lord intend, when he declares, "I am not come to call the righteous, but sinners?" (*o*) If sinners only are admitted, why do we seek to enter by a counterfeit righteousness?

(*g*) Rom. iv. 17. (*h*) Job xli. 11. (*i*) Rom. xi. 35.
(*k*) Ephes. ii. 10. (*l*) 2 Tim. i. 9. (*m*) Titus iii. 4, 5, 7.
(*n*) Rom. xi. 6. (*o*) Matt. ix. 13.

VI. The same thought frequently recurs to me, that I am in danger of injuring the mercy of God, by labouring with so much anxiety in the defence of this doctrine, as though it were doubtful or obscure. But such being our malignity, that, unless it be most powerfully subdued, it never allows to God that which belongs to him, I am constrained to dwell a little longer upon it. But as the Scripture is sufficiently perspicuous on this subject, I shall use its language in preference to my own. Isaiah, after having described the universal ruin of mankind, properly subjoins the method of recovery. "The Lord saw it, and it displeased him that there was no judgment. And he saw that there was no man, and wondered that there was no intercessor: therefore his own arm brought salvation unto him; and his righteousness it sustained him." (*p*) Where are our righteousnesses, if it be true, as the prophet says, that no one assists the Lord in procuring his salvation? So another prophet introduces the Lord speaking of the reconciliation of sinners to himself, saying, "I will betroth thee unto me for ever, in righteousness, and in judgment, and in loving-kindness, and in mercies. I will have mercy upon her that had not obtained mercy." (*q*) If this covenant, which is evidently our first union with God, depend on his mercy, there remains no foundation for our righteousness. And I should really wish to be informed by those, who pretend that man advances to meet God with some righteousness of works, whether there be any righteousness at all, but that which is accepted by God. If it be madness to entertain such a thought, what that is acceptable to God can proceed from his enemies, who, with all their actions, are the objects of his complete abhorrence? And that we are all the inveterate and avowed enemies of our God, till we are justified and received into his friendship, is an undeniable truth. (*r*) If justification be the principle from which love originates, what righteousnesses of works can precede it? To destroy that pestilent arrogance, therefore, John carefully apprizes us that "we did not first love him." (*s*) And the Lord had by his prophet long before taught the same truth: "I will love them freely," saith he, "for mine anger is turned away." (*t*) If his love was spontaneously inclined

(*p*) Isaiah lix. 15, 16. (*q*) Hosea ii. 19, 23.
(*r*) Rom. v. 6, 10. Col. i. 21. (*s*) 1 John iv. 10. (*t*) Hosea xiv. 4.

towards us, it certainly is not excited by works. But the ignorant mass of mankind have only this notion of it—that no man has merited that Christ should effect our redemption; but that towards obtaining the possession of redemption, we derive some assistance from our own works. But however we may have been redeemed by Christ, yet till we are introduced into communion with him by the calling of the Father, we are both heirs of darkness and death, and enemies to God. For Paul teaches, that we are not purified and washed from our pollutions by the blood of Christ, till the Spirit effects that purification within us. (*u*) This is the same that Peter intends, when he declares that the "sanctification of the Spirit" is effectual "unto obedience, and sprinkling of the blood of Jesus Christ." (*x*) If we are sprinkled by the Spirit with the blood of Christ for purification, we must not imagine that before this ablution we are in any other state than that of sinners destitute of Christ. We may be certain, therefore, that the commencement of our salvation is, as it were, a resurrection from death to life; because, when "on the behalf of Christ it is given to us to believe on him," (*y*) we then begin to experience a transition from death to life.

VII. The same reasoning may be applied to the second and third classes of men in the division stated above. For the impurity of the conscience proves, that they are neither of them yet regenerated by the Spirit of God; and their unregeneracy betrays also their want of faith: whence it appears, that they are not yet reconciled to God, or justified in his sight, since these blessings are only attained by faith. What can be performed by sinners alienated from God, that is not execrable in his view? Yet all the impious, and especially hypocrites, are inflated with this foolish confidence. Though they know that their heart is full of impurity, yet if they perform any specious actions, they esteem them too good to be despised by God. Hence that pernicious error, that though convicted of a polluted and impious heart, they cannot be brought to confess themselves destitute of righteousness; but while they acknowledge themselves to be unrighteous, because it cannot be denied, they still arrogate to

---

(*u*) 1 Cor. vi. 11. (*x*) 1 Peter i. 2. (*y*) Phil. i. 29.

themselves some degree of righteousness. This vanity the Lord excellently refutes by the prophet. "Ask now," saith he, "the priests, saying, If one bear holy flesh in the skirt of his garment, and with his skirt do touch bread, or any meat, shall it be holy? And the priests answered and said, No. Then said Haggai, If one that is unclean by a dead body touch any of these, shall it be unclean? And the priests answered and said, It shall be unclean. Then answered Haggai, and said, So is this people, and so is this nation before me, saith the Lord; and so is every work of their hands; and that which they offer there is unclean." (*z*) I wish that this passage might either obtain full credit with us, or be deeply impressed on our memory. For there is no one, however flagitious his whole life may be, who can suffer himself to be persuaded of what the Lord here plainly declares. The greatest sinner, as soon as he has performed two or three duties of the law, doubts not but they are accepted of him for righteousness; but the Lord positively denies that any sanctification is acquired by such actions, unless the heart be previously well purified; and not content with this, he asserts that all the works of sinners are contaminated by the impurity of their hearts. Let the name of righteousness, then, no longer be given to these works which are condemned for their pollution by the lips of God. And by what a fine similitude does he demonstrate this! For it might have been objected that what the Lord had enjoined was inviolably holy. But he shows, on the contrary, that it is not to be wondered at, if those things which are sanctified by the law of the Lord, are defiled by the pollution of the wicked; since an unclean hand cannot touch any thing that has been consecrated, without profaning it.

VIII. He excellently pursues the same argument also in Isaiah: "Bring no more vain oblations; incense is an abomination unto me; your new moons and your appointed feasts my soul hateth; they are a trouble unto me; I am weary to bear them. When ye spread forth your hands, I will hide mine eyes from you; yea, when ye make many prayers, I will not hear: your hands are full of blood. Wash you, make you clean; put away the evil of your doings." (*a*) What is the reason that the Lord is so displeased at

---

(*z*) Hag. ii. 11—14. (*a*) Isaiah i. 13, 16.

an obedience to his law? But, in fact, he here rejects nothing that arises from the genuine observance of the law; the beginning of which, he every where teaches, is an unfeigned fear of his name. (*b*) If that be wanting, all the oblations made to him are not merely trifles, but nauseous and abominable pollutions. Let hypocrites go now, and, retaining depravity concealed in their hearts, endeavour by their works to merit the favour of God. But by such means they will add provocation to provocation; for "the sacrifice of the wicked is an abomination to the Lord; but the prayer of the upright" alone "is his delight." (*c*) We lay it down, therefore, as an undoubted truth, which ought to be well known to such as are but moderately versed in the Scriptures, that even the most splendid works of men not yet truly sanctified, are so far from righteousness in the Divine view, that they are accounted sins. And therefore they have strictly adhered to the truth, who have maintained that the works of a man do not conciliate God's favour to his person; but, on the contrary, that works are never acceptable to God, unless the person who performs them has previously found favour in his sight. And this order, to which the Scripture directs us, is religiously to be observed. Moses relates, that "The Lord had respect unto Abel and to his offering." (*d*) Does he not plainly indicate that the Lord is propitious to men, before he regards their works? Wherefore the purification of the heart is a necessary prerequisite, in order that the works which we perform may be favourably received by God; for the declaration of Jeremiah is always in force, that the "eyes of the Lord are upon the truth." (*e*) And the Holy Spirit has asserted by the mouth of Peter, that it is "by faith" alone that the "heart" is "purified," (*f*) which proves that the first foundation is laid in a true and living faith.

IX. Let us now examine what degree of righteousness is possessed by those whom we have ranked in the fourth class. We admit, that when God, by the interposition of the righteousness of Christ, reconciles us to himself, and having granted us the free remission of our sins, esteems us as righteous persons, to

---

(*b*) Deut. iv. 6. Psalm cxi. 10. Prov. i. 7; ix. 10.
(*c*) Prov. xv. 8. (*d*) Gen. iv. 4.
(*e*) Jer. v. 3. (*f*) Acts xv. 9.

this mercy he adds also another blessing; for he dwells in us by his Holy Spirit, by whose power our carnal desires are daily more and more mortified, and we are sanctified, that is, consecrated to the Lord unto real purity of life, having our hearts moulded to obey his law, so that it is our prevailing inclination to submit to his will, and to promote his glory alone by all possible means. But even while, under the guidance of the Holy Spirit, we are walking in the ways of the Lord,—that we may not forget ourselves, and be filled with pride, we feel such remains of imperfection, as afford us abundant cause for humility. The Scripture declares, that "there is not a just man upon earth, that doeth good and sinneth not." (*g*) What kind of righteousness, then, will even believers obtain from their own works? In the first place, I assert, that the best of their performances are tarnished and corrupted by some carnal impurity and debased by a mixture of some alloy. Let any holy servant of God select from his whole life that which he shall conceive to have been the best of all his actions, and let him examine it with attention on every side; he will undoubtedly discover in it some taint of the corruption of the flesh; since our alacrity to good actions is never what it ought to be, but our course is retarded by great debility. Though we perceive that the blemishes which deform the works of the saints, are not difficult to be discovered, yet suppose we admit them to be very diminutive spots, will they not be at all offensive in the sight of God, in which even the stars are not pure? We have now ascertained, that there is not a single action performed by the saints, which, if judged according to its intrinsic merit, does not justly deserve to be rewarded with shame.

X. In the next place, even though it were possible for us to perform any works completely pure and perfect, yet one sin is sufficient to extinguish and annihilate all remembrance of antecedent righteousness, as is declared by the prophet. (*h*) With him James also agrees: "Whosoever shall offend," says he, "in one point, he is guilty of all." (*i*) Now, since this mortal life is never pure or free from sin, whatever righteousness we might acquire being perpetually corrupted, overpowered, and destroyed by sub-

(*g*) Eccles. vii. 20. (*h*) Ezek. xviii. 24. (*i*) James ii. 10.

sequent sins, it would neither be admitted in the sight of God, nor be imputed to us for righteousness. Lastly, in considering the righteousness of works, we should regard, not any action commanded in the law, but the commandment itself. Therefore, if we seek righteousness by the law, it is in vain for us to perform two or three works; a perpetual observance of the law is indispensably necessary. Wherefore God does not impute to us for righteousness that remission of sins, of which we have spoken, once only, (as some foolishly imagine,) in order that, having obtained pardon for our past lives, we may afterwards seek righteousness by the law; which would be only sporting with us, and deluding us by a fallacious hope. For since perfection is unattainable by us, as long as we are in this mortal body, and the law denounces death and judgment on all whose works are not completely and universally righteous, it will always have matter of accusation and condemnation against us, unless it be prevented by the Divine mercy continually absolving us by a perpetual remission of our sins. Wherefore it will ever be true, as we asserted at the beginning, that if we be judged according to our demerits, whatever be our designs or undertakings, we are nevertheless with all our endeavours and all our pursuits, deserving of death and destruction.

XI. We must strenuously insist on these two points—first, that there never was an action performed by a pious man, which, if examined by the scrutinizing eye of Divine justice, would not deserve condemnation; and secondly, if any such thing be admitted, (though it cannot be the case with any individual of mankind,) yet being corrupted and contaminated by the sins, of which its performer is confessedly guilty, it loses every claim to the Divine favour. And this is the principal hinge on which our controversy [with the Papists] turns. For concerning the beginning of justification, there is no dispute between us and the sounder schoolmen, but we all agree, that a sinner being freely delivered from condemnation obtains righteousness, and that by the remission of his sins; only they, under the term *justification,* comprehend that renovation in which we are renewed by the Spirit of God to an obedience to the law, and so they describe the righteousness of a regenerate man as consisting in this—that a man, after having been once reconciled to God through faith in Christ, is accounted righteous with God on account of his good works, the merit of which is the cause of his acceptance. But the Lord, on the contrary, declares, "that faith was reckoned to Abraham for righteousness," (*k*) not during the time while he yet remained a worshipper of idols, but after he had been eminent during many years for the sanctity of his life. Abraham, then, had for a long time worshipped God from a pure heart, and performed all that obedience to the law, which a mortal man is capable of performing; yet, after all, his righteousness consisted in faith. Whence we conclude, according to the argument of Paul, that it was not of works. So when the prophet says, "The just shall live by his faith," (*l*) he is not speaking of the impious and profane, whom the Lord justifies by converting them to the faith; but his address is directed to believers, and they are promised life by faith. Paul also removes every doubt, when, in confirmation of this sentiment, he adduces the following passage of David: "Blessed are they whose iniquities are forgiven." (*m*) But it is certain that David spake not of impious men, but of believers, whose characters resembled his own; for he spoke from the experience of his own conscience. Wherefore it is necessary for us, not to have this blessing for once only, but to retain it as long as we live. Lastly, he asserts, that the message of a free reconciliation with God, is not only promulgated for a day or two, but is perpetual in the church. (*n*) Believers, therefore, even to the end of their lives, have no other righteousness than that which is there described. For the mediatorial office is perpetually sustained by Christ, by whom the Father is reconciled to us; and the efficacy of whose death is perpetually the same, consisting in ablution, satisfaction, expiation, and perfect obedience, which covers all our iniquities. And Paul does not tell the Ephesians that they are indebted to grace merely for the beginning of their salvation, but that they "are saved by grace, not of works, lest any man should boast." (*o*)

XII. The subterfuges, by which the schoolmen endeavour to evade these arguments, are unavailing. They say, that the sufficiency of good works to justification arises not from their in-

(*k*) Rom. iv. 9. (*l*) Hab. ii. 4. (*m*) Rom. iv. 7.
(*n*) 2 Cor. v. 18, 19. (*o*) Ephes. ii. 8, 9.

trinsic merit, but from the grace through which they are accepted. Secondly, because they are constrained to acknowledge the righteousness of works to be always imperfect in the present state, they admit, that as long as we live we need the remission of our sins, in order to supply the defects of our works; but that our deficiencies are compensated by works of supererogation. I reply, that what they denominate the grace through which our works are accepted, is no other than the free goodness of the Father, with which he embraces us in Christ, when he invests us with the righteousness of Christ, and accepts it as ours, in order that, in consequence of it, he may treat us as holy, pure, and righteous persons. For the righteousness of Christ (which, being the only perfect righteousness, is the only one that can bear the Divine scrutiny) must be produced on our behalf, and judicially presented, as in the case of a surety. Being furnished with this, we obtain by faith the perpetual remission of our sins. Our imperfections and impurities, being concealed by its purity, are not imputed to us, but are as it were buried, and prevented from appearing in the view of Divine justice, till the advent of that hour, when the old man being slain and utterly annihilated in us, the Divine goodness shall receive us into a blessed peace with the new Adam, in that state to wait for the day of the Lord, when we shall receive incorruptible bodies, and be translated to the glories of the celestial kingdom.

XIII. If these things are true, surely no works of ours can render us acceptable to God; nor can the actions themselves be pleasing to him, any otherwise than as a man, who is covered with the righteousness of Christ, pleases God and obtains the remission of his sins. For God has not promised eternal life as a reward of certain work; he only declares, that "he that doeth these things shall live," (*p*) denouncing, on the contrary, that memorable curse against all who continue not in the observance of every one of his commands. (*q*) This abundantly refutes the erroneous notion of a partial righteousness, since no other righteousness is admitted into heaven but an entire observance of the law. Nor is there any more solidity in their pretence of a suffi-

(*p*) Lev. xviii. 5. Rom. x. 5. (*q*) Deut. xxvii. 26. Gal. iii. 10.

cient compensation for inperfections by works of supererogation. For are they not by this perpetually recurring to the subterfuge, from which they have already been driven, that the partial observance of the law constitutes, as far as it goes, a righteousness of works? They unblushingly assume as granted, what no man of sound judgment will concede. The Lord frequently declares, that he acknowledges no righteousness of works, except in a perfect obedience to his law. What presumption is it for us, who are destitute of this, in order that we may not appear to be despoiled of all our glory, or, in other words, to submit entirely to the Lord —what presumption is it for us to boast of I know not what fragments of a few actions, and to endeavour to supply deficiencies by other satisfactions! *Satisfactions* have already been so completely demolished, that they ought not to occupy even a transient thought. I only remark, that those who trifle in this manner, do not consider what an execrable thing sin is in the sight of God; for indeed they ought to know, that all the righteousness of all mankind, accumulated in one mass, is insufficient to compensate for a single sin. We see that man on account of one offence was rejected and abandoned by God, so that he lost all means of regaining salvation. (*r*) They are deprived, therefore, of the power of satisfaction, with which, however they flatter themselves, they will certainly never be able to render a satisfaction to God, to whom nothing will be pleasing or acceptable that proceeds from his enemies. Now, his enemies are all those to whom he determines to impute sin. Our sins, therefore, must be covered and forgiven, before the Lord can regard any of our works. Whence it follows that the remission of sins is absolutely gratuitous, and that it is wickedly blasphemed by those who obtrude any *satisfactions.* Let us, therefore, after the example of the apostle, "forgetting those things which are behind, and reaching forth unto those things which are before, press toward the mark for the prize of our high calling." (*s*)

XIV. But how is the pretence of works of supererogation consistent with this injunction—"When ye shall have done all those things which are commanded you, say, We are unprofitable serv-

---

(*r*) Gen. iii. (*s*) Phil. iii. 13, 14.

ants; we have done that which was our duty to do?" (*t*) This direction does not inculcate an act of simulation or falsehood, but a decision in our mind respecting that of which we are certain. The Lord, therefore, commands us sincerely to think and consider with ourselves, that our services to him are none of them gratuitous, but merely the performance of indispensable duties; and that justly; for we are servants under such numerous obligations as we could never discharge; even though all our thoughts and all our members were devoted to the duties of the law. In saying, therefore, "When ye shall have done all those things which are commanded," he supposes a case of one man having attained to a degree of righteousness beyond what is attained by all the men in the world. How, then, while every one of us is at the greatest distance from this point, can we presume to glory that we have completely attained to that perfect standard? Nor can any one reasonably object, that there is nothing to prevent his efforts from going beyond his necessary obligations, who in any respect fails of doing the duty incumbent on him. For we must acknowledge, that we cannot imagine any thing pertaining either to the service of God or to the love of our neighbour, which is not comprehended in the Divine law. But if it is a part of the law, let us not boast of voluntary liberality, where we are bound by necessity.

XV. It is irrelevant to this subject, to allege the boasting of Paul, (*u*) that among the Corinthians he voluntarily receded from what, if he had chosen, he might have claimed as his right, and not only did what was incumbent on him to do, but afforded them his gratuitous services beyond the requisitions of duty. They ought to attend to the reason there assigned, that he acted thus, "lest he should hinder the gospel of Christ." (*w*) For wicked and fraudulent teachers recommended themselves by this stratagem of liberality, by which they endeavoured, both to conciliate a favourable reception to their own pernicious dogmas, and to fix an odium on the gospel; so that Paul was necessitated either to endanger the doctrine of Christ, or to oppose these artifices. Now, if it be a matter of indifference to a Christian to incur an offence

(*t*) Luke xvii. 10. (*u*) 1 Cor. ix. (*w*) 1 Cor. ix. 12.

when he may avoid it, I confess that the apostle performed for the Lord a work of supererogation; but if this was justly required of a prudent minister of the gospel, I maintain that he did what was his duty to do. Even if no such reason appeared, yet the observation of Chrysostom is always true—that all that we have is on the same tenure as the possessions of slaves, which the law pronounces to be the property of their masters. And Christ has clearly delivered the same truth in the parable, where he inquires whether we thank a servant, when he returns home in the evening, after the various labours of the day. (*x*) But it is possible that he may have laboured with greater diligence than we had ventured to require. This may be granted; yet he has done no more than, by the condition of servitude, he was under an obligation to do; since he belongs to us, with all the ability he has. I say nothing of the nature of the supererogations which these men wish to boast of before God; for they are contemptible trifles, which he has never commanded, which he does not approve, nor, when they render up their account to him, will he accept them. We cannot admit that there are any works of supererogation except such as those of which it is said by the prophet, "Who hath required this at your hand?" (*y*) But let them remember the language of another passage respecting these things: "Wherefore do ye spend money for that which is not bread? and your labour for that which satisfieth not?" (*z*) It is easy, indeed, for these idle doctors to dispute concerning these things in easy chairs; but when the Judge of all shall ascend the judgment seat, all such empty notions must vanish away. The object of our inquiries ought to be, what plea we may bring forward with confidence at his tribunal, not what we can invent in schools and cloisters.

XVI. On this subject our minds require to be guarded chiefly against two pernicious principles—That we place no confidence in the righteousness of our works, and that we ascribe no glory to them. The Scriptures every where drive us from all confidence, when they declare that all our righteousnesses are odious in the Divine view, unless they are perfumed with the holiness of Christ;

(*x*) Luke xvii. 9. (*y*) Isaiah i. 12. (*z*) Isaiah iv. 2.

and that they can only excite the vengeance of God, unless they are supported by his merciful pardon. Thus they leave us nothing to do, but to deprecate the wrath of our Judge with the confession of David, "Enter not into judgment with thy servant; for in thy sight shall no man living be justified." (*a*) And where Job says, "If I be wicked, woe unto me; and if I be righteous, yet will I not lift up my head;" (*b*) though he refers to that consummate righteousness of God, compared to which even the angels are deficient, yet he at the same time shows, that when God comes to judgment, all men must be dumb. For he not only means that he would rather freely recede, than incur the danger of contending with the rigour of God, but signifies that he experiences in himself no other righteousness than what would instantaneously vanish before the Divine presence. When confidence is destroyed, all boasting must of necessity be relinquished. For who can give the praise of righteousness to his works, in which he is afraid to confide in the presence of God? We must therefore have recourse to the Lord, in whom we are assured, by Isaiah, that "all the seed of Israel shall be justified, and shall glory;" (*c*) for it is strictly true, as he says in another place, that we are "the planting of the Lord, that he might be glorified." (*d*) Our minds therefore will then be properly purified, when they shall in no degree confide nor glory in our works. But foolish men are led into such a false and delusive confidence, by the error of always considering their works as the cause of their salvation.

XVII. But if we advert to the four kinds of causes, which the philosophers direct us to consider in the production of effects, we shall find none of them consistent with works in the accomplishment of our salvation. For the Scripture every where proclaims, that the efficient cause of eternal life being procured for us, was the mercy of our heavenly Father, and his gratuitous love towards us; that the material cause is Christ and his obedience, by which he obtained a righteousness for us; and what shall we denominate the formal and instrumental cause, unless it be faith? These three John comprehends in one sentence, when he says, that "God so loved the world that he gave his only begotten Son,

(*a*) Psalm cxliii. 2. (*b*) Job x. 15.
(*c*) Isaiah xlv. 25. (*d*) Isaiah lxi. 3.

that whosoever believeth in him should not perish, but have everlasting life." (*e*) The final cause the apostle declares to be, both the demonstration of the Divine righteousness and the praise of the Divine goodness, in a passage in which he also expressly mentions the other three causes. For this is his language to the Romans: "All have sinned, and come short of the glory of God, being justified freely by his grace:" (*f*) here we have the original source of our salvation, which is the gratuitous mercy of God towards us. It follows, "through the redemption that is in Christ Jesus:" here we have the matter of our justification. "Through faith in his blood:" here he points out the instrumental cause, by which the righteousness of Christ is revealed to us. Lastly, he subjoins the end of all, when he says, "To declare his righteousness; that he might be just, and the justifier of him which believeth in Jesus." And to suggest, by the way, that this righteousness consists in reconciliation or propitiation, he expressly asserts that Christ was "set forth to be a propitiation." So also in the first chapter to the Ephesians, he teaches that we are received into the favour of God through his mere mercy; that it is accomplished by the mediation of Christ; that it is apprehended by faith; and that the end of all is, that the glory of the Divine goodness may be fully displayed. (*g*) When we see that every part of our salvation is accomplished without us, what reason have we to confide or to glory in our works? Nor can even the most inveterate enemies of Divine grace raise any controversy with us concerning the efficient or the final cause, unless they mean altogether to renounce the authority of the Scripture. Over the material and formal causes they superinduce a false colouring; as if our own works were to share the honour of them with faith and the righteousness of Christ. But this also is contradicted by the Scripture, which affirms that Christ is the sole author of our righteousness and life, and that this blessing of righteousness is enjoyed by faith alone.

XVIII. The saints often confirm and console themselves with the remembrance of their own innocence and integrity, and sometimes even refrain not from proclaiming it. Now, this is done for

---

(*e*) John iii. 16. (*f*) Rom. iii. 23, &c. (*g*) Ephes. i. 5—7, 13.

two reasons; either that, in comparing their good cause with the bad cause of the impious, they derive from such comparison an assurance of victory, not so much by the commendation of their own righteousness, as by the just and merited condemnation of their adversaries; or that, even without any comparison with others, while they examine themselves before God, the purity of their consciences affords them some consolation and confidence. To the former of these reasons we shall advert hereafter; let us now briefly examine the consistency of the latter with what we have before asserted, that in the sight of God we ought to place no reliance on the merit of works, nor glory on account of them. The consistency appears in this—that for the foundation and accomplishment of their salvation, the saints look to the Divine goodness alone, without any regard to works. And they not only apply themselves to it above all things, as the commencement of their happiness, but likewise depend upon it as the consummation of their felicity. A conscience thus founded, built up, and established, is also confirmed by the consideration of works; that is, as far as they are evidences of God dwelling and reigning in us. Now, this confidence of works being found in none but those who have previously cast all the confidence of their souls on the mercy of God, it ought not to be thought contrary to that upon which it depends. Wherefore, when we exclude the confidence of works, we only mean that the mind of a Christian should not be directed to any merit of works as a mean of salvation; but should altogether rely on the gratuitous promise of righteousness. We do not forbid him to support and confirm this faith by marks of the Divine benevolence to him.. For if, when we call to remembrance the various gifts which God has conferred on us, they are all as so many rays from the Divine countenance, by which we are illuminated to contemplate the full blaze of supreme goodness,—much more the grace of good works, which demonstrates that we have received the Spirit of adoption.

XIX. When the saints, therefore, confirm their faith, or derive matter of rejoicing from the integrity of their consciences, they only conclude, from the fruits of vocation, that they have been adopted by the Lord as his children. The declaration of Solomon, that "In the fear of the Lord is strong confidence;" (*h*) and the protestation sometimes used by the saints to obtain a favourable audience from the Lord, that "they have walked before" him "in truth and with a perfect heart;" (*i*) these things have no concern in laying the foundation for establishing the conscience; nor are they of any value, except as they are consequences of the Divine vocation. For there nowhere exists that fear of God which can establish a full assurance, and the saints are conscious that their integrity is yet accompanied with many relics of corruption. But as the fruits of regeneration evince that the Holy Spirit dwells in them, this affords them ample encouragement to expect the assistance of God in all their necessities, because they experience him to be their Father in an affair of such vast importance. And even this they cannot attain, unless they have first apprehended the Divine goodness, confirmed by no other assurance but that of the promise. For if they begin to estimate it by their good works, nothing will be weaker or more uncertain; for, if their works be estimated in themselves, their imperfection will menace them with the wrath of God, as much as their purity, however incomplete, testifies his benevolence. In a word, they declare the benefits of God, but in such a way as not to turn away from his gratuitous favour, in which Paul assures us there is "length, and breadth, and depth, and height;" as though he had said, Which way soever the pious turn their views, how high soever they ascend, how widely soever they expatiate, yet they ought not to go beyond the love of Christ, but employ themselves wholly in meditating on it, because it comprehends in itself all dimensions. Therefore he says that it "passeth knowledge," and that when we know how much Christ has loved us, we are "filled with all the fulness of God." (*k*) So also in another place, when he glories that believers are victorious in every conflict, he immediately adds, as the reason of it, "through him that loved us." (*l*)

XX. We see now, that the confidence which the saints have in their works is not such as either ascribes any thing to the merit of them, (since they view them only as the gifts of God, in which

(*h*) Prov. xiv. 26.
(*i*) 2 Kings xx. 3.
(*k*) Ephes. iii. 18, 19.
(*l*) Rom. viii. 37.

they acknowledge his goodness, and as marks of their calling, whence they infer their election,) or derogates the least from the gratuitous righteousness which we obtain in Christ; since it depends upon it, and cannot subsist without it. This is concisely and beautifully represented by Augustine, when he says, "I do not say to the Lord, Despise not the works of my hands. I have sought the Lord with my hands, and I have not been deceived. But I commend not the works of my hands; for I fear that when thou hast examined them, thou wilt find more sin than merit. This only I say, this I ask, this I desire; Despise not the works of thy hands. Behold in me thy work, not mine. For if thou beholdest mine, thou condemnest me; if thou beholdest thine own, thou crownest me. Because whatever good works I have, they are from thee." He assigns two reasons why he ventured not to boast of his works to God; first, that if he has any good ones, he sees nothing of his own in them; secondly, that even these are buried under a multitude of sins. Hence the conscience experiences more fear and consternation than security. Therefore he desires God to behold his best performances, only that he may recognize in them the grace of his own calling, and perfect the work which he has begun.

XXI. The remaining objection is, that the Scripture represents the good works of believers as the causes for which the Lord blesses them. But this must be understood so as not to affect what we have before proved, that the efficient cause of our salvation is the love of God the Father; the material cause, the obedience of the Son; the instrumental cause, the illumination of the Spirit, that is, faith; and the final cause, the glory of the infinite goodness of God. No obstacle arises from these things to prevent good works being considered by the Lord as inferior causes. But how does this happen? Because those whom his mercy has destined to the inheritance of eternal life, he, in his ordinary dispensations, introduces to the possession of it by good works. That which, in the order of his dispensations, precedes, he denominates the cause of that which follows. For this reason he sometimes deduces eternal life from works; not that the acceptance of it is to be referred to them; but because he justifies the objects of his election, that he may finally glorify them; he makes the former favour, which is a step to the succeeding one, in some sense the cause of it. But whenever the true cause is to be assigned, he does not direct us to take refuge in works, but confines our thoughts entirely to his mercy. For what does he teach us by the apostle? "The wages of sin is death; but the gift of God is eternal life through Jesus Christ our Lord." Why does he not oppose righteousness to sin, as well as life to death? Why does he not make righteousness the cause of life, as well as sin the cause of death? For then the antithesis would have been complete, whereas by this variation it is partly destroyed. But the apostle intended by this comparison to express a certain truth—that death is due to the demerits of men, and that life proceeds solely from the mercy of God. Lastly, these phrases denote rather the order of the Divine gifts, than the cause of them. In the accumulation of graces upon graces, God derives from the former a reason for adding the next, that he may not omit any thing necessary to the enrichment of his servants. And while he thus pursues his liberality, he would have us always to remember his gratuitous election, which is the source and original of all. For although he loves the gifts which he daily confers, as emanations from that fountain, yet it is our duty to adhere to that gratuitous acceptance, which alone can support our souls, and to connect the gifts of his Spirit, which he afterwards bestows on us, with the first cause, in such a manner as will not be derogatory to it.

CHAPTER XV

Boasting of the Merit of Works, Equally Subversive of God's Glory in the Gift of Righteousness, and of the Certainty of Salvation

WE HAVE now discussed the principal branch of this subject; that because righteousness, if dependent on works, must inevitably be confounded in the sight of God, therefore it is contained exclusively in the mercy of God and the participation of Christ, and consequently in faith alone. Now, it must be carefully remarked that this is the principal hinge on which the argument turns, that we may not be implicated in the common delusion, which equally affects the learned and the vulgar. For as soon as justification by faith or works becomes the subject of inquiry, they have immediate recourse to those passages which seem to attribute to works some degree of merit in the sight of God; as though justification by works would be fully evinced, if they could be proved to be of any value before God. We have already clearly demonstrated that the righteousness of works consists only in a perfect and complete observance of the law. Whence it follows, that no man is justified by works, but he who, being elevated to the summit of perfection, cannot be convicted even of the least transgression. This, therefore, is a different and separate question, whether, although works be utterly insufficient for the justification of men, they do not, nevertheless, merit the grace of God.

II. In the first place, with respect to the term *merit*, it is necessary for me to premise, that whoever first applied it to human works, as compared with the Divine judgment, showed very little concern for the purity of the faith. I gladly abstain from all controversies about mere words; but I could wish that this sobriety had always been observed by Christian writers, that they had avoided the unnecessary adoption of terms not used in the Scriptures, and calculated to produce great offence, but very little advantage. For what necessity was there for the introduction of the word *merit*, when the value of good works might be significantly expressed without offence by a different term? But the great offence contained in it, appears in the great injury the world has received from it. The consummate haughtiness of its import can only obscure the Divine grace, and taint the minds of men with presumptuous arrogance. I confess, the ancient writers of the Church have generally used it, and I wish that their misuse of one word had not been the occasion of error to posterity. Yet they also declare in some places that they did not intend any thing prejudicial to the truth. For this is the language of Augustine in one passage: "Let human merit, which was lost by Adam, here be silent, and let the grace of God reign through Jesus Christ." Again: "The saints ascribe nothing to their own merits; they will ascribe all, O God, only to thy mercy." In another place: "And when a man sees that whatever good he has, he has it not from himself, but from his God, he sees that all that is commended in him proceeds not from his own merits, but from the Divine mercy." We see how, by divesting man of the power of performing good actions, he likewise destroys the dignity of merit. Chrysostom says, "Our works, if there be any consequent on God's gratuitous vocation, are a retribution and a debt; but the gifts of God are grace, beneficence, and immense liberality." Leaving the name, however, let us rather attend to the thing. I have before cited a passage from Bernard: "As not to presume on our merits is sufficiently meritorious, so to be destitute of merits is sufficient for the judgment." But by the explanation immediately annexed, he properly softens the harshness of these expressions, when he says, "Therefore you should be concerned to have merits; and if you have them, you should know that they are given to you; you should hope for the fruit, the mercy of God; and you have escaped all danger of poverty, ingratitude, and presumption. Happy the Church which is not destitute, either of merits without presumption, or of presumption without merits." And just before he had fully shown how pious his meaning was. "For concerning merits," he says, "why should the Church be solicitous, which has a more firm and secure foundation for glorying in the purpose of God? For God cannot deny himself; he will perform what he has promised. Thus you have no reason for inquiring, on account of what merits we may hope for blessings, especially when you read, 'Not for your sakes, but for my sake;' (*m*) it is sufficiently meritorious to know that merits are insufficient."

III. The Scripture shows what all our works are capable of meriting, when it represents them as unable to bear the Divine scrutiny, because they are full of impurity; and in the next place, what would be merited by the perfect observance of the law, if this could any where be found, when it directs us, "When ye shall have done all those things which are commanded you, say, We are unprofitable servants;" (*n*) because we shall not have conferred any favour on God, but only have performed the duties incumbent on us, for which no thanks are due. Nevertheless, the good works which the Lord has conferred on us, he denominates our own, and declares that he will not only accept, but also reward them. It is our duty to be animated by so great a promise, and to stir up our minds that we "be not weary in well doing," (*o*) and to be truly grateful for so great an instance of Divine goodness. It is beyond a doubt, that whatever is laudable in our works proceeds from the grace of God; and that we cannot properly ascribe the least portion of it to ourselves. If we truly and seriously acknowledge this truth, not only all confidence, but likewise all idea of merit, immediately vanishes. We, I say, do not, like the sophists, divide the praise of good works between God and man, but we preserve it to the Lord complete, entire, and

(*m*) Ezek. xxxvi. 32 (*n*) Luke xvii. 10.
(*o*) Gal. vi. 9. 2 Thess. iii. 13.

uncontaminated. All that we attribute to man, is, that those works which were otherwise good are tainted and polluted by his impurity. For nothing proceeds from the most perfect man, which is wholly immaculate. Therefore let the Lord sit in judgment on the best of human actions, and he will indeed recognize in them his own righteousness, but man's disgrace and shame. Good works, therefore, are pleasing to God, and not unprofitable to the authors of them; and they will moreover receive the most ample blessings from God as their reward; not because they merit them, but because the Divine goodness has freely appointed them this reward. But what wickedness is it, not to be content with that Divine liberality which remunerates works destitute of merit with unmerited rewards, but with sacrilegious ambition still to aim at more, that what entirely originates in the Divine munificence may appear to be a compensation of the merit of works! Here I appeal to the common sense of every man. If he who, by the liberality of another, enjoys the use and profit of an estate, usurp to himself also the title of proprietor, does he not by such ingratitude deserve to lose the possession which he had? So also if a slave, manumitted by his master, conceal his mean condition as a freed-man, and boast that he was free by birth, does he not deserve to be reduced to his former servitude? For this is the legitimate way of enjoying a benefit, if we neither arrogate more than is given us, nor defraud our benefactor of his due praise; but, on the contrary, conduct ourselves in such a manner, that what he has conferred on us may appear, as it were, to continue with himself. If this moderation ought to be observed towards men, let every one examine and consider what is due to God.

IV. I know that the sophists abuse some texts in order to prove that the term *merit* is found in the Scriptures with reference to God. They cite a passage from Ecclesiasticus: "Mercy shall make place for every man according to the merit of his works." (*p*) And from the Epistle to the Hebrews: "To do good, and to communicate, forget not; for with such sacrifices men merit of God." (*q*) My right to reject the authority of Ecclesiasticus I at

(*p*) Ecclus. xvi. 14. (*q*) Heb. xiii. 16.

ever foolish we may be in ourselves, he is our wisdom before God; that however impure we are, he is our purity; that though we are weak and exposed to Satan, yet that power is ours which is given to him in heaven and in earth, (*a*) by which he defeats Satan for us, and breaks the gates of hell; that though we still carry about with us a body of death, yet he is our life; in short, that all that is his belongs to us, and that we have every thing in him, but nothing in ourselves. On this foundation, I say, it is necessary for us to build, if we wish to "grow unto a holy temple in the Lord." (*b*)

VI. But the world has long been taught a different lesson; for I know not what good works of morality have been invented to render men acceptable to God, before they are ingrafted into Christ. As though the Scripture were false in asserting, that "he that hath not the Son of God, hath not life." (*c*) If they are destitute of life, how could they generate any cause of life? As though there were no truth in the declaration, that "whatsoever is not of faith, is sin!" (*d*) as though an evil tree could produce good fruits! But what room have these most pestilent sophists left to Christ for the exertion of his power? They say that he has merited for us the first grace; that is, the opportunity of meriting; and that now it is our part not to miss the offered opportunity. What extreme impudence and impiety! Who would have expected that any persons professing the name of Christ, would presume thus to rob him of his power, and almost to trample him under their feet? It is every where testified of him, that all who believe in him are justified: (*e*) these men tell us, that the only benefit received from him is, that a way is opened for all men to justify themselves. But I wish that they had experienced what is contained in these passages: "He that hath the Son, hath life;" (*f*) "he that believeth is passed from death unto life;" (*g*) "justified by his grace," that we might "be made heirs of eternal life;" (*h*) that believers have Christ abiding in them, by whom they are united to God; (*i*) that they are partakers of his life, and sit with

(*a*) Matt. xxviii. 18. (*b*) Ephes. ii. 21. Titus iii. 7. (*c*) 1 John v. 12.
(*d*) Rom. xiv. 23. (*e*) Acts xiii. 39.
(*f*) 1 John v. 12. (*g*) John v. 24.
(*h*) Rom. iii. 24. (*i*) 1 John iii. 24.

him "in heavenly places;" (*k*) that they are translated into the kingdom of God, and have obtained salvation; (*l*) and innumerable places of similar import. For they do not signify that by faith in Christ we merely gain the ability to attain righteousness or effect our salvation, but that both are bestowed on us. Therefore, as soon as we are ingrafted into Christ by faith, we are already become sons of God, heirs of heaven, partakers of righteousness, possessors of life, and (the better to refute their falsehoods) we have attained, not the opportunity of meriting, but all the merits of Christ; for they are all communicated to us.

VII. Thus the Sorbonic schools, those sources of all kinds of errors, have deprived us of justification by faith, which is the substance of all piety. They grant, indeed, in words, that a man is justified by faith formed; but this they afterwards explain to be, because faith renders good works effectual to justification; so that their mention of faith has almost the appearance of mockery, since it could not be passed over in silence, while the Scripture is so full of it, without exposing them to great censure. And not content with this, they rob God of part of the praise of good works, and transfer it to man. Perceiving that good works avail but little to the exaltation of man, and that they cannot properly be denominated merits if they be considered as the effects of Divine grace, they derive them from the power of free-will; which is like extracting oil from a stone. They contend, that though grace be the principal cause of them, yet that this is not to the exclusion of free-will, from which all merit originates. And this is maintained not only by the latter sophists, but likewise by their master, Lombard, whom, when compared with them, we may pronounce to be sound and sober. Truly wonderful was their blindness, with Augustine so frequently in their mouths, not to see how solicitously he endeavoured to prevent men from arrogating the least degree of glory on account of good works. Before, when we discussed the question of free-will, we cited from him some testimonies to this purpose; and similar ones frequently recur in his writings; as when he forbids us ever to boast of our merits, since even they are the gifts of God; and when he

(*k*) Ephes. ii. 6.

(*l*) Col. i. 13.

says, "that all our merit proceeds from grace alone; that it is not obtained by our sufficiency, but is produced entirely by grace," &c. That Lombard was blind to the light of Scripture, in which he appears not to have been so well versed, need not excite so much surprise. Yet nothing could be wished for more explicit, in opposition to him and his disciples, than this passage of the apostle; who, having interdicted Christians from all boasting, subjoins as a reason why boasting is unlawful, that "we are his (God's) workmanship, created in Christ Jesus unto good works, which God hath before ordained that we should walk in them." (*m*) Since nothing good, then, can proceed from us but as we are regenerated, and our regeneration is, without exception, entirely of God, we have no right to arrogate to ourselves the smallest particle of our good works. Lastly, while they assiduously inculcate good works, they at the same time instruct the consciences of men in such a manner, that they can never dare to be confident that God is propitious and favourable to their works. But, on the contrary, our doctrine, without any mention of merit, animates the minds of believers with peculiar consolation, while we teach them that their works are pleasing to God, and that their persons are undoubtedly accepted by him. And we likewise require, that no man attempt or undertake any work without faith; that is, unless he can previously determine, with a certain confidence of mind, that it will be pleasing to God.

VIII. Wherefore let us not suffer ourselves to be seduced even a hair's breadth from the only foundation, on which, when it is laid, wise architects erect a firm and regular superstructure. For if there be a necessity for doctrine and exhortation, they apprize us, that "for this purpose the Son of God was manifested, that he might destroy the works of the devil; whosoever is born of God doth not commit sin:" (*n*) "the time past of our life may suffice us to have wrought the will of the Gentiles;" (*o*) the elect of God are vessels of mercy selected to honour, and therefore ought to be cleansed from all impurity. (*p*) But every thing is said at once, when it is shown that Christ chooses such for his disciples as will deny themselves, take up their cross, and follow

(*m*) Ephes. ii. 10. (*n*) 1 John iii. 8, 9.
(*o*) 1 Peter iv. 3. (*p*) 2 Tim. ii. 20. Rom. ix. 23.

him. (*q*) He who has denied himself, has laid the axe to the root of all evils, that he may no longer seek those things which are his own; he who has taken up his cross, has prepared himself for all patience and gentleness. But the example of Christ comprehends not only these, but all other duties of piety and holiness. He was obedient to his Father, even to death; he was entirely occupied in performing the works of God; he aspired with his whole soul to promote the glory of his Father; he laid down his life for his brethren; he both acted and prayed for the benefit of his enemies. But if there be need of consolation, these passages will afford it in a wonderful degree: "We are troubled on every side, yet not distressed; we are perplexed, but not in despair; persecuted, but not forsaken; cast down, but not destroyed; always bearing about in the body the dying of the Lord Jesus, that the life also of Jesus might be made manifest in our body." (*r*) "If we be dead with him, we shall also live with him; if we suffer, we shall also reign with him." (*t*) "Being made conformable unto his death; if by any means I might attain unto the resurrection of the dead." (*u*) The Father has predestinated all whom he has chosen in his Son "to be conformed to his image, that he might be the first-born among many brethren;" and therefore "neither death, nor life, nor things present, nor things to come, shall separate us from the love of God which is in Christ Jesus;" (*w*) but "all things shall work together for good" (*x*) to us, and conduce to our salvation. We do not justify men by works before God; but we say, that all who are of God are regenerated and made new creatures, that they may depart from the kingdom of sin into the kingdom of righteousness; and that by this testimony they ascertain their vocation, (*y*) and, like trees, are judged by their fruits.

(*q*) Luke ix. 23. (*r*) 2 Cor. iv. 8—10. (*t*) 2 Tim. ii. 11, 12. (*u*) Phil. iii. 10, 11. (*w*) Rom. viii. 29, 38, 39. (*x*) Rom. viii. 28. (*y*) 2 Peter i. 10.

CHAPTER XVI

A Refutation of the Injurious Calumnies of the Papists Against This Doctrine

THE observation with which we closed the preceding chapter is, of itself, sufficient to refute the impudence of some impious persons, who accuse us, in the first place, of destroying good works, and seducing men from the pursuit of them, when we say that they are not justified by works, nor saved through their own merit; and secondly, of making too easy a road to righteousness, when we teach that it consists in the gratuitous remission of sins; and of enticing men, by this allurement, to the practice of sin, to which they have naturally too strong a propensity. These calumnies, I say, are sufficiently refuted by that one observation; yet I will briefly reply to them both. They allege that justification by faith destroys good works. I forbear any remarks on the characters of these zealots for good works, who thus calumniate us. Let them rail with impunity as licentiously as they infest the whole world with the impurity of their lives. They affect to lament that while faith is so magnificently extolled, works are degraded from their proper rank. What if they be more encouraged and established? For we never dream either of a faith destitute of good works, or of a justification unattended by them: this is the sole difference, that while we acknowledge a necessary connection between faith and good works, we attribute justification, not to works, but to faith. Our reason for this we can readily explain, if we only turn to Christ, towards whom faith is directed, and from whom it receives all its virtue. Why, then, are we justified by faith? Because by faith we apprehend the righteousness of Christ, which is the only medium of our reconciliation to God. But this you cannot attain, without at the same time attaining to sanctification; for he "is made unto us wisdom and righteousness, and sanctification and redemption." (*z*) Christ therefore justifies no one whom he does not also sanctify. For these benefits are perpetually and indissolubly connected, so that whom he illuminates with his wisdom, them he redeems; whom he redeems, he justifies; whom he justifies, he sanctifies. But as the present question relates only to righteousness and sanctification, let us insist upon them. We may distinguish between them, but Christ contains both inseparably in himself. Do you wish, then, to obtain righteousness in Christ? You must first possess Christ; but you cannot possess him without becoming a partaker of his sanctification; for he cannot be divided. Since, then, the Lord affords us the enjoyment of these blessings only in the bestowment of himself, he gives them both together, and never one without the other. Thus we see how true it is that we are justified, not without works, yet not by works; since union with Christ, by which we are justified, contains sanctification as well as righteousness.

II. It is also exceedingly false, that the minds of men are seduced from an inclination to virtue, by our divesting them of all ideas of merit. Here the reader must just be informed, that they impertinently argue from reward to merit, as I shall afterwards more fully explain; because, in fact, they are ignorant of this principal, that God is equally liberal in assigning a reward to good works, as in imparting an ability to perform them. But this I would rather defer to its proper place. It will suffice, at present, to show the weakness of their objection, which shall be done two ways. For, first, when they say that there will be no concern about the proper regulation of our life without a hope of reward being proposed, they altogether deceive themselves. If they only mean that men serve God in expectation of a reward,

---

(*z*) 1 Cor. i. 30.

and hire or sell their services to him, they gain but little; for he will be freely worshipped and freely loved, and he approves of that worshipper who, after being deprived of all hope of receiving any reward, still ceases not to worship him. Besides, if men require to be stimulated, it is impossible to urge more forcible arguments than those which arise from the end of our redemption and calling; such as the word of God adduces, when it inculcates, that it is the greatest and most impious ingratitude not reciprocally to "love him who first loved us;" (*a*) that "by the blood of Christ our consciences are purged from dead works, to serve the living God;" (*b*) that it is a horrible sacrilege, after having been once purged, to defile ourselves with new pollutions, and to profane that sacred blood; (*c*) that we have been "delivered out of the hand of our enemies," that we "might serve him without fear, in holiness and righteousness before him, all the days of our life;" (*d*) that we are made "free from sin," that with a free spirit we might "become the servants of righteousness;" (*e*) "that our old man is crucified," that "we should walk in newness of life." (*f*) Again: "If ye be risen with Christ," as his members indeed are, "seek those things which are above," and conduct yourselves as "pilgrims on the earth;" that you may aspire towards heaven, where your treasure is. (*g*) That "the grace of God hath appeared, teaching us, that denying ungodliness and worldly lusts, we should live soberly, righteously, and godly, in this present world; looking for that blessed hope, and the glorious appearing of the great God and our Saviour." (*h*) Wherefore "God hath not appointed us to wrath, but to obtain salvation by Christ." (*i*) That we are the "temples of the Holy Ghost," which it is unlawful to profane; (*k*) that we are not *darkness,* "but light in the Lord," whom it becomes to "walk as children of the light;" (*l*) that "God hath not called us unto uncleanness, but unto holiness; for this is the will of God, even our sanctification,

(*a*) 1 John iv. 10, 19.
(*b*) Heb. ix. 14.
(*c*) Heb. x. 29.
(*d*) Luke i. 74, 75.
(*e*) Rom. vi. 18.
(*f*) Rom. vi. 4, 6.
(*g*) Col. iii. 1. Heb. xi. 13. 1 Peter ii. 11.
(*h*) Titus ii. 11—13.
(*i*) 1 Thess. v. 9.
(*k*) 1 Cor. iii. 16, 17; vi. 19. Ephes. ii. 21.
(*l*) Ephes. v. 8.

that we should abstain from fornication;" (*m*) that our calling is a holy one, which should be followed by a correspondent purity of life; (*n*) that we are "made free from sin," that we might "become servants of righteousness." (*o*) Can we be incited to charity by any stronger argument than that of John, "If God so loved us, we ought also to love one another?" "in this the children of God are manifest, and the children of the devil;" (*p*) hereby the children of light, by their abiding in love, are distinguished from the children of darkness; or that of Paul, That if we be united to Christ, we are members of one body, and ought to afford each other mutual assistance? (*q*) Or can we be more powerfully excited to holiness, than when we are informed by John, that "every man that hath this hope in him purifieth himself, even as God is pure?" (*r*) Or when Paul says, "Having therefore these promises, (relative to our adoption,) let us cleanse ourselves from all filthiness of the flesh and spirit?" (*s*) or than when we hear Christ proposing himself as our example, that we should follow his steps? (*t*)

III. These few instances, indeed, I have given as a specimen; for if I were disposed to quote every particular passage, I should produce a large volume. The apostles are quite full of admonitions, exhortations, and reproofs, to "furnish the man of God unto all good works," (*u*) and that without any mention of merit. But they rather deduce their principal exhortations from this consideration, That our salvation depends not on any merit of ours, but merely on the mercy of God. As Paul, after having very largely shown that we can have no hope of life, but from the righteousness of Christ, when he proceeds to exhortations, beseeches us "by the mercies of God" with which we have been favoured. (*v*) And indeed this one reason ought to be enough; that God may be glorified in us. (*w*) But if any persons be not so powerfully affected by the glory of God, yet the remembrance of his benefits should be amply sufficient to incite them to rectitude of conduct. But these men, who by the obtrusion of merit

(*m*) 1 Thess. iv. 3, 7. (*n*) 2 Tim. i. 9. 1 Peter i. 15.
(*o*) Rom. vi. 18. (*p*) 1 John iv. 11; iii. 10.
(*q*) 1 Cor. xii. 12, &c. (*r*) 1 John iii. 3.
(*s*) 2 Cor. vii. 1. (*t*) Matt. xi. 29. John xiii. 15.
(*u*) 2 Tim. iii. 17. (*v*) Rom. xii. 1. (*w*) Matt. v. 16

extort some servile and constrained acts of obedience to the law, are guilty of falsehood when they affirm that we have no arguments to enforce the practice of good works, because we do not proceed in the same way; as though, truly, such obedience were very pleasing to God, who declares that he "loveth a cheerful giver;" and forbids any thing to be given "grudgingly, or of necessity." (*x*) Nor do I say this, because I either reject or neglect that kind of exhortation, which the Scripture frequently uses, that no method of animating us to our duty may be omitted. It mentions the reward which "God will render to every man according to his works;" (*y*) but that this is the only argument, or the principal one, I deny. In the next place, I assert that we ought not to begin with it. Moreover, I contend that it has no tendency to establish the merit preached by these men, as we shall afterwards see; and, lastly, that it is entirely useless, unless preceded by this doctrine, That we are justified solely on account of the merit of Christ, apprehended by faith, and not on account of any merit in our own works; because none can be capable of the pursuit of holiness, but such as have previously imbibed this doctrine. This sentiment is beautifully suggested by the Psalmist when he thus addresses the Lord: "There is forgiveness with thee, that thou mayest be feared;" (*z*) for he shows that there is no worship of God without an acknowledgment of his mercy, on which alone it is both founded and established. And this well deserves to be remarked, in order that we may know, not only that the true worship of God arises from a reliance on his mercy, but that the fear of God (which the Papists hold to be meritorious) cannot be dignified with the title of *merit*, because it is founded in the pardon and remission of sins.

IV. But the most futile of all their calumnies is, that men are encouraged to the practice of sin by our maintaining the gratuitous remission of sins, in which we make righteousness to consist. For we say that so great a blessing could never be compensated by any virtue of ours, and that therefore it could never be obtained, unless it were gratuitously bestowed; moreover, that it is gratuitous to us indeed, but not so to Christ, whom it

---

(*x*) 2 Cor. ix. 7. (*y*) Matt. xvi. 27. Rom. ii. 6.
(*z*) Psalm cxxx. 4.

cost so much, even his own most sacred blood, beside which no price sufficiently valuable could be paid to Divine justice. When men are taught in this manner, they are apprized that it is not owing to them that this most sacred blood is not shed as often as they sin. Besides, we learn that such is our pollution, that it can never be washed away, except in the fountain of this immaculate blood. Must not persons who hear these things conceive a greater horror of sin, than if it were said to be cleansed by a sprinkling of good works? And if they have any fear of God, will they not dread, after being once purified, to plunge themselves again into the mire, and thereby to disturb and infect, as far as they can, the purity of this fountain? "I have washed my feet," (says the believing soul in Solomon,) "how shall I defile them?" (*a*) Now, it is plain which party better deserves the charge of degrading the value of remission of sins, and prostituting the dignity of righteousness. They pretend that God is appeased by their frivolous *satisfactions,* which are no better than dung; we assert, that the guilt of sin is too atrocious to be expiated by such insignificant trifles; that the displeasure of God is too great to be appeased by these worthless satisfactions; and therefore that this is the exclusive prerogative of the blood of Christ. They say, that righteousness, if it ever be defective, is restored and repaired by works of satisfaction. We think it so valuable that no compensation of works can be adequate to it; and therefore that for its restitution we must have recourse to the mercy of God alone. The remaining particulars that pertain to the remission of sins may be found in the next chapter.

(*a*) Cant. v. 3.

CHAPTER XVII

The Harmony Between the Promises of the Law and Those of the Gospel

LET us now pursue the other arguments with which Satan by his satellites attempts to destroy or to weaken justification by faith. I think we have already gained this point with these calumniators—that they can no longer accuse us of being enemies to good works. For we reject the notion of justification by works, not that no good works may be done, or that those which are performed may be denied to be good, but that we may neither confide in them, nor glory in them, nor ascribe salvation to them. For this is our trust, this is our glory, and the only anchor of our salvation, That Christ the Son of God is ours, and that we are likewise, in him, sons of God and heirs of the celestial kingdom; being called, not for our worthiness, but by the Divine goodness, to the hope of eternal felicity. But since they assail us besides, as we have observed, with other weapons, let us also proceed to the repulsion of them. In the first place, they return to the legal promises which the Lord gave to the observers of his law, and inquire whether we suppose them to be entirely vain, or of any validity. As it would be harsh and ridiculous to say they are vain, they take it for granted that they have some efficacy. Hence they argue, that we are not justified by faith alone. For thus saith the Lord, "Wherefore it shall come to pass, if ye hearken to these judgments, and keep and do them, that the Lord thy God shall keep unto thee the covenant and the mercy which he sware unto thy fathers; and he will love thee, and bless thee, and multiply thee." (*b*) Again: "If ye thoroughly amend your ways and your doings; if ye thoroughly execute judgment between a man and his neighbour; if ye oppress not, neither walk after other gods; then will I cause you to dwell in this place," &c. (*c*) I am not willing to recite a thousand passages of the same kind, which, not being different in sense, will be elucidated by an explanation of these. The sum of all is declared by Moses, who says that in the law are proposed "a blessing and a curse, life and death." (*d*) Now, they argue, either that this blessing becomes inefficacious and nugatory, or that justification is not by faith alone. We have already shown how, if we adhere to the law, being destitute of every blessing, we are obnoxious to the curse which is denounced on all transgressors. For the Lord promises nothing, except to the perfect observers of his law, of which description not one can be found. The consequence then is, that all mankind are proved by the law to be obnoxious to the curse and wrath of God; in order to be saved from which, they need deliverance from the power of the law, and emancipation from its servitude; not a carnal liberty, which would seduce us from obedience to the law, invite to all kinds of licentiousness, break down the barriers of inordinate desire, and give the reins to every lawless passion; but a spiritual liberty, which will console and elevate a distressed and dejected conscience, showing it to be delivered from the curse and condemnation under which it was held by the law. This liberation from subjection to the law, and manumission, (if I may use the term,) we attain, when we apprehend by faith the mercy of God in Christ, by which we are assured of the remission of sins, by the sense of which the law penetrated us with compunction and remorse.

II. For this reason all the promises of the law would be ineffectual and vain, unless we were assisted by the goodness of God in the gospel. For the condition of a perfect obedience to the law, on which they depend, and in consequence of which alone they are to be fulfilled, will never be performed. Now, the Lord affords this assistance, not by leaving a part of righteous-

(*b*) Deut. vii. 12, 13. (*c*) Jer. vii. 5—7. (*d*) Deut. xi. 26; xxx. 15.

ness in our works, and supplying part from his mercy, but by appointing Christ alone for the completion of righteousness. For the apostle, having said that he and other Jews, "knowing that a man is not justified by the works of the law, believed in Christ," adds as a reason, not that they might be assisted to obtain a complete righteousness by faith in Christ, but "that they might be justified by the faith of Christ, and not by the works of the law." (*e*) If the faithful pass from the law to faith, to find righteousness in the latter, which they perceive to be wanting in the former, they certainly renounce the righteousness of the law. Therefore let whosoever will now amplify the rewards which are said to await the observer of the law; only let him remark, that our depravity prevents us from receiving any benefit from them, till we have obtained by faith another righteousness. Thus David, after having mentioned the reward which the Lord has prepared for his servants, immediately proceeds to the acknowledgment of sins, by which it is annulled. In the nineteenth psalm, likewise, he magnificently celebrates the benefits of the law; but immediately exclaims, "Who can understand his errors? cleanse thou me from secret faults." (*f*) This passage perfectly accords with that before referred to, where, after having said, "All the paths of the Lord are mercy and truth unto such as keep his covenant and his testimonies," he adds, "For thy name's sake, O Lord, pardon mine iniquity; for it is great." (*g*) So we ought also to acknowledge, that the Divine favour is offered to us in the law, if we could purchase it by our works; but that no merit of ours can ever obtain it.

III. What, then, it will be said, were those promises given, to vanish away without producing any effect? I have already declared that this is not my opinion. I assert, indeed, that they have no efficacy with respect to us as long as they are referred to the merit of works; wherefore, considered in themselves, they are in some sense abolished. Thus that grand promise, "Keep my statutes and judgments; which if a man do, he shall live in them;" (*h*) the apostle maintains to be of no value to us, if we rest upon it, and that it will be no more beneficial to us than if

(*e*) Gal. ii. 16.
(*f*) Psalm xix. 12.
(*g*) Psalm xxv. 10, 11.
(*h*) Lev. xviii. 5.

it had never been given; because it is inapplicable to the holiest of God's servants, who are all far from fulfilling the law, and are encompassed with a multitude of transgressions. (*i*) But when these are superseded by the evangelical promises, which proclaim the gratuitous remission of sins, the consequence is, that not only our persons, but also our works, are accepted by God; and not accepted only, but followed by those blessings, which were due by the covenant to the observance of the law. I grant, therefore, that the works of believers are rewarded by those things which the Lord has promised in his law to the followers of righteousness and holiness; but in this retribution it is always necessary to consider the cause, which conciliates such favour to those works. Now, this we perceive to be threefold: The first is, That God, averting his eyes from the actions of his servants, which are invariably more deserving of censure than of praise, receives and embraces them in Christ, and by the intervention of faith alone reconciles them to himself without the assistance of works. The second is, That in his paternal benignity and indulgence, he overlooks the intrinsic worth of these works, and exalts them to such honour, that he esteems them of some degree of value. The third cause is, That he pardons these works as he receives them, not imputing the imperfection with which they are all so defiled, that they might otherwise be accounted rather sins than virtues. Hence it appears how great has been the delusion of the sophists, who thought that they had dexterously avoided all absurdities by saying that works are sufficient to merit salvation, not on account of their own intrinsic goodness, but by reason of the covenant, because the Lord in his mercy has estimated them so highly. But at the same time, they had not observed how far the works, which they styled *meritorious*, fell short of the condition of the promise; unless they were preceded by justification founded on faith alone, and by remission of sins, by which even good works require to be purified from blemishes. Therefore, of the three causes of the Divine goodness, in consequence of which the works of believers are accepted, they only noticed one, and suppressed two others, and those the principal.

(*i*) Rom. x. 5, &c.

IV. They allege the declaration of Peter, which Luke recites in the Acts: "Of a truth I perceive that God is no respecter of persons; but in every nation he that worketh righteousness is accepted with him." (*k*) And hence they conclude, what they think admits of no doubt, that if a man by rectitude of conduct conciliate to himself the favour of God, the grace of God is not the sole cause of his salvation; moreover, that God of his own mercy assists a sinner in such a manner, as to be influenced to the exercise of mercy by his works. But we cannot by any means reconcile the Scriptures with themselves, unless we observe a twofold acceptance of man with God. For God finds nothing in man, in his native condition, to incline him to mercy, but mere misery. If, then, it is evident that man is entirely destitute of all good, and full of every kind of evil, when he is first received by God, by what good qualities shall we pronounce him entitled to the heavenly calling? Let us reject, therefore, all vain imagination of merits, where God so evidently displays his unmerited clemency. The declaration of the angel to Cornelius in the same passage, "Thy prayers and thine alms are come up for a memorial before God," they most wickedly pervert to prove that the practice of good works prepares a man to receive the grace of God. For Cornelius must have been already illuminated with the Spirit of wisdom, since he was endued with the fear of God, which is true wisdom; and he must have been sanctified by the same Spirit, since he was a follower of righteousness, which the apostle represents as one of the Spirit's most certain fruits. (*l*) It was from the grace of God, then, that he derived all these things in which he is said to have pleased him; so far was he from preparing himself to receive it by the exercise of his own powers. There cannot indeed be adduced a single syllable of the Scripture, which is not in harmony with this doctrine; That there is no other cause for God's reception of man into his love, than his knowledge that man, if abandoned by him, would be utterly lost; and because it is not his will to abandon him to perdition, he displays his mercy in his deliverance. Now, we see that this acceptance is irrespective of the righteousness of man, but is an unequivocal

---

(*k*) Acts x. 34, 35. (*l*) Gal. v. 5.

proof of the Divine goodness towards miserable sinners, who are infinitely unworthy of so great a favour.

V. After the Lord has recovered a man from the abyss of perdition, and separated him to himself by the grace of adoption,—because he has regenerated him, and raised him to a new life, he now receives and embraces him, as a new creature, with the gifts of his Spirit. This is the acceptance mentioned by Peter, in which even the works of believers after their vocation are approved by God; for the Lord cannot but love and accept those good effects which are produced in them by his Spirit. But it must always be remembered, that they are accepted by God in consequence of their works, only because, for their sakes and the favour which he bears to them, he deigns to accept whatever goodness he has liberally communicated to their works. For whence proceeds the goodness of their works, but from the Lord's determination to adorn with true purity those whom he has chosen as vessels of honour? And how is it that they are accounted good, as though they were free from all imperfection, except from the mercy of their Father, who pardons the blemishes which adhere to them? In a word, Peter intends nothing else in this passage, but that God accepts and loves his children, in whom he beholds the marks and lineaments of his own countenance; for we have elsewhere shown that regeneration is a reparation of the Divine image in us. Wherever the Lord contemplates his own likeness, he justly both loves and honours it. The life of his children, therefore, being devoted to holiness and righteousness, is truly represented as pleasing to him. But as the faithful, while they are surrounded with mortal flesh, are still sinners, and all their works are imperfect, and tainted with the vices of the flesh, he cannot be propitious either to their persons or to their works, without regarding them in Christ rather than in themselves. It is in this sense that those passages must be understood, which declare God to be merciful and compassionate to the followers of righteousness. Moses said to the Israelites, "The Lord thy God, which keepeth covenant and mercy with them that love him and keep his commandments, to a thousand generations" (*m*)—a sentence which

(*m*) Deut. vii. 9.

was afterwards in frequent use among that people. Thus Solomon, in his solemn prayer: "Lord God of Israel, who keepest covenant and mercy with thy servants that walk before thee with all their heart." (*n*) The same language is also repeated by Nehemiah. (*o*) For as, in all the covenants of his mercy, the Lord stipulates with his servants for integrity and sanctity in their lives, that his goodness may not become an object of contempt, and that no man infected with a vain confidence in his mercy, (*p*) may bless himself in his mind while walking in the depravity of his heart, so he designs by these means to confine to their duty all that are admitted to the participation of his covenant; yet, nevertheless, the covenant is originally constituted and perpetually remains altogether gratuitous. For this reason, David, though he declares that he had been rewarded for the purity of his hands, does not overlook that original source which I have mentioned: "He delivered me, because he delighted in me;" (*q*) where he commends the goodness of his cause, so as not to derogate from the gratuitous mercy which precedes all the gifts that originate from it.

VI. And here it will be useful to remark, by the way, what difference there is between such forms of expression and the legal promises. By legal promises I intend, not all those which are contained in the books of Moses,—since in those books there likewise occur many evangelical ones,—but such as properly pertain to the ministry of the law. Such promises, by whatever appellation they may be distinguished, proclaim that a reward is ready to be bestowed, on condition that we perform what is commanded. But when it is said that "the Lord keepeth covenant and mercy with them that love him," this rather designates the characters of his servants, who have faithfully received his covenant, than expresses the causes of his beneficence to them. Now, this is the way to prove it: As the Lord favours us with the hope of eternal life, in order that he may be loved, reverenced, and worshipped by us, therefore all the promises of mercy contained in the Scriptures are justly directed to this end, that we may revere and worship the Author of our blessings. Whenever, there-

---

(*n*) 1 Kings viii. 23.
(*o*) Neh. i. 5.
(*p*) Deut. xxix. 19, 20.
(*q*) 2 Sam. xxii. 20, 21.

fore, we hear of his beneficence to them who observe his laws, let us remember that the children of God are designated by the duty in which they ought always to be found; and that we are adopted as his children, in order that we may venerate him as our Father. Therefore, that we may not renounce the privilege of our adoption, we ought to aim at that which is the design of our vocation. On the other hand, however, we may be assured, that the accomplishment of God's mercy is independent of the works of believers; but that he fulfils the promise of salvation to them whose vocation is followed by a correspondent rectitude of life, because in them who are directed by his Spirit to good works, he recognizes the genuine characters of his children. To this must be referred what is said of the citizens of the Church: "Lord, who shall abide in thy tabernacle? who shall dwell in thy holy hill? He that walketh uprightly, and worketh righteousness," &c. (*r*) And in Isaiah: "Who shall dwell with the devouring fire? He that walketh righteously, and speaketh uprightly," &c. (*s*) For these passages describe, not the foundation which supports the faithful before God, but the manner in which their most merciful Father introduces them into communion with him, and preserves and confirms them in it. For as he detests sin, and loves righteousness, those whom he unites to him he purifies by his Spirit, in order to conform them to himself and his kingdom. Therefore, if it be inquired what is the first cause which gives the saints an entrance into the kingdom of God, and which makes their continuance in it permanent, the answer is ready; Because the Lord in his mercy has once adopted and perpetually defends them. But if the question relate to the manner in which he does this, it will then be necessary to advert to regeneration and its fruits, which are enumerated in the psalm that we have just quoted.

VII. But there appears to be much greater difficulty in those places which dignify good works with the title of *righteousness*, and assert that a man is justified by them. Of the former kind there are many, where the observance of the commands is denominated *justification* or *righteousness*. An example of the other kind we find in Moses: "And it shall be our righteousness, if we

(*r*) Psalm xv. 1, 2. (*s*) Isaiah xxxiii. 14, 15.

observe to do all these commandments." (*t*) If it be objected that this is a legal promise, which, having an impossible condition annexed to it, proves nothing,—there are other passages which will not admit of a similar reply; such as, "In case thou shalt deliver him the pledge, &c., it shall be righteousness unto thee before the Lord." (*u*) Similar to this is what the Psalmist says, that the zeal of Phinehas in avenging the disgrace of Israel, "was counted unto him for righteousness." (*w*) Therefore the Pharisees of our day suppose that these passages afford ample ground for their clamour against us. For when we say, that if the righteousness of faith be established, there is an end of justification by works,—they argue, in the same manner, that if righteousness be by works, then it is not true that we are justified by faith alone. Though I grant that the precepts of the law are termed *righteousness*, there is nothing surprising in this; for they are so in reality. The reader, however, ought to be apprized that the Hebrew word חקים (*commandments*) is not well translated by the Greek word δικαιωματα, (*righteousness.*) But I readily relinquish all controversy respecting the word. Nor do we deny that the Divine law contains perfect righteousness. For although, being under an obligation to fulfil all its precepts, we should, even after a perfect obedience to it, only be unprofitable servants,—yet, since the Lord has honoured the observance of it with the title of *righteousness*, we would not detract from what he has given. We freely acknowledge, therefore, that the perfect obedience of the law is righteousness, and that the observance of every particular command is a part of righteousness; since complete righteousness consists of all the parts. But we deny that such a kind of righteousness any where exists. And therefore we reject the righteousness of the law; not that it is of itself defective and mutilated, but because, on account of the debility of our flesh, (*x*) it is no where to be found. It may be said, that the Scripture not only calls the Divine precepts *righteousnesses*, but gives this appellation also to the works of the saints. As where it relates of Zacharias and his wife, that "they were both righteous before God, walking in all his commandments:" (*y*) certainly, when it

(*t*) Deut. vi. 25. (*u*) Deut. xxiv. 13. (*w*) Psalm cvi. 30, 31. (*x*) Rom. viii. 3. (*y*) Luke i. 6.

speaks thus, it estimates their works rather according to the nature of the law, than according to the actual condition of the persons. Here it is necessary to repeat the observation which I have just made, that no rule is to be drawn from the incautiousness of the Greek translator. But as Luke has not thought proper to alter the common version, neither will I contend for it. Those things which are commanded in the law, God has enjoined upon man as necessary to righteousness; but that righteousness we do not fulfil without observing the whole law, which is broken by every act of transgression. Since the law, therefore, only prescribes a righteousness, if we contemplate the law itself, all its distinct commands are parts of righteousness; if we consider men, by whom they are performed, they cannot obtain the praise of righteousness from one act, while they are transgressors in many, and while that same act is partly vicious by reason of its imperfection.

VIII. But I proceed to the second class of texts, in which the principal difficulty lies. Paul urges nothing more forcible in proof of justification by faith, than what is stated respecting Abraham—that he "believed God, and it was counted unto him for righteousness." (*z*) Since the action of Phinehas, therefore, is said to have been "counted unto him for righteousness," (*a*) we may also use the same argument concerning works, which Paul insists on respecting faith. Therefore our adversaries, as though they had established the point, determine that we are justified neither without faith, nor by faith alone; and that our righteousness is completed by works. Therefore I conjure believers, if they know that the true rule of righteousness is to be sought in the Scripture alone, to accompany me in a serious and solemn examination how the Scripture may be properly reconciled with itself without any sophistry. Paul, knowing the righteousness of faith to be the refuge of those who are destitute of any righteousness of their own, boldly infers that all who are justified by faith, are excluded from the righteousness of works. It being likewise evident, on the other hand, that this is common to all believers, he with equal confidence concludes that no man is justified by works, but rather, on the contrary, that we are justified independently of all

(*z*) Rom. iv. 3. Gal. iii. 6. (*a*) Psalm cvi. 31.

works. But it is one thing to dispute concerning the intrinsic value of works, and another, to argue respecting the place they ought to hold after the establishment of the righteousness of faith. If we are to determine the value of works by their own worthiness, we say that they are unworthy to appear in the sight of God; that there is nothing in our works of which we can glory before God; and consequently, that being divested of all assistance from works, we are justified by faith alone. Now, we describe this righteousness in the following manner: That a sinner, being admitted to communion with Christ, is by his grace reconciled to God; while, being purified by his blood, he obtains remission of sins, and being clothed with his righteousness, as if it were his own, he stands secure before the heavenly tribunal. Where remission of sins has been previously received, the good works which succeed are estimated far beyond their intrinsic merit; for all their imperfections are covered by the perfection of Christ, and all their blemishes are removed by his purity, that they may not be scrutinized by the Divine judgment. The guilt, therefore, of all transgressions, by which men are prevented from offering any thing acceptable to God being obliterated, and the imperfection, which universally deforms even the good works of believers, being buried in oblivion, their works are accounted righteous, or, which is the same thing, are imputed for righteousness.

IX. Now, if any one urge this to me as an objection, to oppose the righteousness of faith, I will first ask him, Whether a man is reputed righteous on account of one or two holy works, who is in the other actions of his life a transgressor of the law. This would be too absurd to be pretended. I shall next inquire, If he is reputed righteous on account of many good works, while he is found guilty of any instance of transgression. This, likewise, my adversary will not presume to maintain, in opposition to the sanction of the law, which denounces a curse on all those who do not fulfil every one of its precepts. (*b*) I will further inquire, If there is any work which does not deserve the charge of impurity or imperfection. (*c*) But how could this be possible before those

---

(*b*) Deut. xxvii. 26. (*c*) Job iv. 18; xv. 15; xxv. 5.

eyes, in which the stars are not sufficiently pure, nor the angels sufficiently righteous? Thus he will be compelled to concede, that there is not a good work to be found, which is not too much polluted, both by its own imperfection and by the transgressions with which it is attended, to have any claim to the honourable appellation of *righteousness.* Now, if it be evidently in consequence of justification by faith, that works, otherwise impure and imperfect, unworthy of the sight of God, and much more of his approbation, are imputed for righteousness,—why do they attempt, by boasting of the righteousness of works, to destroy the righteousness of faith, from which all righteousness of works proceeds? But do they wish to produce a viperous offspring to destroy the parent? For such is the true tendency of this impious doctrine. They cannot deny that justification by faith is the beginning, foundation, cause, motive, and substance of the righteousness of works; yet they conclude, that a man is not justified by faith because good works also are imputed for righteousness. Let us therefore leave these impertinences, and acknowledge the real state of the case; if all the righteousness which can be attributed to works depends on justification by faith, the latter is not only not diminished, but, on the contrary, is confirmed by it; since its influence appears the more extensive. But let us not suppose that works, subsequent to gratuitous justification, are so highly esteemed, that they succeed to the office of justifying men, or divide that office with faith. For unless justification by faith remain always unimpaired, the impurity of their works will be detected. Nor is there any absurdity in saying, that a man is so justified by faith, that he is not only righteous himself, but that even his works are accounted righteous beyond what they deserve.

X. In this way we will admit, not only a partial righteousness of works, which our opponents maintain, but such as is approved by God, as though it were perfect and complete. A remembrance of the foundation on which it stands will solve every difficulty. For no work is ever acceptable, till it be received with pardon. Now, whence proceeds pardon, but from God's beholding us and all our actions in Christ? When we are ingrafted into Christ, therefore, as our persons appear righteous before God, because our iniquities are covered by his righteousness, so our works are accounted righteous, because the sinfulness otherwise belonging to them is not imputed, being all buried in the purity of Christ. So we may justly assert, that not only our persons, but even our works, are justified by faith alone. Now, if this righteousness of works, whatever be its nature, is consequent and dependent on faith and gratuitous justification, it ought to be included under it, and subordinated to it, as an effect to its cause; so far is it from deserving to be exalted, either to destroy or to obscure the righteousness of faith. Thus Paul, to evince that our blessedness depends on the mercy of God, and not on our works, chiefly urges this declaration of David: "Blessed are they whose iniquities are forgiven, and whose sins are covered. Blessed is the man to whom the Lord will not impute sin." (*d*) If, in opposition to this, the numerous passages be adduced where blessedness seems to be attributed to works; such as, "Blessed is the man that feareth the Lord; (*e*) that hath mercy on the poor; (*f*) that walketh not in the counsel of the ungodly; (*g*) that endureth temptation;" (*h*) "Blessed are they that keep judgment; (*i*) the undefiled, (*k*) the poor in spirit, the meek, the merciful," &c.; (*l*) they will not at all weaken the truth of what is advanced by Paul. For since no man ever attains all these characters, so as thereby to gain the Divine approbation, it appears that men are always miserable till they are delivered from misery by the pardon of their sins. Since all the beatitudes celebrated in the Scriptures are of no avail, and no man can derive any benefit from them, till he has obtained blessedness by the remission of his sins, which then makes room for the other beatitudes, it follows that this is not merely the noblest and principal, but the only blessedness; unless, indeed, we suppose it to be diminished by those which are dependent on it. Now, we have much less reason to be disturbed by the appellation of *righteous*, which is generally given to believers. I acknowledge that they are denominated *righteous* from the sanctity of their lives; but as they rather devote themselves to the pursuit of righteousness than actually attain to righteousness itself, it is

(*d*) Rom. iv. 7, 8. Psalm xxxii. 1, 2.
(*e*) Psalm cxii. 1. (*f*) Prov. xiv. 21. (*g*) Psalm i. 1.
(*h*) James i. 12. (*i*) Psalm cvi. 3.
(*k*) Psalm cxix. 1. (*l*) Matt. v. 3, 5, 7.

proper that this righteousness, such as it is, should be subordinate to justification by faith, from which it derives its origin.

XI. But our adversaries say that we have yet more difficulty with James, since he contradicts us in express terms. For he teaches, that "Abraham was justified by works," and that we are all "justified by works, and not by faith only." (*m*) What then? Will they draw Paul into a controversy with James? If they consider James as a minister of Christ, his declarations must be understood in some sense not at variance with Christ when speaking by the mouth of Paul. The Spirit asserts, by the mouth of Paul, that Abraham obtained righteousness by faith, not by works; we likewise teach, that we are all justified by faith without the works of the law. The same Spirit affirms by James, that both Abraham's righteousness and ours consists in works, and not in faith only. That the Spirit is not inconsistent with himself is a certain truth. But what harmony can there be between these two apparently opposite assertions? Our adversaries would be satisfied, if they could totally subvert the righteousness of faith, which we wish to be firmly established; but to afford tranquillity to the disturbed conscience, they feel very little concern. Hence we perceive, that they oppose the doctrine of justification by faith, but at the same time fix no certain rule of righteousness, by which the conscience may be satisfied. Let them triumph then as they please, if they can boast no other victory but that of having removed all certainty of righteousness. And this miserable victory, indeed, they will obtain, where, after having extinguished the light of truth, they are permitted by the Lord to spread the shades of error. But, wherever the truth of God remains, they will not prevail. I deny, therefore, that the assertion of James, which they hold up against us as an impenetrable shield, affords them the least support. To evince this, we shall first examine the scope of the apostle, and then remark wherein they are deceived. Because there were many persons at that time, and the Church is perpetually infested with similar characters, who, by neglecting and omitting the proper duties of believers, manifestly betrayed their real infidelity, while they continued to glory in the false pretence

(*m*) James ii. 21, 24.

of faith, James here exposes the foolish confidence of such persons. It is not his design, then, to diminish, in any respect, the virtue of true faith, but to show the folly of these triflers, who were content with arrogating to themselves the vain image of it, and securely abandoned themselves to every vice. This statement being premised, it will be easy to discover where lies the error of our adversaries. For they fall into two fallacies; one respecting the word "faith," the other respecting the word "justification." When the apostle gives the appellation of *faith* to a vain notion, widely different from true faith, it is a concession which derogates nothing from the argument; this he shows from the beginning in these words: "What doth it profit, my brethren, though a man say he hath faith, and have not works?" (*n*) He does not say, If any one have faith without works; but, If any one boast of having it. He speaks still more plainly just after, where he ridicules it by representing it as worse than the knowledge of devils; and lastly, when he calls it *dead*. But his meaning may be sufficiently understood from the definition he gives: "Thou believest," says he, "that there is one God." Indeed, if nothing be contained in this creed but a belief of the Divine existence, it is not at all surprising that it is inadequate to justification. And we must not suppose this denial to be derogatory to Christian faith, the nature of which is widely different. For how does true faith justify, but by uniting us to Christ, that, being made one with him, we may participate his righteousness? It does not, therefore, justify us, by attaining a knowledge of God's existence, but by a reliance on the certainty of his mercy.

XII. But we shall not have ascertained the whole scope of the apostle, till we have exposed the other fallacy; for he attributes justification partly to works. If we wish to make James consistent with the rest of the Scriptures, and even with himself, we must understand the word "justify" in a different signification from that in which it is used by Paul. For we are said by Paul to be justified, when the memory of our unrighteousness is obliterated, and we are accounted righteous. If James had alluded to this, it would have been preposterous for him to make that quotation

(*n*) James ii. 14.

from Moses: "Abraham believed God," &c. (*o*) For he introduces it in the following manner: Abraham obtained righteousness by works, because he hesitated not to sacrifice his son at the command of God. And thus was the Scripture fulfilled, which saith, Abraham believed God, and it was imputed unto him for righteousness. If an effect antecedent to its cause be an absurdity, either Moses falsely asserts in that place, that Abraham's faith was imputed to him for righteousness, or Abraham did not obtain righteousness by his obedience, displayed in the oblation of his son. Abraham was justified by faith, while Ishmael, who arrived at adolescence before the birth of Isaac, was not yet conceived. How, then, can we ascribe his justification to an act of obedience performed so long after? Wherefore, either James improperly inverted the order of events, (which it is unlawful to imagine,) or, by saying that Abraham was justified, he did not mean that the patriarch deserved to be accounted righteous. What, then, was his meaning? He evidently appears to speak of a declaration of righteousness before men, and not of an imputation of it in the sight of God; as though he had said, They who are justified by true faith, prove their justification, not by a barren and imaginary resemblance of faith, but by obedience and good works. In a word, he is not disputing concerning the method of justification, but requiring of believers a righteousness manifested in good works. And as Paul contends for justification independent of works, so James will not allow those to be accounted righteous, who are destitute of good works. The consideration of this object will extricate us from every difficulty. For the principal mistake of our adversaries consists in supposing, that James describes the method of justification, while he only endeavours to destroy the corrupt security of those who make vain pretences to faith, in order to excuse their contempt of good works. Into whatever forms, therefore, they pervert the words of James, they will extort nothing but these two truths—that a vain notion of faith cannot justify; and that the faithful, not content with such an imagination, manifest their righteousness by their good works.

XIII. Nor can they derive the least support from a similar

(*o*) James ii. 21—23. Gen. xv. 6.

passage which they cite from Paul, that "Not the hearers of the law, but the doers of the law, shall be justified." (*p*) I have no wish to evade it by the explanation of Ambrose, that this is spoken, because faith in Christ is the fulfilling of the law. For this I conceive to be a mere subterfuge, which is totally unnecessary. The apostle in that place is demolishing the foolish confidence of the Jews, who boasted of possessing the exclusive knowledge of the law, whilst at the same time they were the greatest despisers of it. To prevent such great self-complacence on account of a mere acquaintance with the law, he admonishes them, that if righteousness be sought by the law, it is requisite not only to know but to observe it. We certainly do not question that the righteousness of the law consists in works, nor that this righteousness consists in the worthiness and merit of works. But still it cannot be proved that we are justified by works, unless some person be produced who has fulfilled the law. That Paul had no other meaning, is sufficiently evident from the context. After having condemned the Gentiles and Jews indiscriminately for unrighteousness, he proceeds particularly to inform us, that "as many as have sinned without law shall also perish without law;" which refers to the Gentiles; and that "as many as have sinned in the law shall be judged by the law;" which belongs to the Jews. Moreover, because they shut their eyes against their transgressions, and gloried in their mere possession of the law, he adds, what is exceedingly applicable, that the law was not given that men might be justified merely by hearing its voice, but by obeying it; as though he had said, Do you seek righteousness by the law? Plead not your having heard it, which of itself is a very small advantage, but produce works as an evidence that the law has not been given to you in vain. Since in this respect they were all deficient, they were consequently deprived of their glorying in the law. The meaning of Paul therefore, rather furnishes an opposite argument: Legal righteousness consists in perfect works; no man can boast of having satisfied the law by his works; therefore there is no righteousness by the law.

XIV. Our adversaries proceed to adduce those passages in

(*p*) Rom. ii. 13.

which the faithful boldly offer their righteousness to the examination of Divine justice, and desire to be judged according to it. Such are the following: "Judge me, O Lord, according to my righteousness, and according to mine integrity that is in me." (*q*) Again: "Hear the right, O Lord. Thou hast proved mine heart; thou hast visited me in the night; thou hast tried me, and shalt find nothing." (*r*) Again: "I have kept the ways of the Lord, and have not wickedly departed from my God. I was also upright before him, and I kept myself from mine iniquity. Therefore hath the Lord recompensed me according to my righteousness, according to the cleanness of my hands." (*s*) Again: "Judge me, O Lord, for I have walked in my integrity. I have not sat with vain persons; neither will I go in with dissemblers. Gather not my soul with sinners, nor my life with bloody men; in whose hands is mischief, and their right hand is full of bribes. But as for me, I will walk in mine integrity." (*t*) I have already spoken of the confidence which the saints appear to derive from their works. The passages now adduced will form no objection to our doctrine, when they are explained according to the occasion of them. Now, this is twofold. For believers who have expressed themselves in this manner, have no wish to submit to a general examination to be condemned or absolved according to the whole tenor of their lives, but they bring forward a particular cause to be judged; and they attribute righteousness to themselves, not with reference to the Divine perfection, but in comparison with men of impious and abandoned characters. In the first place, in order to a man's being justified, it is requisite that he should have, not only a good cause in some particular instance, but a perpetual consistency of righteousness through life. But the saints, when they implore the judgment of God in approbation of their innocence, do not present themselves as free from every charge, and absolutely guiltless; but having fixed their dependence on his goodness alone, and confiding in his readiness to avenge the poor who are unlawfully and unjustly afflicted, they supplicate his regard to the cause in which the innocent are oppressed. But when they place themselves and their adversaries before the Divine tribunal, they

(*q*) Psalm vii. 8.
(*r*) Psalm xvii. 1, 3.
(*s*) Psalm xviii. 21, 23, 24.
(*t*) Psalm xxvi. 1, 4, 9—11.

boast not an innocence, which, on a severe examination, would be found correspondent to the purity of God; but knowing that their sincerity, justice, simplicity, and purity, are pleasing and acceptable to God, in comparison with the malice, wickedness, fraud, and iniquity of their enemies, they are not afraid to invoke Him to judge between them. Thus, when David said to Saul, "The Lord render to every man his righteousness and his faithfulness," (*v*) he did not mean that the Lord should examine every individual by himself, and reward him according to his merits; but he called the Lord to witness the greatness of his innocence in comparison with the iniquity of Saul. Nor did Paul, when he gloried in having "the testimony of" his "conscience" that he had conducted himself in the Church "with simplicity and godly sincerity," (*w*) intend to rely on this before God; but the calumnies of the impious constrained him to oppose all their slanderous aspersions by asserting his fidelity and probity, which he knew to be acceptable to the Divine goodness. For we know what he says in another place: "I am conscious to myself of nothing; yet am I not hereby justified." (*x*) Because, indeed, he was certain, that the judgment of God far transcended the narrow comprehension of man. However, therefore, the pious may vindicate their innocence against the hypocrisy of the impious, by invoking God to be their witness and judge, yet in their concerns with God alone, they all with one voice exclaim, "If thou, Lord, shouldst mark iniquities, O Lord, who shall stand?" (*y*) Again: "Enter not into judgment with thy servant, for in thy sight shall no man living be justified." (*z*) And, diffident of their own works, they gladly sing, "Thy loving-kindness is better than life." (*a*)

XV. There are likewise other passages, similar to the preceding, on which some person may yet insist. Solomon says, "The just man walketh in his integrity." (*b*) Again: "In the way of righteousness there is life; and in the pathway thereof there is no death." (*c*) Thus also Ezekiel declares, that he who "doth that which is lawful and right, shall surely live." (*d*) We neither deny nor obscure any of these. But let one of the sons of Adam produce

(*v*) 1 Sam. xxvi. 23. (*w*) 2 Cor. i. 12. (*x*) 1 Cor. iv. 4.
(*y*) Psalm cxxx. 3. (*z*) Psalm cxliii. 2. (*a*) Psalm lxiii. 3.
(*b*) Prov. xx. 7. (*c*) Prov. xii. 28. (*d*) Ez. xxxiii. 14, 15.

such an integrity. If no one can, they must either perish from the presence of God, or flee to the asylum of mercy. Nor do we deny, that to believers their integrity, however imperfect, is a step toward immortality. But what is the cause of this, unless it be that when the Lord has admitted any persons into the covenant of his grace, he does not scrutinize their works according to their intrinsic merit, but embraces them with paternal benignity? By this we mean, not merely what is taught by the schoolmen, "that works receive their value from the grace which accepts them;" for they suppose, that works, otherwise inadequate to the attainment of salvation by the legal covenant, are rendered sufficient for this by the Divine acceptance of them. But I assert, that they are so defiled, both by other transgressions and by their own blemishes, that they are of no value at all, except as the Lord pardons both; and this is no other than bestowing on a man gratuitous righteousness. It is irrelevant to this subject, to allege those prayers of the apostle, in which he desires such perfection for believers, that they may be unblamable and irreprovable in the day of Christ. (*e*) These passages, indeed, the Celestines formerly perverted, in order to prove a perfection of righteousness in the present life. We think it sufficient briefly to reply, with Augustine, "that all the pious ought, indeed, to aspire to this object, to appear one day immaculate and guiltless before the presence of God; but since the highest excellency in this life is nothing more than a progress towards perfection, we shall never attain it, till, being divested at once of mortality and sin, we shall fully adhere to the Lord." Nevertheless, I shall not pertinaciously contend with any person who chooses to attribute to the saints the character of perfection, provided he also defines it in the words of Augustine himself; who says, "When we denominate the virtue of the saints perfect, to this perfection itself belongs the acknowledgment of imperfection, both in truth and in humility."

(*e*) 1 Thess. iii. 13, et alibi.

CHAPTER XVIII

Justification from Works Not to Be Inferred from the Promise of a Reward

LET US now proceed to those passages which affirm that "God will render to every man according to his deeds;" (*f*) that "every one may receive the things done in his body, according to that he hath done, whether it be good or bad." (*g*) "Tribulation and anguish upon every soul that doeth evil; but glory, honour, and peace, to every man that worketh good." (*h*) And, "All shall come forth; they that have done good, unto the resurrection of life; and they that have done evil, unto the resurrection of damnation." (*i*) "Come, ye blessed of my Father; for I was a hungered, and ye gave me meat: I was thirsty, and ye gave me drink," &c. (*k*) And with these let us also connect those which represent eternal life as the reward of works, such as the following: "The recompense of a man's hands shall be rendered unto him." (*l*) "He that feareth the commandment shall be rewarded." (*m*) "Rejoice and be exceeding glad; for great is your reward in heaven." (*n*) "Every one shall receive his own reward, according to his own labour." (*o*) The declaration, that God will render to every one according to his works, is easily ex-

(*f*) Rom. ii. 6. Matt. xvi. 27. (*g*) 2 Cor. v. 10. (*h*) Rom. ii. 9, 10.
(*i*) John v. 29. (*k*) Matt. xxv. 34—36. (*l*) Prov. xii. 14.
(*m*) Prov. xiii. 13. (*n*) Matt. v. 12. Luke vi. 23. (*o*) 1 Cor. iii. 8.

plained. For that phrase indicates the order of events, rather than the cause of them. But it is beyond all doubt, that the Lord proceeds to the consummation of our salvation by these several gradations of mercy: "Whom he hath predestinated, them he calls; whom he hath called, he justifies; and whom he hath justified, he finally glorifies." (*p*) Though he receives his children into eternal life, therefore, of his mere mercy, yet since he conducts them to the possession of it through a course of good works, that he may fulfil his work in them in the order he has appointed, we need not wonder if they are said to be rewarded according to their works, by which they are undoubtedly prepared to receive the crown of immortality. And for this reason, they are properly said to "work out their own salvation," (*q*) while, devoting themselves to good works, they aspire to eternal life; just as in another place they are commanded to "labor for the meat which perisheth not," when they obtain eternal life by believing in Christ; and yet it is immediately added, "which the Son of man shall give unto you." (*r*) Whence it appears that the word *work* is not opposed to grace, but refers to human endeavours; and therefore it does not follow, either that believers are the authors of their own salvation, or that salvation proceeds from their works. But as soon as they are introduced, by the knowledge of the gospel and the illumination of the Holy Spirit, into communion with Christ, eternal life is begun in them. Now, "the good work which" God "hath begun in" them, "he will perform until the day of Jesus Christ." (*s*) And it is performed, when they prove themselves to be the genuine children of God by their resemblance to their heavenly Father in righteousness and holiness.

II. We have no reason to infer from the term *reward*, that good works are the cause of salvation. First, let this truth be established in our minds, that the kingdom of heaven is not the stipend of servants, but the inheritance of children, which will be enjoyed only by those whom the Lord adopts as his children, and for no other cause than on account of this adoption. "For the son of the bond-woman shall not be heir with the son of the free-

(*p*) Rom. viii. 30.
(*q*) Phil. ii. 12.
(*r*) John vi. 27.
(*s*) Phil. i. 6.

woman." (*t*) And, therefore, in the same passages in which the Holy Spirit promises eternal life as the reward of works, by expressly denominating it "an inheritance," he proves it to proceed from another cause. Thus Christ enumerates the works which he compensates by the reward of heaven, when he calls the elect to the possession of it; but at the same time adds, that it is to be enjoyed by right of inheritance. (*v*) So Paul encourages servants, who faithfully discharge their duty, to hope for a reward from the Lord; but at the same time calls it "the reward of the inheritance." (*w*) We see how they, almost in express terms, caution us against attributing eternal life to works, instead of ascribing it to Divine adoption. Why, then, it may be asked, do they at the same time make mention of works? This question shall be elucidated by one example from the Scripture. Before the nativity of Isaac, there had been promised to Abraham a seed in whom all the nations of the earth were to be blessed, a multiplication of his posterity, which would equal the stars of heaven and the sands of the sea, and other similar blessings. (*x*) Many years after, in consequence of a Divine command, Abraham prepares to sacrifice his son. After this act of obedience, he receives this promise: "By myself have I sworn, saith the Lord, for because thou hast done this thing, and hast not withheld thy son, thine only son; that in blessing I will bless thee, and in multiplying I will multiply thy seed as the stars of the heaven, and as the sand which is upon the sea-shore; and thy seed shall possess the gate of his enemies; and in thy seed shall all the nations of the earth be blessed; because thou hast obeyed my voice." (*y*) What? did Abraham by his obedience merit that blessing which had been promised him before the command was delivered? Here, then, it appears, beyond all doubt, that the Lord rewards the works of believers with those blessings which he had already given them before their works were thought of, and while he had no reason for his beneficence, but his own mercy.

III. Nor does the Lord deceive or trifle with us, when he says that he will requite works with what he had freely given previously to the performance of them. For since it is his pleasure that

(*t*) Gal. iv. 30. (*v*) Matt. xxv. 34. (*w*) Col. iii. 24.
(*x*) Gen. xii. 2, 3; xiii. 16; xv. 5. (*y*) Gen. xxii. 16—18.

we be employed in good works, while aspiring after the manifestation or enjoyment of those things which he has promised, and that they constitute the road in which we should travel to endeavour to attain the blessed hope proposed to us in heaven, therefore the fruit of the promises, to the perfection of which fruit those works conduct us, is justly assigned to them. The apostle beautifully expressed both those ideas when he said that the Colossians applied themselves to the duties of charity, "for the hope which was laid up for them in heaven, whereof they heard before in the word, of the truth of the gospel." (*z*) For his assertion, that they knew from the gospel, that there was hope laid up for them in heaven, is equivalent to a declaration that it depended not on any works, but on Christ alone; which perfectly accords with the observation of Peter, that believers "are kept by the power of God through faith unto salvation, ready to be revealed in the last time." (*a*) When it is said that they must labour for it, it implies, that in order to attain to it, believers have a race to run, which terminates only with their lives. But that we might not suppose the reward promised us by the Lord to be regulated according to the proportion of merit, he proposes a parable, in which he has represented himself under the character of a householder, who employs all the persons he meets in the cultivation of his vineyard; some he hires at the first hour of the day, others at the second, others at the third, and some even at the eleventh hour; in the evening he pays them all the same wages. (*b*) A brief and just explanation of this parable is given by the ancient writer, whoever he was, of the treatise "On the Calling of the Gentiles," which bears the name of Ambrose. I shall adopt his words in preference to my own. "By the example of this comparison, (says he,) the Lord has shown a variety of manifold vocation pertaining to the same grace. They who, having been admitted into the vineyard at the eleventh hour, are placed on an equality with them who had laboured the whole day, represent the state of those whom, to magnify the excellence of grace, God, in his mercy, has rewarded in the decline of the day, and at the conclusion of life; not paying them the wages due to their labour,

(*z*) Col. i. 4, 5. (*a*) 1 Peter i. 5. (*b*) Matt. xx. 1, &c.

but sending down the riches of his goodness, in copious effusions, on them whom he has chosen without works; that even they who have laboured the most, and have received no more than the last, may understand theirs to be a reward of grace, not of works." Lastly, it is also worthy of being observed, that in those places where eternal life is called a reward of works, it is not to be understood simply of that communion which we have with God, as the prelude to a happy immortality, when he embraces us in Christ with paternal benevolence, but of the possession or fruition of ultimate blessedness, as the very words of Christ import—"in the world to come, eternal life." (*c*) And in another place, "Come, inherit the kingdom," &c. (*d*) For the same reason, Paul applies the term *adoption* to the revelation of adoption, which shall be made in the resurrection; and afterwards explains it to be "the redemption of our body." (*e*) Otherwise, as alienation from God is eternal death, so when a man is received into the favour of God so as to enjoy communion with him and become united to him, he is translated from death to life; which is solely the fruit of adoption. And if they insist, with their accustomed pertinacity, on the reward of works, we may retort against them that passage of Peter, where eternal life is called "the end (or reward) of faith." (*f*)

IV. Let us not, therefore, imagine, that the Holy Spirit by these promises commends the worthiness of our works, as though they merited such a reward. For the Scripture leaves us nothing that can exalt us in the Divine presence. Its whole tendency is rather to repress our arrogance, and to inspire us with humility, dejection, and contrition. But such promises assist our weakness, which otherwise would immediately slide and fall, if it did not sustain itself by this expectation, and alleviate its sorrows by this consolation. First, let every one reflect, how difficult it is for a man to relinquish and renounce not only all that belong to him, but even himself. And yet this is the first lesson which Christ teaches his disciples, that is to say, all the pious. Afterwards he gives them such tuition during the remainder of their lives, under the discipline of the cross, that their hearts may not fix either their

(*c*) Mark x. 30.
(*d*) Matt. xxv. 34.
(*e*) Rom. viii. 23.
(*f*) 1 Peter i. 9.

desires or their dependence on present advantages. In short, he generally manages them in such a manner, that whithersoever they turn their views throughout the world, nothing but despair presents itself to them on every side; so that Paul says, "If in this life only we have hope in Christ, we are of all men most miserable." (*g*) To preserve them from sinking under these afflictions, they have the presence of the Lord, who encourages them to raise their heads higher, and to extend their views further, by assurances that they will find in him that blessedness which they cannot see in the world. This blessedness he calls *a reward, a recompense;* not attributing any merit to their works, but signifying that it is a compensation for their oppressions, sufferings, and disgrace. Wherefore there is no objection against our following the example of the Scripture in calling eternal life *a reward;* since in that state the Lord receives his people from labor into rest; from affliction into prosperity and happiness; from sorrow into joy; from poverty into affluence; from ignominy into glory; and commutes all the evils which they have endured for blessings of superior magnitude. So, likewise, it will occasion no inconvenience, if we consider holiness of life as the way, not which procures our admission into the glory of the heavenly kingdom, but through which the elect are conducted by their God to the manifestation of it; since it is his good pleasure to glorify them whom he has sanctified. Only let us not imagine a reciprocal relation of merit and reward which is the error into which the sophists fell, for want of considering the end which we have stated. But how preposterous is it, when the Lord calls our attention to one end, for us to direct our views to another! Nothing is clearer, than that the promise of a reward to good works is designed to afford some consolation to the weakness of our flesh, but not to inflate our minds with vain-glory. Whoever, therefore, infers from this, that there is any merit in works, or balances the work against the reward, errs very widely from the true design of God.

V. Therefore, when the Scripture says, that "the Lord, the righteous Judge, shall give" to his people "a crown of righteous-

(*g*) 1 Cor. xv. 19.

ness," (*h*) I not only reply with Augustine—"To whom could the righteous Judge have given a crown, if the Father of mercies had never given grace? and how would it have been an act of righteousness, if not preceded by that grace which justifies the ungodly? how could these due rewards be rendered, unless those unmerited blessings were previously bestowed?" but I further inquire—How could he impute righteousness to our works, unless his indulgent mercy had concealed their unrighteousness? How could he esteem them worthy of a reward, unless his infinite goodness had abolished all their demerit of punishment? Augustine is in the habit of designating eternal life by the word *grace*, because, when it is given as the reward of works, it is conferred on the gratuitous gifts of God. But the Scripture humbles us more, and at the same times exalts us. For beside prohibiting us to glory in works, because they are the gratuitous gifts of God, it likewise teaches us that they are always defiled by some pollutions; so that they cannot satisfy God, if examined according to the rule of his judgment; but it is also added, to prevent our despondency, that they please him merely through his mercy. Now, though Augustine expresses himself somewhat differently from us, yet that there is no real difference of sentiment will appear from his language to Boniface. After a comparison between two men, the one of a life holy and perfect even to a miracle, the other a man of probity and integrity, yet not so perfect but that many defects might be discovered, he at length makes this inference: "The latter, whose character appears inferior to the former, on account of the true faith in God by which he lives, and according to which he accuses himself in all his delinquencies, and in all his good works praises God, ascribing the glory to him, the ignominy to himself, and deriving from him both the pardon of his sins and the love of virtue; this man, I say, when delivered from this life, removes into the presence of Christ. Wherefore, but on account of faith? which, though no man be saved by it without works, (for it is not a reprobate faith, but such as works by love,) yet produces remission of sins, for the just lives by faith; (*i*) but without it, works apparently good are perverted into sins." Here he avows,

---

(*h*) 2 Tim. iv. 8. (*i*) Heb. x. 38.

without any obscurity, that for which we so strenuously contend —that the righteousness of good works depends on their acceptance by the Divine mercy.

VI. Very similar to the foregoing passages is the import of the following: "Make to yourselves friends of the mammon of unrighteousness; that, when ye fail, they may receive you into everlasting habitations." (*k*) "Charge them that are rich in this world, that they be not high-minded, nor trust in uncertain riches, but in the living God; that they do good, that they be rich in good works; laying up in store for themselves a good foundation against the time to come, that they may lay hold on eternal life." (*l*) Here good works are compared to riches, which we may enjoy in the happiness of eternal life. I reply, that we shall never arrive at the true meaning of these passages, unless we advert to the design of the Spirit in such language. If Christ's declaration be true, that "where our treasure is, there will our heart be also," (*m*)—as the children of this world are generally intent on the acquisition of those things which conduce to the comfort of the present life, so it ought to be the concern of believers, after they have been taught that this life will ere long vanish like a dream, to transmit those things which they really wish to enjoy, to that place where they shall possess a perfect and permanent life. It behoves us, therefore, to imitate the conduct of those who determine to migrate to any new situation, where they have chosen to reside during the remainder of their lives; they send their property before them, without regarding the inconvenience of a temporary absence from it; esteeming their happiness the greater in proportion to the wealth which they possess in the place which they intend for their permanent residence. If we believe heaven to be our country, it is better for us to transmit our wealth thither, than to retain it here, where we may lose it by a sudden removal. But how shall we transmit it? Why, if we communicate to the necessities of the poor; whatever is bestowed on them, the Lord considers as given to himself. (*n*) Whence that celebrated promise, "He that hath pity upon the poor, lendeth unto the Lord." (*o*) Again: "He which soweth bountifully shall

(*k*) Luke xvi. 9. (*l*) 1 Tim. vi. 17—19. (*m*) Matt. vi. 21.
(*n*) Matt. xxv. 40. (*o*) Prov. xix. 17.

reap also bountifully." (*p*) For all things that are bestowed on our brethren in a way of charity, are so many deposits in the hand of the Lord; which he, as a faithful depositary, will one day restore with ample interest. Are our acts of duty, then, it will be asked, so valuable in the sight of God, that they are like riches reserved in his hand for us? And who can be afraid to assert this, when the Scripture so frequently and plainly declares it? But if any one, from the mere goodness of God, would infer the merit of works, these testimonies will afford no countenance to such an error. For we can infer nothing from them except the indulgence which God in his mercy is disposed to show us, since, in order to animate us to rectitude of conduct, though the duties we perform are unworthy of the least notice from him, yet he suffers not one of them to go unrewarded.

VII. But they insist more on the words of the apostle, who, to console the Thessalonians under their tribulations, tells them that the design of their infliction is, "that they may be counted worthy of the kingdom of God, for which they also suffer. Seeing," says he, "it is a righteous thing with God to recompense tribulation to them that trouble you; and to you who are troubled, rest with us, when the Lord Jesus shall be revealed from heaven." (*q*) And the author of the Epistle to the Hebrews says, "God is not unrighteous to forget your work and labour of love, which ye have showed toward his name, in that ye have ministered to the saints." (*r*) To the first passage I reply, That it indicates no worthiness of merit; but since it is the will of God the Father, that those whom he has chosen as his children be conformed to Christ his first begotten Son; (*s*) as it was necessary for him first to suffer and then to enter into the glory destined for him; (*t*) so "we must through much tribulation enter into the kingdom of God." (*u*) The tribulations, therefore, which we suffer for the name of Christ, are, as it were, certain marks impressed on us by which God usually distinguishes the sheep of his flock. For this reason, then, we are accounted worthy of the kingdom of God, because we bear in our body the marks of our Lord and Master, (*w*)

(*p*) 2 Cor. ix. 6. (*q*) 2 Thess. i. 5—7. (*r*) Heb. vi. 10.
(*s*) Rom. viii. 21. (*t*) Luke xxiv. 26.
(*u*) Acts xiv. 22. (*w*) Gal. vi. 17.

which are the badges of the children of God. The same sentiment is conveyed in the following passages: "Bearing about in the body the dying of the Lord Jesus, that the life also of Jesus might be made manifest in our body." (*x*) "Being made conformable unto his death, if by any means I might attain unto the resurrection of the dead." (*y*) The reason which the apostle subjoins tends not to establish any merit, but to confirm the hope of the kingdom of God; as though he had said, As it is consistent with the judgment of God to avenge on your enemies those vexations with which they have harassed you, so it is also to grant you respite and repose from those vexations. Of the other passage, which represents it as becoming the righteousness of God not to forget our services, so as almost to imply that he would be unrighteous if he did forget them, the meaning is, that in order to arouse our indolence, God has assured us that the labour which we undergo for the glory of his name shall not be in vain. And we should always remember that this promise, as well as all others, would be fraught with no benefit to us, unless it were preceded by the gratuitous covenant of mercy, on which the whole certainty of our salvation must depend. But relying on that covenant, we may securely confide that our services, however unworthy, will not go without a reward from the goodness of God. To confirm us in that expectation, the apostle asserts that God is not unrighteous, but will perform the promise he has once made. This righteousness, therefore, refers rather to the truth of the Divine promise, than to the equity of rendering to us any thing that is our due. To this purpose there is a remarkable observation of Augustine; and as that holy man has not hesitated frequently to repeat it as deserving of remembrance, so I deem it not unworthy of a constant place in our minds. "The Lord," says he, "is faithful, who has made himself our debtor, not by receiving any thing from us, but by promising all things to us."

VIII. Our Pharisees adduce the following passages of Paul: "Though I have all faith, so that I could remove mountains, and have not charity, I am nothing." Again: "Now abideth faith, hope, charity, these three; but the greatest of these is charity." (*z*)

(*x*) 2 Cor. iv. 10. (*y*) Phil. iii. 10, 11. (*z*) 1 Cor. xiii. 2, 13.

Again: "Above all these things, put on charity, which is the bond of perfectness." (*a*) From the first two passages they contend that we are justified rather by charity than by faith; that is, by the superior virtue, as they express it. But this argument is easily overturned. For we have already shown, that what is mentioned in the first passage, has no reference to true faith. The second we explain to signify true faith, than which he calls charity greater, not as being more meritorious, but because it is more fruitful, more extensive, more generally serviceable, and perpetual in its duration; whereas the use of faith is only temporary. In respect of excellence, the preëminence must be given to the love of God, which is not in this place the subject of Paul's discourse. For the only point which he urges is, that with reciprocal charity we mutually edify one another in the Lord. But let us suppose that charity excels faith in all respects, yet what person possessed of sound judgment, or even of the common exercise of reason, would argue from this that it has a greater concern in justification? The power of justifying, attached to faith, consists not in the worthiness of the act. Our justification depends solely on the mercy of God and the merit of Christ, which when faith apprehends, it is said to justify us. Now, if we ask our adversaries in what sense they attribute justification to charity, they will reply, that because it is a duty pleasing to God, the merit of it, being accepted by the Divine goodness, is imputed to us for righteousness. Here we see how curiously their argument proceeds. We assert that faith justifies, not by procuring us a righteousness through its own merit, but as the instrument by which we freely obtain the righteousness of Christ. These men, passing over in silence the mercy of God and making no mention of Christ, in whom is the substance of righteousness, contend that we are justified by the virtue of charity, because it is more excellent than faith; just as though any one should insist that a king in consequence of his superior rank, is more expert at making a shoe than a shoemaker. This one argument affords an ample proof that all the Sorbonic schools are destitute of the least experience of justification by faith. But if any wrangler should yet inquire,

---

(*a*) Col. iii. 14.

why we understand Paul to use the word *faith* in different acceptations in the same discourse, I am prepared with a substantial reason for such an interpretation. For since those gifts which Paul enumerates, are in some respect connected with faith and hope, because they relate to the knowledge of God, he summarily comprises them all under those two words; as though he had said, The end of prophecy, and of tongues, of knowledge, and of the gift of interpretation, is to conduct us to the knowledge of God. But we know God in this life only by hope and faith. Therefore, when I mention faith and hope, I comprehend all these things under them. "And now abideth faith, hope, charity, these three;" that is, all gifts, whatever may be their variety, are referred to these. "But the greatest of these is charity." From the third passage they infer, that if "charity is the bond of perfectness," it is therefore the bond of righteousness, which is no other than perfection. Now, to refrain from observing that what Paul calls *perfectness,* is the mutual connection which subsists between the members of a well-constituted church, and to admit that charity constitutes our perfection before God; yet what new advantage will they gain? On the contrary, I shall always object, that we never arrive at that perfection, unless we fulfil all the branches of charity; and hence I shall infer, that since all men are at an immense distance from complete charity, they are destitute of all hope of perfection.

IX. I have no inclination to notice all the passages of Scripture, which the folly of the modern Sorbonists seizes as they occur, and without any reason employs against us. For some of them are so truly ridiculous, that I could not even mention them, unless I wished to be accounted a fool. I shall therefore conclude this subject after having explained a sentence uttered by Christ, with which they are wonderfully pleased. To a lawyer, who asked him what was necessary to salvation, he replied, "If thou wilt enter into life, keep the commandments." (*b*) What can we wish more, say they, when the Author of grace himself commands to obtain the kingdom of heaven by an observance of the commandments? As though it were not evident, that Christ adapted

(*b*) Matt. xix. 17.

his replies to those with whom he conversed. Here a doctor of the law inquires the method of obtaining happiness, and that not simply, but what men must *do* in order to attain it. Both the character of the speaker and the inquiry itself induced the Lord to make this reply. The inquirer, persuaded of the righteousness of the law, possessed a blind confidence in his works. Besides, he only inquired what were those works of righeousness by which salvation might be procured. He is therefore justly referred to the law, which contains a perfect mirror of righteousness. We also explicitly declare, that if life be sought by works, it is indispensably requisite to keep the commandments. And this doctrine is necessary to be known by Christians; for how should they flee for refuge to Christ, if they did not acknowledge themselves to have fallen from the way of life upon the precipice of death? And how could they know how far they have wandered from the way of life, without a previous knowledge of what that way of life is? It is then, therefore, that Christ is presented to them as the asylum of salvation, when they perceive the vast difference between their own lives and the Divine righteousness, which consists in the observance of the law. The sum of the whole is, that if we seek salvation by works, we must keep the commandments, by which we are taught perfect righteousness. But to stop here, would be failing in the midst of our course, for to keep the commandments is a task to which none of us are equal. Being excluded, then, from the righteousness of the law, we are under the necessity of resorting to some other refuge, namely, to faith in Christ. Wherefore, as the Lord, knowing this doctor of the law to be inflated with a vain confidence in his works, recalls his attention to the law, that it may teach him his own character as a sinner, obnoxious to the tremendous sentence of eternal death, so, in another place, addressing those who have already been humbled under this knowledge, he omits all mention of the law, and consoles them with a promise of grace—"Come unto me, all ye that labour and are heavy laden, and I will give you rest; and ye shall find rest unto your souls." (*c*)

X. At length, after our adversaries have wearied themselves

(*c*) Matt. xi. 28, 29.

with perversions of Scripture, they betake themselves to subtleties and sophisms. They cavil, that faith is in some places called a work, (*d*) and hence they infer that we improperly oppose faith to works. As though faith procured righteousness for us by its intrinsic merit, as an act of obedience to the Divine will, and not rather because by embracing the Divine mercy, it seals to our hearts the righteousness of Christ, which that mercy offers to us in the preaching of the gospel. The reader will pardon me for not dwelling on the confutation of such follies; for they require nothing to refute them but their own weakness. But I wish briefly to answer one objection, which has some appearance of reason, to prevent its being the source of any difficulty to persons who have had but little experience. Since common sense dictates that opposites are subject to similar rules, and as all sins are imputed to us for unrighteousness, they maintain it to be reasonable, on the other hand, that all good works should be imputed to us for righteousness. Those who reply, that the condemnation of men proceeds from unbelief alone, and not from particular sins, do not satisfy me. I agree with them, that incredulity is the fountain and root of all evils. For it is the original defection from God, which is afterwards followed by particular transgressions of the law. But as they appear to fix one and the same rule for good and evil works in forming a judgment of righteousness or unrighteousness, here I am obliged to dissent from them. For the righteousness of works is the perfect obedience of the law. We cannot therefore be righteous by works, unless we follow this straight line throughout the whole of our lives. The first deviation from it is a lapse into unrighteousness. Hence it appears that righteousness arises not from one or a few works, but from an inflexible and indefatigable observance of the Divine will. But the rule of judging of unrighteousness is very different. For he who has committed fornication or theft, is for one transgression liable to the sentence of death, because he has offended against the divine Majesty. These disputants of ours, therefore, fall into an error for want of adverting to the decision of James, that "whosoever shall keep the whole law, and yet offend in one point,

(*d*) John vi. 29.

he is guilty of all." For he that said, "Do not commit adultery," said also, "Do not kill," &c. (*e*) It ought not, therefore, to be deemed absurd, when we say, that death is the reward justly due to every sin, because they are all and every one deserving of the indignation and vengeance of God. But it will be a weak argument to infer, on the contrary, that one good work will reconcile a man to God, whose wrath he has incurred by a multitude of sins.

(*e*) James ii. 10, 11.

CHAPTER XIX

On Christian Liberty

WE HAVE now to treat of Christian liberty, an explanation of which ought not to be omitted in a treatise which is designed to comprehend a compendious summary of evangelical doctrine. For it is a subject of the first importance, and unless it be well understood, our consciences scarcely venture to undertake any thing without doubting, experience in many things hesitation and reluctance, and are always subject to fluctuations and fears. But especially it is an appendix to justification, and affords no small assistance towards the knowledge of its influence. Hence they who sincerely fear God will experience the incomparable advantage of that doctrine, which impious scoffers pursue with their railleries; because in the spiritual intoxication with which they are seized, they allow themselves the most unbounded impudence. Wherefore this is the proper time to introduce the subject; and though we have slightly touched upon it on some former occasions, yet it was useful to defer the full discussion of it to this place; because, as soon as any mention is made of Christian liberty, then either inordinate passions rage, or violent emotions arise, unless timely opposition be made to those wanton spirits, who most nefariously corrupt things which are otherwise the best. For some, under the pretext of this liberty, cast off all obedience to God, and precipitate themselves into the most unbridled licentiousness; and some despise it, supposing it to be subversive of all moderation, order, and moral distinctions. What can we do in this case, surrounded by such difficulties? Shall we entirely discard Christian liberty, and so preclude the occasion of such dangers? But, as we have observed, unless this be understood, there can be no right knowledge of Christ, or of evangelical truth, or of internal peace of mind. We should rather exert ourselves to prevent the suppression of such a necessary branch of doctrine, and at the same time to obviate those absurd objections which are frequently deduced from it.

II. Christian liberty, according to my judgment, consists of three parts. The first part is, that the consciences of believers, when seeking an assurance of their justification before God, should raise themselves above the law, and forget all the righteousness of the law. For since the law, as we have elsewhere demonstrated, leaves no man righteous, either we must be excluded from all hope of justification, or it is necessary for us to be delivered from it, and that so completely as not to have any dependence on works. For he who imagines, that in order to obtain righteousness he must produce any works, however small, can fix no limit or boundary, but renders himself a debtor to the whole law. Avoiding, therefore, all mention of the law, and dismissing all thought of our own works, in reference to justification, we must embrace the Divine mercy alone, and turning our eyes from ourselves, fix them solely on Christ. For the question is, not how we can be righteous, but how, though unrighteous and unworthy, we can be considered as righteous. And the conscience that desires to attain any certainty respecting this, must give no admission to the law. Nor will this authorize any one to conclude, that the law is of no use to believers, whom it still continues to instruct and exhort, and stimulate to duty, although it has no place in their consciences before the tribunal of God. For these two things, being very different, require to be properly and carefully distinguished by us. The whole life of Christians ought to be an exercise of piety, since they are called to sanctification. (*f*) It is the office of the law to remind them of their duty, and thereby to excite them to the pursuit of holiness and integrity. But when their consciences are solicitous how God may be propitiated, what answer they shall make, and on what they shall rest

(*f*) Ephes. i. 4. 1 Thess. iv. 3, 7.

their confidence, if called to his tribunal, there must then be no consideration of the requisitions of the law, but Christ alone must be proposed for righteousness, who exceeds all the perfection of the law.

III. On this point turns almost the whole argument of the Epistle to the Galatians. For that they are erroneous expositors, who maintain, that Paul there contends only for liberty from ceremonies, may be proved from the topics of his reasoning. Such as these: "Christ hath redeemed us from the curse of the law, being made a curse for us." (*g*) Again: "Stand fast, therefore, in the liberty wherewith Christ hath made us free, and be not entangled again with the yoke of bondage. Behold, I Paul say unto you, that if ye be circumcised, Christ shall profit you nothing. Every man that is circumcised is a debtor to do the whole law. Christ is become of no effect unto you, whosoever of you are justified by the law; ye are fallen from grace." (*h*) These passages certainly comprehend something more exalted than a freedom from ceremonies. I confess, indeed, that Paul is there treating of ceremonies, because he is contending with the false apostles, who attempted to introduce again into the Christian Church the ancient shadows of the law, which had been abolished by the advent of Christ. But for the decision of this question it was necessary to discuss some higher topics, in which the whole controversy lay. First, because the brightness of the gospel was obscured by those Jewish shadows, he shows that in Christ we have a complete exhibition of all those things which were adumbrated by the ceremonies of Moses. Secondly, because these impostors instilled into the people the very pernicious opinion, that this ceremonial obedience was sufficient to merit the Divine favour, he principally contends, that believers ought not to suppose that they can obtain righteousness before God by any works of the law, much less by those inferior elements. And he at the same time teaches, that from the condemnation of the law, which otherwise impends over all men, they are delivered by the cross of Christ, that they may rely with perfect security on him alone—a topic which properly belongs to our present subject. Lastly, he

(*g*) Gal. iii. 13. (*h*) Gal. v. 1—4.

asserts the liberty of the consciences of believers, which ought to be laid under no obligation in things that are not necessary.

IV. The second part of Christian liberty, which is dependent on the first, is, that their consciences do not observe the law, as being under any legal obligation; but that, being liberated from the yoke of the law, they yield a voluntary obedience to the will of God. For being possessed with perpetual terrors, as long as they remain under the dominion of the law, they will never engage with alacrity and promptitude in the service of God, unless they have previously received this liberty. We shall more easily and clearly discover the design of these things from an example. The precept of the law is, "Thou shalt love the Lord thy God with all thine heart, and with all thy soul, and with all thy might." (*i*) That this command may be fulfilled, our soul must be previously divested of every other perception and thought, our heart must be freed from all desires, and our might must be collected and contracted to this one point. Those who, compared with others, have made a very considerable progress in the way of the Lord, are yet at an immense distance from this perfection. For though they love God with their soul, and with sincere affection of heart, yet they have still much of their heart and soul occupied by carnal desires, which retard their progress towards God. They do indeed press forward with strong exertions, but the flesh partly debilitates their strength, and partly attracts it to itself. What can they do in this case, when they perceive that they are so far from observing the law? They wish, they aspire, they endeavour, but they do nothing with the perfection that is required. If they advert to the law, they see that every work they attempt or meditate is accursed. Nor is there the least reason for any person to deceive himself, by concluding that an action is not necessarily altogether evil, because it is imperfect, and that therefore the good part of it is accepted by God. For the law, requiring perfect love, condemns all imperfection, unless its rigour be mitigated. Let him consider his work, therefore, which he wished to be thought partly good, and he will find that very work to be a transgression of the law, because it is imperfect.

(*i*) Deut. vi. 5.

V. See how all our works, if estimated according to the rigour of the law, are subject to its curse. How, then, could unhappy souls apply themselves with alacrity to any work for which they could expect to receive nothing but a curse? On the contrary, if they are liberated from the severe exaction of the law, or rather from the whole of its rigour, and hear God calling them with paternal gentleness, then with cheerfulness and prompt alacrity they will answer to his call and follow his guidance. In short, they who are bound by the yoke of the law, are like slaves who have certain daily tasks appointed by their masters. They think they have done nothing, and presume not to enter into the presence of their masters without having finished the work prescribed to them. But children, who are treated by their parents in a more liberal manner, hesitate not to present to them their imperfect, and in some respects faulty works, in confidence that their obedience and promptitude of mind will be accepted by them, though they have not performed all that they wished. Such children ought we to be, feeling a certain confidence that our services, however small, rude, and imperfect, will be approved by our most indulgent Father. This he also confirms to us by the prophet: "I will spare them," saith he, "as a man spareth his own son that serveth him;" (*k*) where it is evident, from the mention of *service*, that the word *spare* is used to denote indulgence, or an overlooking of faults. And we have great need of this confidence, without which all our endeavours will be vain; for God considers us as serving him in none of our works, but such as are truly done by us to his honour. But how can this be done amidst those terrors, where it is a matter of doubt whether our works offend God or honour him?

VI. This is the reason why the author of the Epistle to the Hebrews refers to faith, and estimates only by faith, all the good works which are recorded of the holy patriarchs. (*l*) On this liberty there is a remarkable passage in the Epistle to the Romans, where Paul reasons that sin ought not to have dominion over us, because we are not under the law, but under grace. (*m*) For after he had exhorted believers, "Let not sin, therefore, reign

---

(*k*) Mal. iii. 17. (*l*) Heb. xi. 2. (*m*) Rom. vi. 14.

in your mortal body; neither yield ye your members as instruments of unrighteousness; but yield yourselves unto God, as those that are alive from the dead, and your members as instruments of righteousness unto God," (*n*)—they might, on the contrary, object that they yet carried about with them the flesh full of inordinate desires, and that sin dwelt in them; but he adds the consolation furnished by their liberty from the law; as though he had said, Although you do not yet experience sin to be destroyed, and righteousness living in you in perfection, yet you have no cause for terror and dejection of mind, as if God were perpetually offended on account of your remaining sin; because by grace you are emancipated from the law, that your works may not be judged according to that rule. But those, who infer that we may commit sin because we are not under the law, may be assured that they have no concern with this liberty, the end of which is to animate us to virtue.

VII. The third part of Christian liberty teaches us, that we are bound by no obligation before God respecting external things, which in themselves are indifferent; but that we may indifferently sometimes use, and at other times omit them. And the knowledge of this liberty also is very necessary for us; for without it we shall have no tranquillity of conscience, nor will there be any end of superstitions. Many in the present age think it a folly to raise any dispute concerning the free use of meats, of days, and of habits, and similar subjects, considering these things as frivolous and nugatory; but they are of greater importance than is generally believed. For when the conscience has once fallen into the snare, it enters a long and inextricable labyrinth, from which it is afterwards difficult to escape; if a man begin to doubt the lawfulness of using flax in sheets, shirts, handkerchiefs, napkins, and table cloths, neither will he be certain respecting hemp, and at last he will doubt of the lawfulness of using tow; for he will consider with himself whether he cannot eat without table cloths or napkins, whether he cannot do without handkerchiefs. If any one imagine delicate food to be unlawful, he will ere long have no tranquillity before God in eating brown bread and common

---

(*n*) Rom. vi. 12, 13.

viands, while he remembers that he might support his body with meat of a quality still inferior. If he hesitate respecting good wine, he will afterwards be unable with any peace of conscience to drink the most vapid; and at last he will not presume even to touch purer and sweeter water than others. In short, he will come to think it criminal to step over a twig that lies across his path. For this is the commencement of no trival controversy; but the dispute is whether the use of certain things be agreeable to God, whose will ought to guide all our resolutions and all our actions. The necessary consequence is, that some are hurried by despair into a vortex of confusion, from which they see no way of escape; and some, despising God, and casting off all fear of him, make a way of ruin for themselves. For all, who are involved in such doubts, which way soever they turn their views, behold something offensive to their consciences presenting itself on every side.

VIII. "I know," says Paul, "that there is nothing unclean of itself; but to him that esteemeth any thing to be unclean, to him it is unclean." (*o*) In these words he makes all external things subject to our liberty, provided that our minds have regard to this liberty before God. But if any superstitious notion cause us to scruple, those things which were naturally pure become contaminated to us. Wherefore he subjoins, "Happy is he that condemneth not himself in that which he alloweth. And he that doubteth is condemned if he eat, because he eateth not of faith; for whatsoever is not of faith is sin." (*p*) Are not they, who in these perplexities show their superior boldness by the security of their presumption, guilty of departing from God? whilst they who are deeply affected with the true fear of God, when they are even constrained to admit many things to which their own consciences are averse, are filled with terror and consternation. No persons of this description receive any of the gifts of God with thanksgiving, by which alone Paul, nevertheless, declares them to be all sanctified to our use. (*q*) I mean a thanksgiving proceeding from a mind which acknowledges the beneficence and goodness of God in the blessings he bestows. For many of them, indeed, apprehend the good things which they use to be from

(*o*) Rom. xiv. 14. (*p*) Rom. xiv. 22, 23. (*q*) 1 Tim. iv. 5.

God, whom they praise in his works; but not being persuaded that they are *given* to them, how could they give thanks to God as the giver of them? We see, in short, the tendency of this liberty, which is, that without any scruple of conscience or perturbation of mind, we should devote the gifts of God to that use for which he has given them; by which confidence our souls may have peace with him, and acknowledge his liberality towards us. For this comprehends all ceremonies, the observation of which is left free, that the conscience may not be bound by any obligation to observe them, but may remember that by the goodness of God it may use them, or abstain from them, as shall be most conducive to edification.

IX. Now, it must be carefully observed, that Christian liberty is in all its branches a spiritual thing; all the virtue of which consists in appeasing terrified consciences before God, whether they are disquieted and solicitous concerning the remission of their sins, or are anxious to know if their works, which are imperfect and contaminated by the defilements of the flesh, be acceptable to God; or are tormented concerning the use of things that are indifferent. Wherefore they are guilty of perverting its meaning, who either make it the pretext of their irregular appetites, that they may abuse the Divine blessings to the purposes of sensuality, or who suppose that there is no liberty but what is used before men, and therefore in the exercise of it totally disregard their weak brethren. The former of these sins is the more common in the present age. There is scarcely any one, whom his wealth permits to be sumptuous, who is not delighted with luxurious splendour in his entertainments, in his dress, and in his buildings; who does not desire a preëminence in every species of luxury; who does not strangely flatter himself on his elegance. And all these things are defended under the pretext of Christian liberty. They allege that they are things indifferent; this I admit, provided they be indifferently used. But where they are too ardently coveted, proudly boasted, or luxuriously lavished, these things, of themselves otherwise indifferent, are completely polluted by such vices. This passage of Paul makes an excellent distinction respecting things which are indifferent: "Unto the pure all things are pure; but unto them that are defiled and unbelieving is nothing pure; but even their mind and conscience is defiled." (*r*) For why are curses denounced on rich men, who "receive their consolation," who are "satiated," who "now laugh," who "lie on beds of ivory," who "join field to field," who "have the harp, and the lyre, and the tabret, and wine in their feasts?" (*s*) Ivory and gold, and riches of all kinds, are certainly blessings of Divine Providence, not only permitted, but expressly designed for the use of men; nor are we any where prohibited to laugh, or to be satiated with food, or to annex new possessions to those already enjoyed by ourselves or by our ancestors, or to be delighted with musical harmony, or to drink wine. This indeed is true; but amidst an abundance of all things, to be immersed in sensual delights, to inebriate the heart and mind with present pleasures, and perpetually to grasp at new ones,— these things are very remote from a legitimate use of the Divine blessings. Let them banish, therefore, immoderate cupidity, excessive profusion, vanity, and arrogance; that with a pure conscience they may make a proper use of the gifts of God. When their hearts shall be formed to this sobriety, they will have a rule for the legitimate enjoyment of them. On the contrary, without this moderation, even common and ordinary pleasures are chargeable with excess. For it is truly observed, that a proud heart frequently dwells under coarse and ragged garments, and that simplicity and humility are sometimes concealed under purple and fine linen. Let all men, in their respective stations, whether of poverty, of competence, or of splendour, live in the remembrance of this truth, that God confers his blessings on them for the support of life, not for luxury; and let them consider this as the law of Christian liberty, that they learn the lesson which Paul had learned, when he said, "I have learned, in whatsoever state I am, therewith to be content. I know both how to be abased, and I know how to abound: every where and in all things I am instructed, both to be full and to be hungry, both to abound and to suffer need." (*t*)

X. Many persons err likewise in this respect, that, as if their liberty would not be perfectly secure unless witnessed by men,

---

(*r*) Titus i. 15. (*s*) Luke vi. 24, 25. Amos vi. 1, &c. Isaiah v. 8, &c.
(*t*) Phil. iv. 11, 12.

they make an indiscriminate and imprudent use of it—a disorderly practice, which occasions frequent offence to their weak brethren. There are some to be found, in the present day, who imagine their liberty would be abridged, if they were not to enter on the enjoyment of it by eating animal food on Friday. Their eating is not the subject of my reprehension; but their minds require to be divested of this false notion; for they ought to consider, that they obtain no advantage from their liberty before men, but with God; and that it consists in abstinence as well as in use. If they apprehend it to be immaterial in God's view, whether they eat animal food or eggs, whether their garments be scarlet or black, it is quite sufficient. The conscience, to which the benefit of this liberty was due, is now emancipated. Therefore, though they abstain from flesh, and wear but one color, during all the rest of their lives, this is no diminution of their freedom. Nay, because they are free, they therefore abstain with a free conscience. But they fall into a very pernicious error in disregarding the infirmity of their brethren, which it becomes us to bear, so as not rashly to do any thing which would give them the least offence. But it will be said, that it is sometimes right to assert our liberty before men. This I confess; yet the greatest caution and moderation must be observed, lest we cast off all concern for the weak, whom God has so strongly recommended to our regards.

XI. I shall now, therefore, make some observations concerning offences; how they are to be discriminated, what are to be avoided, and what are to be disregarded; whence we may afterwards determine what room there is for our liberty in our intercourse with mankind. I approve of the common distinction between an offence given and an offence taken, since it is plainly countenanced by Scripture, and is likewise sufficiently significant of the thing intended to be expressed. If you do any thing at a wrong time or place, or with an unseasonable levity, or wantonness, or temerity, by which the weak and inexperienced are offended, it must be termed an offence given by you; because it arises from your fault. And an offence is always said to be given in any action, the fault of which proceeds from the performer of that action. An offence taken is, when any transaction, not otherwise unseasonable or culpable, is, through malevolence, or some perverse disposition, construed into an occasion of offence. For in this instance the offence is not given, but taken without reason by such perverseness of construction. The first species of offence affects none but the weak; the second is created by moroseness of temper, and Pharisaical superciliousness. Wherefore we shall denominate the former, the offence of the weak, the latter, that of Pharisees; and we shall so temper the use of our liberty, that it ought to submit to the ignorance of weak brethren, but not at all to the austerity of Pharisees. For our duty to the weak, Paul fully shows in many places. "Him that is weak in the faith receive ye." Again: "Let us not therefore judge one another any more; but judge this rather, that no man put a stumbling-block or an occasion to fall in his brother's way;" (*u*) and much more to the same import, which were better examined in its proper connection than recited here. The sum of all is, that "we, then, that are strong, ought to bear the infirmities of the weak, and not to please ourselves. Let every one of us please his neighbour for his good to edification." (*v*) In another place: "But take heed lest by any means this liberty of yours become a stumbling-block to them that are weak." (*w*) Again: "Whatsoever is sold in the shambles, that eat; asking no questions for conscience' sake; conscience, I say, not thine own, but of the other." In short, "Give none offence, neither to the Jews, nor to the Gentiles, nor to the Church of God." (*x*) In another place also: "Brethren, ye have been called unto liberty; only use not liberty for an occasion to the flesh, but by love serve one another." (*y*) The meaning of this is, that our liberty is not given us to be used in opposition to our weak neighbours, to whom charity obliges us to do every possible service; but rather in order that, having peace with God in our minds, we may also live peaceably among men. But how much attention should be paid to an offence taken by Pharisees, we learn from our Lord's injunction, "Let them alone; they be blind leaders of the blind." (*z*) The disciples had informed him, that the Pharisees were offended with his discourse. He replies that they are to be let alone, and their offence disregarded.

XII. But the subject is still pending in uncertainty, unless we

(*u*) Rom. xiv. 1, 13. (*v*) Rom. xv. 1, 2. (*w*) 1 Cor. viii. 9.
(*x*) 1 Cor. x 25, 29, 32. (*y*) Gal. v. 13. (*z*) Matt. xv. 14.

know whom we are to account weak, and whom we are to consider as Pharisees; without which distinction, I see no use of liberty in the midst of offences, but such as must be attended with the greatest danger. But Paul appears to me to have very clearly decided, both by doctrine and examples, how far our liberty should be either moderated or asserted on the occurrence of offences. When he made Timothy his associate, he circumcised him; (*a*) but could not be induced to circumcise Titus. (*b*) Here was a difference in his proceedings, but no change of mind or of purpose. In the circumcision of Timothy, "though he was free from all men, yet he made himself servant unto all;" and says he, "Unto the Jews I became as a Jew, that I might gain the Jews; to them that are under the law, as under the law, that I might gain them that are under the law: I am made all things to all men, that I might by all means save some." (*c*) Thus we have a proper moderation of liberty, if it may be indifferently restricted with any advantage. His reason for resolutely refraining from circumcising Titus, he declares in the following words: "But neither Titus, who was with me, being a Greek, was compelled to be circumcised, and that because of false brethren unawares brought in, who came in privily to spy out our liberty which we have in Christ Jesus, that they might bring us into bondage; to whom we gave place by subjection, no, not for an hour; that the truth of the gospel might continue with you." (*d*) We also are under the necessity of vindicating our liberty, if it be endangered in weak consciences by the iniquitous requisitions of false apostles. We must at all times study charity, and keep in view the edification of our neighbour. "All things (says Paul) are lawful for me, but all things are not expedient: all things are lawful for me, but all things edify not. Let no man seek his own, but every man another's." (*e*) Nothing can be plainer than this rule, that our liberty should be used, if it conduces to our neighbour's edification; but that if it be not beneficial to our neighbour, it should be abridged. There are some, who pretend to imitate the prudence of Paul in refraining from the exercise of liberty, while they are doing any thing but exercising the duties of charity. For to pro-

(*a*) Acts xvi. 3. (*b*) Gal. ii. 3. (*c*) 1 Cor. ix. 19, 20, 22.
(*d*) Gal. ii. 3—5. (*e*) 1 Cor. x. 23, 24.

mote their own tranquillity, they wish all mention of liberty to be buried; whereas it is no less advantageous to our neighbours sometimes to use our liberty to their benefit and edification, than at other times to moderate it for their accommodation. But a pious man considers this liberty in external things as granted him in order that he may be the better prepared for all the duties of charity.

XIII. But whatever I have advanced respecting the avoidance of offences, I wish to be referred to indifferent and unimportant things; for necessary duties must not be omitted through fear of any offence: as our liberty should be subject to charity, so charity itself ought to be subservient to the purity of faith. It becomes us, indeed, to have regard to charity; but we must not offend God for the love of our neighbour. We cannot approve the intemperance of those who do nothing but in a tumultuous manner, and who prefer violent measures to lenient ones. Nor must we listen to those, who, while they show themselves the leaders in a thousand species of impiety, pretend that they are obliged to act in such a manner, that they may give no offence to their neighbours; as though they are not at the same time fortifying the consciences of their neighbours in sin; especially since they are always sticking in the same mire without any hope of deliverance. And whether their neighbour is to be instructed by doctrine or by example, they maintain that he ought to be fed with milk, though they are infecting him with the worst and most pernicious notions. Paul tells the Corinthians, "I have fed you with milk;" (*f*) but if the Popish mass had been then introduced among them, would he have united in that pretended sacrifice in order to feed them with milk? Certainly not; for milk is not poison. They are guilty of falsehood, therefore, in saying that they feed those whom they cruelly murder under the appearance of such flatteries. But admitting that such dissimulation is to be approved for a time, how long will they feed their children with the same milk? For if they never grow, so as to be able to bear even some light meat, it is a clear proof that they were never fed with milk. I am prevented from pushing this controversy with them any further at

(*f*) 1 Cor. iii. 2.

present, by two reasons—first, because their absurdities scarcely deserve a refutation, being justly despised by all men of sound understanding; secondly, having done this at large in particular treatises, I am unwilling to travel the same ground over again. Only let the readers remember, that with whatever offences Satan and the world may endeavour to divert us from the ordinances of God, or to retard our pursuit of what he enjoins, yet we must nevertheless strenuously advance; and moreover, that whatever dangers threaten us, we are not at liberty to deviate even a hair's breadth from his command, and that it is not lawful under any pretext to attempt any thing but what he permits.

XIV. Now, since the consciences of believers, being privileged with the liberty which we have described, have been delivered by the favour of Christ from all necessary obligation to the observance of those things in which the Lord has been pleased they should be left free, we conclude that they are exempt from all human authority. For it is not right that Christ should lose the acknowledgments due to such kindness, or our consciences the benefit of it. Neither is that to be accounted a trivial thing, which we see cost Christ so much; which he estimated not with gold or silver, but with his own blood; (*n*) so that Paul hesitates not to assert, that his death is rendered vain, if we suffer our souls to be in subjection to men. (*o*) For his sole object in some chapters of his Epistle to the Galatians is to prove that Christ is obscured, or rather abolished, with respect to us, unless our consciences continue in their liberty; from which they are certainly fallen, if they can be insnared in the bonds of laws and ordinances at the pleasure of men. (*p*) But as it is a subject highly worthy of being understood, so it needs a more diffuse and perspicuous explanation. For as soon as a word is mentioned concerning the abrogation of human establishments, great tumults are excited, partly by seditious persons, partly by cavillers; as though all obedience of men were at once subverted and destroyed.

XV. To prevent any one from falling into this error, let us therefore consider, in the first place, that man is under two kinds of government—one spiritual, by which the conscience is formed

(*n*) 1 Peter i. 18, 19. (*o*) Gal. v. 1, 4. (*p*) 1 Cor. vii. 23.

to piety and the service of God; the other political, by which a man is instructed in the duties of humanity and civility, which are to be observed in an intercourse with mankind. They are generally, and not improperly, denominated the spiritual and the temporal jurisdiction; indicating that the former species of government pertains to the life of the soul, and that the latter relates to the concerns of the present state; not only to the provision of food and clothing, but to the enactment of laws to regulate a man's life among his neighbours by the rules of holiness, integrity, and sobriety. For the former has its seat in the interior of the mind, whilst the latter only directs the external conduct: one may be termed a spiritual kingdom, and the other a political one. But these two, as we have distinguished them, always require to be considered separately; and while the one is under discussion, the mind must be abstracted from all consideration of the other. For man contains, as it were, two worlds, capable of being governed by various rulers and various laws. This distinction will prevent what the gospel inculcates concerning spiritual liberty from being misapplied to political regulations; as though Christians were less subject to the external government of human laws, because their consciences have been set at liberty before God; as though their freedom of spirit necessarily exempted them from all carnal servitude. Again, because even in those constitutions which seem to pertain to the spiritual kingdom, there may possibly be some deception, it is necessary to discriminate between these also; which are to be accounted legitimate, as according with the Divine word, and which, on the contrary, ought not to be received among believers. Of civil government I shall treat in another place. Of ecclesiastical laws also I forbear to speak at present; because a full discussion of them will be proper in the Fourth Book, where we shall treat of the power of the Church. But we shall conclude the present argument in the following manner: The question, which, as I have observed, is in itself not very obscure or intricate, greatly perplexes many, because they do not distinguish with sufficient precision between the external jurisdiction and the court of conscience. The difficulty is increased by Paul's injunction to obey magistrates "not only for wrath, but also for conscience' sake;" (*q*) from which it should follow, that the conscience also is bound by political laws. But if this were true, it would supersede all that we have already said, or are now about to say, respecting spiritual government. For the solution of this difficulty, it will be of use, first, to know what conscience is. And the definition of it must be derived from the etymology of the word. For as, when men apprehend the knowledge of things in the mind and understanding, they are thence said *scire,* "to know," whence is derived the word *scientia,* "science" or "knowledge;" so when they have a sense of Divine justice, as an additional witness, which permits them not to conceal their sins, or to elude accusation at the tribunal of the supreme Judge, this sense is termed *conscientia,* "conscience." For it is a kind of medium between God and man; because it does not suffer a man to suppress what he knows within himself, but pursues him till it brings him to conviction. This is what Paul means by "their conscience also bearing witness, and their thoughts accusing, or else excusing, one another." (*r*) Simple knowledge might remain, as it were, confined within a man. This sentiment, therefore, which places man before the Divine tribunal, is appointed, as it were, to watch over man, to observe and examine all his secrets, that nothing may remain enveloped in darkness. Hence the old proverb, Conscience is as a thousand witnesses. For the same reason Peter speaks of "the answer of a good conscience towards God," (*s*) to express our tranquillity of mind, when, persuaded of the favour of Christ, we present ourselves with boldness in the presence of God. And the author of the Epistle to the Hebrews expresses absolution or freedom from every future charge of sin, by "having no more conscience of sin." (*t*)

XVI. Therefore, as works respect men, so conscience regards God; so that a good conscience is no other than inward integrity of heart. In which sense Paul says, that "the end of the commandment is charity, out of a pure heart, and of a good conscience, and of faith unfeigned." (*u*) Afterwards also, in the same chapter, he shows how widely it differs from understanding, saying, that "some, having put away a good conscience, con-

(*q*) Rom. xiii. 1, 5. (*r*) Rom. ii. 15. (*s*) 1 Peter iii. 21.
(*t*) Heb. x. 2. (*u*) 1 Tim. i. 5.

cerning faith have made shipwreck." (*w*) For these words indicate that it is a lively inclination to the service of God, and a sincere pursuit of piety and holiness of life. Sometimes, indeed, it is likewise extended to men; as when the same apostle declares, "Herein do I exercise myself, to have always a conscience void of offence toward God and toward men." (*x*) But the reason of this assertion is, that the fruits of a good conscience reach even to men. But in strict propriety of speech it has to do with God alone, as I have already observed. Hence it is that a law, which simply binds a man without relation to other men, or any consideration of them, is said to bind the conscience. For example, God not only enjoins the preservation of the mind chaste and pure from every libidinous desire, but prohibits all obscenity of language and external lasciviousness. The observance of this law is incumbent on my conscience, though there were not another man existing in the world. Thus he who transgresses the limits of temperance, not only sins by giving a bad example to his brethren, but contracts guilt on his conscience before God. Things in themselves indifferent are to be guided by other considerations. It is our duty to abstain from them, if they tend to the least offence, yet without violating our liberty of conscience. So Paul speaks concerning meat consecrated to idols: "If any man say unto you, This is offered in sacrifice to idols, eat not for conscience' sake; conscience, I say, not thine own, but of the other." (*y*) A pious man would be guilty of sin, who, being previously admonished, should, nevertheless, eat such meat. But though, with respect to his brother, abstinence is necessary for him, as it is enjoined by God, yet he ceases not to retain liberty of conscience. We see, then, how this law, though it binds the external action, leaves the conscience free.

(*w*) 1 Tim. i. 19. (*x*) Acts xxiv. 16. (*y*) 1 Cor. x. 28, 29.

CHAPTER XX

On Prayer, the Principal Exercise of Faith, and the Medium of Our Daily Reception of Divine Blessings

FROM the subjects already discussed, we clearly perceive how utterly destitute man is of every good, and in want of all the means of salvation. Wherefore, if he seek for relief in his necessities, he must go out of himself, and obtain it from some other quarter. It has been subsequently stated, that the Lord voluntarily and liberally manifests himself in his Christ, in whom he offers us all felicity instead of our misery, and opulence instead of our poverty; in whom he opens to our view the treasures of heaven, that our faith may be wholly engaged in the contemplation of his beloved Son, that all our expectation may depend upon him, and that in him all our hope may rest and be fully satisfied. This, indeed, is that secret and recondite philosophy, which cannot be extracted from syllogisms; but is well understood by those whose eyes God has opened, that in his light they may see light. But since we have been taught by faith to acknowledge, that whatever we want for the supply of our necessities is in God and our Lord Jesus Christ, in whom it has pleased the Father all the fulness of his bounty should dwell, that we may all draw from it, as from a most copious fountain, it remains for us to seek in him, and by prayers to implore of him, that which we have been informed resides in him. Otherwise to know God as the Lord and Giver of every good, who invites us to supplicate him, but neither to approach him nor to supplicate him, would be equally unprofitable, as for a man to neglect a treasure discovered to him buried in the earth. Wherefore the apostle, to show that true faith cannot but be engaged in calling upon God, has laid down this order—that, as faith is produced by the gospel, so by faith our hearts are brought to invoke the name of the Lord. (*z*) And this is the same as he had a little before said, that the "Spirit of adoption," who seals the testimony of the gospel in our hearts, encourages our spirits, so that they venture to pour out their desires before God, excite "groanings that cannot be uttered," and cry with confidence, "Abba, Father." (*a*) This last subject, therefore, having been before only cursorily mentioned and slightly touched, requires now to be treated more at large.

II. By means of prayer, then, we penetrate to those riches which are reserved with our heavenly Father for our use. For between God and men there is a certain communication; by which they enter into the sanctuary of heaven, and in his immediate presence remind him of his promises, in order that his declarations, which they have implicitly believed, may in time of necessity be verified in their experience. We see, therefore, that nothing is revealed to us, to be expected from the Lord, for which we are not likewise enjoined to pray; so true is it, that prayer digs out those treasures, which the gospel of the Lord discovers to our faith. Now, the necessity and various utility of the exercise of prayer no language can sufficiently explain. It is certainly not without reason that our heavenly Father declares, that the only fortress of salvation consists in invocation of his name; by which we call to our aid the presence of his providence, which watches over all our concerns; of his power, which supports us when weak and ready to faint; and of his goodness, which receives us into favour, though miserably burdened with sins; in which, finally, we call upon him to manifest his presence with us in all his attributes. Hence our consciences derive peculiar peace and

(*z*) Rom. x. 13, 14, 17. (*a*) Rom. viii. 15, 26.

tranquillity; for when the affliction which oppressed us is represented to the Lord, we feel abundant composure even from this consideration—that none of our troubles are concealed from him, whom we know to possess both the greatest readiness and the greatest ability to promote our truest interest.

III. But some will say, Does he not, without information, know both our troubles and our necessities; so that it may appear unnecessary to solicit him with our prayers, as if he were inattentive or sleeping, till aroused by our voice? But such reasoners advert not to the Lord's end in teaching his people to pray; for he has appointed it not so much for his own sake as for ours. It is his pleasure indeed, as is highly reasonable, that his right be rendered to him, by their considering him as the Author of all that is desired and found useful by men, and by their acknowledgments of this in their prayers. But the utility of this sacrifice, by which he is worshipped, returns to us. The greater the confidence, therefore, with which the ancient saints gloried in the Divine benefits to themselves and others, with so much the more earnestness were they incited to pray. The single example of Elijah shall suffice, who, though certain of God's design, having already with sufficient authority promised rain to king Ahab, yet anxiously prays between his knees, and sends his servant seven times to look for it; (*b*) not with an intention to discredit the Divine oracle, but under a conviction of his duty to prevent his faith becoming languid and torpid, by pouring out his prayers before God. Wherefore, although, when we are stupid and insensible to our own miseries, he vigilantly watches and guards us, and sometimes affords us unsolicited succour, yet it highly concerns us assiduously to supplicate him, that our heart may be always inflamed with a serious and ardent desire of seeking, loving, and worshipping him, while we accustom ourselves in all our necessities to resort to him as our sheet anchor. Further, that no desire or wish, which we should be ashamed for him to know, may enter our minds; when we learn to present our wishes, and so to pour out our whole heart in his presence. Next, that we may be prepared to receive his blessings with true gratitude of soul, and even with

(*b*) 1 Kings xviii. 42, &c.

grateful acknowledgments; being reminded by our praying that they come from his hand. Moreover, that when we have obtained what we sought, the persuasion that he has answered our requests may excite us to more ardent meditations on his goodness, and produce a more joyful welcome of those things which we acknowledge to be the fruits of our prayers. Lastly, that use and experience itself may yield our minds a confirmation of his providence in proportion to our imbecility, while we apprehend that he not only promises never to forsake us, and freely opens a way of access for our addressing him in the very moment of necessity; but that his hand is always extended to assist his people, whom he does not feed with mere words, but supports with present aid. On these accounts our most merciful Father, though liable to no sleep or languor, yet frequently appears as if he were sleepy or languid, in order to exercise us, who are otherwise slothful and inactive, in approaching, supplicating, and earnestly importuning him to our own advantage. It is extremely absurd, therefore, in them who, with a view to divert the minds of men from praying to God, pretend that it is useless for us by our interruptions to weary the Divine Providence, which is engaged in the conservation of all things; whereas the Lord declares, on the contrary, that he "is nigh to all that call upon him in truth." (*c*) And equally nugatory is the objection of others, that it is superfluous to petition for those things which the Lord is ready voluntarily to bestow; whereas even those very things, which flow to us from his spontaneous liberality, he wishes us to consider as granted to our prayers. This is evinced by that memorable passage in the Psalms, as well as by many other correspondent texts,—"The eyes of the Lord are upon the righteous, and his ears are open unto their cry;" (*d*) which celebrates the Divine Providence as spontaneously engaged to accomplish the salvation of believers; yet does not omit the exercise of faith, by which sloth is expelled from the minds of men. The eyes of God, then, are vigilant to succour the necessity of the blind; but he is likewise willing to hear our groans, to give a better proof of his love towards us. And thus it is equally true, that "he that keepeth

(*c*) Psalm cxlv. 18. (*d*) Psalm xxxiv. 15.

Israel neither slumbers nor sleeps," and yet that he remains, as it were, forgetful of us, while he beholds us slothful and dumb.

IV. Now, for conducting prayer in a right and proper manner, the first rule is, that our heart and mind be composed to a suitable frame, becoming those who enter into conversation with God. This state of mind we shall certainly attain, if, divested of all carnal cares and thoughts, that tend to divert and seduce it from a right and clear view of God, it not only devotes itself entirely to the solemn exercise, but is likewise as far as possible elevated and carried above itself. Nor do I here require a mind so disengaged as to be disturbed by no solicitude; since there ought, on the contrary, most anxiously to be kindled within us a fervency of prayer, (as we see the holy servants of God discover great solicitude, and even anguish, when they say they utter their complaints to the Lord from the deep abysses of affliction and the very jaws of death.) But I maintain the necessity of dismissing all foreign and external cares, by which the wandering mind may be hurried hither and thither, and dragged from heaven down to earth. It ought to be elevated above itself, that it may not intrude into the Divine presence any of the imaginations of our blind and foolish reason, nor confine itself within the limits of its own vanity, but rise to purity worthy of God.

V. Both these things are highly worthy of observation—first, that whoever engages in prayer, should apply all his faculties and attention to it, and not be distracted, as is commonly the case, with wandering thoughts; nothing being more contrary to a reverence for God than such levity, which indicates a licentious spirit, wholly unrestrained by fear. In this case our exertions must be great in proportion to the difficulty we experience. For no man can be so intent on praying, but he may perceive many irregular thoughts intruding on him, and either interrupting, or by some oblique digression retarding, the course of his devotions. But here let us consider what an indignity it is, when God admits us to familiar intercourse with him, to abuse such great condescension by a mixture of things sacred and profane, while our thoughts are not confined to him by reverential awe; but as if we were conversing with a mean mortal, we quit him in the midst of our prayer, and make excursions on every side. We may be assured, therefore, that none are rightly prepared for the exercise of prayer, but those who are so affected by the Divine Majesty as to come to it divested of all earthly cares and affections. And this is indicated by the ceremony of lifting up the hands, that men may remember that they are at a great distance from God, unless they lift up their thoughts on high. As it is also expressed in the psalm, "Unto thee do I lift up my soul." (*e*) And the Scripture frequently uses this mode of expression, "to lift up one's prayer;" that they, who desire to be heard by God, may not sink into lethargic inactivity. To sum up the whole, the greater the liberality of God towards us, in gently inviting us to disburden ourselves of our cares by casting them on him, the less excusable are we, unless his signal and incomparable favour preponderate with us beyond every thing else, and attract us to him in a serious application of all our faculties and attention to the duty of prayer; which cannot be done unless our mind by strenuous exertion rise superior to every impediment. Our second proposition is, that we must pray for no more than God permits. For though he enjoins us to pour out our hearts before him, (*f*) yet he does not carelessly give the reins to affections of folly and depravity; and when he promises to "fulfil the desire" (*g*) of believers, he does not go to such an extreme of indulgence, as to subject himself to their caprice. But offences against both these rules are common and great; for most men not only presume, without modesty or reverence, to address God concerning their follies, and impudently to utter at his tribunal whatever has amused them in their reveries or dreams, but so great is their folly or stupidity, that they dare to obtrude upon God all their foulest desires, which they would be exceedingly ashamed to reveal to men. Some heathens have ridiculed and even detested this presumption, but the vice itself has always prevailed; and hence it was that the ambitious chose Jupiter as their patron; the avaricious, Mercury; the lovers of learning, Apollo and Minerva; the warlike, Mars; and the libidinous, Venus; just as in the present age (as I have lately hinted) men indulge a greater license to their unlawful desires in their prayers, than if they were con-

(*e*) Psalm xxv. 1. (*f*) Psalm lxii. 8. (*g*) Psalm cxlv. 19.

versing in a jocular manner with their equals. God suffers not his indulgence to be so mocked, but asserts his power, and subjects our devotions to his commands. Therefore we ought to remember this passage in John: "This is the confidence that we have in him, that, if we ask any thing according to his will, he heareth us." (*h*) But as our abilities are very unequal to such great perfection, we must seek some remedy to relieve us. As the attention of the mind ought to be fixed on God, so it is necessary that it should be followed by the affection of the heart. But they both remain far below this elevation; or rather, to speak more consistently with truth, they grow weary and fail in the ascent, or are carried a contrary course. Therefore, to assist this imbecility, God gives us the Spirit, to be the director of our prayers, to suggest what is right, and to regulate our affections. For "the Spirit helpeth our infirmities; for we know not what we should pray for as we ought; but the Spirit itself maketh intercession for us with groanings which cannot be uttered;" (*i*) not that he really prays or groans; but he excites within us confidence, desires, and sighs, to the conception of which our native powers were altogether inadequate. Nor is it without reason that Paul terms those "groanings," which arise from believers under the influence of the Spirit, "unutterable;" because they who are truly engaged in prayers, are not ignorant that they are so perplexed with dubious anxieties, that they can scarcely decide what it is expedient to utter; and even while they are attempting to lisp, they stammer and hesitate; whence it follows that the ability of praying rightly is a peculiar gift. These things are not said in order that we may indulge our own indolence, resigning the office of prayer to the Spirit of God, and growing torpid in that negligence to which we are too prone; according to the impious errors of some, that we should wait in indolent supineness till he call our minds from other engagements and draw them to himself; but rather that, wearied with our sloth and inactivity, we may implore such assistance of the Spirit. Nor does the apostle, when he exhorts us to "pray in the Holy Ghost," (*k*) encourage us to remit our vigilance; signifying, that the inspiration of the

(*h*) 1 John v. 14.   (*i*) Rom. viii. 26.   (*k*) Jude 20. 1 Cor. xiv. 15.

Spirit operates in the formation of our prayers, so as not in the least to impede or retard our own exertions; since it is the will of God to prove in this instance the efficacious influence of faith on our hearts.

VI. Let this be the second rule: That in our supplications we should have a real and permanent sense of our indigence, and seriously considering our necessity of all that we ask, should join with the petitions themselves a serious and ardent desire of obtaining them. For multitudes carelessly recite a form of prayer, as though they were discharging a task imposed on them by God; and though they confess that this is a remedy necessary for their calamities, since it would be certain destruction to be destitute of the Divine aid which they implore, yet that they perform this duty merely in compliance with custom, is evident from the coldness of their hearts, and their inattention to the nature of their petitions. They are led to this by some general and confused sense of their necessity, which nevertheless does not excite them to implore a relief for their great need as a case of present urgency. Now, what can we imagine more odious or execrable to God than this hypocrisy, when any man prays for the pardon of sins, who at the same time thinks he is not a sinner, or at least does not think that he is a sinner? which is an open mockery of God himself. But such depravity, as I have before observed, pervades the whole human race, that as a matter of form they frequently implore of God many things which they either expect to receive from some other source independent of his goodness, or imagine themselves already to possess. The crime of some others appears to be smaller, but yet too great to be tolerated; who, having only imbibed this principle, that God must be propitiated by devotions, mutter over their prayers without meditation. But believers ought to be exceedingly cautious, never to enter into the presence of God to present any petition, without being inflamed with a fervent affection of soul, and feeling an ardent desire to obtain it from him. Moreover, although in those things which we request only for the Divine glory, we do not at the first glance appear to regard our own necessity, yet it is incumbent on us to pray for them with equal fervour and vehemence of desire. As when we pray that his name may be hallowed, or sanctified, we ought (so to speak) ardently to hunger and thirst for that sanctification.

VII. If any man object, that we are not always urged to pray by the same necessity, this I grant, and this distinction is usefully represented to us by James: "Is any among you afflicted? let him pray. Is any merry? let him sing psalms." (*l*) Common sense itself therefore dictates, that because of our extreme indolence, we are the more vigorously stimulated by God to earnestness in prayer according to the exigencies of our condition. And this David calls "a time when God may be found," (*m*) because (as he teaches in many other places) the more severely we are oppressed by troubles, disasters, fears, and other kinds of temptations, we have the greater liberty of access to God, as though he then particularly invited us to approach him. At the same time, it is equally true that we ought to be, as Paul says, "praying always," (*n*) because, how great soever we may believe the prosperity of our affairs, and though we are surrounded on every side by matter of joy, yet there is no moment of time in which our necessity does not furnish incitements to prayer. Does any one abound in wine and corn? Since he cannot enjoy a morsel of bread but by the continual favour of God, his cellars or barns afford no objection to his praying for daily bread. Now, if we reflect how many dangers threaten us every moment, fear itself will teach us that there is no time in which prayer is unsuitable to us. Yet this may be discovered still better in spiritual concerns. For when will so many sins, of which we are conscious, suffer us to remain in security, without humbly deprecating both the guilt and the punishment? When will temptations grant us a truce, so that we need not be in haste to obtain assistance? Besides, an ardent desire of the Divine kingdom and glory ought irresistibly to attract us, not by intervals, but without intermission, rendering every season equally suitable. It is not in vain, therefore, that assiduity in prayer is so frequently enjoined. I speak not yet of perseverance, which shall be mentioned hereafter; but the scriptural admonitions to "pray without ceasing" are so many reproofs of our sloth; because we feel not our need

---

(*l*) James v. 13. (*m*) Psalm xxxii. 6. (*n*) Ephes. vi. 18.

of this care and diligence. This rule precludes and banishes from prayer, hypocrisy, subtilty, and falsehood. God promises that he will be near to all who call upon him in truth, and declares he will be found by those who seek him with their whole heart. But to this, persons pleased with their own impurity never aspire. Legitimate prayer, therefore, requires repentance. Whence it is frequently said in the Scriptures, that God hears not the wicked, and that their prayers are an abomination; as are also their sacrifices; for it is reasonable that they who shut up their own hearts, should find the ears of God closed against them; and God should be inflexible to them who provoke his rigour by their obduracy. In Isaiah, he threatens thus: "When ye make many prayers, I will not hear: your hands are full of blood." (*o*) Again in Jeremiah: "I protested, yet they inclined not their ear. Therefore, though they shall cry unto me, I will not hearken unto them." (*p*) Because he considers himself grossly insulted by the wicked boasting of his covenant, while they are continually dishonouring his sacred name. Wherefore he complains, in Isaiah, "This people draw near me with their mouth, but have removed their heart far from me." (*q*) He does not restrict this solely to prayer; but asserts his abhorrence of hypocrisy in every branch of his worship. Which is the meaning of this passage in James: "Ye ask, and receive not, because ye ask amiss, that ye may consume it upon your lusts." (*r*) It is true, indeed, (as we shall presently again see,) that the prayers of the faithful depend not on their personal worthiness; yet this does not supersede the admonition of John: "Whatsoever we ask, we receive of him, because we keep his commandments;" (*s*) because an evil conscience shuts the gate against us. Whence it follows, that none pray aright, and that no others are heard, but the sincere worshippers of God. Whosoever therefore engages in prayer, should be displeased with himself on account of his sins, and assume, what he cannot do without repentance, the character and disposition of a beggar.

VIII. To these must be added a third rule—That whoever presents himself before God for the purpose of praying to him, must renounce every idea of his own glory, reject all opinion of his

(*o*) Isaiah i. 15. (*p*) Jer. xi. 7, 8, 11. (*q*) Isaiah xxix. 13.
(*r*) James iv. 3. (*s*) 1 John iii. 22.

own merit, and, in a word, relinquish all confidence in himself, giving, by this humiliation of himself, all the glory entirely to God; lest, arrogating any thing, though ever so little, to ourselves, we perish from his presence in consequence of our vanity. Of this submission, which prostrates every high thought, we have frequent examples in the servants of God; of whom the most eminent for holiness feel the greatest consternation on entering into the presence of the Lord. Thus Daniel, whom the Lord himself has so highly commended, said, "We do not present our supplications before thee for our righteousness, but for thy great mercies. O Lord, hear; O Lord, forgive; O Lord, hearken and do; defer not, for thine own sake, O my God; for thy city and thy people are called by thy name." (*t*) Nor does he, as is generally the case, confound himself with the multitude, as one of the people; but makes a separate confession of his own guilt, resorting as a suppliant to the asylum of pardon; as he expressly declares, "Whilst I was confessing my sin, and the sin of my people." (*u*) We are taught the same humility also by the example of David: "Enter not into judgment with thy servant; for in thy sight shall no man living be justified." (*v*) In this manner Isaiah prays: "Behold, thou art wroth; for we have sinned: in thy ways is continuance, and we shall be saved. For we are all as an unclean thing, and all our righteousnesses are as filthy rags; and we all do fade as a leaf; and our iniquities, like the wind, have taken us away. And there is none that calleth upon thy name, that stirreth up himself to take hold of thee; for thou hast hid thy face from us, and hast consumed us, because of our iniquities. But now, O Lord, thou art our Father; we are the clay, and thou our potter; and we all are the work of thy hand. Be not wroth very sore, O Lord, neither remember iniquity for ever; behold, see, we beseech thee, we are all thy people." (*w*) Observe, they have no dependence but this; that considering themselves as God's children, they despair not of his future care of them. Thus Jeremiah: "Though our iniquities testify against us, do thou it for thy name's sake." (*x*) For that is equally consistent with the strictest truth and holiness, which was written by

(*t*) Dan. ix. 18, 19. (*u*) Dan. ix. 20. (*v*) Psalm cxliii. 2. (*w*) Isaiah lxiv. 5—9. (*x*) Jer. xiv. 7.

an uncertain author, but is ascribed to the prophet Baruch: "A soul sorrowful and desolate for the greatness of its sin, bowed down and infirm, a hungry soul and fainting eyes give glory to thee, O Lord. Not according to the righteousnesses of our fathers do we pour out our prayers in thy sight, and ask mercy before thy face, O Lord, our God; but because thou art merciful, have mercy upon us, for we have sinned against thee." (*y*)

IX. Finally, the commencement and even introduction to praying rightly is a supplication for pardon with an humble and ingenuous confession of guilt. For neither is there any hope that even the holiest of men can obtain any blessing of God till he be freely reconciled to him, nor is it possible for God to be propitious to any, but those whom he pardons. It is no wonder, then, if believers with this key open to themselves the gate of prayer; as we learn from many places in the Psalms. For David, when requesting another thing, says, "Remember not the sins of my youth, nor my transgressions: according to thy mercy remember thou me, for thy goodness' sake, O Lord." Again: "Look upon mine affliction and my pain; and forgive all my sins." (*z*) Where we likewise perceive, that it is not sufficient for us to call ourselves to a daily account for recent sins, unless we remember those which might seem to have been long buried in oblivion. For the same Psalmist, in another place, (*a*) having confessed one grievous crime, takes occasion thence to revert to his mother's womb, where he had contracted his original pollution; not in order to extenuate his guilt by the corruption of his nature, but that, accumulating all the sins of his life, he may find God the more ready to listen to his prayers in proportion to the severity of his self-condemnation. But though the saints do not always in express terms pray for remission of sins, yet if we diligently examine their prayers recited in the Scriptures, it will easily appear, as I assert, that they derived their encouragement to pray from the mere mercy of God, and so always began by deprecating his displeasure; for if every man examine his own conscience, he is so far from presuming familiarly to communicate his cares to God, that he trembles at every approach to him, except in a

---

(*y*) Baruch ii. 18. (*z*) Psalm xxv. 7, 18. (*a*) Psalm li. 5.

reliance on his mercy and forgiveness. There is also, indeed, another special confession, when they wish for an alleviation of punishments, which is tacitly praying for the pardon of their sins; because it were absurd to desire the removal of an effect, while the cause remains. For we must beware of imitating foolish patients, who are only solicitous for the cure of the symptoms, but neglect the radical cause of the disease. Besides, we should first seek for God to be propitious to us, previously to any external testimonies of his favour; because it is his own will to observe this order, and it would be of little advantage to us to receive benefits from him, unless a discovery to the conscience of his being appeased towards us rendered him altogether amiable in our view. Of this we are likewise apprized by the reply of Christ; for when he had determined to heal a paralytic person, he said, "Thy sins be forgiven thee;" (*b*) thereby calling our attention to that which ought to be the chief object of desire, that God may receive us into his favour, and then, by affording us assistance, discover the effect of reconciliation. But beside the special confession of present guilt, in which believers implore the pardon of every sin and the remission of every punishment, that general preface, which conciliates a favourable attention to our prayers, is never to be omitted; because, unless they be founded on God's free mercy, they will all be unavailing. To this topic we may refer that passage of John—"If we confess our sins, he is faithful and just to forgive us our sins, and to cleanse us from all unrighteousness." (*c*) Wherefore, under the law, prayers are required to be consecrated by an atonement of blood, to render them acceptable, and to remind the people that they were unworthy of so great and honourable a privilege, till, purified from their pollutions, they should derive confidence in prayer from the mere mercy of God.

X. But when the saints sometimes appear to urge their own righteousness as an argument in their supplications with God, —as when David says, "Preserve my soul; for I am holy;" (*d*) and Hezekiah, "I beseech thee, O Lord, remember now how I have walked before thee in truth, and have done that which is

(*b*) Matt. ix. 2. (*c*) 1 John i. 9. (*d*) Psalm lxxxvi. 2.

good in thy sight," (*e*)—their only design in such modes of expression is, from their regeneration to prove themselves to be servants and sons of God, to whom he declares he will be propitious. He tells us by the Psalmist, (as we have already seen,) that "his eyes are upon the righteous, and that his ears are open unto their cry;" (*f*) and again, by the apostle, that "whatsoever we ask, we receive of him, because we keep his commandments;" (g) in which passages he does not determine the value of prayer according to the merit of works; but intends by them to establish the confidence of those who are conscious to themselves, as all believers ought to be, of unfeigned integrity and innocence. For the observation in John, made by the blind man who received his sight, that "God heareth not sinners," (*h*) is a principle of Divine truth, if we understand the word *sinners*, in the common acceptation of Scripture, to signify those who are all asleep and content in their sins, without any desire of righteousness; since no heart can ever break out into a sincere invocation of God, unaccompanied with aspirations after piety. To such promises, therefore, correspond those declarations of the saints, in which they introduce the mention of their own purity or innocence, that they may experience a manifestation to themselves of what is to be expected by all the servants of God. Besides, they are generally found in the use of this species of prayer, when before the Lord they compare themselves with their enemies, from whose iniquity they desire him to deliver them. Now, in this comparison, we need not wonder, if they produce their righteousness and simplicity of heart, in order to prevail upon him by the justice of their cause to yield the more ready assistance. We object not, therefore, to the pious heart of a good man making use before the Lord of the consciousness of his own purity for his confirmation in the promises which the Lord has given for the consolation and support of his true worshippers; but his confidence of success we wish to be independent of every consideration of personal merit, and to rest solely on the Divine clemency.

XI. The fourth and last rule is, That thus prostrate with true humility, we should nevertheless be animated to pray by the

---

(*e*) 2 Kings xx. 3. (*f*) Psalm xxxiv. 15.
(*g*) 1 John iii. 22. (*h*) John ix. 31.

certain hope of obtaining our requests. It is indeed an apparent contradiction, to connect a certain confidence of God's favour with a sense of his righteous vengeance; though these two things are perfectly consistent, if persons oppressed by their own guilt be encouraged solely by the Divine goodness. For as we have before stated, that repentance and faith, of which one terrifies, and the other exhilarates, are inseparably connected, so their union is necessary in prayer. And this agreement is briefly expressed by David: "I will come (says he) into thy house in the multitude of thy mercy; and in thy fear will I worship toward thy holy temple." (*i*) Under the "goodness of God," he comprehends faith, though not to the exclusion of fear; for his majesty not only commands our reverence, but our own unworthiness makes us forget all pride and security, and fills us with fear. I do not mean a confidence which delivers the mind from all sense of anxiety, and soothes it into pleasant and perfect tranquillity; for such a placid satisfaction belongs to those whose prosperity is equal to their wishes, who are affected by no care, corroded by no desire, and alarmed by no fear. And the saints have an excellent stimulus to calling upon God, when their necessities and perplexities harass and disquiet them, and they are almost despairing in themselves, till faith opportunely relieves them; because, amidst such troubles, the goodness of God is so glorious in their view, that though they groan under the pressure of present calamities, and are likewise tormented with the fear of greater in future, yet a reliance on it alleviates the difficulty of bearing them, and encourages a hope of deliverance. The prayers of a pious man, therefore, must proceed from both these dispositions, and must also contain and discover them both; though he must groan under present evils, and is anxiously afraid of new ones, yet at the same time he must resort for refuge to God, not doubting his readiness to extend the assistance of his hand. For God is highly incensed by our distrust, if we supplicate him for blessings which we have no expectation of receiving. There is nothing, therefore, more suitable to the nature of prayers, than that they be conformed to this rule—not to rush forward

---

(*i*) Psalm v. 7.

with temerity, but to follow the steps of faith. To this principle Christ calls the attention of us all in the following passage: "I say unto you, What things soever ye desire, when ye pray, believe that ye receive them, and ye shall have them." (*k*) This he confirms also in another place: "Whatsoever ye shall ask in prayer, believing, ye shall receive." (*l*) With which James agrees: "If any of you lack wisdom, let him ask of God, that giveth to all men liberally, and upbraideth not. But let him ask in faith, nothing wavering." (*m*) Where, by opposing "faith" to "wavering," he very aptly expresses its nature. And equally worthy of attention is what he adds, that they avail nothing, who call upon God in perplexity and doubt, and are uncertain in their minds whether they shall be heard or not; whom he even compares to waves, which are variously tossed and driven about with the wind. Whence he elsewhere calls a legitimate prayer "the prayer of faith." (*n*) Besides, when God so frequently affirms, that he will give to every man according to his faith, he implies that we can obtain nothing without faith. Finally, it is faith that obtains whatever is granted in answer to prayer. This is the meaning of that famous passage of Paul, to which injudicious men pay little attention: "How shall they call on him, in whom they have not believed? And how shall they believe in him, of whom they have not heard? So then faith cometh by hearing, and hearing by the word of God." (*o*) For by a regular deduction of prayer originally from faith, he evidently contends, that God cannot be sincerely invoked by any, but those to whom his clemency and gentleness have been revealed and familiarly discovered by the preaching of the gospel.

XII. This necessity our adversaries never consider. Therefore, when we inculcate on believers a certain confidence of mind that God is propitious and benevolent towards them, they consider us as advancing the greatest of all absurdities. But if they were in the habit of true prayer, they would certainly understand, that there can be no proper invocation of God without such a strong sense of the Divine benevolence. But since no man can fully discover the power of faith without an experience of it in

(*k*) Mark xi. 24. (*l*) Matt. xxi. 22. (*m*) James i. 5, 6. (*n*) James v. 15. (*o*) Rom. x. 14, 17.

his heart, what advantage can arise from disputing with such men, who plainly prove that they never had any other than a vain imagination? For the value and necessity of that assurance which we require, is chiefly learned by prayer; and he who does not perceive this, betrays great stupidity of conscience. Leaving, then, this class of blinded mortals, let us ever abide by the decision of Paul, that God cannot be called upon, but by those who receive from the gospel a knowledge of his mercy, and a certain persuasion that it is prepared for them. For what kind of an address would this be? "O Lord, I am truly in doubt, whether thou be willing to hear me; but since I am oppressed with anxiety, I flee to thee, that if I be worthy thou mayest assist me." This does not resemble the solicitude of the saints, whose prayers we read in the Scriptures. Nor is it agreeable to the teaching of the Holy Spirit by the apostle, who commands us "to come boldly to the throne of grace, that we may find grace;" (*p*) and informs us, that "we have boldness and access, with confidence, by the faith of Christ." (*q*) This assurance of obtaining what we implore, therefore, which is both commanded by the Lord himself, and taught by the example of the saints, it becomes us to hold fast with all our might, if we would pray to any good purpose. For that prayer alone is accepted by God, which arises (if I may use the expression) from such a presumption of faith, and is founded on an undaunted assurance of hope. He might, indeed, have contented himself with the simple mention of "faith;" yet he has not only added "confidence," but furnished that confidence with liberty or "boldness," to distinguish by this criterion between us and unbelievers, who do indeed pray to God in common with us, but entirely at an uncertainty. For which reason, the whole Church prays in the psalm, "Let thy mercy, O Lord, be upon us, according as we hope in thee." (*r*) The Psalmist elsewhere introduces the same idea: "This I know; for God is for me." (*s*) Again: "In the morning will I direct my prayer unto thee, and will look up." (*t*) For from these words we gather, that prayers are but empty sounds, if unattended by hope, from which, as from a watch-tower, we quietly look out for God. With which corre-

(*p*) Heb. iv. 16. (*q*) Ephes. iii. 12. (*r*) Psalm xxxiii. 22. (*s*) Psalm lvi. 9. (*t*) Psalm v. 3.

sponds the order of Paul's exhortation; for before exhorting believers to "pray always with all prayer and supplication in the Spirit," he first directs them to "take the shield of faith, the helmet of salvation, and the sword of the Spirit, which is the word of God." (*u*) Now, let the reader recollect, what I have before asserted, that faith is not at all weakened by being connected with an acknowledgment of our misery, poverty, and impurity. For believers feel themselves oppressed by a grievous load of sins, while destitute of every thing which could conciliate the favour of God, and burdened with much guilt, which might justly render him an object of their dread; yet they cease not to present themselves before him; nor does this experience terrify them from resorting to him, since there is no other way of access to him. For prayer was instituted, not that we might arrogantly exalt ourselves in the presence of God, or form a high opinion of any thing of our own; but that we might confess our guilt to him, and deplore our miseries with the familiarity of children confiding their complaints to their parents. The immense accumulation of our distresses should operate as so many incitements to urge us to pray; as we are taught likewise by the example of the Psalmist: "Heal my soul; for I have sinned against thee." (*v*) I confess, indeed, that the operation of such incentives would be fatal, were it not for the Divine aid; but our most benevolent Father, in his incomparable mercy, has afforded a timely remedy, that allaying all perturbation, alleviating all cares, and dispelling all fears, he might gently allure us to himself, and facilitate our approach to him, by the removal of every obstacle and every doubt.

XIII. And in the first place, when he enjoins us to pray, the commandment itself implies a charge of impious contumacy, if we disobey it. No command can be more precise than that in the psalm: "Call upon me in the day of trouble." (*w*) But as the Scripture recommends no one of the duties of piety more frequently, it is unnecessary to dwell any longer upon it. "Ask, (says our Lord,) and it shall be given you; knock, and it shall be opened unto you." (*x*) To this precept, however, there is also

---

(*u*) Ephes. vi. 16, 18.
(*v*) Psalm xli. 4.
(*w*) Psalm l. 15.
(*x*) Matt. vii. 7.

annexed a promise, which is very necessary; for though all men acknowledge obedience to be due to a precept, yet the greater part of them would neglect the calls of God, if he did not promise to be propitious to them, and even to advance to meet them. These two positions being proved, it is evident that all those who turn their backs on God, or do not directly approach him, are not only guilty of disobedience and rebellion, but also convicted of unbelief; because they distrust the promises; which is the more worthy of observation, since hypocrites, under the pretext of humility and modesty, treat the command of God with such haughty contempt as to give no credit to his kind invitation, and even defraud him of a principal part of his worship. For after having refused sacrifices, in which all holiness then appeared to consist, he declares the principal and most acceptable part of his service to be, "calling upon him in the day of trouble." Wherefore, when he requires what is due to him, and animates us to a cheerful obedience, there are no pretexts for diffidence or hesitation sufficiently specious to excuse us. The numerous texts of Scripture, therefore, which enjoin us to call upon God, are as so many banners placed before our eyes to inspire us with confidence. It were temerity to rush into the presence of God, without a previous invitation from him. He therefore opens a way for us by his own word: "I will say, It is my people; and they shall say, The Lord is my God." (*y*) We see how he leads his worshippers, and desires them to follow him; and therefore that there is no reason to fear lest the melody, which he dictates, should not be agreeable to him. Let us particularly remember this remarkable character of God, by a reliance on which we shall easily surmount every obstacle: "O thou that hearest prayer, unto thee shall all flesh come." (*z*) For what is more amiable or attractive than for God to bear this character, which assures us, that nothing is more agreeable to his nature, than to grant the requests of humble suppliants? Hence the Psalmist concludes that the way is open, not to a few only, but to all men; because he addresses all in these words: "Call upon me in the day of trouble: I will deliver thee, and thou shalt glorify me." (*a*) Ac-

(*y*) Zech. xiii. 9. (*z*) Psalm lxv. 2. (*a*) Psalm 1. 15.

cording to this rule, David, in order to obtain his request, pleads the promise that had been given him: "Thou, O Lord, hast revealed to thy servant—; therefore hath thy servant found in his heart to pray." (*b*) Whence we conclude that he would have been fearful, had he not been encouraged by the promise. So in another place he furnishes himself with this general doctrine: "He will fulfil the desire of them that fear him." (*c*) In the Psalms we may likewise observe the connection of prayer as it were interrupted, and sudden transitions made, sometimes to the power of God, sometimes to his goodness, and sometimes to the truth of his promises. It might appear as though David mutilated his prayers by an unseasonable introduction of such passages; but believers know by experience, that the ardour of devotion languishes, unless it be supported by fresh supplies; and therefore a meditation on the nature and the word of God is far from being useless in the midst of our prayers. Let us not hesitate, then, to follow the example of David in the introduction of topics calculated to reanimate languid souls with new vigour.

XIV. And it is wonderful that we are no more affected with promises so exceedingly sweet; that the generality of men, wandering through a labyrinth of errors, after having forsaken the fountain of living waters, prefer hewing out for themselves cisterns incapable of containing any water, to embracing the free offers of Divine goodness. "The name of the Lord (says Solomon) is a strong tower: the righteous runneth into it, and is safe." (*d*) And Joel, after having predicted the speedy approach of a dreadful destruction, adds this memorable sentence: "Whosoever shall call on the name of the Lord, shall be delivered;" (*e*) which we know properly refers to the course of the gospel. Scarcely one man in a hundred is induced to advance to meet the Lord. He proclaims by Isaiah, "Before they call, I will answer; and while they are yet speaking, I will hear." (*f*) And in another place he dignifies the whole Church in general with the same honour; as it belongs to all the members of Christ: "He shall call upon me and I will answer him: I will be with him in trouble: I will deliver him." (*g*) As I have before said, however,

(*b*) 2 Sam. vii. 27. (*c*) Psalm cxlv. 19. (*d*) Prov. xviii. 10.
(*e*) Joel ii. 32. (*f*) Isaiah lxv. 24. (*g*) Psalm xci. 15.

my design is not to enumerate all the texts, but to select the most remarkable, from which we may perceive the condescending kindness of God in inviting us to him, and the circumstances of aggravation attending our ingratitude, while our indolence still lingers in the midst of such powerful incitements. Wherefore let these words perpetually resound in our ears: "The Lord is nigh unto all them that call upon him, to all that call upon him in truth;" (*h*) as well as those which we have cited from Isaiah and Joel; in which God affirms, that he is inclined to hear prayers, and is delighted, as with a sacrifice of a sweet savour, when we cast our cares upon him. We derive this singular benefit from the Divine promises, when our prayers are conceived without doubt or trepidation; but in reliance on his word, whose majesty would otherwise terrify us, we venture to call upon him as our Father, because he deigns to suggest to us this most delightful appellation. Favoured with such invitations, it remains for us to know that they furnish us with sufficient arguments to enforce our petitions; since our prayers rest on no intrinsic merit; but all their worthiness, as well as all our hope of obtaining our requests, is founded in, and dependent upon, the Divine promises; so that there is no need of any other support or further anxiety. Therefore we may be fully assured, that though we equal not the sanctity so celebrated in holy patriarchs, prophets, and apostles, yet, since the command to pray is common to us as well as to them, and we are partakers of the same common faith, if we rely on the Divine word, we are associated with them in this privilege. For God's declaration, (already noticed,) that he will be gentle and merciful to all, gives all, even the most miserable, a hope of obtaining the objects of their supplications; and therefore we should remark the general forms of expression, by which no man, from the greatest to the least, is excluded; only let him possess sincerity of heart, self-abhorrence, humility, and faith; and let not our hypocrisy profane the name of God by a pretended invocation of him; our most merciful Father will not reject those whom he exhorts to approach him, and even urges by every possible mode of solicitation. Hence the argument of David's prayer,

---

(*h*) Psalm cxlv. 18.

just recited: "Thou, O Lord, hast revealed to thy servant—; therefore hath thy servant found in his heart to pray this prayer unto thee. And now, O Lord God, thou art that God, and thy words be true, and thou hast promised this goodness unto thy servant:" begin therefore and do it. (*i*) As also in another place: "Let thy kindness be according to thy word unto thy servant." (*k*) And all the Israelites together, whenever they fortify themselves with a recollection of the covenant, sufficiently declare that fear ought to be banished from our devotions, because it is contrary to the Divine injunction; and in this respect they imitated the examples of the patriarchs, particularly of Jacob, who, after having confessed himself "not worthy of the least of all the mercies" he had received from the hand of God, yet declares himself animated to pray for still greater blessings, because God had promised to grant them. (*l*) But whatever be the pretences of unbelievers, for not applying to God under the pressure of every necessity, for not seeking him or imploring his aid, they are equally chargeable with defrauding him of the honour due to him, as if they had fabricated for themselves new gods and idols; for by this conduct, they deny him to be the Author of all their blessings. On the contrary, there is nothing more efficacious to deliver believers from every scruple, than this consideration, that no impediment ought to prevent their acting according to the command of God, who declares that nothing is more agreeable to him than obedience. These observations tend more fully to elucidate what I have advanced before; that a spirit of boldness in prayer is perfectly consistent with fear, reverence, and solicitude; and that there is no absurdity in God's exalting those who are abased. This establishes an excellent agreement between those apparently repugnant forms of expression. Both Jeremiah and Daniel use this phrase: "Make prayers fall" before God; for so it is in the original. (*m*) Jeremiah also: "Let our supplication fall before thee." (*n*) Again: believers are frequently said to "lift up their prayer." (*o*) So says Hezekiah, when requesting the prophet to intercede for him. And David desires that his prayer

(*i*) 2 Sam. vii. 27, 28.
(*k*) Psalm cxix. 76.
(*l*) Gen. xxxii. 10, &c.
(*m*) Jer. xlii. 9. Dan. ix. 18.
(*n*) Jer. xlii. 2.
(*o*) 2 Kings xix. 4.

may ascend "as incense." (*p*) For though, under a persuasion of God's fatherly love, they cheerfully commit themselves to his faithfulness, and hesitate not to implore the assistance he freely promises, yet they are not impudently elated with careless security, but ascend upwards by the steps of the promises, yet in such a manner, that they still continue to be suppliant and self-abased.

XV. Here several questions are started. The Scripture relates that the Lord has complied with some prayers, which nevertheless did not arise from a calm or well-regulated heart. Jotham, for a just cause indeed, but from the impulse of rage, resentment, and revenge, devoted the inhabitants of Shechem to the destruction which afterwards fell upon them: (*q*) the Lord, by fulfilling this curse, seems to approve of such disorderly sallies of passion. Samson also was hurried away by similar fervour when he said, "O Lord, strengthen me, that I may be avenged of the Philistines." (*r*) For though there was some mixture of honest zeal, yet it was a violent, and therefore sinful, avidity of revenge which predominated. God granted the request. Whence it seems deducible, that prayers not conformable to the rules of the Divine word, are nevertheless efficacious. I reply, first, that a permanent rule is not annulled by particular examples; secondly, that peculiar emotions have sometimes been excited in a few individuals, causing a distinction between them and men in general. For the answer of Christ to his disciples, who inconsiderately wished to emulate the example of Elias, "that they knew not what spirit they were of," is worthy of observation. But we must remark, further, that God is not always pleased with the prayers which he grants; but that, as far as examples are concerned, there are undeniable evidences of the Scripture doctrine, that he succours the miserable, and hears the groans of those who under the pressure of injustice implore his aid; that he therefore executes his judgments, when the complaints of the poor arise to him, though they are unworthy of the least favourable attention. For how often, by punishing the cruelty, rapine, violence, lust, and other crimes of the impious, by restraining their audacity and fury, and even subverting their tyrannical power, has he manifestly

---

(*p*) Psalm cxli. 2. (*q*) Judges ix. 20. (*r*) Judges xvi. 28.

assisted the victims of unrighteous oppression, though they have been beating the air with supplications to an unknown God! And one of the Psalmists clearly teaches that some prayers are not ineffectual, which nevertheless do not penetrate into heaven by faith. (*s*) For he collects those prayers which necessity naturally extorts from unbelievers as well as from believers, but to which the event shows God to be propitious. Does he by such condescension testify that they are acceptable to him? No; he designs to amplify or illustrate his mercy by this circumstance, that even the requests of unbelievers are not refused; and likewise to stimulate his true worshippers to greater diligence in prayer, while they see that even the lamentations of the profane are not unattended with advantage. Yet there is no reason why believers should deviate from the rule given them by God, or envy unbelievers, as though they had made some great acquisition when they have obtained the object of their wishes. In this manner we have said that the Lord was moved by the hypocritical penitence of Ahab, in order to prove by this example how ready he is to grant the prayers of his own elect, when they seek reconciliation with him by true conversion. Therefore in the Psalms he expostulates with the Jews, because, after having experienced his propitiousness to their prayers, they had almost immediately returned to their native perverseness. (*t*) It is evident, also, from the history of the Judges, that whenever they wept, though their tears were hypocritical, yet they were delivered from the hands of their enemies. As the Lord, therefore, "maketh his sun to rise on the evil and on the good," (*u*) promiscuously, so he despises not the lamentations of those whose cause is just, and whose afflictions deserve relief. At the same time his attention to them is no more connected with salvation, than his furnishing food to the despisers of his goodness. The question relative to Abraham and Samuel is attended with more difficulty; the former of whom prayed for the inhabitants of Sodom without any Divine direction, and the latter for Saul even contrary to a plain prohibition. (*v*) The same is the case of Jeremiah, who deprecated the destruction of the city. (*w*) For though they suffered a repulse, yet it seems harsh

(*s*) Psalm cvii. (*t*) Psalm cvi. 39. (*u*) Matt. v. 45.
(*v*) Gen. xviii. 23. 1 Sam. xv. 11. (*w*) Jer. xxxii. 16, &c.

to deny them to have been under the influence of faith. But the modest reader will, I hope, be satisfied with this solution; that mindful of the general principles by which God enjoins them to be merciful even to the unworthy, they were not entirely destitute of faith, though in a particular instance their opinion may have disappointed them. Augustine has somewhere this judicious observation: "How do the saints pray in faith, when they implore of God that which is contrary to his decrees? It is because they pray according to his will, not that hidden and immutable will, but that with which he inspires them, that he may hear them in a different way, as he wisely discriminates." This is an excellent remark; because, according to his incomprehensible designs, he so regulates the events of things, that the prayers of the saints, which contain a mixture of faith and error, are not in vain. Yet this no more affords an example for imitation, than a sufficient plea to excuse the saints themselves, whom I admit to have transgressed the bounds of duty. Wherefore, when no certain promise can be found, we should present our supplications to God in a conditional way; which is implied in this petition of David: "Awake to the judgment that thou hast commanded;" (*x*) because he suggests that he was directed by a particular revelation to pray for a temporal blessing.

XVI. It will also be of use to remark, that the things I have delivered concerning the four rules for praying aright, are not required by God with such extreme rigour as to cause the rejection of all prayers, in which he does not find a perfection of faith or repentance, united with ardent zeal and well-regulated desires. We have said, that although prayer is a familiar intercourse between God and pious men, yet reverence and modesty must be preserved, that we may not give a loose to all our wishes, nor even in our desires exceed the Divine permission; and to prevent the majesty of God being lessened in our view, our minds must be raised to a pure and holy veneration of him. This no man has ever performed with the purity required; for, to say nothing of the multitude, how many complaints of David savour of intemperance of spirit! not that he would designedly remon-

(*x*) Psalm vii. 6.

strate with God, or murmur at his judgments; but he faints in consequence of his infirmity, and finds no better consolation than to pour his sorrows into the Divine bosom. Moreover, God bears with our lisping, and pardons our ignorance, whenever any inconsiderate expressions escape us; and certainly without this indulgence there could be no freedom of prayer. But though it was David's intention to submit himself wholly to the Divine will, and his patience in prayer was equal to his desire of obtaining his requests, yet we sometimes perceive the appearance and ebullition of turbulent passions, very inconsistent with the first rule we have laid down. We may discover, particularly from the conclusion of the thirty-ninth psalm, with what vehemence of grief this holy man was hurried away beyond all the bounds of propriety. "O spare me (says he) before I go hence, and be no more." (*y*) One might be ready to say, that the man, being in despair, desires nothing but the removal of God's hand, that he may putrefy in his own iniquities and miseries. He does not intend to rush into intemperance of language, or, as is usual with the reprobate, desire God to depart from him; he only complains that he cannot bear the Divine wrath. In these temptations, also, the saints often drop petitions, not sufficiently conformable to the rule of God's word, and without due reflection on what is right and proper. All prayers polluted with these blemishes deserve to be rejected; yet if the saints mourn, correct themselves, and return to themselves again, God forgives them. Thus they offend likewise against the second rule; because they frequently have to contend with their own indifference; nor do their poverty and misery sufficiently incite them to seriousness of devotion. Now, their minds frequently wander, and are almost absorbed in vanity; and they also need pardon in this respect, lest languid, or mutilated, or interrupted and desultory prayers should meet with a repulse. God has naturally impressed the minds of men with a conviction that prayers require to be attended with an elevation of heart. Hence the ceremony of elevating the hands, as before observed, which has been common in all ages and nations, and still continues; but where is the person, who, while lifting

---

(*y*) Psalm xxxix. 13.

up the hands, is not conscious of dulness, because his heart cleaves to the earth? As to praying for the remission of sins, though none of the faithful omit this article, yet they who have been truly engaged in prayers, perceive that they scarcely offer the tenth part of the sacrifices mentioned by David: "The sacrifices of God are a broken spirit; a broken and a contrite heart, O God, thou wilt not despise." (*z*) Thus they have always to pray for a twofold forgiveness; both because they are conscious of many transgressions, with which they are not so deeply affected as to be sufficiently displeased with themselves, and as they are enabled to advance in repentance and the fear of God, humbled with just sorrow for their offences, they deprecate the vengeance of the Judge. But above all, the weakness or imperfection of their faith would vitiate the prayers of believers, were it not for the Divine indulgence; but we need not wonder that this defect is forgiven by God, who frequently exercises his children with severe discipline, as if he fully designed to annihilate their faith. It is a very sharp temptation, when believers are constrained to cry, "How long wilt thou be angry against the prayer of thy people?" (*a*) as though even their prayers were so many provocations of Divine wrath. So when Jeremiah says, "God shutteth out my prayer," (*b*) he was undoubtedly agitated with severe trouble. Innumerable examples of this kind occur in the Scriptures, from which it appears that the faith of the saints is often mingled and agitated with doubts, so that amidst the exercises of faith and hope, they nevertheless betray some remains of unbelief; but since they cannot attain all that is to be wished, it becomes them to be increasingly diligent, in order that, correcting their faults, they may daily make nearer approaches to the perfect rule of prayer, and at the same time to consider into what an abyss of evils they must have been plunged, who even in their very remedies contract new diseases; since there is no prayer which God would not justly disdain, if he did not overlook the blemishes with which they are all deformed. I mention these things, not that believers may securely forgive themselves any thing sinful, but that, by severely correcting themselves, they

(*z*) Psalm li. 17. (*a*) Psalm lxxx. 4. (*b*) Lam. iii. 8.

may strive to surmount these obstacles; and that, notwithstanding the endeavours of Satan to obstruct them in all their ways, with a view to prevent them from praying, they may nevertheless break through all opposition, certainly persuaded, that, though they experience many impediments, yet God is pleased with their efforts, and approves of their prayers, provided they strenuously aim at that which they do not immediately attain.

XVII. But since there is no one of the human race worthy to present himself to God, and to enter into his presence, our heavenly Father himself, to deliver us at once from shame and fear, which might justly depress all our minds, has given us his Son Jesus Christ our Lord to be our Advocate and Mediator with him; (*c*) introduced by whom we may boldly approach him, confident, with such an Intercessor, that nothing we ask in his name will be denied us, as nothing can be denied to him by his Father. And to this must be referred all that we have hitherto advanced concerning faith; because, as the promise recommends Christ to us as the Mediator, so, unless our hope of success depend on him, it deprives itself of all the benefit of prayer. For as soon as we reflect on the terrible majesty of God, we cannot but be exceedingly afraid, and driven away from him by a consciousness of our unworthiness, till we discover Christ as the Mediator, who changes the throne of dreadful glory into a throne of grace; as the apostle also exhorts us to "come boldly unto the throne of grace, that we may obtain mercy, and find grace to help in time of need." (*d*) And as there is a rule given for calling upon God, as well as a promise that they shall be heard who call upon him, so we are particularly enjoined to invoke him in the name of Christ; and we have an express promise, that what we ask in his name we shall obtain. "Hitherto (says he) ye have asked nothing in my name: ask, and ye shall receive. At that day ye shall ask in my name; and whatsoever ye shall ask in my name, that will I do, that the Father may be glorified in the Son." (*e*) Hence it is plain beyond all controversy, that they who call upon God in any other name than that of Christ, are guilty of a contumacious neglect of his precepts, and a total disregard of his

(*c*) 1 Tim. ii. 5. 1 John ii. 1. (*d*) Heb. v. 16.
(*e*) John xvi. 24, 26; xiv. 13.

will; and that they have no promise of any success. For, as Paul says of Christ, "All the promises of God in him are yea, and in him amen;" that is, are confirmed and fulfilled. (*f*)

XVIII. And we must carefully remark the circumstance of the time when Christ commands his disciples to apply to his intercession, which was to be after his ascension to heaven; "At that day (says he) ye shall ask in my name." It is certain that from the beginning no prayers had been heard but for the sake of the Mediator. For this reason the Lord had appointed in the law, that the priest alone should enter the sanctuary, bearing on his shoulders the names of the tribes of Israel, and the same number of precious stones before his breast; but that the people should stand without in the court, and there unite their prayers with those of the priest. (*g*) The use of the sacrifice was to render their prayers effectual. The meaning, therefore, of that shadowy ceremony of the law was, that we are all banished from the presence of God, and therefore need a mediator to appear in our name, to bear us on his shoulders, and bind us to his breast, that we may be heard in his person; and, moreover, that the sprinkling of his blood purifies our prayers, which have been asserted to be otherwise never free from defilement. And we see that the saints, when they wished to obtain any thing by prayer, founded their hope on the sacrifices; because they knew them to be the confirmations of all their prayers. David says, "The Lord remember all thy offerings, and accept thy burnt-sacrifice." (*h*) Hence we conclude, that God has from the beginning been appeased by the intercession of Christ, so as to accept the devotions of believers. Why, then, does Christ assign a new period, when his disciples shall begin to pray in his name, but because this grace, being now become more illustrious, deserves to be more strongly recommended to us? In this same sense he had just before said, "Hitherto ye have asked nothing in my name; ask." (*i*) Not that they were totally unacquainted with the office of the Mediator, (since all the Jews were instructed in these first principles,) but because they did not yet clearly understand that Christ, on his ascension to heaven, would be more evidently the advocate of the Church

(*f*) 2 Cor. i. 20. (*g*) Exod. xxviii.
(*h*) Psalm xx. 3. (*i*) John xvi. 24.

than he was before. Therefore, to console their sorrow for his absence with some signal advantage, he claims the character of an advocate, and teaches them that they have hitherto wanted the principal benefit, which it shall be given them to enjoy, when they shall call upon God with greater freedom in a reliance on his intercession; as the apostle says that this new way is consecrated by his blood. (*k*) So much the more inexcusable is our perverseness, unless we embrace with the greatest alacrity such an inestimable benefit, which is particularly destined for us.

XIX. Moreover, since he is the only way of access by which we are permitted to approach God, to them who deviate from this road, and desert this entrance, there remains no other way of access to God, nor any thing on his throne but wrath, judgment, and terror. Finally, since the Father has appointed him to be our Head and Leader, they who in any respect decline or turn aside from him, endeavour, as far as they can, to deface and obliterate a character impressed by God. Thus Christ is appointed as the one Mediator, by whose intercession the Father is rendered propitious and favourable to us. The saints have likewise their intercessions, in which they mutually commend each other's interests to God, and which are mentioned by the apostle; (*l*) but these are so far from detracting any thing from the intercession of Christ, that they are entirely dependent on it. For as they arise from the affection of love, reciprocally felt by us towards each other as members of one body, so likewise they are referred to the unity of the Head. Being made also in the name of Christ, what are they but a declaration, that no man can be benefited by any prayers at all, independently of Christ's intercession? And as the intercession of Christ is no objection to our mutually pleading for each other, in our prayers in the Church, so let it be considered as a certain maxim, that all the intercessions of the whole Church should be directed to that principal one. We ought to beware of ingratitude particularly on this head, because God, pardoning our unworthiness, not only permits us to pray each one for himself, but even admits us as intercessors for one another. For, when those who richly deserve to be rejected, if they

(*k*) Heb. x. 20.

(*l*) Ephes. vi. 18, 19. 1 Tim. ii. 1.

should privately pray each for himself, are appointed by God as advocates of his Church, what pride would it betray to abuse this liberality to obscure the honour of Christ!

XX. Now, the cavil of the sophists is quite frivolous, that Christ is the Mediator of redemption, but believers of intercession; as if Christ, after performing a temporary mediation, had left to his servants that which is eternal and shall never die. They who detract so diminutive a portion of honour from him, treat him, doubtless, very favourably. But the Scripture, with the simplicity of which a pious man, forsaking these impostors, ought to be contented, speaks very differently; for when John says, "If any man sin, we have an Advocate with the Father, Jesus Christ," (*m*) does he only mean that he has been heretofore an Advocate for us, or does he not rather ascribe to him a perpetual intercession? What is intended by the assertion of Paul, that he "is even at the right hand of God, and also maketh intercession for us?" (*n*) And when he elsewhere calls him the "one Mediator between God and man," does he not refer to prayers, which he has mentioned just before?" (*o*) For having first asserted that intercessions should be made for all men, he immediately adds, in confirmation of that idea, that all have one God and one Mediator. Consistent with which is the explanation of Augustine, when he thus expresses himself: "Christian men in their prayers mutually recommend each other to the Divine regard. That person, for whom no one intercedes, while he intercedes for all, is the true and only Mediator. The apostle Paul, though a principal member under the Head, yet because he was a member of the body of Christ, and knew the great and true High Priest of the Church had entered, not typically, into the recesses within the veil, the holy of holies, but truly and really into the interior recesses of heaven, into a sanctuary not emblematical, but eternal,—Paul, I say, recommends himself to the prayers of believers. Neither does he make himself a mediator between God and the people, but exhorts all the members of the body of Christ mutually to pray for one another; since the members have a mutual solicitude for each other; and if one member suffers, the rest

(*m*) 1 John ii. 1. (*n*) Rom. viii. 34. (*o*) 1 Tim. ii. 5.

sympathize with it. And so should the mutual prayers of all the members, who are still engaged in the labours of the present state, ascend on each other's behalf to the Head, who is gone before them into heaven, and who is the propitiation for our sins. For if Paul were a mediator, the other apostles would likewise sustain the same character; and so there would be many mediators; and Paul's argument could not be supported, when he says, 'For there is one God, and one Mediator between God and men, the man Christ Jesus; in whom we also are one, if we keep the unity of the Spirit in the bond of peace.'" Again, in another place: "But if you seek a priest, he is above the heavens, where he now intercedes for you, who died for you on earth." Yet we do not dream that he intercedes for us in suppliant prostration at the Father's feet; but we apprehend, with the apostle, that he appears in the presence of God for us in such a manner, that the virtue of his death avails as a perpetual intercession for us; yet so as that, being entered into the heavenly sanctuary, he continually, till the consummation of all things, presents to God the prayers of his people, who remain, as it were, at a distance in the court.

XXI. With respect to the saints who are dead in the flesh, but live in Christ, if we attribute any intercession to them, let us not imagine that they have any other way of praying to God than by Christ, who is the only way, or that their prayers are accepted by God in any other name. Therefore, since the Scripture calls us away from all others to Christ alone,—since it is the will of our heavenly Father to gather together all things in him,—it would be a proof of great stupidity, not to say insanity, to be so desirous of procuring an admission by the saints, as to be seduced from him, without whom they have no access themselves. But that this has been practised in some ages, and is now practised wherever Popery prevails, who can deny? Their merits are frequently obtruded to conciliate the Divine favour; and in general Christ is totally neglected, and God is addressed through their names. Is not this transferring to them that office of exclusive intercession, which we have before asserted to be peculiar to Christ? Again, who, either angel or demon, ever uttered to any of the human race a syllable concerning such an intercession as they pretend? for the Scripture is perfectly silent respecting any such thing.

What reason, then, was there for its invention? Certainly, when the human mind thus seeks assistances for itself, in which it is not warranted by the word of God, it evidently betrays its want of faith. Now, if we appeal to the consciences of all the advocates for the intercession of saints, we shall find that the only cause of it is, an anxiety in their minds, as if Christ could fail of success, or be too severe in this business. By which perplexity they, in the first place, dishonour Christ, and rob him of the character of the only Mediator, which, as it has been given by the Father as his peculiar prerogative, ought therefore not to be transferred to any other. And by this very conduct they obscure the glory of his nativity, and frustrate the benefit of his cross; in a word, they divest and defraud him of the praise which is due to him for all his actions and all his sufferings; since the end of them all is, that he may really be, and be accounted, the sole Mediator. They at the same time reject the goodness of God, who exhibits himself as their Father; for he is not a father to them, unless they acknowledge Christ as their brother. Which they plainly deny, unless they believe themselves to be the objects of his fraternal affection, than which nothing can be more mild or tender. Wherefore the Scripture offers him alone to us, sends us to him, and fixes us in him. "He," says Ambrose, "is our mouth, with which we address the Father; our eye, by which we behold the Father; our right hand, by which we present ourselves to the Father. Without whose mediation, neither we, nor any of all the saints, have the least intercourse with God." If they reply, that the public prayers in the churches are finished by this conclusion, "through Christ our Lord," it is a frivolous subterfuge; because the intercession of Christ is not less profaned when it is confounded with the prayers and merits of the dead, than if it were wholly omitted, and the dead alone mentioned. Besides, in all their litanies, both verse and prose, where every honour is ascribed to dead saints, there is no mention of Christ.

XXII. But their folly rises to such a pitch, that we have here a striking view of the genius of superstition, which, when it has once shaken off the reins, places in general no limits to its excursions. For after men had begun to regard the intercession of saints, they by degrees gave to each his particular attributes, so that sometimes one, sometimes another, might be invoked as intercessor, according to the difference of the cases; then they chose each his particular saint, to whose protection they committed themselves as to the care of tutelary gods. Thus they not only set up (as the prophet anciently accused Israel) gods according to the number of their cities, (*k*) but even according to the multitude of persons. But, since the saints refer all their desires solely to the will of God, and observe it, and acquiesce in it, he must entertain foolish and carnal, and even degrading thoughts of them, who ascribes to them any other prayer, than that in which they pray for the advent of the kingdom of God; very remote from which is what they pretend concerning them—that every one of them is disposed by a private affection more particularly to regard his own worshippers. At length multitudes fell even into horrid sacrilege, by invoking them, not as subordinate promoters, but as principal agents, in their salvation. See how low wretched mortals fall, when they wander from their lawful station, the word of God. I omit the grosser monstrosities of impiety, for which, though they render them detestable to God, angels, and men, they do not yet feel either shame or grief. Prostrate before the statue or picture of Barbara, Catharine, and others, they mutter *Pater Noster*, "Our Father." This madness the pastors are so far from endeavouring to remedy or to restrain, that, allured by the charms of lucre, they approve and applaud it. But though they attempt to remove from themselves the odium of so foul a crime, yet what plea will they urge in defence of this, that Eligius and Medardus are supplicated to look down from heaven on their servants, and to assist them? and the holy Virgin to command her Son to grant their petitions? It was anciently forbidden at the Council of Carthage, that at the altar any prayers should be made directly to the saints; and it is probable that, when those holy men could not wholly subdue the force of depraved custom, they imposed this restraint, that the public prayers might not be deformed by this phrase, "Saint Peter, pray for us." But to how much greater lengths of diabolical absurdity have they proceeded, who hesitate not to transfer to dead men what exclusively belongs to God and Christ!

(*k*) Jer. ii. 28; xi. 13.

XXIII. But when they attempt to make this intercession appear to be founded on the authority of Scripture, they labour in vain. We frequently read, they say, of the prayers of angels; and not only so, but the prayers of believers are said to be carried by their hands into the presence of God. But if they would compare saints deceased to angels, they ought to prove that they are the ministering spirits who are delegated to superintend the concerns of our salvation, whose province it is to keep us in all our ways, who surround us, who advise and comfort us, who watch over us; all of which offices are committed to angels, but not to departed saints. (*l*) How preposterously they include dead saints with angels, fully appears from so many different functions, by which the Scripture distinguishes some from others. No man will presume, without previous permission, to act the part of an advocate before an earthly judge: whence, then, have worms so great a license to obtrude on God as intercessors those who are not recorded to have been appointed to that office? God has been pleased to appoint the angels to attend to our salvation, whence they frequent the sacred assemblies, and the Church is to them a theatre, in which they admire the various and "manifold wisdom of God." (*m*) Those who transfer to others that which is peculiar to them, certainly confound and pervert the order established by God, which ought to be inviolable. With equal dexterity they proceed to cite other testimonies. God said to Jeremiah, "Though Moses and Samuel stood before me, yet my mind could not be toward this people." (*n*) How, they say, could he thus have spoken concerning persons deceased, unless he knew that they were accustomed to intercede for the living? But I, on the contrary, deduce this conclusion—That since it appears that neither Moses nor Samuel interceded for the Israelites, there was then no intercession of the dead. For who of the saints must we believe to be concerned for the salvation of the people, when this ceases to be the case with Moses, who far surpassed all others in this respect while alive? But if they pursue such minute subtleties, that the dead intercede for the living, because the Lord has said, "Though they interceded," I shall argue, with far greater plausi-

(*l*) Heb. i. 14. Psalm xci. 11; xxxiv. 7.
(*m*) Ephes. iii. 10. (*n*) Jer. xv. 1.

bility, in this manner—In the people's extreme necessity, no intercession was made by Moses, of whom it is said, Though he interceded. Therefore it is highly probable, that no intercession is made by any other, since they are all so far from possessing the gentleness, kindness, and paternal solicitude of Moses. This is indeed the consequence of their cavilling, that they are wounded with the same weapons with which they thought themselves admirably defended. But it is very ridiculous, that a plain sentence should be so distorted; only because the Lord declares that he will not spare the crimes of the people, even though their cause had been pleaded by Moses or Samuel, to whose prayers he had shown himself so very propitious. This idea is very clearly deduced from a similar passage of Ezekiel—"Though these three men, Noah, Daniel, and Job, were in the land, they should deliver but their own souls by their righteousness, saith the Lord God;" (*o*) where he undoubtedly meant to signify, if two of them should return to life again; for the third was then alive, namely, Daniel, who is well known to have given an incomparable specimen of his piety, even in the flower of his youth. Let us then leave them, whom the Scripture clearly shows to have finished their course. Therefore Paul, when speaking of David, does not say that he assists posterity by his prayers, but only that "he served his own generation." (*p*)

XXIV. They further object—Shall we then divest them of every benevolent wish, who through the whole course of their lives breathed only benevolence and mercy? Truly, as I do not wish too curiously to inquire into their actions or thoughts, so it is by no means probable that they are agitated by the impulse of particular wishes, but rather that with fixed and permanent desires they aspire after the kingdom of God; which consists no less in the perdition of the impious, than in the salvation of believers. If this be true, their charity also is comprehended within the communion of the body of Christ, and extends no further than the nature of that communion permits. But though I grant that in this respect they pray for us, yet they do not therefore relinquish their own repose, to be distracted with early cares; and much less

(*o*) Ezek. xiv. 14. (*p*) Acts xiii. 36.

are they therefore to be the objects of our invocation. Neither is it a necessary consequence of this, that they must imitate the conduct of men on earth by mutually praying for one another. For this conduces to the cultivation of charity among them, while they divide, as it were, between them, and reciprocally bear their mutual necessities. And in this, indeed, they act according to God's precept, and are not destitute of his promise; which two are always the principal points in prayer. No such considerations have any relation to the dead; whom when the Lord has removed from our society, he has left us no intercourse with them, nor them, indeed, as far as our conjectures can reach, any with us. (*q*) But if any one plead, that they cannot but retain the same charity towards us, as they are united with us by the same faith, yet who has revealed that they have ears long enough to reach our voices, and eyes so perspicacious as to watch over our necessities? They talk in the schools of I know not what refulgence of the Divine countenance irradiating them, in which, as in a mirror, they behold from heaven the affairs of men. But to affirm this, especially with the presumption with which they dare to assert it, what is it but an attempt, by the infatuated dreams of our own brains, forcibly to penetrate into the secret appointments of God, without the authority of his word, and to trample the Scripture under our feet? which so frequently pronounces our carnal wisdom to be hostile to the wisdom of God; totally condemns the vanity of our mind; and directs all our reason to be laid in the dust, and the Divine will to be the sole object of our regard.

XXV. The other testimonies of Scripture which they adduce in defence of this false doctrine, they distort with the greatest perverseness. But Jacob (they say) prays that his own name, and the name of his fathers, Abraham and Isaac, might be named on his posterity. (*r*) Let us first inquire the form of this naming, or calling on their names, among the Israelites; for they do not invoke their fathers to assist them; but they beseech God to remember his servants Abraham, Isaac, and Jacob. Their example, therefore, is no vindication of those who address the saints themselves. But as these stupid mortals understand neither what it is

---

(*q*) Eccles. ix. 5, 6. (*r*) Gen. xlviii. 16.

to name the name of Jacob, nor for what reason it should be named, we need not wonder that they so childishly err even in the form itself. This phraseology more than once occurs in the Scriptures. For Isaiah says, that the name of the husband is "called upon" the wife who lives under his care and protection. The naming or calling, therefore, of the name of Abraham upon the Israelites, consists in their deducing their genealogy from him, and revering and celebrating his memory as their great progenitor. Neither is Jacob actuated by a solicitude for perpetuating the celebrity of his name, but by a knowledge that all the happiness of his posterity consisted in the inheritance of that covenant which God had made with him: and perceiving that this would be the greatest of all blessings to them, he prays that they may be numbered among his children; which is only transmitting to them the succession of the covenant. They, on their part, when they introduce the mention of this in their prayers, do not recur to the intercessions of the dead, but put the Lord in remembrance of his covenant, in which their most merciful Father has engaged to be propitious and beneficent to them, for the sake of Abraham, Isaac, and Jacob. How little the saints depended in any other sense on the merits of their fathers, is evinced by the public voice of the Church in the prophet: "Thou art our Father, though Abraham be ignorant of us, and Israel acknowledge us not: thou, O Lord, art our Father, our Redeemer." (*s*) And when they thus express themselves, they add at the same time, "O Lord, return, for thy servants' sake;" yet not entertaining a thought of any intercession, but adverting to the blessing of the covenant. But now, since we have the Lord Jesus, in whose hand the eternal covenant of mercy is not only made but confirmed to us,—whose name should we rather plead in our prayers? And since these good doctors contend that the patriarchs are in these words represented as intercessors, I wish to be informed by them, why, in such a vast multitude, no place, not even the lowest among them, is allotted to Abraham, the father of the Church? From what vile source they derive their advocates, is well known. Let them answer me by proving it right, that Abraham, whom God has

---

(*s*) Isaiah lxiii. 16.

preferred to all others, and elevated to the highest degree of honour, should be neglected and suppressed. The truth is, that since this practice was unknown in the ancient Church, they thought proper, in order to conceal its novelty, to be silent respecting the ancient fathers; as though the difference of names were a valid excuse for a recent and corrupt custom. But the objection urged by some, that God is entreated to have mercy on the people for the sake of David, is so far from supporting their error, that it is a decisive refutation of it. For if we consider the character sustained by David, he is selected from the whole company of the saints, that God may fulfil the covenant which he made with him; so that it refers to the covenant, rather than to the person, and contains a figurative declaration of the sole intercession of Christ. For it is certain that what was peculiar to David, as being a type of Christ, is inapplicable to any others.

XXVI. But it seems that some are influenced by the frequent declarations which we read, that the prayers of the saints are heard. Why? Truly because they have prayed. "They cried unto thee," says the Psalmist, "and were delivered; they trusted in thee, and were not confounded." (*t*) Therefore, let us likewise pray after their example, that we may obtain a similar audience. But these men preposterously argue, that none will be heard but such as have been once already heard. How much more properly does James say, "Elias was a man subject to like passions as we are, and he prayed earnestly that it might not rain; and it rained not on the earth by the space of three years and six months. And he prayed again, and the heaven gave rain, and the earth brought forth her fruit." (*u*) What! does he infer any peculiar privilege of Elias, to which we should have recourse? Not at all; but he shows the perpetual efficacy of pure and pious prayer, to exhort us to pray in a similar manner. For we put a mean construction on the promptitude and benignity of God in hearing them, unless we be encouraged by such instances to a firmer reliance on his promises; in which he promises to hear, not one or two, or even a few, but all who call upon his name. And this ignorance is so much the less excusable, because they appear almost professedly

(*t*) Psalm xxii. 5.

(*u*) James v. 17, 18.

to disregard so many testimonies of Scripture. David experienced frequent deliverances by the Divine power; was it that he might arrogate it to himself, in order to deliver us by his interposition? He makes some very different declarations: "The righteous shall compass me about; for thou shalt deal bountifully with me." (*x*) Again: "They looked unto him, and were lightened; and their faces were not ashamed. This poor man cried, and the Lord heard him, and saved him out of all his troubles." (*y*) The Psalms contain many such prayers, in which he implores God to grant his requests from this consideration, that the righteous may not be put to shame, but may be encouraged by his example to entertain a good hope. Let us be contented at present with one instance: "For this shall every one that is godly pray unto thee in a time when thou mayest be found;" (*z*) a text which I have the more readily cited, because the hireling and cavilling advocates of Popery have not been ashamed to plead it to prove the intercession of the dead. As though David had any other design than to show the effect which would proceed from the Divine clemency and goodness when his prayers should be heard. And in general it must be maintained, that an experience of the grace of God, both to ourselves and to others, affords no small assistance to confirm our faith in his promises. I do not recite numerous passages, where he proposes to himself the past blessings of God as a ground of present and future confidence, since they will naturally occur to those who peruse the Psalms. Jacob by his example had long before taught the same lesson: "I am not worthy of the least of all the mercies, and of all the truth, which thou hast showed unto thy servant; for with my staff I passed over this Jordan; and now I am become two bands." (*a*) He mentions the promise indeed, but not alone; he likewise adds the effect, that he may in future confide with the greater boldness in the continuance of the Divine goodness towards him. For God is not like mortals, who grow weary of their liberality, or whose wealth is exhausted; but is to be estimated by his own nature, as is judiciously done by David, when he says, "Thou hast redeemed me, O Lord God of truth." (*b*) After ascribing to him the praise of his

(*x*) Psalm cxlii. 7. (*y*) Psalm xxxiv. 5, 6. (*z*) Psalm xxxii. 6.
(*a*) Gen. xxxii. 10. (*b*) Psalm xxxi. 5.

salvation, he adds, that he is a God of truth; because, unless he were perpetually and uniformly consistent with himself, there could not be derived from his benefits a sufficient argument for confiding in him, and praying to him. But when we know that every act of assistance, which he affords us, is a specimen and proof of his goodness and faithfulness, we shall have no reason to fear lest our hopes be confounded or our expectations disappointed.

XXVII. Let us conclude this argument in the following manner: Since the Scripture represents the principal part of Divine worship to be an invocation of God, as he, in preference to all sacrifices, requires of us this duty of piety, no prayer can without evident sacrilege be directed to any other. Wherefore also the Psalmist says, "If we have stretched out our hands to a strange god, shall not God search this out?" (*c*) Besides, since God will only be invoked in faith, and expressly commands prayers to be conformed to the rule of his word; finally, since faith founded on the word is the source of true prayer,—as soon as the least deviation is made from the word, there must necessarily be an immediate corruption of prayer. But it has been already shown, that if the whole Scripture be consulted, this honour is there claimed for God alone. With respect to the office of intercession, we have also seen, that it is peculiar to Christ, and that no prayer is acceptable to God, unless it be sanctified by this Mediator. And though believers mutually pray to God for their brethren, we have proved that this derogates nothing from the sole intercession of Christ; because they all commend both themselves and others to God in a reliance upon it. Moreover we have argued, that this is injudiciously applied to the dead, of whom we nowhere read that they are commanded to pray for us. The Scripture frequently exhorts us to the mutual performance of this duty for each other; but concerning the dead there is not even a syllable; and James, by connecting these two things, "Confess your faults one to another, and pray one for another," tacitly excludes the dead. (*d*) Wherefore, to condemn this error, this one reason is sufficient, that right prayer originates in faith, and that faith is

(*c*) Psalm xliv. 20, 21. (*d*) James v. 16.

produced by hearing the word of God, where there is no mention of this fictitious intercession; for the temerity of superstition has chosen itself advocates, who were not of Divine appointment. For whilst the Scripture abounds with many forms of prayer, there is not to be found an example of this advocacy, without which the Papists believe there can be no prayer at all. Besides, it is evident that this superstition has arisen from a want of faith, because they either were not content with Christ as their intercessor, or entirely denied him this glory. The latter of these is easily proved from their impudence; for they adduce no argument more valid to show that we need the mediation of the saints, than when they object that we are unworthy of familiar access to God. Which indeed we acknowledge to be strictly true; but we thence conclude, that they rob Christ of every thing, who consider his intercession as unavailing without the assistance of George and Hippolytus, and other such phantasms.

XXVIII. But though prayer is properly restricted to wishes and petitions, yet there is so great an affinity between petition and thanksgiving, that they may be justly comprehended under the same name. For the species which Paul enumerates, fall under the first member of this division. In requests and petitions we pour out our desires before God, imploring those things which tend to the propagation of his glory and the illustration of his name, as well as those benefits which conduce to our advantage. In thanksgiving we celebrate his beneficence towards us with due praises, acknowledging all the blessings we have received as the gifts of his liberality. Therefore David has connected these two parts together: "Call upon me in the day of trouble: I will deliver thee, and thou shalt glorify me." (*e*) The Scripture, not without reason, enjoins us the continual use of both; for we have elsewhere said that our want is so great, and experience itself proclaims that we are molested and oppressed on every side with such numerous and great perplexities, that we all have sufficient cause for unceasing sighs, and groans, and ardent supplications to God. For though they enjoy a freedom from adversity, yet the guilt of their sins, and the innumerable assaults of temptation, ought to

(*e*) Psalm l. 15.

stimulate even the most eminent saints to pray for relief. But of the sacrifice of praise and thanksgiving there can be no interruption, without guilt; since God ceases not to accumulate on us his various benefits, according to our respective cases, in order to constrain us, inactive and sluggish as we are, to the exercise of gratitude. Finally, we are almost overwhelmed with such great and copious effusions of his beneficence; we are surrounded, whithersoever we turn our eyes, by such numerous and amazing miracles of his hand, that we never want matter of praise and thanksgiving. And to be a little more explicit on this point, since all our hopes and all our help are in God, (which has already been sufficiently proved,) so that we cannot enjoy prosperity, either in our persons or in any of our affairs, without his benediction,—it becomes us assiduously to commend to him ourselves and all our concerns. Further, whatever we think, speak, or act, let all our thoughts, words, and actions be under his direction, subject to his will, and finally in hope of his assistance. For the curse of God is denounced on all, who deliberate and decide on any enterprise in a reliance on themselves or on any other, who engage in or attempt to begin any undertaking independently of his will, and without invoking his aid. And since it has already been several times observed, that he is justly honoured when he is acknowledged to be the Author of all blessings, it thence follows that they should all be so received from his hand, as to be attended with unceasing thanksgiving; and that there is no other proper method of using the benefits which flow to us from his goodness, but by continual acknowledgments of his praise, and unceasing expressions of our gratitude. For Paul, when he declares that they are "sanctified by the word of God and prayer," at the same time implies, that they are not at all holy and pure to us without the word and prayer; (*f*) the word being metonymically used to denote faith. Wherefore David, after experiencing the goodness of the Lord, beautifully declares, "He hath put a new song in my mouth;" (*g*) in which he certainly implies that we are guilty of a criminal silence, if we omit to praise him for any benefit; since, in every blessing he bestows on us, he gives

(*f*) 1 Tim. iv. 5. (*g*) Psalm xl. 3.

us additional cause to bless his name. Thus also Isaiah, proclaiming the unparalleled grace of God, exhorts believers to a new and uncommon song. (*h*) In which sense David elsewhere says, "O Lord, open thou my lips; and my mouth shall show forth thy praise." (*i*) Hezekiah likewise, and Jonah, declare that the end of their deliverance shall be to sing the Divine goodness in the temple. (*k*) David prescribes the same general rule for all the saints. "What shall I render (says he) unto the Lord for all his benefits towards me? I will take the cup of salvation, and call upon the name of the Lord." (*l*) And this is followed by the Church in another psalm: "Save us, O Lord our God, to give thanks unto thy holy name, and to triumph in thy praise." (*m*) Again: "He will regard the prayer of the destitute, ard not despise their prayer. This shall be written for the generation to come; and the people which shall be created shall praise the Lord. To declare the name of the Lord in Zion, and his praise in Jerusalem." (*n*) Moreover, whenever believers entreat the Lord to do any thing "for his name's sake," as they profess themselves unworthy to obtain any blessing on their own account, so they lay themselves under an obligation to thanksgiving; and promise that the Divine beneficence shall be productive of this proper effect on them, even to cause them to celebrate its fame. Thus Hosea, speaking of the future redemption of the Church, addresses the Lord: "Take away all iniquity, and receive us graciously; so will we render the calves of our lips." (*o*) Nor do the Divine blessings only claim the praises of the tongue, but naturally conciliate our love. "I love the Lord (says David) because he hath heard my voice and my supplications." (*p*) In another place also, enumerating the assistances he had experienced, "I will love thee, O Lord, my strength." (*q*) Nor will any praises ever please God, but such as flow from this ardour of love. We must likewise remember the position of Paul, that all petitions, to which thanksgiving is not annexed, are irregular and faulty. For thus he speaks: "In every thing by prayer and supplication with thanks-

(*h*) Isaiah xlii. 10. (*i*) Psalm li. 15.
(*k*) Isaiah xxxviii. 20. Jonah ii. 9.
(*l*) Psalm cxvi. 12, 13. (*m*) Psalm cvi. 47. (*n*) Psalm cii. 17, &c.
(*o*) Hosea xiv. 2. (*p*) Psalm cxvi. 1. (*q*) Psalm xviii. 1.

giving, let your requests be made known unto God." (*r*) For since moroseness, weariness, impatience, pungent sorrow and fear, impel many to mutter petitions, he enjoins such a regulation of the affections, that believers may cheerfully bless God, even before they have obtained their requests. If this connection ought to exist in circumstances apparently adverse, God lays us under a still more sacred obligation to sing his praises, whenever he grants us the enjoyment of our wishes. But as we have asserted that our prayers, which had otherwise been defiled, are consecrated by the intercession of Christ, so the apostle, when he exhorts us "by Christ to offer the sacrifice of praise," (*s*) admonishes us that our lips are not sufficiently pure to celebrate the name of God, without the intervention of the priesthood of Christ. Whence we infer, how prodigious must be the fascination of the Papists, the majority of whom wonder that Christ is called an Advocate. This is the reason why Paul directs to "pray without ceasing," and "in every thing to give thanks;" (*t*) because he desires that all men, with all possible assiduity, at every time and in every place, and in all circumstances and affairs, may direct their prayers to God, expecting all from him, and ascribing to him the praise of all, since he affords us perpetual matter of prayer and praise.

XXIX. But this diligence in prayer, although it chiefly respects the particular and private devotions of each individual, has, notwithstanding, some reference also to the public prayers of the Church. But these cannot be unceasing, nor ought they to be conducted otherwise than according to the polity which is appointed by the common consent. This, indeed, I confess. For therefore also certain hours are fixed and prescribed, though indifferent with God, yet necessary to the customs of men, that the benefit of all may be regarded, and all the affairs of the Church be administered, according to the direction of Paul, "decently and in order." (*u*) But this by no means prevents it from being the duty of every Church often to stimulate themselves to a greater frequency of prayer, and also to be inflamed with more ardent devotion on the pressure of any necessity unusually great. But

(*r*) Phil. iv. 6.
(*s*) Heb. xiii. 15.
(*t*) 1 Thess. v. 17, 18.
(*u*) 1 Cor. xiv. 40.

the place to speak of perseverance, which is nearly allied to unceasing diligence, will be towards the end. Moreover these things afford no encouragement to those vain repetitions which Christ has chosen to interdict us; (*x*) for he does not forbid us to pray long or frequently, or with great fervour of affection; but he forbids us to confide in our ability to extort any thing from God by stunning his ears with garrulous loquacity, as though he were to be influenced by the arts of human persuasion. For we know that hypocrites, who do not consider that they are concerned with God, are as pompous in their prayers as in a triumph. For that Pharisee, who thanked God that he was not like other men, (*y*) undoubtedly flattered himself in the eyes of men, as if he wished to gain by his prayer the reputation of sanctity. Hence that βαττολογια (*vain repetition*) which from a similar cause at present prevails among the Papists; while some vainly consume the time by reiterating the same oraisons, and others recommend themselves among the vulgar by a tedious accumulation of words. Since this garrulity is a puerile mocking of God, we need not wonder that it is prohibited in the Church, that nothing may be heard there but what is serious, and proceeds from the very heart. Very similar to this corrupt practice is another, which Christ condemns at the same time; that hypocrites, for the sake of ostentation, seek after many witnesses of their devotions, and rather pray in the market-place, than that their prayers should want the applause of the world. But as it has been already observed that the end of prayer is to elevate our minds towards God, both in a confession of his praise and in a supplication of his aid, we may learn from this that its principal place is in the mind and heart; or, rather, that prayer itself is the desire of the inmost heart, which is poured out and laid before God the searcher of hearts. Wherefore our heavenly Teacher, as has already been mentioned, when he intended to deliver the best rule respecting prayer, gave the following command: "Enter into thy closet, and when thou hast shut thy door, pray to thy Father which is in secret; and thy Father which seeth in secret shall reward thee openly." (*z*) For when he has dissuaded from imitating the ex-

(*x*) Matt. vi. 7. (*y*) Luke xviii. 11. (*z*) Matt. vi. 6.

ample of hypocrites, who endeavoured by the ambitious ostentation of their prayers to gain the favour of men, he immediately adds a better direction, which is, to enter into our closet, and there to pray with the door shut. In which words, as I understand them, he has taught us to seek retirement, that we may be enabled to descend into our own hearts, with all our powers of reflection, and promised us that God, whose temples our bodies ought to be, will accede to the desires of our souls. For he did not intend to deny the expediency of praying also in other places; but shows that prayer is a kind of secret thing, which lies principally in the heart, and requires a tranquillity of mind undisturbed by all cares. It was not without reason, therefore, that the Lord himself, when he would engage in an unusual vehemence of devotion, retired to some solitary place, far from the tumult of men; but with a view to admonish us by his own example, that we ought not to neglect these helps, by which our hearts, naturally too inconstant, are more intensely fixed on the devotional exercise. But notwithstanding, as he did not refrain from praying even in the midst of a multitude, if at any time the occasion required it, so we, in all places where it may be necessary, should "lift up holy hands." (*a*) And so it is to be concluded, that whoever refuses to pray in the solemn assembly of the saints, knows nothing of private prayer, either solitary or domestic. And again, that he who neglects solitary and private prayer, how sedulously soever he may frequent the public assemblies, only forms there such as are mere wind, because he pays more deference to the opinion of men than to the secret judgment of God. In the mean time, that the common prayers of the Church might not sink into contempt, God anciently distinguished them by splendid titles, especially when he called the temple a "house of prayer." (*b*) For by this expression he taught both that the duty of prayer is a principal part of his worship, and that the temple had been erected as a standard for believers, in order that they might engage in it with one consent. There was also added a remarkable promise: "Praise waiteth for thee, O God, in Sion; and unto thee shall the vow be performed;" (*c*) in which words the Psalmist informs us that

(*a*) 1 Tim. ii. 8. (*b*) Isaiah lvi. 7. (*c*) Psalm lxv. 1.

the prayers of the Church are never in vain, because the Lord supplies his people with perpetual matter of praise and joy. But though the legal shadows have ceased, yet since it has been the Divine will by this ceremony to maintain a unity of faith among us also, the same promise undoubtedly belong to us, Christ having confirmed it with his own mouth, and Paul having represented it as perpetually valid.

XXX. Now, as God in his word commands believers to unite in common prayers, so also it is necessary that public temples be appointed for performing them; where they who refuse to join with the people of God in their devotions, have no just reason for abusing this pretext, that they enter into their closets, in obedience to the Divine mandate. For he who promises to grant whatever shall be implored by two or three persons convened in his name, (*d*) proves that he is far from despising prayers offered in public; provided they be free from ostentation and a desire of human applause, and accompanied with a sincere and real affection dwelling in the secret recesses of the heart. If this be the legitimate use of temples, as it certainly is, there is need of great caution, lest we either consider them as the proper habitations of the Deity, where he may be nearer to us to hear our prayers,—an idea which has begun to be prevalent for several ages,—or ascribe to them I know not what mysterious sanctity, which might be supposed to render our devotions more holy in the Divine view. For since we are ourselves the true temples of God, we must pray within ourselves, if we wish to invoke him in his holy temple. But let us, who are directed to worship the Lord "in spirit and in truth," (*e*) without any difference of place, relinquish those gross ideas of religion to the Jews or pagans. There was, indeed, anciently a temple dedicated, by Divine command, to the oblation of prayers and sacrifices: at that time the truth was figuratively concealed under such shadows; but now, having been plainly discovered to us, it no longer permits an exclusive attachment to any material temple. Nor, indeed, was the temple recommended to the Jews that they might enclose the Divine presence within its walls, but that they might be employed in contemplating a rep-

---

(*d*) Matt. xviii. 20. (*e*) John iv. 23.

resentation of the true temple. Therefore Isaiah and Stephen have sharply reprehended those who suppose that God dwells in any respect "in temples made with hands." (*f*)

XXXI. Hence it is moreover clearly evident, that neither voice nor singing, if used in prayer, has any validity, or produces the least benefit with God, unless it proceed from the inmost desire of the heart. But they rather provoke his wrath against us, if they be only emitted from the lips and throat; since that is an abuse of his sacred name, and a derision of his majesty; as we conclude from the words of Isaiah, which, though their meaning be more extensive, contain also a reproof of this offence: "The Lord said, Forasmuch as this people draw near me with their mouth, and with their lips do honour me, but have removed their heart far from me, and their fear toward me is taught by the precept of men,—therefore, behold, I will proceed to do a marvellous work among this people, even a marvellous work and a wonder; for the wisdom of their wise men shall perish, and the understanding of their prudent men shall be hid." (*g*) Nor do we here condemn the use of the voice, or singing, but rather highly recommend them, provided they accompany the affection of the heart. For they exercise the mind in Divine meditation, and fix the attention of the heart; which by its lubricity and versatility is easily relaxed and distracted to a variety of objects, unless it be supported by various helps. Besides, as the glory of God ought in some respect to be manifested in every part of our bodies, to this service, both in singing and in speaking, it becomes us especially to addict and devote our tongues, which were created for the express purpose of declaring and celebrating the Divine praises. Nevertheless the principal use of the tongue is in the public prayers which are made in the congregations of believers; the design of which is, that with one common voice, and as it were with the same mouth, we may all at once proclaim the glory of God, whom we worship in one spirit and with the same faith; and this is publicly done, that all interchangeably, each one of his brother, may receive the confession of faith, and be invited and stimulated by his example.

XXXII. Now, the custom of singing in churches (to speak of

(*f*) Isaiah lxvi. 1. Acts vii. 48. (*g*) Isaiah xxix. 13, 14. Matt. xv. 8, 9.

it by the way) not only appears to be very ancient, but that it was even used by the apostles, may be concluded from these words of Paul: "I will sing with the spirit, and I will sing with the understanding also." (*h*) Again, to the Colossians: "Teaching and admonishing one another in psalms, and hymns, and spiritual songs, singing with grace in your hearts to the Lord." (*i*) For in the former passage he inculcates singing with the voice and with the heart; and in the latter he recommends spiritual songs, which may conduce to the mutual edification of the saints. Yet that it was not universal is proved by Augustine, who relates that in the time of Ambrose, the church at Milan first adopted the practice of singing, when, during the persecution of the orthodox faith by Justina, the mother of Valentinian, the people were unusually assiduous in their vigils; and that the other Western churches followed. For he had just before mentioned that this custom had been derived from the churches of the East. He signifies also, in the second book of his Retractions, that in his time it was received in Africa. "One Hilary, (says he,) who held the tribunitial office, took every opportunity of loading with malicious censures the custom which was then introduced at Carthage, that hymns from the Book of Psalms should be sung at the altar, either before the oblation, or while that which had been offered was distributed to the people. In obedience to the commands of my brethren, I answered him." And certainly if singing be attempered to that gravity which becomes the presence of God and of angels, it adds a dignity and grace to sacred actions, and is very efficacious in exciting the mind to a true concern and ardour of devotion. Yet great caution is necessary, that the ears be not more attentive to the modulation of the notes, than the mind to the spiritual import of the words. With which danger Augustine confesses himself to have been so effected, as sometimes to have wished for the observance of the custom instituted by Athanasius, who directed that the reader should sound the words with such a gentle inflection of voice, as would be more nearly allied to rehearsing than to singing. But when he recollected the great benefit which himself had received from singing, he inclined to the other side.

(*h*) 1 Cor. xiv. 15. (*i*) Col. iii. 16.

With the observance, therefore, of this limitation, it is without doubt an institution of great solemnity and usefulness. As, on the reverse, whatever music is composed only to please and delight the ear, is unbecoming the majesty of the Church, and cannot but be highly displeasing to God.

XXXIII. Hence also it plainly appears, that public prayers are to be composed, not in Greek among the Latins, nor in Latin among the French or English, as has hitherto been universally practised; but in the vernacular tongue, which may be generally understood by the whole congregation; for it ought to be conducted to the edification of the whole Church, to whom not the least benefit can result from sounds which they do not understand. But they who disregard the voice both of charity and of humanity, ought at least to discover some little respect for the authority of Paul, whose words are free from all ambiguity: "When thou shalt bless with the Spirit, how shall he that occupieth the room of the unlearned say Amen at thy giving of thanks, seeing he understandeth not what thou sayest? For thou verily givest thanks well, but the other is not edified." (*k*) Who, then, can sufficiently wonder at the unbridled license of the Papists, who, notwithstanding this apostolic caution against it, are not afraid to bellow their verbose prayers in a foreign language, of which they neither sometimes understand a syllable themselves, nor wish a syllable to be understood by others! But Paul directs to a different practice: "What is it then? (says he) I will pray with the spirit, and I will pray with the understanding also: I will sing with the spirit, and I will sing with the understanding also." (*l*) Signifying by the word *spirit* the peculiar gift of tongues, which was abused by some of its possessors, when they separated it from understanding. Thus it must be fully admitted, that both in public and in private prayer, the tongue, unaccompanied by the heart, cannot but be highly displeasing to God; and likewise that the mind ought to be incited, in the ardour of meditation, to rise to a much higher elevation than can ever be attained by the expression of the tongue; lastly, that the tongue is indeed not necessary to private prayer, any further than as the mind is insufficient to

---

(*k*) 1 Cor. xiv. 16, 17. (*l*) 1 Cor. xiv. 15.

arouse itself, or as the vehemence of its emotions irresistibly carries the tongue along with them. For though some of the best prayers are not vocal, yet it is very common, under strong emotions, for the tongue to break forth into sounds, and the other members into gestures, without the least ostentation. Hence the uncertain muttering of Hannah, (*m*) somewhat similar to which is experienced by the saints in all ages, when they break forth into abrupt and imperfect sounds. The corporeal gestures usually observed in prayer, such as kneeling and uncovering the head, are customs designed to increase our reverence of God.

XXXIV. Now, we must learn not only a certain rule, but also the form of praying; even that which our heavenly Father has given us by his beloved Son; (*n*) in which we may recognize his infinite goodness and clemency. For beside advising and exhorting us to seek him in all our necessities, as children, whenever they are afflicted with any distress, are accustomed to have recourse to the protection of their parents; seeing that we did not sufficiently perceive how great was our poverty, what it was right to implore, or what would be suitable to our condition, he has provided a remedy even for this our ignorance, and abundantly supplied the deficiencies of our capacity. For he has prescribed for us a form, in which he gives a statement of all that it is lawful to desire of him, all that is conducive to our benefit, and all that it is necessary to ask. From this kindness of his, we derive great consolation in the persuasion that we pray for nothing absurd, nothing injurious or unseasonable; in a word, nothing but what is agreeable to him; since our petitions are almost in his own words. Plato, observing the ignorance of men in presenting their supplications to God, which if granted were frequently very detrimental to them, pronounces this to be the best method of praying, borrowed from an ancient poet: "King Jupiter, give us those things which are best, whether we pray for them or not; but command evil things to remain at a distance from us, even though we implore them." And indeed the wisdom of that heathen is conspicuous in this instance, since he considers it as very dangerous to supplicate the Lord to gratify all the dictates of

---

(*m*) 1 Sam. i. 13. (*n*) Matt. vi. 9. Luke xi. 2.

our appetites; and at the same time discovers our infelicity, who cannot, without danger, even open our mouths in the presence of God, unless we be instructed by the Spirit in the right rule of prayer. (*o*) And this privilege deserves to be the more highly valued by us, since the only begotten Son of God puts words into our mouths, which may deliver our minds from all hesitation.

XXXV. This form or rule of prayer, whichever appellation be given to it, is composed of six petitions. For my reason for not agreeing with those who divide it into seven parts is, that the Evangelist appears, by the insertion of the adversative conjunction, to connect together these two clauses; as though he had said, Suffer us not to be oppressed with temptation, but rather succour our weakness, and deliver us, that we may not fall. The ancient writers of the Church also are of our opinion; so that what is now added in Matthew in the seventh place, must be explained as belonging to the sixth petition. Now, though the whole prayer is such, that in every part of it the principal regard must be paid to the glory of God, yet to this the first three petitions are particularly devoted, and to this alone we ought to attend in them, without any consideration of our own interest. The remaining three concern ourselves, and are expressly assigned to supplications for those things which tend to our benefit. As when we pray that God's name may be hallowed, since he chooses to prove whether our love and worship of him be voluntary, or dictated by mercenary motives, we must then think nothing of our own interest, but his glory must be proposed as the only object of our fixed attention; nor is it lawful for us to be differently affected in the other petitions of this class. And this indeed conduces to our great benefit; because, when the Divine name is hallowed or sanctified as we pray, it becomes likewise our sanctification. But our eyes should overlook, and be, as it were, blind to such advantage, so as not to pay the least regard to it. And even if we were deprived of all hope of private benefit, yet this hallowing, and the other things which pertain to the glory of God, ought still to be the objects of our desires and of our prayers. This is conspicuous in the ex-

(*o*) Rom. viii. 26, 27.

amples of Moses and Paul, (*p*) who felt a pleasure in averting their minds and eyes from themselves, and in praying with vehement and ardent zeal for their own destruction, that they might promote the kingdom and glory of God even at the expense of their own happiness. On the other hand, when we pray that our daily bread may be given us, although we wish for what is beneficial to ourselves, yet here also we ought principally to aim at the glory of God, so as not even to ask it, unless it tend to his glory. Now, let us attempt an explanation of the prayer itself.

XXXVI. Our Father, who art in heaven, &c. The first idea that occurs is, what we have before asserted, that we ought never to present a prayer to God but in the name of Christ, since no other name can recommend it to his regard. For by calling God our Father, we certainly plead the name of Christ. For with what confidence could any one call God his Father? who could proceed to such a degree of temerity, as to arrogate to himself the dignity of a son of God, if we had not been adopted as the children of his grace in Christ? who, being his true Son, has been given by him to us as our brother, that the character which properly belongs to him by nature, may become ours by the blessing of adoption, if we receive this inestimable favour with a steady faith; as John says, that to them is given "power to become the sons of God, even to them that believe on the name of the only begotten of the Father." (*q*) Therefore he denominates himself our Father, and wishes us to give him the same appellation; delivering us from all diffidence by the great sweetness of this name, since the affection of love can nowhere be found in a stronger degree than in the heart of a father. Therefore he could not give us a more certain proof of his infinite love towards us, than by our being denominated the sons of God. But his love to us is as much greater and more excellent than all the love of our parents, as he is superior to all men in goodness and mercy; (*r*) so that though all the fathers in the world, divested of every emotion of paternal affection, should leave their children destitute, he will never forsake us, because "he cannot deny himself." (*s*) For we

(*p*) Exod. xxxii. 32. Rom. ix. 3. (*q*) John i. 12, 14.
(*r*) 1 John iii. 1. Psalm xxvii. 10. Isaiah lxiii. 16. (*s*) 2 Tim. ii. 13.

have his promise, "If ye, then, being evil, know how to give good gifts unto your children, how much more shall your Father which is in heaven?" (*t*) Again, in the prophet: "Can a woman forget her child? Yea, they may forget, yet will I not forget thee." (*u*) But if we are his sons, then, as a son cannot commit himself to the protection of a stranger and an alien, without at the same time complaining of the cruelty or poverty of his father, so neither can we seek supplies for our wants from any other quarter than from him, without charging him with indigence and inability or with cruelty and excessive austerity.

XXXVII. Neither let us plead that we are justly terrified by a consciousness of our sins, which may cause even a merciful, kind Father to be daily offended with us. For if, among men, a son can conduct his cause with his father by no better advocate, can conciliate and recover his lost favour by no better mediator, than by approaching him as an humble suppliant, acknowledging his own guilt, and imploring his father's mercy, (for the bowels of a father could not conceal their emotions at such supplications,) what will he do, who is "the Father of mercies, and the God of all comfort?" (*x*) Will he not hear the cries and groans of his children when they deprecate his displeasure for themselves, especially since it is to this that he invites and exhorts us; rather than attend to any intercessions of others, to which they resort in great consternation, not without some degree of despair, arising from a doubt of the kindness and clemency of their Father? Of this exuberance of paternal kindness, he gives us a beautiful representation in a parable; (*y*) where a father meets and embraces a son who had alienated himself from his family, who had dissolutely lavished his substance, who had grievously offended him in every respect: nor does he wait till he actually supplicates for pardon, but anticipates him, recognizes him when returning at a great distance, voluntarily runs to meet him, consoles him, and receives him into favour. For by proposing to our view an example of such great kindness in a man, he intended to teach us how much more abundant compassion we ought, notwithstanding our ingratitude, rebellion, and wickedness, to ex-

(*t*) Matt. vii. 11.
(*u*) Isaiah xlix. 15.
(*x*) 2 Cor. i. 3.
(*y*) Luke xv. 11, &c.

pect from him, who is not only our Father, but the most benevolent and merciful of all fathers, provided we only cast ourselves on his mercy. And to give us the more certain assurance that he is such a Father, if we be Christians, he will be called not only "Father," but expressly "Our Father;" as though we might address him in the following manner: O Father, whose affection towards thy children is so strong, and whose readiness to pardon them is so great, we thy children invoke thee and pray to thee, under the assurance and full persuasion that thou hast no other than a paternal affection towards us, how unworthy soever we are of such a Father. But because the contracted capacities of our minds cannot conceive of a favour of such immense magnitude, we not only have Christ as the pledge and earnest of adoption, but as a witness of this adoption he gives us the Spirit, by whom we are enabled with a loud voice freely to cry, "Abba, Father." (*z*) Whenever, therefore, we may be embarrassed by any difficulty, let us remember to supplicate him, that he will correct our timidity, and give us this spirit of magnanimity to enable us to pray with boldness.

XXXVIII. But since we are not instructed, that every individual should appropriate him to himself exclusively as his Father, but rather that we should all in common call him Our Father, we are thereby admonished how strong a fraternal affection ought to prevail among us, who, by the same privilege of mercy and free grace, are equally the children of such a Father. For if we all have one common Father, (*a*) from whom proceeds every blessing we enjoy, there ought to be nothing exclusively appropriated by any among us, but what we should be ready to communicate to each other with the greatest alacrity of heart, whenever necessity requires. Now, if we desire, as we ought, to exert ourselves for our mutual assistance, there is nothing in which we can better promote the interests of our brethren, than by commending them to the providential care of our most benevolent Father, with whose mercy and favour no other want can be experienced. And, indeed, this is a debt which we owe to our Father himself. For as he who truly and cordially loves any father

(*z*) Gal. iv. 6. (*a*) Matt. xxiii. 9.

of a family, feels likewise a love and friendship for his whole household, in the same manner, our zeal and affection towards this heavenly Father must be shown towards his people, his family, his inheritance, whom he has dignified with the honourable appellation of the "fulness" of his only begotten Son. (*b*) Let a Christian, then, regulate his prayers by this rule, that they be common, and comprehend all who are his brethren in Christ; and not only those whom he at present sees and knows to be such, but all men in the world; respecting whom, what God has determined is beyond our knowledge; only that to wish and hope the best concerning them, is equally the dictate of piety and of humanity. It becomes us, however, to exercise a peculiar and superior affection "unto them who are of the household of faith;" whom the apostle has in every case recommended to our particular regards. (*c*) In a word, all our prayers ought to be such, as to respect that community which our Lord has established in his kingdom and in his family.

XXXIX. Yet this is no objection to the lawfulness of particular prayers, both for ourselves and for other certain individuals; provided our minds be not withdrawn from a regard to this community, nor even diverted from it, but refer every thing to this point. For though the words of them be singular, yet as they are directed to this end, they cease not to be common. All this may be rendered very intelligible by a similitude. God has given a general command to relieve the wants of all the poor; and yet this is obeyed by them who to that end succour the indigence of those whom they either know or see to be labouring under poverty; even though they pass by multitudes who are oppressed with necessities equally severe, because neither their knowledge nor ability can extend to all. In the same manner, no opposition is made to the Divine will by them who, regarding and considering this common society of the Church, present such particular prayers, in which, with a public spirit, but in particular terms, they recommend to God themselves or others, whose necessity he has placed within their more immediate knowledge. However, there is not a perfect similarity in every respect between prayer

(*b*) Ephes. i. 23. (*c*) Gal. vi. 10.

and donation of alms, for munificence cannot be exercised but towards them whose wants we have perceived; but we may assist by our prayers even the greatest strangers, and those with whom we are the most unacquainted, how distant soever they may be from us. This is done by that general form of prayer, which comprehends all the children of God, among whom they also are numbered. To this may be referred the exhortation which Paul gives believers of his age, "that men pray every where, lifting up holy hands without wrath;" (*d*) because by admonishing them, that discord shuts the gate against prayers, he advises them unanimously to unite all their petitions together.

XL. It is added, THAT HE IS IN HEAVEN. From which it is not hastily to be inferred, that he is included and circumscribed within the circumference of heaven, as by certain barriers. For Solomon confesses, that "the heaven of heavens cannot contain" him. (*e*) And he says himself, by the prophet, "The heaven is my throne, and the earth is my footstool." (*f*) By which he clearly signifies that he is not limited to any particular region, but diffused throughout all space. But because the dulness of our minds could not otherwise conceive of his ineffable glory, it is designated to us by the heaven, than which we can behold nothing more august or more majestic. Since, then, wherever our senses apprehend any thing, there they are accustomed to fix it, God is represented as beyond all place, that when we seek him we may be elevated above all reach of both body and soul. Moreover, by this form of expression, he is exalted above all possibility of corruption or mutation: finally, it is signified, that he comprehends and contains the whole world, and governs the universe by his power. Wherefore, this is the same as if he had been said to be possessed of an incomprehensible essence, infinite magnitude or sublimity, irresistible power, and unlimited immortality. But when we hear this, our thoughts must be raised to a higher elevation when God is mentioned; that we may not entertain any terrestrial or carnal imaginations concerning him, that we may not measure him by our diminutive proportions, or

(*d*) 1 Tim. ii. 8. (*e*) 1 Kings viii. 27.
(*f*) Isaiah lxvi. 1. Acts vii. 49; xvii. 24.

judge of his will by our affections. We should likewise be encouraged to place the most implicit reliance on him, by whose providence and power we understand both heaven and earth to be governed. To conclude: under the name of "Our Father" is represented to us, that God who has appeared to us in his own image, that we might call upon him with a steady faith; and the familiar appellation of Father is not only adapted to produce confidence, but also efficacious to prevent our minds from being seduced to dubious or fictitious deities, and to cause them to ascend from the only begotten Son to the common Father of angels and of saints; moreover, when his throne is placed in heaven, we are reminded by his government of the world, that it is not in vain for us to approach to him who makes us the objects of his present and voluntary care. "He that cometh to God (says the apostle) must believe that he is, and that he is a rewarder of them that diligently seek him." (*g*) Christ asserts both these of his Father, that we may have first a firm faith in his existence, and then a certain persuasion that, since he deigns to extend his providence to us, he will not neglect our salvation. By these principles, Paul prepares us for praying in right manner; for his exhortation, "Let your requests be made known unto God," is thus prefaced: "The Lord is at hand. Be careful for nothing." (*h*) Whence it appears, that their prayers must be attended with great doubt and perplexity of mind, who are not well established in this truth, that "the eyes of the Lord are upon the righteous." (*i*)

XLI. The first petition is, THAT GOD'S NAME MAY BE HALLOWED; the necessity of which is connected with our great disgrace. For what is more shameful, than that the Divine glory should be obscured partly by our ingratitude, partly by our malignity, and, as far as possible, obliterated by our presumption, infatuation, and perverseness? Notwithstanding all the sacrilegious rage and clamours of the impious, yet the refulgence of holiness still adorns the Divine name. Nor does the Psalmist without reason exclaim, "According to thy name, O God, so is thy praise unto the ends of the earth." (*k*) For wherever God may

---

(*g*) Heb. xi. 6. (*h*) Phil. iv. 5, 6.
(*i*) Psalm xxxiv. 15; xxxiii. 18. (*k*) Psalm xlviii. 10.

be known, there must necessarily be a manifestation of his perfections of power, goodness, wisdom, righteousness, mercy, and truth, which command our admiration and excite us to celebrate his praise. Therefore, because God is so unjustly robbed of his holiness on earth, if it is not in our power to assert it for him, we are at least commanded to regard it in our prayers. The substance of it is, that we wish God to receive all the honour that he deserves, that men may never speak or think of him but with the highest reverence; to which is opposed that profanation, which has always been too common in the world, as it continues to be in the present age. And hence the necessity of this petition, which, if we were influenced by only a tolerable degree of piety, ought to be superfluous. But if the name of God be truly hallowed, when separated from all others it breathes pure glory, we are here commanded to pray, not only that God will vindicate his holy name from all contempt and ignominy, but also that he will constrain all mankind to revere it. Now, as God manifests himself to us partly by his word, and partly by his works, he is no otherwise hallowed by us, than if we attribute to him in both instances that which belongs to him, and so receive whatever proceeds from him; ascribing, moreover, equal praise to his severity and to his clemency; since on the multiplicity and variety of his works he has impressed characters of his glory, which should draw from every tongue a confession of his praise. Thus will the Scripture obtain a just authority with us, nor will any event obstruct the benedictions which God deserves in the whole course of his government of the world. The tendency of the petition is, further, that all impiety which sullies this holy name, may be utterly abolished; that whatever obscures or diminishes this hallowing, whether detraction or derision, may disappear; and that while God restrains all sacrilege, his majesty may shine with increasing splendour.

XLII. The second petition is, THAT THE KINGDOM OF GOD MAY COME; which, though it contains nothing new, is yet not without reason distinguished from the first; because, if we consider our inattention in the most important of all concerns, it is useful for that which ought of itself to have been most intimately known to us, to be inculcated in a variety of words.

Therefore, after we have been commanded to pray to God to subdue, and at length utterly to destroy, every thing that sullies his holy name, there is now added another petition, similar and almost identically the same—That his kingdom may come. Now, though we have already given a definition of this kingdom, I now briefly repeat, that God reigns when men, renouncing themselves and despising the world and the present state, submit themselves to his righteousness, so as to aspire to the heavenly state. Thus this kingdom consists of two parts; the one, God's correcting by the power of his Spirit all our carnal and depraved appetites, which oppose him in great numbers; the other, his forming all our powers to an obedience to his commands. No others therefore observe a proper order in this petition, but they who begin from themselves, that is, that they may be purified from all corruptions which disturb the tranquillity, or violate the purity, of God's kingdom. Now, since the Divine word resembles a royal sceptre, we are commanded to pray that he will subdue the hearts and minds of all men to a voluntary obedience to it. This is accomplished, when, by the secret inspiration of his Spirit, he displays the efficacy of his word, and causes it to obtain the honour it deserves. Afterwards, it is our duty to descend to the impious, by whom his authority is resisted with the perseverance of obstinacy and the fury of despair. God therefore erects his kingdom on the humiliation of the whole world, though his methods of humiliation are various; for he restrains the passions of some, and breaks the unsubdued arrogance of others. It ought to be the object of our daily wishes, that God would collect churches for himself from all the countries of the earth, that he would enlarge their numbers, enrich them with gifts, and establish a legitimate order among them; that, on the contrary, he would overthrow all the enemies of the pure doctrine and religion, that he would confound their counsels, and defeat their attempts. Whence it appears that the desire of a daily progress is not enjoined us in vain; because human affairs are never in such a happy situation, as that all defilement of sin is removed, and purity can be seen in full perfection. This perfection is deferred till the last advent of Christ, when, the apostle says, "God will be all in all." (*l*)

(*l*) 1 Cor. xv. 28.

And so this petition ought to withdraw us from all the corruptions of the world, which separate us from God, and prevent his kingdom from flourishing within us; it ought likewise to inflame us with an ardent desire of mortifying the flesh, and finally to teach us to bear the cross; since these are the means which God chooses for the extension of his kingdom. Nor should we be impatient that the outward man is destroyed, provided the inward man be renewed. For this is the order of the kingdom of God, that, when we submit to his righteousness, he makes us partakers of his glory. This is accomplished, when, discovering his light and truth with perpetual accession of splendour, before which the shades and falsehoods of Satan and of his kingdom vanish and become extinct, he by the aids of his Spirit directs his children into the path of rectitude, and strengthens them to perseverance; but defeats the impious conspiracies of his enemies, confounds their insidious and fraudulent designs, disappoints their malice, and represses their obstinacy, till at length "he" will "consume" Antichrist "with the spirit of his mouth, and destroy" all impiety "with the brightness of his coming." (*m*)

XLIII. The third petition is, THAT THE WILL OF GOD MAY BE DONE ON EARTH AS IT IS IN HEAVEN; which, though it is an appendage to his kingdom, and cannot be disjoined from it, is yet not without reason separately mentioned, on account of our ignorance, which does not apprehend with facility what it is for God to reign in the world. There will be nothing absurd, then, in understanding this as an explanation, that God's kingdom will then prevail in the world, when all shall submit to his will. Now, we speak not here of his secret will, by which he governs all things, and appoints them to fulfil his own purposes. For though Satan and men oppose him with all the violence of rage, yet his incomprehensible wisdom is able, not only to divert their impetuosity, but to overrule it for the accomplishment of his decrees. But the Divine will here intended, is that to which voluntary obedience corresponds; and therefore heaven is expressly compared with the earth, because the angels, as the Psalmist says, spontaneously "do his commandments, hearkening unto the voice

(*m*) 2 Thess. ii. 8.

of his word." (*n*) We are therefore commanded to desire that, as in heaven nothing is done but according to the Divine will, and the angels are placidly conformed to every thing that is right, so the earth, all obstinacy and depravity being annihilated, may be subject to the same government. And in praying for this, we renounce our own carnal desires; because, unless we resign all our affections to God, we are guilty of all the opposition in our power to his will, for nothing proceeds from us but what is sinful. And we are likewise habituated by this petition to a renunciation of ourselves, that God may rule us according to his own pleasure; and not only so, but that he may also create in us new minds and new hearts, annihilating our own, that we may experience no emotion of desire within us, but a mere consent to his will; in a word, that we may have no will of our own, but that our hearts may be governed by his Spirit, by whose internal teachings we may learn to love those things which please him, and to hate those which he disapproves; consequently, that he may render abortive all those desires which are repugnant to his will. These are the three first clauses of this prayer, in praying which we ought solely to have in view the glory of God, omitting all consideration of ourselves, and not regarding any advantage of our own, which, though they largely contribute to it, should not be our end in these petitions. But though all these things, even if we never think of them, nor wish for them, nor request them, must nevertheless happen in their appointed time, yet they ought to be the objects of our wishes, and the subjects of our prayers. And such petitions it will be highly proper for us to offer, that we may testify and profess ourselves to be the servants and sons of God manifesting the sincerest devotedness, and making the most zealous efforts in our power for advancing the honour which is due to him, both as a Master and as a Father. Persons, therefore, who are not incited, by this ardent zeal for promoting the glory of God, to pray, that his name may be hallowed, that his kingdom may come, and that his will may be done, are not to be numbered among his sons and servants; and as all these things will be accomplished in opposition to their inclinations, so they will contribute to their confusion and destruction.

(*n*) Psalm ciii. 20.

XLIV. Next follows the second part of the prayer, in which we descend to our own interests; not that we must dismiss all thoughts of the Divine glory, (which, according to Paul, (*o*) should be regarded even in eating and drinking,) and only seek what is advantageous to ourselves; but we have already announced that this is the distinction—that God, by exclusively claiming three petitions, absorbs us entirely in the consideration of himself, that thus he may prove our piety; afterwards he permits us to attend to our own interests, yet on this condition, that the end of all our requests be the illustration of his glory, by whatever benefits he confers on us, since nothing is more reasonable than that we live and die to him. But the first petition of the second part, GIVE US THIS DAY OUR DAILY BREAD, is a general request to God for a supply of all our corporeal wants in the present state, not only for food and clothing, but also for every thing which he sees to be conducive to our good, that we may eat our bread in peace. By this we briefly surrender ourselves to his care, and commit ourselves to his providence, that he may feed, nourish, and preserve us. For our most benevolent Father disdains not to receive even our body into his charge and protection, that he may exercise our faith in these minute circumstances, while we expect every thing from him, even down to a crumb of bread and a drop of water. For since it is a strange effect of our iniquity, to be affected and distressed with greater solicitude for the body than for the soul, many, who venture to confide to God the interests of their souls, are nevertheless still solicitous concerning the body, still anxious what they shall eat and what they shall wear; and unless they have an abundance of corn, wine, and oil, for the supply of their future wants, tremble with fear. Of so much greater importance to us is the shadow of this transitory life, than that eternal immortality. But they who, confiding in God, have once cast off that anxiety for the concerns of the body, expect likewise to receive from him superior blessings, even salvation and eternal life. It is therefore no trivial exercise of faith, to expect from God those things which otherwise fill us with so much anxiety; nor is it a small proficiency when we have

---

(*o*) 1 Cor. x. 31.

divested ourselves of this infidelity, which is almost universally interwoven with the human constitution. The speculations of some, concerning supernatural bread, appear to me not very consonant to the meaning of Christ; for if we did not ascribe to God the character of our Supporter even in this transitory life, our prayer would be defective. The reason which they allege has too much profanity; that it is unbecoming for the children of God, who ought to be spiritual, not only to devote their own attention to terrestrial cares, but also to involve God in the same anxieties with themselves; as though, truly, his benediction and paternal favour were not conspicuous even in our sustenance; or there were no meaning in the assertion, that "godliness hath promise of the life that now is, and of that which is to come." (*p*) Now, though remission of sins is of much greater value than corporeal aliments, yet Christ has given the first place to the inferior blessing, that he might gradually raise us to the two remaining petitions, which properly pertain to the heavenly life; in which he has consulted our dulness. We are commanded to ask "our bread," that we may be content with the portion which our heavenly Father deigns to allot us, nor practise any illicit arts for the love of lucre. In the mean time, it must be understood that it becomes ours by a title of donation; because neither our industry, nor our labour, nor our hands, (as is observed by Moses,) (*q*) acquire any thing for us of themselves, when unattended by the Divine blessing; and that even an abundance of bread would not be of the least service to us, unless it were by the Divine power converted into nourishment. And therefore this liberality of God is equally as necessary to the rich as to the poor; for though their barns and cellars were full, they would faint with hunger and thirst, unless through his goodness they enjoyed their food. The expression "this day," or "day by day," as it is in the other Evangelist, and the epithet *daily*, restrain the inordinate desire of transitory things, with which we are often violently inflamed, and which leads to other evils; since if we have a greater abundance, we fondly lavish it away in pleasure, delights, ostentation, and other kinds of luxury. Therefore we are enjoined to ask only as

---

(*p*) 1 Tim. iv. 8. (*q*) Lev. xxvi. 20.

much as will supply our necessity, and as it were for the present day, with this confidence, that our heavenly Father, after having fed us to-day, will not fail us to-morrow. Whatever affluence, then, we possess, even when our barns and cellars are full, yet it behoves us always to ask for our daily bread; because it must be considered as an undeniable truth, that all property is nothing, any further than the Lord, by the effusions of his favour, blesses it with continual improvement; and that even what we have in our possession is not our own, any further than as he hourly bestows on us some portion of it, and grants us the use of it. Since the pride of man does not easily suffer itself to be convinced of this, the Lord declares that he has given to all ages an eminent proof of it, by feeding his people with manna in the desert, in order to apprize us "that man doth not live by bread only, but by every word that proceedeth out of his mouth;" (*r*) which implies, that it is his power alone by which our life and strength are sustained, although he communicates it to us by corporeal means; as he is accustomed to teach us likewise by an opposite example, when he breaks, at his pleasure, the strength (and, as he himself calls it, "the staff") of bread, so that though men eat they pine with hunger, and though they drink are parched with thirst. (*s*) Now, they who are not satisfied with daily bread, but whose avidity is insatiable, and whose desires are unbounded, and they who are satiated with their abundance, and think themselves secure amid their immense riches, and who nevertheless supplicate the Divine Being in this petition, are guilty of mocking him. For the former ask what they would not wish to obtain, and even what most of all they abominate, that is, daily bread only; they conceal from God, as much as they can, their avaricious disposition; whereas true prayer ought to pour out before him the whole mind, and all the inmost secrets of the soul; and the latter implore what they are far from expecting to receive from him, what they think they have in their own possession. In its being called "ours," the Divine goodness is, as we have observed, the more conspicuous, since it makes that *ours,* to which we have no claim of right. Yet we must not reject the explanation

(*r*) Deut. viii. 3. Matt. iv. 4.

(*s*) Lev. xxvi. 26.

which I have likewise hinted at, that it intends also such as is acquired by just and innocent labour, and not procured by acts of deception and rapine; because, whatever we acquire by any criminal methods, is never our own, but belongs to others. Our praying that it may be "given" to us signifies that it is the simple and gratuitous donation of God, from what quarter soever we receive it; even when it most of all appears to be obtained by our own skill and industry, and to be procured by our own hands; since it is solely the effect of his blessing, that our labours are attended with success.

XLV. It follows—FORGIVE US OUR DEBTS; in which petition, and the next, Christ has comprised whatever relates to the heavenly life; as in these two parts consists the spiritual covenant which God has made for the salvation of his Church—"I will write my law in their hearts, and will pardon their iniquities" (*t*) Here Christ begins with remission of sins: immediately after, he subjoins a second favour—that God would defend us by the power, and support us by the aid, of his Spirit, to enable us to stand unconquered against all temptations. Sins he calls debts, because we owe the penalty of them—a debt we are altogether incapable of discharging, unless we are released by this remission, which is a pardon flowing from his gratuitous mercy, when he freely cancels these debts without any payment from us, being satisfied by his own mercy in Christ, who has once given himself for our redemption. Those, therefore, who rely on God's being satisfied with their own merits, or the merits of others, and persuade themselves that remission of sins is purchased by these satisfactions, have no interest in this gratuitous forgiveness; and while they call upon God in this form, they are only subscribing their own accusation, and even sealing their condemnation with their own testimony. For they confess themselves debtors, unless they are discharged by the benefit of remission, which nevertheless they accept not, but rather refuse, while they obtrude upon God their own merits and satisfactions. For in this way they do not implore his mercy, but appeal to his judgment. They who amuse themselves with dreams of perfection, superseding the

(*t*) Jer. xxxi. 33, 34; xxxiii. 8.

necessity of praying for pardon, may have disciples whom itching ears lead into delusions; but it must be clear that all whom they gain are perverted from Christ, since he teaches all to confess their guilt, and receives none but sinners; not that he would flatter and encourage sins, but because he knew that believers are never wholly free from the vices of their flesh, but always remain obnoxious to the judgment of God. It ought, indeed, to be the object of our desires and strenuous exertions, that, having fully discharged every part of our duty, we may truly congratulate ourselves before God on being pure from every stain; but as it pleases God to restore his image within us by degrees, so that some contagion always remains in our flesh, the remedy ought never to be neglected. Now, if Christ, by the authority given him by the Father, enjoins us, as long as we live, to have recourse to prayer for the pardon of guilt, who will tolerate the new teachers, who endeavour to dazzle the eyes of the simple with a visionary phantom of perfect innocence, and fill them with a confidence in the possibility of their being delivered from all sin? which, according to John, is no other than making God a liar. (*u*) At the same time, also, these worthless men, by obliterating one article, mutilate, and so totally invalidate, the covenant of God, in which we have seen our salvation is contained; being thus guilty not only of sacrilege by separating things so united, but also of impiety and cruelty, by overwhelming miserable souls with despair, and of treachery to themselves and others, by contracting a habit of carelessness, in diametrical opposition to the Divine mercy. The objection of some, that in wishing the advent of God's kingdom, we desire at the same time the abolition of sin, is too puerile; because, in the first part of the prayer, we have an exhibition of the highest perfection, but here of infirmity. Thus these two things are perfectly consistent, that in aspiring towards the mark we may not neglect the remedies required by our necessity. Lastly, we pray that we may be forgiven AS WE FORGIVE OUR DEBTORS; that is, as we forgive and pardon all who have ever injured us, either by unjust actions or by contumelious language. Not that it is our province to forgive the guilt of sin and trans-

---

(*u*) 1 John i. 10.

gression; this is the prerogative of God alone: our forgiveness consists in divesting the mind of anger, enmity, and desire of revenge, and losing the memory of injuries by a voluntary forgetfulness. Wherefore we must not pray to God for forgiveness of sins, unless we also forgive all the offences and injuries of others against us, either present or past. But if we retain any enmities in our minds, meditate acts of revenge, and seek opportunities of annoyance, and even if we do not endeavour to obtain reconciliation with our enemies, to oblige them by all kind offices, and to render them our friends,—we beseech God, by this petition, not to grant us remission of sins. For we supplicate him to grant to us what we grant to others. This is praying him not to grant it to us, unless we grant it also. What do persons of this description gain by their prayers but a heavier judgment? Lastly, it must be observed, that this is not a condition, that he would forgive us as we forgive our debtors, because we can merit his forgiveness of us by our forgiveness of others, as though it described the cause of his forgiveness; but, by this expression, the Lord intended, partly to comfort the weakness of our faith; for he has added this as a sign, that we may be as certainly assured of remission of sins being granted us by him, as we are certain and conscious of our granting it to others; if, at the same time, our minds be freed and purified from all hatred, envy, and revenge; partly by this, as a criterion, he expunges from the number of his children, those who, hasty to revenge and difficult to forgive, maintain inveterate enmities, and cherish in their own hearts towards others, that indignation which they deprecate from themselves, that they may not presume to invoke him as their Father. Which is also clearly expressed by Luke in Christ's own words.

XLVI. The sixth petition is, LEAD US NOT INTO TEMPTATION, BUT DELIVER US FROM EVIL. This, as we have said, corresponds to the promise respecting the law of God to be engraven in our hearts. But because our obedience to God is not without continual warfare, and severe and arduous conflicts, we here pray for arms, and assistance to enable us to gain the victory. This suggests to us our necessity, not only of the grace of the Spirit within us to soften, bend, and direct our hearts to obedience to God, but also of his aid to render us invincible, in opposition to all the stratagems and violent assaults of Satan. Now, the forms of temptations are many and various. For the corrupt conceptions of the mind, provoking us to transgressions of the law, whether suggested by our own concupiscence or excited by the devil, are temptations; and things not evil in themselves, nevertheless become temptations through the subtlety of the devil, when they are obtruded on our eyes in such a manner that their intervention occasions our seduction or declension from God. And these temptations are either from prosperous, or from adverse events. From prosperous ones, as riches, power, honours; which generally dazzle men's eyes by their glitter and external appearance of goodness, and insnare them with their blandishments, that, caught with such delusions and intoxicated with such delights, they forget their God. From unpropitious ones, as poverty, reproaches, contempt, afflictions, and other things of this kind; overcome with the bitterness and difficulty of which, they fall into despondency, cast away faith and hope, and at length become altogether alienated from God. To both these kinds of temptations which assail us, whether kindled within us by our concupiscence, or presented to us by the craft of Satan, we pray our heavenly Father not to permit us to yield, but rather to sustain and raise us up with his hand, that, strong in his might, we may be able to stand firm against all the assaults of our malignant enemy, whatever imaginations he may inject into our minds; and also, that whatever is presented to us on either quarter, we may convert it to our benefit; that is, by not being elated with prosperity or dejected with adversity. Yet we do not here pray for an entire exemption from all temptations, which we very much need, to excite, stimulate, and animate us, lest we should grow torpid with too much rest. For it was not without reason that David wished to be tempted or tried; nor is it without cause that the Lord daily tries his elect, chastising them by ignominy, poverty, tribulation, and the cross in various forms. But the temptations of God are widely different from those of Satan. Satan tempts to overthrow, condemn, confound, and destroy. But God, that, by proving his people, he may make a trial of their sincerity, to confirm their strength by exercising it, to mortify, purify, and refine their flesh, which, without such restraints, would run into the greatest excesses. Besides, Satan attacks persons unarmed and unprepared, to overwhelm the unwary. "God, with the temptation, also makes a way to escape, that they may be able to bear" whatever he brings upon them. (*y*) By the word *evil*, whether we understand the devil or sin, is of little importance. Satan himself, indeed, is the enemy that lies in wait for our life; but sin is the weapon with which he seeks our destruction. Our petition therefore is, that we may not be overwhelmed and conquered by any temptations, but that we may stand, strong in the power of the Lord, against all adverse powers that assault us, which is not to submit to temptations; that being taken into his custody and charge, and being secure in his protection, we may persevere unconquered, and rise superior to sin, death, the gates of hell, and the whole kingdom of the devil. This is being delivered from evil. Here it must also be carefully remarked, that it is not in our power to contend with so powerful an enemy as the devil, and sustain the violence of his assaults. Otherwise it would be useless, or insulting, to supplicate from God what we already possessed in ourselves. Certainly, they who prepare themselves for such a combat with self-confidence, are not sufficiently aware of the skill and prowess of the enemy that they have to meet. Now, we pray to be delivered from his power, as from the mouth of a ravenous and raging lion, just about to tear us with his teeth and claws, and to swallow us down his throat, unless the Lord snatch us from the jaws of death; knowing, at the same time, that if the Lord shall be present and fight for us while we are silent, in his strength "we shall do valiantly." (*z*) Let others confide as they please in the native abilities and powers of free-will, which they suppose themselves to possess,—let it be sufficient for us, to stand and be strong in the power of God alone. But this petition comprehends more than at first appears. For if the Spirit of God is our strength for fighting the battle with Satan, we shall not be able to gain the victory, till, being full of him, we shall have laid aside all the infirmity of our flesh. When we pray for deliverance from Satan and sin, therefore, we pray to be frequently enriched with new accessions

---

(*y*) 1 Cor. x. 13. (*z*) Psalm lx. 12.

of Divine grace; till, being quite filled with them, we may be able to triumph over all evil. To some there appears a difficulty and harshness in our petition to God, that he will not lead us into temptation, whereas, according to James, it is contrary to his nature for him to tempt us. (*a*) But this objection has already been partly answered, because our own lust is properly the cause of all the temptations that overcome us, and therefore we are charged with the guilt. Nor does James intend any other than to assert the futility and injustice of transferring to God the vices which we are constrained to impute to ourselves, because we are conscious of our being guilty of them. But notwithstanding this, God may, when he sees fit, deliver us to Satan, abandon us to a reprobate mind and sordid passions, and so lead us into temptations, by a righteous yet often secret judgment; the cause being frequently concealed from man, but, at the same time, well known to him. Whence it is inferred, that there is no impropriety in this mode of expression, if we are persuaded that there is any meaning in his frequent threatenings, that he will manifest his vengeance on the reprobate, by smiting them with blindness and hardness of heart.

XLVII. These three petitions, in which we particularly commend to God ourselves and all our concerns, evidently prove, what we have before asserted, that the prayers of Christians ought to be public, and to regard the public edification of the Church, and the advancement of the communion of believers. For each individual does not supplicate the gift of any favour to himself in particular; but we all in common pray for our bread, the remission of our sins, that we may not be led into temptation, that we may be delivered from evil. The cause is likewise subjoined, which gives us such great boldness in asking, and confidence of obtaining; which, though not to be found in the Latin copies, yet appears too apposite to this place to be omitted—namely, HIS IS THE KINGDOM, AND THE POWER, AND THE GLORY FOR EVER. This is a solid and secure basis for our faith; for if our prayers were to be recommended to God by our own merit, who could dare to utter a word in his presence? Now, all miserable, unworthy,

(*a*) James i. 13, 14.

and destitute as we are of every recommendation, yet we shall never want an argument or plea for our prayers: our confidence can never forsake us; for our Father can never be deprived of his kingdom, power, and glory. The whole is concluded with AMEN; which expresses our ardent desire to obtain the blessings supplicated of God, and confirms our hope that all these things are already obtained, and will certainly be granted to us; because they are promised by God, who is incapable of deception. And this agrees with that form of petition already quoted—"Do this, O Lord, for thy name's sake, not for our sake, or for our righteousness;" in which the saints not only express the end of their prayers, but acknowledge that they are unworthy to obtain it, unless God derive the cause from himself, and that their confidence of success arises solely from his nature.

XLVIII. Whatever we ought, or are even at liberty, to seek from God, is stated to us in this model and directory for prayer, given by that best of masters, Christ, whom the Father has set over us as our Teacher, and to whom alone he has enjoined us to listen. (*b*) For he was always his eternal wisdom, and being made man, was given to men as the Angel of great counsel. (*c*) And this prayer is so comprehensive and complete, that whatever addition is made of any thing extraneous or foreign, not capable of being referred to it, is impious and unworthy of the approbation of God. For in this summary he has prescribed what is worthy of him, what is acceptable to him, what is necessary for us, and, in a word, what he chooses to bestow. Wherefore those who presume to go beyond it, and to ask of God any thing else, in the first place, are determined to make some addition of their own to the wisdom of God, which cannot be done without folly and blasphemy; in the next place, despising the limits fixed by the will of God, they are led far astray by their own irregular desires; and in the last place, they will never obtain any thing, since they pray without faith. And there is no doubt that all prayers of this kind are made without faith, because they are not sanctioned by the word of God, the only basis on which faith can stand. But they who neglect the Master's rule, and indulge their own desires,

(*b*) Matt. xvii. 5. (*c*) Isaiah xi. 2.

not only deviate from the word of God, but make all possible opposition against it. With equal beauty and truth, therefore, Tertullian has called this a *legitimate prayer*, tacitly implying, that all others are irregular and unlawful.

XLIX. We would not here be understood, as if we were confined to this form of prayer, without the liberty of changing a word or syllable. For the Scriptures contain many prayers, expressed in words very different from this, yet written by the same Spirit, and very profitable for our use. Many, which have little verbal resemblance to it, are continually suggested to believers by the same Spirit. We only mean by these observations, that no one should even seek, expect, or ask for any thing that is not summarily comprehended in this prayer, though there may be a diversity of expression, without any variation of sense. As it is certain that all the prayers contained in the Scriptures, or proceeding from pious hearts, are referred to this, so it is impossible to find one any where which can surpass or even equal the perfection of this. Here is nothing omitted which ought to be recollected for the praises of God, nothing that should occur to the mind of man for his own advantage; and the whole is so complete, as justly to inspire universal despair of attempting any improvement. To conclude; let us remember, that this is the teaching of Divine wisdom, which taught what it willed, and willed what is needful.

L. But though we have before said that we ought to be always aspiring towards God with our minds, and praying without intermission, yet as our weakness requires many assistances, and our indolence needs to be stimulated, we ought every one of us, for the sake of regularity, to appoint particular hours which should not elapse without prayer, and which should witness all the affections of the mind entirely engaged in this exercise; as, when we rise in the morning, before we enter on the business of the day, when we sit down to meat, when we have been fed by the Divine blessing, when we retire to rest. This must not be a superstitious observance of hours, by which, as if discharging our debt to God, we may fancy ourselves discharged from all obligation for the remaining hours; but a discipline for our weakness, which may thus, from time to time, be exercised and stimulated. It must especially be the object of our solicitous care, whenever we are oppressed, or see others oppressed, with adversity, immediately to resort to him with celerity, not of body, but of mind; secondly, to suffer no prosperity of our own or others to pass without testifying our acknowledgment of his hand by praise and thanksgiving; lastly, we must carefully observe this in every prayer, that we entertain not the thought of binding God to certain circumstances, or prescribing to him the time, the place, or the manner of his proceedings. As we are taught by this prayer to fix no law, to impose no condition on him, but to leave it to his will to do what he intends, in the manner, at the time, and in the place he pleases, therefore, before we form a petition for ourselves, we first pray that his will may be done; thereby submitting our will to his, that, being, as it were, bridled and restrained, it may not presume to regulate God, but may constitute him the arbiter and ruler of all its desires.

LI. If, with minds composed to this obedience, we suffer ourselves to be governed by the laws of Divine Providence, we shall easily learn to persevere in prayer, and with suspended desires to wait patiently for the Lord; assured, though he does not discover himself, yet that he is always near us, and in his own time will declare that his ears have not been deaf to those prayers which, to human apprehension, seemed to be neglected. Now, this, if God do not at any time answer our first prayers, will be an immediate consolation, to prevent our sinking into despair, like those who, actuated only by their own ardour, call upon God in such a manner, that if he do not attend to their first transports, and afford them present aid, they at once imagine him to be displeased and angry with them, and, casting away all hope of succeeding in their prayers, cease to call upon him. But deferring our hope with a well-tempered equanimity, let us rather practise the perseverance so highly recommended to us in the Scriptures. For in the Psalms we may frequently observe how David and other faithful men, when, almost wearied with praying, they seemed to beat the air, and God seemed deaf to their petitions, yet did not desist from praying; because the authority of the Divine word is not maintained, unless it be fully credited, notwithstanding the appearance of any circumstances to the contrary. Nor let us tempt God, and provoke him against us by wearying him with our presumption; which is the practice of many who merely bargain with God on a certain condition, and as though he were subservient to their passions, bind him with laws of their own stipulation; with which unless he immediately complies, they give way to anger and fretfulness, to cavils, and murmurs, and rage. To such persons, therefore, he frequently grants in his wrath what he denies in mercy to others. This is exemplified in the children of Israel, for whom it had been better for the Lord not to have heard them, than for them to swallow his indignation with the meat that he sent them. (*d*)

LII. But if, after long waiting, our sense neither understands what advance we have made by praying, nor experiences any advantage resulting from it, yet our faith will assure us, what cannot be perceived by sense, that we have obtained what was expedient for us, since the Lord so frequently and so certainly promises to take care of our troubles when they have been once deposited in his bosom. And thus he will cause us to possess abundance in poverty, and consolation in affliction. For though all things fail us, yet God will never forsake us; he cannot disappoint the expectation and patience of his people. He will amply compensate us for the loss of all others, for he comprehends in himself all blessings, which he will reveal to us at the day of judgment, when his kingdom will be fully manifested. Besides, though God grants our prayers, he does not always answer them according to the express form of the request; but seeming to keep us in suspense, shows by unknown means that our prayers were not in vain. This is the meaning of these words of John: "If we know that he heareth us, whatsoever we ask, we know that we have the petitions that we desired of him." (*e*) This seems to be a feeble superfluity of expression, but is in reality a very useful declaration, that God, even when he does not comply with our desires, is nevertheless favourable and propitious to our prayers, so that a hope depending upon his word can never disappoint us. Now, this patience is very necessary to support believers, who would not long stand unless they relied upon it. For the Lord

---

(*d*) Num. xi. 18, 33. (*e*) 1 John v. 15.

proves his people with heavy trials, and exercises them with severity; frequently driving them to various kinds of extremities, and suffering them to remain in them a long time before he grants them any enjoyment of his grace; and as Hannah says, "The Lord killeth, and maketh alive; he bringeth down to the grave, and bringeth up." (*f*) In such distresses must they not inevitably faint in their minds, and fall into despair, unless, in the midst of their affliction and desolation, and almost death, they were revived by this reflection, that God regards them, and that the end of their present evils is approaching? But though they rely on the certainty of this hope, they at the same time cease not to pray; because, without constant perseverance in prayer, we pray to no purpose.

(*f*) 1 Sam. ii. 6.

CHAPTER XXI

Eternal Election, or God's Predestination of Some to Salvation, and of Others to Destruction

THE covenant of life not being equally preached to all, and among those to whom it is preached not always finding the same reception, this diversity discovers the wonderful depth of the Divine judgment. Nor is it to be doubted that this variety also follows, subject to the decision of God's eternal election. If it be evidently the result of the Divine will, that salvation is freely offered to some, and others are prevented from attaining it,—this immediately gives rise to important and difficult questions, which are incapable of any other explication, than by the establishment of pious minds in what ought to be received concerning election and predestination—a question, in the opinion of many, full of perplexity; for they consider nothing more unreasonable, than that, of the common mass of mankind, some should be predestinated to salvation, and others to destruction. But how unreasonably they perplex themselves will afterwards appear from the sequel of our discourse. Besides, the very obscurity which excites such dread, not only displays the utility of this doctrine, but shows it to be productive of the most delightful benefit. We shall never be clearly convinced as we ought to be, that our salvation flows from the fountain of God's free mercy, till we are acquainted with his eternal election, which illustrates the grace of God by this comparison, that he adopts not all promiscuously to the hope of salvation, but gives to some what he refuses to others. Ignorance of this principle evidently detracts from the Divine glory, and diminishes real humility. But according to Paul, what is so necessary to be known, never can be known, unless God, without any regard to works, chooses those whom he has decreed. "At this present time also, there is a remnant according to the election of grace. And if by grace, then it is no more of works; otherwise, grace is no more grace. But if it be of works, then it is no more grace; otherwise, work is no more work." (*g*) If we need to be recalled to the origin of election, to prove that we obtain salvation from no other source than the mere goodness of God, they who desire to extinguish this principle, do all they can to obscure what ought to be magnificently and loudly celebrated, and to pluck up humility by the roots. In ascribing the salvation of the remnant of the people to the election of grace, Paul clearly testifies, that it is then only known that God saves whom he will of his mere good pleasure, and does not dispense a reward to which there can be no claim. They who shut the gates to prevent any one from presuming to approach and taste this doctrine, do no less injury to man than to God; for nothing else will be sufficient to produce in us suitable humility, or to impress us with a due sense of our great obligations to God. Nor is there any other basis for solid confidence, even according to the authority of Christ, who, to deliver us from all fear, and render us invincible amidst so many dangers, snares, and deadly conflicts, promises to preserve in safety all whom the Father has committed to his care. Whence we infer, that they who know not themselves to be God's peculiar people will be tortured with continual anxiety; and therefore, that the interest of all believers, as well as their own, is very badly consulted by those who, blind to the three advantages we have remarked, would wholly remove the foundation of our salvation. And hence the Church rises to our view, which otherwise, as Bernard justly observes, could neither be discovered nor recognized among creatures, being in two respects wonderfully concealed in the bosom of a blessed

---

(*g*) Rom. xi. 5, 6.

predestination, and in the mass of a miserable damnation. But before I enter on the subject itself, I must address some preliminary observations to two sorts of persons. The discussion of predestination—a subject of itself rather intricate—is made very perplexed, and therefore dangerous, by human curiosity, which no barriers can restrain from wandering into forbidden labyrinths, and soaring beyond its sphere, as if determined to leave none of the Divine secrets unscrutinized or unexplored. As we see multitudes every where guilty of this arrogance and presumption, and among them some who are not censurable in other respects, it is proper to admonish them of the bounds of their duty on this subject. First, then, let them remember that when they inquire into predestination, they penetrate the inmost recesses of Divine wisdom, where the careless and confident intruder will obtain no satisfaction to his curiosity, but will enter a labyrinth from which he will find no way to depart. For it is unreasonable that man should scrutinize with impunity those things which the Lord has determined to be hidden in himself; and investigate, even from eternity, that sublimity of wisdom which God would have us to adore and not comprehend, to promote our admiration of his glory. The secrets of his will which he determined to reveal to us, he discovers in his word; and these are all that he foresaw would concern us or conduce to our advantage.

II. "We are come into the way of faith," says Augustine; "let us constantly pursue it. It conducts into the king's palace, in which are hidden all the treasures of wisdom and knowledge. For the Lord Christ himself envied not his great and most select disciples when he said, 'I have many things to say unto you, but ye cannot bear them now.' We must walk, we must improve, we must grow, that our hearts may be able to understand those things of which we are at present incapable. If the last day finds us improving, we shall then learn what we never could learn in the present state." If we only consider that the word of the Lord is the only way to lead us to an investigation of all that ought to be believed concerning him, and the only light to enlighten us to behold all that ought to be seen of him, this consideration will easily restrain and preserve us from all presumption. For we shall know that when we have exceeded the limits of the word, we shall get into a devious and darksome course, in which errors, slips, and falls will often be inevitable. Let us, then, in the first place, bear in mind, that to desire any other knowledge of predestination than what is unfolded in the word of God, indicates as great folly, as a wish to walk through unpassable roads, or to see in the dark. Nor let us be ashamed to be ignorant of some things relative to a subject in which there is a kind of learned ignorance. Rather let us abstain with cheerfulness from the pursuit of that knowledge, the affectation of which is foolish, dangerous, and even fatal. But if we are stimulated by the wantonness of intellect, we must oppose it with a reflection calculated to repress it, that as "it is not good to eat much honey, so for men to search their own glory, is not glory." (*h*) For there is sufficient to deter us from that presumption, which can only precipitate us into ruin.

III. Others, desirous of remedying this evil, will have all mention of predestination to be as it were buried; they teach men to avoid every question concerning it as they would a precipice. Though their moderation is to be commended, in judging that mysteries ought to be handled with such great sobriety, yet, as they descend too low, they have little influence on the mind of man, which refuses to submit to unreasonable restraints. To observe, therefore, the legitimate boundary on this side also, we must recur to the word of the Lord, which affords a certain rule for the understanding. For the Scripture is the school of the Holy Spirit, in which, as nothing necessary and useful to be known is omitted, so nothing is taught which it is not beneficial to know. Whatever, therefore, is declared in the Scripture concerning predestination, we must be cautious not to withhold from believers, lest we appear either to defraud them of the favor of their God, or to reprove and censure the Holy Spirit for publishing what it would be useful by any means to suppress. Let us, I say, permit the Christian man to open his heart and his ears to all the discourses addressed to him by God, only with this moderation, that as soon as the Lord closes his sacred mouth, he shall also

(*h*) Prov. xxv. 27.

desist from further inquiry. This will be the best barrier of sobriety, if in learning we not only follow the leadings of God, but as soon as he ceases to teach, we give up our desire of learning. Nor is the danger they dread, sufficient to divert our attention from the oracles of God. It is a celebrated observation of Solomon, that "it is the glory of God to conceal a thing." (*i*) But, as both piety and common sense suggest that this is not to be understood generally of every thing, we must seek for the proper distinction, lest we content ourselves with brutish ignorance under the pretext of modesty and sobriety. Now, this distinction is clearly expressed in a few words by Moses. "The secret things," he says, "belong unto the Lord our God; but those things which are revealed belong unto us, and to our children for ever, that we may do all the words of this law." (*k*) For we see how he enforces on the people attention to the doctrine of the law only by the celestial decree, because it pleased God to promulgate it; and restrains the same people within those limits with this single reason, that it is not lawful for mortals to intrude into the secrets of God.

IV. Profane persons, I confess, suddenly lay hold of something relating to the subject of predestination, to furnish occasion for objections, cavils, reproaches, and ridicule. But if we are frightened from it by their impudence, all the principal articles of the faith must be concealed, for there is scarcely one of them which such persons as these leave unviolated by blasphemy. The refractory mind will discover as much insolence, on hearing that there are three persons in the Divine essence, as on being told, that when God created man, he foresaw what would happen concerning him. Nor will they refrain from derision on being informed, that little more than five thousand years have elapsed since the creation of the world. They will ask why the power of God was so long idle and asleep. Nothing can be advanced which they will not endeavour to ridicule. Must we, in order to check these sacrileges, say nothing of the Divinity of the Son and Spirit, or pass over in silence the creation of the world? In this instance, and every other, the truth of God is too powerful to

---

(*i*) Prov. xxv. 2. (*k*) Deut. xxix. 29.

dread the detraction of impious men; as is strenuously maintained by Augustine, in his treatise on the Perseverance of the Faithful. We see the false apostles, with all their defamation and accusation of the true doctrine of Paul, could never succeed to make him ashamed of it. Their assertion, that all this discussion is dangerous to pious minds, because it is inconsistent with exhortations, shakes their faith, and disturbs and discourages the heart itself, is without any foundation. Augustine admits, that he was frequently blamed, on these accounts, for preaching predestination too freely; but he readily and amply refutes them. But as many and various absurdities are crowded upon us here, we prefer reserving every one to be refuted in its proper place. I only desire this general admission, that we should neither scrutinize those things which the Lord has left concealed, nor neglect those which he has openly exhibited, lest we be condemned for excessive curiosity on the one hand, or for ingratitude on the other. For it is judiciously remarked by Augustine, that we may safely follow the Scripture, which proceeds as with the pace of a mother stooping to the weakness of a child, that it may not leave our weak capacities behind. But persons who are so cautious or timid, as to wish predestination to be buried in silence, lest feeble minds should be disturbed,—with what pretext, I ask, will they gloss over their arrogance, which indirectly charges God with foolish inadvertency, as though he foresaw not the danger which they suppose they have had the penetration to discover. Whoever, therefore, endeavours to raise prejudices against the doctrine of predestination, openly reproaches God, as though something had inconsiderately escaped from him that is pernicious to the Church.

V. Predestination, by which God adopts some to the hope of life, and adjudges others to eternal death, no one, desirous of the credit of piety, dares absolutely to deny. But it is involved in many cavils, especially by those who make foreknowledge the cause of it. We maintain, that both belong to God; but it is preposterous to represent one as dependent on the other. When we attribute foreknowledge to God, we mean that all things have ever been, and perpetually remain, before his eyes, so that to his knowledge nothing is future or past, but all things are present; and present in such a manner, that he does not merely conceive of them from ideas formed in his mind, as things remembered by us appear present to our minds, but really beholds and sees them as if actually placed before him. And this foreknowledge extends to the whole world, and to all the creatures. Predestination we call the eternal decree of God, by which he has determined in himself, what he would have to become of every individual of mankind. For they are not all created with a similar destiny; but eternal life is foreordained for some, and eternal damnation for others. Every man, therefore, being created for one or the other of these ends, we say, he is predestinated either to life or to death. This God has not only testified in particular persons, but has given a specimen of it in the whole posterity of Abraham, which should evidently show the future condition of every nation to depend upon his decision. "When the Most High divided the nations, when he separated the sons of Adam, the Lord's portion was his people; Jacob was the lot of his inheritance." (*l*) The separation is before the eyes of all: in the person of Abraham, as in the dry trunk of a tree, one people is peculiarly chosen to the rejection of others: no reason for this appears, except that Moses, to deprive their posterity of all occasion of glorying, teaches them that their exaltation is wholly from God's gratuitous love. He assigns this reason for their deliverance, that "he loved their fathers, and chose their seed after them." (*m*) More fully in another chapter: "The Lord did not set his love upon you, nor choose you, because you were more in number than any people; but because the Lord loved you." (*n*) He frequently repeats the same admonition: "Behold, the heaven is the Lord's thy God, the earth also, with all that therein is. Only the Lord had a delight in thy fathers to love them, and he chose their seed after them." (*o*) In another place, sanctification is enjoined upon them, because they were chosen to be a peculiar people. (*p*) And again, elsewhere, love is asserted to be the cause of their protection. It is declared by the united voice of the faithful, "He hath chosen our inheritance for us, the excellency of Jacob, whom he loved." (*q*) For the gifts conferred on them by

(*l*) Deut. xxxii. 8, 9.
(*m*) Deut. iv. 37.
(*n*) Deut. vii. 7, 8.
(*o*) Deut. x. 14, 15.
(*p*) Deut. xxiii.
(*q*) Psalm xlvii. 4.

God, they all ascribe to gratuitous love, not only from a consciousness that these were not obtained by any merit of theirs, but from a conviction, that the holy patriarch himself was not endued with such excellence as to acquire the privilege of so great an honour for himself and his posterity. And the more effectually to demolish all pride, he reproaches them with having deserved no favour, being "a stiff-necked and rebellious people." (*r*) The prophets also frequently reproach the Jews with the unwelcome mention of this election, because they had shamefully departed from it. Let them, however, now come forward, who wish to restrict the election of God to the desert of men, or the merit of works. When they see one nation preferred to all others,—when they hear that God had no inducement to be more favourable to a few, and ignoble, and even disobedient and obstinate people,—will they quarrel with him because he has chosen to give such an example of mercy? But their obstreperous clamours will not impede his work, nor will the reproaches they hurl against Heaven, injure or affect his justice; they will rather recoil upon their own heads. To this principle of the gracious covenant, the Israelites are also recalled whenever thanks are to be rendered to God, or their hopes are to be raised for futurity. "He hath made us, and not we ourselves," says the Psalmist: "we are his people, and the sheep of his pasture." (*s*) It is not without reason that the negation is added, "not we ourselves," that they may know that of all the benefits they enjoy, God is not only the Author, but derived the cause from himself, there being nothing in them deserving of such great honour. He also enjoins them to be content with the mere good pleasure of God, in these words: "O ye seed of Abraham his servant, ye children of Jacob his chosen." And after having recounted the continual benefits bestowed by God as fruits of election, he at length concludes that he had acted with such liberality, "because he remembered his covenant." (*t*) Consistent with this doctrine is the song of the whole Church: "Thy right hand, and thine arm, and the light of thy countenance, gave our fathers the land, because thou hadst a favour unto them." (*u*) It must be observed that where men-

(*r*) Deut. ix. 6, 7.
(*s*) Psalm c. 3.
(*t*) Psalm cv. 6, 8.
(*u*) Psalm xliv. 3.

tion is made of the land, it is a visible symbol of the secret separation, which comprehends adoption. David, in another place, exhorts the people to the same gratitude: "Blessed is the nation whose God is the Lord; and the people whom he hath chosen for his own inheritance." (*x*) Samuel animates to a good hope: "The Lord will not forsake his people, for his great name's sake; because it hath pleased the Lord to make you his people." (*y*) David, when his faith is assailed, thus arms himself for the conflict: "Blessed is the man whom thou choosest, and causest to approach unto thee; he shall dwell in thy courts." (*z*) But since the election hidden in God has been confirmed by the first deliverance, as well as by the second and other intermediate blessings, the word *choose* is transferred to it in Isaiah: "The Lord will have mercy on Jacob, and will yet choose Israel;" (*a*) because, contemplating a future period, he declares that the collection of the residue of the people, whom he had appeared to have forsaken, would be a sign of the stable and sure election, which had likewise seemed to fail. When he says also, in another place, "I have chosen thee, and not cast thee away," (*b*) he commends the continual course of his signal liberality and paternal benevolence. The angel, in Zechariah, speaks more plainly: "The Lord shall choose Jerusalem again;" (*c*) as though his severe chastisement had been a rejection, or their exile had been an interruption of election; which, nevertheless, remains inviolable, though the tokens of it are not always visible.

VI. We must now proceed to a second degree of election, still more restricted, or that in which the Divine grace was displayed in a more special manner, when of the same race of Abraham God rejected some, and by nourishing others in the Church, proved that he retained them among his children. Ishmael at first obtained the same station as his brother Isaac, for the spiritual covenant was equally sealed in him by the symbol of circumcision. He is cut off; afterwards Esau; lastly, an innumerable multitude, and almost all Israel. In Isaac the seed was called; the same calling continued in Jacob. God exhibited a similar ex-

---

(*x*) Psalm xxxiii. 12.
(*y*) 1 Sam. xii. 22.
(*z*) Psalm lxv. 4.
(*a*) Isaiah xiv. 1.
(*b*) Isaiah xli. 9.
(*c*) Zech ii. 12.

ample in the rejection of Saul, which is magnificently celebrated by the Psalmist: "He refused the tabernacle of Joseph, and chose not the tribe of Ephraim, but chose the tribe of Judah;" (*d*) and this the sacred history frequently repeats, that the wonderful secret of Divine grace may be more manifest in that change. I grant, it was by their own crime and guilt that Ishmael, Esau, and persons of similar characters, fell from the adoption; because the condition annexed was, that they should faithfully keep the covenant of God, which they perfidiously violated. Yet it was a peculiar favour of God, that he deigned to prefer them to other nations; as it is said in the Psalms: "He hath not dealt so with any nation; and as for his judgments, they have not known them." (*e*) But I have justly said that here are two degrees to be remarked; for in the election of the whole nation, God has already shown that in his mere goodness he is bound by no laws, but is perfectly free, so that none can require of him an equal distribution of grace, the inequality of which demonstrates it to be truly gratuitous. Therefore Malachi aggravates the ingratitude of Israel, because, though not only elected out of the whole race of mankind, but also separated from a sacred family to be a peculiar people, they perfidiously and impiously despised God their most beneficent Father. "Was not Esau Jacob's brother? saith the Lord: yet I loved Jacob, and I hated Esau." (*f*) For God takes it for granted, since both were sons of a holy father, successors of the covenant, and branches from a sacred root, that the children of Jacob were already laid under more than common obligations by their admission to that honour; but Esau the first-born having been rejected, and their father, though inferior by birth, having been made the heir, he proves them guilty of double ingratitude, and complains of their violating this twofold claim.

VII. Though it is sufficiently clear, that God, in his secret counsel, freely chooses whom he will, and rejects others, his gratuitous election is but half displayed till we come to particular individuals, to whom God not only offers salvation, but assigns it in such a manner, that the certainty of the effect is liable

(*d*) Psalm lxxviii. 67, 68. (*e*) Psalm cxlvii. 20. (*f*) Mal. i. 2, 3.

to no suspense or doubt. These are included in that one seed mentioned by Paul; for though the adoption was deposited in the hand of Abraham, yet many of his posterity being cut off as putrid members, in order to maintain the efficacy and stability of election, it is necessary to ascend to the head, in whom their heavenly Father has bound his elect to each other, and united them to himself by an indissoluble bond. Thus the adoption of the family of Abraham displayed the favour of God, which he denied to others; but in the members of Christ there is a conspicuous exhibition of the superior efficacy of grace; because, being united to their head, they never fail of salvation. Paul, therefore, justly reasons from the passage of Malachi which I have just quoted, that where God, introducing the covenant of eternal life, invites any people to himself, there is a peculiar kind of election as to part of them, so that he does not efficaciously choose all with indiscriminate grace. The declaration, "Jacob have I loved," respects the whole posterity of the patriarch, whom the prophet there opposes to the descendants of Esau. Yet this is no objection to our having in the person of one individual a specimen of the election, which can never fail of attaining its full effect. These, who truly belong to Christ, Paul correctly observes, are called "a remnant;" for experience proves, that of a great multitude the most part fall away and disappear, so that often only a small portion remains. That the general election of a people is not always effectual and permanent, a reason readily presents itself, because, when God covenants with them, he does not also give them the spirit of regeneration to enable them to persevere in the covenant to the end; but the external call, without the internal efficacy of grace, which would be sufficient for their preservation, is a kind of medium between the rejection of all mankind and the election of the small number of believers. The whole nation of Israel was called "God's inheritance," though many of them were strangers; but God, having firmly covenanted to be their Father and Redeemer, regards that gratuitous favour rather than the defection of multitudes; by whom his truth was not violated, because his preservation of a certain remnant to himself, made it evident that his calling was without repentance. For God's collection of a Church for himself, from time to time, from the children of Abraham, rather than from the profane nations, was in consideration of his covenant, which, being violated by the multitude, he restricted to a few, to prevent its total failure. Lastly, the general adoption of the seed of Abraham was a visible representation of a greater blessing, which God conferred on a few out of the multitude. This is the reason that Paul so carefully distinguishes the descendants of Abraham according to the flesh, from his spiritual children called after the example of Isaac. Not that the mere descent from Abraham was a vain and unprofitable thing, which could not be asserted without depreciating the covenant; but because to the latter alone the immutable counsel of God, in which he predestinated whom he would, was of itself effectual to salvation. But I advise my readers to adopt no prejudice on either side, till it shall appear from adduced passages of Scripture what sentiments ought to be entertained. In conformity, therefore, to the clear doctrine of the Scripture, we assert, that by an eternal and immutable counsel, God has once for all determined, both whom he would admit to salvation, and whom he would condemn to destruction. We affirm that this counsel, as far as concerns the elect, is founded on his gratuitous mercy, totally irrespective of human merit; but that to those whom he devotes to condemnation, the gate of life is closed by a just and irreprehensible, but incomprehensible, judgment. In the elect, we consider calling as an evidence of election, and justification as another token of its manifestation, till they arrive in glory, which constitutes its completion. As God seals his elect by vocation and justification, so by excluding the reprobate from the knowledge of his name and the sanctification of his Spirit, he affords an indication of the judgment that awaits them. Here I shall pass over many fictions fabricated by foolish men to overthrow predestination. It is unnecessary to refute things which, as soon as they are advanced, sufficiently prove their own falsehood. I shall dwell only on those things which are subjects of controversy among the learned, or which may occasion difficulty to simple minds, or which impiety speciously pleads in order to stigmatize the Divine justice.

CHAPTER XXII

Testimonies of Scripture in Confirmation of This Doctrine

ALL the positions we have advanced are controverted by many, especially the gratuitous election of believers, which nevertheless cannot be shaken. It is a notion commonly entertained, that God, foreseeing what would be the respective merits of every individual, makes a correspondent distinction between different persons; that he adopts as his children such as he foreknows will be deserving of his grace, and devotes to the damnation of death others, whose dispositions he sees will be inclined to wickedness and impiety. Thus they not only obscure election by covering it with the veil of foreknowledge, but pretend that it originates in another cause. Nor is this commonly received notion the opinion of the vulgar only, for it has had great advocates in all ages; which I candidly confess, that no one may cherish a confidence of injuring our cause by opposing us with their names. For the truth of God on this point is too certain to be shaken, too clear to be overthrown by the authority of men. Others, neither acquainted with the Scripture, nor deserving of any attention, oppose the sound doctrine with extreme presumption and intolerable effrontery. God's sovereign election of some, and preterition of others, they make the subject of formal accusation against him. But if this is the known fact, what will they gain by quarrelling with God? We teach nothing but what experience has proved, that God has always been at liberty to bestow his grace on whom he chooses. I will not inquire how the posterity of Abraham excelled other nations, unless it was by that favour, the cause of which can only be found in God. Let them answer why they are men, and not oxen or asses: when it was in God's power to create them dogs, he formed them after his own image. Will they allow the brute animals to expostulate with God respecting their condition, as though the distinction were unjust? Their enjoyment of a privilege which they have acquired by no merits, is certainly no more reasonable than God's various distribution of his favours according to the measure of his judgment. If they make a transition to persons where the inequality is more offensive to them, the example of Christ at least ought to deter them from carelessly prating concerning this sublime mystery. A mortal man is conceived of the seed of David: to the merit of what virtues will they ascribe his being made, even in the womb, the Head of angels, the only begotten Son of God, the Image and Glory of the Father, the Light, Righteousness, and Salvation of the world? It is judiciously remarked by Augustine, that there is the brightest example of gratuitous election in the Head of the Church himself, that it may not perplex us in the members; that he did not become the Son of God by leading a righteous life, but was gratuitously invested with this high honour, that he might afterwards render others partakers of the gifts bestowed upon him. If any one inquire, why others are not all that he was, or why we are all at such a vast distance from him,—why we are all corrupt, and he purity itself,—he will betray both folly and impudence. But if they persist in the wish to deprive God of the uncontrollable right of choosing and rejecting, let them also take away what is given to Christ. Now, it is of importance to attend to what the Scripture declares respecting every individual. Paul's assertion, that we were "chosen in Christ before the foundation of the world," (*g*) certainly precludes any consideration of merit in us; for it is as though he had said, our heavenly Father, finding nothing worthy of his choice in all the posterity

---

(*g*) Ephes. i. 4.

of Adam, turned his views towards his Christ, to choose members from his body whom he would admit to the fellowship of life. Let believers, then, be satisfied with this reason, that we were adopted in Christ to the heavenly inheritance, because in ourselves we were incapable of such high dignity. He has a similar remark in another place, where he exhorts the Colossians to "give thanks unto the Father, who had made them meet to be partakers of the inheritance of the saints." (*h*) If election precedes this grace of God, which makes us meet to obtain the glory of the life to come, what will God find in us to induce him to elect us? Another passage from this apostle will still more clearly express my meaning. "He hath chosen us," he says, "before the foundation of the world, according to the good pleasure of his will, that we should be holy, and without blame before him;" (*i*) where he opposes the good pleasure of God to all our merits whatsoever.

II. To render the proof more complete, it will be useful to notice all the clauses of that passage, which, taken in connection, leave no room for doubt. By the appellation of the *elect* or *chosen,* he certainly designates believers, as he soon after declares: wherefore it is corrupting the term by a shameful fiction to restrict it to the age in which the gospel was published. By saying that they were elected before the creation of the world, he precludes every consideration of merit. For what could be the reason for discrimination between those who yet had no existence, and whose condition was afterward to be the same in Adam? Now, if they are chosen in Christ, it follows, not only that each individual is chosen out of himself, but also that some are separated from others; for it is evident, that all are not members of Christ. The next clause, stating them to have been "chosen that they might be holy," fully refutes the error which derives election from foreknowledge; since Paul, on the contrary, declares that all the virtue discovered in men is the effect of election. If any inquiry be made after a superior cause, Paul replies, that God thus "predestinated," and that it was "according to the good pleasure of his will." This overturns any means of election which

(*h*) Col. i. 12. (*i*) Ephes. i. 4, 5.

men imagine in themselves; for all the benefits conferred by God for the spiritual life, he represents as flowing from this one source, that God elected whom he would, and, before they were born, laid up in reserve for them the grace with which he determined to favor them.

III. Wherever this decree of God reigns, there can be no consideration of any works. The antithesis, indeed, is not pursued here; but it must be understood, as it is amplified by the same writer in another place: "Who hath called us with a holy calling, not according to our works, but according to his own purpose and grace, which was given us in Christ Jesus, before the world began." (*k*) And we have already shown that the following clause, "that we should be holy," removes every difficulty. For say, Because he foresaw they would be holy, therefore he chose them, and you will invert the order of Paul. We may safely infer, then, If he chose us that we should be holy, his foresight of our future holiness was not the cause of his choice. For these two propositions, That the holiness of believers is the fruit of election, and, That they attain it by means of works, are incompatible with each other. Nor is there any force in the cavil to which they frequently resort, that the grace of election was not God's reward of antecedent works, but his gift to future ones. For when it is said, that believers were elected that they should be holy, it is fully implied, that the holiness they were in future to possess had its origin in election. And what consistency would there be in asserting, that things derived from election were the causes of election? A subsequent clause seems further to confirm what he had said—"according to his good pleasure, which he purposed in himself." (*l*) For the assertion, that God purposed in himself, is equivalent to saying, that he considered nothing out of himself, with any view to influence his determination. Therefore he immediately subjoins, that the great and only object of our election is, "that we should be to the praise of" Divine "grace." Certainly the grace of God deserves not the sole praise of our election, unless this election be gratuitous. Now, it could not be gratuitous, if, in choosing his people, God himself con-

(*k*) 2 Tim. i. 9. (*l*) Ephes. i. 9.

sidered what would be the nature of their respective works. The declaration of Christ to his disciples, therefore, is universally applicable to all believers: "Ye have not chosen me, but I have chosen you;" (*m*) which not only excludes past merits, but signifies that they had nothing in themselves to cause their election, independently of his preventing mercy. This also is the meaning of that passage of Paul, "Who hath first given to him, and it shall be recompensed unto him again? (*n*) For his design is to show, that God's goodness altogether anticipates men, finding nothing in them, either past or future, to conciliate his favour towards them.

IV. In the Epistle to the Romans, where he goes to the bottom of this argument, and pursues it more at length, he says, "They are not all Israel which are" born "of Israel;" (*o*) because though all were blessed by hereditary right, yet the succession did not pass to all alike. This controversy originated in the pride and vain-glorying of the Jewish people, who, claiming for themselves the title of the Church, would make the faith of the gospel to depend on their decision; just as, in the present day, the Papists with this false pretext would substitute themselves in the place of God. Paul, though he admits the posterity of Abraham to be holy in consequence of the covenant, yet contends that most of them are strangers to it; and that not only because they degenerate, from legitimate children becoming spurious ones, but because the preëminence and sovereignty belong to God's special election, which is the sole foundation of the validity of their adoption. If some were established in the hope of salvation by their own piety, and the rejection of others were owing wholly to their own defection, Paul's reference of his readers to the secret election would indeed be weak and absurd. Now, if the will of God, of which no cause appears or must be sought out of himself, discriminates some from others, so that the children of Israel are not all true Israelites, it is in vain pretended that the condition of every individual originates with himself. He pursues the subject further under the example of Jacob and Esau; for being both children of Abraham, and both enclosed in their

---

(*m*) John xv. 16. (*n*) Rom. xi. 35. (*o*) Rom. ix. 6.

mother's womb, the transfer of the honour of primogeniture to Jacob was by a preternatural change, which Paul, however, contends indicated the election of the one and the reprobation of the other. The origin and the cause are inquired, which the champions of foreknowledge maintain to be exhibited in the virtues and the vices of men. For this is their short and easy doctrine— That God has showed in the person of Jacob, that he elects such as are worthy of his grace; and in the person of Esau, that he rejects those whom he foresees to be unworthy. This, indeed, they assert with confidence; but what is the testimony of Paul? "The children being not yet born, neither having done any good or evil, that the purpose of God according to election might stand, not of works, but of him that calleth, it was said, The elder shall serve the younger; as it is written, Jacob have I loved, but Esau have I hated." (*p*) If this distinction between the brothers was influenced by foreknowledge, the mention of the time must certainly be unnecessary. On the supposition that Jacob was elected, because that honour was acquired by his future virtues, to what purpose could Paul remark that he was not yet born? It would not have been so proper to add, that he had not yet done any good; for it will be immediately replied, that nothing is concealed from God, and therefore the piety of Jacob must have been present before him. If grace be the reward of works, they ought to have had their just value attributed to them before Jacob was born, as much as if he were already grown to maturity. But the apostle proceeds in unravelling the difficulty, and teaches that the adoption of Jacob flowed not from works, but from the calling of God. In speaking of works, he introduces no time, future or past, but positively opposes them to the calling of God, intending the establishment of the one, and the absolute subversion of the other; as though he had said, We must consider the good pleasure of God, and not the productions of men. Lastly, the very terms, *election* and *purpose*, certainly exclude from this subject all the causes frequently invented by men, independently of God's secret counsel.

V. Now, what pretexts will be urged to obscure these argu-

(*p*) Rom. ix. 11—13.

ments, by those who attribute to works, either past or future, any influence on election? For this is nothing but an evasion of the apostle's argument, that the distinction between the two brothers depends not on any consideration of works, but on the mere calling of God, because it was fixed between them when they were not yet born. Nor would their subtilty have escaped him, if there had been any solidity in it; but well knowing the impossibility of God's foreseeing any good in man, except what he had first determined to bestow by the benefit of his election, he resorts not to the preposterous order of placing good works before their cause. We have the apostle's authority that the salvation of believers is founded solely on the decision of Divine election, and that that favour is not procured by works, but proceeds from gratuitous calling. We have also a lively exhibition of this truth in a particular example. Jacob and Esau are brothers, begotten of the same parents, still enclosed in the same womb, not yet brought forth into light; there is in all respects a perfect equality between them; yet the judgment of God concerning them is different. For he takes one, and rejects the other. The primogeniture was the only thing that gave one a right of priority to the other. But that also is passed by, and on the younger is bestowed what is refused to the elder. In other instances, also, God appears always to have treated primogeniture with designed and decided contempt, to cut off from the flesh all occasion of boasting. He rejects Ishmael, and favours Isaac. He degrades Manasseh, and honours Ephraim.

VI. If it be objected, that from these inferior and inconsiderable benefits, it must not be concluded respecting the life to come, that he who has been raised to the honour of primogeniture is therefore to be considered as adopted to the inheritance of heaven,—for there are many who spare not Paul, as though in his citation of Scripture testimonies he had perverted them from their genuine meaning,—I answer as before, that the apostle has neither erred through inadvertency, nor wilfully perverted testimonies of Scripture. But he saw, what they cannot bear to consider, that God intended by an earthly symbol to declare the spiritual election of Jacob, which otherwise lay concealed behind his inaccessible tribunal. For unless the primogeniture granted him had reference to the future world, it was a vain and ridiculous kind of blessing, which produced him nothing but various afflictions and adversities, grievous exile, numerous cares, and bitter sorrows. Discerning, beyond all doubt, that God's external blessing was an indication of the spiritual and permanent blessing he had prepared for his servant in his kingdom, Paul hesitated not to argue from the former in proof of the latter. It must also be remembered, that to the land of Canaan was annexed the pledge of the celestial residence; so that it ought not to be doubted that Jacob was ingrafted with angels into the body of Christ, that he might be a partaker of the same life. While Esau is rejected, therefore, Jacob is elected, and distinguished from him by God's predestination, without any difference of merit. If you inquire the cause, the apostle assigns the following: "For he saith to Moses, I will have mercy on whom I will have mercy, and I will have compassion on whom I will have compassion." (*q*) And what is this but a plain declaration of the Lord, that he finds no cause in men to induce him to show favour to them, but derives it solely from his own mercy; and therefore that the salvation of his people is his work? When God fixes your salvation in himself alone, why will you descend into yourself? When he assigns you his mere mercy, why will you have recourse to your own merits? When he confines all your attention to his mercy, why will you divert part of it to the contemplation of your own works? We must therefore come to that more select people, whom Paul in another place tells us "God foreknew," (*r*) not using this word, according to the fancy of our opponents, to signify a prospect, from a place of idle observation, of things which he has no part in transacting, but in the sense in which it is frequently used. For certainly, when Peter says that Christ was "delivered" to death "by the determinate counsel and foreknowledge of God," (*s*) he introduces God not as a mere spectator, but as the Author of our salvation. So the same apostle, by calling believers, to whom he writes, "elect according to the foreknowledge of God," (*t*) properly expresses that secret predestination by which God has marked out whom he would as his chil-

(*q*) Rom. ix. 15.
(*r*) Rom. xi. 2.
(*s*) Acts ii. 23.
(*t*) 1 Pet. i. 2.

dren. And the word *purpose,* which is added as a synonymous term, and in common speech is always expressive of fixed determination, undoubtedly implies that God, as the Author of our salvation, does not go out of himself. In this sense Christ is called, in the same chapter, the "Lamb foreknown before the foundation of the world." For what can be more absurd or uninteresting, than God's looking from on high to see from what quarter salvation would come to mankind? The people, therefore, whom Paul describes as "foreknown," (*u*) are no other than a small number scattered among the multitude, who falsely pretend to be the people of God. In another place also, to repress the boasting of hypocrites assuming before the world the preëminence among the godly, Paul declares, "The Lord knoweth them that are his." (*x*) Lastly, by this expression Paul designates two classes of people, one consisting of the whole race of Abraham, the other separated from it, reserved under the eyes of God, and concealed from the view of men. And this, without doubt, he gathered from Moses, who asserts that God will be merciful to whom he will be merciful; though he is speaking of the chosen people, whose condition was, to outward appearance, all alike; as though he had said, that the common adoption includes in it peculiar grace towards some, who resemble a more sacred treasure; that the common covenant prevents not this small number being exempted from the common lot; and that, determined to represent himself as the uncontrolled dispenser and arbiter in this affair, he positively denies that he will have mercy on one rather than another, from any other motive than his own pleasure; because, when mercy meets a person who seeks it, though he suffers no repulse, yet he either anticipates or in some degree obtains for himself that favour, of which God claims to himself all the praise.

VII. Now, let the supreme Master and Judge decide the whole matter. Beholding in his hearers such extreme obduracy, that his discourses were scattered among the multitude almost without any effect, to obviate this offence, he exclaims, "All that the Father giveth me, shall come to me. And this is the Father's will, that

---

(*u*) Rom. xi. 2. (*x*) 2 Tim. ii. 19.

of all which he hath given me, I should lose nothing." (*y*) Observe, the origin is from the donation of the Father, that we are given into the custody and protection of Christ. Here, perhaps, some one may argue in a circle, and object, that none are considered as the Father's peculiar people, but those whose surrender has been voluntary, arising from faith. But Christ only insists on this point—that notwithstanding the defections of vast multitudes, shaking the whole world, yet the counsel of God will be stable and firmer than the heavens, so that election can never fail. They are said to have been the elect of the Father, before he gave them to his only begotten Son. Is it inquired whether this was by nature? No, he draws those who were strangers, and so makes them his children. The language of Christ is too clear to be perplexed by the quibbles of sophistry: "No man can come to me, except the Father draw him. Every man that hath heard and learned of the Father, cometh unto me." (*z*) If all men promiscuously submitted to Christ, election would be common: now, the fewness of believers discovers a manifest distinction. Having asserted his disciples therefore, who were given to him, to be the peculiar portion of the Father, Christ a little after adds, "I pray not for the world, but for them which thou hast given me, for they are thine;" (*a*) which shows that the whole world does not belong to its Creator; only that grace delivers from the curse and wrath of God, and from eternal death, a few, who would otherwise perish, but leaves the world in its destruction, to which it has been destined. At the same time, though Christ introduces himself in his mediatorial capacity, yet he claims to himself the right of election, in common with the Father. "I speak not of all," he says; "I know whom I have chosen." (*b*) If it be inquired whence he chose them, he elsewhere answers, "out of the world," (*c*) which he excludes from his prayers, when he commends his disciples to the Father. It must be admitted, that when Christ asserts his knowledge of whom he has chosen, it refers to a particular class of mankind, and that they are distinguished, not by the nature of their virtues, but by the decree of Heaven. Whence it follows, that none attain any excellence by their own

---

(*y*) John vi. 37, 39. (*z*) John vi. 44, 45. (*a*) John xvii. 9. (*b*) John xiii. 18. (*c*) John xv. 19.

ability or industry, since Christ represents himself as the author of election. His enumeration of Judas among the elect, though he was a devil, only refers to the apostolical office, which, though an illustrious instance of the Divine favour, as Paul so frequently acknowledges in his own person, yet does not include the hope of eternal salvation. Judas, therefore, in his unfaithful exercise of the apostleship, might be worse than a devil; but of those whom Christ has once united to his body, he will never suffer one to perish; for in securing their salvation, he will perform what he has promised, by exerting the power of God, who is greater than all. What he says in another place, "Those that thou gavest me I have kept, and none of them is lost, but the son of perdition," is a mode of expression, called *catachresis*, but the sense is sufficiently plain. The conclusion is, that God creates whom he chooses to be his children by gratuitous adoption; that the cause of this is wholly in himself; because he exclusively regards his own secret determination.

VIII. But, it will be said, Ambrose, Origen, and Jerome believed that God dispenses his grace among men, according to his foreknowledge of the good use which every individual will make of it. Augustine also was once of the same sentiment; but when he had made a greater proficiency in scriptural knowledge, he not only retracted, but powerfully confuted it. And after his retractation, rebuking the Pelagians for persisting in this error, he says, "Who but must wonder that this most ingenious sense should escape the apostle? For after proposing what was calculated to excite astonishment respecting those children yet unborn, he started to himself, by way of objection, the following question: What, then, is there unrighteousness with God? It was the place for him to answer, that God foresaw the merits of each of them; yet he says nothing of this, but resorts to the decrees and mercy of God." And in another place, after having discarded all merits antecedent to election, he says, "Here undoubtedly falls to the ground the vain reasoning of those who defend the foreknowledge of God in opposition to his grace, and affirm that we were elected before the foundation of the world, because God foreknew that we would be good, not that he himself would make us good. This is not the language of him who says, 'Ye have not chosen me, but

I have chosen you.' (*d*) For if he elected us because he foreknew our future good, he must also have foreknown our choice of him;" and more to the like purpose. This testimony should have weight with those who readily acquiesce in the authority of the fathers. Though Augustine will not allow himself to be disunited from the rest, but shows by clear testimonies the falsehood of that discordance, with the odium of which he was loaded by the Pelagians, he makes the following quotations from Ambrose's book on predestination: "Whom Christ has mercy on, him he calls. Those who were indevout he could, if he would, have made devout. But God calls whom he pleases, and makes whom he will religious." If I were inclined to compile a whole volume from Augustine, I could easily show my readers, that I need no words but his; but I am unwilling to burden them with prolixity. But come, let us suppose them to be silent; let us attend to the subject itself. A difficult question was raised—Whether it was a just procedure in God to favour with his grace certain particular persons. This Paul could have decided by a single word, if he had pleaded the consideration of works. Why, then, does he not do this, but rather continue his discourse involved in the same difficulty? Why, but from necessity? for the Holy Spirit, who spoke by his mouth, never laboured under the malady of forgetfulness. Without any evasion or circumlocution, therefore, he answers, that God favours his elect because he will, and has mercy because he will. For this oracle, "I will be gracious to whom I will be gracious, and will show mercy on whom I will show mercy," (*e*) is equivalent to a declaration, that God is excited to mercy by no other motive than his own will to be merciful. The observation of Augustine therefore remains true, "that the grace of God does not find men fit to be elected, but makes them so."

IX. We shall not dwell upon the sophistry of Thomas Aquinas, "that the foreknowledge of merits is not the cause of predestination in regard to the act of him who predestinates; but that with regard to us, it may in some sense be so called, according to the particular consideration of predestination; as when God is said to predestinate glory for man according to merits, because he

(*d*) John xv. 16. (*e*) Exod. xxxiii. 19.

decreed to give him grace by which glory is merited." For since the Lord allows us to contemplate nothing in election but his mere goodness, the desire of any one to see any thing more is a preposterous disposition. But if we were inclined to a contention of subtilty, we should be at no loss to refute this petty sophism of Aquinas. He contends that glory is in a certain sense predestinated for the elect according to their merits, because God predestinates to them the grace by which glory is merited. What if I, on the contrary, reply, that predestination to grace is subordinate to election to life, and attendant upon it? that grace is predestinated to those to whom the possession of glory has been already assigned; because it pleases the Lord to conduct his children from election to justification? For hence it will follow, that predestination to glory is rather the cause of predestination to grace, than the contrary. But let us dismiss these controversies; they are unnecessary with those who think they have wisdom enough in the word of God. For it was truly remarked by an ancient ecclesiastical writer, That they who ascribe God's election to merits, are wiser than they ought to be.

X. It is objected by some, that God will be inconsistent with himself, if he invites all men universally to come to him, and receives only a few elect. Thus, according to them, the universality of the promises destroys the discrimination of special grace; and this is the language of some moderate men, not so much for the sake of suppressing the truth, as to exclude thorny questions, and restrain the curiosity of many. The end is laudable, but the means cannot be approved; for disingenuous evasion can never be excused; but with those who use insult and invective, it is a foul cavil or a shameful error. How the Scripture reconciles these two facts, that by external preaching all are called to repentance and faith, and yet that the spirit of repentance and faith is not given to all, I have elsewhere stated, and shall soon have occasion partly to repeat. What they assume, I deny as being false in two respects. For he who threatens drought to one city while it rains upon another, and who denounces to another place a famine of doctrine, (*f*) lays himself under no positive obligation to call all

(*f*) Amos iv. 7; viii. 11.

men alike. And he who, forbidding Paul to preach the word in Asia, and suffering him not to go into Bithynia, calls him into Macedonia, (*g*) demonstrates his right to distribute this treasure to whom he pleases. In Isaiah, he still more fully declares his destination of the promises of salvation exclusively for the elect; for of them only, and not indiscriminately of all mankind, he declares that they shall be his disciples. (*h*) Whence it appears, that when the doctrine of salvation is offered to all for their effectual benefit, it is a corrupt prostitution of that which is declared to be reserved particularly for the children of the church. At present let this suffice, that though the voice of the gospel addresses all men generally, yet the gift of faith is bestowed on few. Isaiah assigns the cause, that "the arm of the Lord" is not "revealed" to all. (*i*) If he had said, that the gospel is wickedly and perversely despised, because many obstinately refuse to hear it, perhaps there would be some colour for this notion of the universal call. The design of the prophet is not to extenuate the guilt of men, when he states that the source of blindness is God's not deigning to reveal his arm to them; he only suggests that their ears are in vain assailed with external doctrine, because faith is a peculiar gift. I would wish to be informed by these teachers, whether men become children of God by mere preaching, or by faith. Surely, when John declares that all who believe in God's only begotten Son, are themselves made the children of God, (*k*) this is not said of all the hearers of the word in a confused mass, but a particular rank is assigned to believers, "which were born, not of blood, nor of the will of the flesh, nor of the will of man, but of God." (*l*) But they say, there is a mutual agreement between faith and the word. This is the case wherever there is any faith; but it is no new thing for the seed to fall among thorns or in stony places; not only because most men are evidently in actual rebellion against God, but because they are not all endued with eyes and ears. Where, then, will be the consistency of God's calling to himself such as he knows will never come? Let Augustine answer for me: "Do you wish to dispute with me? Rather unite with me in admiration, and exclaim, O the depth! Let us

(*g*) Acts xvi. 6—10. (*h*) Isaiah viii. 16, &c. (*i*) Isaiah liii. 1. (*k*) John i. 12. (*l*) John i. 13.

both agree in fear, lest we perish in error." Besides, if election is, as Paul represents it, the parent of faith, I retort that argument upon them, that faith cannot be general, because election is special. For from the connection of causes and effects, it is easily inferred, when Paul says, "God hath blessed us with all spiritual blessings, according as he hath chosen us before the foundation of the world;" that therefore these treasures are not common to all, because God has chosen only such as he pleased. This is the reason why, in another place, he commends "the faith of God's elect;" (*m*) that none may be supposed to acquire faith by any exertion of their own, but that God may retain the glory of freely illuminating the objects of his previous election. For Bernard justly observes, "Friends hear each one for himself when he addresses them, 'Fear not, little flock, for to you it is given to know the mystery of the kingdom of heaven.' Who are these? Certainly those whom he has foreknown and predestinated to be conformed to the image of his Son. The great and secret counsel has been revealed. The Lord knows who are his, but what was known to God is manifested to men. Nor does he favour any others with the participation of so great a mystery, but those particular individuals whom he foreknew, and predestinated to be his own." A little after he concludes, "The mercy of God is from everlasting to everlasting upon them that fear him; from everlasting in predestination, to everlasting in beatification; the one knowing no beginning; the other, no end." But what necessity is there for citing the testimony of Bernard, since we hear from the Master's own mouth, that "no man hath seen the Father, save he which is of God," (*n*) which implies, that all who are not regenerated by God, are stupefied with the splendour of his countenance. Faith, indeed, is properly connected with election, provided it occupies the second place. This order is clearly expressed in these words of Christ: "This is the Father's will, that of all which he hath given me, I should lose nothing. And this is the will of him that sent me, that every one which believeth on the Son, may have everlasting life." (*o*) If he willed the salvation of all, he would give them

(*m*) Titus i. 1. (*n*) John vi. 46. (*o*) John vi. 39, 40.

all into the custody of his Son, and unite them all to his body by the sacred bond of faith. Now, it is evident, that faith is the peculiar pledge of his paternal love, reserved for his adopted children. Therefore Christ says in another place, "The sheep follow the shepherd, for they know his voice; and a stranger will they not follow, for they know not the voice of strangers." (*p*) Whence arises this difference, but because their ears are divinely penetrated? For no man makes himself a sheep, but is created such by heavenly grace. Hence also the Lord proves the perpetual certainty and security of our salvation, because it is kept by the invincible power of God. (*q*) Therefore he concludes that unbelievers are not his sheep, because they are not of the number of those whom God by Isaiah promised to him for his future disciples. (*r*) Moreover, the testimonies I have cited, being expressive of perseverance, are so many declarations of the invari[illegible] perpetuity of election.

XI. Now, with respect to the reprobate, whom the apostle introduces in the same place; as Jacob, without any merit yet acquired by good works, is made an object of grace, so Esau, while yet unpolluted by any crime, is accounted an object of hatred. (*s*) If we turn our attention to works, we insult the apostle, as though he saw not that which is clear to us. Now, that he saw none, is evident, because he expressly asserts the one to have been elected and the other rejected while they had not done any good or evil; in order to prove the foundation of Divine predestination not to be in works. (*t*) Secondly, when he raises the objection whether God is unjust, he never urges, what would have been the most absolute and obvious defence of his justice, that God rewarded Esau according to his wickedness; but contents himself with a different solution, that the reprobate are raised up for this purpose, that the glory of God may be displayed by their means. Lastly, he subjoins a concluding observation, that "God hath mercy on whom he will have mercy, and whom he will he hardeneth." (*u*) You see how he attributes both

---

(*p*) John x. 4; 5.
(*q*) John x. 29.
(*r*) John x. 26.
(*s*) Rom. ix. 13.
(*t*) Rom. ix. 11.
(*u*) Rom. ix. 18.

to the mere will of God. If, therefore, we can assign no reason why he grants mercy to his people but because such is his pleasure, neither shall we find any other cause but his will for the reprobation of others. For when God is said to harden or show mercy to whom he pleases, men are taught by this declaration to seek no cause beside his will.

CHAPTER XXIII

A Refutation of the Calumnies Generally, But Unjustly, Urged Against This Doctrine

WHEN the human mind hears these things, its petulance breaks all restraint, and it discovers as serious and violent agitation as if alarmed by the sound of a martial trumpet. Many, indeed, as if they wished to avert odium from God, admit election in such a way as to deny that any one is reprobated. But this is puerile and absurd, because election itself could not exist without being opposed to reprobation. God is said to separate those whom he adopts to salvation. To say that others obtain by chance, or acquire by their own efforts, that which election alone confers on a few, will be worse than absurd. Whom God passes by, therefore, he reprobates, and from no other cause than his determination to exclude them from the inheritance which he predestines for his children. And the petulance of men is intolerable, if it refuses to be restrained by the word of God, which treats of his incomprehensible counsel, adored by angels themselves. But now we have heard that hardening proceeds from the Divine power and will, as much as mercy. Unlike the persons I have mentioned, Paul never strives to excuse God by false allegations; he only declares that it is unlawful for a thing formed to quarrel with its maker. (*x*) Now, how will those, who admit not that any are reprobated by God, evade this declaration of Christ: "Every plant which my heavenly Father hath not planted, shall be rooted up?" (*y*) Upon all whom our heavenly Father has not deigned to plant as sacred trees in his garden, they hear destruction plainly denounced. If they deny this to be a sign of reprobation, there is nothing so clear as to be capable of proof to such persons. But if they cease not their clamour, let the sobriety of faith be satisfied with this admonition of Paul, that there is no cause for quarrelling with God, if, on the one hand, willing to show his wrath, and to make his power known, he endures, "with much long-suffering, the vessels of wrath fitted to destruction;" and on the other, makes "known the riches of his glory on the vessels of mercy, whom he had afore prepared unto glory." (*z*) Let the reader observe that, to preclude every pretext for murmurs and censures, Paul ascribes supreme dominion to the wrath and power of God; because it is unreasonable for those deep judgments, which absorb all our faculties, to be called in question by us. It is a frivolous reply of our adversaries, that God does not wholly reject the objects of his long-suffering, but remains in suspense towards them, awaiting the possibility of their repentance; as though Paul attributed patience to God, in expectation of the conversion of those whom he asserts to be fitted to destruction. For Augustine, in expounding this passage, where power is connected with patience, justly observes, that God's power is not permissive, but influential. They observe, also, that it is not said without meaning, that the vessels of wrath are fitted to destruction, but that God prepared the vessels of mercy; since by this mode of expression, he ascribes and challenges to God the praise of salvation, and throws the blame of perdition upon those who by their choice procure it to themselves. But though I concede to them, that Paul softens the asperity of the former clause by the difference of phraseology, yet it is not at all consistent to transfer the preparation for destruction to any other than the secret counsel of God; which is also asserted just before in the context, that "God raised up Pharaoh,

(*x*) Rom. ix. 20. (*y*) Matt. xv. 13. (*z*) Rom. ix. 22, 23.

and whom he will he hardeneth." Whence it follows, that the cause of hardening is the secret counsel of God. This, however, I maintain, which is observed by Augustine that when God turns wolves into sheep, he renovates them by more powerful grace to conquer their obduracy; and therefore the obstinate are not converted, because God exerts not that mightier grace of which he is not destitute, if he chose to display it.

II. These things will amply suffice for persons of piety and modesty, who remember that they are men. But as these virulent adversaries are not content with one species of opposition, we will reply to them all as occasion shall require. Foolish mortals enter into many contentions with God, as though they could arraign him to plead to their accusations. In the first place they inquire, by what right the Lord is angry with his creatures who had not provoked him by any previous offence; for that to devote to destruction whom he pleases, is more like the caprice of a tyrant than the lawful sentence of a judge; that men have reason, therefore, to expostulate with God, if they are predestinated to eternal death without any demerit of their own, merely by his sovereign will. If such thoughts ever enter the minds of pious men, they will be sufficiently enabled to break their violence by this one consideration, how exceedingly presumptuous it is only to inquire into the causes of the Divine will; which is in fact, and is justly entitled to be, the cause of every thing that exists. For if it has any cause, then there must be something antecedent, on which it depends; which it is impious to suppose. For the will of God is the highest rule of justice; so that what he wills must be considered just, for this very reason, because he wills it. When it is inquired, therefore, why the Lord did so, the answer must be, Because he would. But if you go further, and ask why he so determined, you are in search of something greater and higher than the will of God, which can never be found. Let human temerity, therefore, desist from seeking that which is not, lest it should fail of finding that which is. This will be a sufficient restraint to any one disposed to reason with reverence concerning the secrets of his God. Against the audaciousness of the impious, who are not afraid openly to rail against God, the Lord will sufficiently defend himself by his own justice, without any vindication by us, when, depriving their consciences of every subterfuge, he shall convict them and bind them with a sense of their guilt. Yet we espouse not the notion of the Romish theologians concerning the absolute and arbitrary power of God, which, on account of its profaneness, deserves our detestation. We represent not God as lawless, who is a law to himself; because, as Plato says, laws are necessary to men, who are the subjects of evil desires; but the will of God is not only pure from every fault, but the highest standard of perfection, even the law of all laws. But we deny that he is liable to be called to any account; we deny also that we are proper judges, to decide on this cause according to our own apprehension. Wherefore, if we attempt to go beyond what is lawful, let us be deterred by the Psalmist, who tells us, that God will be clear when he is judged by mortal man. (*a*)

III. Thus God is able to check his enemies by silence. But that we may not suffer them to deride his holy name with impunity, he supplies us from his word with arms against them. Therefore, if any one attack us with such an inquiry as this, why God has from the beginning predestinated some men to death, who, not yet being brought into existence, could not yet deserve the sentence of death,—we will reply by asking them, in return, what they suppose God owes to man, if he chooses to judge of him from his own nature. As we are all corrupted by sin, we must necessarily be odious to God, and that not from tyrannical cruelty, but in the most equitable estimation of justice. If all whom the Lord predestinates to death are in their natural condition liable to the sentence of death, what injustice do they complain of receiving from him? Let all the sons of Adam come forward; let them all contend and dispute with their Creator, because by his eternal providence they were previously to their birth adjudged to endless misery. What murmur will they be able to raise against this vindication, when God, on the other hand, shall call them to a review of themselves. If they have all been taken from a corrupt mass, it is no wonder that they are subject to condemnation. Let them not, therefore, accuse God of injustice, if his eternal decree has destined them to death, to which they feel themselves, what-

(*a*) Psalm li. 4.

ever be their desire or aversion, spontaneously led forward by their own nature. Hence appears the perverseness of their disposition to murmur, because they intentionally suppress the cause of condemnation, which they are constrained to acknowledge in themselves, hoping to excuse themselves by charging it upon God. But though I ever so often admit God to be the author of it, which is perfectly correct, yet this does not abolish the guilt impressed upon their consciences, and from time to time recurring to their view.

IV. They further object, Were they not, by the decree of God, antecedently predestinated to that corruption which is now stated as the cause of condemnation? When they perish in their corruption, therefore, they only suffer the punishment of that misery into which, in consequence of his predestination, Adam fell, and precipitated his posterity with him. Is he not unjust, therefore, in treating his creatures with such cruel mockery? I confess, indeed, that all the descendants of Adam fell by the Divine will into that miserable condition in which they are now involved; and this is what I asserted from the beginning, that we must always return at last to the sovereign determination of God's will, the cause of which is hidden in himself. But it follows not, therefore, that God is liable to this reproach. For we will answer them thus in the language of Paul: "O man, who art thou that repliest against God? Shall the thing formed say to him that formed it, Why hast thou made me thus? Hath not the potter power over the clay, of the same lump, to make one vessel unto honour and another unto dishonour?" (*b*) They will deny this to be in reality any vindication of God's justice, and call it a subterfuge, such as is commonly resorted to by persons destitute of a sufficient defence. For what appears to be the meaning of this, but that God possesses power, that cannot be resisted, of doing any thing whatsoever according to his pleasure? But it is very different. For what stronger reason can be alleged, than when we are directed to consider who God is? How could any injustice be committed by him who is the Judge of the world? If it is the peculiar property of the nature of God to do justice, then he naturally loves right-

(*b*) Rom. ix. 20, 21.

eousness and hates iniquity. The apostle, therefore, has not resorted to sophistry, as if he were in danger of confutation, but has shown that the reason of the Divine justice is too high to be measured by a human standard, or comprehended by the littleness of the human mind. The apostle, indeed, acknowledges that there is a depth in the Divine judgments sufficient to absorb the minds of all mankind, if they attempt to penetrate it. But he also teaches how criminal it is to reduce the works of God to such a law, that on failing to discover the reason of them, we presume to censure them. It is a well known observation of Solomon, though few rightly understand it, that "the great God, that formed all things, both rewardeth the fool, and rewardeth transgressors." (*c*) For he is proclaiming the greatness of God, whose will it is to punish fools and transgressors, although he favours them not with his Spirit. And men betray astonishing madness in desiring to comprehend immensity within the limits of their reason. The angels who stood in their integrity, Paul calls "elect;" (*d*) if their constancy rested on the Divine pleasure, the defection of the others argues their being forsaken—a fact for which no other cause can be assigned than the reprobation hidden in the secret counsel of God.

V. Now, to any follower of Manes or Celestius, a calumniator of Divine Providence, I reply with Paul, that no account ought to be given of it, for its greatness far surpasses our understanding. What wonder or absurdity is there in this? Would he have the Divine power so limited, as to be unable to execute more than his little capacity can comprehend? I say, with Augustine, that the Lord created those who, he certainly foreknew, would fall into destruction, and that this was actually so because he willed it; but of his will it belongs not to us to demand the reason, which we are incapable of comprehending; nor is it reasonable that the Divine will should be made the subject of controversy with us, which, whenever it is discussed, is only another name for the highest rule of justice. Why, then, is any question started concerning injustice, where justice is evidently conspicuous? Nor let us be ashamed to follow the example of Paul, and stop the mouths

(*c*) Prov. xxvi. 10. (*d*) 1 Tim. v. 21.

of unreasonable and wicked men in this manner, repeating the same answer as often as they shall dare to repeat their complaints. Who are you, miserable mortals, preferring an accusation against God, because he accommodates not the greatness of his works to your ignorance? as though they were necessarily wrong, because they are concealed from carnal view. Of the immensity of God's judgments you have the clearest evidences. You know they are called "a great deep." Now, examine your contracted intellects, whether they can comprehend God's secret decrees. What advantage or satisfaction do you gain from plunging yourselves, by your mad researches, into an abyss that reason itself pronounces will be fatal to you? Why are you not at least restrained by some fear of what is contained in the history of Job and the books of the prophets, concerning the inconceivable wisdom and terrible power of God? If your mind is disturbed, embrace without reluctance the advice of Augustine: "You, a man, expect an answer from me, who am also a man. Let us, therefore, both hear him, who says, O man, who art thou? Faithful ignorance is better than presumptuous knowledge. Seek merits; you will find nothing but punishment. O the depth! Peter denies; the thief believes; O the depth! Do you seek a reason? I will tremble at the depth. Do you reason? I will wonder. Do you dispute? I will believe. I see the depth, I reach not the bottom. Paul rested, because he found admiration. He calls the judgments of God unsearchable; and are you come to scrutinize them? He says, his ways are past finding out; and are you come to investigate them?" We shall do no good by proceeding any further; it will not satisfy their petulance; and the Lord needs no other defence than what he has employed by his Spirit, speaking by the mouth of Paul; and we forget to speak well when we cease to speak with God.

VI. Impiety produces also a second objection, which directly tends, not so much to the crimination of God, as to the vindication of the sinner; though the sinner whom God condemns cannot be justified without the disgrace of the Judge. For this is their profane complaint, Why should God impute as a fault to man those things which were rendered necessary by his predestination? What should they do? Should they resist his decrees? This would be vain, for it would be impossible. Therefore they are not justly punished for those things of which God's predestination is the principal cause. Here I shall refrain from the defence commonly resorted to by ecclesiastical writers, that the foreknowledge of God prevents not man from being considered as a sinner, since God foresees man's evils, not his own. For then the cavil would not stop here; it would rather be urged, that still God might, if he would, have provided against the evils he foresaw, and that not having done this, he created man expressly to this end, that he might so conduct himself in the world; but if, by the Divine Providence, man was created in such a state as afterwards to do whatever he actually does, he ought not to be charged with guilt for things which he cannot avoid, and to which the will of God constrains him. Let us see, then, how this difficulty should be solved. In the first place, the declaration of Solomon ought to be universally admitted, that "the Lord hath made all things for himself; yea, even the wicked for the day of evil." (*e*) Observe; all things being at God's disposal, and the decision of salvation or death belonging to him, he orders all things by his counsel and decree in such a manner, that some men are born devoted from the womb to certain death, that his name may be glorified in their destruction. If any one pleads, that no necessity was imposed on them by the providence of God, but rather that they were created by him in such a state in consequence of his foresight of their future depravity,—it will amount to nothing. The old writers used, indeed, to adopt this solution, though not without some degree of hesitation. But the schoolmen satisfy themselves with it, as though it admitted of no opposition. I will readily grant, indeed, that mere foreknowledge lays no necessity on the creatures, though this is not universally admitted; for there are some who maintain it to be the actual cause of what comes to pass. But Valla, a man otherwise not much versed in theology, appears to me to have discovered superior acuteness and judiciousness, by showing that this controversy is unnecessary, because both life and death are acts of God's will, rather than of his foreknowledge. If God simply foresaw the fates of men, and did not also dispose and fix them by his determination, there

(*e*) Prov. xvi. 4.

would be room to agitate the question, whether his providence or foresight rendered them at all necessary. But since he foresees future events only in consequence of his decree that they shall happen, it is useless to contend about foreknowledge, while it is evident that all things come to pass rather by ordination and decree.

VII. They say it is nowhere declared in express terms, that God decreed Adam should perish by his defection; as though the same God, whom the Scripture represents as doing whatever he pleases, created the noblest of his creatures without any determinate end. They maintain, that he was possessed of free choice, that he might be the author of his own fate, but that God decreed nothing more than to treat him according to his desert. If so weak a scheme as this be received, what will become of God's omnipotence, by which he governs all things according to his secret counsel, independently of every person or thing besides? But whether they wish it or dread it, predestination exhibits itself in Adam's posterity. For the loss of salvation by the whole race through the guilt of one parent, was an event that did not happen by nature. What prevents their acknowledging concerning one man, what they reluctantly grant concerning the whole species? Why should they lose their labour in sophistical evasions? The Scripture proclaims, that all men were, in the person of their father, sentenced to eternal death. This, not being attributable to nature, it is evident must have proceeded from the wonderful counsel of God. The perplexity and hesitation discovered at trifles by these pious defenders of the justice of God, and their facility in overcoming great difficulties, are truly absurd. I inquire again, how it came to pass that the fall of Adam, independent of any remedy, should involve so many nations with their infant children in eternal death, but because such was the will of God. Their tongues, so loquacious on every other point, must here be struck dumb. It is an awful decree, I confess; but no one can deny that God foreknew the future final fate of man before he created him, and that he did foreknow it because it was appointed by his own decree. If any one here attacks God's foreknowledge, he rashly and inconsiderately stumbles. For what ground of accusation is there against the heavenly Judge for not being ignorant of futurity? If there is any just or plausible complaint, it lies against predestination. Nor should it be thought absurd to affirm, that God not only foresaw the fall of the first man, and the ruin of his posterity in him, but also arranged all by the determination of his own will. For as it belongs to his wisdom to foreknow every thing future, so it belongs to his power to rule and govern all things by his hand. And this question also, as well as others, is judiciously discussed by Augustine. "We most wholesomely confess, what we most rightly believe, that the God and Lord of all things, who created every thing very good, and foreknew that evil would arise out of good, and knew that it was more suitable to his almighty goodness to bring good out of evil than not to suffer evil to exist, ordained the life of angels and men in such a manner as to exhibit in it, first, what free-will was capable of doing, and afterwards, what could be effected by the blessings of his grace, and the sentence of his justice."

VIII. Here they recur to the distinction between will and permission, and insist that God permits the destruction of the impious, but does not will it. But what reason shall we assign for his permitting it, but because it is his will? It is not probable, however, that man procured his own destruction by the mere permission, and without any appointment, of God; as though God had not determined what he would choose to be the condition of the principal of his creatures. I shall not hesitate, therefore, to confess plainly with Augustine, "that the will of God is the necessity of things, and that what he has willed will necessarily come to pass; as those things are really about to happen which he has foreseen." Now, if either Pelagians, or Manichæans, or Anabaptists, or Epicureans, (for we are concerned with these four sects on this argument,) in excuse for themselves and the impious, plead the necessity with which they are bound by God's predestination,—they allege nothing applicable to the case. For if predestination is no other than a dispensation of Divine justice,—mysterious indeed, but liable to no blame,—since it is certain they were not unworthy of being predestinated to that fate, it is equally certain, that the destruction they incur by predestination is consistent with the strictest justice. Besides, their perdition depends on the Divine predestination in such a manner, that the cause and matter of it are found in themselves. For the first man fell because the Lord had determined it was so expedient. The reason of this determination is unknown to us. Yet it is certain that he determined thus, only because he foresaw it would tend to the just illustration of the glory of his name. Whenever you hear the glory of God mentioned, think of his justice. For what deserves praise must be just. Man falls, therefore, according to the appointment of Divine Providence; but he falls by his own fault. The Lord had a little before pronounced "every thing that he had made" to be "very good." Whence, then, comes the depravity of man to revolt from his God? Lest it should be thought to come from creation, God had approved and commended what had proceeded from himself. By his own wickedness, therefore, he corrupted the nature he had received pure from the Lord, and by his fall he drew all his posterity with him into destruction. Wherefore let us rather contemplate the evident cause of condemnation, which is nearer to us in the corrupt nature of mankind, than search after a hidden and altogether incomprehensible one in the predestination of God. And we should feel no reluctance to submit our understanding to the infinite wisdom of God, so far as to acquiesce in its many mysteries. To be ignorant of things which it is neither possible nor lawful to know, is to be learned: an eagerness to know them, is a species of madness.

IX. Some one perhaps will say, that I have not yet adduced a sufficient answer to that sacrilegious excuse. I confess it is impossible ever wholly to prevent the petulance and murmurs of impiety; yet I think I have said what should suffice to remove not only all just ground, but every plausible pretext, for objection. The reprobate wish to be thought excusable in sinning, because they cannot avoid a necessity of sinning; especially since this necessity is laid upon them by the ordination of God. But we deny this to be a just excuse; because the ordination of God, by which they complain that they are destined to destruction, is guided by equity, unknown indeed to us, but indubitably certain. Whence we conclude, that they sustain no misery that is not inflicted upon them by the most righteous judgment of God. In the next place, we maintain that they act preposterously, who, in seeking for the origin of their condemnation, direct their views to the secret recesses of the Divine counsel, and overlook the corruption of nature, which is its real source. The testimony God gives to his creation prevents their imputing it to him. For though, by the eternal providence of God, man was created to that misery to which he is subject, yet the ground of it he has derived from himself, not from God; since he is thus ruined solely in consequence of his having degenerated from the pure creation of God to vicious and impure depravity.

X. The doctrine of God's predestination is calumniated by its adversaries, as involving a third absurdity. For when we attribute it solely to the determination of the Divine will, that those whom God admits to be heirs of his kingdom are exempted from the universal destruction, from this they infer, that he is a respecter of persons, which the Scripture uniformly denies; that, therefore, either the Scripture is inconsistent with itself, or in the election of God regard is had to merits. In the first place, the Scripture denies that God is a respecter of persons, in a different sense from that in which they understand it; for by the word *person,* it signifies not a man, but those things in a man, which, being conspicuous to the eyes, usually conciliate favour, honour, and dignity, or attract hatred, contempt, and disgrace. Such are riches, wealth, power, nobility, magistracy, country, elegance of form, on the one hand; and on the other hand, poverty, necessity, ignoble birth, slovenliness, contempt, and the like. Thus Peter and Paul declare that God is not a respecter of persons, because he makes no difference between the Jew and Greek, to reject one and receive the other, merely on account of his nation. (*f*) So James uses the same language when he means to assert, that God in his judgment pays no regard to riches. (*g*) And Paul, in another place, declares, that in judging, God has no respect to liberty or bondage. (*h*) There will, therefore, be no contradiction in our affirming, that according to the good pleasure of his will, God chooses whom he will as his children, irrespective of all merit, while he rejects and reprobates others. Yet, for the sake of further satisfaction, the matter may be explained in the following manner: They ask how it happens, that of two persons distinguished

---

(*f*) Acts x. 34. Rom. ii. 11. Gal. iii. 28.
(*g*) James ii. 5. (*h*) Col. iii. 25. Eph. vi. 9.

from each other by no merit, God, in his election, leaves one and takes another. I, on the other hand, ask them, whether they suppose him that is taken to possess any thing that can attract the favour of God. If they confess that he has not, as indeed they must, it will follow, that God looks not at man, but derives his motive to favour him from his own goodness. God's election of one man, therefore, while he rejects another, proceeds not from any respect of man, but solely from his own mercy; which may freely display and exert itself wherever and whenever it pleases. For we have elsewhere seen also that, from the beginning, not many noble, or wise, or honourable were called, (*i*) that God might humble the pride of flesh; so far is his favour from being confined to persons.

XI. Wherefore some people falsely and wickedly charge God with a violation of equal justice, because, in his predestination, he observes not the same uniform course of proceeding towards all. If he finds all guilty, they say, let him punish all alike; if innocent, let him withhold the rigour of justice from all. But they deal with him just as if either mercy were forbidden him, or, when he chooses to show mercy, he were constrained wholly to renounce justice. What is it that they require? If all are guilty, that they shall all suffer the same punishment. We confess the guilt to be common, but we say, that some are relieved by Divine mercy. They say, Let it relieve all. But we reply, Justice requires that he should likewise show himself to be a just judge in the infliction of punishment. When they object to this, what is it but attempting to deprive God of the opportunity to manifest his mercy, or to grant it to him, at least, on the condition that he wholly abandon his justice? Wherefore there is the greatest propriety in these observations of Augustine: "The whole mass of mankind having fallen into condemnation in the first man, the vessels that are formed from it to honour, are not vessels of personal righteousness, but of Divine mercy; and the formation of others to dishonour, is to be attributed, not to iniquity, but to the Divine decree," &c. While God rewards those whom he rejects with deserved punishment, and to those whom he calls, freely

(*i*) 1 Cor. i. 26.

gives undeserved grace, he is liable to no accusation, but may be compared to a creditor, who has power to release one, and enforce his demands on another. The Lord, therefore, may give grace to whom he will, because he is merciful, and yet not give it to all, because he is a just judge; may manifest his free grace, by giving to some what they never deserve, while, by not giving to all, he declares the demerit of all. For when Paul says, that "God hath concluded all under sin, that he might have mercy upon all," (*l*) it must, at the same time, be added, that he is debtor to none; for no man "hath first given to him," to entitle him to demand a recompense. (*m*)

XII. Another argument often urged to overthrow predestination is, that its establishment would destroy all solicitude and exertion for rectitude of conduct. For who can hear, they say, that either life or death is appointed for him by God's eternal and immutable decree, without immediately concluding that it is of no importance how he conducts himself; since no action of his can in any respect either impede or promote the predestination of God? Thus all will abandon themselves to despair, and run into every excess to which their licentious propensities may lead them. And truly this objection is not altogether destitute of truth; for there are many impure persons who bespatter the doctrine of predestination with these vile blasphemies, and with this pretext elude all admonitions and reproofs: God knows what he has determined to do with us: if he has decreed our salvation, he will bring us to it in his own time; if he has destined us to death, it will be in vain for us to strive against it. But the Scripture, while it inculcates superior awe and reverence of mind in the consideration of so great a mystery, instructs the godly in a very different conclusion, and fully refutes the wicked and unreasonable inferences of these persons. For the design of what it contains respecting predestination is, not that, being excited to presumption, we may attempt, with nefarious temerity, to scrutinize the inaccessible secrets of God, but rather that, being humbled and dejected, we may learn to tremble at his justice and admire his mercy. At this object believers will aim. But the impure

(*l*) Gal. iii. 22. Rom. xi. 32.

(*m*) Rom. xi. 35.

cavils of the wicked are justly restrained by Paul. They profess to go on securely in their vices; because if they are of the number of the elect, such conduct will not prevent their being finally brought into life. But Paul declares the end of our election to be, that we may lead a holy and blameless life. (*n*) If the object of election be holiness of life, it should rather awaken and stimulate us to a cheerful practice of it, than be used as a pretext for slothfulness. But how inconsistent is it to cease from the practice of virtue because election is sufficient to salvation, while the end proposed in election is our diligent performance of virtuous actions! Away, then, with such corrupt and sacrilegious perversions of the whole order of election. They carry their blasphemies much further, by asserting, that any one who is reprobated by God will labour to no purpose if he endeavour to approve himself to him by innocence and integrity of life; but here they are convicted of a most impudent falsehood. For whence could such exertion originate but from election? Whoever are of the number of the reprobate, being vessels made to dishonour, cease not to provoke the Divine wrath against them by continual transgressions, and to confirm by evident proofs the judgment of God already denounced against them; so that their striving with him in vain is what can never happen.

XIII. This doctrine is maliciously and impudently calumniated by others, as subversive of all exhortations to piety of life. This formerly brought great odium upon Augustine, which he removed by his Treatise on Correction and Grace, addressed to Valentine, the perusal of which will easily satisfy all pious and teachable persons. Yet I will touch on a few things, which I hope will convince such as are honest and not contentious. How openly and loudly gratuitous election was preached by Paul, we have already seen; was he therefore cold in admonitions and exhortations? Let these good zealots compare his vehemence with theirs; theirs will be found ice itself in comparison with his incredible fervour. And certainly every scruple is removed by this principle, that "God hath not called us to uncleanness, but that every one should know how to possess his vessel in sanctifica-

---

(*n*) Ephes. i. 4.

tion and honour;" (*o*) and again, that "we are his workmanship, created in Christ Jesus unto good works, which God hath before ordained, that we should walk in them." (*p*) Indeed, a slight acquaintance with Paul will enable any one to understand, without tedious arguments, how easily he reconciles things which they pretend to be repugnant to each other. Christ commands men to believe in him. Yet his limitation is neither false nor contrary to his command, when he says, "No man can come unto me, except it were given unto him of my Father." (*q*) Let preaching therefore have its course to bring men to faith, and by a continual progress to promote their perseverance. Nor let the knowledge of predestination be prevented, that the obedient may not be proud as of any thing of their own, but may glory in the Lord. Christ had some particular meaning in saying, "Who hath ears to hear, let him hear." (*r*) Therefore when we exhort and preach, persons endued with ears readily obey; and those who are destitute of them exhibit an accomplishment of the Scripture, that hearing they hear not. (*s*) "But why (says Augustine) should some have ears, and others not? 'Who hath known the mind of the Lord?' (*t*) Must that which is evident be denied, because that which is concealed cannot be comprehended?" These observations I have faithfully borrowed from Augustine; but as his words will perhaps have more authority than mine, I will proceed to an exact quotation of them. "If, on hearing this, some persons become torpid and slothful, and exchanging labour for lawless desire, pursue the various objects of concupiscence, must what is declared concerning the foreknowledge of God be therefore accounted false? If God foreknew that they would be good, will they not be so, in whatever wickedness they now live? and if he foreknew that they would be wicked, will they not be so, in whatever goodness they now appear? Are these, then, sufficient causes why the truths which are declared concerning the foreknowledge of God should be either denied or passed over in silence? especially when the consequence of silence respecting these would be the adoption of other errors. The reason of concealing the truth (he says) is one thing, and the necessity of declaring it is another.

(*o*) 1 Thess. iv. 4, 7. (*p*) Ephes. ii. 10. (*q*) John vi. 65.
(*r*) Matt. xiii. 9. (*s*) Isaiah vi. 9. (*t*) Rom. xi. 34.

It would be tedious to inquire after all the reasons for passing the truth over in silence; but this is one of them; lest those who understand it not should become worse, while we wish to make those who understand it better informed; who, indeed, are not made wiser by our declaring any such thing, nor are they rendered worse. But since the truth is of such a nature, that when we speak of it, he becomes worse who cannot understand it, and when we are silent about it, he who can understand it becomes worse,—what do we think ought to be done? Should not the truth rather be spoken, that he who is capable may understand it, than buried in silence; the consequence of which would be, not only that neither would know it, but even the more intelligent of the two would become worse, who, if he heard and understood it, would also teach it to many others? And we are unwilling to say what we are authorized to say by the testimony of Scripture. For we are afraid, indeed, lest by speaking we may offend him who cannot understand, but are not afraid lest in consequence of our silence, he who is capable of understanding the truth may be deceived by falsehood." And condensing this sentiment afterwards into a smaller compass, he places it in a still stronger light. "Wherefore, if the apostles and the succeeding teachers of the Church both piously treated of God's eternal election, and held believers under the discipline of a pious life, what reason have these our opponents, when silenced by the invincible force of truth, to suppose themselves right in maintaining that what is spoken of predestination, although it be true, ought not to be preached to the people? But it must by all means be preached, that he who has ears to hear may hear. But who has them, unless he receives them from him who has promised to bestow them? Certainly he who receives not may reject, provided he who receives, takes and drinks, drinks and lives. For as piety must be preached that God may be rightly worshipped, so also must predestination, that he who has ears to hear of the grace of God, may glory in God, and not in himself."

XIV. And yet, being peculiarly desirous of edification, that holy man regulates his mode of teaching the truth, so that offence may as far as possible be prudently avoided. For he suggests that whatever is asserted with truth may also be delivered in a suitable manner. If any one address the people in such a way as this, If you believe not, it is because you are by a Divine decree already destined to destruction,—he not only cherishes slothfulness, but even encourages wickedness. If any one extend the declaration to the future, that they who hear will never believe because they are reprobated,—this would be rather imprecation than instruction. Such persons, therefore, as foolish teachers, or inauspicious, ominous prophets, Augustine charges to depart from the Church. In another place, indeed, he justly maintains, "that a man then profits by correction, when he, who causes whom he pleases to profit even without correction, compassionates and assists. But why some in one way, and some in another? Far be it from us to ascribe the choice to the clay instead of the potter." Again afterwards: "When men are either introduced or restored into the way of righteousness by correction, who works salvation in their hearts, but he who gives the increase, whoever plants and waters? he whose determination to save is not resisted by any freewill of man. It is beyond all doubt, therefore, that the will of God, who has done whatever he has pleased in heaven and in earth, and who has done even things that are yet future, cannot possibly be resisted by the will of man, so as to prevent the execution of his purposes; since he controls the wills of men according to his pleasure." Again: "When he designs to bring men to himself, does he bind them by corporeal bonds? He acts inwardly; he inwardly seizes their hearts; he inwardly moves their hearts, and draws them by their wills, which he has wrought in them." But he immediately subjoins, what must by no means be omitted; "that because we know not who belongs, or does not belong, to the number of the predestinated, it becomes us affectionately to desire the salvation of all. The consequence will be, that whomsoever we meet we shall endeavour to make him a partaker of peace. But our peace shall rest upon the sons of peace. On our part, therefore, salutary and severe reproof, like a medicine, must be administered to all, that they may neither perish themselves nor destroy others; but it will be the province of God to render it useful to them whom he had foreknown and predestinated."

CHAPTER XXIV

Election Confirmed by the Divine Call. The Destined Destruction of the Reprobate Procured by Themselves

But, in order to a further elucidation of the subject, it is necessary to treat of the calling of the elect, and of the blinding and hardening of the impious. On the former I have already made a few observations, with a view to refute the error of those who suppose the generality of the promises to put all mankind on an equality. But the discriminating election of God, which is otherwise concealed within himself, he manifests only by his calling, which may therefore with propriety be termed the testification or evidence of it. "For whom he did foreknow, he also did predestinate to be conformed to the image of his Son. Moreover, whom he did predestinate, them he also called; and whom he called, them he also justified," in order to their eventual glorification. (*u*) Though by choosing his people, the Lord has adopted them as his children, yet we see that they enter not on the possession of so great a blessing till they are called; on the other hand, as soon as they are called, they immediately enjoy some communication of his election. On this account Paul calls the Spirit received by

(*u*) Rom. viii. 29, 30.

them, both "the Spirit of adoption, and the seal and earnest of the future inheritance;" (*x*) because, by his testimony, he confirms and seals to their hearts the certainty of their future adoption. For though the preaching of the gospel is a stream from the source of election, yet, being common also to the reprobate, it would of itself be no solid proof of it. For God effectually teaches his elect, to bring them to faith, as we have already cited from the words of Christ: "He which is of God, he," and he alone, "hath seen the Father." (*y*) Again: "I have manifested thy name unto the men which thou gavest me." (*z*) For he says in another place, "No man can come to me, except the Father draw him." (*a*) This passage is judiciously explained by Augustine in the following words: "If, according to the declaration of truth, every one that has learned comes, whosoever comes not, certainly has not learned. It does not necessarily follow that he who can come actually comes, unless he has both willed and done it; but every one that has learned of the Father, not only can come, but also actually comes; where there is an immediate union of the advantage of possibility, the inclination of the will, and the consequent action." In another place he is still clearer: "Every one that hath heard and learned of the Father, cometh unto me. Is not this saying, There is no one that hears and learns of the Father, and comes not unto me? For if every one that has heard and learned of the Father comes, certainly every one that comes not has neither heard nor learned of the Father; for if he had heard and learned, he would come. Very remote from carnal observation is this school, in which men hear and learn of the Father to come to the Son." Just after he says, "This grace, which is secretly communicated to the hearts of men, is received by no hard heart; for the first object of its communication is, that hardness of heart may be taken away. When the Father is heard within therefore, he takes away the heart of stone, and gives a heart of flesh. For thus he forms children of promise and vessels of mercy whom he has prepared for glory. Why, then, does he not teach all, that they may come to Christ, but because all whom he teaches, he teaches in mercy? but whom he teaches not, he teaches not in

(*x*) Rom. viii. 15, 16. Ephes. i. 13, 14. (*y*) John vi. 46.
(*z*) John xvii. 6. (*a*) John vi. 44.

judgment; for he hath mercy on whom he will have mercy, and whom he will he hardeneth." Those whom God has chosen, therefore, he designates as his children, and determines himself to be their Father. By calling, he introduces them into his family, and unites them to himself, that they may be one. By connecting calling with election, the Scripture evidently suggests that nothing is requisite to it but the free mercy of God. For if we inquire whom he calls, and for what reason, the answer is, those whom he had elected. But when we come to election, we see nothing but mercy on every side. And so that observation of Paul is very applicable here—"It is not of him that willeth, nor of him that runneth, but of God that showeth mercy;" but not as it is commonly understood by those who make a distribution between the grace of God, and the will and exertion of man. For they say, that human desires and endeavours have no efficacy of themselves, unless they are rendered successful by the grace of God; but maintain that, with the assistance of his blessing, these things have also their share in procuring salvation. To refute their cavil, I prefer Augustine's words to my own. "If the apostle only meant that it is not of him that wills, or of him that runs, without the assistance of the merciful Lord, we may retort the converse proposition, that it is not of mercy alone without the assistance of willing and running." If this be manifestly impious, we may be certain that the apostle ascribes every thing to the Lord's mercy, and leaves nothing to our wills or exertions. This was the opinion of that holy man. Nor is the least regard due to their paltry sophism, that Paul would not have expressed himself so, if we had no exertion or will. For he considered not what was in man; but seeing some persons attribute salvation partly to human industry, he simply condemned their error in the former part of the sentence, and in the latter, vindicated the claim of Divine mercy to the whole accomplishment of salvation. And what do the prophets, but perpetually proclaim the gratuitous callings of God?

II. This point is further demonstrated by the very nature and dispensation of calling, which consists not in the mere preaching of the word, but in the accompanying illumination of the Spirit. To whom God offers his word, we are informed in the prophet: "I am sought of them that asked not for me: I am found of them that sought me not: I said, Behold me, behold me, unto a nation that was not called by my name." (*b*) And lest the Jews should suppose that this clemency extended only to the Gentiles, he recalls to their remembrance the situation from which he took their father Abraham, when he deigned to draw him to himself; that was from the midst of idolatry, in which he and all his family were sunk. (*c*) When he first shines upon the undeserving with the light of his word, he thereby exhibits a most brilliant specimen of his free goodness. Here, then, the infinite goodness of God is displayed, but not to the salvation of all; for heavier judgment awaits the reprobate, because they reject the testimony of Divine love. And God also, to manifest his glory, withdraws from them the efficacious influence of his Spirit. This internal call, therefore, is a pledge of salvation, which cannot possibly deceive. To this purpose is that passage of John—"Hereby we know that he abideth in us, by the Spirit which he hath given us." (*d*) And lest the flesh should glory in having answered at least to his call, and accepted his free offers, he affirms that men have no ears to hear, or eyes to see, but such as he has formed; and that he acts in this, not according to individual gratitude, but according to his own election. Of this fact Luke gives us an eminent example, where Jews and Gentiles in common heard the preaching of Paul and Barnabas. Though they were all instructed on that occasion with the same discourse, it is narrated that "as many as were ordained to eternal life, believed." (e) With what face, then, can we deny the freeness of calling, in which election reigns alone, even to the last?

III. Here two errors are to be avoided. For some suppose man to be a coöperator with God, so that the validity of election depends on his consent; thus, according to them, the will of man is superior to the counsel of God. As though the Scripture taught, that we are only given an ability to believe, and not faith itself. Others, not thus enervating the grace of the Holy Spirit, yet induced by I know not what mode of reasoning, suspend election on that which is subsequent to it; as though it were doubtful and ineffectual till it is confirmed by faith. That this is its confirma-

---

(*b*) Isaiah lxv. 1. (*c*) Joshua xxiv. 2, 3.
(*d*) 1 John iii. 24. (*e*) Acts xiii. 48.

tion *to us* is very clear; that it is the manifestation of God's secret counsel before concealed, we have already seen; but all that we are to understand by this, is that what was before unknown is verified, and as it were ratified with a seal. But it is contrary to the truth to assert, that election has no efficacy till after we have embraced the gospel, and that this circumstance gives it all its energy. The certainty of it, indeed, we are to seek here; for if we attempt to penetrate to the eternal decree of God, we shall be ingulfed in the profound abyss. But when God has discovered it to us, we must ascend to loftier heights, that the cause may not be lost in the effect. For what can be more absurd and inconsistent, when the Scripture teaches that we are illuminated according as God has chosen us, than that our eyes should be so dazzled with the blaze of this light as to refuse to contemplate election? At the same time I admit that, in order to attain an assurance of our salvation, we ought to begin with the word, and that with it our confidence ought to be satisfied, so as to call upon God as our Father. For some persons, to obtain certainty respecting the counsel of God, "which is nigh unto us, in our mouth and in our heart," (*f*) preposterously wish to soar above the clouds. Such temerity, therefore, should be restrained by the sobriety of faith, that we may be satisfied with the testimony of God in his external word respecting his secret grace; only the channel, which conveys to us such a copious stream to satisfy our thirst, must not deprive the fountain-head of the honour which belongs to it.

IV. As it is erroneous, therefore, to suspend the efficacy of election upon the faith of the gospel, by which we discover our interest in election, so we shall observe the best order, if, in seeking an assurance of our election, we confine our attention to those subsequent signs which are certain attestations of it. Satan never attacks believers with a more grievous or dangerous temptation, than when he disquiets them with doubts of their election, and stimulates to an improper desire of seeking it in a wrong way. I call it seeking in a wrong way, when miserable man endeavours to force his way into the secret recesses of Divine wisdom, and to penetrate even to the highest eternity, that he may discover what is

---

(*f*) Deut. xxx. 14.

determined concerning him at the tribunal of God. Then he precipitates himself to be absorbed in the profound of an unfathomable gulf; then he entangles himself in numberless and inextricable snares; then he sinks himself in an abyss of total darkness. For it is right that the folly of the human mind should be thus punished with horrible destruction, when it attempts by its own ability to rise to the summit of Divine wisdom. This temptation is the more fatal, because there is no other to which men in general have a stronger propensity. For there is scarcely a person to be found, whose mind is not sometimes struck with this thought—Whence can you obtain salvation but from the election of God? And what revelation have you received of election? If this has once impressed a man, it either perpetually excruciates the unhappy being with dreadful torments, or altogether stupefies him with astonishment. Indeed, I should desire no stronger argument to prove how extremely erroneous the conceptions of such persons are respecting predestination, than experience itself; since no error can affect the mind, more pestilent than such as disturbs the conscience, and destroys its peace and tranquillity towards God. Therefore, if we dread shipwreck, let us anxiously beware of this rock, on which none ever strike without being destroyed. But though the discussion of predestination may be compared to a dangerous ocean, yet, in traversing over it, the navigation is safe and serene, and I will also add pleasant, unless any one freely wishes to expose himself to danger. For as those who, in order to gain an assurance of their election, examine into the eternal counsel of God without the word, plunge themselves into a fatal abyss, so they who investigate it in a regular and orderly manner, as it is contained in the word, derive from such inquiry the benefit of peculiar consolation. Let this, then, be our way of inquiry; to begin and end with the calling of God. Though this prevents not believers from perceiving, that the blessings they daily receive from the hand of God descend from that secret adoption; as Isaiah introduces them, saying, "Thou hast done wonderful things; thy counsels of old are faithfulness and truth;" (*g*) for by adoption, as by a token, God chooses to confirm to us

---

(*g*) Isaiah xxv. 1.

all that we are permitted to know of his counsel. Lest this should be thought a weak testimony, let us consider how much clearness and certainty it affords us. Bernard has some pertinent observations on this subject. After speaking of the reprobate, he says, "The counsel of God stands, the sentence of peace stands, respecting them who fear him, concealing their faults and rewarding their virtues; so that to them, not only good things, but evil ones also, coöperate for good. Who shall lay any thing to the charge of God's elect? It is sufficient for me, for all righteousness, to possess his favour alone, against whom alone I have sinned. All that he has decreed not to impute to me, is just as if it had never been." And a little after: "O place of true rest, which I might not improperly call a bed-chamber, in which God is viewed, not as disturbed with anger, or filled with care, but where his will is proved to be good, and acceptable, and perfect. This view is not terrifying, but soothing; it excites no restless curiosity, but allays it; it fatigues not the senses, but tranquillizes them. Here true rest is enjoyed. A tranquil God tranquillizes all things; and to behold rest, is to enjoy repose."

V. In the first place, if we seek the fatherly clemency and propitious heart of God, our eyes must be directed to Christ, in whom alone the Father is well pleased. (*h*) If we seek salvation, life, and the immortality of the heavenly kingdom, recourse must be had to no other; for he alone is the Fountain of life, the Anchor of salvation, and the Heir of the kingdom of heaven. Now, what is the end of election, but that, being adopted as children by our heavenly Father, we may by his favour obtain salvation and immortality? Consider and investigate it as much as you please, you will not find its ultimate scope extend beyond this. The persons, therefore, whom God has adopted as his children, he is said to have chosen, not in themselves, but in Christ; because it was impossible for him to love them, except in him; or to honour them with the inheritance of his kingdom, unless previously made partakers of him. But if we are chosen in him, we shall find no assurance of our election in ourselves; nor even in God the Father, considered alone, abstractedly from the Son. Christ, therefore, is

---

(*h*) Matt. iii. 17.

the mirror, in which it behoves us to contemplate our election; and here we may do it with safety. For as the Father has determined to unite to the body of his Son all who are the objects of his eternal choice, that he may have, as his children, all that he recognizes among his members, we have a testimony sufficiently clear and strong, that if we have communion with Christ, we are written in the book of life. And he gave us this certain communion with himself, when he testified by the preaching of the gospel, that he was given to us by the Father, to be ours with all his benefits. We are said to put him on, and to grow up into him, that we may live because he lives. This doctrine is often repeated. "God spared not his only begotten Son, that whosoever believeth in him should not perish." (*i*) "He that believeth on him, is passed from death unto life." (*k*) In which sense he calls himself "The bread of life, he that eateth which, shall live for ever." (*l*) He, I say, is our witness, that all who receive him by faith shall be considered as the children of his heavenly Father. If we desire any thing more than being numbered among the sons and heirs of God, we must rise above Christ. If this is our highest limit, what folly do we betray in seeking out of him, that which we have already obtained in him, and which can never be found any where else! Besides, as he is the Father's eternal Wisdom, immutable Truth, and determined Counsel, we have no reason to fear the least variation in the declarations of his word from that will of the Father, which is the object of our inquiry; indeed, he faithfully reveals it to us, as it has been from the beginning, and will ever continue to be. This doctrine ought to have a practical influence on our prayers. For though faith in election animates us to call upon God, yet it would be preposterous to obtrude it upon him when we pray, or to stipulate this condition—O Lord, if I am elected, hear me; since it is his pleasure that we should be satisfied with his promises, and make no further inquiries whether he will be propitious to our prayers. This prudence will extricate us from many snares, if we know how to make a right use of what has been rightly written; but we must not inconsiderately apply to various purposes, what ought to be restricted to the object particularly designed.

(*i*) Rom. viii. 32. John iii. 15, 16.
(*k*) John v. 24. (*l*) John vi. 35—58.

VI. For the establishment of our confidence, there is also another confirmation of election, which, we have said, is connected with our calling. For those whom Christ illuminates with the knowledge of his name, and introduces into the bosom of his Church, he is said to receive into his charge and protection. And all whom he receives are said to be committed and intrusted to him by the Father, to be kept to eternal life. What do we wish for ourselves? Christ loudly proclaims that all whose salvation was designed by the Father, had been delivered by him into his protection. (*m*) If, therefore, we want to ascertain whether God is concerned for our salvation, let us inquire whether he has committed us to Christ, whom he constituted the only Saviour of all his people. Now, if we doubt whether Christ has received us into his charge and custody, he obviates this doubt, by freely offering himself as our Shepherd, and declaring that if we hear his voice, we shall be numbered among his sheep. We therefore embrace Christ, thus kindly offered to us and advancing to meet us; and he will number us with his sheep, and preserve us enclosed in his fold. But yet we feel anxiety for our future state; for as Paul declares that "whom he predestinated, them he also called," (*n*) so Christ informs us that "many are called, but few chosen." (*o*) Besides, Paul himself also, in another place, cautions against carelessness, saying, "Let him that thinketh he standeth, take heed lest he fall." (*p*) Again: "Art thou grafted among the people of God? Be not high-minded, but fear. God is able to cut thee off again, and graft in others." (*q*) Lastly, experience itself teaches us that vocation and faith are of little value, unless accompanied by perseverance, which is not the lot of all. But Christ has delivered us from this anxiety, for these promises undoubtedly belong to the future: "All that the Father giveth me, shall come to me; and him that cometh to me, I will in no wise cast out. And this is the Father's will which hath sent me, that of all which he hath given me, I should lose nothing, but should raise it up again at the last day." (*r*) Again: "My sheep hear my voice, and I know them, and they follow me. And I give unto them eternal life, and they shall never perish, neither shall any pluck them out of my

(*m*) John vi. 37, 39; xvii. 6, 12. (*n*) Rom. viii. 30. (*o*) Matt. xxii. 14.
(*p*) 1 Cor. x. 12. (*q*) Rom. xi. 17—23. (*r*) John vi. 37, 39.

hand. My Father, which gave them me, is greater than all; and none is able to pluck them out of my Father's hand." (*s*) Besides, when he declares, "Every plant which my heavenly Father hath not planted, shall be rooted up," (*t*) he fully implies on the contrary, that those who are rooted in God, can never by any violence be deprived of salvation. With this corresponds that passage of John, "If they had been of us, they would no doubt have continued with us." (*u*) Hence also that magnificent exultation of Paul, in defiance of life and death, of things present and future; which must necessarily have been founded in the gift of perseverance. (*x*) Nor can it be doubted that he applies this sentiment to all the elect. The same apostle in another place says, "He which hath begun a good work in you, will perform it until the day of Jesus Christ." (*y*) This also supported David when his faith was failing: "Thou wilt not forsake the work of thine own hands." (*z*) Nor is it to be doubted, that when Christ intercedes for all the elect, he prays for them the same as for Peter, that their faith may never fail. Hence we conclude, that they are beyond all danger of falling away, because the intercessions of the Son of God for their perseverance in piety have not been rejected. What did Christ intend we should learn from this, but confidence in our perpetual security, since we have once been introduced into the number of his people?

VII. But it daily happens, that they who appeared to belong to Christ, fall away from him again, and sink into ruin. Even in that very place, where he asserts that none perish of those who were given to him by the Father, he excepts the son of perdition. This is true; but it is equally certain, that such persons never adhered to Christ with that confidence of heart which, we say, gives us an assurance of our election. "They went out from us," says John, "but they were not of us; for if they had been of us, they would no doubt have continued with us." (*a*) I dispute not their having similar signs of calling with the elect; but I am far from admitting them to possess that certain assurance of election which I enjoin believers to seek from the word of the gospel.

(*s*) John x. 27—29. (*t*) Matt. xv. 13. (*u*) 1 John ii. 19.
(*x*) Rom. viii. 35—39. (*y*) Phil. i. 6.
(*z*) Psalm cxxxviii. 8. (*a*) 1 John ii. 19.

Wherefore, let not such examples move us from a tranquil reliance on our Lord's promise, where he declares, that all who receive him by faith were given him by the Father, and that since he is their Guardian and Shepherd, not one of them shall perish. Of Judas we shall speak afterwards. Paul is dissuading Christians, not from all security, but from supine, unguarded, carnal security, which is attended with pride, arrogance, and contempt of others, extinguishes humility and reverence of God, and produces forgetfulness of favours received. For he is addressing Gentiles, teaching them that the Jews should not be proudly and inhumanly insulted because they had been rejected, and the Gentiles substituted in their place. He also inculcates fear; not such a fear as produces terror and uncertainty, but such as teaches humble admiration of the grace of God, without any diminution of confidence in it; as has been elsewhere observed. Besides, he is not addressing individuals, but distinct parties generally. For as the Church was divided into two parties, and emulation gave birth to dissension, Paul admonishes the Gentiles, that their substitution in the place of the holy and peculiar people ought to be a motive to fear and modesty. There were, however, many clamorous people among them, whose empty boasting it was necessary to restrain. But we have already seen that our hope extends into futurity, even beyond the grave, and that nothing is more contrary to its nature than doubts respecting our final destiny.

VIII. The declaration of Christ, that "many are called, and few chosen," is very improperly understood. For there will be no ambiguity in it, if we remember what must be clear from the foregoing observations, that there are two kinds of calling. For there is a universal call, by which God, in the external preaching of the word, invites all, indiscriminately, to come to him, even those to whom he intends it as a savour of death, and an occasion of heavier condemnation. There is also a special call, with which he, for the most part, favours only believers, when, by the inward illumination of his Spirit, he causes the word preached to sink into their hearts. Yet sometimes he also communicates it to those whom he only enlightens for a season, and afterwards forsakes on account of their ingratitude, and strikes with greater blindness. Now, the Lord, seeing the gospel published far and wide, held in contempt by the generality of men, and justly appreciated by few, gives us a description of God, under the character of a king, who prepares a solemn feast, and sends out his messengers in every direction, to invite a great company, but can only prevail on very few, every one alleging impediments to excuse himself; so that at length he is constrained by their refusal to bring in all who can be found in the streets. Thus far, every one sees, the parable is to be understood of the external call. He proceeds to inform us, that God acts like a good master of a feast, walking round the tables, courteously receiving his guests; but that if he finds any one not adorned with a nuptial garment, he suffers not the meanness of such a person to disgrace the festivity of the banquet. I confess, this part is to be understood of those who enter into the Church by a profession of faith, but are not invested with the santification of Christ. Such blemishes, and, as it were, cankers of his Church, God will not always suffer, but will cast them out of it, as their turpitude deserves. Few, therefore, are chosen out of a multitude that are called, but not with that calling by which we say believers ought to judge of their election. For the former is common also to the wicked; but the latter is attended with the Spirit of regeneration, the earnest and seal of the future inheritance, which seals our hearts to the day of the Lord. (*b*) In short, though hypocrites boast of piety as if they were true worshippers of God, Christ declares that he will finally cast them out of the place which they unjustly occupy. Thus the Psalmist says, "Who shall abide in thy tabernacle? He that worketh righteousness, and speaketh the truth in his heart." (*c*) Again: "This is the generation of them that seek him, that seek thy face, O Jacob." (*d*) And thus the Spirit exhorts believers to patience, that they may not be disturbed by Ishmaelites being united with them in the Church, since the mask will at length be torn off, and they will be cast out with disgrace.

IX. The same reasoning applies to the exception lately cited, where Christ says, that "none of them is lost, but the son of perdition." (*e*) Here is, indeed, some inaccuracy of expression, but the meaning is clear. For he was never reckoned among the sheep of Christ, as being really such, but only as he occupied the place of

(*b*) Ephes. i. 13, 14. (*c*) Psalm xv. 1.
(*d*) Psalm xxiv. 6. (*e*) John xvii. 12.

one. When the Lord declares he was chosen by himself with the other apostles, it only refers to the ministerial office. "Have not I chosen you twelve," says he, "and one of you is a devil?" (*f*) That is, he had chosen him to the office of an apostle. But when he speaks of election to salvation, he excludes him from the number of the elect: "I speak not of you all; I know whom I have chosen." (*g*) If any one confound the term *election* in these passages, he will miserably embarrass himself; if he make a proper distinction, nothing is plainer. It is therefore a very erroneous and pernicious assertion of Gregory, that we are only conscious of our calling, but uncertain of our election; from which he exhorts all to fear and trembling, using also this argument, that though we know what we are to-day, yet we know not what we may be in future. But the context plainly shows the cause of his error on this point. For as he suspended election on the merit of works, this furnished abundant reason for discouragement to the minds of men: he could never establish them, for want of leading them from themselves to a confidence in the Divine goodness. Hence believers have some perception of what we stated at the beginning, that predestination, rightly considered, neither destroys nor weakens faith, but rather furnishes its best confirmation. Yet I will not deny, that the Spirit sometimes accommodates his language to the limited extent of our capacity, as when he says, "They shall not be in the assembly of my people, neither shall they be written in the writing of the house of Israel." (*h*) As though God were beginning to write in the book of life those whom he numbers among his people, whereas we know from the testimony of Christ, that the names of God's children have been written in the book of life from the beginning. (*i*) But these expressions only signify the rejection of those who seemed to be the chief among the elect; as the Psalmist says, "Let them be blotted out of the book of the living, and not be written with the righteous." (*k*)

X. Now, the elect are not gathered into the fold of Christ by calling, immediately from their birth, nor all at the same time, but according as God is pleased to dispense his grace to them. Before they are gathered to that chief Shepherd, they go astray,

(*f*) John vi. 70. (*g*) John xiii. 18. (*h*) Ezek. xiii. 9.
(*i*) Luke x. 20. (*k*) Psalm lxix. 28.

scattered in the common wilderness, and differing in no respect from others, except in being protected by the special mercy of God from rushing down the precipice of eternal death. If you observe them, therefore, you will see the posterity of Adam partaking of the common corruption of the whole species. That they go not to the most desperate extremes of impiety, is not owing to any innate goodness of theirs, but because the eye of God watches over them, and his hand is extended for their preservation. For those who dream of I know not what seed of election sown in their hearts from their very birth, always inclining them to piety and the fear of God, are unsupported by the authority of Scripture, and refuted by experience itself. They produce, indeed, a few examples to prove that certain elect persons were not entire strangers to religion, even before they were truly enlightened; that Paul lived blameless in his Pharisaism; (*l*) that Cornelius, with his alms and prayers, was accepted of God, (*m*) and if there are any other similar ones. What they say of Paul, we admit; but respecting Cornelius, we maintain that they are deceived; for it is evident, he was then enlightened and regenerated, and wanted nothing but a clear revelation of the gospel. But what will they extort from these very few examples? that the elect have always been endued with the spirit of piety? This is just as if any one, having proved the integrity of Aristides, Socrates, Xenocrates, Scipio, Curius, Camillus, and other heathens, should conclude from this, that all who were left in the darkness of idolatry, were followers of holiness and virtue. But this is contradicted in many passages of Scripture. Paul's description of the state of the Ephesians prior to regeneration, exhibits not a grain of this seed. "Ye were dead," he says, "in trespasses and sins, wherein in time past ye walked according to the course of this world, according to the prince of the power of the air, the spirit that now worketh in the children of disobedience; among whom also we all had our conversation in times past, in the lusts of our flesh, fulfilling the desires of the flesh and of the mind, and were by nature the children of wrath, even as others." (*n*) Again: "Remember that at that time ye were without hope, and without God in the world." (*o*) Again: "Ye

(*l*) Phil. iii. 5. 6.
(*m*) Acts x. 2.
(*n*) Ephes. ii. 1—3.
(*o*) Ephes. ii. 11, 12.

were sometimes darkness, but now are ye light in the Lord; walk as children of light." (*p*) But perhaps they will plead, that these passages refer to that ignorance of the true God, in which they acknowledge the elect to be involved previously to their calling. Though this would be an impudent cavil, since the apostle's inferences from them are such as these: "Put away lying; and let him that stole, steal no more." (*q*) But what will they reply to other passages? such as that where, after declaring to the Corinthians, that "Neither fornicators, nor idolaters, nor adulterers, nor effeminate, nor abusers of themselves with mankind, nor thieves, nor covetous, nor drunkards, nor revilers, nor extortioners, shall inherit the kingdom of God;" he immediately adds, "And such were some of you; but ye are washed, but ye are sanctified, but ye are justified in the name of the Lord Jesus, and by the Spirit of our God." (*r*) And another passage, addressed to the Romans: "As ye have yielded your members servants to uncleanness, and to iniquity unto iniquity; even so now yield your members servants to righteousness. What fruit had ye then in those things whereof ye are now ashamed?" (*s*)

XI. What kind of seed of election was springing up in them, who were all their lives contaminated with various pollutions, and with desperate wickedness wallowed in the most nefarious and execrable of all crimes? If he had intended to speak according to these teachers, he ought to have shown how much they were obliged to the goodness of God, which had preserved them from falling into such great pollutions. So likewise the persons whom Peter addressed, he ought to have exhorted to gratitude on account of the perpetual seed of election. But, on the contrary, he admonishes them, "that the time past may suffice to have wrought the will of the Gentiles." (*t*) What if we come to particular examples? What principle of righteousness was there in Rahab the harlot before faith? (*u*) in Manasseh, when Jerusalem was dyed, and almost drowned, with the blood of the prophets? (*x*) in the thief, who repented in his dying moments? (*y*) Away, then, with these arguments, which men of presumptuous curosity raise to them-

(*p*) Ephes. v. 8; iv. 18. (*q*) Ephes. iv. 25, 28. (*r*) 1 Cor. vi. 9—11.
(*s*) Rom. vi. 19, 21. (*t*) 1 Peter iv. 3. (*u*) Josh. ii. 1, &c.
(*x*) 2 Kings xxi. 16. (*y*) Luke xxiii. 40—42.

selves without regarding the Scripture. Let us rather abide by the declaration of the Scripture, that "all we like sheep have gone astray; we have turned every one to his own way," (*z*) that is, destruction. Those whom the Lord has determined to rescue from this gulf of perdition, he defers till his appointed season; before which he only preserves them from falling into unpardonable blasphemy.

XII. As the Lord, by his effectual calling of the elect, completes the salvation to which he predestinated them in his eternal counsel, so he has his judgments against the reprobate, by which he executes his counsel respecting them. Those, therefore, whom he has created to a life of shame and a death of destruction, that they might be instruments of his wrath, and examples of his severity, he causes to reach their appointed end, sometimes depriving them of the opportunity of hearing the word, sometimes, by the preaching of it, increasing their blindness and stupidity. Of the former there are innumerable examples: let us only select one that is more evident and remarkable than the rest. Before the advent of Christ, there passed about four thousand years, in which the Lord concealed the light of the doctrine of salvation from all the Gentiles. If it be replied, that he withheld from them the participation of so great a blessing because he esteemed them unworthy, their posterity will be found equally unworthy of it. The truth of this, to say nothing of experience, is sufficiently attested by Malachi, who follows his reproofs of unbelief and gross blasphemies by an immediate prediction of the coming of the Messiah. Why, then, is he given to the posterity rather than to their ancestors? He will torment himself in vain, who seeks for any cause of this beyond the secret and inscrutable counsel of God. Nor need we be afraid lest any disciple of Porphyry should be imboldened to calumniate the justice of God by our silence in its defence. For while we assert that all deserve to perish, and it is of God's free goodness that any are saved, enough is said for the illustration of his glory, so that every subterfuge of ours is altogether unnecessary. The supreme Lord, therefore, by depriving of the communication of his light, and leaving in darkness, those whom he has reprobated,

---

(*z*) Isaiah liii. 6.

makes way for the accomplishment of his predestination. Of the second class, the Scriptures contain many examples, and others present themselves every day. The same sermon is addressed to a hundred persons; twenty receive it with the obedience of faith; the others despise, or ridicule, or reject, or condemn it. If it be replied, that the difference proceeds from their wickedness and perverseness, this will afford no satisfaction; because the minds of others would have been influenced by the same wickedness, but for the correction of Divine goodness. And thus we shall always be perplexed, unless we recur to Paul's question—"Who maketh thee to differ?" (*a*) In which he signifies, that the excellence of some men beyond others, is not from their own virtue, but solely from Divine grace.

XIII. Why, then, in bestowing grace upon some, does he pass over others? Luke assigns a reason for the former, that they "were ordained to eternal life." What conclusion, then, shall we draw respecting the latter, but that they are vessels of wrath to dishonour? Wherefore let us not hesitate to say with Augustine, "God could convert to good the will of the wicked, because he is omnipotent. It is evident that he could. Why, then, does he not? Because he would not. Why he would not, remains with himself." For we ought not to aim at more wisdom than becomes us. That will be much better than adopting the evasion of Chrysostom, "that he draws those who are willing, and who stretch out their hands for his aid;" that the difference may not appear to consist in the decree of God, but wholly in the will of man. But an approach to him is so far from being a mere effort of man, that even pious persons, and such as fear God, still stand in need of the peculiar impulse of the Spirit. Lydia, the seller of purple, feared God, and yet it was necessary that her heart should be opened, to attend to, and profit by, the doctrine of Paul. This declaration is not made respecting a single female, but in order to teach us that every one's advancement in piety is the secret work of the Spirit. It is a fact not to be doubted, that God sends his word to many whose blindness he determines shall be increased. For with what design does he direct so many commands to be delivered to Pharaoh?

(*a*) 1 Cor. iv. 7.

Was it from an expectation that his heart would be softened by repeated and frequent messages? Before he began, he knew and foretold the result. He commanded Moses to go and declare his will to Pharaoh, adding at the same time, "But I will harden his heart, that he shall not let the people go." (*b*) So, when he calls forth Ezekiel, he apprizes him that he is sending him to a rebellious and obstinate people, that he may not be alarmed if they refuse to hear him. (*c*) So Jeremiah foretells that his word will be like fire, to scatter and destroy the people like stubble. (*d*) But the prophecy of Isaiah furnishes a still stronger confirmation; for this is his mission from the Lord: "Go and tell this people, Hear ye, indeed, but understand not, and see ye, indeed, but perceive not. Make the heart of this people fat, and make their ears heavy, and shut their eyes; lest they see with their eyes, and hear with their ears, and understand with their heart, and convert, and be healed." (*e*) Observe, he directs his voice to them, but it is that they may become more deaf; he kindles a light, but it is that they may be made more blind; he publishes his doctrine, but it is that they may be more besotted; he applies a remedy, but it is that they may not be healed. John, citing this prophecy, declares that the Jews could not believe, because this curse of God was upon them. (*f*) Nor can it be disputed, that to such persons as God determines not to enlighten, he delivers his doctrine involved in enigmatical obscurity, that its only effect may be to increase their stupidity. For Christ testifies that he confined to his apostles the explanations of the parables in which he had addressed the multitude; "because to you it is given to know the mysteries of the kingdom of heaven, but to them it is not given." (*g*) What does the Lord mean, you will say, by teaching those by whom he takes care not to be understood? Consider whence the fault arises, and you will cease the inquiry; for whatever obscurity there is in the word, yet there is always light enough to convince the consciences of the wicked.

XIV. It remains now to be seen why the Lord does that which it is evident he does. If it be replied, that this is done because men have deserved it by their impiety, wickedness, and ingratitude, it

(*b*) Exod. iv. 21. (*c*) Ezek. ii. 3; xii. 2. (*d*) Jer. v. 14.
(*e*) Isaiah vi. 9, 10. (*f*) John xii. 39, 40. (*g*) Matt. xiii. 11.

will be a just and true observation; but as we have not yet discovered the reason of this diversity, why some persist in obduracy while others are inclined to obedience, the discussion of it will necessarily lead us to the same remark that Paul has quoted from Moses concerning Pharaoh: "Even for this same purpose have I raised thee up, that I might show my power in thee, and that my name might be declared throughout all the earth." (*h*) That the reprobate obey not the word of God, when made known to them, is justly imputed to the wickedness and depravity of their hearts, provided it be at the same time stated, that they are abandoned to this depravity because they have been raised up, by a just but inscrutable judgment of God, to display his glory in their condemnation. So, when it is related of the sons of Eli, that they listened not to his salutary admonitions, "because the Lord would slay them," (*i*) it is not denied that their obstinacy proceeded from their own wickedness, but it is plainly implied that though the Lord was able to soften their hearts, yet they were left in their obstinacy, because his immutable decree had predestinated them to destruction. To the same purpose is that passage of John, "Though he had done so many miracles before them, yet they believed not on him; that the saying of Esaias the prophet might be fulfilled, which he spake, 'Lord, who hath believed our report?' " (*k*) For though he does not acquit the obstinate from the charge of guilt, yet he satisfies himself with this reason, that the grace of God has no charms for men till the Holy Spirit gives them a taste for it. And Christ cites the prophecy of Isaiah, "They shall be all taught of God," (*l*) with no other design than to show, that the Jews are reprobate and strangers to the Church, because they are destitute of docility; and he adduces no other reason for it than that the promise of God does not belong to them; which is confirmed by that passage of Paul, where "Christ crucified, unto the Jews a stumbling-block, and unto the Greeks foolishness," is said to be "unto them which are called, the power of God, and the wisdom of God." (*m*) For, after remarking what generally happens whenever the gospel is preached, that it exasperates some, and is despised by others, he represents it as duly appreciated

(*h*) Rom. ix. 17. (*i*) 1 Sam. ii. 25. (*k*) John xii. 37, 38. (*l*) John vi. 45. (*m*) 1 Cor. i. 23, 24.

only by "those who are called." A little before he had mentioned "them that believe;" not that he had an intention to deny its proper place to the grace of God, which precedes faith, but he seems to add this second description by way of correction, in order that those who had received the gospel might ascribe the praise of their faith to the Divine call. And so, likewise, in a subsequent sentence, he represents them as the objects of Divine election. When the impious hear these things, they loudly complain that God, by a wanton exercise of power, abuses his wretched creatures for the sport of his cruelty. But we, who know that all men are liable to so many charges at the Divine tribunal, that of a thousand questions they would be unable to give a satisfactory answer to one, confess that the reprobate suffer nothing but what is consistent with the most righteous judgment of God. Though we cannot comprehend the reason of this, let us be content with some degree of ignorance where the wisdom of God soars into its own sublimity.

XV. But as objections are frequently raised from some passages of Scripture, in which God seems to deny that the destruction of the wicked is caused by his decree, but that, in opposition to his remonstrances, they voluntarily bring ruin upon themselves,—let us show by a brief explication that they are not at all inconsistent with the foregoing doctrine. A passage is produced from Ezekiel, where God says, "I have no pleasure in the death of the wicked, but that the wicked turn from his way and live." (*n*) If this is to be extended to all mankind, why does he not urge many to repentance, whose minds are more flexible to obedience than those of others, who grow more and more callous to his daily invitations? Among the inhabitants of Nineveh and Sodom, Christ himself declares that his evangelical preaching and miracles would have brought forth more fruit than in Judea. How is it, then, if God will have all men to be saved, that he opens not the gate of repentance to those miserable men who would be more ready to receive the favour? Hence we perceive it to be a violent perversion of the passage, if the will of God, mentioned by the prophet, be set in opposition to his eternal counsel, by which he has distin-

---

(*n*) Ezek. xxxiii. 11.

guished the elect from the reprobate. Now, if we inquire the genuine sense of the prophet, his only meaning is to inspire the penitent with hopes of pardon. And this is the sum, that it is beyond a doubt that God is ready to pardon sinners immediately on their conversion. Therefore he wills not their death, inasmuch as he wills their repentance. But experience teaches, that he does not will the repentance of those whom he externally calls, in such a manner as to affect all their hearts. Nor should he on this account be charged with acting deceitfully; for, though his external call only renders those who hear without obeying it inexcusable, yet it is justly esteemed the testimony of God's grace, by which he reconciles men to himself. Let us observe, therefore, the design of the prophet in saying that God has no pleasure in the death of a sinner; it is to assure the pious of God's readiness to pardon them immediately on their repentance, and to show the impious the aggravation of their sin in rejecting such great compassion and kindness of God. Repentance, therefore, will always be met by Divine mercy; but on whom repentance is bestowed, we are clearly taught by Ezekiel himself, as well as by all the prophets and apostles.

XVI. Another passage adduced is from Paul, where he states that "God will have all men to be saved;" (*o*) which, though somewhat different from the passage just considered, yet is very similar to it. I reply, in the first place, that it is evident from the context, how God wills the salvation of all; for Paul connects these two things together, that he "will have all men to be saved, and to come unto the knowledge of the truth." If it was fixed in the eternal counsel of God, that they should receive the doctrine of salvation, what is the meaning of that question of Moses, "What nation is there so great, who hath God so nigh unto them as we have?" (*p*) How is it that God has deprived many nations of the light of the gospel, which others enjoyed? How is it that the pure knowledge of the doctrine of piety has never reached some, and that others have but just heard some obscure rudiments of it? Hence it will be easy to discover the design of Paul. He had enjoined Timothy to make solemn prayers in the

---

(*o*) 1 Tim. ii. 4. (*p*) Deut. iv. 7.

Church for kings and princes; but as it might seem somewhat inconsistent to pray to God for a class of men almost past hope,—for they were not only strangers to the body of Christ, but striving with all their power to ruin his kingdom,—he subjoins, that "this is good and acceptable in the sight of God, who will have all men to be saved;" which only imports, that God has not closed the way of salvation against any order of men, but has diffused his mercy in such a manner that he would have no rank to be destitute of it. The other texts adduced are not declarative of the Lord's determination respecting all men in his secret counsel: they only proclaim that pardon is ready for all sinners who sincerely seek it. (*q*) For if they obstinately insist on its being said that God is merciful to all, I will oppose to them, what is elsewhere asserted, that "our God is in the heavens; he hath done whatsoever he hath pleased." (*r*) This text, then, must be explained in a manner consistent with another, where God says, "I will be gracious to whom I will be gracious, and I will show mercy on whom I will show mercy." (*s*) He who makes a selection of objects for the exercise of his mercy, does not impart that mercy to all. But as it clearly appears that Paul is there speaking, not of individuals, but orders of men, I shall forbear any further argument. It must be remarked, however, that Paul is not declaring the actual conduct of God at all times, in all places, and to all persons, but merely representing him as at liberty to make kings and magistrates at length partakers of the heavenly doctrine, notwithstanding their present rage against it in consequence of their blindness. There is more apparent plausibility in their objection, from the declaration of Peter, that "the Lord is not willing that any should perish, but that all should come to repentance." (*t*) But the second clause furnishes an immediate solution of this difficulty; for the willingness that they should come to repentance must be understood in consistence with the general tenor of Scripture. Conversion is certainly in the power of God; let him be asked, whether he wills the conversion of all, when he promises a few individuals to give them "a heart of flesh," while he leaves others with "a heart of stone." (*u*) If he were not ready to receive those who implore his mercy, there

(*q*) Psalm cxlv. 9. (*r*) Psalm cxv. 3. (*s*) Exod. xxxiii. 19.
(*t*) 2 Peter iii. 9. (*u*) Ezek. xxxvi. 26.

would indeed be no propriety in this address, "Turn ye unto me, and I will turn unto you;" (*x*) but I maintain that no mortal ever approaches God without being divinely drawn. But if repentance depended on the will of man, Paul would not have said, "If God peradventure will give them repentance." (*y*) And if God, whose voice exhorts all men to repentance, did not draw the elect to it by the secret operation of his Spirit, Jeremiah would not have said, "Turn thou me, and I shall be turned; for thou art the Lord my God. Surely after that I was turned, I repented." (*z*)

XVII. If this be correct, it will be said there can be but little faith in the promises of the gospel, which, in declaring the will of God, assert that he wills what is repugnant to his inviolable decree. But this is far from a just conclusion. For if we turn our attention to the effect of the promises of salvation, we shall find that their universality is not at all inconsistent with the predestination of the reprobate. We know the promises to be effectual to us only when we receive them by faith; on the contrary, the annihilation of faith is at once an abolition of the promises. If this is their nature, we may perceive that there is no discordance between these two things—God's having appointed from eternity on whom he will bestow his favour and exercise his wrath, and his proclaiming salvation indiscriminately to all. Indeed, I maintain that there is the most perfect harmony between them. For his sole design in thus promising, is to offer his mercy to all who desire and seek it, which none do but those whom he has enlightened, and he enlightens all whom he has predestinated to salvation. These persons experience the certain and unshaken truth of the promises; so that it cannot be pretended that there is the least contrariety between God's eternal election and the testimony of his grace offered to believers. But why does he mention all? It is in order that the consciences of the pious may enjoy the more secure satisfaction, seeing that there is no difference between sinners, provided they have faith; and, on the other hand, that the impious may not plead the want of an asylum to flee to from the bondage of sin, while they ungratefully reject that which is offered to them. When the mercy of God is offered to both by the gospel, it is faith, that

(*x*) Zech. i. 3. (*y*) 2 Tim. ii. 25. (*z*) Jer. xxxi. 18, 19.

is, the illumination of God, which distinguishes between the pious and impious; so that the former experience the efficacy of the gospel, but the latter derive no benefit from it. Now, this illumination is regulated by God's eternal election. The complaint and lamentation of Christ, "O Jerusalem, Jerusalem, how often would I have gathered thy children together, and ye would not," (*a*) however they cite it, affords them no support. I confess, that Christ here speaks not merely in his human character, but that he is upbraiding the Jews for having in all ages rejected his grace. But we must define the will of God which is here intended. It is well known how sedulously God laboured to preserve that people to himself, and with what extreme obstinacy, from the first to the last, they refused to be gathered, being abandoned to their own wandering desires; but this does not authorize the conclusion, that the counsel of God was frustrated by the wickedness of men. They object, that nothing is more inconsistent with the nature of God than to have two wills. This I grant them, provided it be rightly explained. But why do they not consider the numerous passages, where, by the assumption of human affections, God condescends beneath his own majesty. He says, "I have spread out my hands all the day unto a rebellious people;" (*b*) early and late endeavouring to bring them to himself. If they are determined to accommodate all this to God, and disregard the figurative mode of expression, they will give rise to many needless contentions, which may be settled by this one solution, that what is peculiar to man is transferred to God. The solution, however, elsewhere stated by us, is fully sufficient—that though to our apprehension the will of God is manifold and various, yet he does not in himself will things at variance with each other, but astonishes our faculties with his various and "manifold wisdom," according to the expression of Paul, till we shall be enabled to understand, that he mysteriously wills what now seems contrary to his will. They impertinently object, that God being the Father of all, it is unjust for him to disinherit any but such as have previously deserved this punishment by their own guilt. As if the goodness of God did not extend even to dogs and swine. But if the question relates to the human race, let them

(*a*) Matt. xxiii. 37. (*b*) Isaiah lxv. 2.

answer why God allied himself to one people as their Father; why he gathered even from them but a very small number, as the flower of them. But their rage for slander prevents these railers from considering that God "maketh his sun to rise on the evil and on the good," (*c*) but that the inheritance is reserved for the few, to whom it shall one day be said, "Come, ye blessed of my Father, inherit the kingdom prepared for you from the foundation of the world." (*d*) They further object, that God hates nothing he has made; which though I grant them, the doctrine I maintain still remains unshaken, that the reprobate are hated by God, and that most justly, because, being destitute of his Spirit, they can do nothing but what is deserving of his curse. They further allege, that there is no difference between the Jew and the Gentile, and therefore that the grace of God is offered indiscriminately to all: I grant it; only let them admit, according to the declaration of Paul, that God calls whom he pleases, both of the Jews and of the Gentiles, (*e*) so that he is under no obligations to any. In this way also we answer their arguments from another text, which says, that "God hath concluded them all in unbelief, that he might have mercy upon all;" (*f*) which imports that he will have the salvation of all who are saved ascribed to his mercy, though this blessing is not common to all. Now, while many arguments are advanced on both sides, let our conclusion be to stand astonished with Paul at so great a mystery, and amidst the clamour of petulant tongues let us not be ashamed of exclaiming with him, "O man, who art thou that repliest against God?" For, as Augustine justly contends, it is acting a most perverse part, to set up the measure of human justice as the standard by which to measure the justice of God.

(*c*) Matt. v. 48. (*d*) Matt. xxv. 34.
(*e*) Rom. ix. 24. (*f*) Rom. xi. 32.

CHAPTER XXV

The Final Resurrection

THOUGH Christ, the Sun of Righteousness, after having "abolished death," is declared by Paul to have "brought life and immortality to light," shining upon us "through the gospel," (*g*) whence also in believing we are said to have "passed from death unto life," (*h*) being "no more strangers and foreigners, but fellow-citizens with the saints, and of the household of God," (*i*) who "hath made us sit together in heavenly places" with his only begotten Son, (*k*) that nothing may be wanting to our complete felicity,—yet, lest we should find it grievous to be still exercised with a severe warfare, as though we derived no benefit from the victory gained by Christ, we must remember what is stated in another place concerning the nature of hope. For "since we hope for that we see not," (*l*) and, according to another text, "faith is the evidence of things not seen;" (*m*) as long as we are confined in the prison of the flesh, "we are absent from the Lord." (*n*) Wherefore the same apostle says, "Ye are dead, and your life is hid with Christ in God;" and "when Christ, who is our life, shall appear, then shall ye also appear with him in glory." (*o*) This, then, is our condition, "that we should live soberly, righteously, and godly, in this present world, looking for that blessed hope, and the glorious appearing of the great God and our Saviour Jesus Christ." (*p*) Here we have need of more than common patience,

(*g*) 2 Tim. i. 10. (*h*) John v. 24. (*i*) Ephes. ii. 19.
(*k*) Ephes. ii. 6. (*l*) Rom. viii. 24. (*m*) Heb. xi. 1.
(*n*) 2 Cor. v. 6. (*o*) Col. iii. 3, 4. (*p*) Titus ii. 12, 13.

lest, being wearied, we pursue a retrograde course, or desert the station assigned us. All that has hitherto been stated, therefore, concerning our salvation, requires minds elevated towards heaven, that, according to the suggestion of Peter, we may love Christ, whom we have not seen, and, believing in him, may "rejoice with joy unspeakable and full of glory," till we receive "the end of our faith." (*q*) For which reason, Paul represents the faith and hope of believers as having respect to "the hope that is laid up in heaven." (*r*) When we are thus looking towards heaven, with our eyes fixed upon Christ, and nothing detains them on earth from carrying us forward to the promised blessedness, we realize the fulfilment of that declaration, "Where your treasure is, there will your heart be also." (*s*) Hence it is, that faith is so scarce in the world; because to our sluggishness nothing is more difficult than to ascend through innumerable obstacles, "pressing toward the mark, for the prize of the high calling." (*t*) To the accumulation of miseries which generally oppress us, are added the mockeries of the profane, with which our simplicity is assailed; while voluntarily renouncing the allurements of present advantage or pleasure, we seem to pursue happiness, which is concealed from our view, like a shadow that continually eludes our grasp. In a word, above and below, before and behind, we are beset by violent temptations, which our minds would long ago have been incapable of sustaining, if they had not been detached from terrestrial things, and attached to the heavenly life, which is apparently at a remote distance. He alone, therefore, has made a solid proficiency in the gospel who has been accustomed to continual meditation on the blessed resurrection.

II. The supreme good was a subject of anxious dispute, and even contention, among the ancient philosophers; yet none of them, except Plato, acknowledge the chief good of man to consist in his union with God. But of the nature of this union he had not even the smallest idea; and no wonder, for he was totally uninformed respecting the sacred bond of it. We know what is the only and perfect happiness even in this earthly pilgrimage; but it daily inflames our hearts with increasing desires after it, till we shall be

(*q*) 1 Peter i. 8, 9.
(*r*) Col. i. 5.
(*s*) Matt. vi. 21.
(*t*) Phil. iii. 14.

satisfied with its full fruition. Therefore I have observed that the advantage of Christ's benefits is solely enjoyed by those who elevate their minds to the resurrection. Thus Paul also sets before believers this object, towards which he tells us he directs all his own efforts, forgetting every thing else, "if by any means he may attain unto it." (*u*) And it behoves us to press forward to the same point with the greater alacrity, lest, if this world engross our attention, we should be grievously punished for our sloth. He therefore characterizes believers by this mark, "Our conversation is in heaven, from whence also we look for the Saviour." (*x*) And that their minds may not flag in this course, he associates with them all creatures as their companions. For as ruin and deformity are visible on every side, he tells us that all things in heaven and earth are tending to renovation. For the fall of Adam having deranged the perfect order of nature, the bondage to which the creatures have been subjected by the sin of man is grievous and burdensome to them; not that they are endued with any intelligence, but because they naturally aspire to the state of perfection from which they have fallen. Paul therefore attributes to them groaning and travailing pains, (*y*) that we who have received the first-fruits of the Spirit may be ashamed of remaining in our corruption, and not imitating at least the inanimate elements which bear the punishment of the sin of others. But as a still stronger stimulus to us, he calls the second advent of Christ "our redemption." It is true, indeed, that all the parts of our redemption are already completed; but because "Christ was once offered to bear the sins of many, he shall appear the second time without sin unto salvation." (*z*) Whatever calamities oppress us, this redemption should support us even till its full consummation.

III. Let the importance of the object sharpen our pursuit. Paul justly argues, that "if there be no resurrection of the dead," the whole gospel is vain and fallacious; for we should be "of all men the most miserable," being exposed to the hatred and reproaches of mankind, "standing in jeopardy every hour," (*a*) and being even like sheep destined to the slaughter; and therefore its authority would fall to the ground not in one point only, but in every

(*u*) Phil. iii. 8—11. (*x*) Phil. iii. 20. (*y*) Rom. viii. 19—23. (*z*) Heb. ix. 28. (*a*) 1 Cor. xv. 13, &c.

thing it contains relating to adoption and the accomplishment of our salvation. To this subject, the most important of all, let us give an attention never to be wearied by length of time. With this view I have deferred what I shall briefly say of it to this place, that the reader, after receiving Christ as the Author of complete salvation, may learn to soar higher, and may know that he is invested with heavenly glory and immortality, in order that the whole body may be conformed to the Head; as in his person the Holy Spirit frequently gives an example of the resurrection. It is a thing difficult to be believed, that bodies, after having been consumed by corruption, shall at length, at the appointed time, be raised again. Therefore, while many of the philosophers asserted the immortality of the soul, the resurrection of the body was admitted by few. And though this furnishes no excuse, yet it admonishes us that this truth is too difficult to command the assent of the human mind. To enable faith to surmount so great an obstacle, the Scripture supplies us with two assistances: one consists in the similitude of Christ, the other in the omnipotence of God. Now, whenever the resurrection is mentioned, let us set before us the image of Christ, who, in our nature, which he assumed, finished his course in this mortal life in such a manner, that, having now obtained immortality, he is the pledge of future resurrection to us. For in the afflictions that befall us, "we bear about in the body the dying of the Lord Jesus, that the life also of Jesus might be made manifest in our body." (*b*) And to separate him from us, is not lawful, nor indeed possible, without rending him asunder. Hence the reasoning of Paul: "If there be no resurrection of the dead, then is Christ not risen;" (*c*) for he assumes this as an acknowledged principle, that Christ neither fell under the power of death, nor triumphed over it in his resurrection, for himself as a private individual; but that all this was a commencement in the Head of what must be fulfilled in all the members, according to every one's order and degree. For it would not be right, indeed, for them to be in all respects equal to him. It is said in the Psalms, "Thou wilt not suffer thine Holy One to see corruption." (*d*) Though a portion of this confidence belongs to us, according to the measure be-

---

(*b*) 2 Cor. iv. 10. (*c*) 1 Cor. xv. 13. (*d*) Psalm xvi. 10.

stowed upon us, yet the perfect accomplishment has been seen in Christ alone, who had his body restored to him entire, free from all corruption. Now that we may have no doubt of our fellowship with Christ in his blessed resurrection, and may be satisfied with this pledge, Paul expressly affirms that the design of his session in heaven, and his advent in the character of Judge at the last day, is to "change our vile body, that it may be fashioned like unto his glorious body." (*e*) In another place also, he shows that God raised his Son from the dead, not in order to display a single specimen of his power, but to exert on believers the same energy of his Spirit, whom he therefore calls "our life" while he dwells in us, because he was given for this very purpose, "to quicken our mortal bodies." (*f*) I am but briefly glancing at things which would admit of a fuller discussion, and are deserving of more elegance of style; but I trust the pious reader will find in a small compass sufficient matter for the edification of his faith. Christ, therefore, rose again, that we might be the companions of his future life. He was raised by the Father, inasmuch as he was the Head of the church, from which he does not suffer him to be separated. He was raised by the power of the Spirit, who is given to us also for the purpose of quickening us. In a word, he was raised that he might be "the resurrection and the life." But as we have observed that this mirror exhibits to us a lively image of our resurrection, so it will furnish a firm foundation for our minds to rest upon, provided we are not wearied or disturbed by the long delay; because it is not ours to measure the moments of time by our own inclination, but to wait patiently for God's establishment of his kingdom in his own appointed time. To this purpose is the expression of Paul, "Christ the first-fruits, afterward they that are Christ's at his coming." (*g*) But that no doubt might be entertained of the resurrection of Christ, on which the resurrection of us all is founded, we see in how many and various ways he has caused it to be attested to us. Scorners will ridicule the history narrated by the evangelists, as a childish mockery. For what weight, they ask, is there in the message brought by some women in a fright, and afterwards confirmed by the disciples half dead

(*e*) Phil. iii. 21. (*f*) Col. iii. 4. Rom. viii. 11. (*g*) 1 Cor. xv. 23.

with fear? Why does not Christ rather set up the splendid trophies of his victory in the midst of the temple and the public places? Why does he not make a formidable entrance into the presence of Pilate? Why does he not prove himself to be again alive, to the priests and all the inhabitants of Jerusalem? Profane men will scarcely believe the persons selected by him to be competent witnesses. I reply, notwithstanding the contemptible weakness evident in these beginnings, yet all this was conducted by the admirable providence of God, that they who were lately dispirited with fear, were hurried away to the sepulchre, partly by love to Christ and pious zeal, partly by their own unbelief, not only to be eye-witnesses of the fact, but to hear from the angels the same as they saw with their eyes. How can we suspect the authority of those who considered what they heard from the women "as idle tales," till they had the fact clearly before them? (*h*) As to the people at large, and the governor himself, it is no wonder that after the ample conviction they had, they were denied a sight of Christ, or any other proofs. The sepulchre is sealed, a watch is set, the body is not found on the third day. The soldiers, corrupted by bribes, circulate a rumour that he was stolen away by his disciples; (*i*) as if they had power to collect a strong force, or were furnished with arms, or were even accustomed to such a daring exploit. But if the soldiers had not courage enough to repulse them, why did they not pursue them, that with the assistance of the people they might seize some of them? The truth is, therefore, that Pilate by his zeal attested the resurrection of Christ; and the guards who were placed at the sepulchre, either by their silence or by their falsehood, were in reality so many heralds to publish the same fact. In the mean time, the voice of the angels loudly proclaimed, "He is not here, but is risen." (*k*) Their celestial splendour evidently showed them to be angels, and not men. After this, if there was any doubt still remaining, it was removed by Christ himself. More than once, his disciples saw, and even felt and handled him; and their unbelief has eminently contributed to the confirmation of our faith. He discoursed among them concerning the mysteries of the kingdom of God, and at length they saw him

---

(*h*) Luke xxiv. 11. (*i*) Matt. xxvii. 66; xxviii. 11, &c.
(*k*) Luke xxiv. 4—6. Matt. xxviii. 3—6.

ascend to heaven. (*l*) Nor was this spectacle exhibited only to the eleven apostles, but "he was seen of above five hundred brethren at once." (*m*) By the mission of the Holy Spirit he gave an undeniable proof, not only of his life, but also of his sovereign dominion; according to his prediction, "It is expedient for you that I go away; for if I go not away, the Comforter will not come unto you; but if I depart, I will send him unto you." (*n*) Paul, in his way to Damascus, was not prostrated to the ground by the influence of a dead man, but felt that the person whom he was opposing was armed with supreme power. He appeared to Stephen for another reason—to overcome the fear of death by an assurance of life. (o) To refuse credit to testimonies so numerous and authentic, is not diffidence, but perverse and unreasonable obstinacy.

IV. The remark we have made, that in proving the resurrection, vile body, that it may be fashioned like unto his glorious body, according to the working whereby he is able even to subdue all briefly suggested in these words of Paul: "Who shall change our our minds should be directed to the infinite power of God, is things unto himself." (*p*) It would therefore be extremely unreasonable here, to consider what could possibly happen in the ordinary course of nature, when the object proposed to us is an inestimable miracle, the magnitude of which absorbs all our faculties. Yet Paul adduces an example from nature to reprove the folly of those who deny the resurrection. "Thou fool," says he, "that which thou sowest is not quickened, except it die." (*q*) He tells us that seed sown displays an image of the resurrection, because the corn is reproduced from putrefaction. Nor would it be a thing so difficult to believe, if we paid proper attention to the miracles which present themselves to our view in all parts of the world. But let us remember, that no man will be truly persuaded of the future resurrection, but he who is filled with admiration, and ascribes to the power of God the glory that is due to it. Transported with this confidence, Isaiah exclaims, "Thy dead men shall live; together with my dead body shall they arise; awake and sing,

(*l*) Acts i. 3, 9.
(*m*) 1 Cor. xv. 6.
(*n*) John xvi. 7.
(*o*) Acts vii. 55.
(*p*) Phil. iii. 21.
(*q*) 1 Cor. xv. 36.

ye that dwell in dust." (*r*) Surrounded by desperate circumstances, he has recourse to God, the Author of life, unto whom, as the Psalmist says, "belong the issues from death." (*s*) Even reduced to a state resembling a dead carcass more than a living man, yet relying on the power of God, just as if he were in perfect health, Job looks forward without any doubts to that day. "I know," says he, "that my Redeemer liveth, and that he shall stand at the latter day upon the earth," there to display his power; "and though after my skin, worms destroy this body, yet in my flesh shall I see God; whom I shall see for myself, and not another." (*t*) For though some persons employ great subtilty to pervert these texts, as if they ought not to be understood of the resurrection, they nevertheless confirm what they wish to destroy; since holy men, in the midst of calamities, seek consolation from no other quarter than from the similitude of the resurrection; which more fully appears from a passage in Ezekiel. (*u*) For when the Jews rejected the promise of their restoration, and objected, that there was no more probability of a way being opened for their return, than of the dead coming forth from their sepulchres, a vision is presented to the prophet, of a field full of dry bones, and God commands them to receive flesh and nerves. Though this figure is intended to inspire the people with a hope of restoration, he borrows the argument for it from the resurrection; as it is to us also the principal model of all the deliverances which believers experience in this world. So Christ, after having declared that the voice of the gospel communicates life, in consequence of its rejection by the Jews, immediately adds, "Marvel not at this; for the hour is coming, in the which all that are in the graves shall hear his voice, and shall come forth." (*x*) After the example of Paul, therefore, let us even now triumphantly exult in the midst of our conflicts, that he who has promised us a life to come "is able to keep that which we have committed to him;" and thus let us glory that "there is laid up for us a crown of righteousness, which the righteous Judge shall give us." (*y*) The consequence of this will be, that all the troubles we suffer will point us to the life to come, "seeing it is a righteous thing with God," and agreeable to his

(*r*) Isaiah xxvi. 19. (*s*) Psalm lxviii. 20. (*t*) Job xix. 25, 27.
(*u*) Ezek. xxxvii. 1—14. (*x*) John v. 28, 29. (*y*) 2 Tim. i. 12; iv. 8.

nature, "to recompense tribulation to them that trouble us, and to us who are" unjustly "troubled, rest, when the Lord Jesus shall be revealed, with his mighty angels, in flaming fire." (*z*) But we must remember what immediately follows, that "he shall come to be glorified in his saints, and to be admired in all them that believe," because they believe the gospel.

V. Now, though the minds of men ought to be continually occupied with the study of this subject, yet as if they expressly intended to abolish all remembrance of the resurrection, they have called death the end of all things, and the destruction of man. For Solomon certainly speaks according to a common and received opinion, when he says, "A living dog is better than a dead lion." (*a*) And again: "Who knows whether the spirit of man goeth upward, and the spirit of the beast goeth downward?" (*b*) This brutish stupidity has infected all ages of the world, and even forced its way into the Church; for the Sadducees had the audacity publicly to profess, that there is no resurrection, and that souls are mortal. But that none might be excused by this gross ignorance, the very instinct of nature has always set before the eyes of unbelievers an image of the resurrection. For what is the sacred and inviolable custom of interring the dead, but a pledge of another life? Nor can it be objected that this originated in error; for the rites of sepulture were always observed among the holy fathers; and it pleased God that the same custom should be retained among the Gentiles, that their torpor might be roused by the image of the resurrection thereby set before them. Though this ceremony produced no good effects upon them, yet it will be useful to us, if we wisely consider its tendency; for it is no slight refutation of unbelief, that all united in professing a thing that none of them believed. But Satan has not only stupefied men's minds, to make them bury the memory of the resurrection together with the bodies of the dead, but has endeavoured to corrupt this point of doctrine by various fictions, with an ultimate view to its total subversion. Not to mention that he began to oppose it in the days of Paul, not long after arose the Millenarians, who limited the reign of Christ to a thousand years. Their fiction is too puerile to

---

(*z*) 2 Thess. i. 6—8, 10. (*a*) Eccl. ix. 4. (*b*) Eccl. iii. 21.

require or deserve refutation. Nor does the Revelation, which they quote in favour of their error, afford them any support; for the term of a thousand years, there mentioned, (*c*) refers not to the eternal blessedness of the Church, but to the various agitations which awaited the Church in its militant state upon earth. But the whole Scripture proclaims that there will be no end of the happiness of the elect, or the punishment of the reprobate. Now, all those things which are invisible to our eyes, or far above the comprehension of our minds, must either be believed on the authority of the oracles of God, or entirely rejected. Those who assign the children of God a thousand years to enjoy the inheritance of the future life, little think what dishonour they cast on Christ and his kingdom. For if they are not invested with immortality, neither is Christ himself, into the likeness of whose glory they will be transformed, received up into immortal glory. If their happiness will have any end, it follows that the kingdom of Christ, on the stability of which it rests, is temporary. Lastly, either these persons are extremely ignorant of all Divine things, or they are striving, with malignant perverseness, to overturn all the grace of God and power of Christ; and these can never be perfectly fulfilled till sin is abolished, and death swallowed up, and eternal life completely established. But the folly of being afraid that too much cruelty is attributed to God, if the reprobate are doomed to eternal punishment, is even evident to the blind. Will the Lord do any injury by refusing the enjoyment of his kingdom to persons whose ingratitude shall have rendered them unworthy of it? But their sins are temporary. This I grant; but the majesty of God, as well as his justice, which their sins have violated, is eternal. Their iniquity, therefore, is justly remembered. Then the punishment is alleged to be excessive, being disproportioned to the crime. But this is intolerable blasphemy, when the majesty of God is so little valued, when the contempt of it is considered of no more consequence than the destruction of one soul. But let us pass by these triflers; lest, contrary to what we have before said, we should appear to consider their reveries as worthy of refutation.

VI. Beside these wild notions, the perverse curiosity of man

(*c*) Rev. xx. 4.

has introduced two others. Some have supposed that the whole man dies, and that souls are raised again together with bodies; others, admitting the immortality of souls, suppose they will be clothed with new bodies, and thereby deny the resurrection of the flesh. As I have touched on the former of these notions in the creation of man, it will be sufficient again to apprize my readers, that it is a brutish error, to represent the spirit, formed after the image of God, as a fleeting breath which animates the body only during this perishable life, and to annihilate the temple of the Holy Spirit; in short, to despoil that part of us in which Divinity is eminently displayed, and the characters of immortality are conspicuous, of this property; so that the condition of the body must be better and more excellent than that of the soul. Very different is the doctrine of Scripture, which compares the body to a habitation, from which we depart at death; because it estimates us by that part of our nature which constitutes the distinction between us and the brutes. Thus Peter, when near his death, says, "Shortly I must put off this my tabernacle." (*d*) And Paul, speaking of believers, having said that "if our earthly house of this tabernacle were dissolved, we have a building in the heavens," adds that "whilst we are at home in the body, we are absent from the Lord, and willing rather to be absent from the body, and to be present with the Lord." (*e*) Unless our souls survive our bodies, what is it that is present with God when separated from the body? But the apostle removes all doubt when he says that we are "come to the spirits of just men made perfect." (*f*) By which expression he means, that we are associated with the holy fathers, who, though dead, still maintain the same piety with us, so that we cannot be members of Christ without being united with them. If souls separated from bodies did not retain their existence so as to be capable of glory and felicity, Christ would not have said to the thief, "To-day shalt thou be with me in paradise." (*g*) Supported by such undeniable testimonies, let us not hesitate, after the example of Christ, when we die, to commend our spirits to God; or, like Stephen, to resign them to the care of Christ, who is justly called the faithful "Shepherd and Bishop of

(*d*) 2 Peter i. 14. (*e*) 2 Cor. v. 1, 8.
(*f*) Heb. xii. 23. (*g*) Luke xxiii. 43.

souls." Over-curious inquiry respecting their intermediate state is neither lawful nor useful. Many persons exceedingly perplex themselves by discussing what place they occupy, and whether they already enjoy the glory of heaven, or not. But it is folly and presumption to push our inquiries on unknown things beyond what God permits us to know. The Scripture declares that Christ is present with them, and receives them into paradise, where they enjoy consolation, and that the souls of the reprobate endure the torments which they have deserved; but it proceeds no further. Now, what teacher or doctor shall discover to us that which God has concealed? The question respecting place is equally senseless and futile; because we know that the soul has no dimensions like the body. The blessed assemblage of holy spirits being called the bosom of Abraham, teaches us that it is enough for us, at the close of this pilgrimage, to be received by the common Father of believers, and to participate with him in the fruit of his faith. In the mean while, as the Scripture uniformly commands us to look forward with eager expectation to the coming of Christ, and defers the crown of glory which awaits us till that period, let us be content within these limits which God prescribes to us—that the souls of pious men, after finishing their laborious warfare, depart into a state of blessed rest, where they wait with joy and pleasure for the fruition of the promised glory; and so, that all things remain in suspense till Christ appears as the Redeemer. And there is no doubt that the condition of the reprobate is the same as Jude assigns to the devils, who are confined and bound in chains till they are brought forth to the punishment to which they are doomed.

VII. Equally monstrous is the error of those who imagine that souls will not resume the bodies which at present belong to them, but will be furnished with others altogether different. It was the very futile reasoning of the Manichæans, that it is absurd to expect that the flesh which is so impure will ever rise again. As if there were no impurity attached to the souls, which they nevertheless encouraged to entertain hopes of a heavenly life. It was therefore just as if they had maintained, that any thing infected with the contagion of sin is incapable of being purified by the power of God; for that reverie, that the flesh was created by the devil, and therefore naturally impure, I at present forbear to notice; and only observe, that whatever we have in us now unworthy of heaven, will not hinder the resurrection. In the first place, when Paul exhorts believers to "cleanse" themselves "from all filthiness of the flesh and spirit," (*h*) thence follows the judgment he elsewhere denounces, "that every one" shall "receive the things done in his body, according to that he hath done, whether it be good or bad;" (*i*) with which agrees another passage, "that the life also of Jesus might be made manifest in our body." (*k*) Wherefore in another place, he prays to God that the whole person may "be preserved blameless unto the coming of our Lord Jesus Christ," even the "body," as well as the "soul and spirit." (*l*) And no wonder; for that those bodies which God has dedicated as temples for himself, should sink into corruption, without any hope of resurrection, would be absurd in the extreme. What is to be concluded from their being members of Christ? (*m*) from God's enjoining every part of them to be sanctified to himself, requiring their tongues to celebrate his name, their hands to be lifted up with purity to him (*n*) and their bodies altogether to be presented to him as "living sacrifices?" (*o*) This part of our nature therefore being degnified with such illustrious honour by the heavenly Judge, what madness is betrayed by a mortal man, in asserting it to be reduced to ashes without any hope of restoration! And Paul, when he gives us this exhortation, "Glorify God in your body, and in your spirit, which are God's," (*p*) certainly does not countenance consigning to eternal corruption that which he asserts to be consecrated to God. Nor is there any point more clearly established in Scripture, than the resurrection of our present bodies. "This corruptible," says Paul, "must put on incorruption, and this mortal must put on immortality." (*q*) If new bodies were to be formed by God, what would become of this change of quality? If it had been said, that we must be renewed, the ambiguity of the expression might have given occasion for cavil: now, when he particularly designates the bodies that surround us, and promises that they shall be "raised in incorruption," it is a

---

(*h*) 2 Cor. vii. 1. (*i*) 2 Cor. v. 10. (*k*) 2 Cor. iv. 10.
(*l*) 1 Thess. v. 23. (*m*) 1 Cor. vi. 15. (*n*) 1 Tim. ii. 8.
(*o*) Rom. xii. 1. (*p*) 1 Cor. vi. 20. (*q*) 1 Cor. xv. 54.

sufficient denial of the formation of new ones. "He could not indeed," says Tertullian, "have spoken more expressly, unless he had held his own skin in his hand." Nor will any cavil evade the declaration of Isaiah, cited by the apostle, respecting Christ as the future Judge of the world: "As I live, saith the Lord, every knee shall bow to me;" (*r*) for he plainly declares to the persons addressed by him, that they shall be obliged to give an account of their lives; which would not be reasonable, if new bodies were to be placed at the tribunal. There is no obscurity in the language of Daniel: "Many of them that sleep in the dust of the earth shall awake, some to everlasting life, and some to shame and everlasting contempt." (*s*) For God does not collect fresh materials from the four elements for the fabrication of men, but calls the dead out of their sepulchres. And this the plainest reason dictates. For if death, which originated in the fall of man, be adventitious, and not necessary to our nature, the restoration effected by Christ belongs to the same body which was thus rendered mortal. From the ridicule of the Athenians, when Paul asserted the resurrection, it is easy to infer the nature of his doctrine; and that ridicule is of no small weight for the confirmation of our faith. The injunction of Christ also is worthy of attention: "Fear not them which kill the body, but are not able to kill the soul; but rather fear him which is able to destroy both soul and body in hell." (*t*) For there would be no reason for this fear, if the body which we now carry about were not liable to punishment. Another of Christ's declarations is equally plain: "The hour is coming, in the which all that are in the graves shall hear his voice, and shall come forth, they that have done good, unto the resurrection of life, and they that have done evil, unto the resurrection of damnation." (*u*) Shall we say that souls rest in graves, and will there hear the voice of Christ, and not rather that bodies at his command will return to the vigour they had lost? Besides, if we are to receive new bodies, where will be the conformity between the Head and members? Christ rose; was it by making himself a new body? No, but according to his prediction, "Destroy this temple, and in three days I will raise it up." (*x*) The mortal body which he

(*r*) Rom. xiv. 11, 12. (*s*) Dan. xii. 2. (*t*) Matt. x. 28. (*u*) John v. 28, 29. (*x*) John ii. 19.

before possessed, he again assumed. For it would have conducted but little to our benefit, if there had been a substitution of a new body, and an annihilation of that which had been offered as an atoning sacrifice. We must, therefore, maintain the connection stated by the apostle—that we shall rise, because Christ has risen; (*y*) for nothing is more improbable, than that our body, in which "we bear about the dying of the Lord Jesus," (*z*) should be deprived of a resurrection similiar to his. There was an illustrious example of this immediately on Christ's resurrection, when "the graves were opened, and many bodies of the saints which slept arose." (*a*) For it cannot be denied, that this was a prelude, or rather an earnest, of the final resurrection, which we expect; such as was exhibited before in Enoch and Elias, whom Tertullian speaks of as "the candidates of the resurrection," because they were taken into the immediate care of God, with an entire exemption from corruption in body and soul.

VIII. I am ashamed of consuming so many words on so clear a subject; but my readers will cheerfully unite with me in submitting to this trouble, that no room may be left for men of perverse and presumptuous minds to deceive the unwary. The unsteady spirits I am now opposing, bring forward a figment of their own brains, that at the resurrection there will be a creation of new bodies. What reason can induce them to adopt this sentiment, but a seeming incredibility, in their apprehension, that a body long consumed by corruption can ever return to its pristine state? Unbelief, therefore, is the only source of this opinion. In the Scripture, on the contrary, we are uniformly exhorted by the Spirit of God to hope for the resurrection of our body. For this reason, baptism is spoken of by Paul as a seal of our future resurrection; (*b*) and we are as clearly invited to this confidence by the sacred Supper, when we receive into our mouths the symbols of spiritual grace. And certainly the exhortation of Paul, to "yield our members as instruments of righteousness unto God," (*c*) would lose all its force, if unaccompanied by what he afterwards subjoins: "He that raised up Christ from the dead, shall also quicken your mortal bodies." (*d*) For what would it avail to devote our feet,

(*y*) 1 Cor. xv. 12, &c. (*z*) 2 Cor. iv. 10. (*a*) Matt. xxvi. 52.
(*b*) Col. ii. 12. (*c*) Rom. vi. 13. (*d*) Rom. viii. 11.

hands, eyes, and tongues to the service of God, if they were not to participate the benefit and reward? This is clearly confirmed by the following passage of Paul: "The body is not for fornication, but for the Lord; and the Lord for the body. And God hath both raised up the Lord, and will also raise up us by his own power." (*e*) The following passages are still plainer—that our bodies are the "temples of the Holy Ghost," and "members of Christ." (*f*) In the mean time, we see how he connects the resurrection with chastity and holiness; and so he just after extends the price of redemption to our bodies. Now, it would be extremely unreasonable that the body of Paul, in which he "bore the marks of the Lord Jesus," (*g*) and in which he eminently glorified Christ, should be deprived of the reward of the crown. Hence also that exultation: "We look for the Saviour from heaven, who shall change our vile body, that it may be fashioned like unto his glorious body." (*h*) And if it be true, "that we must through much tribulation enter into the kingdom of God," (*i*) there can be no reason for prohibiting this entrance to the bodies, which God trains under the banner of the cross, and honours with the glory of victory. Therefore no doubt has ever been entertained by the saints, whether they should hope to be companions of Christ hereafter; who transfers to his own person all the afflictions with which we are tried, to teach us that they are conducting us to life. And God also established the holy fathers under the law in this faith by an external ceremony. For to what purpose was the rite of sepulture, as we have already seen, but to instruct them that another life was prepared for the interred bodies? The same was suggested by the spices and other symbols of immortality, which, like the sacrifices under the law, assisted the obscurity of direct instruction. Nor did this custom arise from superstition; for we find the Holy Spirit as diligent in mentioning the sepultures, as in insisting on the principal mysteries of faith. And Christ commends this as no mean office; (*k*) certainly for no other reason, but because it raises our eyes from the view of the grave, which corrupts and dissolves all things, to the spectacle of future renovation. Besides the very careful observance of this ceremony,

(*e*) 1 Cor. vi. 13, 14. (*f*) 1 Cor. vi. 15, 19, 20. (*g*) Gal. vi. 17.
(*h*) Phil. iii. 20, 21. (*i*) Acts xiv. 22. (*k*) Matt. xxvi. 10, 12.

which is commended in the fathers, sufficiently proves it to have been an excellent and valuable assistance to faith. Nor would Abraham have discovered such solicitous concern about the sepulchre of his wife, if he had not been actuated by motives of religion, and the prospect of more than worldly advantage; that by adorning her dead body with the emblems of the resurrection, he might confirm his own faith, and that of his family. (*l*) There is yet a clearer proof of this in the example of Jacob; who, to testify to his posterity that the hope of the promised land did not forsake his heart even in death, commands his bones to be reconveyed thither. (*m*) If he was to be furnished with a new body, would not this have been a ridiculous command concerning dust that was soon to be annihilated? Wherefore, if the authority of the Scripture has any weight with us, no clearer or strong proof of any doctrine can possibly be desired. Even children understand this to be the meaning of the term "resurrection;" for we never apply this term to any instance of original creation; nor would it be consistent with that declaration of Christ, "Of all which the Father hath given me, I shall lose nothing, but will raise it up again at the last day." (*n*) The same is implied in the word "sleeping," which is only applicable to the body. Hence the appellation of *cemetery*, or *sleeping-place*, given to places of burial. It remains for me to touch a little on the manner of the resurrection. And I shall but just hint at it; because Paul, by calling it a mystery, exhorts us to sobriety, and forbids all licentiousness of subtle and extravagant speculation. In the first place, let it be remembered, as we have observed, that we shall rise again with the same bodies we have now, as to the substance, but that the quality will be different; just as the very body of Christ which had been offered as a sacrifice was raised again, but with such new and superior qualities, as though it had been altogether different. Paul represents this by some familiar examples. For as the flesh of man and of brutes is the same in substance, but not in quality; as the matter of all the stars is the same, but they differ in glory; so, though we shall retain the substance of our body, he tells us there will be a change, which will render its condition far

(*l*) Gen. xxiii. 3—19. (*m*) Gen. xlvii. 30. (*n*) John vi. 39, 40.

more excellent. (*o*) The "corruptible" body, therefore, will neither perish nor vanish, in order to our resurrection; but having laid aside corruption, will "put on incorruption." (*p*) God, having all the elements subject to his control, will find no difficulty in commanding the earth, the water, and the fire, to restore whatever they appear to have consumed. This is declared in figurative language by Isaiah: "Behold, the Lord cometh out of his place to punish the inhabitants of the earth for their iniquity; the earth also shall disclose her blood, and shall no more cover her slain." (*q*) But we must remark the difference between those who shall have been already dead, and those whom that day shall find alive. "We shall not all sleep," says Paul, "but we shall all be changed;" (*r*) that is, there will be no necessity for any distance of time to intervene between death and the commencement of the next life; for "in a moment, in the twinkling of an eye, the trumpet shall sound, and the dead shall be raised incorruptible," and the living transformed by a sudden change into the same glory. So in another Epistle he comforts believers who were to die, that those "which are alive and remain unto the coming of the Lord, shall not prevent them which are asleep," but that "the dead in Christ shall rise first." (*s*) If it be objected that the apostle says, "It is appointed unto men once to die," (*t*) the answer is easy,—that where the state of the nature is changed, it is a species of death, and may without impropriety be so called; and therefore there is a perfect consistence between these things, that all will be removed by death when they put off the mortal body, but that a separation of the body and soul will not be necessary, where there will be an instantaneous change.

IX. But here arises a question of greater difficulty. How can the resurrection, which is a peculiar benefit of Christ, be common to the impious and the subjects of the Divine curse? We know that in Adam all were sentenced to death; (*u*) Christ comes as "the resurrection and the life;" (*x*) but was it to bestow life promiscuously on all mankind? But what would be more improbable, than that they should attain, in their obstinate blindness, what the pious

(*o*) 1 Cor. xv. 39—41. (*p*) 1 Cor. xv. 53. (*q*) Isaiah xxvi. 21.
(*r*) 1 Cor. xv. 51, 52. (*s*) 1 Thess. iv. 15, 16. (*t*) Heb. ix. 27.
(*u*) Rom. v. 12. (*x*) John xi. 25.

worshippers of God recover by faith alone? Yet it remains certain, that one will be a resurrection to judgment, the other to life; and that Christ will come to "separate the sheep from the goats." (*y*) I reply, we ought not to think that so very strange, which we see exemplified in our daily experience. We know that in Adam we lost the inheritance of the whole world, and have no more right to the enjoyment of common ailments, than to the fruit of the tree of life. How is it, then, that God not only "maketh his sun to rise on the evil and on the good," (*z*) but that, for the accommodations of the present life, his inestimable liberality is diffused in the most copious abundance? Hence we see, that things which properly belong to Christ and his members, are also extended to the impious; not to become their legitimate possession, but to render them more inexcusable. Thus impious men frequently experience God's beneficence in remarkable instances, which sometimes exceed all the blessings of the pious, but which, nevertheless, are the means of aggravating their condemnation. If it be objected, that the resurrection is improperly compared with fleeting and terrestrial advantages, I reply again, that when men were first alienated from God, the Fountain of life, they deserved the ruin of the devil to be altogether destroyed; yet the wonderful counsel of God devised a middle state, that without life they might live in death. It ought not to be thought more unreasonable, if the impious are raised from the dead, in order to be dragged to the tribunal of Christ, whom they now refuse to hear as their Master and Teacher. For it would be a slight punishment to be destroyed by death, if they were not to be brought before the Judge whose infinite and endless vengeance they have incurred, to receive the punishments due to their rebellion. But though we must maintain what we have asserted, and what is asserted by Paul in his celebrated confession before Felix, "that there shall be a resurrection of the dead, both of the just and unjust," (*a*) yet the Scripture more commonly exhibits the resurrection to the children of God alone, in connection with the glory of heaven; because, strictly speaking, Christ will come, not for the destruction of the world,

(*y*) Matt. xxv. 32. (*z*) Matt. v. 45. (*a*) Acts xxiv. 15.

but for purposes of salvation. This is the reason that the Creed mentions only the life of blessedness.

X. But, as the prophecy of "death being swallowed up in victory," shall then, and not till then, be fully accomplished,—let us always reflect on eternal felicity as the end of the resurrection; of the excellence of which, if every thing were said that could be expressed by all the tongues of men, yet the smallest part of it would scarcely be mentioned. For though we are plainly informed, that the kingdom of God is full of light, joy, felicity, and glory, yet all that is mentioned remains far above our comprehension, and enveloped, as it were, in enigmatical obscurity, till the arrival of that day, when he shall exhibit his glory to us face to face. "Now are we the sons of God, (says John,) and it doth not yet appear what we shall be; but we know, that when he shall appear, we shall be like him; for we shall see him as he is." (*b*) Wherefore the prophets, because they could not describe that spiritual blessedness by any terms expressive of its sublime nature, generally represented it under corporeal images. Yet, as any intimation of that happiness must kindle in us a fervour of desire, let us chiefly dwell on this reflection—If God, as an inexhaustible fountain, contains within himself a plenitude of all blessings, nothing beyond him can ever be desired by those who aspire to the supreme good, and a perfection of happiness. This we are taught in various passages of Scripture. "Abraham," says God, "I am thy exceeding great reward." (*c*) With this David agrees: "The Lord is the portion of mine inheritance; the lines are fallen unto me in pleasant places." (*d*) Again: "I will behold thy face; I shall be satisfied." (*e*) Peter declares, that believers are called, "that they might be partakers of the Divine nature." (*f*) How will this be? Because "he shall be glorified in his saints, and admired in all them that believe." (*g*) If the Lord will make the elect partakers of his glory, strength, and righteousness, and will even bestow himself upon them to be enjoyed, and, what is better than this, to be in some sense united to them,—let us remember, that in this favour every kind of felicity is comprised. And after we have made considerable progress in this meditation, we may still

(*b*) 1 John iii. 2. (*c*) Gen. xv. 1. (*d*) Psalm xvi. 5, 6.
(*e*) Psalm xvii. 15. (*f*) 2 Peter i. 4. (*g*) 2 Thess. i. 10.

acknowledge the conceptions of our minds to be extremely low, in comparison with the sublimity of this mystery. Sobriety, therefore, is the more necessary for us on this subject, lest, forgetful of our slender capacity, we presumptuously soar to too high an elevation, and are overwhelmed with the blaze of celestial glory. We perceive, likewise, how we are actuated by an inordinate desire of knowing more than is right; which gives rise to a variety of questions, both frivolous and pernicious. I call those frivolous, from which no advantage can possible be derived. But those of the second class are worse, involving persons, who indulge them, in injurious speculations, and therefore I call them pernicious. What is taught in the Scriptures, we ought to receive without any controversy; that as God, in the various distribution of his gifts to the saints in this world, does not equally enlighten them all, so in heaven, where God will crown those gifts, there will be an inequality in the degrees of their glory. The language of Paul is not indiscriminately applicable to all—"Ye are our glory and joy at our Lord's coming;" (*h*) nor Christ's address to his apostles—"Ye shall sit judging the twelve tribes of Israel." (*i*) But Paul, who knew that according as God enriches the saints with spiritual gifts on earth, so he adorns them with glory in heaven, doubts not that there is in reserve for him a peculiar crown in proportion to his labours. And Christ commends to his apostles the dignity of the office with which they were invested, by assuring them that the reward of it was laid up in heaven. (*k*) Thus also Daniel: "They that be wise, shall shine as the brightness of the firmament; and they that turn many to righteousness, as the stars, for ever and ever." (*l*) And an attentive consideration of the Scriptures will convince us, that they not only promise eternal life generally to believers, but also a special reward to each individual. Whence that expression of Paul—"The Lord reward him according to his works." (*m*) It is also confirmed by the promise of Christ that his disciples should receive a hundred-fold more in eternal life. (*n*) In a word, as Christ begins the glory of his body by a manifold variety of gifts in this world, and enlarges it by degrees, in the same manner he will also perfect it in heaven.

(*h*) 1 Thess. ii. 19, 20. (*i*) Matt. xix. 29. (*k*) Matt. v. 12.
(*l*) Dan. xii. 3. (*m*) 2 Tim. iv. 14. (*n*) Matt. xix. 29.

XI. As all the pious will receive this with one consent, because it is sufficiently attested in the word of God, so, on the other hand, dismissing abstruse questions, which they know to be obstructions to them, they will not transgress the limits prescribed to them. For myself, I not only refrain as an individual from the unnecessary investigation of useless questions, but think it my duty to be cautious, lest I encourage the vanity of others by answering them. Men, thirsting after useless knowledge, inquire what will be the distance between the prophets and apostles, and between the apostles and martyrs; and how many degrees of difference there will be between those who have married and those who have lived and died in celibacy; in short, they leave not a corner of heaven unexplored. The next object of their inquiry is, what end will be answered by the restoration of the world; since the children of God will want nothing of all its vast and incomparable abundance, but will be like the angels of God, whose freedom from all animal necessities is the symbol of eternal blessedness. I reply, there will be such great pleasantness in the very prospect, and such exquisite sweetness in the mere knowledge, without any use of it, that this felicity will far exceed all the accommodations afforded us in the present state. Let us suppose ourselves placed in some region the most opulent in the world, and furnished with every pleasure; who would not sometimes be prevented by disease from making use of the bounties of God? who would not often have his enjoyment of them interrupted by the consequences of intemperance? Hence it follows, that calm and serene enjoyment, pure from every vice and free from all defect, although there should be no use of a corruptible life, is the perfection of happiness. Others go further, and inquire, whether dross and all impurities in metals are not removed from that restoration, and incompatible with such a state. Though I in some measure grant this, I expect, with Paul, a reparation of all the evils caused by sin, for which he represents the creatures as groaning and travailing. They proceed further still, and inquire, what better state awaits the human race, when the blessing of posterity shall no longer be enjoyed. The solution of this question also is easy. The splendid commendations of it in the Scriptures relate to that progressive increase, by which God is continually carrying forward the system of nature to its consummation. But as the unwary are easily caught by such temptations, and are afterwards drawn further into the labyrinth, till, at length, every one being pleased with his own opinion, there is no end to disputes,—the best and shortest rule for our conduct, is to content ourselves with "seeing through a glass darkly," till we shall "see face to face." (*o*) For very few persons are concerned about the way that leads to heaven, but all are anxious to know, before the time, what passes there. Men in general are slow, and reluctant to engage in the conflict and yet portray to themselves imaginary triumphs.

XII. Now, as no description can equal the severity of the Divine vengeance on the reprobate, their anguish and torment are figuratively represented to us under corporeal images; as, darkness, weeping, and gnashing of teeth, unextinguishable fire, a worm incessantly gnawing the heart. (*p*) For there can be no doubt but that, by such modes of expression, the Holy Spirit intended to confound all our faculties with horror; as when it is said, that "Tophet is ordained of old; the pile thereof is fire and much wood: the breath of the Lord, like a stream of brimstone, doth kindle it." (*q*) As these representations should assist us in forming some conception of the wretched condition of the wicked, so they ought principally to fix our attention on the calamity of being alienated from the presence of God; and in addition to this, experiencing such hostility from the Divine majesty as to be unable to escape from its continual pursuit. For, in the first place, his indignation is like a most violent flame, which devours and consumes all that it touches. In the next place, all the creatures so subserve the execution of his judgment, that those to whom the Lord will thus manifest his wrath, will find the heaven, the earth, and the sea, the animals, and all that exists, inflamed, as it were, with dire indignation against them, and all armed for their destruction. It is no trivial threatening, therefore, denounced by the apostle, that unbelievers "shall be punished with everlasting destruction from the presence of the Lord, and from the glory of his power." (*r*) And when the prophets excite terror by corporeal

(*o*) 1 Cor. xiii. 12.

(*p*) Matt. iii. 12; viii. 12; xxii. 13. Mark ix. 43, 44. Isaiah lxvi. 24.

(*q*) Isaiah xxx. 33. (*r*) 2 Thess. i. 9.

figures, though they advance nothing hyperbolical for our dull understandings, yet they mingle preludes of the future judgment with the sun, the moon, and the whole fabric of the world. Wherefore miserable consciences find no repose, but are harassed and agitated with a dreadful tempest, feel themselves torn asunder by an angry God, and transfixed and penetrated by mortal stings, are terrified at the thunderbolts of God, and broken by the weight of his hand; so that to sink into any gulfs and abysses would be more tolerable than to stand for a moment in these terrors. How great and severe, then, is the punishment, to endure the never ceasing effects of his wrath! On which subject there is a memorable passage in the ninetieth psalm; that though by his countenance he scatters all mortals, and turns them to destruction, yet he encourages his servants in proportion to their timidity in this world, to excite them, though under the burden of the cross, to press forward, till he shall be all in all.

Book IV

On the External Means or Aids by Which God Calls Us Into Communion with Christ, and Retains Us in It

ARGUMENT

THREE parts of the Apostles' Creed, respecting God the Creator, Redeemer, and Sanctifier, have been explained in the former books. This last book is an exposition of what remains, relating to the Holy Catholic Church, and the Communion of Saints.

The chapters contained in it may be conveniently arranged in three grand divisions:—

I. The Church.
II. The Sacraments.
III. Civil Government.

The First Division, extending to the end of the thirteenth chapter, contains many particulars, which, however, may all be referred to four principal heads:—

I. The marks of the Church, or the criteria by which it may be distinguished; since we must cultivate union with it—Chap. I–II.

II. The government of the church—Chap. III–VII.
   1. The order of government in the church—Chap. III.
   2. The form practised by the ancient Christians—Chap. IV.

3. The nature of the present ecclesiastical government under the Papacy—Chap. V. The primacy of the Pope—Chap. VI. And the degrees of his advancement to this tyrannical power—Chap. VII.

III. The power of the church—Chap. VIII–XI.

1. Relating to articles of faith,—which resides either in the respective bishops—Chap. VIII.—or in the church at large, represented in councils—Chap. IX.
2. In making laws—Chap. X.
3. In ecclesiastical jurisdiction—Chap. XI.

IV. The discipline of the Church—Chap. XII–XIII.

1. The principal use of it—Chap. XII.
2. The abuse of it—Chap. XIII.

The Second Division, relating to the sacraments, contains three parts.

I. The sacraments in general—Chap. XIV.

II. Each sacrament in particular—Chap. XV–XVIII.

1. Baptism—Chap. XV. Distinct discussion of Pædobaptism —Chap. XVI.
2. The Lord's Supper—Chap. XVII.—and its profanation—Chap. XVIII.

III. The five other ceremonies, falsely called sacraments—Chap. XIX.

The Third Division regards civil government.

I. This government in general.

II. Its respective branches.

1. The magistrates.
2. The laws.
3. The people.

CHAPTER I

The True Church, and the Necessity of Our Union with Her, Being the Mother of All the Pious

THAT by the faith of the gospel Christ becomes ours, and we become partakers of the salvation procured by him, and of eternal happiness, has been explained in the preceding Book. But as our ignorance and slothfulness, and, I may add, the vanity of our minds, require external aids, in order to the production of faith in our hearts, and its increase and progressive advance even to its completion, God has provided such aids in compassion to our infirmity; and that the preaching of the gospel might be maintained, he has deposited this treasure with the Church. He has appointed pastors and teachers, that his people might be taught by their lips; he has invested them with authority; in short, he has omitted nothing that could contribute to a holy unity of faith, and to the establishment of good order. (*a*) First of all, he has instituted Sacraments, which we know by experience to be means of the greatest utility for the nourishment and support of our faith. For as, during our confinement in the prison of our flesh, we have not yet attained to the state of angels, God has, in his wonderful providence, accommodated himself to our capacity, by prescribing a way in which we might approach him, notwith-

(*a*) Ephes. iv. 11—16.

standing our immense distance from him. Wherefore the order of instruction requires us now to treat of the Church and its government, orders, and power; secondly, of the Sacraments; and lastly, of Civil Government; and at the same time to call off the pious readers from the abuses of the Papacy, by which Satan has corrupted every thing that God had appointed to be instrumental to our salvation. I shall begin with the Church, in whose bosom it is God's will that all his children should be collected, not only to be nourished by her assistance and ministry during their infancy and childhood, but also to be governed by her maternal care, till they attain a mature age, and at length reach the end of their faith. For it is not lawful to "put asunder" those things "which God hath joined together;" (*b*) that the Church is the mother of all who have him for their Father; and that not only under the law, but since the coming of Christ also, according to the testimony of the apostle, who declares the new and heavenly Jerusalem to be "the mother of us all." (*c*)

II. That article of the Creed, in which we profess to believe THE CHURCH, refers not only to the visible Church of which we are now speaking, but likewise to all the elect of God, including the dead as well as the living. The word BELIEVE is used, because it is often impossible to discover any difference between the children of God and the ungodly, between his peculiar flock and wild beasts. The particle IN, interpolated by many is not supported by any probable reason. I confess that it is generally adopted at present, and is not destitute of the suffrage of antiquity, being found in the Nicene Creed, as it is transmitted to us in ecclesiastical history. Yet it is evident from the writings of the fathers, that it was anciently admitted without controversy to say, "I believe the Church," not "*in* the Church." For not only is this word not used by Augustine and the ancient writer of the work "On the Exposition of the Creed," which passes under the name of Cyprian, but they particularly remark that there would be an impropriety in the expression, if this preposition were inserted; and they confirm their opinion by no trivial reason. For we declare that we believe *in God* because our mind depends

(*b*) Mark x. 9. (*c*) Gal. iv. 26.

upon him as true, and our confidence rests in him. But this would not be applicable to the Church, any more than to "the remission of sins," or the "resurrection of the body." Therefore, though I am averse to contentions about words, yet I would rather adopt a proper phraseology adapted to express the subject than affect forms of expression by which the subject would be unnecessarily involved in obscurity. The design of this clause is to teach us, that though the devil moves every engine to destroy the grace of Christ, and all the enemies of God exert the most furious violence in the same attempt, yet his grace cannot possibly be extinguished, nor can his blood be rendered barren, so as not to produce some fruit. Here we must regard both the secret election of God, and his internal vocation; because he alone "knoweth them that are his;" and keeps them enclosed under his "seal," to use the expression of Paul; (*d*) except that they bear his impression, by which they may be distinguished from the reprobate. But because a small and contemptible number is concealed among a vast multitude, and a few grains of wheat are covered with a heap of chaff, we must leave to God alone the knowledge of his Church whose foundation is his secret election. Nor is it sufficient to include in our thoughts and minds the whole multitude of the elect, unless we conceive of such a unity of the Church, into which we know ourselves to be truly ingrafted. For unless we are united with all the other members under Christ our Head, we can have no hope of the future inheritance. Therefore the Church is called CATHOLIC, or universal; because there could not be two or three churches, without Christ being divided, which is impossible. But all the elect of God are so connected with each other in Christ, that as they depend upon one head, so they grow up together as into one body, compacted together like members of the same body; being made truly one, as living by one faith, hope, and charity, through the same Divine Spirit, being called not only to the same inheritance of eternal life, but also to a participation of one God and Christ. Therefore, though the melancholy desolation which surrounds us, seems to proclaim that there is nothing left of the Church, let us remember that the death of Christ is

(*d*) 2 Tim. ii. 19.

fruitful, and that God wonderfully preserves his Church as it were in hiding-places; according to what he said in Elijah: "I have reserved to myself seven thousand men, who have not bowed the knee to Baal." (*e*)

III. This article of the creed, however, relates in some measure to the external Church, that every one of us may maintain a brotherly agreement with all the children of God, may pay due deference to the authority of the Church, and, in a word, may conduct himself as one of the flock. Therefore we add THE COMMUNION OF SAINTS—a clause which, though generally omitted by the ancients, ought not to be neglected, because it excellently expresses the character of the Church; as though it had been said that the saints are united in the fellowship of Christ on this condition, that whatever benefits God confers upon them, they should mutually communicate to each other. This destroys not the diversity of grace, for we know that the gifts of the Spirit are variously distributed; nor does it disturb the order of civil polity, which secures to every individual the exclusive enjoyment of his property, as it is necessary for the preservation of the peace of society that men should have peculiar and distinct possessions. But the community asserted is such as Luke describes, that "the multitude of them that believed were of one heart and of one soul;" (*f*) and Paul, when he exhorts the Ephesians to be "one body, and one spirit, even as they were called in one hope." (*g*) Nor is it possible, if they are truly persuaded that God is a common Father to them all, and Christ their common Head, but that, being united in brotherly affection, they should mutually communicate their advantages to each other. Now, it highly concerns us to know what benefit we receive from this. For we believe the Church, in order to have a certain assurance that we are members of it. For thus our salvation rests on firm and solid foundations, so that it cannot fall into ruin, though the whole fabric of the world should be dissolved. First, it is founded on the election of God, and can be liable to no variation or failure, but with the subversion of his eternal providence. In the next place, it is united with the stability of Christ, who will no more

(*e*) Rom. xi. 4. 1 Kings xix. 18. (*f*) Acts iv. 32. (*g*) Ephes. iv. 4.

INSTITVTIO CHRI-
ſtianæ religionis, in libros qua-
tuor nunc primùm digeſta, certíſque diſtincta capitibus, ad aptiſſimam methodum: aucta etiam tam magna acceſſione vt propemodum opus nouum haberi poſſit.

IOHANNE CALVINO AVTHORE.

Oliua Roberti Stephani.

GENEVAE.

M. D. LIX.

Title-Page of Definitive Edition of 1559

suffer his faithful people to be severed from him, than his members to be torn in pieces. Besides, we are certain, as long as we continue in the bosom of the Church, that we shall remain in possession of the truth. Lastly, we understand these promises to belong to us: "In mount Zion shall be deliverance." (*h*) God is in the midst of her; she shall not be moved." (*i*) Such is the effect of union with the Church, that it retains us in the fellowship of God. The very word *communion* likewise contains abundant consolation; for while it is certain that whatever the Lord confers upon his members and ours belong to us, our hope is confirmed by all the benefits which they enjoy. But in order to embrace the unity of the Church in this manner, it is unnecessary, as we have observed, to see the Church with our eyes, or feel it with our hands; on the contrary, from its being an object of faith, we are taught that it is no less to be considered as existing, when it escapes our observation, than if it were evident to our eyes. Nor is our faith the worse, because it acknowledges the Church which we do not fully comprehend; for we are not commanded here to distinguish the reprobate from the elect, which is not our province, but that of God alone; we are only required to be assured in our minds, that all those who, by the mercy of God the Father, through the efficacious influence of the Holy Spirit, have attained to the participation of Christ, are separated as the peculiar possession and portion of God; and that being numbered among them, we are partakers of such great grace.

IV. But as our present design is to treat of the *visible* Church, we may learn even from the title of *mother*, how useful and even necessary it is for us to know her; since there is no other way of entrance into life, unless we are conceived by her, born of her, nourished at her breast, and continually preserved under her care and government till we are divested of this mortal flesh, and "become like the angels." (*k*) For our infirmity will not admit of our dismission from her school; we must continue under her instruction and discipline to the end of our lives. It is also to be remarked, that out of her bosom there can be no hope of remission

---

(*h*) Joel ii. 32. Obad. 17. (*i*) Psalm xlvi. 5. (*k*) Matt. xxii. 30.

of sins, or any salvation, according to the testimony of Joel and Isaiah; (*l*) which is confirmed by Ezekiel, (*m*) when he denounces that those whom God excludes from the heavenly life, shall not be enrolled among his people. So, on the contrary, those who devote themselves to the service of God, are said to inscribe their names among the citizens of Jerusalem. For which reason the Psalmist says, "Remember me, O Lord, with the favour that thou bearest unto thy people: O visit me with thy salvation; that I may see the good of thy chosen; that I may rejoice in the gladness of thy nation; that I may glory with thine inheritance." (*n*) In these words the paternal favour of God, and the peculiar testimony of the spiritual life, are restricted to his flock, to teach us that it is always fatally dangerous to be separated from the Church.

V. But let us proceed to state what belongs to this subject. Paul writes, that Christ, "that he might fill all things, gave some apostles, and some prophets, and some evangelists, and some pastors and teachers; for the perfecting of the saints, for the work of the ministry, for the edifying of the body of Christ: till we all come in the unity of the faith, and of the knowledge of the Son of God, unto a perfect man, unto the measure of the stature of the fulness of Christ." (*o*) We see that though God could easily make his people perfect in a single moment, yet it was not his will that they should grow to mature age, but under the education of the Church. We see the means expressed; the preaching of the heavenly doctrine is assigned to the pastors. We see that all are placed under the same regulation, in order that they may submit themselves with gentleness and docility of mind to be governed by the pastors who are appointed for this purpose. Isaiah had long before described the kingdom of Christ by this character: "My Spirit that is upon thee, and my words which I have put in thy mouth, shall not depart out of thy mouth, nor out of the mouth of thy seed, nor out of the mouth of thy seed's seed, from henceforth and for ever." (*p*) Hence it follows, that all who reject the spiritual food for their souls, which is extended to them by the hands of the Church, deserve to perish with hunger

(*l*) Isaiah xxxvii. 35. Joel ii. 32. (*m*) Ezek. xiii. 9.
(*n*) Psalm cvi. 4, 5. (*o*) Ephes. iv. 10—13. (*p*) Isaiah lix. 21.

and want. It is God who inspires us with faith, but it is through the instrumentality of the gospel, according to the declaration of Paul, "that faith cometh by hearing." (*q*) So also the power to save resides in God, but, as the same apostle testifies in another place, he displays it in the preaching of the gospel. With this design, in former ages he commanded solemn assemblies to be held in the sanctuary, that the doctrine taught by the mouth of the priest might maintain the unity of the faith; and the design of those magnificent titles, where the temple is called God's "rest," his "sanctuary," and "dwelling-place," where he is said to "dwell between the cherubim," (*r*) was no other than to promote the esteem, love, reverence, and dignity of the heavenly doctrine; which the view of a mortal and despised man would otherwise greatly diminish. That we may know, therefore, that we have an inestimable treasure communicated to us from earthen vessels, (*s*) God himself comes forward, and as he is the Author of this arrangement, so he will be acknowledged as present in his institution. Therefore, after having forbidden his people to devote themselves to auguries, divinations, magical arts, necromancy, and other superstitions, he adds, that he will give them what ought to be sufficient for every purpose, namely, that he will never leave them without prophets. Now, as he did not refer his ancient people to angels, but raised up earthly teachers who truly discharged the office of angels, so, in the present day, he is pleased to teach us by the instrumentality of men. And as formerly he was not content with the written law, but appointed the priests as interpreters, at whose lips the people might inquire its true meaning, so, in the present day, he not only requires us to be attentive to reading, but has appointed teachers for our assistance. This is attended with a twofold advantage. For on the one hand, it is a good proof of our obedience when we listen to his ministers, just as if he were addressing us himself; and on the other, he has provided for our infirmity, by choosing to address us through the medium of human interpreters, that he may sweetly allure us to him, rather than to drive us away from him by his thunders. And the propriety of this familiar manner

(*q*) Rom. x. 17. (*r*) Psalm cxxxii. 14; lxxx. 1. (*s*) 2 Cor. iv. 7.

of teaching, is evident to all the pious, from the terror with which the majesty of God justly alarms them. Those who consider the authority of the doctrine as weakened by the meanness of the men who are called to teach it, betray their ingratitude; because among so many excellent gifts with which God has adorned mankind, it is a peculiar privilege, that he deigns to consecrate men's lips and tongues to his service, that his voice may be heard in them. Let us not therefore, on our parts, be reluctant to receive and obey the doctrine of salvation proposed to us at his express command; for though the power of God is not confined to external means, yet he has confined us to the ordinary manner of teaching, the fanatical rejecters of which necessarily involve themselves in many fatal snares. Many are urged by pride, or disdain, or envy, to persuade themselves that they can profit sufficiently by reading and meditating in private, and so to despise public assemblies, and consider preaching as unnecessary. But since they do all in their power to dissolve and break asunder the bond of unity, which ought to be preserved inviolable, not one of them escapes the just punishment of this impious breach, but they all involve themselves in pestilent errors and pernicious reveries. Wherefore, in order that the pure simplicity of faith may flourish among us, let us not be reluctant to use this exercise of piety, which the Divine institution has shown to be necessary, and which God so repeatedly commends to us. There has never been found, among the most extravagant of mortals, one insolent enough to say that we ought to shut our ears against God; but the prophets and pious teachers, in all ages, have had a difficult contest with the wicked, whose arrogance can never submit to be taught by the lips and ministry of men. Now, this is no other than effacing the image of God, which is discovered to us in the doctrine. For the faithful under the former dispensation were directed to seek the face of God in the sanctuary; (*t*) and this is so frequently repeated in the law, for no other reason, but because the doctrine of the law and the exhortations of the prophets exhibited to them a lively image of God; as Paul declares that his preaching displayed "the glory of God in the

(*t*) Psalm cv. 4.

face of Jesus Christ." (*v*) And in so much the greater detestation ought we to hold those apostates, who make it their study to cause divisions in churches, as if they would drive away the sheep from the fold, and throw them into the jaws of wolves. But let us remember what we have quoted from Paul—that the Church can only be edified by the preaching of this word, and that the saints have no common bond of union to hold them together, any longer than, while learning and profiting with one accord, they observe the order which God has prescribed for the Church. It was principally for this end, as I have already stated, that the faithful under the law were commanded to resort to the sanctuary; because Moses not only celebrates it as the residence of God, but likewise declares it to be the place where God has fixed the record of his name; (*w*) which without the doctrine of piety, he plainly suggests, would be of no use. And it is undoubtedly for the same reason that David complains, with great bitterness of soul, of being prevented from access to the tabernacle by the tyrannical cruelty of his enemies. (*x*) To many persons perhaps this appears to be a puerile lamentation, because it could be but a very trivial loss, and not a privation of much satisfaction to be absent from the court of the temple, provided he were in the possession of other pleasures. But by this one trouble, anxiety, and sorrow, he complains that he is grieved, tormented, and almost consumed; because nothing is more valued by believers than this assistance, by which God gradually raises his people from one degree of elevation to another. For it is also to be remarked, that God always manifested himself to the holy fathers, in the mirror of his doctrine, in such a manner that their knowledge of him was spiritual. Hence the temple was not only called his *face*, but in order to guard against all superstition, was also designated as his *footstool*. (*y*) And this is that happy conjunction in the unity of the faith spoken of by Paul, when all, from the highest to the lowest, are aspiring towards the head. All the temples which the Gentiles erected to God with any other design, were nothing but a profanation of his worship—a crime which, though not to an equal extent, was also frequently com-

(*v*) 2 Cor. iv. 6. (*w*) Exod. xx. 24.
(*x*) Psalm lxxxiv. (*y*) Psalm cxxxii. 7; xcix. 5.

mitted by the Jews. Stephen reproaches them for it in the language of Isaiah: "The Most High dwelleth not in temples made with hands; as saith the prophet, Heaven is my throne, and earth is my footstool," (*z*) because God alone sanctifies temples by his word, that they may be legitimately used for his worship. And if we presumptuously attempt any thing without his command, the evil beginning is immediately succeeded by further inventions, which multiply the mischief without end. Xerxes, however, acted with great indiscretion, when, at the advice of the magi, he burned or demolished all the temples of Greece, from an opinion of the absurdity that gods, to whom all space ought to be left perfectly free, should be enclosed within walls and roofs. As if it were not in the power of God to descend in any way to us, and yet at the same time not to make any change of place, or to confine us to earthly means, but rather to use them as vehicles to elevate us towards his celestial glory, which fills all things with its immensity, as well as transcends the heavens in its sublimity.

VI. Now, as the present age has witnessed a violent dispute respecting the efficacy of the ministry, some exaggerating its dignity beyond measure, and others contending that it is a criminal transfer to mortal man of what properly belongs to the Holy Spirit, to suppose that ministers and teachers penetrate the mind and heart, so as to correct the blindness of the one, and the hardness of the other,—we must proceed to a decision of this controversy. The arguments advanced on both sides may be easily reconciled by a careful observation of the passages, in which God, the Author of preaching, connecting his Spirit with it, promises that it shall be followed with success; or those in which, separating himself from all external aids, he attributes the commencement of faith, as well as its subsequent progress, entirely and exclusively to himself. The office of the second Elias, according to Malachi, was to illuminate the minds and to "turn the hearts of the fathers to the children," and the disobedient to the wisdom of the just. (*a*) Christ declares that he sent his disciples, that they "should bring forth fruit" (*b*) from

(*z*) Acts vii. 48, 49. (*a*) Mal. iv. 6. (*b*) John xv. 16.

their labours. What that fruit was, is briefly defined by Peter, when he says that we are "born again, not of corruptible seed, but of incorruptible." (*c*) Therefore Paul glories that he had "begotten" the Corinthians "through the gospel," and that they were "the seal of his apostleship;" (*d*) and even that he was not a minister of the letter," merely striking the ear with a vocal sound, but that the energy of the Spirit had been given to him to render his doctrine efficacious. (*e*) In the same sense, he affirms, in another Epistle, that his "gospel came not in word only, but also in power." (*f*) He declares also to the Galatians, that they "received the Spirit by the hearing of faith." (*g*) In short, there are several places, in which he not only represents himself as a "labourer together with God," (*h*) but even attributes to himself the office of communicating salvation. He certainly never advanced all these things, in order to arrogate to himself the least praise independent of God, as he briefly states in other passages: "Our entrance in unto you was not in vain." (*i*) "I labour, striving according to his working, which worketh in me mightily." (*k*) "He that wrought effectually in Peter to the apostleship of the circumcision, the same was mighty in me toward the Gentiles." (*l*) Besides, it is evident, from other places, that he leaves ministers possessed of nothing, considered in themselves: "Neither is he that planteth any thing, neither he that watereth; but God that giveth the increase." (*m*) Again: "I laboured more abundantly than they all; yet not I, but the grace of God which was with me." (*n*) And it is certainly necessary to bear in memory those passages, in which God ascribes to himself the illumination of the mind and renovation of the heart, and thereby declares it to be sacrilege for man to arrogate to himself any share in either. Yet every one who attends with docility of mind to the ministers whom God has appointed, will learn from the beneficial effect, that this mode of teaching has not in vain been pleasing to God, and that this yoke of modesty has not without reason been imposed upon believers.

(*c*) 1 Peter i. 23. (*d*) 1 Cor. iv. 15; ix. 2. (*e*) 2 Cor. iii. 6.
(*f*) 1 Thess. i. 5. (*g*) Gal. iii. 2. (*h*) 1 Cor. iii. 9; xv. 10. 2 Cor. vi. 1.
(*i*) 1 Thess. ii. 1. (*k*) Col. i. 29. (*l*) Gal. ii. 8.
(*m*) 1 Cor. iii. 7. (*n*) 1 Cor. xv. 10.

VII. From what has been said, I conceive it must now be evident what judgment we ought to form respecting the Church, which is visible to our eyes, and falls under our knowledge. For we have remarked that the word *Church* is used in the sacred Scriptures in two senses. Sometimes, when they mention the Church, they intend that which is really such in the sight of God, into which none are received but those who by adoption and grace are the children of God, and by the sanctification of the Spirit are the true members of Christ. And then it comprehends not only the saints at any one time resident on earth, but all the elect who have lived from the beginning of the world. But the word *Church* is frequently used in the Scriptures to designate the whole multitude, dispersed all over the world, who profess to worship one God and Jesus Christ, who are initiated into his faith by baptism, who testify their unity in true doctrine and charity by a participation of the sacred supper, who consent to the word of the Lord, and preserve the ministry which Christ has instituted for the purpose of preaching it. In this Church are included many hypocrites, who have nothing of Christ but the name and appearance; many persons ambitious, avaricious, envious, slanderous, and dissolute in their lives, who are tolerated for a time, either because they cannot be convicted by a legitimate process, or because discipline is not always maintained with sufficient vigour. As it is necessary, therefore, to believe that Church, which is invisible to us, and known to God alone, so this Church, which is visible to men, we are commanded to honour, and to maintain communion with it.

VIII. As far, therefore, as was important for us to know it, the Lord has described it by certain marks and characters. It is the peculiar prerogative of God himself to "know them that are his," (*o*) as we have already stated from Paul. And to guard against human presumption ever going to such an extreme, the experience of every day teaches us how very far his secret judgments transcend all our apprehensions. For those who seemed the most abandoned, and were generally considered past all hope, are recalled by his goodness into the right way; while some, who

(*o*) 2 Tim. ii. 19.

seemed to stand better than others, fall into perdition. "According to the secret predestination of God," therefore as Augustine observes, "there are many sheep without the pale of the Church, and many wolves within." For he knows and seals those who know not either him or themselves. Of those who externally bear his seal, his eyes alone can discern who are unfeignedly holy, and will persevere to the end; which is the completion of salvation. On the other hand, as he saw it to be in some measure requisite that we should know who ought to be considered as his children, he has in this respect accommodated himself to our capacity. And as it was not necessary that on this point we should have an assurance of faith, he has substituted in its place a judgment of charity, according to which we ought to acknowledge as members of the Church all those who by a confession of faith, an exemplary life, and a participation of the sacraments, profess the same God and Christ with ourselves. But the knowledge of the body itself being more necessary to our salvation, he has distinguished it by more clear and certain characters.

IX. Hence the visible Church rises conspicuous to our view. For wherever we find the word of God purely preached and heard, and the sacrements administered according to the institution of Christ, there, it is not to be doubted, is a Church of God; for his promise can never deceive—"where two or three are gathered together in my name, there am I in the midst of them." (*p*) But, that we may have a clear understanding of the whole of this subject, let us proceed by the following steps: That the universal Church is the whole multitude, collected from all nations, who, though dispersed in countries widely distant from each other, nevertheless consent to the same truth of Divine doctrine, and are united by the bond of the same religion; that in this universal Church are comprehended particular churches, distributed according to human necessity in various towns and villages; and that each of these respectively is justly distinguished by the name and authority of a church; and that individuals, who, on a profession of piety, are enrolled among Churches of the same description, though they are really strangers to any par-

---

(*p*) Matt. xviii. 20.

ticular Church, do nevertheless in some respect belong to it, till they are expelled from it by a public decision. There is some difference, however, in the mode of judging respecting private persons and churches. For it may happen, in the case of persons whom we think altogether unworthy of the society of the pious, that, on account of the common consent of the Church, by which they are tolerated in the body of Christ, we may be obliged to treat them as brethren, and to class them in the number of believers. In our private opinion we approve not of such persons as members of the Church, but we leave them the station they hold among the people of God, till it be taken away from them by legitimate authority. But respecting the congregation itself, we must form a different judgment. If they possess and honour the ministry of the word, and the administration of the sacraments, they are, without all doubt, entitled to be considered as a Church; because it is certain that the word and sacraments cannot be unattended with some good effects. In this manner, we preserve the unity of the universal Church, which diabolical spirits have always been endeavouring to destroy; and at the same time without interfering with the authority of those legitimate assemblies, which local convenience has distributed in different places.

X. We have stated that the marks by which the Church is to be distinguished, are, the preaching of the word and the administration of the sacraments. For these can nowhere exist without bringing forth fruit, and being prospered with the blessing of God. I assert not that wherever the word is preached, the good effects of it immediately appear; but that it is never received so as to obtain a permanent establishment, without displaying some efficacy. However this may be, where the word is heard with reverence, and the sacraments are not neglected, there we discover, while that is the case, an appearance of the Church, which is liable to no suspicion of uncertainty, of which no one can safely despise the authority or reject the admonitions, or resist the counsels, or slight the censures, much less separate from it and break up its unity. For so highly does the Lord esteem the communion of his Church, that he considers every one as a traitor and apostate from religion, who perversely withdraws himself from any Christian society which preserves the true ministry of the word and sacraments. He commends the authority of the Church, in such a manner as to account every violation of it an infringement of his own. For it is not a trivial circumstance, that the Church is called "the house of God, the pillar and ground of truth." (*q*) For in these words Paul signifies that in order to keep the truth of God from being lost in the world, the Church is its faithful guardian; because it has been the will of God, by the ministry of the Church, to preserve the pure preaching of his word, and to manifest himself as our affectionate Father, while he nourishes us with spiritual food, and provides all things conducive to our salvation. Nor is it small praise, that the Church is chosen and separated by Christ to be his spouse, "not having spot or wrinkle," (*r*) to be "his body, the fulness of him that filleth all in all." (*s*) Hence it follows, that a departure from the Church is a renunciation of God and Christ. And such a criminal dissension is so much the more to be avoided, because, while we endeavour, as far as lies in our power, to destroy the truth of God, we deserve to be crushed with the most powerful thunders of his wrath. Nor is it possible to imagine a more atrocious crime, than that sacrilegious perfidy, which violates the conjugal relation that the only begotten Son of God has condescended to form with us.

XI. Let us, therefore, diligently retain those characters impressed upon our minds, and estimate them according to the judgment of God. For there is nothing that Satan labours more to accomplish, than to remove and destroy one or both of them; at one time to efface and obliterate these marks, and so to take away all true and genuine distinction of the Church; at another to inspire us with contempt of them, and so to drive us out of the Church by an open separation. By his subtlety it has happened, that in some ages the pure preaching of the word has altogether disappeared; and in the present day he is labouring with the same malignity to overturn the ministry; which, however, Christ has ordained in his Church, so that if it were taken away, the edification of the Church would be quite at an end. How dangerous, then, how fatal is the temptation, when it even enters into

---

(*q*) 1 Tim. iii. 15. (*r*) Eph. v. 27. (*s*) Eph. i. 23.

the heart of a man to withdraw himself from that congregation, in which he discovers those signs and characters which the Lord has deemed sufficiently descriptive of his Church! We see, however, that great caution requires to be observed on both sides. For, to prevent imposture from deceiving us, under the name of the Church, every congregation assuming this name should be brought to that proof, like gold to the touchstone. If it have the order prescribed by the Lord in the word and sacraments, it will not deceive us; we may securely render to it the honour due to all churches. On the contrary, if it pretend to the name of a Church, without the word and sacraments, we ought to beware of such delusive pretensions, with as much caution as, in the other case, we should use in avoiding presumption and pride.

XII. When we affirm the pure ministry of the word, and pure order in the celebration of the sacraments, to be a sufficient pledge and earnest, that we may safely embrace the society in which both these are found, as a true Church, we carry the observation to this point, that such a society should never be rejected as long as it continues in those things, although in other respects it may be chargeable with many faults. It is possible, moreover, that some fault may insinuate itself into the preaching of the doctrine, or the administration of the sacraments, which ought not to alienate us from its communion. For all the articles of true doctrine are not of the same description. Some are so necessary to be known, that they ought to be universally received as fixed and indubitable principles, as the peculiar maxims of religion; such as, that there is one God; that Christ is God and the Son of God; that our salvation depends on the mercy of God; and the like. There are others, which are controverted among the churches, yet without destroying the unity of the faith. For why should there be a division on this point, if one church be of opinion, that souls, at their departure from their bodies, are immediately removed to heaven; and another church venture to determine nothing respecting their local situation, but be nevertheless firmly convinced, that they live to the Lord; and if this diversity of sentiment on both sides be free from all fondness for contention and obstinacy of assertion? The language of the apostle is, "Let us therefore, as many as be perfect, be thus minded; and if in any thing ye be otherwise minded,

God shall reveal even this unto you." (*t*) Does not this sufficiently show, that a diversity of opinion respecting these non-essential points ought not to be a cause of discord among Christians? It is of importance, indeed, that we should agree in every thing; but as there is no person who is not enveloped with some cloud of ignorance, either we must allow of no church at all, or we must forgive mistakes in those things, of which persons may be ignorant, without violating the essence of religion, or incurring the loss of salvation. Here I would not be understood to plead for any errors, even the smallest, or to recommend their being encouraged by connivance or flattery. But I maintain, that we ought not, on account of every trivial difference of sentiment, to abandon the Church, which retains the saving and pure doctrine that insures the preservation of piety, and supports the use of the sacraments instituted by our Lord. In the mean time, if we endeavour to correct what we disapprove, we are acting in this case according to our duty. And to this we are encouraged by the direction of Paul: "If any thing be revealed to another that sitteth by, let the first hold his peace." (*v*) From which it appears, that every member of the Church is required to exert himself for the general edification, according to the measure of his grace, provided he do it decently and in order; that is to say, that we should neither forsake the communion of the Church, nor, by continuing in it, disturb its peace and well regulated discipline.

XIII. But in bearing with imperfections of life, we ought to carry our indulgence a great deal further. For this is a point in which we are very liable to err, and here Satan lies in wait to deceive us with no common devices. For there have always been persons, who, from a false notion of perfect sanctity, as if they were already become disembodied spirits, despised the society of all men in whom they could discover any remains of human infirmity. Such, in ancient times, were the Cathari, and also the Donatists, who approached to the same folly. Such, in the present day, are some of the Anabaptists, who would be thought to have made advances in piety beyond all others. There are others who err, more from an inconsiderate zeal for righteousness, than from

---

(*t*) Phil. iii. 15.   (*v*) 1 Cor. xiv. 30.

this unreasonable pride. For when they perceive, that among those to whom the gospel is preached, its doctrine is not followed by correspondent effects in the life, they immediately pronounce, that there no church exists. This is, indeed, a very just ground of offence, and one for which we furnish more than sufficient occasion in the present unhappy age; nor is it possible to excuse our abominable inactivity, which the Lord will not suffer to escape with impunity, and which he has already begun to chastise with heavy scourges. Woe to us, therefore, who, by the dissolute licentiousness of our crimes, cause weak consciences to be wounded on our account! But, on the other hand, the error of the persons of whom we now speak, consists in not knowing how to fix any limits to their offence. For where our Lord requires the exercise of mercy, they entirely neglect it, and indulge themselves in immoderate severity. Supposing it impossible for the Church to exist, where there is not a perfect purity and integrity of life, through a hatred of crimes they depart from the true Church, while they imagine themselves to be only withdrawing from the factions of the wicked. They allege, that the Church of Christ is holy. But that they may also understand, that it is composed of good and bad men mingled together, let them hear that parable from the lips of Christ, where it is compared to a net, in which fishes of all kinds are collected, and no separation is made till they are exposed on the shore. (*w*) Let them hear another parable, comparing the Church to a field, which, after having been sown with good seed, is, by the craft of an enemy, corrupted with tares, from which it is never cleared till the harvest is brought into the barn. (*x*) Lastly, let them hear another comparison of the Church to a threshing-floor, in which the wheat is collected in such a manner, that it lies concealed under the chaff, till, after being carefully purged, by winnowing and sifting, it is at length laid up in the garner. (*y*) But if our Lord declares, that the Church is to labour under this evil, and to be encumbered with a mixture of wicked men, even till the day of judgment, it is vain to seek for a Church free from every spot.

XIV. But they exclaim, that it is an intolerable thing that the

(*w*) Matt. xiii. 47. (*x*) Matt. xiii. 24. (*y*) Matt. iii. 12.

pestilence of crimes so generally prevails. I grant it would be happy if the fact were otherwise; but in reply, I would present them with the judgment of the apostle. Among the Corinthians, more than a few had gone astray, and the infection had seized almost the whole society; there was not only one species of sin, but many; and they were not trivial faults, but dreadful crimes; and there was not only a corruption of morals, but also of doctrine. In this case, what is the conduct of the holy apostle, the organ of the heavenly Spirit, by whose testimony the Church stands or falls? Does he seek to separate from them? Does he reject them from the kingdom of Christ? Does he strike them with the thunderbolt of the severest anathema? He not only does none of these things, but, on the contrary, acknowledges and speaks of them as a Church of Christ and a society of saints. If there remained a church among the Corinthians, where contentions, factions, and emulations were raging; where cupidity, disputes, and litigations were prevailing; where a crime held in execration even among the Gentiles, was publicly sanctioned; where the name of Paul, whom they ought to have revered as their father, was insolently defamed; where some ridiculed the doctrine of the resurrection, with the subversion of which the whole gospel would be annihilated; where the graces of God were made subservient to ambition, instead of charity; where many things were conducted without decency and order; (*z*) and if there still remained a Church, because the ministry of the word and sacraments was not rejected—who can refuse the name of a Church to those who cannot be charged with a tenth part of those crimes? And those who display such violence and severity against the Churches of the present age, I ask, how would they have conducted themselves towards the Galatians, who almost entirely deserted the gospel, but among whom, nevertheless, the same apostle found Churches? (*a*)

XV. They object that Paul bitterly reproves the Corinthians for admitting an atrocious offender into their company, and follows this reproof with a general declaration, that with a man of scandalous life it is not lawful even to eat. (*b*) Here they exclaim,

(*z*) 1 Cor. i. 11; iii. 3; v. 1; vi. 7; ix. 1; xiv. 26, 40; xv. 12.
(*a*) Gal. i. 6; iii. 1; iv. 11.
(*b*) 1 Cor. v. 2, 11, 12.

If it be not lawful to eat common bread with him, how can it be lawful to unite with him in eating the bread of the Lord? I confess it is a great disgrace, if persons of immoral lives occupy places among the children of God; and if the sacred body of Christ be prostituted to them, the disgrace is vastly increased. And, indeed, if Churches be well regulated, they will not suffer persons of abandoned characters among them, nor will they promiscuously admit the worthy and the unworthy to that sacred supper. But because the pastors are not always so diligent in watching over them, and sometimes exercise more indulgence than they ought, or are prevented from exerting the severity they would wish, it happens that even those who are openly wicked are not always expelled from the society of the saints. This I acknowledge to be a fault, nor have I any inclination to extenuate it, since Paul sharply reproves it in the Corinthians. But though the Church may be deficient in its duty, it does not therefore follow that it is the place of every individual to pass judgment of separation for himself. I admit that it is the duty of a pious man to withdraw himself from all private intimacy with the wicked, and not to involve himself in any voluntary connection with them. But it is one thing to avoid familiar intercourse with the wicked; and another thing, from hatred of them, to renounce the communion of the Church. And persons who deem it sacrilege to participate with them the bread of the Lord, are in this respect far more rigid than Paul. For when he exhorts us to a pure and holy participation of it, he requires not one to examine another, or every one to examine the whole Church, but each individual to prove himself. If it were unlawful to communicate with an unworthy person, Paul would certainly have enjoined us to look around us, to see whether there were not some one in the multitude by whose impurity we might be contaminated. But as he only requires every one to examine himself, he shows that it is not the least injury to us if some unworthy persons intrude themselves with us. And this is fully implied in what he afterwards subjoins: "He that eateth and drinketh unworthily, eateth and drinketh judgment to himself." (*c*) He says, not to others, but to himself,

(*c*) 1 Cor. xi. 28, 29.

and with sufficient reason. For it ought not to be left to the judgment of every individual *who* ought to be admitted into the Church, and *who* ought to be expelled from it. This authority belongs to the whole Church, and cannot be exercised without legitimate order, as will be stated more at large hereafter. It would be unjust, therefore, that any individual should be contaminated with the unworthiness of another, whose approach it is neither in his power nor his duty to prevent.

XVI. But though this temptation sometimes arises even to good men, from an inconsiderate zeal for righteousness, yet we shall generally find that excessive severity is more owing to pride and haughtiness, and a false opinion which persons entertain of their own superior sanctity, than to true holiness, and a real concern for its interests. Those, therefore, who are most daring in promoting a separation from the Church, and act, as it were, as standard-bearers in the revolt, have in general no other motive than to make an ostentatious display of their own superior excellence, and their contempt for all others. Augustine correctly and judiciously observes—"Whereas the pious rule and method of ecclesiastical discipline ought principally to regard the unity of the Spirit in the bond of peace, which the apostle enjoined to be preserved by mutual forbearance, and which not being preserved, the medicinal punishment is evinced to be not only superfluous, but even pernicious, and therefore to be no longer medicinal; those wicked children, who, not from a hatred of the iniquities of others, but from a fondness for their own contentions, earnestly endeavor to draw the simple and uninformed multitude wholly after them, by entangling them with boasting of their own characters, or at least to divide them; those persons, I say, inflated with pride, infuriated with obstinacy, insidious in the circulation of calumnies, and turbulent in raising seditions, conceal themselves under the mast of a rigid severity, lest they should be proved to be destitute of the truth; and those things which in the Holy Scriptures are commanded to be done with great moderation, and without violating the sincerity of love, or breaking the unity of peace, for the correction of the faults of our brethren, they pervert to the sacrilege of schism, and an occasion of separation from the Church." To pious and peaceable persons he gives this advice: that they should correct in mercy whatever they can; that what they cannot, they should patiently bear, and affectionately lament, till God either reform and correct it, or, at the harvest, root up the tares and sift out the chaff. All pious persons should study to fortify themselves with these counsels, lest, while they consider themselves as valiant and strenuous defenders of righteousness, they depart from the kingdom of heaven, which is the only kingdom of righteousness. For since it is the will of God that the communion of his Church should be maintained in this external society, those who, from an aversion of wicked men, destroy the token of that society, enter on a course in which they are in great danger of falling from the communion of saints. Let them consider, in the first place, that in a great multitude there are many who escape their observation, who, nevertheless, are truly holy and innocent in the sight of God. Secondly, let them consider, that of those who appear subject to moral maladies, there are many who by no means please or flatter themselves in their vices, but are oftentimes aroused, with a serious fear of God, to aspire to greater integrity. Thirdly, let them consider that judgment ought not to be pronounced upon a man from a single act, since the holiest persons have sometimes most grievous falls. Fourthly, let them consider, that the ministry of the word, and the participation of the sacraments, have too much influence in preserving the unity of the Church, to admit of its being destroyed by the guilt of a few impious men. Lastly, let them consider, that in forming an estimate of the Church, the judgment of God is of more weight than that of man.

XVII. When they allege that there must be some reason why the Church is said to be holy, it is necessary to examine the holiness in which it excels; lest by refusing to admit the existence of a Church without absolute and sinless perfection, we should leave no Church in the world. It is true, that, as Paul tells us, "Christ loved the Church, and gave himself for it, that he might sanctify and cleanse it, by the washing of water by the word, that he might present it to himself a glorious Church, not having spot, or wrinkle, or any such thing." (*d*) It is nevertheless equally true,

(*d*) Ephes. v. 25—27.

that the Lord works from day to day in smoothing its wrinkles, and purging away its spots; whence it follows, that its holiness is not yet perfect. The Church, therefore, is so far holy, that it is daily improving, but has not yet arrived at perfection; that it is daily advancing, but has not yet reached the mark of holiness; as in another part of this work will be more fully explained. The predictions of the prophets, therefore, that "Jerusalem shall be holy, and there shall no strangers pass through her any more," and that the way of God shall be a "way of holiness, over which "the unclean shall not pass," (*e*) are not to be understood as if there were no blemish remaining in any of the members of the Church; but because they aspire with all their souls towards perfect holiness and purity, the goodness of God attributes to them that sanctity to which they have not yet fully attained. And though such evidences of sanctification are oftentimes rarely to be found among men, yet it must be maintained, that, from the foundation of the world, there has never been a period in which God had not his Church in it; and that, to the consummation of all things, there never will be a time in which he will not have his Church. For although, in the very beginning of time, the whole human race was corrupted and defiled by the sin of Adam; yet, from this polluted mass, God always sanctifies some vessels to honour, so that there is no age which has not experienced his mercy. This he has testified by certain promises, such as the following: "I have made a covenant with my chosen: I have sworn unto David, my servant, They seed will I establish for ever, and build up thy throne to all generations." (*f*) Again: "The Lord hath chosen Zion; he hath desired it for his habitation. This is my rest for ever." (*g*) Again: "Thus saith the Lord, which giveth the sun for a light by day, and the ordinances of the moon and of the stars for a light by night: If those ordinances depart from before me, saith the Lord, then the seed of Israel also shall cease from being a nation before me for ever." (*h*)

XVIII. Of this truth Christ himself, the apostles, and almost all the prophets, have given us an example. Dreadful are those descriptions in which Isaiah, Jeremiah, Joel, Habakkuk, and

---

(*e*) Joel iii. 17. Isaiah xxxv. 8. (*f*) Psalm lxxxix. 3, 4.
(*g*) Psalm cxxxii. 13, 14. (*h*) Jer. xxxi. 35, 36.

others, deplore the disorders of the Church of Jerusalem. There was such general and extreme corruption in the people, in the magistrates, and in the priests, that Isaiah does not hesitate to compare Jerusalem to Sodom and Gomorrah. Religion was partly despised, partly corrupted. Their manners were generally disgraced by thefts, robberies, treacheries, murders, and similar crimes. Nevertheless, the prophets on this account neither raised themselves new churches, nor built new altars for the oblation of separate sacrifices; but whatever were the characters of the people, yet because they considered that God had deposited his word among that nation, and instituted the ceremonies in which he was there worshipped, they lifted up pure hands to him even in the congregation of the impious. If they had thought that they contracted any contagion from these services, surely they would have suffered a hundred deaths rather than have permitted themselves to be dragged to them. There was nothing therefore to prevent their departure from them, but the desire of preserving the unity of the Church. But if the holy prophets were restrained by a sense of duty from forsaking the Church on account of the numerous and enormous crimes which were practised, not by a few individuals, but almost by the whole nation,—it is extreme arrogance in us, if we presume immediately to withdraw from the communion of a Church where the conduct of all the members is not compatible either with our judgment, or even with the Christian profession.

XIX. Now, what kind of an age was that of Christ and his apostles? Yet the desperate impiety of the Pharisees, and the dissolute lives every where led by the people, could not prevent *them* from using the same sacrifices, and assembling in the same temple with others, for the public exercises of religion. How did this happen, but from a knowledge that the society of the wicked could not contaminate those who with pure consciences united with them in the same solemnities? If any one pay no deference to the prophets and apostles, let him at least acquiesce in the authority of Christ. Cyprian has excellently remarked, "Although tares, or impure vessels, are found in the Church, yet this is not a reason why we should withdraw from it. It only behoves us to labour that we may be the wheat, and to use our utmost endeavours and exertions, that we may be vessels of gold or of silver. But to break in pieces the vessels of earth belongs to the Lord alone, to whom a rod of iron is also given. Nor let any one arrogate to himself what is exclusively the province of the Son of God, by pretending to fan the floor, clear away the chaff, and separate all the tares by the judgment of man. This is proud obstinacy and sacrilegious presumption, originating in a corrupt frenzy." Let these two points, then, be considered as decided; first, that he who voluntarily deserts the external communion of the Church where the word of God is preached, and the sacraments are administered, is without any excuse; secondly, that the faults either of few persons or of many, form no obstacles to a due profession of our faith in the use of the ceremonies instituted by God; because the pious conscience is not wounded by the unworthiness of any other individual, whether he be a pastor or a private person; nor are the mysteries less pure and salutary to a holy and upright man, because they are received at the same time by the impure.

XX. Their severity and haughtiness go to still greater lengths. Acknowledging no church but such as is pure from the smallest blemishes, they are even angry with honest teachers, because, by exhorting believers to progressive improvements, they teach them to groan under the burden of sins, and to seek for pardon all their lifetime. For hereby, they pretend, the people are drawn away from perfection. I confess, that in urging men to perfection, we ought to labour with unremitting ardour and diligence; but to inspire their minds with a persuasion that they have already attained it, while they are yet in the pursuit of it, I maintain to be a diabolical invention. Therefore, in the Creed, *the communion of saints* is immediately followed by *the forgiveness of sins*, which can only be obtained by the citizens and members of the Church, as we read in the prophet. (*i*) The heavenly Jerusalem, therefore, ought first to be built, in which this favour of God may be enjoyed, that whoever shall enter it, their iniquity shall be blotted out. Now, I affirm that this ought first to be built; not that there can ever be any Church without remission of sins, but because

(*i*) Isaiah xxxiii. 24.

God has not promised to impart his mercy, except in the communion of saints. Our first entrance, therefore, into the Church and kingdom of God, is the remission of sins, without which we have no covenant or union with God. For thus he speaks by the prophet: "In that day will I make a covenant for them with the beasts of the field, and with the fowls of heaven, and with the creeping things of the ground; and I will break the bow and the sword, and the battle out of the earth, and will make them to lie down safely. And I will betroth thee unto me for ever; yea, I will betroth thee unto me in righteousness, and in judgment, and in loving-kindness, and in mercies." (*k*) We see how God reconciles us to himself by his mercy. So in another place, where he foretells the restoration of the people whom he had scattered in his wrath, he says, "I will cleanse them from all their iniquity, whereby they have sinned against me." (*l*) Wherefore it is by the sign of ablution, that we are initiated into the society of his Church; by which we are taught that there is no admittance for us into the family of God, unless our pollution be first taken away by his goodness.

XXI. Nor does God only once receive and adopt us into his Church by the remission of sins; he likewise preserves and keeps us in it by the same mercy. For to what purpose would it be, if we obtained a pardon which would afterwards be of no use? And that the mercy of the Lord would be vain and delusive, if it were only granted for once, all pious persons can testify to themselves; for every one of them is all his life-time conscious of many infirmities, which need the Divine mercy. And surely it is not without reason, that God particularly promises this grace to the members of his family, and commands the same message of reconciliation to be daily addressed to them. As we carry about with us the relics of sin, therefore, as long as we live, we shall scarcely continue in the Church for a single moment, unless we are sustained by the constant grace of the Lord in forgiving our sins. But the Lord has called his people to eternal salvation; they ought, therefore, to believe that his grace is always ready to pardon their sins. Wherefore it ought to be held as a certain conclusion, that from

---

(*k*) Hos. ii. 18, 19. (*l*) Jerem. xxxiii. 8.

the Divine liberality, by the intervention of the merit of Christ, through the sanctification of the Spirit, pardon of sins has been, and is daily, bestowed upon us, who have been admitted and ingrafted into the body of the Church.

XXII. It was to dispense this blessing to us, that the keys were given to the Church. (*m*) For, when Christ gave commandment to his apostles, and conferred on them the power of remitting sins, (*n*) it was not with an intention that they should merely absolve from their sins those who were converted from impiety to the Christian faith, but rather that they should continually exercise this office among the faithful. This is taught by Paul, when he says, that the message of reconciliation was committed to the ministers of the Church, that in the name of Christ they might daily exhort the people to be reconciled to God. (*o*) In the communion of saints, therefore, sins are continually remitted to us by the ministry of the Church, when the presbyters or bishops, to whom this office is committed, confirm pious consciences, by the promises of the gospel, in the hope of pardon and remission; and that as well publicly as privately, according as necessity requires. For there are many persons who, on account of their infirmity stand in need of separate and private consolation. And Paul tells us that he "taught," not only publicly, but also "from house to house, testifying repentance toward God, and faith toward our Lord Jesus Christ;" (*p*) and admonished every individual separately respecting the doctrine of salvation. Here are three things, therefore, worthy of our observation. First, that whatever holiness may distinguish the children of God, yet such is their condition as long as they inhabit a mortal body, that they cannot stand before God without remission of sins. Secondly, that this benefit belongs to the Church; so that we cannot enjoy it unless we continue in its communion. Thirdly, that it is dispensed to us by the ministers and pastors of the Church, either in the preaching of the gospel, or in the administration of the sacraments; and that this is the principal exercise of the power of the keys, which the Lord has conferred on the society of believers. Let every one of us, therefore, consider it as his duty, not to seek remission of

(*m*) Matt. xvi. 19; xviii. 18. (*n*) John xx. 23.
(*o*) 2 Cor. v. 18—20. (*p*) Acts xx. 20, 21.

sins any where but where the Lord has placed it. Of public reconciliation, which is a branch of discipline, we shall speak in its proper place.

XXIII. But as those fanatic spirits, of whom I spoke, endeavour to rob the Church of this sole anchor of salvation, our consciences ought to be still more strongly fortified against such a pestilent opinion. The Novatians disturbed the ancient Churches with this tenet; but the present age also has witnessed some of the Anabaptists, who resemble the Novatians by falling into the same follies. For they imagine that by baptism the people of God are regenerated to a pure and angelic life, which cannot be contaminated by any impurities of the flesh. And if any one be guilty of sin after baptism, they leave him no prospect of escaping the inexorable judgment of God. In short, they encourage no hope of pardon in any one who sins after having received the grace of God; because they acknowledge no other remission of sins than that by which we are first regenerated. Now, though there is no falsehood more clearly refuted in the Scripture than this, yet because its advocates find persons to submit to their impositions, as Novatus formerly had numerous followers, let us briefly show how very pernicious their error is both to themselves and to others. In the first place, when the saints obey the command of the Lord by a daily repetition of this prayer, "forgive us our debts," (*q*) they certainly confess themselves to be sinners. Nor do they pray in vain, for our Lord has not enjoined the use of any petitions, but such as he designed to grant. And after he had declared that the whole prayer would be heard by the Father, he confirmed this absolution by a special promise. What do we want more? The Lord requires from the saints a confession of sins, and that daily as long as they live, and he promises them pardon. What presumption is it either to assert that they are exempt from sin, or, if they have fallen, to exclude them from all grace! To whom does he enjoin us to grant forgiveness seventy times seven times? Is it not to our brethren? And what was the design of this injunction, but that we might imitate his clemency? He pardons,

(*q*) Matt. vi. 12.

therefore, not once or twice, but as often as the sinner is alarmed with a sense of his sins, and sighs for mercy.

XXIV. But to begin from the infancy of the Church: the patriarchs had been circumcised, admitted to the privileges of the covenant, and without doubt instructed in justice and integrity by the care of their father, when they conspired to murder their brother. This was a crime to be abominated even by the most desperate and abandoned robbers. At length, softened by the admonitions of Judah, they sold him for a slave. This also was an intolerable cruelty. Simon and Levi, in a spirit of nefarious revenge, condemned even by the judgment of their father, murdered the inhabitants of Sichem. Reuben was guilty of execrable incest with his father's concubine. Judah, with an intention of indulging a libidinous passion, violated the law of nature by a criminal connection with his son's wife. Yet they are so far from being expunged out of the number of the chosen people, that, on the contrary, they are constituted the heads of the nation. (*r*) What shall we say of David? Though he was the official guardian of justice, how scandalously did he prepare the way for the gratification of a blind passion, by the effusion of innocent blood! He had already been regenerated, and among the regenerate had been distinguished by the peculiar commendations of the Lord; yet he perpetrated a crime even among heathens regarded with horror, and yet he obtained mercy. (*s*) And not to dwell any longer on particular examples, the numerous promises which the law and the prophets contain, of Divine mercy towards the Israelites, are so many proofs of the manifestation of God's placability to the offences of his people. For what does Moses promise to the people in case of their return to the Lord, after having fallen into idolatry? "Then the Lord thy God will turn thy captivity, and have compassion upon thee, and will return and gather thee from all the nations, whither the Lord thy God hath scattered thee. If any of thine be driven out unto the outmost parts of heaven, from thence will the Lord thy God gather thee." (*t*)

XXV. But I am unwilling to commence an enumeration which would have no end. For the prophets are full of such promises,

(*r*) Gen. xxxvii. 18, 28; xxxiv. 25; xxxv. 22; xxxviii. 16.
(*s*) 2 Sam. xi. 4, 15; xii. 13.
(*t*) Deut. xxx. 3, 4.

which offer mercy to the people, though covered with innumerable crimes. What sin is worse than rebellion? It is described as a divorce between God and the Church: yet this is overcome by the goodness of God. Hear his language by the mouth of Jeremiah: "If a man put away his wife, and she go from him, and become another man's, shall he return unto her again? Shall not that land be greatly polluted? But thou hast played the harlot with many lovers, and thou hast polluted the land with thy whoredoms and with thy wickedness. Yet return again to me, thou backsliding Israel, saith the Lord, and I will not cause mine anger to fall upon you; for I am merciful, saith the Lord, and will not keep anger for ever." (*v*) And surely there cannot possibly be any other disposition in him who affirms, that he "hath no pleasure in the death of the wicked, but that the wicked turn from his way and live." (*w*) Therefore, when Solomon dedicated the temple, he appointed it also for this purpose, that prayers, offered to obtain pardon of sins, might there be heard and answered. His words are, "If they sin against thee, (for there is no man that sinneth not,) and thou be angry with them, and deliver them to the enemy, so that they carry them away captives unto the land of the enemy, far or near; yet if they shall bethink themselves, and repent in the land whither they were carried captives, and repent and make supplication unto thee in the land of those that carried them captives, saying, We have sinned, and have done perversely, we have committed wickedness; and pray unto thee toward the land which thou gavest unto their fathers, the city which thou hast chosen, and the house which I have built for thy name; then hear thou their prayer and their supplication in heaven, and forgive thy people that have sinned against thee, and all their transgressions wherein they have transgressed against thee." (*x*) Nor was it without cause that in the law the Lord ordained daily sacrifices for sins; for unless he had foreseen that his people would be subject to the maladies of daily sins, he would never have appointed these remedies. (*y*)

XXVI. Now, I ask whether, by the advent of Christ, in whom the fulness of grace was displayed, believers have been deprived

(*v*) Jer. iii. 1, 2, 12.
(*w*) Ezek. xxxiii. 11.
(*x*) 1 Kings viii. 46—50.
(*y*) Numb. xxviii. 3.

of this benefit, so that they can no longer presume to supplicate for the pardon of their sins; so that if they offend against the Lord, they can obtain no mercy. What would this be but to affirm, that Christ came for the destruction of his people, and not for their salvation; if the loving-kindness of God, in the pardon of sins, which was continually ready to be exercised to the saints under the Old Testament, be maintained to be now entirely withdrawn? But if we give any credit to the Scriptures, which proclaim that in Christ the grace and philanthropy of God have at length been fully manifested, that his mercy has been abundantly diffused, and reconciliation between God and man accomplished, (*z*) we ought not to doubt that the clemency of our heavenly Father is displayed to us in greater abundance, rather than restricted or diminished. Examples to prove this are not wanting. Peter, who had been warned that he who would not confess the name of Christ before men would be denied by him before angels, denied him three times in one night, and accompanied the denial with execrations; yet he was not refused pardon. (*a*) Those of the Thessalonians who led disorderly lives, are reprehended by the apostle, in order to be invited to repentance. (*b*) Nor does Peter drive Simon Magus himself to despair, but rather directs him to cherish a favourable hope, when he persuades him to pray for forgiveness. (*c*)

XXVII. What are we to say of cases in which the most enormous sins have sometimes seized whole Churches? From this situation Paul rather mercifully reclaimed them, than abandoned them to the curse. The defection of the Galatians was no trivial offence. (*d*) The Corinthians were still less excusable, their crimes being more numerous and equally enormous. (*e*) Yet neither are excluded from the mercy of the Lord: on the contrary, the very persons who had gone beyond all others in impurity, unchastity, and fornication, are expressly invited to repentance. For the covenant of the Lord will ever remain eternal and inviolable, which he has made with Christ, the antitype of

---

(*z*) 2 Tim. i. 9, 10. Tit. ii. 11; iii. 4—7.
(*a*) Matt. x. 33. Mark viii. 38. Matt. xxvi. 69, &c.
(*b*) 2 Thess. iii. 6, 11, 12. (*c*) Acts viii. 22.
(*d*) Gal. i. 6; iii. 1; iv. 9. (*e*) 1 Cor. i. 11, 12; v. 1. 2 Cor. xii. 21.

Solomon, and with all his members, in these words: "If his children forsake my law, and walk not in my judgments; if they break my statutes, and keep not my commandments; then will I visit their transgression with the rod, and their iniquity with stripes. Nevertheless my loving-kindness will I not utterly take from him." (*f*) Finally, the order of the Creed teaches us that pardon of sins ever continues in the Church of Christ, because, after having mentioned the Church, it immediately adds *the forgiveness of sins.*

XXVIII. Some persons, who are a little more judicious, perceiving the notion of Novatus to be so explicitly contradicted by the Scripture, do not represent every sin as unpardonable, but only voluntary transgression, into which a person may have fallen with the full exercise of his knowledge and will. These persons admit of no pardon for any sins, but such as may have been the mere errors of ignorance. But as the Lord, in the law, commanded some sacrifices to be offered to expiate the voluntary sins of believers, and others to atone for sins of ignorance, what extreme presumption is it to deny that there is any pardon for voluntary transgression! I maintain, that there is nothing more evident, than that the one sacrifice of Christ is available for the remission of the voluntary sins of the saints, since the Lord has testified the same by the legal victims, as by so many types. Besides, who can plead ignorance as an excuse for David, who was evidently so well acquainted with the law? Did not David know that adultery and murder were great crimes, which he daily punished in others? Did the patriarchs consider fratricide as lawful? Had the Corinthians learned so little that they could imagine impurity, incontinence, fornication, animosities, and contentions, to be pleasing to God? Could Peter, who had been so carefully warned, be ignorant how great a crime it was to abjure his Master? Let us not, therefore, by our cruelty, shut the gate of mercy which God has so liberally opened.

XXIX. I am fully aware that the old writers have explained those sins, which are daily forgiven to believers, to be the smaller faults, which are inadvertently committed through the infirmity

(*f*) Psalm lxxxix 30—33.

of the flesh; but solemn repentance, which was then required for greater offences, they thought, was no more to be repeated than baptism. This sentiment is not to be understood as indicating their design, either to drive into despair such persons as had relapsed after their first repentance, or to extenuate those errors, as if they were small in the sight of God. For they knew that the saints frequently stagger through unbelief; that they sometimes utter unnecessary oaths; that they occasionally swell into anger, and even break out into open reproaches; and that they are likewise chargeable with other faults, which the Lord holds in the greatest abomination. They expressed themselves in this manner, to distinguish between private offences and those public crimes which were attended with great scandal in the Church. But the difficulty, which they made, of forgiving those who had committed any thing deserving of ecclesiastical censure, did not arise from an opinion that it was difficult for them to obtain pardon from the Lord; they only intended by this severity to deter others from rashly running into crimes, which would justly be followed by their exclusion from the communion of the Church. The word of the Lord, however, which ought to be our only rule in this case, certainly prescribes greater moderation. For it teaches, that the rigour of discipline ought not to be carried to such an extent, as to overwhelm with sorrow the person whose benefit we are required to regard as its principal object; as we have before shown more at large.

CHAPTER II

The True and False Church Compared

WE HAVE already stated the importance which we ought to attach to the ministry of the word and sacraments, and the extent to which our reverence for it ought to be carried, so as to account it a perpetual mark and characteristic of the Church. That is to say, that wherever *that* exists entire and uncorrupted, no errors and irregularities of conduct form a sufficient reason for refusing the name of a Church. In the next place, that the ministry itself is not so far vitiated by smaller errors, as to be considered on that account less legitimate. It has further been shown, that the errors which are entitled to this forgiveness are those by which the grand doctrine of religion is not injured, which do not suppress the points in which all believers ought to agree as articles of faith, and which, in regard to the sacraments, neither abolish nor subvert the legitimate institution of their Author. But as soon as falsehood has made a breach in the fundamentals of religion, and the system of necessary doctrine is subverted, and the use of the sacraments fails, the certain consequence is the ruin of the Church, as there is an end of a man's life when his throat is cut, or his heart is mortally wounded. And this is evident from the language of Paul, when he declares the Church to be "built upon the foundation of the apostles and prophets, Jesus Christ himself being the chief corner-stone." (*h*) If the foundation of the Church be the doctrine of the prophets and apostles, which en-

(*h*) Ephes. ii. 20.

joins believers to place their salvation in Christ alone, how can the edifice stand any longer, when that doctrine is taken away? The Church, therefore, must of necessity fall, where that system of religion is subverted which alone is able to sustain it. Besides, if the true Church be "the pillar and ground of truth," (*i*) that certainly can be no Church where delusion and falsehood have usurped the dominion.

II. As this is the state of things under the Papacy, it is easy to judge how much of the Church remains there. Instead of the ministry of the word, there reigns a corrupt government, composed of falsehoods, by which the pure light is suppressed or extinguished. An execrable sacrilege has been substituted for the supper of the Lord. The worship of God is deformed by a multifarious and intolerable mass of superstitions. The doctrine, without which Christianity cannot exist, has been entirely forgotten or exploded. The public assemblies have become schools of idolatry and impiety. In withdrawing ourselves, therefore, from the pernicious participation of so many enormities, there is no danger of separating ourselves from the Church of Christ. The communion of the Church was not instituted as a bond to confine us in idolatry, impiety, ignorance of God, and other evils; but rather as a mean to preserve us in the fear of God, and obedience of the truth. I know that the Papists give us the most magnificent commendations of their Church, to make us believe that there is no other in the world; and then, as if they had gained their point, they conclude all who dare to withdraw themselves from that Church which they describe, to be schismatics, and pronounce all to be heretics who venture to open their mouths in opposition to its doctrine. But by what reasons do they prove theirs to be the true Church? They allege from ancient records what formerly occurred in Italy, in France, in Spain; that they are descended from those holy men, who by sound doctrine founded and raised the Churches in these countries, and confirmed their doctrine and the edification of the Church by their blood; and that the Church, thus consecrated among them, both by spiritual gifts, and by the blood of martyrs, has been preserved by a perpetual succession

---

(*i*) 1 Tim. iii. 15.

of bishops, that it might never be lost. They allege the importance attached to this succession by Irenæus, Tertullian, Origen, Augustine, and others. To those who are willing to attend me in a brief examination of these allegations, I will clearly show that they are frivolous, and manifestly ridiculous. I would likewise exhort those who advance them, to pay a serious attention to the subject, if I thought my arguments could produce any effect upon them; but as their sole object is to promote their own interest by every method in their power, without any regard to truth, I shall content myself with making a few observations, with which good men, and inquirers after truth, may be able to answer their cavils. In the first place, I ask them, why they allege nothing respecting Africa, and Egypt, and all Asia. It is because, in all those countries, there has been a failure of this sacred succession of bishops, by virtue of which they boast that the Church has been preserved among them. They come to this point, therefore, that they have the true Church, because from its commencement it has never been destitute of bishops, for that some have been succeeded by others in an uninterrupted series. But what if I oppose them with the example of Greece? I ask them again, therefore, why they assert that the Church has been lost among the Greeks, among whom there has never been any interruption of that succession of bishops, which they consider as the sole guard and preservative of the Church? They call the Greeks schismatics. For what reason? Because, it is pretended, they have lost their privilege by revolting from the Apostolical see. But do not they much more deserve to lose it, who have revolted from Christ himself? It follows, therefore, that their plea of uninterrupted succession is a vain pretence, unless the truth of Christ, which was transmitted from the fathers, be permanently retained pure and uncorrupted by their posterity.

III. The pretensions of the Romanists, therefore, in the present day, are no other than those which appear to have been formerly set up by the Jews, when they were reproved by the prophets of the Lord for blindness, impiety, and idolatry. For as the Jews boasted of the temple, the ceremonies, and the priesthood, in which things they firmly believed the Church to consist; so, instead of the Church, the Papists produce certain external forms, which are often at a great distance from the Church, and are not at all necessary to its existence. Wherefore we need no other argument to refute them, than that which was urged by Jeremiah against that foolish confidence of the Jews: "Trust ye not in lying words, saying, The temple of the Lord, the temple of the Lord, the temple of the Lord, are these." (*k*) For the Lord acknowledges no place as his temple, where his word is not heard and devoutly observed. So, though the glory of God resided between the cherubim in the sanctuary, and he had promised his people that he would make it his permanent seat, yet when the priests had corrupted his worship by perverse superstitions, he departed, and left the place without any sanctity. If that temple which appeared to be consecrated to the perpetual residence of God, could be forsaken and desecrated by him, there can be no reason for their pretending that God is so attached to persons or places, or confined to external observances, as to be constrained to remain among those who have nothing but the name and appearance of the Church. And this is the argument which is maintained by Paul in the Epistle to the Romans, from the ninth chapter to the twelfth. For it had violently disturbed weak consciences, to observe that, while the Jews appeared to be the people of God, they not only rejected, but also persecuted, the doctrine of the gospel. Therefore, after having discussed that doctrine, he removes this difficulty; and denies the claim of those Jews, who were enemies of the truth, to be considered as the Church, though in other respects they wanted nothing that could be requisite to its external form. And the only reason for this denial was, because they did not receive Christ. He speaks rather more explicitly in the Epistle to the Galatians, (*l*) where, in a comparison between Ishmael and Isaac, he represents many as occupying a place in the Church, who have no right to the inheritance, because they are not the children of a free mother. Hence he proceeds to a contrast of the two Jerusalems, because as the law was given on Mount Sinai, but the gospel came forth from Jerusalem, so many who have been born and educated in bondage, confidently boast of being the children of God and of the Church, and though they

(*k*) Jer. vii. 4. (*l*) Gal. iv.

are themselves a spurious offspring, look down with contempt on his genuine and legitimate children. But as for us, on the contrary, who have once heard it proclaimed from heaven, "Cast out the bondwoman and her son," let us confide in this inviolable decree, and resolutely despise their ridiculous pretensions. For if they pride themselves on an external profession, Ishmael also was circumcised. If they depend on antiquity, he was the first born. Yet we see that he was rejected. If the cause of this be inquired, Paul tells us that none are accounted children but those who are born of the pure and legitimate seed of the word. (*m*) According to this reason, the Lord declares that he is not confined to impious priests, because he had made a covenant with their father Levi to be his angel or messenger. (*n*) He even retorts on them their false boasting, with which they were accustomed to oppose the prophets, that the dignity of the priesthood ought to be held in peculiar estimation. This he readily admits, and argues with them on this ground, because he was prepared to observe the covenant, whereas they failed of discharging the correspondent obligations, and therefore deserved to be rejected. See, then, what such succession is worth, unless it be connected with a continual imitation and conformity. Without this, the descendants, who are convicted of a departure from their predecessors, must immediately be deprived of all honour; unless, indeed, because Caiaphas was the successor of many pious priests, and there had been an uninterrupted series even from Aaron to him, that execrable assembly be deemed worthy to be called the Church. But it would not be tolerated even in earthly governments, that the tyranny of Caligula, Nero, Heliogabalus, and others, should be called the true state of the republic, because they succeeded the Bruti, the Scipios, and the Camilli. But in regard to the government of the Church, nothing can be more frivolous than to place the succession in the persons, to the neglect of the doctrine. And nothing was further from the intentions of the holy doctors, whose authority they falsely obtrude upon us, than to prove that Churches existed by a kind of hereditary right, wherever there has been a constant succession of bishops. But as it was

(*m*) Rom. ix. 6—8. (*n*) Mal. ii. 1—9.

beyond all doubt that, from the beginning even down to their times, no change had taken place in the doctrine, they assumed, what would suffice for the confutation of all new errors, that they were repugnant to the doctrine which had been constantly and unanimously maintained even from the days of the apostles. They will gain nothing, therefore, by persisting to disguise themselves under the name of the Church. The Church we regard with becoming reverence; but when they come to the definition, they are miserably embarrassed, for they substitute an execrable harlot in the place of the holy spouse of Christ. That we may not be deceived by such a substitution, beside other admonitions, let us remember this of Augustine; for, speaking of the Church, he says, "It is sometimes obscured and beclouded by a multitude of scandals; sometimes it appears quiet and unmolested in a season of tranquillity, and is sometimes disturbed and overwhelmed with the waves of tribulations and temptations." He produces examples, that those who were its firmest pillars, have either undauntedly suffered banishment on account of the faith, or secluded themselves from all society.

IV. In the same manner, the Romanists in the present day harass us, and terrify ignorant persons with the name of the Church, though there are no greater enemies to Christ than themselves. Although they may pretend therefore to the temple, the priesthood, and other similar forms, this vain glitter, which dazzles the eyes of the simple, ought by no means to induce us to admit the existence of a Church, where we cannot discover the word of God. For this is the perpetual mark by which our Lord has characterized his people: "Every one that is of the truth heareth my voice." (*o*) And, "I am the good Shepherd, and know my sheep, and am known of mine." "My sheep hear my voice, and I know them, and they follow me." He had just before said, "The sheep follow their shepherd; for they know his voice; and a stranger will they not follow, but will flee from him, for they know not the voice of strangers." (*p*) Why, then, do we wilfully run into error in forming a judgment of the Church, since Christ has designated it by an unequivocal character, that

(*o*) John xviii. 37. (*p*) John x. 4, 5, 14, 27.

wherever it is discovered, it infallibly assures us of the existence of a Church, and wherever it is wanting, there is no real evidence of a Church left. For Paul declares the Church to be founded, not upon the opinions of men, not upon the priesthood, but upon the "doctrine of the apostles and prophets." (*q*) And Jerusalem is to be distinguished from Babylon, the Church of Christ from the synagogue of Satan, by this difference, by which Christ has discriminated them from each other. "He that is of God, heareth God's words; ye therefore hear them not, because ye are not of God." (*r*) In fine, as the Church is the kingdom of Christ, and he reigns only by his word, can any person doubt the falsehood of those pretensions, which represent the kingdom of Christ as destitute of his sceptre, that is, of his holy word?

V. With respect to the charge which they bring against us of heresy and schism, because we preach a different doctrine from theirs, and submit not to their laws, and hold separate assemblies for prayers, for baptism, for the administration of the Lord's supper, and other sacred exercises, it is indeed a most heavy accusation, but such as by no means requires a long or laborious defence. The appellations of heretics and schismatics are applied to persons who cause dissension, and destroy the communion of the Church. Now, this communion is preserved by two bonds—agreement in sound doctrine, and brotherly love. Between heretics and schismatics, therefore, Augustine makes the following distinction—that the former corrupt the purity of the faith by false doctrines, and that the latter break the bond of affection, sometimes even while they retain the same faith. But it is also to be remarked, that this union of affection is dependent on the unity of faith, as its foundation, end, and rule. Let us remember, therefore, that, whenever the unity of the Church is enjoined upon us in the Scripture, it is required, that, while our minds hold the same doctrines in Christ, our wills should likewise be united in mutual benevolence in Christ. Therefore, Paul, when he exhorts us to it, assumes as a foundation, that there is "one Lord, one faith, and one baptism." (*s*) And when he inculcates our being "like-minded, and having the same love, being of one accord, of one

(*q*) Ephes. ii. 20. (*r*) John viii. 47. (*s*) Ephes. iv. 5.

mind," (*t*) he immediately adds, that this should be in Christ, or according to Christ; signifying that all union which is formed without the word of the Lord, is a faction of the impious, and not an association of believers.

VI. Cyprian, also, after the example of Paul, deduces the origin of all ecclesiastical concord from the supreme bishopric of Christ. He afterwards subjoins, "There is but one Church, which is widely extended into a multitude by the offspring of its fertility; just as there are many rays of the sun, but the light is one; and a tree has many branches, but only one trunk, fixed on a firm root. And when many rivers issue from one source, though by its exuberant abundance the stream is multiplied into numerous currents, yet the unity of the fountain still remains. Separate a ray from the body of the sun, and its unity sustains no division. Break off a branch from a tree, and the broken branch can never bud. Cut off a river from the source, and it immediately dries up. So the Church, overspread with the light of the Lord, is extended over the whole world: yet it is one and the same light which is universally diffused." No representation could be more elegant to express that inseparable connection which subsists between all the members of Christ. We see how he continually recalls us to the fountain-head. Therefore he pronounces the origin of heresies and schisms to be, that men neither return to the source of truth, nor seek the Head, nor attend to the doctrine of the heavenly Master. Now, let the Romanists exclaim that we are heretics, because we have withdrawn from their church; while the sole cause of our secession has been, that theirs cannot possibly be the pure profession of the truth. I say nothing of their having expelled us with anathemas and execrations. But this reason is more than sufficient for our exculpation, unless they are determined to pronounce sentence of schism also against the apostles, with whom we have but one common cause. Christ, I say, foretold to his apostles, that for his name's sake they should be cast out of the synagogues. (*v*) Now, those synagogues, of which he spoke, were then accounted legitimate Churches. Since it is evident, then, that we have been cast out, and we are prepared to prove that this

(*t*) Phil. ii. 2, 5. (*v*) John xvi. 2.

has been done for the name of Christ, it is necessary to inquire into the cause, before any thing be determined respecting us, either on one side or the other. But this point I readily relinquish to them. It is sufficient for me that it was necessary for us to withdraw from them, in order to approach to Christ.

VII. But it will be still more evident, in what estimation we ought to hold all the Churches who have submitted to the tyranny of the Roman pontiff, if we compare them with the ancient Church of Israel, as delineated by the prophets. There was a true Church among the Jews and the Israelites, while they continued to observe the laws of the covenant; because they then obtained from the favour of God those things which constitute a Church. They had the doctrine of truth in the law; the ministry of it was committed to the priests and prophets; they were initiated into the Church by the sign of circumcision; and were exercised in other sacraments for the confirmation of their faith. There is no doubt that the commendations, with which the Lord has honoured his Church, truly belonged to their society. But after they deserted the law of the Lord, and fell into idolatry and superstition, they partly lost this privilege. For who would dare to refuse the title of a Church to those among whom God deposited the preaching of his word, and the observance of his mysteries? On the other hand, who would dare to give the appellation of a Church, without any exception, to that society, where the word of God is openly and fearlessly trampled under foot; where its ministry, the principal sinew, and even the soul of the Church, is discontinued?

VIII. What, then, it will be said, was there no particle of a Church left among the Jews from the moment of their defection to idolatry? The answer is easy. In the first place, I observe, that in this defection there were several degrees. Nor will we maintain the fall of Judah, and that of Israel, to have been exactly the same, at the time when they both began to depart from the pure worship of God. When Jeroboam made the calves, in opposition to the express prohibition of God, and dedicated a place which it was not lawful to use for the oblation of sacrifices, in this case religion was totally corrupted. The Jews polluted themselves with practical impieties and superstitions, before they made any unlawful changes in the external forms of religion. For though they generally adopted many corrupt ceremonies in the time of Rehoboam, yet as the doctrine of the law, and the priesthood, and the rites which God had instituted, were still preserved at Jerusalem, believers had in that kingdom a tolerable form of a Church. Among the Israelites, there was no reformation down to the reign of Ahab, and in his time there was an alteration for the worse. Of the succeeding kings, even to the subversion of the kingdom, some resembled Ahab, and others, who would be a little better, followed the example of Jeroboam; but all, without exception, were impious idolaters. In Judah there were various changes; some kings corrupted the worship of God with false and groundless superstitions, and others restored religion from its abuses; till, at length, the priests themselves polluted the temple of God with idolatrous and abominable rites.

IX. Now, however the Papists may extenuate their vices, let them deny, if they can, that the state of religion is as corrupt and depraved among them, as it was in the kingdom of Israel, in the time of Jeroboam. But they practise a grosser idolatry, and their doctrine is equally, if not more, impure. God is my witness, and all men who are endued with moderate judgment, and the fact itself declares, that in this I am guilty of no exaggeration. Now, when they try to drive us into the communion of their Church, they require two things of us—first, that we should communicate in all their prayers, sacraments, and ceremonies; secondly, that whatever honour, power, and jurisdiction, Christ has conferred upon his Church, we should attribute the same to theirs. With respect to the first point, I confess that the prophets who were at Jerusalem, when the state of affairs there was very corrupt, neither offered up sacrifices apart from others, nor held separate assemblies for prayer. For they had the express command of God, that they were to assemble in the temple of Solomon; and they knew that the Levitical priests, because they had been ordained by the Lord as ministers of the sacrifices, and had not been deposed, however unworthy they might be of such honour, still retained the lawful possession of that place. But, what is the principal point of the whole controversy, they were not constrained to join in any superstitious worship; on the contrary, they engaged in no service that was not of Divine institution. But what resemblance is there to this among the Papists? We can scarcely assemble with them on a single occasion, without polluting ourselves with open idolatry. The principal bond of their communion is certainly the mass, which we abominate as the greatest sacrilege. Whether we are right or wrong in this, will be seen in another place. It is sufficient, at present, to show that, in this respect, our case is different from that of the prophets, who, though they were present at the sacrifices of impious persons, were never compelled to use, or to witness, any ceremonies but those which God had instituted. And if we wish to have an example entirely similar, we must take it from the kingdom of Israel. According to the regulations of Jeroboam, circumcision continued, sacrifices were offered, the law was regarded as sacred, the people invoked the same God whom their fathers had worshipped; yet, on account of novel ceremonies invented in opposition to the Divine prohibitions, God disapproved and condemned all that was done there. Show me a single prophet, or any pious man, who even once worshipped or offered sacrifice at Bethel. They knew that they could not do it without contaminating themselves with sacrilege. We have established this point, therefore, that the attachment of pious persons to the communion of the Church, ought not to be carried to such an extent, as to oblige them to remain in it, if it degenerated into profane and impure rites.

X. But against their second requisition, wc contend upon still stronger ground. For if the Church be held in such consideration that we are required to revere its judgment, to obey its authority, to receive its admonitions, to fall under its censures, and scrupulously and uniformly to adhere to its communion, we cannot allow their claim to the character of the Church, without necessarily obliging ourselves to subjection and obedience. Yet we readily concede to them what the prophets conceded to the Jews and Israelites of their time, when things among them were in a similar, or even in a better state. But we see how they frequently exclaim, that their assemblies were iniquitous meetings, (*w*) a concurrence in which were as criminal as a renunciation of God. And certainly, if those assemblies were Churches, it follows that

(*w*) Isaiah i. 13, 14.

Elijah, Micaiah, and others in Israel, were strangers to the Church of God; and the same would be true of Isaiah, Jeremiah, Hosea, and others of that description in Judah, whom the false prophets, priests, and people of their day, hated and execrated as if they had been worse than any heathens. If such assemblies were Churches, then the Church is not the pillar of truth, but a foundation of falsehood, not the sanctuary of the living God, but a receptacle of idols. They found themselves under a necessity, therefore, of withdrawing from all connection with those assemblies, which were nothing but a conspiracy against God. For the same reason, if any one acknowledges the assemblies of the present day, which are contaminated with idolatry, superstition, and false doctrine, as true Churches, in full communion with which a Christian man ought to continue, and in whose doctrine he ought to coincide, this will be a great error. For if they be Churches, they possess the power of the keys; but the keys are inseparably connected with the word, which is exploded from among them. Again, if they be Churches, that promise of Christ must be applicable to them—"Whatsoever ye shall bind on earth shall be bound in heaven, and whatsoever ye shall loose on earth shall be loosed in heaven." (*x*) On the contrary, all who sincerely profess themselves to be the servants of Christ, they expel from their communion. Either, therefore, the promise of Christ must be vain, or in this respect they are not Churches. Lastly, instead of the ministry of the word, they have schools of impiety, and a gulf of every species of errors. Either, therefore, in this respect they are not Churches, or no mark will be left to distinguish the legitimate assemblies of believers from the conventions of Turks.

XI. Nevertheless, as in former times the Jews continued in possession of some peculiar privileges of the Church, so we refuse not to acknowledge, among the Papists of the present day, those vestiges of the Church which it has pleased the Lord should remain among them after its removal. When God had once made his covenant with the Jews, it continued among them, rather because it was supported by its own stability in opposition to their impiety, than in consequence of their observance of it. Such,

---

(*x*) Matt. xviii. 18.

therefore, was the certainty and constancy of the Divine goodness, the covenant of the Lord remained among them; his faithfulness could not be obliterated by their perfidy; nor could circumcision be so profaned by their impure hands, but that it was always the true sign and sacrament of his covenant. Hence the children that were born to them, God calls his own, (*y*) though they could not have belonged to him but by a special benediction. So after he had deposited his covenant in France, Italy, Germany, Spain, and England, when those countries were oppressed by the tyranny of Antichrist, still, in order that the covenant might remain inviolable, as a testimony of that covenant, he preserved baptism among them, which, being consecrated by his lips, retains its virtue in opposition to all the impiety of men. He also, by his providence, caused other vestiges of the Church to remain, that it might not be entirely lost. And as buildings are frequently demolished in such a manner as to leave the foundations and ruins remaining, so the Lord has not suffered Antichrist either to subvert his Church from the foundation, or to level it with the ground; though, to punish the ingratitude of men who despised his word, he has permitted a dreadful concussion and dilapidation to be made; yet, amidst this devastation, he has been pleased to preserve the edifice from being entirely destroyed.

XII. While we refuse, therefore, to allow to the Papists the title of the Church, without any qualification or restriction, we do not deny that there are Churches among them. We only contend for the true and legitimate constitution of the Church, which requires not only a communion in the sacraments, which are the signs of a Christian profession, but above all, an agreement in doctrine. Daniel and Paul had predicted that Antichrist would sit in the temple of God. (*z*) The head of that cursed and abominable kingdom, in the Western Church, we affirm to be the Pope. When his seat is placed in the temple of God, it suggests, that his kingdom will be such, that he will not abolish the name of Christ, or the Church. Hence it appears, that we by no means deny that Churches may exist, even under his tyranny; but he has profaned them by sacrilegious impiety, afflicted them by cruel des-

---

(*y*) Ezek. xiv. 20. (*z*) Dan. ix. 27. 2 Thess. ii. 3, 4.

potism, corrupted and almost terminated their existence by false and pernicious doctrines, like poisonous potions; in such Churches, Christ lies half buried, the gospel is suppressed, piety exterminated, and the worship of God almost abolished; in a word, they are altogether in such a state of confusion, that they exhibit a picture of Babylon, rather than of the holy city of God. To conclude, I affirm that they are Churches, inasmuch as God has wonderfully preserved among them a remnant of his people, though miserably dispersed and dejected, and as there still remain some marks of the Church, especially those, the efficacy of which neither the craft of the devil nor the malice of men can ever destroy. But, on the other hand, because those marks, which we ought chiefly to regard in this controversy, are obliterated, I affirm, that the form of the legitimate Church is not to be found either in any one of their congregations, or in the body at large.

CHAPTER III

The Teachers and Ministers of the Church; Their Election and Office

WE MUST now treat of the order which it has been the Lord's will to appoint for the government of his Church. For although he alone ought to rule and reign in the Church, and to have all preëminence in it, and this government ought to be exercised and administered solely by his word,—yet, as he dwells not among us by a visible presence, so as to make an audible declaration of his will to us, we have stated, that for this purpose he uses the ministry of men whom he employs as his delegates, not to transfer his right and honour to them, but only that he may himself do his work by their lips; just as an artificer makes use of an instrument in the performance of his work. Some observations which I have made already, are necessary to be repeated here. It is true that he might do this either by himself, without any means or instruments, or even by angels; but there are many reasons why he prefers making use of men. For, in the first place, by this method he declares his kindness towards us, since he chooses from among men those who are to be his ambassadors to the world, to be the interpreters of his secret will, and even to act as his personal representatives. And thus he affords an actual proof, that when he so frequently calls us his temples, it is not an unmeaning appellation, since he gives answers to men, even from the mouths of men, as from a sanctuary. In the second place, this is a most excellent and beneficial method to train us to humility, since he accustoms us to obey his word, though it is preached to us by men like ourselves, and sometimes even of inferior rank. If he were himself to speak from heaven, there would be no wonder if his sacred oracles were instantly received with reverence, by the ears and hearts of all mankind. For who would not be awed by his present power? who would not fall prostrate at the first view of infinite Majesty? who would not be confounded by that overpowering splendour? But when a contemptible mortal, who had just emerged from the dust, addresses us in the name of God, we give the best evidence of our piety and reverence towards God himself, if we readily submit to be instructed by his minister, who possesses no personal superiority to ourselves. For this reason, also, he has deposited the treasure of his heavenly wisdom in frail and earthen vessels, (*a*) in order to afford a better proof of the estimation in which we hold it. Besides, nothing was more adapted to promote brotherly love, than a mutual connection of men by this bond, while one is constituted the pastor to teach all the rest, and they who are commanded to be disciples, receive one common doctrine from the same mouth. For if each person were sufficient for himself, and had no need of the assistance of another, such is the pride of human nature, every one would despise others, and would also be despised by them. The Lord, therefore, has connected his Church together, by that which he foresaw would be the strongest bond for the preservation of their union, when he committed the doctrine of eternal life and salvation to men, that by their hands it might be communicated to others. Paul had this in view when he wrote to the Ephesians, "There is one body, and one Spirit, even as ye are called in one hope of your calling; one Lord, one faith, one baptism, one God and Father of all, who is above all, and through all, and in you all. But unto every one of us is given grace according to the measure of the gift of Christ. Wherefore he saith, When he ascended up on high, he led captivity captive, and gave gifts unto men. (Now that he ascended, what is it but that he also descended first into the lower parts of the earth? He that descended is the same also that ascended up far above all heavens, that he might fill all

(*a*) 2 Cor. iv. 7.

things.) And he gave some, apostles; and some, prophets; and some, evangelists; and some, pastors and teachers; for the perfecting of the saints, for the work of the ministry, for the edifying of the body of Christ; till we all come in the unity of the faith, and of the knowledge of the Son of God, unto a perfect man, unto the measure of the stature of the fulness of Christ; that we henceforth be no more children, tossed to and fro, and carried about with every wind of doctrine, by the sleight of men, and cunning craftiness, whereby they lie in wait to deceive; but, speaking the truth in love, may grow up into him in all things, which is the head, even Christ; from whom the whole body fitly joined together, and compacted by that which every joint supplieth, according to the effectual working in the measure of every part, maketh increase of the body unto the edifying of itself in love." (*b*)

II. In this passage he shows that the ministry of men, which God employs in his government of the Church, is the principal bond which holds believers together in one body. He also indicates that the Church cannot be preserved in perfect safety, unless it be supported by these means which God has been pleased to appoint for its preservation. Christ, he says, "ascended up far above all heavens, that he might fill all things." (*c*) And this is the way in which he does it. By means of his ministers, to whom he has committed this office, and on whom he has bestowed grace to discharge it, he dispenses and distributes his gifts to the Church, and even affords some manifestation of his own presence, by exerting the power of his Spirit in this his institution, that it may not be vain or ineffectual. Thus is the restoration of the saints effected; thus is the body of Christ edified; thus we grow up unto him who is our Head in all things, and are united with each other; thus we are all brought to the unity of Christ; if prophecy flourishes among us, if we receive the apostles, if we despise not the doctrine which is delivered to us. Whoever, therefore, either aims to abolish or undervalue this order, of which we are treating, and this species of government, attempts to disorganize the Church, or rather to subvert and destroy it altogether. For neither

---

(*b*) Eph. iv. 4—16. (*c*) Eph. iv. 10.

the light and heat of the sun, nor any meat and drink, are so necessary to the nourishment and sustenance of the present life, as the apostolical and pastoral office is to the preservation of the Church in the world.

III. Therefore I have already remarked, that God has frequently commended its dignity to us by every possible encomium, in order that we might hold it in the highest estimation and value, as more excellent than every thing else. That he confers a peculiar favour upon men by raising up teachers for them, he fully signifies, when he commands the prophet to exclaim, "How beautiful are the feet of him that publisheth peace;" (*d*) and when he calls the apostles "the light of the world," and "the salt of the earth." (*e*) Nor could that office be more splendidly distinguished than when he said to them, "He that heareth you, heareth me." (*f*) But there is no passage more remarkable than that in Paul's Second Epistle to the Corinthians, where he professedly discusses this question. He contends, that there is nothing more excellent or glorious than the ministry of the gospel in the Church, inasmuch as it is the ministration of the Spirit, and of righteousness, and of eternal life. (*g*) The tendency of these and similar passages, is to preserve that mode of governing the Church by its ministers, which the Lord appointed to be of perpetual continuance, from sinking into disesteem, and, at length, falling into disuse through mere contempt. And how exceedingly necessary it is, he has not only declared in words, but shown by examples. When he was pleased to illuminate Cornelius more fully with the light of his truth, he despatched an angel from heaven to send Peter to him. When he designs to call Paul to the knowledge of himself, and to introduce him into the Church, he does not address him with his own voice, but sends him to a man to receive the doctrine of salvation, and the sanctification of baptism. If it was not without sufficient reason, that an angel, who is the messenger of God, refrains from announcing the Divine will himself, and directs a man to be sent for in order to declare it,—and that Christ, the sole Teacher of believers, committed Paul to the instruction of a man, the same Paul whom he had determined to elevate into the third heaven,

(*d*) Isaiah lii. 7.
(*e*) Matt. v. 13, 14.
(*f*) Luke x. 16.
(*g*) 2 Cor. iii. 6, &c.

and to favour with a miraculous revelation of things unspeakable, —who can now dare to despise that ministry, or to neglect it as unnecessary, the utility and necessity of which God has been pleased to evince by such examples?

IV. Those who preside over the government of the Church, according to the institution of Christ, are named by Paul, first, "apostles;" secondly, "prophets;" thirdly, "evangelists;" fourthly, "pastors;" lastly, "teachers." (*h*) Of these, only the two last sustain an ordinary office in the Church: the others were such as the Lord raised up at the commencement of his kingdom, and such as he still raises up on particular occasions, when required by the necessity of the times. The nature of the apostolic office is manifest from this command: "Go preach the gospel to every creature." (*i*) No certain limits are prescribed, but the whole world is assigned to them, to be reduced to obedience to Christ; that by disseminating the gospel wherever they could, they might erect his kingdom in all nations. Therefore Paul, when he wished to prove his apostleship, declares, not merely that he had gained some one city for Christ, but that he had propagated the gospel far and wide, and that he had not built upon the foundation of others, but had planted Churches where the name of the Lord had never been heard before. The "apostles," therefore, were missionaries, who were to reduced the world from their revolt to true obedience to God, and to establish his kingdom universally by the preaching of the gospel. Or, if you please, they were the first architects of the Church, appointed to lay its foundations all over the world. Paul gives the appellation of "prophets," not to all interpreters of the Divine will, but only to those who were honoured with some special revelation. Of these, either there are none in our day, or they are less conspicuous. By "evangelists," I understand those who were inferior to the apostles in dignity, but next to them in office, and who performed similar functions. Such were Luke, Timothy, Titus, and others of that description; and perhaps also the seventy disciples, whom Christ ordained to occupy the second station from the apostles. (*k*) According to this interpretation, which appears to me perfectly consistent with the

---

(*h*) Eph. iv. 11. (*i*) Mark xvi. 15. (*k*) Luke x. 1.

language and meaning of the apostle, those three offices were not instituted to be of perpetual continuance in the Church, but only for that age when Churches were to be raised where none had existed before, or were at least to be conducted from Moses to Christ. Though I do not deny, that, even since that period, God has sometimes raised up apostles or evangelists in their stead, as he has done in our own time. For there was a necessity for such persons to recover the Church from the defection of Antichrist. Nevertheless, I call this an extraordinary office, because it has no place in well-constituted Churches. Next follow "pastors" and "teachers," who are always indispensable to the Church. The difference between them I apprehend to be this—that teachers have no official concern with the discipline, or the administration of the sacraments, or with admonitions and exhortations, but only with the interpretation of the Scripture, that pure and sound doctrine may be retained among believers; whereas the pastoral office includes all these things.

V. We have now ascertained what offices were appointed to continue for a time in the government of the Church, and what were instituted to be of perpetual duration. If we connect the evangelists with the apostles, as sustaining the same office, we shall then have two offices of each description, corresponding to each other. For our pastors bear the same resemblance to the apostles, as our teachers do to the ancient prophets. The office of the prophets was more excellent, on account of the special gift of revelation, by which they were distinguished; but the office of teachers is executed in a similar manner, and has precisely the same end. So those twelve individuals, whom the Lord chose to promulgate the first proclamation of his gospel to the world, preceded all others in order and dignity. For although, according to the meaning and etymology of the word, all the ministers of the Church may be called apostles, because they are all sent by the Lord, and are his messengers, yet, as it was of great importance to have a certain knowledge of the mission of persons who were to announce a thing new and unheard before, it was necessary that those twelve, together with Paul, who was afterwards added to their number, should be distinguished beyond all others by a peculiar title. Paul himself, indeed, gives this name to "Andronicus and Junia who," he says, "are of note among the apostles;" (*l*) but when he means to speak with strict propriety, he never applies that name except to those of the first order that we have mentioned. And this is the common usage of the Scripture. But the province of pastors is the same as that of the apostles, except that they preside over particular Churches respectively committed to each of them. Of the nature of their functions let us now proceed to a more distinct statement.

VI. Our Lord, when he sent forth his apostles, commissioned them, as we have just remarked, to preach the gospel, and to baptize all believers for the remission of sins. (*m*) He had already commanded them to distribute the sacred symbols of his body and blood according to his own example. (*n*) Behold the sacred, inviolable, and perpetual law imposed upon those who call themselves successors of the apostles; it commands them to preach the gospel, and to administer the sacraments. Hence we conclude, that those who neglect both these duties have no just pretensions to the character of apostles. But what shall we say of pastors? Paul speaks not only of himself, but of all who bear that office, when he says, "Let a man so account of us, as of the ministers of Christ, and stewards of the mysteries of God." (*o*) Again: "A bishop must hold fast the faithful word as he hath been taught, that he may be able, by sound doctrine, both to exhort and to convince the gainsayers." (*p*) From these and similar passages, which frequently occur, we may infer that the preaching of the gospel, and the administration of the sacraments, constitute the two principal parts of the pastoral office. Now, the business of teaching is not confined to public discourses, but extends also to private admonitions. Thus Paul calls upon the Ephesians to witness the truth of his declaration, "I have kept back nothing that was profitable unto you, but have showed you, and have taught you publicly, and from house to house, testifying both to the Jews, and also to the Greeks, repentance toward God, and faith toward our Lord Jesus Christ." And a little after: "I ceased not to warn every one, night and day, with tears." (*q*) But it is no part of my present design, to enumerate all the excellences of a good

(*l*) Rom. xvi. 7. (*m*) Matt. xxviii. 19. (*n*) Luke xxii. 19.
(*o*) 1 Cor. iv. 1. (*p*) Titus i. 7, 9. (*q*) Acts xx. 20, 21, 31.

pastor, but only to show what is implied in the profession of those who call themselves pastors; namely, that they preside over the Church in that station, not that they may enjoy a respectable sinecure, but to instruct the people in true piety by the doctrine of Christ, to administer the holy mysteries, to maintain and exercise proper discipline. For the Lord denounces to all those who have been stationed as watchmen in the Church, that if any one perish in ignorance through their negligence, he will require the blood of such a person at their hands. (*r*) What Paul says of himself, belongs to them all: "Woe is unto me, if I preach not the gospel," because "a dispensation of the gospel is committed unto me." (*s*) Lastly, what the apostles did for the whole world, that every individual pastor ought to do for his flock to which he is appointed.

VII. While we assign to them all respectively their distinct Churches, yet we do not deny that a pastor, who is connected with one Church, may assist others, either when any disputes arise, which may require his presence, or when his advice is asked upon any difficult subject. But because, in order to preserve the peace of the Church, there is a necessity for such a regulation as shall clearly define to every one what duty he has to do, lest they should all fall into disorder, run hither and thither in uncertainty without any call, and all resort to one place; and lest those who feel more solicitude for their personal accommodation than for the edification of the Church, should, without any cause but their own caprice, leave the Churches destitute,—this distribution ought as far as possible to be generally observed, that every one may be content with his own limits, and not invade the province of another. Nor is this an invention of men, but an institution of God himself. For we read that Paul and Barnabas "ordained elders in the respective Churches of Lystra, Iconium, and Antioch;" (*t*) and Paul himself directed Titus to "ordain elders in every city." (*v*) So in other passages he mentions "the bishops at Philippi," (*w*) and Archippus, the bishop of the Colossians. (*x*) And a remarkable speech of his is preserved by Luke, addressed to "the elders of the Church of Ephesus." (*y*) Whoever, therefore,

(*r*) Ezek. iii. 17, 18. (*s*) 1 Cor. ix. 16, 17. (*t*) Acts xiv. 21, 23.
(*v*) Titus i. 5. (*w*) Phil. i. 1.
(*x*) Col. iv. 17. (*y*) Acts xx. 17, &c.

has undertaken the government and charge of one Church, let him know that he is bound to this law of the Divine call; not that he is fixed to his station so as never to be permitted to leave it in a regular and orderly manner, if the public benefit should require it; but he who has been called to one place, ought never to think either of departing from his situation, or relinquishing the office altogether, from any motive of personal convenience or advantage. But if it be expedient that he should remove to another station, he ought not to attempt this on his own private opinion, but to be guided by public authority.

VIII. In calling those who preside over Churches by the appellations of bishops, elders, pastors, and ministers, without any distinction, I have followed the usage of the Scripture, which applies all these terms to express the same meaning. For to all who discharge the ministry of the word, it gives the title of "bishops." So when Paul enjoins Titus to "ordain elders in every city," he immediately adds, "For a bishop must be blameless." (*z*) So in another Epistle he salutes more bishops than one in one Church. (*a*) And in the Acts he is declared to have sent for the elders of the Church of Ephesus, whom, in his address to them, he calls "bishops." (*b*) Here it must be observed, that we have enumerated only those offices which consist in the ministry of the word; nor does Paul mention any other in the fourth chapter of the Epistle to the Ephesians, which we have quoted. But in the Epistle to the Romans, and the First Epistle to the Corinthians, he enumerates others, as "powers," "gifts of healing," "interpretation of tongues," "governments," "care of the poor." (*c*) Those functions which were merely temporary, I omit, as foreign to our present subject. But there are two which perpetually remain—"government," and "the care of the poor." "Governors" I apprehend to have been persons of advanced years, selected from the people, to unite with the bishops in giving admonitions and exercising discipline. For no other interpretation can be given of that injunction, "He that ruleth, let him do it with diligence." (*d*) Therefore, from the beginning, every Church has had its senate or

---

(*z*) Titus i. 5, 7. (*a*) Phil. i. 1. (*b*) Acts xx. 17, 28, ἐπισκοπους.
(*c*) 1 Cor. xii. 28, δυναμεις, χαρισματα ιαματων, γενη γλωσσων, κυβερνησεις.
(*d*) Rom. xii. 8.

council, composed of pious, grave, and holy men, who were invested with that jurisdiction in the correction of vices, of which we shall soon treat. Now, that this regulation was not of a single age, experience itself demonstrates. This office of government is necessary, therefore, in every age.

IX. The care of the poor was committed to the "deacons." The Epistle to the Romans, however, mentions two functions of this kind. "He that giveth," says the apostle, "let him do it with simplicity: he that showeth mercy, with cheerfulness." (*e*) Now, as it is certain that he there speaks of the public offices of the Church, it follows that there were two distinct orders of deacons. Unless my judgment deceive me, the former clause refers to the deacons who administered the alms; and the other to those who devoted themselves to the care of poor and sick persons; such as the widows mentioned by Paul to Timothy. (*f*) For women could execute no other public office, than by devoting themselves to the service of the poor. If we admit this,—and it ought to be fully admitted,—there will be two classes of deacons, of whom one will serve the Church in dispensing the property given to the poor, the other in taking care of the poor themselves.—Though the word itself (διακονια) is of more extensive signification, yet the Scripture particularly gives the title of "deacons" to those whom the Church has appointed to dispense the alms and take care of the poor, and constituted stewards, as it were, of the common treasury of the poor; and whose origin, institution, and office, are described in the Acts of the Apostles. For "when there arose a murmuring of the Grecians against the Hebrews because their widows were neglected in the daily ministration," (*g*) the apostles pleaded their inability to discharge both offices, of the ministry of the word and the service of tables, and said to the multitude, "Wherefore, brethren, look ye out among you seven men of honest report, full of the Holy Ghost and wisdom, whom we may appoint over this business." See what were the characters of the deacons in the apostolic Church, and what ought to be the characters of ours, in conformity to the primitive example.

X. Now, as "all things" in the Church are required to "be done decently and in order," (*h*) there is nothing in which this ought

(*e*) Rom. xii. 8, *μεταδιδους, εν ἁπλοτητι, ὁ ελεων, εν ἱλαροτητι.*

(*f*) 1 Tim. v. 9, 10. (*g*) Acts vi. 1—3. (*h*) 1 Cor. xiv. 40.

to be more diligently observed, than the constitution of its government; because there would be more danger from disorder in this case than in any other. Therefore, that restless and turbulent persons may not presumptuously intrude themselves into the office of teaching or of governing, it is expressly provided, that no one shall assume a public office in the Church without a call. In order, therefore, that any one may be accounted a true minister of the Church, it is necessary, in the first place, that he be regularly called to it, and, in the second place, that he answer his call; that is, by undertaking and executing the office assigned to him. This may frequently be observed in Paul; who, when he wishes to prove his apostleship, almost always alleges his call, together with his fidelity in the execution of the office. If so eminent a minister of Christ dare not arrogate to himself an authority to require his being heard in the Church, but in consequence of his appointment to it by a Divine commission, and his faithful discharge of the duty assigned him,—what extreme impudence must it be, if any man, destitute of both these characters, should claim such an honour for himself! But having already spoken of the necessity of discharging the office, let us now confine ourselves to the call.

XI. Now, the discussion of this subject includes four branches: what are the qualifications of ministers; in what manner they are to be chosen; by whom they ought to be appointed; and with what rite or ceremony they are to be introduced into their office. I speak of the external and solemn call, which belongs to the public order of the Church; passing over that secret call, of which every minister is conscious to himself before God, but which is not known to the Church. This secret call, however, is the honest testimony of our heart, that we accept the office offered to us, not from ambition or avarice, or any other unlawful motive, but from a sincere fear of God, and an ardent zeal for the edification of the Church. This, as I have hinted, is indispensable to every one of us, if we would approve our ministry in the sight of God. In the view of the Church, however, he who enters on his office with an evil conscience, is nevertheless duly called, provided his iniquity be not discovered. It is even common to speak of private persons as called to the ministry, who appear to be adapted and qualified for the discharge of its duties; because learning, connected with piety and other endowments of a good pastor, constitutes a kind of preparation for it. For those whom the Lord has destined to so important an office, he first furnishes with those talents which are requisite to its execution, that they may not enter upon it empty and unprepared. Hence Paul, in his Epistle to the Corinthians, when he intended to treat of the offices themselves, first enumerated the gifts which ought to be possessed by the persons who sustain those offices. (*i*) But as this is the first of the four points which I have proposed, let us now proceed to it.

XII. The qualifications of those who ought to be chosen bishops, are stated at large by Paul in two passages. (*k*) The sum of all he says is, that none are to be chosen but men of sound doctrine and a holy life, not chargeable with any fault that may destroy their authority, or disgrace their ministry. The same rule is laid down for the deacons and governors. Constant care is required, that they be not unequal to the burden imposed upon them, or, in other words, that they be endowed with those talents which are necessary to the discharge of their duty. So, when Christ was about to send forth his apostles, he furnished them with such means and powers as were indispensable to their success. (*l*) And Paul, after having delineated the character of a good and genuine bishop, admonishes Timothy not to contaminate himself by the appointment of any one of a different description. (*m*) The question relating to the *manner* in which they are to be chosen, I refer not to the form of election, but to the religious awe which ought to be observed in it. Hence the fasting and prayer, which Luke states to have been practised by the faithful at the ordination of elders. (*n*) For knowing themselves to be engaged in a business of the highest importance, they dared not attempt any thing but with the greatest reverence and solicitude. And above all things, they were earnest in prayers and supplications to God for the spirit of wisdom and discretion.

XIII. The third inquiry we proposed was, by whom ministers

(*i*) 1 Cor. xii. 7, &c. (*k*) 1 Tim. iii. 1, &c. Titus i. 7, &c.
(*l*) Luke xxi. 15; xxiv. 49. Acts i. 8. (*m*) 1 Tim. v. 22.
(*n*) Acts xiv. 23.

are to be chosen. Now, for this no certain rule can be gathered from the appointment of the apostles, which was a case somewhat different from the common call of other ministers. For as theirs was an extraordinary office, it was necessary, in order to render it conspicuous by some eminent character, that they who were to sustain it should be called and appointed by the mouth of the Lord himself. The apostles, therefore, entered upon their work, not in consequence of any human election, but empowered by the sole command of God and of Christ. Hence, when they wish to substitute another in the place of Judas, they refrain from a certain appointment of any one, but nominate two, that the Lord may declare by lot which of them he wills to be his successor. (*o*) In the same sense must be understood the declaration of Paul, that he had been created "an apostle, not of men, neither by man, but by Jesus Christ, and God the Father." (*p*) The first clause, *not of men,* was applicable to him in common with all pious ministers of the word; for no man can lawfully exercise this ministry without having been called by God. The other clause was special and peculiar to himself. When he glories in this, therefore, he not only claims what belongs to a true and lawful pastor, but likewise brings forward an evidence of his apostleship. For whereas there were, among the Galatians, some who, from an eagerness to diminish his authority, represented him as a common disciple deputed by the primary apostles,—in order to vindicate the dignity of his preaching, against which he knew these artifices were directed, he found it necessary to show that he was not inferior to the other apostles in any respect. Wherefore he affirms, that he had not been elected by the judgment of men, like some ordinary bishop, but by the mouth and clear revelation of the Lord himself.

XIV. But that the election and appointment of bishops by men is necessary to constitute a legitimate call to the office, no sober person will deny, while there are so many testimonies of Scripture to establish it. Nor is it contradicted by that declaration of Paul, that he was "an apostle, not of men, nor by man," (*q*) since he is not speaking in that passage of the ordinary election of ministers, but claiming to himself what was the special privilege

(*o*) Acts i. 23. (*p*) Gal. i. 1. (*q*) Gal. i. 1.

of the apostles. The immediate designation of Paul, by the Lord himself, to this peculiar privilege, was nevertheless accompanied with the form of an ecclesiastical call, for Luke states, that "As they ministered to the Lord, and fasted, the Holy Ghost said, Separate me Barnabas and Saul for the work whereunto I have called them." (*r*) What end could be answered by this separation and imposition of hands after the Holy Spirit had testified their election, unless it was the preservation of the order of the Church in designating ministers by men? God could not sanction that order, therefore, by a more illustrious example than when, after having declared that he had constituted Paul the apostle of the Gentiles, he nevertheless directed him to be designated by the Church. The same may be observed in the election of Matthias. (*s*) For the apostolic office being of such high importance that they could not venture to fill up their number by the choice of any one person from their own judgment, they appointed two, one of whom was to be chosen by lot; that so the election might obtain a positive sanction from Heaven, and yet that the order of the Church might not be altogether neglected.

XV. Here it is inquired, whether a minister ought to be chosen by the whole Church, or only by the other ministers and the elders who preside over the discipline, or whether he may be appointed by the authority of an individual. Those who attribute this right to any one man, quote what Paul says to Titus: "For this cause I left thee in Crete, that thou shouldst ordain elders in every city;" (*t*) and to Timothy: "Lay hands suddenly on no man." (*v*) But they are exceedingly mistaken, if they suppose that either Timothy at Ephesus, or Titus in Crete, exercised a sovereign power to regulate every thing according to his own pleasure. For they presided over the people, only to lead them by good and salutary counsels, not to act alone to the exclusion of all others. But that this may not be thought to be an invention of mine, I will prove it by a similar example. For Luke relates, that elders were ordained in the Churches by Paul and Barnabas, but at the same time he distinctly marks the manner in which this was done,—namely, by the suffrages or votes of the people; for

(*r*) Acts xiii. 2. (*s*) Acts i. 23.
(*t*) Titus i. 5. (*v*) 1 Tim. v. 22.

this is the meaning of the term he there employs—χειροτονησαντες πρεσβυτερους κατ' ἐκκλησιαν. (*w*) Those two apostles, therefore, ordained them; but the whole multitude, according to the custom observed in elections among the Greeks, declared by the elevation of their hands who was the object of their choice. So the Roman historians frequently speak of the consul, who held the assemblies, as *appointing* the new magistrates, for no other reason but because he received the suffrages and presided at the election. Surely it is not credible that Paul granted to Timothy and Titus more power than he assumed to himself; but we see that he was accustomed to ordain bishops according to the suffrages of the people. The above passages, therefore, ought to be understood in the same manner, to guard against all infringement of the common right and liberty of the Church. It is a good remark, therefore, of Cyprian, when he contends, "that it proceeds from Divine authority, that a priest should be elected publicly in the presence of all the people, and that he should be approved as a worthy and fit person by the public judgment and testimony." In the case of the Levitical priests, we find it was commanded by the Lord, that they should be brought forward in the view of the people before their consecration. Nor was Matthias added to the number of the apostles, nor were the seven deacons appointed, without the presence and approbation of the people.—"These examples," says Cyprian, "show that the ordination of a priest ought not to be performed but with the knowledge and concurrence of the people, in order that the election which shall have been examined by the testimony of all, may be just and legitimate." We find, therefore, that it is a legitimate ministry according to the word of God, when those who appear suitable persons are appointed with the consent and approbation of the people; but that other pastors ought to preside over the election, to guard the multitude from falling into any improprieties, through inconstancy, intrigue, or confusion.

XVI. There remains the Form of ordination, which is the last point that we have mentioned relative to the call of ministers. Now, it appears that when the apostles introduced any one into

(*w*) Acts xiv. 23.

the ministry, they used no other ceremony than imposition of hands. This rite, I believe, descended from the custom of the Hebrews, who, when they wished to bless and consecrate any thing, presented it to God by imposition of hands. Thus, when Jacob blessed Ephraim and Manasseh, he laid his hands upon their heads. (*x*) This custom was followed by our Lord, when he prayed over infants. (*y*) It was with the same design, I apprehend, that the Jews were directed in the law to lay their hands upon their sacrifices. Wherefore the imposition of the hands of the apostle was an indication that they offered to God the person whom they introduced into the ministry. They used the same ceremony over those on whom they conferred the visible gifts of the Spirit. But, be that as it may, this was the solemn rite invariably practised, whenever any one was called to the ministry of the Church. Thus they ordained pastors and teachers, and thus they ordained deacons. Now, though there is no express precept for the imposition of hands, yet since we find it to have been constantly used by the apostles, such a punctual observance of it by them ought to have the force of a precept with us. And certainly this ceremony is highly useful both to recommend to the people the dignity of the ministry, and to admonish the person ordained that he is no longer his own master, but devoted to the service of God and the Church. Besides, it will not be an unmeaning sign, if it be restored to its true origin. For if the Spirit of God institutes nothing in the Church in vain, we shall perceive that this ceremony, which proceeded from him, is not without its use, provided it be not perverted by a superstitious abuse. Finally, it is to be remarked, that the imposition of hands on the ministers was not the act of the whole multitude, but was confined to the pastors. It is not certain whether this ceremony was, in all cases, performed by more pastors than one, or whether it was ever the act of a single pastor. The former appears to have been the fact in the case of the seven deacons, of Paul and Barnabas, and some few others. (*z*) But Paul speaks of himself as having laid hands upon Timothy, without any mention of many others having united with him. "I put thee in remembrance, that thou

(*x*) Gen. xlviii. 14. (*y*) Matt. xix. 15. (*z*) Acts vi. 6; xiii. 3.

stir up the gift of God which is in thee, by the putting on of my hands." (*a*) His expression, in the other Epistle, of "the laying on of the hands of the presbytery," (*b*) I apprehend not to signify a company of elders, but to denote the ordination itself; as if he had said, Take care that the grace which thou receivedst by the laying on of hands, when I ordained thee a presbyter, be not in vain.

(*a*) 2 Tim. i. 6. (*b*) 1 Tim. iv. 14.

CHAPTER IV

The State of the Ancient Church, and the Mode of Government Practised Before the Papacy

HITHERTO we have treated of the mode of government in the Church, as it has been delivered to us by the pure word of God, and of the offices in it, as they were instituted by Christ. Now, that all these things may be more clearly and familiarly displayed, and more deeply impressed upon our minds, it will be useful to examine what was the form of the ancient Church, in these particulars. It will place before our eyes an actual exemplification of the Divine institution. For though the bishops of those times published many canons, in which they seemed to express more than had been expressed in the Holy Scriptures, yet they were so cautious in framing their whole economy according to the sole standard of the word of God, that in this respect scarcely any thing can be detected among them inconsistent with that word. But though there might be something to be regretted in their regulations, yet because they directed their sincere and zealous efforts to preserve the institution of God, without deviating from it to any considerable extent, it will be highly useful in this place to give a brief sketch of what their practice was. As we have stated that there are three kinds of ministers recommended to us in the Scripture, so the ancient Church divided all the ministers it had into three orders. For from the order of presbyters, they chose some for pastors and teachers; the others presided over the discipline and corrections. To the deacons was committed the care of the poor and the distribution of the alms. *Readers* and *Acolytes* were not names of certain offices, but young men, to whom they also gave the name of *clergy*, whom they accustomed from their youth to certain exercises in the service of the Church, that they might better understand to what they were destined, and might enter upon their office better prepared for it in due time; as I shall soon show more at large. Therefore Jerome, after having mentioned five orders of the Church, enumerates bishops, presbyters, deacons, the faithful, or believers at large, and catechumens, or persons who had not yet been baptized, but had applied for instruction in the Christian faith. Thus he assigns no particular place to the rest of the clergy and the monks.

II. All those to whom the office of teaching was assigned, were denominated presbyters. To guard against dissension, the general consequence of equality, the presbyters in each city chose one of their own number, whom they distiguished by the title of *bishop*. The bishop, however, was not so superior to the rest in honour and dignity, as to have any dominion over his colleagues; but the functions performed by a consul in the senate, such as, to propose things for consideration, to collect the votes, to preside over the rest in the exercise of advice, admonition, and exhortation, to regulate all the proceedings by his authority, and to carry into execution whatever had been decreed by the general voice;—such were the functions exercised by the bishop in the assembly of the presbyters. And that this arrangement was introduced by human agreement, on account of the necessity of the times, is acknowledged by the ancient writers themselves. Thus Jerome, on the Epistle to Titus, says, "A presbyter is the same as a bishop. And before dissensions in religion were produced by the instigation of the devil, and one said, I am of Paul, and another, I am of Cephas, the Churches were governed by a common council of presbyters. Afterwards, in order to destroy the seeds of dissensions, the whole charge was committed to one. Therefore, as the presbyters know that according to the custom of the Church they are subject to the bishop who presides over them, so let the bishops know that their superiority to the presbyters is more from custom than from the appointment of the Lord, and they ought to unite together in the government of the Church." In another place, he shows the antiquity of this institution; for he says, that at Alexandria, even from Mark the Evangelist to Heraclas and Dionysius, the presbyters always chose one of their body to preside over them, whom they called their bishop. Every city, therefore, had its college of presbyters, who were pastors and teachers. For they all executed the duties of teaching, exhorting, and correcting, among the people, as Paul enjoins bishops to do; (*c*) and in order to leave successors behind them, they laboured in training young men, who had enlisted themselves in the sacred warfare. To every city was assigned a certain district, which received presbyters from it, and was reckoned as a part of that Church. Every assembly, as I have stated, for the sole purpose of preserving order and peace, was under the direction of one bishop, who, while he had the precedence of all others in dignity, was himself subject to the assembly of the brethren. If the territory placed under his episcopate was too extensive to admit of his discharging all the duties of a bishop in every part of it, presbyters were appointed in certain stations, to act as his deputies in things of minor importance. These were called *chorepiscopi*, or *country bishops,* because in the country they represented the bishop.

III. But with respect to the office of which we are now treating, the bishops and presbyters were equally required to employ themselves in the dispensation of the word and sacraments. For at Alexandria only, because Arius had disturbed the Church there, it was ordained that no presbyter should preach to the people; as is asserted by Socrates in the ninth book of his Tripartite History, with which Jerome hesitates not to express his dissatisfaction. It would certainly have been regarded as a prodigy, if any man had claimed the character of a bishop, who had not shown himself really such in his conduct. Such was the strictness of those times, that all ministers were constrained to discharge the duties which the Lord requires of them. I refer not to the custom of one age only; for even in the time of Gregory, when the Church was

(*c*) Titus i. 9.

almost extinct, or at least had considerably degenerated from its ancient purity, it would not have been permitted for any bishop to abstain from preaching. Gregory somewhere says, "A priest dies, if his sound be not heard; (*d*) for he provokes the wrath of the invisible Judge against him, if he go without the sound of preaching." And in another place: "When Paul declares that he is 'pure from the blood of all,' (*e*) by this declaration, we, who are called priests, are convicted, confounded, and declared to be guilty, who to all our own crimes add the deaths of others; for we are chargeable with slaying all those whom we daily behold advancing to death, while we are indifferent and silent." He calls himself and others silent, because they were less assiduous in their work than they ought to be. Since he spares not those who performed half of their duty, what is it probable he would have done, if any one had neglected it altogether? It was therefore long maintained in the Church, that the principal office of a bishop was to feed the people with the word of God, or to edify the Church both in public and private with sound doctrine.

IV. The establishment of one archbishop over all the bishops of each province, and the appointment of patriarchs at the Council of Nice, with rank and dignity superior to the archbishops, were regulations for the preservation of discipline. In this disquisition, however, what was of the least frequent use cannot be wholly omitted. The principal reason, therefore, for the institution of these orders was, that if any thing should take place in any Church which could not be settled by a few persons, it might be referred to a provincial synod. If the magnitude or difficulty of the case required a further discussion, the patriarchs were called to unite with the synods; and from them there could be no appeal but to a general council. This constitution of government some called a *hierarchy*—a name, in my opinion, improper, and certainly not used in the Scriptures. For it has been the design of the Holy Spirit, in every thing relating to the government of the Church, to guard against any dreams of principality or dominion. But if we look at the *thing*, without regarding the *term*, we shall find that the ancient bishops had no intention of contriving a form

(*d*) Exod. xxxviii. 35. (*e*) Acts xx. 26.

of government for the Church, different from that which God has prescribed in his word.

V. Nor was the situation of deacons at that time at all different from what it had been under the apostles. For they received the daily contributions of believers and the annual revenues of the Church, to apply them to their proper uses, that is, to distribute part to the ministers, and part for the support of the poor; subject, however, to the authority of the bishop, to whom they also rendered an account of their administration every year. For when the canons invariably represent the bishop as the dispenser of all the benefactions of the Church, it is not to be understood as if he executed that charge himself, but because it belonged to him to give directions to the deacon, who were to be entirely supported from the funds of the Church, to whom the remainder was to be distributed, and in what proportion to each person; and because he had the superintendence over the deacon, to examine whether he faithfully discharged his office. Thus the canons, ascribed to the apostles, contain the following injunction: "We ordain that the bishop do have the property of the Church in his own power. For if the souls of men, which are of superior value, have been intrusted to him, there is far greater propriety in his taking charge of the pecuniary concerns; so that all things may be distributed to the poor by his authority through the presbyters and deacons, and that they may be administered with reverence, and all concern." And in the Council of Antioch it was decreed, that those bishops should be censured who managed the pecuniary concerns of the Church without the concurrence of the presbyters and deacons. But it is unnecessary to argue this point any further, since it is evident from many epistles of Gregory, that even in his time, when the administration of the Church was in other respects become very corrupt, yet this custom was still retained, that the deacons were the stewards for the relief of the poor, under the authority of the bishop. It is probable that subdeacons were at first attached to the deacons, to assist them in transacting the business of the poor; but this distinction was soon lost. Archdeacons were first erected when the extent of the property required a new and more accurate mode of administration; though Jerome states that there were such offices even in his time. In their hands was placed the amount of the annual revenues, of the possessions, and of the household furniture, and the management of the daily contributions. Whence Gregory denounces to the archdeacon of Thessalonica, that he would be held guilty, if any of the property of the Church should be lost by him, either through negligence or fraud. Their appointment to read the gospel, and to exhort the people to pray, and their admission to the administration of the cup in the sacred supper, were intended to dignify their office, that they might discharge it with the more piety, in consequence of being admonished by such ceremonies, that they were not executing some profane stewardship, but that their function was spiritual and dedicated to God.

VI. Hence it is easy to judge what use was made of the property of the Church, and in what manner it was dispensed. We often find it stated, both in the decrees of the councils, and by the ancient writers, that whatever the Church possessed, whether in lands or in money, was the patrimony of the poor. The bishops and deacons, therefore, are continually reminded that they are not managing their own treasures, but those destined to supply the necessity of the poor, which if they unfaithfully withhold or embezzle, they will be guilty of murder. Hence they are admonished to distribute this property to the parties entitled to it, with the greatest caution and reverence, as in the sight of God, and without respect of persons. Hence also the solemn protestations of Chrysostom, Ambrose, Augustine, and other bishops, assuring the people of their integrity. Now, since it is perfectly equitable, and sanctioned by the law of the Lord, that those who are employed in the service of the Church should be maintained at the public expense of the Church,—and even in that age some presbyters consecrated their patrimonies to God, and reduced themselves to voluntary poverty,—the distribution was such, that neither were the ministers left without support, nor were the poor neglected. Yet, at the same time, care was taken that the ministers themselves who ought to set an example of frugality to others, should not have enough to be abused to the purposes of splendour or delicacy, but only what would suffice to supply their necessities. "For," says Jerome, "those of the clergy who are able to maintain themselves from their own patrimony, if they take what belongs to the poor, are guilty of sacrilege, and by such an abuse, they eat and drink judgment to themselves."

VII. At first the administration was free and voluntary, the bishops and deacons acting with spontaneous fidelity, and integrity of conscience and innocence of life supplying the place of laws. Afterwards, when the cupidity or corrupt dispositions of some gave birth to evil examples, in order to correct these abuses, canons were made, which divided the revenues of the Church into four parts, assigning the first to the clergy, the second to the poor, the third to the reparation of Churches and other buildings, the fourth to poor strangers. For, though other canons assign this last part to the bishop, this forms no variation from the division which I have mentioned. For the intention was that it should be appropriated to him, neither for his own exclusive consumption, nor for lavish or arbitrary distribution, but to enable him to support the hospitality which Paul requires of persons in that office. (*f*) And so it is explained by Gelasius and Gregory. For Gelasius adduces no other reason why the bishop should claim any thing for himself, than to enable him to communicate to captives and strangers. And Gregory is still more explicit. He says, "It is the custom of the apostolic see, at the ordination of a bishop, to command him that all the revenue received by him be divided into four portions; namely, one for the bishop and his family, for the support of hospitality and entertainment; the second for the clergy; the third for the poor; the fourth for the reparation of Churches." It was unlawful for the bishop, therefore, to take for his own use any thing more than was sufficient for moderate and frugal sustenance and clothing. If any one began to transgress the due limits, either in luxury, or in ostentation and pomp, he was immediately admonished by his colleagues; and if he would not comply with the admonition, he was deposed from his office.

VIII. The portion which they applied to ornament the sacred edifices, at first was very small; and even after the Church was become a little more wealthy, they did not exceed moderation in this respect: whatever money was so employed, still continued

---

(*f*) 1 Tim. iii. 2, 3.

to be held in reserve for the poor, if any pressing necessity should occur. Thus, when famine prevailed in the province of Jerusalem, and there was no other way of relieving their wants, Cyril sold the vessels and vestments, and expended the produce in purchasing sustenance for the poor. In like manner, when vast numbers of the Persians were almost perishing with hunger, Acatius, bishop of Amida, after having convoked his clergy, and made that celebrated speech, "Our God has no need of dishes or cups, because he neither eats nor drinks," melted down the vessels, and converted them into money, to redeem the wretched, and buy food for them. Jerome also, while he inveighs against the excessive splendour of the temples, makes honourable mention of Exuperius, at that time bishop of Thoulouse, who administered the emblem of our Lord's body in a wicker basket, and the emblem of his blood in a glass, but suffered no poor person to endure hunger. The same that I have just said of Acatius, Ambrose relates of himself; for when he was censured by the Arians for having broken up the sacred vessels to pay the ransom of some captives, he made the following most excellent defence: "He who sent forth the apostles without gold, gathered Churches together likewise without gold. The Church has gold, not to keep, but to expend, and to furnish relief in necessities. What need is there to keep that which is of no service? Do not we know how much gold and silver the Assyrians plundered from the temple of the Lord? Is it not better that it should be melted down by the priest for the sustenance of the poor, if other resources are wanting, than that it should be carried away by a sacrilegious enemy? Will not the Lord say, Wherefore hast thou suffered so many poor to die with hunger, and at the same time hadst gold, with which thou mightest have supplied them with food? Why have so many been carried away into captivity, and never been redeemed? Why have so many been slain by the enemy? It would have been better to preserve the vessels of living beings, than those of metals. To these questions you could make no answer. For what would you say? I was afraid that the temple of God would be destitute of ornament. God would reply, The sacraments require no gold, nor is gold any recommendation of that which is not purchased with gold. The ornament of the sacraments is the redemption of captives." In short, we see that it was very true which was observed by the same writer in another place, "that whatever the Church possessed at that time, was appropriated to the relief of the necessitous," and "that all that a bishop had, belonged to the poor."

IX. These, which we have enumerated, were the offices of the ancient Church. Others, which are mentioned by ecclesiastical historians, were rather exercises and preparations, than certain offices. For to form a seminary, which should provide the Church with future ministers, those holy men took under their charge, protection, and discipline, such youths as, with the consent and sanction of their parents, enlisted themselves in the spiritual warfare; and so they educated them from an early age, that they might not enter on the discharge of their office ignorant and unprepared. All who were trained in this manner, were called by the general name of *clergy*. I could wish, indeed, that some other more appropriate name had been given them; for this appellation originated in error, or at least in some improper views; for Peter calls the whole Church *the clergy*, that is, *the inheritance of the Lord.* (*g*) The institution itself, however, was pious and eminently beneficial; that those who wished to consecrate themselves and their labours to the Church, should be educated under the care of the bishop; that no one might minister in the Church but one who had received sufficient previous instruction, who from his early youth had imbibed sound doctrine, who from a strict discipline had acquired a certain habitual gravity, and more than common sanctity of life, who had been abstracted from secular occupations, and accustomed to spiritual cares and studies. Now, as young soldiers by counterfeit battles are trained to real and serious warfare, so the clergy were prepared by certain probationary exercises, before they were actually promoted to offices. At first they were charged with the care of opening and shutting the temples, and they were called *ostiarii*, or *door-keepers.* Afterwards they were called *acoluthi*, or *followers*, waiting upon the bishop in domestic services, and accompanying him on all occasions, at first

(*g*) 1 Peter v. 3.

in a way of honour, and afterwards to prevent all suspicion; moreover, that by degrees they might become known to the people, and might acquire some consideration among them, and at the same time that they might learn to bear the presence of all, and have courage to speak before them, that after being made presbyters, when they should come to preach, they might not be confounded with shame, therefore they were appointed to read the Scriptures from the pulpit. In this manner they were promoted by degrees, that they might approve their diligence in the respective exercises, till they were made subdeacons. I only contend, that these were rather preparations for pupils, than functions reckoned among the real offices of the Church.

X. We have said, that the first point in the election of ministers related to the qualifications of the persons to be chosen, and the second to the religious reverence with which the business ought to be conducted. In both these points, the ancient Church followed the direction of Paul and the examples of the apostles. For it was their custom to assemble for the election of pastors with the greatest reverence and solemn invocation of the name of God. They had likewise a form of examination, in which they tried the life and doctrine of the candidates by that standard of Paul. Only they ran into the error of immoderate severity, from a wish to require in a bishop more than Paul requires, and especially, in process of time, by enjoining celibacy. In other things their practice was in conformity with the description of Paul. (*h*) In the third point which we have mentioned, namely, by whom ministers ought to be chosen, they did not always observe the same order. In the primitive times there was no one admitted among the number of the clergy, without the consent of all the people; so that Cyprian makes a laboured defence of his having appointed one Aurelius a reader, without consulting the Church, because he departed in this instance from the general custom, though not without reason. He begins in the following manner: "In appointing the clergy, my very dear brethren, we are accustomed first to consult you, and to weigh the morals and merits of every one of them in the general assembly." But as there was not much

---

(*h*) 1 Tim. iii. 2—7.

danger in these inferior exercises, because they were admitted to a long probation, and not to a high office, the consent of the people ceased to be asked. Afterwards, in the other offices also, except the episcopate, the people generally left the judgment and choice to the bishop and presbyters, so that they determined who were capable and deserving; except when new presbyters were appointed to the parishes, for then it was necessary to have the express consent of the body of the people at each place. Nor is it any wonder that the people were not very solicitous for the preservation of their right in this case. For no one was made a subdeacon, who had not been tried for a considerable time as one of the *clergy*, under the severe discipline which was then practised. After he had been tried in that station, he was constituted a deacon; in which if he conducted himself with fidelity, he obtained the rank of a presbyter. Thus no one was promoted who had not really undergone an examination for many years, under the eyes of the people. And there were many canons for the punishment of their faults; so that the Church could not be troubled with wicked presbyters or deacons, unless it neglected the remedies within its reach. The election of presbyters, however, always required the consent of the inhabitants of the place; which is testified by the first canon, which is attributed to Anacletus. And all ordinations took place at stated times of the year, that no one might be introduced clandestinely, without the consent of the faithful, or be promoted with too much facility, without any attestation to his character.

XI. The right of voting in the election of bishops was retained by the people for a long time, that no one might be obtruded who was not acceptable to all. The Council of Antioch therefore decreed, that no bishop should be appointed without the consent of the people, which Leo the First expressly confirms. Hence the following injunctions: "Let him be chosen who shall be called for by the clergy and people, or at least by the majority of them." Again: "Let him who is to preside over all, be chosen by all." For he who is appointed without having been previously known and examined, must of necessity be intruded by force. Again: "Let him be elected who shall have been chosen by the clergy and desired by the people; and let him be consecrated by the bishops of that province, with the authority of the metropolitan. So careful were the holy fathers that this liberty of the people should not by any means be infringed, that when the general council, assembled at Constantinople, appointed Nectarius, they would not do it without the approbation of all the clergy and people; as is evident from their epistle to the Council of Rome. Wherefore, when any bishop appointed his successor, the appointment was not confirmed but by the suffrages of all the people. Of such a circumstance we have not only an example, but the particular form in Augustine's nomination of Eradius. And Theodoret, when he states that Peter was nominated by Athanasius as his successor, immediately adds, that this was confirmed by the clergy, and ratified by the acclamations of the magistracy, the nobility, and all the people.

XII. I confess that there was the greatest propriety in the decree of the Council of Laodicea, that the election should not be left to the populace. For it scarcely ever happens that so many heads concur in one opinion for the settlement of any business; and almost every case verifies the observation, that the uncertain vulgar are divided by contrary inclinations. But to this danger was applied an excellent remedy. For in the first place, the clergy alone made their choice, and presented the person they had chosen to the magistracy, or to the senate and governors. They deliberated on the election, and if it appeared to them a proper one, confirmed it, or otherwise chose another person whom they preferred. Then the business was referred to the multitude, who, though they were nor bound to concur in these previous opinions, yet were less ıikely to be thrown into disorder. Or if the business commenced with the multitude, this method was adopted in order to discover who was the principal object of their wishes; and after hearing the wishes of the people, the clergy proceeded to the election. Thus the clergy were neither at liberty to elect whom they pleased, nor under a necessity of complying with the foolish desires of the people. This order is stated by Leo in another place, when he says, "It is requisite to have the votes of the citizens, the testimonies of the people, the authority of the governors, and the election of the clergy." Again: "Let there be the testimony of the governors, the subscription of the clergy, the consent of the senate and people. Reason permits it not to be done in any other way." Nor is there any other meaning in that decree of the Council of Laodicea, than that the clergy and governors should not suffer themselves to be carried away by the inconsiderate multitude, but by their prudence and gravity should check, on every necessary occasion, the folly and violence of popular desires.

XIII. This mode of election was still practised in the time of Gregory, and it is probable that it continued long after. There are many of his epistles which furnish sufficient evidence of this fact. For in every case relating to the creation of a new bishop in any place, he was accustomed to write to the clergy, the senate, and the people; and sometimes to the duke, according to the constitution of the government in the place to which he was writing. And if, on account of disturbances or dissensions in any Church, he confides the superintendence of the election to some neighbouring bishop, yet he invariably requires a solemn decree confirmed by the subscriptions of all. Even when one Constantius was created bishop of Milan, and on account of the incursions of the barbarians, many of the Milanese had retired to Genoa, he thought the election would not be legitimate, unless they also were called together, and gave their united consent. And what is more, it was within the last five hundred years that Pope Nicholas made this decree respecting the election of the Roman pontiff; that the cardinals should take the lead, that in the next place they should unite with them the rest of the clergy, and lastly that the election should be confirmed by the consent of the people. And at the conclusion he recites that decree of Leo, which I have just quoted, and commands it to be observed in future. If the cabals of the wicked should go to such a length as to constrain the clergy to quit the city in order to make a proper election, still he ordains that some of the people should be present at the same time. The consent of the emperor, as far as I can discover, was required only in two Churches, at Rome and at Constantinople, because they were the two capitals of the empire. For when Ambrose was sent to Milan with authority from Valentinian to preside at the election of a new bishop, that was an extraordinary measure, in consequence of the grievous factions which raged among the citizens. At Rome the authority of the emperor had anciently so much influence in the creation of a bishop, that Gregory speaks of himself as having been appointed to the government of the Church by the sole command of the emperor, notwithstanding he had been formally chosen by the people. But the custom was, that when any one had been chosen by the senate, clergy, and people, it was immediately reported to the emperor, that he might either ratify the election by his approbation, or rescind it by his negative. Nor is there any thing repugnant to this custom in the decrees collected by Gratian; which only say, that it is by no means to be suffered that a king should supersede all canonical election by appointing a bishop at his own pleasure, and that the metropolitans ought not to consecrate any one who shall thus have been promoted by the violence of power. For it is one thing to spoil the Church of its right, by transferring the whole to the caprice of an individual, and another to give a king or an emperor the honour of confirming a legitimate election by his authority.

XIV. It remains for us to state, by what ceremony the ministers of the ancient Church, after their election, were initiated into their office. This the Latins have called *ordination* or *consecration.* The Greeks have called it χειροτονια, *extension* or *elevation of hands*, and sometimes χειροθεσια, *imposition of hands;* though the former word properly signifies that kind of election in which the suffrages are declared by the lifting up of the hands. There is a decree of the Council of Nice, that the metropolitan should meet with all the bishops of the province, to ordain him who shall have been elected; but that if any of them be prevented by the length of the journey, by sickness, or by any other necessary cause, at least three should meet, and those who are absent should testify their consent by letters. And when this canon from disuse had grown obsolete, it was renewed in various councils. Now, the reason why all, or at least as many as had no sufficient excuse, were commanded to be present, was that there might be a more solemn examination into the learning and morals of the person to be ordained; for the business was not completed without examination. And it appears from the epistles of Cyprian, that in the beginning the bishops were not invited after the election, but used to be present at the election, and that for the purpose of acting as moderators, that nothing turbulent might take place among the multitude. For after having said that the people have the power either to choose the worthy for priests, or to reject the unworthy, he adds, "Wherefore it is to be carefully held and observed as a Divine and apostolical tradition, (which is observed among us, and in almost all the provinces,) that for the due performance of ordinations, all the neighbouring bishops of the same province should meet with the people over whom a bishop is to be ordained, and that the bishop should be chosen in the presence of the people." But because such an assembly was sometimes very slowly collected, and there was danger that such a delay might be abused by some for the purposes of intrigue, it was deemed sufficient, if they assembled after the election was made, and upon due examination consecrated the person who had been chosen.

XV. This was the universal practice, without any exception. By degrees a different custom was introduced, and the persons elected went to the metropolitan city to seek ordination. This change arose from ambition and a corruption of the ancient institution, rather than from any good reason. And not long after, when the authority of the see of Rome had increased, another custom obtained, which was still worse; almost all the bishops of Italy went to Rome to be consecrated. This may be seen by the epistles of Gregory. Only a few cities, which did not so easily yield, preserved their ancient right; of which there is an example recorded by him in the case of Milan. Perhaps the metropolitan cities were the only ones that retained their privilege. For almost all the provincial bishops used to assemble in the metropolitan city to consecrate their archbishop. The ceremony was imposition of hands. For I read of no other ceremony practised, except that in the public assembly the bishops had some dress to distinguish them from the rest of the presbyters. Presbyters and deacons also were ordained solely by imposition of hands. But every bishop ordained his own presbyters, in conjunction with the assembly of the other presbyters of his diocese. Now, though they all united in the same act, yet because the bishop took the lead, and the ceremony was performed under his direction, therefore it was called his ordination. Wherefore it is often remarked by the ancient writers, that a presbyter differs from a bishop in no other respect, than that he does not possess the power of ordination.

CHAPTER V

The Ancient Form of Government Entirely Subverted by the Papal Tyranny

Now, it is proper to exhibit the system of ecclesiastical government at present maintained by the see of Rome, and all its dependencies, with a full view of that hierarchy which is perpetually in their mouths, and to compare it with the description we have given of the primitive and ancient Church. This comparison will show what kind of a Church there is among those who fiercely arrogate this exclusive title, in order to oppress, or rather to overwhelm us. Now, it is best to begin with the vocation, that we may see who and what kind of men are called to the ministry, and how they are introduced to it. We shall then consider how faithfully they discharge their duty. We shall give the first place to the bishops; and I wish it might be to their honour to hold the first rank in this disquisition. But the subject itself will not permit me to touch on this argument ever so slightly, without involving their deepest disgrace. I shall remember, however, the nature of the work in which I am now engaged, and shall not suffer my discourse, which ought to be confined to simple doctrine, to exceed its proper bounds. But let some one of those who have not lost all shame, answer me; What kind of bishops are now generally chosen? To examine into their learning, is too obsolete; and if any regard be paid to it, they choose some lawyer, who understands pleading in a court, better than preaching in a Church. It is evident, that for a hundred years, scarcely one in a hundred that has been chosen, had any knowledge of the Holy Scripture. I say nothing of the preceding ages; not that they were much better, but because our business is only with the present Church. If we inquire into their morals, we shall find that there have been few or none who would not have been judged unworthy by the ancient canons. He who has not been a drunkard, has been a fornicator; and he who has been free from both these vices, has been either a gambler or a hunter, or dissolute in some part of his life. For the old canons exclude a man from the episcopal office for smaller vices than these. But the greatest absurdity of all is, that even boys, scarcely ten years of age, have by the permission of the pope been made bishops. And to such lengths of impudence and stupidity have they proceeded, as not to be afraid of that extreme and monstrous enormity, which is altogether repugnant to the common sense of nature. Hence it appears how solemn and conscientious must have been their elections, which were marked with such extreme negligence.

II. All the right of the people to choose has been entirely taken away. Their suffrages, assent, subscriptions, and every thing of this kind, have disappeared. All the power is transferred to the canons. They confer the bishopric on whom they please, and then produce him before the people, but to be adored, not to be examined. Leo, on the contrary, exclaims that no reason permits this, and pronounces it to be a violent imposition. When Cyprian declares it to be of Divine right, that an election should not be made without the consent of the people, he shows that a different method is repugnant to the word of God. The decrees of various councils most severely prohibit it to be done in any other way, and if it be done, command it to be void. If these things be true, there is now no canonical election remaining in all the Papacy, either according to Divine or ecclesiastical right. Now, though there were no other evil, how will they be able to excuse themselves for having thus deprived the Church of her right? But they say, the corruption of the times required, that as the people and magistrates, in the choice of bishops, were rather carried away by antipathies and partialities than governed by an honest and correct judgment, the decision of this business should be intrusted to a few. Let it be admitted that this was an extreme remedy for a disease under desperate circumstances. Yet as the medicine has been found more injurious than the disease itself, why is there no remedy provided against this new malady? They reply, The canons themselves have been particularly directed what course they ought to pursue in an election. But do we doubt, that the people formerly understood themselves to be bound by the most sacred laws, when they saw the word of God proposed as their rule, whenever they assembled for the election of a bishop? For that one declaration of God, in which he describes the true character of a bishop, ought to have more weight than millions of canons. Yet, corrupted by a most sinful disposition, they paid no regard to law or equity. So in the present day, though there are the best written laws, yet they remain buried in paper. At the same time, it has been the general practice, and, as if it were founded in reason, has obtained the general approbation, that drunkards, fornicators, and gamblers, have been promoted to this honour I do not say enough. Bishoprics are the rewards of adulterers and panders. For when they are given to hunters and fowlers, the business must be considered as well managed. To attempt any excuse of such flagitious proceedings is abominable. The people, I say, had a most excellent canon, in the direction of the word of God, that "a bishop must be blameless, apt to teach, no striker," &c. (*i*) Why, then, was the right of election transferred from the people to the canons? They reply, Because the word of God was not attended to, amidst the tumults and factions of the people. And why should it not now be again transferred from them, who not only violate all laws, but, casting off all shame, mingle and confound heaven and earth together, by their lust, avarice, and ambition?

III. But it is a false pretence when they say, that the present practice was introduced as a remedy. We read that in the early times, cities were frequently thrown into confusion at the election of their bishops; yet no one ever dared to think of depriving the citizens of their right. For they had other ways, either of guarding

---

(*i*) 1 Tim. iii. 2—7.

against these evils, or of correcting them when they occurred. But I will state the real truth of the case. When the people began to be negligent about choosing, and, considering this care as less suitable to themselves, left it to the presbyters, the latter abused this occasion to usurp a tyrannical power, which they afterwards confirmed to themselves by new canons. Their form of ordination is no other than a mere mockery. For the appearance of examination which they display in it, is so frivolous and jejune, that it is even destitute of all plausibility. The power of nominating bishops, therefore, which some princes have obtained by stipulation with the Roman pontiff, has caused no new injury to the Church, because the election has only been taken from the canons, who had seized, or rather stolen, it without any just claim. It is certainly a most disgraceful example, that courtiers are made bishops, and sent from the court to seize upon the Churches; and it ought to be the concern of all pious princes to refrain from such an abuse. For it is an impious robbery of the Church, whenever a bishop is imposed upon any people, who have not desired, or at least freely approved of him. But the disorderly custom which has long prevailed in the Churches, has given occasion to princes to assume the presentation of bishops to themselves. For they would rather have this at their own disposal, than in the hands of those who had no more right to it, and by whom it was not less abused.

IV. This is the goodly calling, in consequence of which bishops boast of being successors of the apostles. The power of creating presbyters, they say, belongs exclusively to them. But this is a gross corruption of the ancient institution; for by their ordination they create, not presbyters to rule and feed the people, but priests to offer sacrifice. So when they consecrate deacons, they have nothing to do with their true and proper office, but only ordain them to certain ceremonies about the chalice and patine. In the Council of Chalcedon, on the contrary, it was decreed, that there should be no absolute ordinations, that is, without some place being at the same time assigned to the persons ordained, where they were to exercise their office. This decree was highly useful, for two reasons—first, that the Churches might not be burdened with an unnecessary charge, and the money which ought to be distributed to the poor consumed upon idle men; secondly, that the persons ordained might consider themselves not as promoted to an honour, but as intrusted with an office to the discharge of which they were bound by a solemn engagement. But the Romish doctors, who think their belly ought to be all their care, even in matters of religion, first explain the requisite title to consist in an income sufficient for their support, whether arising from their own patrimony or from a benefice. Therefore, when they ordain a deacon or a presbyter, without giving themselves any concern where he is to officiate, they readily admit him, if he be only rich enough to maintain himself. But who can admit this, that the title which the decree of the council requires is a competent annual income? And because the more recent canons condemned the bishops to maintain those whom they had ordained without a sufficient title, in order to prevent their too great facility in the admission of candidates, they have even contrived a way to evade this penalty. For the person ordained mentions any title whatever, and promises that he will be content with it. By this engagement he is debarred from an action for maintenance. I say nothing of a thousand frauds practised in this business; as when some falsely exhibit empty titles of benefices, from which they could not derive five pence a year; others, under a secret stipulation, borrow benefices which they promise to return immediately, but which, in many instances, are never returned; and other similar mysteries.

V. But even though these grosser abuses were removed, is it not always absurd to ordain a presbyter without assigning him any station? For they ordain no one, but to offer sacrifice. Now, the legitimate ordination of a presbyter consists in a call to the government of the Church, and that of a deacon to the collection of the alms. They adorn their procedure, indeed, with many pompous ceremonies, that its appearance may gain the veneration of the simple; but with judicious persons, what can be gained by those appearances unaccompanied by any solidity or truth? For they use ceremonies either derived from Judaism, or invented among themselves, from which it would be better to refrain. But as to any real examination, the consent of the people, and other necessary things, they are not mentioned. The shadow they retain of these things, I consider not worthy of notice. By shadow, I mean those ridiculous gesticulations, used as a dull and foolish imitation of antiquity. The bishops have their vicars, to inquire before an ordination, into the learning of the candidates. But in what manner? They interrogate them, whether they can read their masses; whether they know how to decline some common noun that may occur in reading, or to conjugate a verb, or to tell the meaning of a word; for it is not necessary for them to know how to give the sense of a verse. And yet none are rejected from the priesthood, who are deficient even in these puerile elements, provided they bring some present or recommendation to favour. In the same spirit it is, that when the persons to be ordained present themselves at the altar, some one inquires three times, in a language not understood, whether they are worthy of that honour. One (who never saw them before, but, that no part of the process might be wanting, acts his part in the farce) answers, They are worthy. What accusation is there against these venerable fathers, but that by sporting with such manifest sacrileges they are guilty of unblushing mockery of God and men? But because they have been long in possession of it, they suppose it is now become right. For whoever ventures to open his mouth against these glaring and atrocious enormities, they hurry him away to execution, as if he had committed a capital crime. Would they do this if they believed that there was any God?

VI. Now, how much better do they conduct themselves in the collation of benefices?—a thing formerly connected with ordination, but now entirely separated from it. The ways in which this business is managed, are various. For the bishops are not the only persons who confer benefices, and in those the collation of which is ascribed to them, they do not always possess the full power, but while they retain the name of the collation for the sake of honour, the presentation belongs to others. Besides these, there are nominations from the colleges, resignations either absolute or made for the sake of exchange, commendatory rescripts, preventions, and the like. But they all conduct themselves in such a manner, that no one can reproach another for any thing. I maintain that scarcely one benefice in a hundred, in all the Papacy, is at present conferred without simony, according to the definition which the ancients gave of that crime. I do not say that they all purchase with ready money; but show me one in twenty who obtains a benefice without any indirect recommendation. Some are promoted by relationship, others by alliance, others by the influence of parents, others gain favour by their services. In short, the end for which sacerdotal offices are conferred, is not to provide for the Churches, but for the persons to whom they are given. And therefore they call them *benefices,* a name by which they sufficiently declare that they view them in no other light than as donatives of princes, by which they either conciliate the favour of their soldiers, or reward their services. I forbear to remark that these rewards are conferred upon barbers, cooks, muleteers, and other dregs of the people. And, in the present day, scarcely any litigations make more noise in the courts of justice than those respecting benefices; so that they may be considered as a mere prey thrown out for dogs to hunt after. Is it tolerable even to hear the name of *pastors* given to men who have forced themselves into the possession of a Church, as into an enemy's farm; who have obtained it by a legal process; who have purchased it with money; who have gained it by dishonourable services; who, while infants just beginning to lisp, succeeded to it as an inheritance transmitted by their uncles and cousins, and sometimes even by fathers to their illegitimate children?

VII. Would the licentiousness of the people, however corrupt and lawless, ever have proceeded to such a length? But it is still more monstrous that one man—I say nothing of his qualifications, only a man not capable of governing himself—should preside over the government of five or six Churches. We may now see, in the courts of princes, young men who hold one archbishopric, two bishoprics, and three abbeys. It is a common thing for canons to be loaded with five, six, or seven benefices, of which they take not the least care, except in receiving the revenues. I will not object that this is every where condemned by the word of God, which has long ceased to have the least weight with them. I will not object that various councils have made many very severe decrees against such disorder; for these also, whenever they please, they fearlessly treat with contempt. But I maintain, that both these things are execrable enormities, utterly repugnant to God, to nature, and to the government of the Church—that one robber should engross several Churches at once, and that the name of *pastor* should be given to one who could not be present with his flock, even if he would; and yet, such is their impudence, they cover these abominable impurities with the name of the Church, in order to exempt them from all censure. And, moreover, that inviolable succession, to the merit of which they boast that the Church owes its perpetual preservation, is included in these iniquities.

VIII. Now, let us see how faithfully they exercise their office, which is the second mark by which we are to judge of a legitimate pastor. Of the priests whom they create, some are *monks*, others are called *seculars*. The former of these classes was unknown to the ancient Church, and to hold such a place in the Church was so incompatible with the monastic profession, that anciently, when any one was chosen from a monastery to be one of the clergy, he ceased to be a monk. And even Gregory, in whose time there was much corruption, yet suffered not this confusion to take place. For he enjoined, that they who became abbots should be divested of their clerical character; for that no one could be a monk and a clergyman at the same time, because the one would be an impediment to the other. Now, if I inquire how that man can duly discharge his office, whom the canons declare to be unfit for it, what answer will they make? I suppose they will cite those abortive decrees of Innocent and Boniface, by which monks are admitted to the honour and authority of the priesthood, so that they may still remain in their monasteries. But what reason is there, that any illiterate ass, as soon as he has once occupied the see of Rome, should by one diminutive word overturn all the usages of antiquity? But of this we shall say more hereafter. Suffice it at present to remark, that during the purer times of the Church, it was deemed a great absurdity for a monk to hold the office of a priest. For Jerome denies that he performed the office of a priest while he lived among the monks; but represents himself as one of the people who ought to be governed by the priests. But if we grant them this point, how do they execute their office? There are some of the mendicants, and a few of the others, who preach. All the rest of the monks either chant or mutter over masses in their cloisters, as if it were the design of Jesus Christ that presbyters should be appointed for this purpose, or as if the nature of their office admitted of it. While the Scripture clearly testifies that it is the duty of a presbyter to govern his own Church, (*k*) is it not an impious profanation to transfer to another object, or rather to make a total change in, God's sacred institution? For when they are ordained monks, they are expressly forbidden to do things which the Lord enjoins upon all presbyters. This direction is given to them: Let a monk be content in his cloister, and not presume to administer the sacraments, or to execute any other branch of public duty. Let them deny, if they can, that it is a glaring mockery of God, to create a presbyter in order that he may refrain from discharging his true and genuine office, and to give a man the name, who cannot possess the thing.

IX. I proceed to the seculars; of whom some are called *beneficiaries*, that is, they have benefices by which they are maintained; others hire themselves to labour by the day, in saying mass or singing, and live on the wages which they gain from these employments. Benefices are either attended with cure of souls, as bishoprics and parishes; or they are the stipends of delicate men, who gain a livelihood by chanting, as prebends, canonries, dignities, chaplainships, and the like. But in the confusion which has been introduced, abbeys and priories are conferred not only on secular priests, but also on boys, by privilege, that is, by common and ordinary custom. As to the mercenaries, who seek their daily sustenance, how could they act otherwise than they do, that is, to offer themselves to hire in a mean and shameful manner; especially among such a vast multitude as now swarms in the world? Therefore, when they are ashamed of open begging, or think they should gain but little by that practice, they run about like hungry dogs, and by their importunity, as by barking, extort from reluctant hands some morsels to put into their mouths. Here if I should endeavour to describe what a great disgrace it is to the Church, that the office and dignity of the presbytery has been so degraded, there would be no end. My readers, therefore, have

---

(*k*) Acts xx. 28.

no reason to expect from me a long discourse, corresponding to such a flagitious enormity. I only assert, in few words, that if it be the duty of a presbyter, as the word of God prescribes, and the ancient canons require, to feed the Church and administer the spiritual kingdom of Christ, (*l*) all those priests who have no work or wages, except in making merchandise of masses, not only fail of executing their office, but have no legitimate office to execute. For there is no place assigned to them to teach; they have no people to govern. In short, nothing remains to them but the altar upon which to offer up Christ in sacrifice; and this is not sacrificing to God, but to demons, as we shall see in another place.

X. Here I touch not on the external vices, but only on the intestine evil which is deeply rooted in their institution, and cannot be separated from it. I shall add a remark, which will sound harshly in their ears, but because it is true, it must be expressed —that canons, deans, chaplains, provosts, and all who are supported by sinecures, are to be considered in the same light. For what service can they perform for the Church? They have discarded the preaching of the word, the superintendence of discipline, and the administration of the sacraments, as employments attended with too much labour and trouble. What have they remaining, then, to boast of as true presbyters? They have chanting and the pomp of ceremonies. But what is all this to the purpose? If they plead custom, usage, prescription of long continuance, I will confront them with the decision of Christ, where he has given us a description of true presbyters, and what qualifications ought to be possessed by those who wish to be considered as such. If they cannot bear so hard a law as to submit themselves to the rule of Christ, let them at least allow this cause to be decided by the authority of the primitive Church. But their condition will not be at all better, if we judge of their state by the ancient canons. Those who have degenerated into canons, ought to be presbyters, as they were in former times, to govern the Church in common with the bishop, and to be his colleagues in the pastoral office. These *chapter dignities*, as they call them, have nothing to do with the government of the Church; much less have the chaplainships,

---

(*l*) 1 Cor. iv. 1.

and the other dregs of similar offices. In what estimation, then, shall we hold them all? It is certain that the word of Christ and the practice of the ancient Church agree in excluding them from the honour of the presbytery. They contend, however, that they are presbyters; but the mask must be torn off. Then we shall find, that their whole profession is most foreign and remote from the office of presbyters, which is described to us by the apostles, and which was required in the primitive Church. All such orders, therefore, by whatever titles they may be distinguished, since they are of modern invention, or at least are not supported by the institution of God, or the ancient usage of the Church, ought to have no place in a description of the spiritual government, which the Church has received, consecrated by the mouth of the Lord himself. Or, if they wish me to use plainer language, since chaplains, canons, deans, provosts, and other idlers of this description, do not even with their little fingers touch a particle of that duty which is necessarily required in presbyters, it is not to be endured that they should falsely usurp the honour, and thus violate the sacred institution of Jesus Christ.

XI. There remain the bishops and the rectors of parishes, who would afford me great pleasure if they exerted themselves to support their office. For we would readily admit to them, that they have a pious and honourable office, provided they discharged it. But when they wish to be considered as pastors, notwithstanding they desert the churches committed to them, and transfer the care of them to others, they act just as if the office of a pastor consisted in doing nothing. If a usurer, who never stirred his foot out of the city, should profess himself a ploughman or vinedresser,—if a soldier, who had spent all his time in the camp and in the field of battle, and had never seen a court of justice or books, should offer himself as a lawyer,—who could endure such gross absurdities? But these men act in a manner still more absurd, who wish to be accounted and called legitimate pastors of the Church, and yet are not willing to be so in reality. For how few of them are there, who execute the government of their Churches even in appearance! Many of them all their lifetime devour the revenues of Churches, which they never approach even to look at them. Others either go themselves, or send an agent once every year, that nothing may be lost by farming them out. When this abuse first intruded itself, they who wished to enjoy this kind of vacation from duty, exempted themselves by special privileges. Now, it is a rare case for any one to reside in his own Church; for they consider their Churches as no other than farms, over which they place their vicars, as bailiffs or stewards. But it is repugnant to common sense, that a man should be pastor of a flock, who never saw one of the sheep.

XII. It appears that some seeds of this evil had sprung up in the time of Gregory, and that the rectors of Churches began to be negligent in preaching and teaching; for he heavily complains of it in the following passages: "The world is full of priests; but yet there are few labourers found in the harvest; because we undertake the sacerdotal office, but perform not the work of the office." Again: "Because they have no bowels of charity, they wish to be considered as lords; they do not acknowledge themselves to be fathers. They change the place of humility into an aggrandizement of dominion." Again: "But, O ye pastors, what are we doing, who receive the wages and are not labourers? We have fallen into extraneous employments; we undertake one thing, and perform another. We relinquish the office of preaching; and it is our misfortune, I conceive, that we are called bishops, since we hold a title of honour, but not of virtue." Since he uses such severity of language against those who were only chargeable with a want of sufficient assiduity, or diligence, in their office, what would he have said, if he had seen scarcely any, or very few of the bishops, and among the rest hardly one in a hundred, ascend a pulpit once in their lives? For things are come to such a pitch of frenzy, that it is generally esteemed beneath the dignity of a bishop to deliver a sermon to a congregation. In the time of Bernard there had been some declension; but we see how sharply he reproves and inveighs against the whole body of the clergy, who, it is probable, however, were far less corrupt in that age than they are in the present.

XIII. Now, if any one will closely observe and strictly examine this whole form of ecclesiastical government, which exists at the present day under the Papacy, he will find it a nest of the most lawless and ferocious banditti in the world. Every thing in it is clearly so dissimilar and repugnant to the institution of Christ, so degenerated from the ancient regulations and usages of the Church, so at variance with nature and reason, that no greater injury can be done to Christ, than by pleading his name in defence of such a disorderly government. We (they say) are the pillars of the Church, the prelates of religion, the vicars of Christ, the heads of the faithful, because we have succeeded to the power and authority of the apostles. They are perpetually vaunting of these fooleries, as if they were talking to blocks of wood; but whenever they repeat these boasts, I will ask them in return, what they have in common with the apostles. For the question is not respecting any hereditary honour, which may be given to men while they are asleep, but of the office of preaching, which they so carefully avoid. So, when we assert that their kingdom is the tyranny of Antichrist, they immediately reply, that it is that venerable hierarchy, which has been so often commended by great and holy men. As though the holy fathers, when they praised the ecclesiastical hierarchy, or spiritual government, as it had been delivered to them by the hands of the apostles, ever dreamed of this chaos of deformity and desolation, where the bishops for the most part are illiterate asses, unacquainted with the first and plainest rudiments of the faith, or, in some instances, are children just out of leading-strings; and if any be more learned,—which, however, is a rare case,—they consider a bishopric to be nothing but a title of splendour and magnificence; where the rectors of Churches think no more of feeding the flock, than a shoemaker does of ploughing; where all things are confounded with a dispersion worse than that of Babel, so that there can no longer be seen any clear vestige of the administration practised in the time of the fathers.

XIV. What if we proceed to inquire into their manners? "Where is that light of the world," which Christ requires? where that "salt of the earth?" (*m*) where that sanctity, which might serve as a perpetual example to others? There is no class of men in the present day more infamous for profusion, delicacy, luxury, and profligacy of every kind; no class of men contains more

(*m*) Matt. v. 13, 14.

apt or expert masters of every species of imposture, fraud, treachery, and perfidy; nowhere can be found equal cunning or audacity in the commission of crime. I say nothing of their pride, haughtiness, rapacity, and cruelty; I say nothing of the abandoned licentiousness of every part of their lives;—enormities which the world is so wearied with bearing, that there is no room for the least apprehension lest I should be charged with excessive exaggeration. One thing I assert, which it is not in their power to deny —that there is scarcely one of the bishops, and not one in a hundred of the parochial clergy, who, if sentence were to be passed upon his conduct according to the ancient canons, would not be excommunicated, or, at the very least, deposed from his office. That ancient discipline, which required a more accurate investigation to be made into the conduct of the clergy, has so long been obsolete, that I may be considered as making an incredible assertion; but such is the fact. Now, let all, who fight under the standards and auspices of the Roman see, go and boast of their sacerdotal order. It is evident that the order which they have is not derived from Christ, from his apostles, from the fathers, or from the ancient Church.

XV. Now, let the deacons come forward, with that most sacred distribution which they have of the property of the Church. They do not at present, however, create their deacons for any such purpose; for they enjoin them nothing but to serve at the altar, to say or chant the gospel, and do I know not what trifles. Nothing of the alms, nothing of the care of the poor, nothing of the whole function which they executed in primitive times. I speak of the institution itself. For if we advert to the fact, it is now become no office at all, but only a step towards the priesthood. In one circumstance, those who act the part of a deacon at the mass, exhibit a useless and frivolous resemblance of antiquity, in receiving the offerings before the consecration. Now, it was the ancient custom, that before the communion of the supper, the faithful kissed each other, and then offered their alms at the altar; thus they expressed their charity, first by a sign, and then by active beneficence. The deacon, who was steward for the poor, received what was given, in order to distribute it. Of the alms given at present, no more reaches the poor than if they were thrown into the sea. This false appearance of deaconship, therefore, is a mockery of the Church. It contains nothing resembling the apostolic institution, or the ancient usage. Even the distribution of the property they have turned into another channel; and have ordered it in such a way, that it is impossible to imagine any thing more disorderly. For as robbers, after having murdered some ill-fated travellers, divide the plunder among themselves, so these men, after having extinguished the light of God's word, and, as it were, cut the throat of the Church, have concluded that whatever had been dedicated to sacred uses, was abandoned to plunder and rapine. They have therefore made a division of it, and every one has seized as large a share as he could.

XVI. Here, all the ancient usages which we have described, have not only been disturbed, but entirely expunged and abolished. The principal part of this plunder was seized by the bishops and the presbyters of cities, who, being enriched by it, were converted into canons. That the partition was made in confusion is evident from the contentions which prevail among them, even to this day, about their respective limits. But, however it may be managed, they have taken care that not a penny of all the property of the Church should reach the poor, who were at least entitled to half of it. For the canons expressly allot them one fourth part, and assign another fourth part to the bishops to be laid out in hospitality and other offices of charity. I say nothing of what the clergy ought to do with their portion, and to what use they ought to apply it. The residue, which is appropriated to the reparation of temples, edifices, and other expenses, it has been sufficiently shown, ought to be at the service of the poor in time of necessity. If they had a single spark of the fear of God in their hearts, could they bear this reflection of conscience, that every thing they eat, and drink, and wear, is the fruit of robbery, and even of sacrilege? But though they are little affected with the judgment of God, they should at least consider that those, whom they wish to persuade into a belief of their possession of such an excellent and well regulated system in their Church as they are accustomed to boast, are men endued with sense and reason. Let them answer me, in a word, whether deaconship be a license for theft and robbery? If they deny this, they will also be obliged to confess, that they have no such office left; seeing that among them the whole administration of the revenues of the Church has been openly perverted into a system of sacrilegious depredation.

XVII. But here they advance a most plausible plea. They allege that the dignity of the Church is becomingly sustained by this magnificence. And such is the impudence of some of their faction, that they dare to boast in express terms, that this princely state of the priesthood constitutes the only fulfilment of those predictions in which the ancient prophets describe the splendour of the kingdom of Christ. It is not in vain, they say, that God has made the following promises to his Church: "The kings of Tarshish and of the isles shall bring presents; the kings of Sheba and Seba shall offer gifts. Yea, all kings shall fall down before him." (*n*) "Awake, awake; put on thy strength, O Zion; put on thy beautiful garments, O Jerusalem." (*o*) "All they from Sheba shall come; they shall bring gold and incense; and they shall show forth the praises of the Lord. All the flocks of Kedar shall be gathered together unto thee." (*p*) If I should dwell long on a refutation of this presumption, I fear I should expose myself to the charge of folly. Therefore I am not inclined to spend my words in vain. But I ask, if any Jew were to abuse these passages in the same manner, what reply would they make to him? There is no doubt but they would reprove his stupidity, in transferring to the flesh and the world things which are spiritually spoken of the spiritual kingdom of the Messiah. For we know that, under the image of earthly things, the prophets have represented to us the heavenly glory of God, which ought to shine in the Church. For of those external blessings which their words express, the Church never had less abundance than in the days of the apostles; and yet it is acknowledged by all that the kingdom of Christ then flourished in its greatest vigour. What, then, it will be asked, is the meaning of these passages? I reply, that every thing precious, high, and excellent, ought to be in subjection to the Lord. In regard to the express declaration, that kings shall submit their sceptres to Christ, cast their crowns at his feet, and consecrate their wealth to the Church, when (they will say) was it more truly

---

(*n*) Psalm lxxii. 10, 11. (*o*) Isaiah iii. 1. (*p*) Isaiah lx. 6, 7.

and fully exemplified, than when Theodosius, casting off the purple robes, and relinquishing the ensigns of imperial majesty, submitted himself, like one of the common people, to do solemn penance before God and the Church? than when he and other such pious princes devoted their cares and exertions to the preservation of pure doctrine in the Church, and to the support and protection of sound teachers? But how far the priests of that age were from rioting in superfluous riches, a single expression of the Council of Aquileia, at which Ambrose presided, sufficiently declares. "Poverty is honourable in the priests of the Lord." It is true that the bishops at that time had some wealth, which they might have employed to display the honour of the Church, if they had considered them as the Church's real ornaments. But knowing that there was nothing more inconsistent with the office of pastors, than to display and to pride themselves on the luxury of their tables, the splendour of their apparel, a large retinue, and magnificent palaces, they followed and maintained the humility and modesty, and even the poverty which Christ has consecrated in all his ministers.

XVIII. But not to dwell too long on this point, let us again collect into a brief summary, how very much the present dispensation, or rather dissipation, of the property of the Church, differs from that true office of deacons, which the word of God commends to us, and which the ancient Church observed. That portion which is employed in the ornaments of temples, I assert, is grossly misapplied, if it be not regulated by that moderation which the nature of sacred things requires, and which the apostles and holy fathers have prescribed both by precept and by examples. But what is there seen like this, in the temples at the present day? Whatever is conformable, I do not say to that primitive frugality, but to any honourable mediocrity, is rejected. Nothing pleases, but what savours of the profusion and corruption of the present times. At the same time they are so far from feeling any just concern for the living temples, that they would suffer thousands of the poor to perish with hunger, rather than convert the smallest chalice or silver pitcher into money, to relieve their wants. And, not of myself to pronounce any thing more severe, I would only request my pious readers to indulge this one reflection. If it could happen that Exuperius,—that bishop of Toulouse whom we have mentioned,—if Acacius, if Ambrose, or any other such,—should be raised from the dead, what would they say? In such extreme necessity of the poor, they surely would not approve of the riches of the Church being applied to another use, and that an unnecessary one. I forbear to remark, that these purposes for which they are employed, even if there were no poor, are in many respects injurious, but of no utility whatever. But I will not appeal to the authority of men. The property has been dedicated to Christ, and therefore ought to be dispensed according to his will. It will be useless for them to allege, that this portion has been employed for Christ, which they have squandered in a manner inconsistent with his command. To confess the truth, however, there is not much of the ordinary revenue of the Church lost in these expenses. For there are no bishoprics so opulent, no abbeys so rich, in short, no benefices so numerous or ample, as to satisfy the voraciouness of the priests. Wishing to spare themselves, therefore, they induce the people, from superstitious motives, to take what ought to be bestowed upon the poor, and apply it to the building of temples, the erection of statues, the purchase of chalices and shrines for relics, and the provision of costly vestments. This is the gulf which swallows up all the daily alms.

XIX. Of the revenue which they derive from lands and possessions, what can I say more than I have already said, and which is evident to the observation of all men? We see with what fidelity the principal portion is disposed of by those who are called bishops and abbots. What folly is it to seek here for any ecclesiastical order! Was it reasonable that they, whose life ought to be an eminent example of frugality, modesty, temperance, and humility, should emulate the pomp of princes, in the number of their attendants, the splendour of their palaces, the elegance of their apparel, and the luxury of their tables? And how very inconsistent it was with the office of those whom the eternal and inviolable decree of God forbids to be greedy of filthy lucre, (*q*) and commands to be content with simple fare, not only to lay

(*q*) Titus i. 7.

their hands upon towns and castles, but to seize on the largest provinces, and even to assume the reins of empire! If they despise the word of God, what reply will they make to those ancient decrees of councils, by which it is ordained that a bishop shall have a small house near the Church, a frugal table, and humble furniture? What will they say to that sentence of the Council of Aquileia, which declares poverty to be honourable in the priests of the Lord? For the direction given by Jerome to Nepotian, that poor persons and strangers, and Christ among them, should be familiar guests at his table, they will perhaps reject as too austere. But they will be ashamed to contradict what he immediately subjoins—"that it is the glory of a bishop to provide for the poor, and the disgrace of all priests to seek to enrich themselves." Yet they cannot receive this, but they must all condemn themselves to ignominy. But it is not necessary to pursue them with any further severity at present, as it was only my intention to show, that the legitimate office of deacon has long been entirely abolished among them, to prevent their continuing to pride themselves on this title, for the purpose of recommending their Church. And this design, I think, I have fully accomplished.

CHAPTER VI

The Primacy of the Roman See

HITHERTO we have treated of those ecclesiastical orders which existed in the government of the ancient Church, but which afterwards, in process of time, being corrupted and gradually more and more perverted, now in the Papal Church merely retain their names, while in reality there are nothing but masks. And this we have done, that by the comparison the pious reader might judge what sort of a Church the Romanists have, for the sake of which they represent us as guilty of schism, because we have separated from it. But the head and summit of the whole establishment, that is, the primacy of the Roman see, by which they endeavour to prove that the Catholic Church is exclusively theirs, we have not yet touched on; because it originated neither in the institution of Christ nor in the usage of the ancient Church, as did the other offices, which we have shown were handed down from antiquity, but since, through the corruption of the times, have degenerated, and even assumed altogether a new form. And yet they endeavour to persuade the world, that the principal and almost only bond of the unity of the Church is adherence to the see of Rome, and perseverance in obedience to it. This is the foundation on which they principally rest, when they wish to deny us all claim to the Church, and to arrogate it to themselves; that they retain the head, on which the unity of the Church depends, and without which it must be torn asunder and crumble to pieces. For their notion is, that the Church is like a mutilated and headless body, unless it be subject to the Roman see as its head. Therefore, when they dispute respecting their hierarchy, they always commence with this axiom, that the Roman pontiff, as the vicar of Christ, who is Head of the Church, presides over the universal Church in his stead, and that the Church cannot be well constituted, unless that see holds the primacy above all others. Wherefore it is necessary to discuss this subject also, that nothing belonging to the good government of the Church may be omitted.

II. Let the question, therefore, be stated thus: Whether it be necessary to the true system of what they call the hierarchy or government of the Church, that one see should have the preëminence above all the rest in dignity and power, so as to be the head of the whole body. Now, we subject the Church to very unreasonable laws, if we impose this necessity upon it without the word of God. Therefore, if our adversaries wish to gain their cause, it is necessary for them, in the first place, to show that this economy was instituted by Christ. For this purpose they allege the high-priesthood ordained in the law, and the supreme jurisdiction of the high-priest which God appointed at Jerusalem. But it is easy to give an answer to this, or, indeed, various answers, if they would not be satisfied with one. In the first place, there is no reason for extending to the whole world what was useful in a single nation; on the contrary, the case of a single nation and that of the whole world are widely different. Because the Jews were surrounded on all sides with idolaters, God, in order to prevent their being distracted by a variety of religions, fixed the seat of his worship in the centre of the country, and there he set over them one principal priest, to whom they were all to be subject, for the better preservation of unity among them. Now, when the true religion has been diffused over the whole world, who does not perceive it to be utterly absurd to assign the government of the east and west to one man? It is just as if it were contended, that the whole world ought to be governed by one magistrate, because there is only one in a small district. But there is another reason why this ought not to be made a precedent for imitation. Every one knows that the Jewish high-priest was a type of Christ: now that the priesthood has been transferred, that right must also be transferred. To whom, then, is it transferred? Certainly not to the pope, as he impudently presumes to boast, when he assumes this title to himself; but to Christ, who exercises that office alone without vicar or successor, and resigns the honour to no other. For this priesthood, which was prefigured in the law, consists not only in preaching or doctrine, but in the propitiation of God, which Christ effected in his death, and in that intercession which he is now making with the Father.

III. There is no reason, therefore, why they should confine us to this example, as if it were a law perpetually binding, whereas we see it was only of temporary duration. From the New Testament they have nothing to adduce in support of their opinion, but that it was said to one, "Thou art Peter; and upon this rock I will build my Church." (*r*) Again: "Peter, lovest thou me? Feed my sheep." (*s*) But to render these proofs substantial, it is necessary for them first to show that he who is commanded to feed the flock of Christ is invested with authority over all Churches, and that binding and loosing are no other than governing the whole world. But as Peter had received the command from the Lord to feed the Church, so he exhorts all other presbyters to do the same. (*t*) Hence it is easy to infer, that this charge of Christ conferred nothing peculiar upon Peter beyond others, or that Peter communicated equally to others the right which he had received. But, not to dispute to no purpose, we have in another place, from the mouth of Christ himself, a clear explanation of what he intends by *binding* and *loosing*, namely, "remitting and retaining sins." (*v*) The manner of *binding* and *loosing* is shown by the whole tenor of Scripture, and particularly by Paul, when he says that the ministers of the gospel have received a commission to reconcile men to God, (*w*) and that they have authority to inflict punishment on those who shall reject this favour. (*x*)

IV. How grossly they pervert those passages which make mention of binding and loosing, I have hinted before, and shall hereafter have to state more at large. At present it is worth while to see what they can extract from that celebrated answer of Christ to Peter. He promised him "the keys of the kingdom of heaven." He said, "Whatsoever thou shalt bind on earth, shall be bound

(*r*) Matt. xvi. 18. (*s*) John xxi. 16. (*t*) 1 Peter v. 2.
(*v*) John xx. 23. (*w*) 2 Cor. v. 18. (*x*) 2 Cor. x. 6.

in heaven." (*y*) If we can agree respecting the word *keys,* and the manner of *binding,* all dispute will immediately cease. For the pope himself will readily relinquish the charge committed to the apostles, which, being full of labour and trouble, would deprive him of his pleasures without yielding him any profit. Since it is the doctrine of the gospel that opens heaven to us, it is beautifully expressed by the metaphorical appellation of *keys.*—There is no other way in which men are *bound* and *loosed,* than when some are reconciled to God by faith, and others are more firmly bound by their unbelief. If the pope assumed nothing but this to himself, I am persuaded there is no man who would either envy him or contend with him.—But this succession being laborious, and by no means lucrative, and, therefore, not at all satisfactory to the pope, hence arises a controversy on the meaning of Christ's promise to Peter. Therefore I infer from the subject itself, that it only denotes the dignity of the apostolic office, which cannot be separated from the burden of it. For if the definition which I have given be admitted,—and it cannot without the greatest effrontery be rejected,—then here is nothing given to Peter that was not also common to his colleagues; because otherwise there would not only be a personal injury done to them, but the majesty of the doctrine would be diminished. This our adversaries strenuously oppose. But what does it avail them to strike upon this rock? For they can never prove, but that as the preaching of the same gospel was enjoined upon all the apostles, so they were all equally armed with the power of binding and loosing. They allege that Christ, when he promised to give the keys to Peter, constituted him head of the universal Church. But what he there promised to one, he in another passage confers upon all the rest together, and delivers it, as it were, into their hands. (*z*) If the same power, which had been promised to one, was granted to all, in what respect is he superior to his colleagues? His preëminence, they say, consists in this—that he receives separately by himself, as well as in common with them, that which is only given to the others in common. What if I reply, with Cyprian and Augustine, that Christ did this, not to prefer one man before others, but to

---

(*y*) Matt. xvi. 19. (*z*) Matt. xviii. 18. John xx. 23.

display the unity of the Church? For this is the language of Cyprian: "That in the person of one man God gave the keys to them all, to signify the unity of them all; that, therefore, the rest were, the same as Peter, endued with an equal participation both of honour and of power; but that Christ commences with one, to show that the Church is one." Augustine says, "If there had not been in Peter a mysterious representation of the Church, the Lord would not have said to him, I will give thee the keys; for if this was said to Peter alone, the Church possesses them not; but if the Church has the keys, Peter, when he received them, must have represented the whole Church." And in another place: "When a question was put to them all, Peter alone answers, Thou art the Christ; and to him Christ says, I will give thee the keys, as if the power of binding and loosing had been conferred upon him alone; whereas he made that answer on behalf of all, and received this power in common with all, as sustaining the character of unity. He is mentioned, therefore, one for all, because there is unity in all."

V. But this declaration, "Thou art Peter, and upon this rock I will build my Church," (*a*) they say, is no where to be found addressed to any other. As if in this passage Christ affirmed any thing respecting Peter, different from what Paul, and even Peter himself asserts, respecting all Christians. For Paul makes "Christ the chief corner-stone," upon which they are built who "grow unto a holy temple in the Lord." (*b*) And Peter enjoins us to be "as lively stones," who, being founded on that "corner-stone, elect and precious," (*c*) are by this connection at once united to our God and to each other. This belongs to Peter, they say, above the rest, because it is expressly attributed to him in particular. I readily allow Peter the honour of being placed among the first in the structure of the Church, or, if they insist upon it, the very first of all the faithful; but I will not permit them to infer from this that he possessed a primacy over the rest. For what kind of reasoning is this: he excels the rest in ardour of zeal, in doctrine, in magnanimity; therefore he possesses authority over them? As though we might not with greater plausibility conclude that An-

---

(*a*) Matt. xvi. 18. (*b*) Eph. ii. 21, 22. (*c*) 1 Peter ii. 4, 5.

drew was superior to Peter, because he preceded him in time, and introduced him to Christ; (*d*) but this I pass over. I am willing that Peter should have the precedence, but there is a great difference between the honour of preceding others, and authority over them. We see that the apostles generally paid this deference to Peter, that he used to speak first in their assembly, and took the lead in proposing, exhorting, and admonishing; but we read not a word of his power.

VI. We are not yet, however, come to that question; I only mean at present to show, that they have no solid argument, when they wish to erect an empire over the universal church upon no other foundation than the name of Peter. For those antiquated fooleries with which they endeavoured at first to impose on the world, are not worthy of a relation, much less of a refutation—that the Church was founded on Peter, because it is said, "Upon this rock I will build my Church." (*e*) They allege in their defence, that it has been so explained by some of the fathers. But when this is contradicted by the whole tenor of Scripture, what avails it to set up their authority in opposition to God? And why do we dispute about the meaning of those words, as though they were ambiguous or obscure? whereas nothing can be expressed with greater clearness or precision. Peter, in his own name and that of his brethren, had confessed that Christ was "the Son of God." (*f*) Upon this rock Christ builds his Church, because it is the only foundation, as Paul says, "other" than which "can no man lay." (*g*) Nor do I reject the authority of the fathers in this case, from a want of testimonies in their writings to support what I maintain, if I were inclined to adduce them. But as I have observed, I am unwilling to be unnecessarily tedious to my readers in arguing so clear a subject; especially as it has been long ago discussed with sufficient copiousness and care by other writers on our side of the question.

VII. Yet, in fact, we can obtain no better decision of this point than from the Scripture itself, if we compare all the places where it shows what office and power Peter held among the apostles, how he conducted himself, and in what manner he was received

(*d*) John i. 40—42.
(*e*) Matt. xvi. 18.
(*f*) Matt. xvi. 16.
(*g*) 1 Cor. iii. 11.

by them. On an examination of the whole, we shall only find that he was one of the twelve, equal to the rest, their companion, not their master. He proposes to the assembly indeed, if there be any thing to be done, and delivers his opinion on what is necessary to be done; but he hears the observations of others, and not only gives them the opportunity of speaking their sentiments, but leaves them to decide, and when they have determined, he follows and obeys. (*h*) When he writes to pastors, he does not command them with authority like a superior; but makes them his colleagues, and exhorts them with a courteousness which is usual among equals. (*i*) When he is accused for having associated with the Gentiles, though this is an unjust accusation, yet he answers it, and vindicates himself. (*k*) Commanded by his colleagues to go with John to Samaria, he refuses not. (*l*) The apostles, by sending him, declared that they did not consider him as their superior. By his compliance and undertaking the commission intrusted to him, he confessed that he was a colleague with them, but had no authority over them. If none of these facts had remained upon record, yet the Epistle to the Galatians might alone easily remove every doubt; where Paul devotes nearly two whole chapters to the sole purpose of showing that he was equal to Peter in the dignity of the apostleship. Hence he relates that he went to Peter, not to profess subjection to him, but to testify to all the harmony of their doctrine; and that Peter required no such thing as submission, but gave him the right hand of fellowship, that they might labour together in the vineyard of the Lord; that no less grace had been conferred upon him among the Gentiles, than upon Peter among the Jews; and lastly, that when Peter acted with some degree of unfaithfulness, he was reproved by him, and stood corrected by the reproof. (*m*) All these things fully prove, either that there was an equality between Paul and Peter, or at least that Peter had no more power over the rest than they had over him. And this, as I have already observed, is the professed object of Paul—to prevent his being considered as inferior in his apostolic character to Peter or John, who were his colleagues, not his masters.

(*h*) Acts xv. 6—29. (*i*) 1 Peter v. 1. (*k*) Acts xi. 2, &c. (*l*) Acts viii. 14, 15. (*m*) Gal. i. 2.

VIII. But though I grant them what they require respecting Peter, by admitting that he was the chief of the apostles, and superior in dignity to all the others, yet there is no reason why they should convert a particular instance into a universal rule, and make what was done but once a perpetual precedent; for the cases are widely different. There was one chief among the apostles; doubtless because they were few in number. If there be one president over twelve men, will it therefore follow that there ought to be but one president over a hundred thousand men? That twelve should have one among them to preside over the rest, is no wonder. For this is consistent with nature, and the common sense of mankind requires, that in every assembly, even though they are all equal in power, yet there should be one to act as moderator, by whom the others should be regulated. There is no court, council, parliament, or assembly of any description, which has not its president or chairman. So there would be no absurdity, if we acknowledged that the apostles gave this pre-eminence to Peter. But that which obtains among a small company is not immediately to be applied to the whole world, to the government of which no one man is sufficient. But the whole economy of nature, they say, teaches us, that there ought to be one supreme head over all. And in proof of this they adduce the example of cranes and bees, which always choose for themselves one leader, and no more. I admit the examples which they produce; but do bees collect together from all parts of the world to choose one king? Each king is content with his own hive. So, among cranes, every flock has its own leader. What will they prove from this, but that every Church ought to have its own bishop? Next they call us to consider examples from civil governments. They quote an observation from Homer, that it is not good to have many governors, with similar passages of other profane writers in commendation of monarchy. The answer is easy; for monarchy is not praised by Ulysses in Homer, or by any others, from an opinion that one king ought to govern the whole world. Their meaning is, that one kingdom does not admit of two kings, and that no prince can bear a partner in his throne.

IX. But supposing it to be, as they contend, good and useful that the whole world should be comprehended in one monarchy, which, however, is a monstrous absurdity; but if this were admitted, I should not, therefore, grant the same system to be applicable to the government of the Church. For the Church has Christ for its sole Head, under whose sovereignty we are all united together, according to that order and form of government which he himself has prescribed. They offer a gross insult to Christ, therefore, when they assign the preëminence over the universal Church to one man, under the pretence that it may not be destitute of a head. For "Christ is the head; from whom the whole body, fitly joined together, and compacted by that which every joint supplieth, according to the effectual working in the measure of every part, maketh increase of the body." (*n*) We see how he places all men, without exception, in the *body*, reserving to Christ alone the honour and name of *head*. We see how he assigns to all the members respectively a certain measure, and a determinate and limited function; so that the perfection of grace, as well as the supreme power of government, resides in Christ alone. I am aware of their usual cavil in evasion of this argument—that Christ is properly styled the sole Head, because he alone governs by his own authority and in his own name, but that this is no reason why there may not be under him another *ministerial head*, as their phrase is, to act as his vicegerent on earth. But they gain nothing by this cavil, except they first prove that this ministry was ordained by Christ. For the apostle teaches, that all the subordinate ministration is distributed among the members, but that the power proceeds from that one heavenly Head. (*o*) Or, if they wish me to speak in plainer terms, since the Scripture declares Christ to be the Head, and ascribes this honour to him alone, it ought not to be transferred to any other, except to one whom Christ himself has appointed his representative. But such an appointment is not only nowhere to be found, but may be abundantly refuted by various passages.

X. Paul gives us a lively description of the church on various occasions, but without making any mention of its having one head upon earth. On the contrary, from the description which he gives, we may rather infer that such a notion is foreign from the

(*n*) Eph. iv. 15, 16. (*o*) Eph. i. 22; iv. 15; v. 23. Col. i. 18; ii. 10.

institution of Christ. Christ, at his ascension, withdrew from us his visible presence; nevertheless "he ascended that he might fill all things." (*p*) He is still, therefore, present, and will always continue present with the Church. With a view to show us the manner in which he manifests himself, Paul calls our attention to the offices which he employs. There is "one Lord," he says, "in you all. But unto every one of us is given grace according to the measure of the gift of Christ. And he gave some, apostles; and some, evangelists; and some, pastors and teachers." (*q*) Why does he not say, that he has appointed one to preside over all as his vicegerent? For his subject absolutely required it, and it ought by no means to have been omitted, if it had been true. "Christ," he says, "is present with us." How? "By the ministry of men whom he has appointed to the government of the Church." Why not rather, "By the ministerial head, to whom he has delegated his authority?" He mentions a unity; but it is in God, and in the faith of Christ. He attributes nothing to men but a common ministry, and to every individual his particular share. In that commendation of unity, after having said, "There is one body, one Spirit, one hope of your calling, one Lord, one faith, one baptism," (*r*) why has he not likewise immediately added, "one supreme pontiff to preserve the Church in unity?" For if it had been true, nothing could have been more proper. Let that passage be duly considered. There is no doubt that he intends there a representation of the sacred and spiritual government of the Church, which has since received the name of *hierarchy*. Monarchy among ministers, or the government of one over all the rest, he not only does not mention, but indicates that there is no such thing. There is no doubt also that he meant to express the nature of the union, by which the faithful are connected with Christ their Head. Now, he not only makes no mention of any ministerial head, but attributes to every one of the members a particular operation, according to the measure of grace distributed to each. Nor is there any foundation for their far-fetched argument from a comparison of the heavenly and earthly hierarchy; for, in judgment of the former, it is not safe to go beyond

(*p*) Eph. iv. 10. (*q*) Eph. iv. 5—7, 11. (*r*) Eph. iv. 4, 5.

the discoveries of the Scripture, and in constituting the latter, it is not right to follow any other model than that which the Lord himself has delineated in his word.

XI. Now, though I should make them another concession, which they will never obtain from judicious persons, that the primacy of the Church was established in Peter, and to be continued by a perpetual succession, how will they prove that its seat was fixed at Rome, so that whoever is bishop of that city must preside over the whole world? By what right do they restrict to one place this dignity, which was conferred without the mention of any place? Peter, they say, lived and died at Rome. What shall we say of Christ himself? Was it not at Jerusalem that he exercised the office of a bishop while he lived, and fulfilled the priestly office by his death? The Prince of pastors, the supreme Bishop, the Head of the Church, could not obtain this honour for the place where he lived and died; how then could Peter, who was far inferior to him? Are not these follies worse than puerile? Christ gave the honour of primacy to Peter; Peter settled at Rome; therefore he fixed the seat of the primacy in that city. For the same reason the ancient Israelites ought to have fixed the seat of their primacy in the desert, because it was there that Moses, their chief teacher, and the prince of their prophets, exercised his ministry, and died.

XII. Let us see how wretchedly they reason. Peter, they say, had the preëminence among the apostles. Therefore, the Church in which he settled ought to have this privilege. But where was he first stationed? They reply, at Antioch. Then I infer that the Church of Antioch is justly entitled to the primacy. They confess that it was originally the first, but allege that Peter, on his removal from it, transferred the honour which was attached to him to Rome. For there is an epistle of Pope Marcellus to the presbyters of Antioch, in which he says, "The see of Peter was at first among you, but at the command of the Lord was afterwards removed to this city." So the Church of Antioch, which was originally the first, has given place to the see of Rome. But I ask, By what oracle did that wise pope know that the Lord had commanded this? For if this cause is to be decided on the footing of right, it is necessary for them to answer, whether this privilege be personal, or real, or mixed. It must be one of these. If they affirm it to be personal, then it has nothing to do with the place. If they allege it to be real, then when it has once been given to a place, it cannot be taken away from it by the death or removal of the person. It remains, therefore, for them to declare it to be mixed; and then it will not be sufficiently simple to consider the place, unless there be an agreement also with respect to the person. Let them choose which they will, I shall immediately conclude, and will easily prove, that the assumption of the primacy by the see of Rome is without any foundation.

XIII. Let us suppose the case, however, that the primacy was, as they pretend transferred from Antioch to Rome. Why did not Antioch retain the second place? For, if Rome has the preëminence of all other sees, because Peter presided there till the close of his life, to what city shall the second place be assigned, but to that which was his first see? How came Alexandria, then, to have the precedence of Antioch? Is it reasonable that the Church of a mere disciple should be superior to the see of Peter? If honour be due to every Church according to the dignity of its founder, what shall we say of the other Churches? Paul mentions three apostles, "who seemed to be pillars, James, Peter, and John." (*s*) If the first place be given to the see of Rome, in honour of Peter, are not the second and third places due to Ephesus and Jerusalem, the sees of John and James? But among the patriarchates, Jerusalem had the last place; Ephesus could not be allowed even the farthest corner. Other Churches also, as well those which were founded by Paul, as those over which the other apostles presided, were left without any distinction. The see of Mark, who was only one of the disciples, obtained the honour. Either let them confess that this was a preposterous arrangement, or let them concede to us, that it is not a perpetual rule, that every Church should be entitled to the degree of honour which was enjoyed by its founder.

XIV. All that they say of the settlement of Peter in the Church of Rome appears to me of very questionable authority. The statement of Eusebius, that he presided there twenty-five years, may be refuted without any difficulty. For it appears, from the first

---

(*s*) Gal. ii. 9.

and second chapter to the Galatians, that about twenty years after the death of Christ, he was at Jerusalem, and that from thence he went to Antioch, where he remained for some time, but it is not certain how long. Gregory says seven years, and Eusebius twenty-five. But from the death of Christ to the end of the reign of Nero, under whom they affirm Peter to have been slain, there were only thirty-seven years. For our Lord suffered in the eighteenth year of the reign of Tiberius. If we deduct twenty years, during which, according to the testimony of Paul, Peter dwelt at Jerusalem, there will remain only seventeen years, which must now be divided between those two bishoprics. If he continued long at Antioch, he could not have resided at Rome, except for a very short time. This point is susceptible of still clearer proof. Paul wrote his Epistle to the Romans on a journey when he was going to Jerusalem, (*t*) where he was seized, and from whence he was sent to Rome. It is probable, therefore, that this Epistle was written four years before his arrival at Rome. Yet it contains no mention of Peter; which ought on no account to have been omitted, if he had presided over that Church. And in the conclusion, where he recites a long catalogue of pious persons to whom he sends his salutations, where, in short, he enumerates all that were known to him, he still says not a word of Peter. (*v*) It is unnecessary to use any long or laboured arguments with persons of sound judgment; for the case itself, and the whole argument of the Epistle proclaims, that if Peter had been at Rome, he ought not to have been omitted.

XV. Paul was afterwards brought as a prisoner to Rome. Luke says that he was received by the brethren, but says nothing of Peter. (*w*) From that city Paul wrote to several Churches. In some of these epistles he introduces salutations, in the names of certain brethren who were with him; but they contain not a single word implying that Peter was there at that time. Who will think it incredible that, if he had been there, Paul could have passed him over in total silence? Moreover, in his Epistle to the Philippians, after having said that he had no one who discovered such sincere concern respecting the work of the Lord as Timothy, he

(*t*) Rom. xv. 25. (*v*) Rom. xvi. (*w*) Acts xxviii. 15.

complains that "all seek their own." (*x*) And to Timothy himself he makes yet a heavier complaint: "At my first answer no man stood with me, but all men forsook me." (*y*) Where was Peter then? For if they say that he was at Rome, how deep is the ignominy which Paul fixes upon him, that he was a deserter of the gospel? For he is speaking of the faithful, because he adds his prayer, "that it may not be laid to their charge." How long, then, and at what time, did Peter hold that see? It will be said, it is the uniform opinion of ancient writers, that he governed that Church till his death. But those writers themselves are not agreed who was his successor. Some say it was Linus; and others, Clement. They likewise relate many absurd and fabulous stories respecting the disputation held between him and Simon Magus. And Augustine, when treating of superstitions, acknowledges that the custom, which obtained at Rome, of not fasting on the day on which Peter gained the victory over Simon Magus, arose from an opinion entertained without any sufficient authority. In the last place, the transactions of that age are so perplexed by a variety of representations, that we must not give implicit credit to every thing that is recorded. Yet, in consequence of this agreement of the ancient writers, I will not dispute his having died at Rome; but that he was bishop there, and especially for any considerable time, is what I cannot be persuaded to believe. Nor am I anxious respecting this point, because Paul testifies that the apostleship of Peter particularly belonged to the Jews, and that his own was directed to us. To add our confirmation, therefore, to the compact which they established between themselves, or rather to admit the validity of the ordinance of the Holy Spirit, it becomes us rather to look up to the apostleship of Paul than to that of Peter. For their different provinces were allotted to them by the Holy Spirit, who sent Peter to the Jews, and Paul to us. The Romanists, therefore, may seek for their primacy elsewhere, but not in the word of God, which affords not the least foundation for it.

XVI. Let us now proceed to show, that our adversaries have no more reason for boasting of the authority of the ancient

(*x*) Phil. ii. 20, 21. (*y*) 2 Tim. iv. 16.

Church than of the testimony of the word of God. For when they bring forward this principle, that the unity of the Church cannot be preserved, unless it have one supreme head upon earth, to whom all the members should be subject, and that, therefore, the Lord gave the primacy to Peter, and afterwards by right of succession, to the see of Rome that it might remain there to the end of time,—they also assert that this has been the usage from the beginning. Now, as they grossly pervert various testimonies, I would first make this preliminary remark. I do not deny that the ancient writers uniformly give great honour to the Roman Church, and speak of it in respectful terms. This I consider as arising principally from three causes. In the first place, that opinion which, I know not how, had been received, that it had been founded and settled by the ministry of Peter operated very powerfully to gain it credit and authority, and, therefore, among the Western churches it was called *the Apostolic See.* In the second place, because it was the capital of the empire; and on this account it is probable that it contained men superior in learning and prudence, skill and experience, to those of any other place; due regard was paid to this circumstance, that the glory of the city and other far more excellent gifts of God might not appear to be undervalued. In the third place, while the Eastern and Greek Churches, and even those in Africa, were agitated by numerous dissensions of opinion among themselves, the Church of Rome was more peaceable and less disturbed. Hence it happened, that pious and holy bishops, on being expelled from their sees, frequently resorted thither, as to an asylum or port of safety. For as the people of Europe have less subtlety and activity of mind than the inhabitants of Asia and Africa, so they are not so volatile or desirous of novelty. It considerably increased the authority of the Church of Rome, therefore, that in those uncertain times it was not so much agitated as the other Churches, and was more tenacious of the doctrine which it had once received than all the rest, as we shall presently show more at large. On account of these three causes, I say, it was held in more than common respect, and received many honourable testimonies from ancient writers.

XVII. But when our adversaries wish to make this a reason for ascribing to that Church the primacy and sovereign power over other Churches, they run, as I have already observed, into a gross error. To make this the more evident, I will first briefly show what the ancient writers thought respecting this unity, on which our opponents so urgently insist. Jerome, writing to Nepotian, after having enumerated many examples of unity, at length descends to the hierarchy of the Church. "Every Church," he says, "has its distinct bishop, archpresbyter, and archdeacon, and all the order of the Church depends upon its governors." This is the language of a Roman priest, recommending unity in the order of the Church. Why does he not mention that all Churches are connected together under one head, as by a common bond? Nothing would have been more in favour of his argument; nor can it be pretended that he omitted it for want of recollection; he would most readily have mentioned it, if the fact had permitted him. It is beyond all doubt, therefore, that he saw this to be the true kind of unity, which is most excellently described by Cyprian in the following passage: "There is only one bishopric, of which every bishop holds an integral part; and there is but one Church, which is widely extended into a multitude by the offspring of its fertility. As the sun has many rays, but only one light; as a tree has many branches, but only one trunk, fixed on a firm root; and as many rivers issue from one spring, and notwithstanding the number of the streams in which its overflowing abundance is diffused, yet the unity of the source remains the same;—so also the Church, illuminated with the light of the Lord, extends its rays over the whole earth, yet it is one and the same light which is universally diffused, nor is the unity of the body destroyed. It stretches its branches, it pours out its ample streams, all over the world; yet there is but one root, and one source." Again: "The spouse of Christ cannot be corrupted; she acknowledges one Master, and preserves her fidelity to him inviolate." We see how he attributes the universal bishopric, which comprehends the whole Church, to Christ alone, and says that integral portions of it are confided to all those who discharge the episcopal office under this head. Where is the primacy of the see of Rome, if the universal bishopric be vested in Christ alone, and every bishop hold an integral portion of it? My object, in these quotations, has been, to convince the reader, by the way, that this principle, which the Romanists assume as an admitted and indubitable maxim, namely, that the unity of the Church requires the supremacy of some earthly head, was altogether unknown to the ancients.

CHAPTER VII

The Rise and Progress of the Papal Power to Its Present Eminence, Attended with the Loss of Liberty to the Church, and the Ruin of All Moderation

IN SUPPORT of the antiquity of the primacy of the see of Rome, there is nothing to be found anterior to the decree of the Council of Nice, by which the bishop of Rome is allotted the first place among the patriarchs, and is directed to superintend the neighbouring Churches. When the council makes a distinction between him and the other patriarchs, so as to assign to all their respective limits, it clearly does not constitute him the head of them all, but only makes him one of the principal. Vitus and Vincentius attended the council on the behalf of Julius, who at that time presided over the Church of Rome. They were seated in the fourth place. If Julius had been acknowledged as the head of the Church, would his representatives have been degraded to the fourth seat? Would Athanasius have presided in a general council, where the form of the hierarchical system ought most particularly to have been observed? In the council of Ephesus, it appears that Celestine, who was then bishop of Rome, made use of a disingenuous artifice to secure the dignity of his see. For when he sent his legates thither, he requested Cyril, patriarch of Alexandria, who was otherwise to preside, to act on his behalf. For what purpose could this request be made, but that his name might, at any rate, occupy the first place? For his legates sat in a lower station, were asked their sentiments among others, and subscribed in their order; at the same time the patriarch of Alexandria united Celestine's name with his own. What shall I say of the second Council of Ephesus, where, though the legates of Leo were present, yet Dioscorus, patriarch of Alexandria, presided as in his own right? They will object, that this was not an orthodox council, because it condemned Flavianus, a holy man, bishop of Constantinople, and acquitted Eutyches, and sanctioned his heresy. But when the council was assembled, and the bishops took their respective seats, it is certain that the legates of the Roman Church were present among the others, as in a holy and legitimate council. Yet they contended not for the first place, but yielded it to another, which they would not have done if they had considered it as belonging to them. For the bishops of Rome have never been ashamed of raising the greatest contentions for their dignity, and they have not hesitated, on this account alone, to harass and agitate the Church with various and pernicious controversies. But because Leo saw that it would be too presumptuous a demand to require the first place for his legates, therefore he waived it.

II. Next follows the Council of Chalcedon, in which, by the permission of the emperor, the legates of the Roman Church occupied the first place. But Leo himself confessed that this was an extraordinary privilege. For when he requested it from Marcian the emperor, and Pulcheria the empress, he did not pretend it to be his right, but only alleged, in support of his claim, that the Eastern bishops who presided in the Council of Ephesus had thrown every thing into confusion, and abused their power. Since it was necessary, therefore, to have a discreet moderator, and it was improbable that those who had once been so unsteady and disorderly would be fit for the office, he requested that, on account of the misconduct and incompetence of the others, the task of presiding should be transferred to him. That which is sought as a special privilege and an exception to a common custom, certainly does not arise from a general rule. Where the only pretext is, that it was necessary to have a new president, because the former ones had violated their duty, it is evident that this had not been the case before, and it ought not to be perpetual, but was merely done in the contemplation of present danger. The bishop of Rome, therefore, had the first place in the Council of Chalcedon, not because it was the right of his see, but because the council was in want of a discreet and suitable president, in consequence of those to whom that honour belonged having excluded themselves from it by their own intemperance and violence. And what I say was proved, in fact, by Leo's successor. For when he sent his legates to the fifth Council of Constantinople, which was held a considerable time after, he contended not for the first seat, but without any difficulty suffered it to be taken by Menna, patriarch of Constantinople. So in the Council of Carthage, at which Augustine was present, the place of president was filled by Aurelius, archbishop of that city, and not by the legates of the Roman see, though the express object of their attendance was to support the authority of the Roman pontiff. And, moreover, there was a general council held in Italy, at which the bishop of Rome was not present. This was the Council of Aquileia, at which Ambrose presided, who was then in high credit with the emperor. There was no mention made of the bishop of Rome. We see, therefore, that the dignity of Ambrose caused the see of Milan at that time to have the precedence above that of Rome.

III. With respect to the title of primacy, and other titles of pride, of which the pope now strangely boasts, it is not difficult to judge when and in what manner they were introduced. Cyprian, bishop of Carthage, makes frequent mention of Cornelius, who was bishop of Rome. He distinguishes him by no other appellation than that of *brother,* or *fellow bishop,* or *colleague.* But when he writes to Stephen, the successor of Cornelius, he not only treats him as equal to himself and others, but even addresses him with considerable severity, charging him at one time with arrogance, and at another with ignorance. Since the time of Cyprian, we know what was the decision of the whole African Church on this subject. For the Council of Carthage prohibited that any one should be called "the prince of priests," or "the first bishop," but only "the bishop of the first see." But any one who examines the more ancient records, will find that at that time the bishop of Rome was content with the common appellation of *brother*. It is certain that as long as the Church retained its true and uncorrupted form, all those names of pride, which in succeeding times have been insolently usurped by the Roman see, were altogether unknown: nothing was heard of a supreme pontiff or a sole head of the Church upon earth. And if the bishop of Rome had been presumptuous enough to make any such assumption, there were judicious men who would immediately have repressed his folly. Jerome, being a Roman presbyter, was not reluctant to assert the dignity of his Church as far as matter of fact and the state of the times admitted; yet we see how he also reduces it to an equality with others. "If it be a question of authority," he says, "the world is greater than a city. Why do you allege to me the custom of a single city? Why do you set up a few instances, which have given rise to pride, against the laws of the Church? Wherever there is a bishop, whether at Rome, at Eugubium, at Constantinople, or at Rhegium, he is of the same dignity and of the same priesthood. The power of riches, or the abasement of poverty, makes no bishop superior or inferior to another."

IV. Respecting the title of *universal bishop*, the first contention arose in the time of Gregory, and was occasioned by the ambition of John, bishop of Constantinople. For he wanted to make himself universal bishop—an attempt which had never been made by any one before. In that controversy Gregory does not plead against this as the assumption of a right which belonged to himself, but resolutely protests against it altogether, as a profane and sacrilegious application, and even as the forerunner of Antichrist. He says, "If he who is called *universal* falls, the foundation of the whole Church sinks at once." In another place: "It is a most melancholy thing to hear with any patience, that our brother and companion in the episcopal office should look down with contempt on all others and be called *sole bishop*. But what does this pride of his indicate, but that the times of Antichrist are already at hand? For indeed he imitates him, who, despising the society of angels, endeavoured to usurp supreme power to himself." In another place, writing to Eulogius, bishop of Alexandria, and Anastasius, bishop of Antioch, he says, "None of my predecessors would ever use this profane word. For if one patriarch be called *universal,* the name of patriarch is taken away from all the rest. But far be it from any Christian heart to wish to arrogate to himself any thing that would in the least degree diminish the honour of his brethren. To consent to that execrable term is no other than to destroy the faith. Our obligation to preserve the unity of the faith is one thing, and to repress the haughtiness of pride is another. But I confidently assert, that whoever calls himself *universal bishop,* or desires to be so called, in such aggrandizement is the precursor of Antichrist, because he proudly sets up himself above all others." Again, to Anastasius, bishop of Antioch: "I have said that the bishop of Constantinople can have no peace with us, unless he would correct the haughtiness of that superstitious and proud title which has been invented by the first apostate; and to say nothing of the injury done to your dignity, if one bishop be called *universal,* when he falls, the whole Church sinks at once." But his assertion that this honour was offered to Leo in the Council of Chalcedon has not the least appearance of truth. For there is not a word of this in the acts of that council. And Leo himself, who in many of his epistles censures the decree passed there in favour of the see of Constantinople, would certainly not have passed over this argument, which would have been the most plausible of all, if that honour had really been offered to him, and he had refused it; and, having otherwise an immoderate thirst for honour, he would not readily have omitted a circumstance so much to his praise. Gregory was mistaken, therefore, in supposing that title to have been given to the see of Rome by the Council of Chalcedon. I forbear to remark how ridiculous it is for him to assert that the holy council conferred such a title, which he at the same time declares was profane, execrable, abominable, proud, and sacrilegious, and even invented by the devil, and published by the herald of Antichrist. And yet he adds that his predecessor refused it, lest, by the dignity given to one individual, all other bishops should be deprived of the honour due to them. In another place he says, "No one has ever wished to be called by such a name; no one has arrogated to himself this presumptuous title; lest, by assuming to himself the exclusive dignity of supreme bishop, he might seem to deny the episcopal honour to all his brethren."

V. I come now to the jurisdiction which the Roman pontiff asserts that he indisputably holds over all churches. I know what violent contentions there were in ancient times on this subject. For there has never been a period when the Roman see did not aspire to some authority over other Churches. And it will not be unsuitable to the present occasion to investigate the means by which it gradually rose to some power. I am not yet speaking of that unbounded empire which it has more recently usurped; that I shall defer to its proper place. But here it will be necessary to point out in a few words in what manner and by what methods it formerly exalted itself, so as to assume any jurisdiction over other Churches. When the Eastern Churches were disturbed and divided by the factions of the Arians, in the reign of Constantius and Constans, sons of Constantine the Great, and Athanasius, the principal defender of the orthodox faith, was driven from his see, that calamity constrained him to go to Rome, in order that, by the authority of the Roman see, he might in some degree repress the rage of his enemies, and confirm the faithful, who were in extreme distress. He was honourably received by Julius, then bishop of Rome, and prevailed on the bishops of the West to undertake the defence of his cause. Thus the pious in the Eastern Churches, finding themselves in great want of foreign aid, and seeing that their principal succour was to be obtained from the Church of Rome, readily ascribed to it all the authority that they possibly could. But all this amounted to nothing more than that communion with it was held in high estimation, and it was accounted ignominious to be excommunicated from it. This dignity was afterwards considerably augmented by men of wicked and abandoned lives; for to escape the punishments which they deserved, they resorted thither as to a common asylum. Therefore, if a priest was condemned by his bishop, or a bishop by the synod of his province, they immediately appealed to Rome. And the bishops of Rome received such appeals with culpable eagerness, considering it as a kind of extraordinary power to interfere in the concerns of distant Churches. Thus when Eutyches was condemned by Flavianus, patriarch of Constantinople, he complained to Leo that he had been treated with injustice. Leo, without any delay, but with equal temerity and expedition, undertook the patronage of a bad cause, issued bitter invectives against Flavianus, as if he had condemned an innocent man without hearing his defence, and by this ambitious conduct he for some time afforded considerable support to the impiety of Eutyches. It appears that similar circumstances frequently happened in Africa. For as soon as any wicked man was convicted before the ordinary tribunal, he flew to Rome, and brought various false accusations against his superiors; and the see of Rome was always ready to interpose. This presumption constrained the African bishops to pass a decree that no one should appeal beyond the sea on pain of excommunication.

VI. But however this might be, let us examine what jurisdiction or power the Roman see then possessed. Now, ecclesiastical power consists in these four things—the ordination of bishops, the calling of councils, the hearing of appeals, or jurisdiction, and corrective admonitions, or censures. All the ancient councils command bishops to be ordained by their own metropolitans; and they never direct the bishop of Rome to be called to this office except in his own province. By degrees, however, a custom was introduced for all the bishops of Italy to go to Rome to be consecrated, except the metropolitans, who did not suffer themselves to be subjected to this bondage. But when any metropolitan was to be ordained, the bishop of Rome sent one of his priests to assist at the ceremony, but not to preside. There is an example of this in an epistle of Gregory, respecting the consecration of Constantius, archbishop of Milan, after the death of Laurentius. I do not suppose, however, that this was a very ancient practice. It is probable that at first they sent legates to each other, from a principle of respect and affection, to witness the ordination, and testify their mutual communion; and that what was originally voluntary, was afterwards considered as necessary. However this may be, it is evident that in ancient times the bishop of Rome did not possess the power of consecrating bishops, except in his own province, that is, in the Churches dependent upon his see; as is declared by one of the canons of the Council of Nice. Consecration was followed by the sending of a synodical epistle; and in this the bishop of Rome had no superiority over others. It was the custom of the patriarchs, immediately after their consecration, to make a solemn declaration of their faith in a written communication to their brethren, professing their adherence to the doctrine of the holy and orthodox councils. Thus, by making a confession of their faith, they mutually approved themselves to each other. If the bishop of Rome had received such a confession from others, and not given it to other bishops in his turn, this would have been an instance of acknowledged superiority; but, as he was under the same obligation to give it as to require it, and was subject to the common law, it was certainly a token of equality, and not of dominion. We have examples of this in the epistles of Gregory to Anastasius and Cyriacus of Constantinople, and to all the patriarchs together.

VII. Next follow admonitions or censures, which, as the bishops of Rome formerly employed them towards others, they also received from others in their turn. Irenæus, bishop of Lyons, sharply reproved Victor, bishop of Rome, for having raised a pernicious dissension in the Church on subjects of no importance. Victor submitted to the reproof without any opposition. It was a liberty at that time commonly used by the holy bishops to exercise the privilege of brethren towards the bishop of Rome, by admonishing and reproving him whenever he committed any fault. He, in like manner, when occasion required, admonished others of their duty, and reproved them for their faults. For Cyprian, when he exhorts Stephen, bishop of Rome, to admonish the bishops of France, argues not from any superior authority, but from the common rights which priests enjoy among each other. If Stephen had then possessed any authority over France, would not Cyprian have said, You should chastise them, because they are subject to you? But he expresses himself in a very different manner. "This fraternal union," says he, "by which we are connected together, requires us to administer to each other mutual admonition." And we see with what severity of language, though otherwise a man of a mild disposition, he censures even Stephen himself, when he considered him assuming too much consequence. In this respect, also, there is yet no appearance of the bishop of Rome having been invested with any jurisdiction over those who were not of his province.

VIII. With respect to the calling of councils, it was the duty of every metropolitan, at stated seasons, to summon a provincial synod. There the bishop of Rome had no authority. But a universal council could only be called by the emperor. For if any one of the bishops had attempted this, not only he would not have been obeyed by those who were out of his province, but such an attempt would have led to immediate confusion. Therefore the emperor sent a summons to attend to all of them alike. Socrates, indeed, in his Ecclesiastical History, states that Julius, bishop of Rome, expostulated with the Eastern bishops, for not having invited him to the Council of Antioch; whereas the canons had forbidden that any thing should be decreed without the knowledge of the bishop of Rome. But who does not see that this is to be understood of those decrees which bind the universal Church? Now, it is no wonder if there was so much respect paid to the antiquity and eminence of the city, and to the dignity of the see, as to determine that no general decree respecting religion should be passed in the absence of the bishop of Rome, unless he refused to be present. But what is this towards dominion over the whole Church? For we do not deny that the bishop of Rome was one of the principal, but we will not admit, what the Romanists now contend, that he had the authority over all.

IX. There remains the fourth kind of ecclesiastical power, which consists in appeals. It is evident that he possesses supreme authority, to whose tribunal appeals are made. Many often appealed to the bishop of Rome; and he also attempted to assume the cognizance of causes; but he always became an object of derision whenever he exceeded his proper limits. I shall say nothing of the East, or of Greece; but it appears that the bishops of France strenuously resisted him, when he discovered an inclination to usurp authority over them. In Africa, this subject occasioned a long controversy. For when the Council of Milevum, at which Augustine was present, had denounced excommunication against all who should appeal beyond the sea, the bishop of Rome endeavoured to get this decree rescinded. He sent legates to state that this privilege had been given to him by the Council of

Nice. The legates produced certain acts which they alleged to be the acts of the Council of Nice, and which they had brought from the archives of their Church. They were resisted by the Africans, who denied that the bishop of Rome ought to be credited in his own cause. They therefore determined to send to Constantinople, and other cities of Greece, to obtain copies liable to less suspicion. It was found that these copies contained no such passages as the Roman legates had pretended. So the decree was confirmed, which had taken the supreme cognizance of appeals from the bishop of Rome. This transaction discovered the scandalous impudence of the Roman pontiff. For when he had fraudulently substituted the council of Sardis for that of Nice, he was disgracefully detected in a manifest falsehood. But still greater wickedness and effrontery were betrayed by those who added to the acts of the council a forged epistle, in which a bishop of Carthage condemns the arrogance of his predecessor, Aurelius, for having dared to withdraw himself from obedience to the apostolic see, presents the submission of himself and his Church, and humbly supplicates for pardon. These are the glorious monuments of antiquity upon which the majesty of the Roman see is founded; while, under the pretext of antiquity, they advance such puerile falsehoods, as require not the least penetration to detect. "Aurelius," says this famous epistle, "elated with diabolical audacity and obstinacy, was a rebel against Christ and St. Peter, and therefore deserved to be anathematized." But what said Augustine? What said all the fathers who were present at the Council of Milevum? But what necessity is there for spending many words to refute that stupid fabrication, which even the Romanists themselves, if they have any modesty left, cannot look at without being exceedingly ashamed? So Gratian, the compiler of the decretal,—whether from wickedness or ignorance I know not,—after having recited that canon, that those who appealed beyond the sea should be excommunicated, adds this exception, unless they appeal to the see of Rome. What can be done with such men, who are so destitute of common sense as to make that one case an exception to a law, to guard against which every one sees that the law was made? For the council, in condemning appeals beyond the sea, only prohibited any one from appealing to Rome; and this admirable expositor excepts Rome from the general prohibition!

X. But to put an end at once to this question, a single transaction, related by Augustine, will be sufficient to show what kind of jurisdiction was anciently possessed by the bishop of Rome. Donatus, bishop of Casæ Nigræ, had accused Cæcilianus, bishop of Carthage. The accused was condemned without a hearing; for, knowing that the bishops had conspired against him, he would not appear. The matter was then brought before the Emperor Constantine. With a view to have the cause decided by an ecclesiastical judgment, he referred the cognizance of it to Melchiades, bishop of Rome, with whom he associated some other bishops from Italy, France, and Spain. If it was part of the ordinary jurisdiction of the see of Rome to hear an appeal in an ecclesiastical cause, why did Melchiades suffer any colleagues to be appointed with him at the pleasure of the Emperor? and, moreover, why did he himself undertake the business rather at the command of the Emperor than from his own authority? But let us hear what took place afterwards. Cæcilianus was victorious. Donatus of Casæ Nigræ was convicted of calumny. He appealed. Constantine referred the appeal to the bishop of Arles. He sat in judgment on the decision of the bishop of Rome. If the Roman see possessed the supreme jurisdiction, subject to no appeal, how did Melchiades submit to such an insult, as for the bishop of Arles to be preferred before him? And who was the Emperor that did this? It was Constantine the Great, of whom they boast that he not only devoted all his attention, but employed almost all the power of his empire, to exalt the dignity of their see. We see, then, how very far the bishop of Rome was at that time from that supreme dominion which he pretends to have been given him by Christ over all Churches, and which he falsely boasts of having exercised in all ages with the consent of the whole world.

XI. I know what numerous epistles, and rescripts, and edicts, there are, in which the pontiffs have confidently advanced the most extravagant claims respecting this power. But it is also known to every person, possessed of the least sense or learning, that most things contained in them are so extremely absurd, that it is easy to discover at the first glance from what source they have proceeded. For what man of sound judgment, and in his sober senses, can suppose that Anacletus was the author of that curious interpretation, which Gratian quotes under his name—that Cephas means a head? There are many such fooleries collected together by Gratian without any judgment, which the Romanists in the present day employ against us in defence of their see; and such phantoms with which they used to delude the ignorant in the darkest times, they still persist in bringing forward amidst all the light of the present age. But I have no intention to devote much labour to the refutation of such things, which manifestly refute themselves by their extreme absurdity. I confess that there are also genuine epistles of the ancient pontiffs, in which they extol the majesty of their see by the most magnificent titles. Such are some epistles of Leo; who, though he was a man of learning and eloquence, had likewise an immoderate thirst for glory and dominion; but whether the Churches at that time gave credit to his testimony when he thus exalted himself, is a subject of inquiry. Now, it appears that many were offended at his ambition, and resisted his claims. In one epistle he deputes the bishop of Thessalonica to act as his representative in Greece and other adjacent countries; in another he delegates the bishop of Arles, or some other bishop, to be his vicar in France. So he appoints Hormisdas, bishop of Seville, his vicar in Spain. But in all cases he mentions, by way of exception, that he makes such appointments on condition that they shall in no respect infringe the ancient privileges of the metropolitans. But Leo himself declares this to be one of their privileges, that if any difficulty should arise, the metropolitan was to be consulted in the first place. These delegations, therefore, were accompanied with this condition—that there was to be no interference with any bishop in his ordinary jurisdiction, with any metropolitan in hearing appeals, or with any provincial synod in the regulation of the Churches. Now, what was this but to abstain from all jurisdiction, and only to interpose for the settlement of disputes, as far as was consistent with the law and nature of ecclesiastical communion?

XII. In the time of Gregory, this ancient custom had already undergone a considerable change. For when the empire was convulsed and torn asunder, when France and Spain were afflicted with repeated and numerous wars and distresses, Illyricum laid waste, Italy harassed, and Africa almost ruined with incessant calamities,—in order to preserve the unity of the faith amidst such a violent convulsion of civil affairs, or at least to prevent its total destruction, all the bishops round about connected themselves more closely with the bishop of Rome. The consequence was, that the power as well as the dignity of that see was greatly increased. I am not much concerned, however, respecting the methods by which this was effected. It is at least evident, that it was greater at that period than in the preceding ages. And even then it was very far from an unlimited dominion, for one man to govern all others according to his own pleasure. But the see of Rome was held in such reverence, that its authority would repress and correct the refractory and obstinate, who could not be confined to their duty by the other bishops. For Gregory embraces every opportunity of protesting, that he as faithfully maintained the rights of others, as he required them to maintain his. "Nor under the influence of ambition," says he, "do I withhold from any one that which is his right; but I desire to honour my brethren in all things."—There is not a sentence in his writings which contains a prouder boast of the majesty of his primacy than the following: "I know no bishop who is not subject to the apostolic see, when he is found in fault." But he immediately adds, "Where there is no fault to require subjection, all are equal by right of humility." He attributes to himself the authority to correct those who have transgressed; if all do their duty, he places himself on an equality with them. But he assumed this authority to himself, and they who were willing consented to it, while others, who disapproved of it, were at liberty to oppose it with impunity; and this, it is notorious, was the conduct of the majority. Besides, it is to be remarked, that he is there speaking of the primate of Constantinople, who had been condemned by a provincial synod, and had disregarded the united judgment of the assembly. His colleagues complained to the emperor of his obstinacy. The emperor appointed Gregory to decide the cause. We see, then, that he made no attempt to interfere with the ordinary jurisdiction; and that the very thing which he does for the assistance of others, he does only at the command of the emperor.

XIII. This, therefore, was all the power which was then possessed by the bishop of Rome,—to oppose rebellious and refractory persons, in cases which required some extraordinary remedy, and that in order to assist, not to hinder, other bishops. Therefore he assumes to himself no more power over others than he grants to all others over himself, when he professes that he is ready to be reproved by all, and to be corrected by all. So in another epistle he commands the bishop of Aquileia to come to Rome to plead his cause in a controversy which had arisen between him and his neighbours, respecting an article of faith; nevertheless he gives this command, not from his own authority, but in consequence of the mandate of the emperor. Nor does he announce himself as the sole judge, but promises to assemble a synod to judge of the whole affair. But though there was still such moderation, that the power of the Roman see had its certain limits, which it was not permitted to exceed, and the bishop of Rome himself no more presided over others than he was subject to them, yet it appears how very displeasing this situation was to Gregory. For he frequently complains, that under the name of being a bishop, he was forced back to the world, and that he was more involved in secular cares than ever he had been while he was a layman; so that in that honour he was oppressed with the tumult of worldly business. In another passage he says, "Such a vast burden of occupations presses me down, that my mind is incapacitated for any elevation towards things above. I am tossed about with numerous causes, like so many waves; and after my former seasons of retirement and tranquillity, I am disquieted with the tempests of a tumultuous life; so that I may truly say, I am come into the depth of the sea, and the tempest has drowned me." Judge, then, what he would have said, if he had fallen upon these times. If he did not fulfil the office of a pastor, yet he was employed in it. He refrained from all interference in the civil government, and acknowledged himself to be subject to the emperor in common with others. He never intruded into the care of other Churches, except when he was constrained by necessity. And yet he considered himself to be in a labyrinth, because he could not wholly devote himself to the exclusive duties of a bishop.

XIV. The bishop of Constantinople, as we have already stated, was at that time engaged in a contest with the bishop of Rome, respecting the primacy. For after the seat of the empire was fixed at Constantinople, the majesty of the government seemed to require that Church to be the next in dignity to the Church of Rome. And indeed at the beginning nothing contributed more to establish the primacy in the Church of Rome than the circumstance of that city being then the capital of the empire. Gratian recites a rescript under the name of Pope Lucinus, in which he says that the distinction of cities appointed to be the residence of metropolitans and primates, was regulated by no other rule than the nature of the civil government previously established in them. There is another similar rescript, also, under the name of Pope Clement, in which he says, that patriarchs had been appointed in those cities which had anciently been the stations of arch-flamens. This statement, though erroneous, approaches to the truth. For it is certain, that in order to make as little change as possible, the provinces were divided according to the existing state of things, and that primates and metropolitans were placed in those cities which had precedence of the rest in dignity and power. Therefore, in the Council of Turin, it was decreed, that those which were the chief cities of the respective provinces in the civil government, should be the principal sees of bishops; and that if the honour of the civil government should happen to be transferred from one city to another, the seat of the metropolitan should be removed to the same place. But Innocent, the Roman pontiff, seeing the ancient dignity of his city beginning to decline, after the translation of the seat of the empire to Constantinople, and trembling for the honour of his see, enacted a contrary law; in which he denies the necessity of a change of the ecclesiastical capitals, in consequence of a change of the imperial capitals. But the authority of a council ought to be preferred to the sentence of an individual, and we may justly suspect Innocent himself in his own cause. He proves by his decree, however, that the original regulation had been for the seats of metropolitans to be disposed according to the civil rank of the respective cities.

XV. According to this ancient ordinance, it was decreed in the first Council of Constantinople, that the bishop of that city should have the next rank and dignity to the bishop of Rome, because that was a new Rome. But when a similar decree was passed long after in the Council of Chalcedon, Leo strenuously opposed it. And he not only took the liberty of pouring contempt on what had been decided by upwards of six hundred bishops, but likewise heavily reproached them with having taken from other sees the honour which they had ventured to confer on the Church of Constantinople. Now, what could incite him to disturb the world for so insignificant a cause, but mere ambition? He says, that what had once been determined by the Council of Nice, ought to have been maintained inviolable. As if the Christian faith were endangered by the preference of one Church to another, or as if the patriarchates had been distributed by the Council of Nice with any other view than the preservation of external order. Now, we know that external order admits, and even requires, various changes according to the various circumstances of different periods. It is a futile pretence, therefore, of Leo, that the honour, which the authority of the Nicene council had given to the see of Alexandria, ought not to be conferred on that of Constantinople. For common sense dictates, that this was such a decree as might be abolished according to the state of the times. And besides, the repeal met with no opposition from the bishops of the East, who were most interested in the matter. Proterius, who had been appointed bishop of Alexander instead of Dioscorus, was present; as were other patriarchs, whose dignity was lessened by this measure. It was for them to oppose it, and not Leo, who retained his original station unaltered. When they all suffered it to pass without any objection, and even assented to it, and the bishop of Rome was the only one who resisted it, it is easy to judge by what motive he was influenced. He foresaw, what actually came to pass not long after, that as the glory of Rome was declining, Constantinople would not be content with the second place, but would contend for the primacy. Yet all his clamour was unavailing; the decree of the council was confirmed. Therefore his successors, seeing themselves vanquished, peaceably refrained from such obstinacy; for they decreed that he should be accounted the second patriarch.

XVI. But a little while after, John, who presided over the Church of Constantinople while Gregory was bishop of Rome, had the arrogance to assume the title of universal patriarch. Gregory, not afraid of defending his see in a good cause, resolutely opposed this assumption. And certainly it betrayed intolerable pride and folly in John to wish to make the limits of his bishopric the same with those of the empire. Now, Gregory did not claim to himself what he denied to another; but execrated the title, by whomsoever it might be usurped, as wicked and impious. In one of his epistles he expresses his displeasure with Eulogius, bishop of Alexandria, for having complimented him with such a title. "Behold," says he, "in the preface of the epistle which you have directed to myself, who have forbidden it, you have taken care to introduce that appellation of pride, by calling me universal pope. Which I entreat that your holiness will not do any more; because all that you give to another beyond what is reasonable, is deducted from yourself. I consider nothing an honour to me, by which I see the honour of my brethren diminished. For my honour is the honour of the universal Church, and the perfect vigour of my brethren. If your holiness calls me universal pope, this is denying that you have any share in that which is wholly attributed to me." Gregory's was a good and honourable cause; but John, being supported by the favour of Mauritius the emperor, could not be diverted from his purpose; and Cyriacus, his successor, was equally inflexible.

XVII. At length Phocas, who ascended the throne after the murder of Mauritius, being more favourable to the Romans,—for what reason I know not, unless because he had been crowned at Rome without any difficulty,—granted to Boniface the Third what Gregory had never demanded,—that Rome should be the head of all Churches. Thus the controversy was decided. Yet this grant of the emperor could not have been so much to the advantage of the see of Rome, if it had not been followed by other things. For Greece and all Asia soon after separated from its communion. France reverenced it only so far as not to carry its obedience beyond its inclinations; nor was it reduced to entire subjection, till Pepin had usurped the crown. For after Zachary, the Roman pontiff, had assisted Pepin in the commission of treason and robbery, in deposing his lawful sovereign, and taking possession of the throne, he was rewarded by having the see of Rome invested with jurisdiction over the Gallican Churches. As robbers are accustomed to divide their common booty, so those worthy persons concerted together, that Pepin should have the temporal and civil sovereignty after the deposition of the rightful monarch, and that Zachary should be made the head over all bishops, and enjoy the spiritual power. At first this was feeble, as is generally the case with new establishments; but it was afterwards confirmed by the authority of Charlemagne, and almost from a similar cause; for he also was indebted to the Roman pontiff, for his exertions in raising him to the dignity of emperor. Now, though it is probable that the Churches, before that time, had in general been greatly disfigured, it is evident that in France and Germany the ancient form of the Church was then entirely obliterated. The archives of the parliament of Paris still contain brief registers of those times, which, in relating ecclesiastical events, make frequent mention of the treaties both of Pepin and Charlemagne with the Roman pontiff; from which it may be concluded that an alteration was then made in the ancient state of the Church.

XVIII. From that time, as things daily became worse and worse, the tyranny of the Roman see was gradually established and increased, and that partly through the ignorance, and partly through the indolence, of the bishops. For while the Roman pontiff was usurping every thing to himself, and proceeding from one assumption to another, without any limits, in defiance of law and justice, the bishops did not exert themselves with the zeal which became them to repress his cupidity, and where there was no want of inclination, they were destitute of real learning and knowledge, so that they were not at all equal to such an important undertaking. We see, therefore, what a horrible profanation of every thing sacred, and what a total disorganization of the Church there was at Rome in the days of Bernard. He complains that the ambitious, the avaricious, the simoniacal, the sacrilegious, the adulterous, the incestuous, and all who were chargeable with the most atrocious crimes, from every part of the world, resorted to Rome, in order to procure or to retain ecclesiastical honours by the apostolical authority; and that fraud, circumvention, and violence, were generally practised. He says, that the judicial process which was then pursued was execrable, and not only unbecoming of the Church, but disgraceful to any civil court. He exclaims, that the Church is full of ambitious men, and that there is not one who is any more afraid of perpetrating the most flagitious crimes, than robbers in their den when they are distributing the plunder which they have seized on the highway. "Few," he says, "regard the mouth of the legislator; they all look at his hands, and that not without cause, for those hands transact all that is done by the pope. What a business it is, that they are bought with the spoils of the Church, who say to you, Well done, well done! The life of the poor is sown in the streets of the rich; silver glitters in the mire; people run to it from all parts, it is borne away, not by the poorest, but by the strongest, or perhaps by him who runs fastest. This custom, or rather this mortal corruption, commenced not with you; I wish it may end with you. In these circumstances you, a pastor, are proceeding, covered with abundant and costly attire. If I might dare to use the expression, these are rather the pastors of devils than of sheep. Did Peter act in this manner? Was Paul guilty of such trifling? Your court has been accustomed to receive men good, more than to make them so. For the wicked are not improved in it, but the good are corrupted." The abuses of appeals which he relates, no pious person can read without the greatest horror. At length, respecting the insatiable cupidity of the see of Rome in the usurpation of jurisdiction, he concludes in the following manner: "I speak the murmur and common complaint of the Churches. They exclaim that they are divided and dismembered. There are few or none of them who do not either bewail or dread this plague. Do you inquire what plague? Abbots are torn away from their bishops, bishops from their archbishops. It is wonderful if this can be excused. By such conduct you prove that you have a plenitude of power, but not of justice. You act thus because you can, but the question is whether you ought. You are appointed to preserve to all their respective honour and rank, and not to envy them." These few passages I have thought proper to recite, out of a great many, partly that the readers may see how sadly the Church had then declined, and partly that they may know into what sorrow and lamentation all good men were plunged by this calamity.

XIX. But though we should grant to the Roman pontiff in the present day the same eminence and extent of jurisdiction which this see possessed in the middle ages, as in the times of Leo and Gregory, what is that to the Papacy in its present state? I am not yet referring to the temporal and secular power, which we shall afterwards examine in its proper place; but the spiritual government itself of which they boast, what resemblance has it to the condition of those times? For the Romanists designate the pope no otherwise than as the supreme head of the Church on earth, and universal bishop of the whole world. And the pontiffs themselves, when they speak of their authority, pronounce with great superciliousness, that they have the power to command, and that to others is only left the necessity to obey; that all their decrees are to be received as if they were confirmed by the voice of St. Peter; that for want of their presence, provincial synods have no authority; that they have the power to ordain priests and deacons for all the Churches, and to summon to their see those who have been elsewhere ordained. In the Decretal of Gratian there are innumerable pretensions of this kind, which I forbear to recite lest I should be too tedious to my readers. But the sum of them all comes to this; that the Roman pontiff alone has the supreme cognizance of all ecclesiastical causes, whether in judging and determining doctrines, in enacting laws, in regulating discipline, or in exercising jurisdiction. It would also be tedious and superfluous to enumerate the prvileges which they assume to themselves in reservations, as they call them. But what is the most intolerable of all, they leave no judgment on earth to curb or restrain their cupidity, if they abuse such unlimited power. "It cannot be lawful," they say, "for any one to reject the judgment of this see, on account of the primacy of the Roman Church." Again: "The judge shall not be judged, either by the emperor or by kings, or by all the clergy, or by the people." This is arrogance beyond all bounds, for one man to constitute himself judge of all, and to refuse to submit to the judgment of any. But what if he exercise tyranny over the people of God, if he divide and desolate the kingdom of Christ, if he disturb and overturn the whole Church, if he pervert the pastoral office into a system of robbery? Even though he should go to the greatest extremes of profligacy and mischief, he denies that he is at all accountable for his conduct. For these are the very words of the pontiffs: "God has been pleased to decide the causes of other men by the judgment of men, but the prelate of this see he has, without all question, reserved to his own judgment." Again, "The actions of our subjects are judged by us; but ours by God alone."

XX. And that such edicts might have the more weight, they have falsely substituted the names of ancient pontiffs, as if things had been so regulated from the beginning; whereas it is very certain, that every thing, which attributes to the Roman pontiff more than we have stated to have been given him by the ancient councils, is a novel and recent fabrication. They have even gone to such a pitch of impudence as to publish a rescript, under the name of Anastasius, patriarch of Constantinople, which declares that it had been ordained by the ancient canons, that nothing should be done even in the remotest provinces, without being first reported to the Roman see. Beside the notorious falsehood of this, what man will think it credible, that such a eulogium of the Roman see proceeded from the adversary and rival of its honour and dignity? But it was necessary that these Antichrists should be carried to such an extreme of madness and blindness, that their iniquity may be evident to all men of sound understanding, who only choose to open their eyes. But the Decretal Epistles, complied by Gregory the Ninth, as well as the Constitutions of Clement the Fifth, and the Decrees of Martin, still more openly and expressly betray, in every page, the inhuman ferocity and tyranny of barbarous kings. But these are the oracles from which the Romanists wish their Papacy to be appreciated. Hence proceeded those famous axioms, which at the present day are universally received by them as oracles: That the pope cannot err; that the pope is superior to all councils; that the pope is the universal bishop of all Churches, and supreme head of the

Church upon earth. I pass over the far greater absurdities, which foolish canonists maintain in their schools; which, however, the Roman theologians not only assent to, but even applaud, in order to flatter their idol.

XXI. I shall not treat them with all the severity which they deserve. To this consummate insolence, another person would oppose the declaration of Cyprian among the bishops at the Council of Carthage, of which he was president: "No one of us calls himself bishop of bishops, or, by tyrannical fear, constrains his colleagues to the necessity of obeying him." He would object what was decreed at Carthage some time after, "That no one should be called *prince of priests, or first bishop.*" He would collect many testimonies from histories, many canons of councils, and various passages from the writings of the fathers, by which the Roman pontiff would be reduced to the rank of other bishops. I pass over these things, however, that I may not appear to lay too much stress upon them. But let the most able advocates of the Roman see answer me, with what face they can dare to defend the title of *universal bishop,* which they find to have been so often anathematized by Gregory. If the testimony of Gregory be entitled to any credit, they cannot make their pontiff universal bishop without thereby declaring him to be Antichrist. Nor was the title of *head* any more in use at that time; for in one of his epistles he says, "Peter is the principal member in the body; John, Andrew, and James, were heads of particular people. Yet they are all members of the Church under one head. Even the saints before the law, the saints under the law, the saints under grace, are all placed among the members, and no one ever wished himself to be called *universal.*" The arrogant pretensions of the pontiff to the power of commanding are very inconsistent with an observation made by Gregory in another passage. For when Eulogius, bishop of Alexandria, had represented himself as commanded by him, he replies in the following manner:—"I beseech you, let me not hear the word *command* mentioned again; for I know what I am, and what you are. In station, you are my brethren; in holiness, you are my fathers. Therefore I gave no command, but intended to suggest to you such things as appeared to be useful." By extending his jurisdiction, as he does, without any limits, the pope does a grievous and atrocious injury, not only to other bishops, but to all other Churches, which he distracts and divides by such conduct, in order to establish his own see upon their ruins. But when he exempts himself from all the judgments of others, and determines to reign in such a tyrannical manner as to have no law but his own pleasure, this is certainly so unbecoming, and foreign from the order of the Church, that it is altogether intolerable, and incapable of any defence. For it is utterly repugnant, not only to every sentiment of piety, but even of humanity.

XXII. But that I may not be obliged to pursue and discuss every particular point, I again appeal to those of my contemporaries, who would be considered as the most able and faithful advocates of the Roman see, whether they are not ashamed to defend the present state of the Papacy, which is evidently a hundred times more corrupt than it was in the times of Gregory and Bernard, but which even then so exceedingly displeased those holy men. Gregory every where complains, that he was excessively distracted with occupations unsuitable to his office; that under the name of being a bishop, he was carried back to the world; that he was involved in secular cares, to a greater extent than he could remember to have been while he was a layman; that he was oppressed with the tumult of worldly business, so that his mind was incapacitated for any elevation towards things above; that he was tossed about with numerous causes like so many waves, and disquieted with the tempests of a tumultuous life, so that he might justly say, "I am come into the depth of the sea." Amidst these worldly avocations, however, he could still instruct the people by public preaching, give private admonition and reproof to those who required it, regulate his Church, give advice to his colleagues, and exhort them to their duty; besides these things, he had some time left for writing; yet he deplores his calamity, in being plunged into the depth of the sea. If the administration of that age was a sea, what must be said of the Papacy in its present state? For what resemblance is there between them? Here we find no sermons preached, no attention to discipline, no concern for the Churches, no spiritual function performed; in a word, nothing but the world. Yet this labyrinth is praised, as though nothing could be found better constituted, or better administered. What complaints are poured out by Bernard, what lamentations does he utter, when he beholds the vices of his times? What would he say, then, if he could behold this our iron, or, if possible, worse than iron age? What impudence is it, not only pertinaciously to defend as sacred and Divine what all the holy fathers have reprobated with one voice but also to abuse their testimony in vindication of the Papacy, which it is evident was utterly unknown to them! In the time of Bernard, however, I confess the corruption was so great that there was no great difference between that age and the present; but those who adduce any plea for the existing state of things from the time of Leo, Gregory, and others in that middle period, must be destitute of all shame. This conduct resembles that of any one, who, to vindicate the monarchy of the Roman emperors, should commend the ancient state of the Roman government; which would be no other than borrowing the praises of liberty to adorn a system of tyranny.

XXIII. Lastly, though all these things were conceded to them, they would be called to a new controversy, when we deny that there exists at Rome a Church in which such privileges can reside, or a bishop capable of exercising these dignified prerogatives. Supposing, therefore, all these things to be true, which, however, we have already refuted,—that, by the voice of Christ, Peter had been constituted head of the universal Church; that the honour vested in him he had committed to the Roman see; that this had been established by the authority of the ancient Church, and confirmed by long usage; that all men, with one consent, had invariably acknowledged the supreme power of the Roman pontiff; that he had been the judge in all causes and of all men, and had been subject to the judgment of none;—though they should have all these concessions, and any more that they wished, yet I reply in one word, that none of them would be of any avail, unless there be at Rome a Church and a bishop. They must of necessity allow, that Rome cannot be the mother of Churches, unless it be itself a Church, and that he cannot be the prince of bishops, who is not a bishop himself. Do they wish, then, to make Rome the apostolic see? Let them show me a true and legitimate apostleship. Do they wish to have the supreme pontiff? Let them show me a bishop. But where will they show us any form or appearance of a Church? They mention it, indeed, and have it frequently in their mouths. But the Church is known by certain marks, and a bishopric is a name of office. I am not now speaking of the people, but of the government itself, which ought always to appear in the Church. Where is the ministry, such as Christ's institution requires? Let us remember what has already been said of the office of presbyters and bishops. If we bring the office of cardinals to that rule, we shall confess that they have no resemblance to presbyters. And I should wish to know what resemblance the pontiff himself bears to a bishop. The first duty of the episcopal office is to instruct the people from the word of God; the second duty, closely connected with the first, is to administer the sacraments; the third is to admonish, exhort, and reprove those who offend, and to regulate the people by holy discipline. Which of these duties does he perform? Which of them does he even pretend to perform? Let them tell me, then, upon what principle they require him to be considered as a bishop, who never, even in appearance, with his little finger touches the least portion of the duty.

XXIV. The case of a bishop is different from that of a king, who still retains the honour and title of a king, though he execute none of the royal functions. But in judging of a bishop, regard is to be paid to the commission of Christ, which ought always to continue in force in the Church. Let the Romanists, therefore, furnish me with a solution of this difficulty. I deny that their pontiff is the chief of bishops, because he is not a bishop himself. Now, they must prove this second member of my position to be false, if they will obtain the victory in the first. But what must be the conclusion, if he not only has no characteristic of a bishop, but every thing contrary to it? But here where shall I begin? with his doctrine, or his conduct? What shall I say? What shall I omit? Where shall I stop? I will make this assertion—that as the world is at present filled with so many corrupt and impious doctrines, loaded with such various kinds of superstitions, blinded with such numerous errors, and immerged in such profound idolatry,—there is not one of these evils which has not originated from the see of Rome, or at least been confirmed by it. Nor is there any other cause for the violent rage of the pontiffs against the revived doctrine of the gospel, and for their exertion of all their power to crush it, and their instigation of all kings and princes to persecute it, but that they see that their whole kingdom will decline and fall to the ground, where the primitive gospel of Christ shall be received. Leo was cruel; Clement was sanguinary; Paul is ferocious. But it is not so much that nature has impelled them to impugn the truth, as that this was the only way to defend their power. As they cannot be safe, therefore, without ruining Christ, they labour in this cause as if it were in the defence of their religion, their habitations, their lives. What, then, shall we consider that as the apostolic see, where we behold nothing but a horrible apostasy? Shall he be regarded as the vicar of Christ, who, by his furious exertions in persecuting the gospel, unequivocally declares himself to be Antichrist? Shall he be deemed Peter's successor, who rages with fire and sword to demolish all that Peter built? Shall we acknowledge him to be head of the Church, who, after severing the Church from Christ, its only true Head, divides and tears it in pieces? Though it be admitted that Rome was once the mother of all Churches, yet from the time when it began to be the seat of Antichrist, it has ceased to be what it was before.

XXV. Some persons think us too severe and censorious, when we call the Roman pontiff Antichrist. But those who are of this opinion do not consider that they bring the same charge of presumption against Paul himself, after whom we speak, and whose language we adopt. And lest any one should object, that we improperly pervert to the Roman pontiff those words of Paul, which belong to a different subject, I shall briefly show that they are not capable of any other interpretation than that which applies them to the Papacy. Paul says, that Antichrist "sitteth in the temple of God." (*z*) In another place, also, the Holy Spirit, describing his image in the person of Antiochus, declares that his kingdom will consist in "speaking great words," or blasphemies, "against the Most High." (*a*) Hence we conclude, that it is rather a tyranny over the souls of men, than over their bodies, which is erected in opposition to the spiritual kingdom

(*z*) 2 Thess. ii. 4. (*a*) Dan. vii. 25.

of Christ. And in the next place, that this tyranny is one which does not abolish the name of Christ or of his Church, but rather abuses the authority of Christ, and conceals itself under the character of the Church, as under a mask. Now, though all the heresies and schisms which have existed from the beginning belong to the kingdom of Antichrist, yet when Paul predicts an approaching apostasy, he signifies by this description that that seat of abomination shall then be erected, when a universal defection shall have seized the Church, notwithstanding many members, dispersed in different places, persevere in the unity of the faith. But when he adds, that even in his days "the mystery of inquity" did "already work" (*b*) in secret what it was afterwards to effect in a more public manner, he gives us to understand that this calamity was neither to be introduced by one man, nor to terminate with one man. Now, when he designates Antichrist by this character,—that he would rob God of his honour in order to assume it to himself,—this is the principal indication which we ought to follow in our inquiries after Antichrist, especially where such pride proceeds to a public desolation of the Church. As it is evident therefore that the Roman pontiff has impudently transferred to himself some of the peculiar and exclusive prerogatives of God and Christ, it cannot be doubted that he is the captain and leader of this impious and abominable kingdom.

XXVI. Now, let the Romanists go and object antiquity against us; as if, in such a subversion of every thing, the honour of the see could remain, where no see exists. Eusebius relates that God, in order to make way for his vengeance, removed the Church from Jerusalem to Pella. What we are informed did happen once, may have happened oftener. Therefore to attach the honour of the primacy to any particular place, so that he who is in fact the most inveterate enemy of Christ, the greatest adversary of the gospel, the desolater and destroyer of the Church, the most cruel murderer and butcher of all the saints, must nevertheless be accounted the vicar of Christ, the successor of Peter, the chief prelate of the Church, merely because he occupies what was anciently the first see, is a thing extremely ridiculous and absurd.

(*b*) 2 Thess. ii. 7.

I forbear to remark the immense difference between the pope's chancery, and a well regulated administration of the Church; though this one thing is sufficient to remove every difficulty on this subject. For no man in his sound senses will include the episcopal office in lead and in bulls, much less in that school of frauds and chicaneries, in which the pope's spiritual government consists. It has justly been remarked, therefore, that the Roman Church which is boasted of, has long ago been converted into a secular court, which is all that is now to be seen at Rome. Nor am I here accusing the vices of individuals, but proving that the Papacy itself is diametrically opposite to the legitimate order of the Church.

XXVII. But if we proceed to persons, it is well known what kind of men we shall find sustaining the character of vicars of Christ. Julius, and Leo, and Clement, and Paul, will be pillars of the Christian faith, and the principal oracles of religion, who never knew any thing of Christ, except what they had learned in the school at Lucian. But why do I enumerate three or four pontiffs, as though it were doubtful what kind of religion the pontiffs and the whole college of cardinals have professed long ago, and profess in the present day? For of the secret theology which prevails among them, the first article is, that there is no God; the second, that all that is written and preached concerning Jesus Christ is falsehood and imposture; the third, that the doctrine of a future life, and that of the final resurrection, are mere fables. This opinion, I confess, is not entertained by all, and is expressed by few of them; yet it long ago began to be the ordinary religion of the pontiffs. Though this is notorious to all who are acquainted with Rome, yet the Roman theologians persist in boasting that the possibility of error in the pope has been prevented by the privilege of Christ, because he said to Peter, "I have prayed for thee, that thy faith fail not." (*c*) What can they gain by such impudent mockery, except it be to convince the whole world of their having arrived at such an extreme of presumption, that they neither fear God nor regard men?

XXVIII. But let us suppose the impiety of those pontiffs whom

---

(*c*) Luke xxii. 32.

I have mentioned, to be concealed, because they have not published it by sermons or by writings, but only betrayed it in their chambers and at their tables, or at least within the walls of their palaces. But if they wish to establish this privilege to which they pretend, they must expunge from the number of the pontiffs John the Twenty-second, who publicly maintained that souls are mortal, and that they perish together with the bodies till the day of resurrection. And to show that the whole see, with its principal pillars, was then entirely overturned, not one of the cardinals resisted this capital error; but the university of Paris urged the king of France to compel the pope to a retraction. The king interdicted his subjects from all communion with him, unless he should speedily repent; and he caused this to be proclaimed, in the usual manner, by a herald. Compelled by necessity, the pontiff abjured his error. This example renders it unnecessary for me to dispute any longer against the assertion of our adversaries, that the see of Rome and its pontiffs cannot err respecting the faith, because Christ said to Peter, "I have prayed for thee, that thy faith fail not." John certainly fell from the true faith in so disgraceful a manner, that he might furnish to posterity a signal proof, that those who succeed Peter in his bishopric are not all Peters. The argument itself, however, is too puerile to need any answer. For if they are determined to apply to Peter's successors every thing that was said to Peter, it will follow that they are all Satans, because the Lord also said to Peter, "Get thee behind me, Satan; thou art an offence unto me." (*d*) It will be as easy for us to retort this passage against them, as it is for them to object the other against us.

XXIX. But it affords me no pleasure to contend with them in such fooleries, and therefore I return from the digression. To confine Christ, and the Holy Spirit, and the Church, to one particular place, so that whoever presides there, even though he be a devil, must, nevertheless, be deemed the vicar of Christ and the head of the Church, because that place was formerly the see of Peter, I maintain to be not only impious and dishonourable to Christ, but altogether absurd and repugnant to common sense.

(*d*) Matt. xvi. 23.

The Roman pontiffs for a long time have either been totally indifferent to religion, or have shown themselves its greatest enemies. They are no more made the vicars of Christ, therefore, by the see which they occupy, than an idol is to be taken for God, because it is placed in his temple. Now, if a judgment is to be formed on their conduct, let the pontiffs answer for themselves in what part of it they can at all be recognized as bishops. In the first place, the mode of life generally pursued at Rome, not only without any opposition from them, but with their connivance, and even tacit approbation, is altogether disgraceful to bishops, whose duty it is to restrain the licentiousness of the people by a rigid discipline. I will not, however, be so severe against them as to charge them with the faults of other persons. But while both themselves and their families, with almost the whole college of cardinals, and the whole host of their clergy, are so abandoned to all kinds of debauchery, impurity, and obscenity, and to every species of enormity and crime, that they resemble monsters rather than men, they prove themselves to have no just claim to the character of bishops. They need not be afraid, however, that I shall proceed to a further disclosure of their turpitude. For it is unpleasant to meddle with such abominable pollution, and it is necessary to spare chaste ears. Besides, I conceive, I have more than sufficiently proved what I intended, that even if Rome had anciently been the head of all Churches, yet at the present day she is not worthy of being accounted one of the smallest toes of the Church's feet.

XXX. With respect to the cardinals, as they are called, I know not how it has come to pass that they have so suddenly risen to such high dignity. In the time of Gregory, this title was exclusively applied to bishops; for whenever he mentions cardinals, he speaks of them not only as belonging to the Church of Rome, but to any other Churches; so that, in short, a cardinal priest is no other than a bishop. I find no such title at all in the writers of any preceding age; and at that time, I observe, they were far inferior to bishops, to whom they are now so far superior. This passage of Augustine is well known: "Though, according to the titles of honour which have long been used in the Church, a bishop is superior to a presbyter, yet Augustine is in many things inferior to Jerome." He clearly makes not the least distinction between a presbyter of the Roman Church and those of other Churches, but places them all alike below the bishops. And this order was so long observed, that in the Council of Carthage, when two legates attended from the Roman see, one a bishop, the other a presbyter, the presbyter was obliged to take the lowest seat. But not to go too far into antiquity for examples, we have the acts of a council held under Gregory at Rome, at which the presbyters sat in the lowest place, and subscribed separately; and the deacons were not allowed to subscribe at all. And, indeed, the priests had no other office at that time, than to attend and assist the bishop in the ministry of the word and the administration of the sacraments. Now, their condition is so changed, that they are become the cousins of kings and emperors. And there is no doubt but they rose by degrees, together with their head, till they reached their present high dignity. This also I have thought proper to suggest by the way in a few words, that the reader may more fully understand, that the Roman see, in its present circumstances, is widely different from its ancient state, under the pretext of which it is now maintained and defended. But whatever they may have been in former times, since they have now no true and legitimate office in the Church, and only retain a mere name and useless mask of one, and since every thing belonging to them is quite contrary to it, it was necessary that what Gregory often forebodes should actually befall them: "I say it with tears, I denounce it with groans, that since the sacerdotal order is fallen within, it will not long be able to stand without." Or rather it was necessary that what Malachi declares of similar characters should be fulfilled in them: "Ye are departed out of the way; ye have caused many to stumble at the law; ye have corrupted the covenant of Levi, saith the Lord of hosts. Therefore have I also made you contemptible and base before all the people." (*e*) I now leave it to all pious persons to consider the nature of the lofty fabric of the Roman hierarchy, to which the Papists, with nefarious impudence, and without any hesitation, sacrifice even the word of God itself, which ought to have been held venerable and sacred by heaven and earth, by men and angels.

(*e*) Mal. ii. 8, 9.

CHAPTER VIII

The Power of the Church Respecting Articles of Faith, and Its Licentious Perversion, Under the Papacy, to the Corruption of All Purity of Doctrine

The next subject is the power of the Church, which is to be considered as residing, partly in the respective bishops, partly in councils, and those either provincial or general. I speak only of the spiritual power which belongs to the Church. Now, it consists either in doctrine, in legislation, or jurisdiction. The subject of doctrine contains two parts—the authority to establish doctrines, and the explication of them. Before we enter on the particular discussion of each of these points, we would apprize the pious readers, that whatever is asserted respecting the power of the Church, they should be mindful to refer to the end for which Paul declares it to have been given, namely, "to edification, and not to destruction;" (*f*) and all who make a legitimate use of it, consider themselves as nothing more than "servants of Christ," (*g*) and the people's "servants for Jesus' sake." (*h*) Now, the only way to edify the Church is, for the ministers themselves to study

(*f*) 2 Cor. x. 8; xiii. 10. (*g*) Phil. i. 1. (*h*) 2 Cor. iv. 5.

to preserve to Jesus Christ his rightful authority, which can no longer be secure than while he is left in possession of what he has received from the Father, that is, to be the sole Master in the Church. (*i*) For of him alone, and of no other, is it said, "Hear ye him." (*k*) The power of the Church, therefore, is not to be depreciated, yet it must be circumscribed by certain limits, that it may not be extended in every direction, according to the caprice of men. It will, therefore, be highly useful to observe how it is described by the prophets and apostles. For if we simply grant to men the power which they may be pleased to assume, it must be obvious to every one, what a door will be opened for tyranny, which ought never to be seen in the Church of Christ.

II. Here, therefore, it is necessary to remember, that whatever authority and dignity is attributed by the Holy Spirit, in the Scripture, either to the priests and prophets under the law, or to the apostles and their successors, it is all given, not in a strict sense to the persons themselves, but to the ministry over which they were appointed, or, to speak more correctly, to the word, the ministration of which was committed to them. For if we examine them all in succession, we shall not find that they were invested with any authority to teach or to answer inquiries, but in the name and word of the Lord. For when they were called to their office, it was at the same time enjoined that they should bring forward nothing of themselves, but should speak from the mouth of the Lord. Nor did he send them forth in public to address the people, before he had instructed them what they should say, that they might speak nothing beside his word. Moses himself, the prince of all the prophets, was to be heard above all others; but he was first furnished with his commission, that he might not be able to announce any thing except from the Lord. Therefore the people, when they received his doctrine, were said to "believe the Lord and his servant Moses." (*l*) The authority of the priests also, that it might not fall into contempt, was confirmed by the severest punishments. (*m*) But, on the other hand, the Lord shows on what condition they were to be heard, when he says, "My covenant was with Levi. The law of truth was in his mouth."

(*i*) Matt. xxiii. 8.
(*k*) Matt. xvii. 5.
(*l*) Exod. xiv. 31.
(*m*) Deut. xvii. 8—12.

And just afterwards, "The priest's lips should keep knowledge, and they should seek the law at his mouth; for he is the messenger of the Lord of hosts." (*n*) Therefore, if a priest would be heard, it was necessary for him to prove himself the messenger of God, by faithfully communicating the commands which he had received from his master; and where attention to the priests is enjoined, it is expressly stated, that "they shall teach the sentence of the law" (*o*) of God.

III. The power of the prophets is fully and beautifully described in Ezekiel. "Son of man," says the Lord, "I have made thee a watchman unto the house of Israel; therefore hear the word at my mouth, and give them warning from me." (*p*) When he is commanded to hear from the mouth of the Lord, is he not prohibited to invent any thing of himself? And what is it to give warning from the Lord, but, to speak in such a manner as to be able to declare with confidence that the message he has brought is not his own, but the Lord's? The Lord expresses the same thing in other words in the prophecy of Jeremiah: "The prophet that hath a dream, let him tell a dream; and he that hath my word, let him speak my word faithfully." (*q*) He clearly delivers a law for them all; its import is, that he permits no one to teach more than he has been commanded; and he afterwards gives the appellation of "chaff" to every thing that has not proceeded from himself alone. Not one of the prophets opened his mouth, therefore, without having first received the words from the Lord. Hence their frequent use of these expressions: "The word of the Lord," "The burden of the Lord," "Thus saith the Lord," "The mouth of the Lord hath spoken;" and this was highly necessary; for Isaiah exclaimed, "I am a man of unclean lips;" (*r*) and Jeremiah said, "Behold, I cannot speak, for I am a child." (*s*) What could proceed from the pollution of the one, and the folly of the other, but impure and foolish speeches, if they had spoken their own words? But their lips were holy and pure, when they began to be the organs of the Holy Spirit. While the prophets were bound by this law to deliver nothing but what they had received, they were likewise adorned with eminent power and splendid titles. For

(*n*) Mal. ii. 4—7. (*o*) Deut. xvii. 1. (*p*) Ezek. iii. 17.
(*q*) Jer. xxiii. 28. (*r*) Isaiah vi. 5. (*s*) Jer. i. 6.

when the Lord declares, "See, I have this day set thee over the nations, and over the kingdoms, to root out, and to pull down, and to destroy, and to throw down, and to build, and to plant," he at the same times assigns the reason—"Behold, I have put my words in thy mouth." (*t*)

IV. If we advert to the apostles, they are certainly honoured with many extraordinary characters. It is said that they are "the light of the world," and "the salt of the earth;" (*v*) that "he that heareth" them "heareth Christ;" (*w*) that "whatsoever" they "shall bind on earth shall be bound in heaven, and whatsoever" they "shall loose on earth shall be loosed in heaven." (*x*) But their very name shows what degree of liberty they were allowed in their office; that if they were apostles, they were not to declaim according to their own pleasure, but to deliver with strict fidelity the commands of him who had sent them. And the language of Christ is sufficiently clear, in which he has defined their message by the following commission: "Go ye, and teach all nations whatsoever I have commanded you." (*y*) He had even received and imposed on himself the same law, in order that no one might refuse to submit to it. "My doctrine," says he, "is not mine, but his that sent me." (*z*) He who was always the eternal and only counsellor of the Father, and was constituted by the Father the Lord and Master of all, yet because he sustained the office of a teacher, prescribed, by his own example, the rule which all ministers ought to follow in their teaching. The power of the Church, therefore, is not unlimited, but subject to the word of the Lord, and, as it were, included in it.

V. But whereas it has been a principle received in the Church from the beginning, and ought to be admitted in the present day, that the servants of God should teach nothing which they have not learned from him, yet they have had different modes of receiving instruction from him, according to the variety of different periods; and the present mode differs from those which have preceded it. In the first place, if the assertion of Christ be true, that "no man knoweth the Father except the Son, and he to whom-

(*t*) Jer. i. 9, 10.
(*v*) Matt. v. 13, 14.
(*w*) Luke x. 16.
(*x*) Matt. xviii. 18.
(*y*) Matt. xxviii. 19, 20.
(*z*) John vii. 16.

soever the Son will reveal him," (*a*) it must always have been necessary for those who would arrive at the knowledge of God, to be directed by that eternal wisdom. For how could they have comprehended the mysteries of God, or how could they have declared them, except by the teaching of him, to whom alone the secrets of the Father are intimately known? The saints in former ages, therefore, had no other knowledge of God than what they obtained by beholding him in the Son, as in a mirror. By this observation I mean that God never manifested himself to man in any other way than by his son, his only wisdom, light, and truth. From this fountain Adam, Noah, Abraham, Isaac, Jacob, and others, drew all the knowledge which they possessed of heavenly doctrine; from this fountain the prophets themselves drew all the celestial oracles which they spoke and wrote. But this wisdom has not always manifested itself in the same way. With the patriarchs God employed secret revelations; for the confirmation of which, however, he at the same time added such signs that they could not entertain the least doubt that it was God who spake to them. What the patriarchs had received, they transmitted from hand to hand to their posterity; for the Lord had committed it to them on the express condition that they should so propagate it. Succeeding generations, from the testimony of God in their hearts, knew that what they heard was from heaven, and not from the earth.

VI. But when it pleased God to raise up a more visible form of a church, it was his will that his word should be committed to writing, in order that the priests might derive from it whatever they would communicate to the people, and that all the doctrine which should be delivered might be examined by that rule. Therefore, after the promulgation of the law, when the priests were commanded to teach "out of the mouth of the Lord," the meaning is, that they should teach nothing extraneous, or different from that system of doctrine which the Lord had comprised in the law; it was not lawful for them to add to it or to diminish from it. Afterwards followed the prophets, by whom God published new oracles, which were to be added to the law; yet they were not so new but that they proceeded from the law, and bore a

(*a*) Matt. xi. 27.

relation to it. For in regard to doctrine, the prophets were merely interpreters of the law, and added nothing to it except prophecies of things to come. Except these, they brought forward nothing but pure explication of the law. But because it pleased God that there should be a more evident and copious doctrine, for the better satisfaction of weak consciences, he directed the prophecies also to be committed to writing, and to be accounted a part of his word. To these likewise were added the histories, which were the productions of the prophets, but composed under the dictation of the Holy Spirit. I class the Psalms with the prophecies, because what we attribute to the prophecies is common to the Psalms. That whole body of Scripture, therefore, consisting of the Law, the Prophets, the Psalms, and the Histories, was the word of God to the ancient Church; and to this standard the priests and teachers, even to the coming of Christ, were bound to conform their doctrine; nor was it lawful for them to deviate either to the right hand or to the left, because their office was wholly confined within these limits, that they should answer the people from the mouth of God. And this may be inferred from that remarkable passage of Malachi, where he commands the Jews to remember the law, and to be attentive to it, even till the publication of the gospel. (*b*) For in that injunction he drives them off from all adventitious doctrines, and prohibits even the smallest deviation from the path which Moses had faithfully showed them. And it is for this reason that David so magnifies the excellence of the law, and recounts so many of its praises; to prevent the Jews from desiring any addition to it, since it contained every thing necessary for them to know.

VII. But when, at length, the Wisdom of God was manifested in the flesh, it openly declared to us all that the human mind is capable of comprehending, or ought to think, concerning the heavenly Father. Now, therefore, since Christ, the Sun of Righteousness, has shone upon us, we enjoy the full splendour of Divine truth, resembling the brightness of noonday, whereas the light enjoyed before was a kind of twilight. For certainly the apostle intended to state no unimportant fact when he said, that "God,

(*b*) Mal. iv. 4.

who, at sundry times, and in divers manners, spake in time past unto the fathers by the prophets, hath in these last days spoken unto us by his Son;" (*c*) for he here suggests, and even plainly declares, that God will not in future, as in ages past, speak from time to time by one and another, that he will not add prophecies to prophecies, or revelations to revelations, but that he has completed all the branches of instruction in his Son, so that this is the last and eternal testimony that we shall have from him; for which reason this whole period of the New Testament, from the appearance of Christ to us in the first promulgation of his gospel, even to the day of judgment, is designated as "the last time," "the last times," "the last days;" in order that, being content with the perfection of the doctrine of Christ, we may learn neither to invent any thing new or beyond it ourselves, nor to receive any such thing from the invention of others. It is not without cause, therefore, that the Father has given us his Son by a peculiar privilege, and appointed him to be our teacher, commanding attention to be paid to him, and not to any mere man. He has recommended his tuition to us in few words, when he says, "Hear ye him;" (*d*) but there is more weight and energy in them than is commonly imagined; for they call us away from all the instructions of men, and place us before him alone; they command us to learn from him alone all the doctrine of salvation, to depend upon him, to adhere to him, in short, as the words express, to listen solely to his voice. And, indeed, what ought now to be either expected or desired from man, when the Word of Life himself has familiarly presented himself before us? It is rather necessary that the mouths of all men should be shut, since he has once spoken, in whom it has pleased the heavenly Father that all the treasures of wisdom and knowledge should be hidden, (*e*) and has spoken in a manner becoming the wisdom of God, in which there is no imperfection, and the Messiah, who was expected to reveal all things; (*f*) that is, has spoken in such a manner as to leave nothing to be said by others after him.

VIII. Let us lay down this, then, as an undoubted axiom, that nothing ought to be admitted in the Church as the word of God,

(*c*) Heb. i. 1, 2.
(*d*) Matt. xvii. 5.
(*e*) Col. i. 19; ii. 3.
(*f*) John iv. 25.

but what is contained first in the law and the prophets, and secondly in the writings of the apostles, and that there is no other method of teaching aright in the Church than according to the direction and standard of that word. Hence we conclude, also, that the apostles were allowed no more discretion than the prophets before them—namely, to expound the ancient Scripture, and to show that the things delivered in it were accomplished in Christ; but this they were only to do from the Lord, that is to say, under the guidance and dictation of the Spirit of Christ. For Christ limited their mission by this condition, when he ordered them to go and teach, not the fabrications of their own presumption, but whatsoever he had commanded them. (*g*) And nothing could be more explicit than what he said on another occasion: "Be not ye called Rabbi; for one is your Master, even Christ." (*h*) To fix this more deeply in their minds, he repeats it twice in the same place. And because their weakness was such that they were unable to comprehend the things which they had heard and learned from the lips of their Master, the Spirit of truth was promised to them, to lead them into the true understanding of all things. (*i*) For that restriction is to be attentively remarked, which assigns to the Holy Spirit the office of suggesting to their minds all that Christ had before taught them with his mouth.

IX. Therefore Peter, who had been fully taught by his Master how far his office extended, represents nothing as left for himself or others, but to dispense the doctrine committed to them by God. "If any man speak," says he, "let him speak as the oracles of God;" (*k*) that is, not with hesitation or uncertainty, like persons conscious of no sufficient authority, but with the noble confidence which becomes a servant of God furnished with his certain commission. What is this but rejecting all the inventions of the human mind, from whatever head they may proceed, in order that the pure word of God may be taught and learned in the Church of believers? What is this but removing all the decrees, or rather inventions of men, whatever be their station, that the ordinances of God alone may be observed? These are the spiritual "weapons, mighty through God to the pulling down of strong-

(*g*) Matt. xxviii. 19, 20.
(*h*) Matt. xxiii. 8, 10.
(*i*) John xiv. 26; xvi. 13.
(*k*) 1 Peter iv. 11.

holds," by which the faithful soldiers of God "cast down imaginations, and every high thing that exalteth itself against the knowledge of God, and bring into captivity every thought to the obedience of Christ." (*l*) This is the extent of the power with which the pastors of the Church, by whatever name they may be distinguished, ought to be invested;—that by the word of God they may venture to do all things with confidence; may constrain all the strength, glory, wisdom, and pride of the world to obey and submit to his majesty; supported by his power, may govern all mankind, from the highest to the lowest; may build up the house of Christ, and subvert the house of Satan; may feed the sheep, and drive away the wolves; may instruct and exhort the docile; may reprove, rebuke, and restrain the rebellious and obstinate; may bind and loose; may discharge their lightnings and thunders, if necessary; but all in the word of God. Between the apostles and their successors, however, there is, as I have stated, this difference—that the apostles were the certain and authentic amanuenses of the Holy Spirit, and therefore their writings are to be received as the oracles of God; but succeeding ministers have no other office than to teach what is revealed and recorded in the sacred Scriptures. We conclude, then, that it is not now left to faithful ministers to frame any new doctrine, but that it behoves them simply to adhere to the doctrine to which God has made all subject, without any exception. In making this observation, my design is to show, not only what is lawful to individuals, but also to the universal Church. With respect to particular persons, Paul had certainly been appointed by the Lord an apostle to the Corinthians; yet he denies that he had any dominion over their faith. (*m*) Who can now dare to arrogate to himself a dominion which Paul testifies did not belong to him? If he had sanctioned such a license of teaching, that whatever the pastor delivered, he might require, as a matter of right, that the same should be implicitly believed, he would never have recommended to the same Corinthians such a regulation as this: "Let the prophets speak two or three, and let the other judge. If any thing be revealed to another that sitteth by, let the first hold his peace." (*n*) For here he ex-

(*l*) 2 Cor. x. 4, 5. (*m*) 2 Cor. i. 24. (*n*) 1 Cor. xiv. 29, 30.

empted none, but made the authority of every one subject to the control of the word of God. But the case of the universal Church, it will be said, is different. I reply—Paul has obviated this objection in another place, when he says that "faith cometh by hearing, and hearing, by the word of God." (*o*) But if it be the word of God alone upon which faith is suspended, towards which it looks, and on which it relies, I ask what is there left for the word of the whole world? Here it will be impossible for any man to hesitate who has really known what faith is. For it ought to rest on such firm ground as to stand invincible and undismayed in opposition to Satan, to all the machinations of hell, and to all the assaults of the world. This stability we shall find in the word of God alone. Besides the reason which we are here required to consider is of universal application—that God denies to man the right of promulgating any new article of faith, in order that he alone may be our Master in spiritual doctrine, as he alone is true beyond all possibility of deceiving or being deceived. This reason is no less applicable to the whole Church than to every individual believer.

X. But if this power, which we have shown to belong to the Church, be compared with that which has now for some ages past been claimed over the people of God by the spiritual tyrants who have falsely called themselves bishops and prelates of religion, there will be no more resemblance than there is between Christ and Belial. It is not my intention here to expose the shameful methods in which they have exercised their tyranny: I shall only state the doctrine, which they defend in the present age, not only by their writings, but also by fire and sword. As they take it for granted that a universal council is the true representative of the Church, having assumed this principle, they at once determine, as beyond all doubt, that such councils are under the immediate direction of the Holy Spirit, and therefore cannot err. Now, as they themselves influence the councils, and even constitute them, the fact is, that they assume to themselves all that they contend for as belonging to the councils. They wish our faith, therefore, to stand or fall at their pleasure, that whatever they may have

(*o*) Rom. x. 17.

determined on one side or the other, may be implicitly received by our minds as fully decided; so that if they approve of any thing, we must approve of the same without any hesitation, and if they condemn any thing, we must unite in the condemnation of it. At the same time, according to their own caprice, and in contempt of the word of God, they fabricate doctrines which, for no other reason than this, they require to be believed. For they acknowledge no man as a Christian, who does not fully assent to all their dogmas, affirmative as well as negative, if not with an explicit, at least with an implicit faith, because they pretend that the Church has authority to make new articles of faith.

XI. First, let us hear by what arguments they prove this authority to have been given to the Church; and then we shall see how far their allegations respecting the Church contribute to support their cause. The Church, they say, has excellent promises, that she is never to be forsaken by Christ, her spouse, but will be led by his Spirit into all truth. (*p*) But of the promises which they are accustomed to allege, many are given no less to each believer in particular, than collectively to the whole Church. For though the Lord was addressing the twelve apostles when he said, "Lo, I am with you alway, even unto the end of the world;" (*q*) and "I will pray the Father, and he shall give you another comforter, even the Spirit of truth;" (*r*) he made these promises not only to the apostles considered as a body, but to every one of the number, and even to the other disciples whom he had already received, or who were afterwards to be added to them. Now, when they interpret these promises, replete with peculiar consolation, in such a sense as if they were given to no individual Christian, but only to the whole Church collectively, what is this but depriving all Christians of the confidence with which such promises ought to animate them? Here I do not deny that the whole society of believers, being adorned with a manifold variety of gifts, possesses a more ample and precious treasure of heavenly wisdom, than each particular individual; nor do I intend that these things are spoken of believers in common, as if they were all equally endued with the spirit of understanding and doctrine;

(*p*) John xvi. 13. (*q*) Matt. xxviii. 20. (*r*) John xiv. 16, 17.

but we must not allow the adversaries of Christ, in defence of a bad cause, to wrest the Scripture to a sense which it was not intended to convey. Leaving this remark, I freely acknowledge that the Lord is continually present with his servants, and that he guides them by his Spirit; that this is not a spirit of error, ignorance, falsehood, or darkness, but "the spirit of wisdom, and revelation, and truth," from whom they may certainly learn "the things that are given to" them "of God," or, in other words, "may know what is the hope of his calling, and what the riches of the glory of his inheritance in the saints." (*s*) But as it is nothing more than the first fruits, a kind of foretaste of that Spirit that is enjoyed by believers in the present state, even by those of them who are favoured with more excellent graces than others, there remains nothing for them, but that, conscious of their imbecility, they solicitously confine themselves within the limits of the word of God; lest, if they proceed far by their own sense, they should wander from the right way, in consequence of being not yet fully enlightened by that Spirit, by whose teaching alone truth is distinguished from falsehood. For all confess with Paul, that they have not yet attained the mark; therefore they rather press on towards daily improvement, than boast of perfection. (*t*)

XII. But they will object, that whatever is partially attributed to every one of the saints, completely and perfectly belongs to the whole Church. Notwithstanding the plausibility of this position, yet I deny it to be true. I admit that God distributes the gifts of his Spirit by measure to every member of his Church, in such a manner that nothing necessary is wanting to the whole body, when those gifts are bestowed in common. But the riches of the Church are always such as to be very far from that consummate perfection boasted by our adversaries. Yet the Church is not left destitute in any respect, but that it always has what is sufficient; for the Lord knows what its necessity requires. But to restrain it within the bounds of humility and pious modesty, he bestows no more than he sees to be expedient. Here, I know, they are accustomed to object, that the Church has been "cleansed by the washing of water by the word, that he might present it to himself a

(*s*) Ephes. i. 17, 18. John xiv. 17. 1 Cor. ii. 12.
(*t*) Phil. iii. 12—14.

glorious Church, not having spot, or wrinkle, or any such thing, but that it should be holy and without blemish;" (*u*) and that for this reason it is called "the pillar and ground of the truth." (*v*) But the former of these passages rather indicates what Christ is daily performing in his Church, than any thing that he has already accomplished. For if he is daily sanctifying, purifying, polishing, and cleansing his people, it must be evident that they still have some spots and wrinkles, and that something is still wanting to their sanctification. How vain and visionary is it to imagine the Church already perfectly holy and immaculate, while all its members are the subjects of corruption and impurity! It is true that the Church is sanctified by Christ, but it is only the commencement of their sanctification that is seen in the present state; the end and perfect completion of it will be when Christ, the Holy of Holies, shall fill it truly and entirely with his holiness. It is likewise true that its spots and wrinkles are effaced, but in such a manner that they are in a daily course of obliteration, till Christ at his coming shall entirely efface all that remains. For, unless we admit this, we must of necessity assert, with the Pelagians, that the righteousness of believers is perfect in the present life, and with the Cathari and Donatists, must allow no infirmity in the Church. The other passage, as we have already seen, has a meaning totally different from what they pretend. For after Paul had instructed Timothy in the true nature of the office of a bishop, he says, "These things I write unto thee, that thou mayest know how thou oughtest to behave thyself in the house of God;" and to enforce his conscientious attention to this object, he adds, that the Church itself is "the pillar and ground of the truth." (*w*) Now, what is the meaning of this expression, but that the truth of God is preserved in the Church, and that by the ministry of preaching? As in another place he states, that Christ "gave some apostles, and some prophets, and some evangelists, and some pastors and teachers, that we be no more carried about with every wind of doctrine," or deluded by men, but that, being enlightened with the true knowledge of the Son of God, we may "all come into the unity of the faith." (*x*) The preserva-

(*u*) Ephes. v. 26, 27.
(*v*) 1 Tim. iii. 15.
(*w*) 1 Tim. iii. 14, 15.
(*x*) Ephes. iv. 11, 13, 14.

tion of the truth, therefore, from being extinguished in the world, is in consequence of the Church being its faithful guardian, by whose efforts and ministry it is maintained. But if this guardianship consists in the ministry of the prophets and apostles, it follows that it wholly depends on the faithful preservation of the purity of the word of God.

XIII. And that the readers may better understand upon what point this question principally turns, I will briefly state what our adversaries require, and wherein we oppose them. When they assert that the Church cannot err, their meaning is, as they themselves explain it, that as it is governed by the Spirit of God, it may safely proceed without the word; that whithersoever it goes, it can neither think nor speak any thing that is not true; and, therefore, that if it determine any thing beyond or beside the Divine word, the same is to be considered in no other light than as a certain oracle of God. If we grant the first point, that the Church cannot err in things essential to salvation, our meaning is, that its security from error is owing to its renouncing all its own wisdom, and submitting itself to the Holy Spirit, to be taught by means of the word of God. This, then, is the difference between us. They ascribe to the Church an authority independent of the word; we maintain it to be annexed to the word, and inseparable from it. And what is there surprising that the spouse and disciple of Christ is subject to her Lord and Master, so as to be assiduously and sedulously awaiting his commands and instructions? For it is the order of a well regulated family, for the wife to obey the command of the husband; it is the order of a well disciplined school, that nothing be heard there but the instructions of the master. Wherefore let not the Church be wise of itself, nor think any thing of itself, but let it fix the boundary of its wisdom where Christ has made an end of speaking. In this manner it will distrust all the inventions of its own reason; but in those things in which it is supported by the word of God, it will not waver with any distrust or hesitation, but will rest upon it with strong certainty and unshaken constancy. Thus confiding in the amplitude of the promises it has received, it will have an excellent support for its faith, so that it cannot doubt that the Holy Spirit, the best guide in the right way, is always present with it; but, at the same time, it will remember what advantage the Lord intends should be received from his Spirit. "The Spirit," says he, "whom I will send from the Father, will guide you into all truth." But how will this be done? Christ says, "He shall bring all things to your remembrance, whatsoever I have said unto you." (*y*) He announces, therefore, that nothing more is to be expected from his Spirit, than that he will enlighten our minds to discover the truth of his doctrine. Wherefore it is very judiciously observed by Chrysostom, that "many boast of the Holy Spirit; but in those who speak from themselves this is a false pretence. As Christ testified that he spake not of himself, because he spake from the law and the prophets, so, if, under the name of the Spirit, any thing be obtruded that is not contained in the gospel, let us not believe it. For as Christ is the accomplishment of the law and the prophets, so is the Spirit, of the gospel." These are the words of Chrysostom. Now, it is easy to infer how great is the error of our adversaries, who boast of the Holy Spirit for no other purpose than to recommend, under his name, doctrines strange and inconsistent with the word of God, whereas it is his determination to be connected with the word by an indissoluble bond; and this was declared by Christ when he promised him to his Church. And so he is, in point of fact. The sobriety which the Lord has once prescribed to his Church, he will have to be perpetually observed; and he has forbidden the Church to add any thing to his word, or to diminish any thing from it. This is the inviolable decree of God and of the Holy Spirit, which our adversaries endeavour to abrogate, when they pretend that the Church is governed by the Spirit without the word.

XIV. Here, again, they cavil, that it was necessary for the Church to add some things to the writings of the apostles, or at least for the apostles themselves afterwards to supply in their discourses what they had not so explicitly delivered in their writings, because Christ declared to them, "I have yet many things to say unto you, but ye cannot bear them now;" (*z*) and that these are the ordinances which have been received by usage and custom without the Scripture. But what effrontery is here

(*y*) John xiv. 26; xv. 26; xvi. 13. (*z*) John xvi. 12.

betrayed! I confess that the disciples were ignorant, and not very docile, when the Lord made this declaration to them; but they were not so stupid, when they committed their doctrine to writing, as to render it necessary for them afterwards to supply in their discourses what they had from ignorance omitted in their writings. But if, when they published their writings, they had already been led by the Spirit into all truth, what hindered them from comprising and leaving on record in those writings a perfect system of evangelical doctrine? Let us grant our opponents, however, what they ask: only let them enumerate those things which require to be revealed, and are not contained in the apostolical writings. If they dare to attempt this, I will reply in the words of Augustine, "Where the Lord has been silent, which of us can say, These things or those are intended; and if he dare to say so, how will he prove it?" But why do I contend a point that is unnecessary? For even children know that the apostolic writings, which these men represent as incomplete and essentially defficient, contain the fruit of that revelation which the Lord then promised them.

XV. What, say they, did not Christ place the doctrines and decrees of the Church beyond all controversy, when he commanded him who should dare to contradict it, to be regarded "as a heathen man and a publican?" (*a*) In the first place, Christ in that text makes no mention of doctrine, but only asserts the authority of the Church in pronouncing censures for the correction of vices, in order that its judgment may not be opposed by any who are admonished or reproved. But leaving this remark, it is astonishing, that they have no more modesty than to presume to boast of that passage. For what will they extort from it, but that it is unlawful to despise the consent of the Church, which never consents to any thing except the truth of the word of God? The Church is to be heard, they say. Who denies it? For it pronounces nothing but from the word of the Lord. If they require any thing further, let them know that these words of Christ afford them no support. Nor ought it to be esteemed too contentious in me to insist so strenuously on this point—That it is not lawful for the

(*a*) Matt. xviii. 17.

Church to invent any new doctrine, or to teach and deliver, as of Divine authority, any thing more than the Lord has revealed in his word. All persons of sound judgment perceive how exceedingly dangerous it would be if so much power were once granted to any man. For they see how wide a door is opened to the scoffs and cavils of the impious, if we assert that the decisions of men are to be received by Christians as articles of faith. It is also to be remarked, that Christ spoke according to the established order of his own time, and gave this name to the Sanhedrim, that his disciples might learn afterwards to reverence the solemn assemblies of the Church. And thus, on the principle of our adversaries, every city and village would have an equal liberty to frame new articles of faith.

XVI. The examples which they allege are nothing to the purpose. They say that the baptism of infants arose, not so much from any express command of Scripture, as from the decree of the Church. It would be a most miserable asylum, if, in defence of infant baptism, we were compelled to have recourse to the mere authority of the Church; but it will be shown in another place, that the fact is very different. So when they object, that the Scriptures nowhere affirm what was pronounced in the Council of Nice, that the Son is of the same substance with the Father, they do great injury to the fathers of that council, as if they had presumptuously condemned Arius for having refused to subscribe to their language, while he professed all the doctrine which is contained in the writings of the prophets and apostles. The word *consubstantial* (ὁμοουσιος,) I confess, is not to be found in the Scripture; but while, on the one hand, it is so often affirmed that there is but one God, and, on the other, Christ is so frequently called the true and eternal God, one with the Father, what have the Nicene fathers done, but simply expressed the natural sense of the Scripture, in declaring the Father and the Son to be of one and the same substance? And Theodoret the historian states, that Constantine the emperor opened that council with the following preliminary address: "In disputes on Divine subjects, we are to adhere to the doctrine of the Holy Spirit; the books of the evangelists and apostles, with the oracles of the prophets, fully reveal to us the will of God. Wherefore, laying aside all discord, let us take the decision of all questions in debate from the words of the Spirit." There was no one at that time who opposed these holy admonitions. No one objected, that the Church might add something of its own, that the Spirit had not revealed every thing to the apostles, or, at least, that they had not transmitted the whole to posterity in writing, or any thing of the like nature. If what our adversaries contend for be true, in the first place, Constantine acted unjustly in depriving the Church of its power; and in the next place, when none of the bishops rose to vindicate that power, their silence was not be excused from treachery, for on that occasion they must have betrayed the rights of the Church. But from the statement of Theodoret, that they readily received what was said by the emperor, it is evident that this novel dogma of our adversaries was at that time altogether unknown.

CHAPTER IX

Councils; Their Authority

THOUGH I should concede to our adversaries all the claims which they set up on behalf of the Church, yet this would effect but little towards the attainment of their object. For whatever is said respecting the Church, they immediately transfer to the councils, which they consider as representing the Church; and it may further be affirmed, that their violent contentions for the power of the Church, are with no other view than to ascribe all that they can extort, to the Roman pontiff and his satellites. Before I enter on the discussion of this question, it is necessary for me to premise two brief observations. First, if in this chapter I am rather severe on our opponents, it is not that I would show the ancient councils less honour than they deserve. I venerate them from my heart, and wish them to receive from all men the honour to which they are entitled; but here some limits must be observed, that we may derogate nothing from Christ. Now, it is the prerogative of Christ to preside over all councils, and to have no mortal man associated with him in that dignity. But I maintain, that he really presides only where he governs the whole assembly by his word and Spirit. Secondly, when I attribute to the councils less than our adversaries require, I am not induced to do this from any fear that the councils would favour their cause and oppose ours. For as we are sufficiently armed by the word of the Lord, and need not seek any further assistance for the complete establishment of our doctrine, and the total subversion of Popery, so, on the other hand, if it were necessary, the ancient councils would furnish us in a great measure with sufficient arguments for both these objects.

II. Let us now come to the subject itself. If it be inquired what is the authority of councils according to the Scriptures, there is no promise more ample or explicit than this declaration of Christ: "Where two or three are gathered together in my name, there am I in the midst of them." (*b*) But this belongs no less to every particular congregation than to a general council. The main stress of the question, however, does not lie in this, but in the annexed condition,—that Christ will be in the midst of a council, then, and then only, when it is assembled in his name. Wherefore, though our adversaries mention councils of bishops a thousand times, they will gain but little ground; nor will they prevail upon us to believe what they pretend,—that such councils are directed by the Holy Spirit,—till it shall have been proved, that they are assembled in the name of Christ. For it is equally as possible for impious and unfaithful bishops to conspire against Christ, as for pious and upright bishops to assemble together in his name. Of this we have ample proof in numerous decrees which have been issued by such councils; as will be seen in the course of this discussion. At present I only reply in one word, that the promise of Christ is exclusively restricted to those who "are gathered together in his name." Let us, therefore, define wherein this consists. I deny that they are assembled in the name of Christ, who, rejecting the command of God, which prohibits any diminution of his word, or the smallest addition to it, (*c*) determine every thing according to their own pleasure; who, not content with the oracles of the Scripture, which constitute the only rule of perfect wisdom, invent something new out of their own heads. Since Christ has not promised to be present in all councils, but has added a particular mark to discriminate true and legitimate councils from others, it certainly behoves us by no means to neglect this distinction. This was the covenant which God anciently made with the Levitical priests, that they should teach their people from his mouth; (*d*) he always required the same of the prophets; and we see that a similar law was imposed upon the apostles. Those who violate this covenant, God neither dignifies with the

(*b*) Matt. xviii. 20. (*c*) Deut. iv. 2. Rev. xxii. 18, 19. (*d*) Mal. ii. 5—7.

honour of the priesthood, nor invests with any authority. Let our adversaries solve this difficulty, if they wish me to submit my faith to the decrees of men, independently of the word of God.

III. For their supposition, that no truth remains in the Church, unless it be found among the pastors, and that the Church itself stands, no longer than it appears in general councils, is very far from having been always correct, if the prophets have left us any authentic records of their times. In the days of Isaiah, there was a Church at Jerusalem, which God had not yet forsaken: nevertheless he speaks of the priests in the following manner: "His watchmen are blind; they are all ignorant; they are all dumb dogs, they cannot bark; sleeping, lying down, loving to slumber: they are shepherds that cannot understand: they all look to their own way, every one for his gain, from his quarter." (*e*)—Hosea speaks in a similar manner: "The watchman of Ephraim was with my God; but the prophet is a snare of a fowler in all his ways, and hatred in the house of his God." (*f*) By thus ironically connecting them with God, he shows that their priesthood was a vain pretence. The Church continued also to the time of Jeremiah. Let us hear what he says of the pastors. "From the prophet even unto the priest, every one dealeth falsely." (*g*) Again: "the prophets prophesy lies in my name; I sent them not, neither have I commanded them." (*h*) And to avoid too much prolixity in reciting his words, I would recommend my readers to peruse the whole of the twenty-third and fortieth chapters. Nor were the same persons treated with less severity by Ezekiel: "There is a conspiracy of her prophets in the midst thereof, like a roaring lion ravening the prey; they have devoured souls; they have taken the treasure and precious things; they have made her many widows in the midst thereof. Her priests have violated my law, and have profaned mine holy things, they have put no difference between the holy and profane. Her prophets have daubed them with untempered mortar, seeing vanity, and divining lies unto them, saying, Thus saith the Lord God, when the Lord hath not spoken." (*i*) Similar complaints abound in all the prophets, so that there is nothing of more frequent recurrence.

(*e*) Isaiah lvi. 10, 11. (*f*) Hosea ix. 8. (*g*) Jer. vi. 13. (*h*) Jer. xiv. 14. (*i*) Ezek. xxii. 25, 26, 28.

IV. But it will be said, though such may have been the case among the Jews, our age is exempt from so great a calamity. I sincerely wish that it were so; but the Holy Spirit has denounced that the event would be very different. The language of Peter is clear: "There were false prophets also among the people, even as there shall be false teachers among you, who privily shall bring in damnable heresies." (*k*) Observe how he declares that danger will arise, not from the common people, but from those who will assume to themselves the name of pastors and teachers. Besides, how often is it predicted by Christ and his apostles, that the greatest dangers would be brought upon the Church by its pastors! (*l*) Paul expressly denounces that Antichrist will "sit in the temple of God;" (*m*) by which he signifies, that the dreadful calamity of which he speaks, will arise from the very persons who will sit as pastors in the Church. And in another place, he shows that the commencement of the mischief was then near at hand. For addressing the bishops of the Church of Ephesus, he says, "I know this, that after my departing shall grievous wolves enter in among you, not sparing the flock; also of your own selves shall men arise, speaking perverse things, to draw away disciples after them." (*n*) If the pastors could so degenerate in a very short space of time, what enormous corruption might be introduced among them in a long series of years! And not to occupy much room with an enumeration, we are taught by the examples of almost all ages, that neither is the truth always maintained in the bosom of the pastors, nor the safety of the Church dependent on their stability. They ought, indeed, to be the guardians and defenders of the peace and safety of the Church, for the preservation of which they are appointed; but it is one thing to perform a duty which we owe, and another, to owe a duty which we do not perform.

V. Let no person conclude from what I have said, that I am inclined on all occasions, and without any discrimination, to weaken the authority of pastors, and bring it into contempt. I only mean to suggest the necessity of discriminating between some pastors and others, that we may not immediately consider

---

(*k*) 2 Peter ii. 1.
(*l*) Matt. xxiv. 11, 24.
(*m*) 2 Thess. ii. 4.
(*n*) Acts xx. 29, 30.

persons as pastors because they bear that title. But the pope and all his bishops, for no other reason but because they are called pastors, casting off all obedience to the word of God, disturb and confound every thing at their own pleasure; while they labour to persuade us that it is impossible for them to be destitute of the light of truth, that the Spirit of God perpetually resides in them, and that with them the Church lives and dies. As though the Lord had now no judgments, to inflict upon the world, in the present day, the same kind of punishment, with which he once visited the ingratitude of his ancient people; (*o*) namely, to smite the pastors with astonishment, madness, and blindness. And such is their extreme stupidity, they are not aware that they are acting the same part which was acted by those who resisted the word of the Lord in ancient times. For thus the enemies of Jeremiah fortified themselves in opposition to the truth: "Come, and let us devise devices against Jeremiah; for the law shall not perish from the priest, nor counsel from the wise, nor the word from the prophet." (*p*)

VI. Hence it is easy to reply to another plea in behalf of general councils. That a true Church existed among the Jews in the time of the prophets, cannot be denied. But if a general council of the priests had been convened, what appearance of a Church would such a council have displayed? We hear what God denounces, not against two or three of them, but against the whole body: "The priests shall be astonished, and the prophets shall wonder." (*q*) Again: "The law shall perish from the priest, and counsel from the ancients." (*r*) Again: "Night shall be unto you, that ye shall not have a vision; and it shall be dark unto you, that ye shall not divine; and the sun shall go down over the prophets, and the day shall be dark over them." (*s*) Now, if these priests and prophets had all been collected together, what spirit would have presided in their assembly? This is remarkably exemplified in the council convoked by Ahab. Four hundred prophets were present. But because they were assembled with no other intention than to flatter that impious monarch, Satan was sent by the Lord to be a lying spirit in all their mouths. (*t*)

(*o*) Zech. xii. 4. (*p*) Jer. xviii. 18. (*q*) Jer. iv. 9.
(*r*) Ezek. vii. 26. (*s*) Micah iii. 6. (*t*) 1 Kings xxii. 6, 22, 24, 27.

There the truth was rejected with one consent; Micaiah was condemned as a heretic, beaten, and cast into prison. Jeremiah received the same treatment, and other prophets experienced similar injustice.

VII. But one example, which is more memorable than the rest, may suffice as a specimen of all. In the council which the chief priests and Pharisees convened at Jerusalem against Christ, what was there wanting in point of external form? For if there had then been no Church at Jerusalem, Christ would never have united in their sacrifices and other ceremonies. A solemn summons was issued; the high priest presided; all the priests attended; yet there Christ was condemned, and his doctrine rejected. This act proves that the Church was not contained in that council. But, it will be said, there is no danger of such a circumstance happening to us. Who has assured us of this? For to be too confident in a matter of such great importance, is culpable stupidity. But while the Spirit has expressly predicted, by the mouth of Paul, that there shall come an apostasy, which cannot take place without the pastors being the first to revolt from God, (*v*) why do we wilfully shut our eyes to our own ruin? Wherefore it is by no means to be conceded, that the Church consists in the assembly of the pastors, respecting whom God has nowhere promised that they should always be good, but, on the contrary, has denounced that they would sometimes be wicked. Now, when he warns us of a danger, his design is to make us more cautious.

VIII. What, then, it will be said, shall the decisions of councils have no authority? Yes, certainly; for I am not contending that all councils ought to be condemned, or that all their acts ought to be rescinded and cancelled at once. Still I shall be told, that I degrade their authority, so as to leave it to the option of every individual to receive or reject whatever a council shall have determined. By no means; but whenever a decree of any council is brought forward, I would wish, first, that a diligent inquiry should be made, at what time, for what cause, and with what design it was held, and what kind of persons were present; secondly, that the subject discussed in it should be examined by

(*v*) 2 Thess. ii. 3. 1 Tim. iv. 1.

the standard of the Scripture; and this in such a manner that the determination should have its weight, and be considered as a precedent or case formerly decided, but that it should not preclude the examination which I have mentioned. I sincerely wish that every person would observe the method recommended by Augustine in his third book against Maximinus. For, with a view to silence the contentions of that heretic respecting the decrees of councils, he says, "I ought not to object to you the Council of Nice, nor ought you to object to me the Council of Ariminum, to preclude each other's judgment by a previous decision. I am not bound by the authority of the latter, nor you by that of the former. Let cause contend with cause, and argument with argument, on the ground of scriptural authorities, which exclusively belong to neither party, but are common to both." The consequence of such a mode of proceeding would be, that councils would retain all the majesty which is due to them, while at the same time the Scripture would hold the preëminence, so that every thing would be subject to its standard. Upon this principle, those ancient councils, such as the Council of Nice, of Constantinople, the first of Ephesus, that of Chalcedon, and others like them, which were held for the condemnation of errors, we cheerfully receive and reverence as sacred, as far as respects the articles of faith which they have defended; for they contain nothing but the pure and natural interpretation of the Scripture, which the holy fathers, with spiritual prudence, applied to the discomfiture of the enemies of religion who arose in those days. In some of the succeeding councils, likewise, we discover a true zeal for piety, and evident proofs of sense, learning, and prudence. But as the progress of the world is generally from worse to worse, it is easy to see, from the more recent councils, how much the Church has gradually degenerated from the purity of that golden age. Even in these more corrupt ages, I doubt not, the councils have been partly composed of some bishops of a better character; but the same observation may be applied to their acts, which was formerly made in a way of complaint against the decrees of the Roman senate, by the senators themselves. Where opinions prevail according to their number, and not according to the weight of argument by which they are supported, the better part of the assembly must of necessity be frequently overcome by the majority. And councils have certainly issued many impious decrees. It is unnecessary here to produce particular examples, as well because this would carry us to too great a length, as because it has already been done by others with a diligence which scarcely admits of any addition.

IX. Now, what need is there to enumerate the repugnances between councils and councils, and how decrees passed by one have been rescinded by another? Here it must not be alleged, that where there is such variance between two councils, one or the other is not legitimate. For how shall we determine this? The only way I know, is to ascertain from the Scriptures that its decrees are not orthodox; for there is no other certain rule of decision. It is now about nine hundred years ago, that the Council of Constantinople, assembled under the emperor Leo, decreed that all images placed in churches should be thrown down and broken to pieces. Soon after, the Council of Nice, which the empress Irene convened in opposition to the former, decreed that they should be restored. Which of these two shall we acknowledge as a legitimate council? This character has generally been attributed to the latter, which gave images a place in the Churches. But Augustine declares that this cannot be done without imminent danger of idolatry. Epiphanius, a more ancient writer, expresses himself in terms of much greater severity; he says that it is abominable wickedness for images to be seen in the temples of Christians. Would the fathers who speak in this manner approve of that council, if they were now living? But if the accounts of historians be true, and credit be given to the acts themselves, that council not only admitted of images, but determined that they were to be worshipped. Now, it is evident that such a decree must have originated from Satan. What shall we say to their perversions and mutilations of the Scripture, which demonstrate that they held it all in contempt, as I have already proved? We shall never be able to discriminate between the numerous councils, which dissent from and contradict each other, unless we examine them all by the word of God, which is the universal standard for men and angels. On this ground, we reject the second Council of Ephesus, and receive the Council of Chalcedon, because the latter council condemned the impiety of Eutyches, which the former had sanctioned. This judgment of the Council of Chalcedon was formed from the Scriptures by holy men, whom we imitate in forming our judgment, as the word of God which enlightened them continues to give light to us. Now, let the Romanists go and boast, as they are accustomed to do, that the Holy Spirit is inseparably attached to their councils.

X. Even in the earliest and purest councils, however, there is something to complain of—either that the bishops who composed them, though men of learning and prudence, being perplexed with the subjects immediately before them, did not extend their views to many other things; or that while they were occupied with more weighty and serious concerns, things of inferior moment escaped their notice; or merely that, being men, they were liable to ignorance and error; or that they were sometimes hurried into precipitancy by the violence of their passions. Of the truth of the last observation, which seems the severest of all, there is a remarkable example in the Council of Nice; the dignity of which has been universally and justly held in the highest veneration. For though the principal article of our faith was endangered, and they had to contend with Arius, the enemy of it, who was there in readiness for the contest,—though it was of the greatest importance that harmony should be maintained among those who came with a design to confute the error of Arius,—notwithstanding that, careless of such great dangers, forgetful of gravity, modesty, and every thing like good manners, dropping the controversy between them as if they had assembled with an express view to the gratification of Arius, they began to counteract themselves with intestine dissensions, and to direct against each other the pen which ought to have been employed against Arius. The foulest accusations were heard, defamatory libels were circulated, and there would have been no end of the contentions till they had murdered one another, if it had not been for the interference of the emperor Constantine, who protested that a scrutiny into their lives was a thing beyond his cognizance, and repressed this intemperate conduct with praise rather than with censure. In how many instances is it probable that errors were committed by other succeeding councils? Nor does this require any long proof; for whoever peruses their acts, will discover many infirmities, not to mention any thing worse.

XI. And Leo, the Roman pontiff, hesitates not to bring a charge of ambition and inconsiderate temerity against the Council of Chalcedon, which he at the same time acknowledges to have been orthodox in points of doctrine. He does not deny it to have been a legitimate council, but he unequivocally asserts that it was possible for it to err. It may be thought, perhaps, that I betray a want of judgment in taking pains to point out such errors; since our adversaries confess that councils might err in things not essential to salvation. This labour, however, is not unnecessary. For though they find themselves obliged to confess this in words, yet when they obtrude upon us the decision of every council on every subject, without any discrimination, as an oracle of the Holy Spirit, they require of us, in fact, more than they had first assumed. What is the language of such conduct, but that councils cannot err, or that, if they do err, it is unlawful for us to discover the truth, or to refuse assent to errors? And I intend to draw no other conclusion from these facts, than that the Holy Spirit governed pious and Christian councils in such a manner, as at the same time to permit them to betray something of human infirmity, that we might not place too much confidence in men. This sentiment is far more favourable than that of Gregory of Nazianzum, "that he never saw a good end of any council." For he who affirms that all without exception terminated ill, leaves them but little authority. It is unnecessary here to take distinct notice of provincial councils, since it is easy to judge from the general councils, what authority they ought to possess in framing articles of faith, and receiving whatever kind of doctrine they pleased.

XII. But our Romanists, when they find all the supports of reason fail them in the defence of their cause, have recourse to that last and wretched subterfuge—That although the persons themselves betray the greatest stupidity in their understandings and pleas, and act from the most iniquitous motives and designs, still the word of God remains, which commands us to obey our governors. (*v*) But what if I deny that such persons are our

(*v*) Heb. xiii. 17.

governors? For they ought not to arrogate to themselves more than belonged to Joshua, who was a prophet of the Lord and an excellent pastor. Now, let us hear with what language he was inaugurated into his office by the Lord: "This book of the law shall not depart out of thy mouth; but thou shalt meditate therein day and night: turn not from it to the right hand or to the left, that thou mayest prosper whithersoever thou goest." (*w*) We shall consider them as our spiritual governors, therefore, who deviate not from the word of God, either to the right hand or to the left. If the doctrine of all pastors ought to be received without any hesitation, why have we such frequent and earnest admonitions from the mouth of the Lord himself, not to listen to the speeches of false prophets? "Hearken not," says he by Jeremiah, "unto the words of the prophets that prophesy unto you; they make you vain; they speak a vision of their own hearts, and not out of the mouth of the Lord." (*x*) Again: "Beware of false prophets, which come to you in sheep's clothing, but inwardly they are ravening wolves." (*y*) The exhortation given us by John would also have been useless: "Try the spirits, whether they are of God;" (*z*) though from this examination the very angels are not exempted, much less Satan with all his falsehoods. How are we to understand this caution of our Lord? "If the blind lead the blind, both shall fall into the ditch." (*a*) Does it not sufficiently declare, that it is of the highest importance what kind of pastors are heard, and that they are not all entitled to the same attention? Wherefore there is no reason why they should overawe us with their titles, to make us partakers of their blindness, while we see, on the contrary, that the Lord has taken peculiar care to deter us from suffering ourselves to be seduced by the error of other men, under whatever mask or name it may be concealed. For if the answer of Christ be true, all blind guides, whether they are denominated priests, prelates, or pontiffs, can do nothing but precipitate their followers into the same ruin with themselves. Impressed, therefore, by these warnings, both of precepts and of examples, no names of pastors, bishops, or councils, which are as capable of being falsely claimed as rightly assumed, ought ever to

(*w*) Joshua i. 7, 8. (*x*) Jer. xxiii. 16. (*y*) Matt. vii. 15. (*z*) 1 John iv. 1. (*a*) Matt. xv. 14.

prevent us from examining all the spirits by the rule of the Divine word, in order to "try whether they are of God."

XIII. Having proved that the Church has received no power to frame any new doctrine, let us now speak of the power which our opponents attribute to it in the interpretation of the Scripture. We have not the least objection to admit, that if a controversy arise respecting any doctrine, there is no better or more certain remedy than to assemble a council of true bishops, in which the controverted doctrine may be discussed. For such a decision, formed by the common consent of the pastors of the Churches, after an invocation of the Spirit of Christ, will have far greater weight, than if every one of them separately were to maintain it in preaching to his people, or if it were the result of a private conference between a few individuals. Besides, when bishops are collected in one assembly, they deliberate together with greater advantage on what they ought to teach, and the manner in which their instructions should be conveyed, so as to guard against offence arising from diversity. In the third place, Paul prescribes this method of determining respecting doctrines. For while he attributes to every distinct Church a power "to judge," (*b*) he shows what ought to be the order of proceeding in more important cases; namely, that the Churches should undertake the common cognizance of them. And so the dictate of piety itself teaches us, that if any one disturb the Church with a new doctrine, and the matter be carried so far as to cause danger of a more grievous dissension, the Churches should first assemble, should examine the question proposed to them, and after a sufficient discussion of it, should announce a decision taken from the Scriptures, which would put an end to all doubt among the people, and shut the mouths of refractory and ambitious persons, so as to check their further presumption. Thus, when Arius arose, the Council of Nice was assembled, and by its authority defeated the pernicious attempts of that impious man, restored peace to the Churches which he had disturbed, and asserted the eternal deity of Christ in opposition to his sacrilegious dogma. Some time after, when Eunomius and Macedonius raised new contentions, their frenzy

(*b*) 1 Cor. xiv. 29.

was opposed with a similar remedy by the Council of Constantinople. The impiety of Nestorius was condemned in the first Council of Ephesus. In short, this has been the ordinary method of the Church from the beginning, for the preservation of unity, whenever Satan has begun to make any attempt against it. But let it be remembered, that neither every age, nor every place, can produce an Athanasius, a Basil, a Cyril, and other such champions of the true doctrine, as the Lord raised up at those periods. Let it also be recollected what happened at the second Council of Ephesus, in which the heresy of Eutyches prevailed. Flavianus, a bishop of irreproachable memory, was banished, together with other pious men, and many similar enormities were committed, because it was Dioscorus, a factious and ill-disposed man, and not the Spirit of the Lord, that presided in that council. But that council, it will be said, was not the Church. I admit it: for I am firmly persuaded of this, that the truth is not extinct in the Church, though it may be oppressed by one council, but that it is wonderfully preserved by the Lord, to arise and triumph again in his own time. But I deny it to be an invariable rule, that every interpretation which may have been approved by a council is the true and certain sense of the Scripture.

XIV. But the Romanists have a further design in maintaining that councils possess the power of interpreting the Scripture, and that without appeal. For it is a false pretence, when every thing that has been determined in councils is called an interpretation of the Scripture. Of purgatory, the intercession of saints, auricular confession, and similar fooleries, the Scriptures contain not a single syllable. But, because all these things have been sanctioned by the authority of councils, or, to speak more correctly, have been admitted into the general belief and practice, therefore every one of them is to be taken for an interpretation of Scripture. And not only so; but if a council determine in direct opposition to the Scripture, it will still be called an interpretation of it. Christ commands all to drink of the cup which he presents to them in the sacred supper. (*c*) The Council of Constance prohibited it to be given to the laity, and determined that none but

(*c*) Matt. xxvi. 27.

the priest should drink of it. Yet this, which is so diametrically repugnant to the institution of Christ, they wish us to receive as an interpretation of it. Paul calls "forbidding to marry" a "doctrine of devils;" (*d*) and the Holy Spirit, in another place, pronounces that "marriage is honourable in all, and the bed undefiled." (*e*) The prohibition, which they have since denounced, of the marriage of priests, they wish us to consider as the true and natural interpretation of the Scriptures, though nothing can be imagined more repugnant to it. If any one dare to open his mouth to the contrary, he is condemned as a heretic, because the determination of the Church is without appeal, and the truth of its interpretation cannot be doubted without impiety. What further requires to be urged against such consummate effrontery? The mere exhibition of it is a sufficient refutation. Their pretensions to confirm the Scripture by the authority of the Church, I purposely pass over. To subject the oracles of God to the authority of men, so as to make their validity dependent on human approbation, is a blasphemy unworthy of being mentioned; beside which, I have touched on this subject already I will only ask them one question: If the authority of the Scripture be founded on the approbation of the Church, what decree of any council can they alleged to this point? I believe, none at all. Why, then, did Arius suffer himself to be vanquished at Nice by testimonies adduced from the Gospel of John? According to the argument of our opponents, he was at liberty to reject them, as not having yet received the approbation of any general council. They allege an ancient catalogue, which is called the Canon of Scripture, and which they say proceeded from the decision of the Church. I ask them again, in what council that canon was composed. To this they can make no reply. Yet I would wish to be further informed, what kind of a canon they suppose it to be. For I see that the ancient writers were not fully agreed respecting it. And if any weight be attached to the testimony of Jerome, the two books of the Maccabees, the history of Tobit, Ecclesiasticus, and other books, will be considered as apocryphal; to which our opponents will by no means consent.

(*d*) 1 Tim. iv. 1, 3.   (*e*) Heb. xiii. 4.

CHAPTER X

The Power of Legislation, in Which the Pope and His Adherents Have Most Cruelly Tyrannized Over the Minds, and Tortured the Bodies, of Men

We now proceed to the second branch of the power of the Church, which the Romanists represent as consisting in legislation—a source from which have issued innumerable human traditions, the most pestilent and fatal to wretched souls. For they have made no more scruple than the scribes and Pharisees to "lay on other men's shoulders burdens which they themselves would not touch with one of their fingers." (*f*) I have shown in another place the extreme cruelty of their injunctions concerning auricular confession. None of their other laws discover such enormous violence; but those which appear the most tolerable of them all, are tyrannically oppressive to the conscience. I forbear to remark how they adulterate the worship of God, and despoil God himself, who is the sole Legislator, of the right which belongs to him. This power is now to be examined—whether the Church has authority to make laws which shall bind

(*f*) Matt. xxiii. 4. Luke xi. 46.

the consciences of men. This question has nothing to do with political order; the only objects of our present attention are, that God may be rightly worshipped according to the rule he has prescribed, and that our spiritual liberty which relates to God may be preserved entire. Whatever edicts have been issued by men respecting the worship of God, independently of his word, it has been customary to call *human traditions.* Against such laws we contend, and not against the holy and useful constitutions of the Church, which contribute to the preservation of discipline, or integrity, or peace. The object for which we contend, is, to restrain that overgrown and barbarous empire, which is usurped over men's souls by those who wish to be accounted the pastors of the Church, but who in reality are its most savage butchers. For they say that the laws which they make are spiritual, pertaining to the soul, and they affirm them to be necessary to eternal life. Thus, as I have lately hinted, the kingdom of Christ is invaded; thus the liberty given by him to the consciences of believers is altogether subverted and destroyed. I forbear to remark at present with what great impiety they enforce the observance of their laws, while they teach men to seek the pardon of their sins and righteousness and salvation from it, and while they make the whole of religion and piety to consist in it. I only contend for this one point, that no necessity ought to be imposed upon consciences in things in which they have been set at liberty by Christ; and without this liberty, as I have before observed, they can have no peace with God. They must acknowledge Christ their Deliverer as their only King, and must be governed by one law of liberty, even the sacred word of the gospel, if they wish to retain the grace which they have once obtained in Christ; they must submit to no slavery; they must be fettered by no bonds.

II. These sapient legislators, indeed, pretend that their constitutions are laws of liberty, an easy yoke, a light burden. But who does not see that these are gross falsehoods? The hardship of their laws is not at all felt by themselves, who have rejected the fear of God, and securely and boldly disregard all laws, human and divine. But persons who are impressed with any concern for their salvation, are far from considering themselves at liberty as long as they are entangled in these snares. We see what great caution Paul used in this respect, to avoid "casting a snare upon" men in a single instance; (*g*) and that not without cause; for he saw what a deep wound would be made in their consciences, by the imposition of any necessity upon them in those things in which the Lord had left them at liberty. On the contrary, it is scarcely possible to enumerate the constitutions, which these men have most rigorously enforced with the denunciation of eternal death, and which they require to be most minutely observed as necessary to salvation. Among these, there are many exceedingly difficult to be fulfilled; but when they are all collected together in one body, so immense is the accumulation, the observance of the whole is utterly impracticable. How, then, can it be possible for those who are loaded with such a vast weight of difficulty, not to be perplexed and tortured with extreme anxiety and terror? My design at present, then, is, to oppose constitutions of this kind, which tend to bind souls internally before God, and to fill them with scruples, as if they enjoined things necessary to salvation.

III. The generality of men, therefore, are embarrassed with this question, for want of distinguishing with sufficient exactness between the outward judgment of men and the court of conscience. The difficulty is increased by the injunction of Paul, that the magistrate is to be obeyed, "not only for wrath, but also for conscience' sake;" (*h*) whence it follows, that consciences are bound by political laws. If this were the case, all that we said in the last chapter, and are about to say in this, on the subject of spiritual government, would fall to the ground. To solve this difficulty, it is first of all necessary to understand what is conscience. The definition may be derived from the etymology of the word. *Science*, or *knowledge*, is the apprehension which men have of things in their mind and understanding. So, when they have an apprehension of the judgment of God, as a witness that suffers them not to conceal their sins, but forces them as criminals before the tribunal of the judge, this apprehension is called *conscience*. For it is something between God and man, which permits not a man to suppress what he knows within himself, but pursues

(*g*) 1 Cor. vii. 35. (*h*) Rom. xiii. 5.

him till it brings him to a sense of his guilt. This is what Paul means, when he speaks of men's "conscience also bearing witness, and their thoughts the mean while accusing, or else excusing, one another" (*i*) before God. A simple knowledge might remain in man, as it were, in a state of concealment. Therefore this sentiment, which places men before the tribunal of God, is like a keeper appointed over man to watch and observe all his secrets, that nothing may remain buried in darkness. Hence that old proverb, that conscience is equal to a thousand witnesses. For the same reason, Peter speaks of "the answer of a good conscience towards God," (*k*) to denote our tranquillity of mind, when, persuaded of the grace of Christ, we present ourselves before God without fear. And the author of the Epistle to the Hebrews speaks of persons "having no more conscience of sins," (*l*) to signify their being liberated, or absolved, so as to feel no more remorse or compunction for sin.

IV. Therefore, as works have respect to man, so the conscience is referred to God. A good conscience is no other than an internal purity of heart. In this sense Paul says that "the end of the commandment is charity, out of a pure heart, and of a good conscience, and of faith unfeigned." (*m*) In a subsequent part of the same chapter, he shows how widely it differs from simple knowledge, when he says, that "some having put away a good conscience, concerning faith have made shipwreck." (*n*) For in these words he implies that it is a lively zeal for the worship of God, and a sincere desire and endeavour to live a pious and holy life. Sometimes, indeed, it is likewise extended to men, as when Luke states Paul to have made this declaration—"I exercise myself, to have always a conscience void of offence toward God and toward men." (*o*) The apostle expressed himself in this manner, because the benefits proceeding from a good conscience do reach even to man. But strictly speaking, the conscience has respect to God alone, as I have already observed. Hence it is, that a law is said to bind the conscience, which simply binds a man without any observation or consideration of other men. For example, God not only commands the heart to be preserved chaste

---

(*i*) Rom. ii. 15. (*k*) 1 Peter iii. 21. (*l*) Heb. x. 2.
(*m*) 1 Tim. i. 5. (*n*) 1 Tim. i. 19. (*o*) Acts xxiv. 16.

and pure from every libidinous desire, but prohibits all obscenity of language and external lasciviousness. My conscience is bound to observe this law, even though not another man existed in the world. The person, therefore, who commits any breach of chastity, not only sins by setting a bad example to his brethren, but brings his conscience into a state of guilt before God. The case of things, in themselves indifferent, stands not on the same ground; for we ought to abstain from whatever is likely to give offence, but with a free conscience. Thus Paul speaks of meat consecrated to idols: "If any man say unto you, This is offered in sacrifice to idols, eat not for his sake, and for conscience' sake. Conscience, I say, not thine own, but of the other." (*p*) A faithful man, who, after previous admonition, should eat such meat, would be guilty of sin. But though such abstinence is enjoined on him by God as necessary on account of his brother, he still retains his liberty of conscience. We see how this law, while it binds the external act, leaves the conscience free.

V. Let us now return to human laws. If they are designed to introduce any scruple into our minds, as though the observance of them were essentially necessary, we assert, that they are unreasonable impositions on the conscience. For our consciences have to do, not with men, but with God alone. And this is the meaning of the well known distinction, maintained in the schools, between a human tribunal and the court of conscience. When the whole world was enveloped in the thickest shades of ignorance, this little spark of light still remained unextinguished, so that they acknowledged the conscience of man to be superior to all human judgments. It is true that what they confessed in one word, they afterwards overturned in fact; yet it was the will of God that even at that time there should remain some testimony in favour of Christian liberty, to rescue the conscience from the tyranny of men. But we have not yet solved the difficulty which arises from the language of Paul. For if princes are to be obeyed, "not only for wrath, but also for conscience' sake," (*q*) it seems to follow, that the laws of princes have dominion over the conscience. If this be true, the same must be affirmed of the laws of

---

(*p*) 1 Cor. x. 28, 29.

(*q*) Rom. xiii. 5.

the Church. I reply, In the first place, it is necessary to distinguish between the *genus* and the *species*. For the conscience is not affected by every particular law; yet we are bound by the general command of God, which establishes the authority of magistrates. And this is the hinge upon which Paul's argument turns, that magistrates are to be honoured because they are "ordained of God." (*r*) At the same time he is far from insinuating that the laws enacted by them have any thing to do with the internal government of the soul; for he every where extols the service of God and the spiritual rule of a holy life, above all the statutes and decrees of men. A second consideration worthy of notice, which is a consequence of the first, is, that human laws,—I mean such as are good and just, whether enacted by magistrates or by the Church,—though they are necessary to be observed, are not on this account binding on the conscience; because all the necessity of observing them has reference to the general object of laws, but does not consist in the particular things which are commanded. There is an immense distance between laws of this description, and those which prescribe any new form for the worship of God, and impose a necessity in things that were left free and indifferent.

VI. Such are the *Ecclesiastical Constitutions*, as they are now called, in the Papacy, which are obtruded as necessary to the true worship of God; and as they are innumerable, they are so many bonds to entrap and insnare souls. Though we have touched on them a little in the exposition of the law, yet as this is a more suitable place to discuss them at large, I shall now endeavour to collect a summary of the whole, in the best order I can. And as we have already said what appeared sufficient respecting the tyrannical power, which the false bishops arrogate to themselves, of teaching whatever doctrines they please, I shall at present pass over all that subject, and confine myself to a discussion of the power which they say they have, to make laws. Our false bishops, therefore, burden men's consciences with new laws under this pretext—that the Lord has constituted them spiritual legislators, by committing to them the government of the Church. Wherefore

(*r*) Rom. xiii. 1.

they contend, that all the commands and ordinances ought of necessity to be observed by all Christian people, and that whoever violates them is guilty of double disobedience, because he is a rebel both against God and the Church. Certainly, if they were true bishops, I would allow them some authority of this kind; not all that they demand, but all that is requisite to the maintenance of good order in the Church. But as they bear no resemblance of the character to which they pretend, the least they can possibly assume is more than their right. Yet as this has been already proved, let us admit the supposition at present, that whatever power true bishops are entitled to, belongs to them. Still I deny that they are therefore appointed as legislators over believers, with power to prescribe a rule of life according to their own pleasure, or to constrain the people committed to them to submit to their decrees. By this observation I mean, that they have no authority to enjoin upon the observance of the Church any thing that they may have invented themselves, independently of the word of God. As this power was unknown to the apostles, and was so frequently interdicted to the ministers of the Church by the mouth of the Lord, I wonder how they have dared to usurp it, and still dare to maintain it contrary to the example of the apostles, and in defiance of the express prohibition of God.

VII. Every thing pertaining to the perfect rule of a holy life, the Lord has comprehended in his law, so that there remains nothing for men to add to that summary. And he has done this, first, that, since all rectitude of life consists in the conformity of all our actions to his will, as their standard, we might consider him as the sole Master and Director of our conduct; and secondly, to show that he requires of us nothing more than obedience. For this reason, James says, "He that judgeth his brother, judgeth the law; but if thou judge the law, thou art not a doer of the law, but a judge. There is one lawgiver, who is able to save and to destroy." (*s*) We hear that God asserts this as his peculiar and exclusive prerogative; to govern us by the empire and laws of his word. And the same sentiment had before been expressed by Isaiah, though in terms not quite so explicit: "The Lord is our

(*s*) James iv. 11, 12.

Judge, the Lord is our Lawgiver, the Lord is our King, he will save us." (*t*) Both passages imply, that he who has authority over the soul, is the Arbiter of life and death; and James even clearly expresses it. No man can assume this to himself. It follows therefore, that God ought to be acknowledged as the only King of souls, who alone has power to save and to destroy, or, in the language of Isaiah, as the King, Judge, Legislator, and Saviour. Wherefore Peter, when he admonishes pastors of their duty, exhorts them "to feed the flock not as being lords over God's heritage," (*v*) or the company of believers. If we duly consider this point, that it is not lawful to transfer to man that which God appropriates solely to himself, we shall understand that this cuts off all the power which is claimed by those who wish to exalt themselves to command any thing in the Church, unsanctioned by the word of God.

VIII. Now, as the whole argument rests here, that, if God is the sole legislator, it is not lawful for men to assume this honour to themselves,—we ought also to bear in mind the two reasons which we have stated, why God asserts this exclusively to himself. The first is, that his will may be received as the perfect rule of all righteousness and holiness, and so that an acquaintance with it may be all the knowledge necessary to a good life. The second is, that with respect to the mode of worshipping him aright, he may exercise the sole empire over our souls, to whom we are under the strongest obligation to obey his authority and await his commands. When these two reasons are kept in view, it will be easy to judge what constitutions of men are contrary to the word of God. Now, of this description are all those which are pretended to belong to the true worship of God, and to be obligatory on men's consciences as necessary to be observed. Let us remember, therefore, that all human laws are to be weighed in this balance, if we would have a certain and infallible test. The first of these reasons is urged by Paul in his Epistle to the Colossians, in opposition to the false apostles, who endeavoured to oppress the Churches with fresh burdens. In a similar argument, in the Epistle to the Galatians, he insists more on the second reason. In the

(*t*) Isaiah xxxiii. 22. (*v*) 1 Peter v. 2, 3.

Epistle to the Colossians, he contends that the doctrine of the true worship of God is not to be sought from men, because the Lord has faithfully and fully instructed us how we ought to worship him. To prove this, in the first chapter he states that all the wisdom by which the man of God is made perfect in Christ is contained in the gospel. In the beginning of the second chapter, he declares that "in Christ are hid all the treasures of wisdom and knowledge;" from which he concludes that believers should "beware lest any man spoil them through philosophy and vain deceit, after the tradition of men." At the end of the chapter, he still more confidently condemns all "will worship;" (*w*) this includes all those fictitious services which men either invent for themselves or receive from others, together with all the precepts by which they presume to regulate the worship of God. Thus we have ascertained the impiety of all those constitutions, in the observance of which the worship of God is pretended to consist. The passages in the Epistle to the Galatians, in which he argues that snares ought not to be imposed on consciences, which are subject to the government of God alone, are too plain to be mistaken; especially in the fifth chapter. (*x*) It will therefore be sufficient to have mentioned them.

IX. But as the whole of this subject will be better elucidated by examples, before I proceed any further, it will be useful to apply this doctrine to our own times. We affirm that the Ecclesiastical Constitutions, with which the pope and his satellites oppress the Church, are pernicious and impious; our adversaries assert them to be holy and useful. Now, they are of two classes: some regard rites and ceremonies, others have more relation to discipline. Is there just cause, then, to induce us to reject both? There certainly is juster cause than we would desire. In the first place, do not the authors of them explicitly declare that the very essence of the worship of God consists in them? To what end do they refer their ceremonies, but that God may be worshipped through them? And this arises not from the mere error of the uninformed multitude, but from the approbation of those who sustain the office of teachers. I am not yet referring to the gross abominations by

(*w*) Col. i. 27, 28; ii. 3, 8, 23. (*x*) Gal. v. 1—18.

which they have attempted to overturn all piety; but they would never pretend a failure in any one of the most insignificant traditions to be such an atrocious crime, unless they made the worship of God subject to their inventions. Wherein are we guilty of any offence, then, if we cannot bear in our day what was declared to be intolerable by Paul: namely, that the legitimate mode of worshipping God should be regulated by the will of men; especially when they enjoin a worship "after the rudiments of the world," which Paul asserts to be "not after Christ." (*y*) It is well known also, with what rigorous necessity they bind men's consciences to observe every thing that they command. In our opposition to this, we unite in a common cause with Paul, who would by no means allow the consciences of believers to be subjected to the bondage of men. (*z*)

X. Moreover, this worst of consequences ensues; that when men have begun to place religion in such vain figments, that perversion is immediately followed by another execrable corruption, with which Christ reproached the Pharisees. "Ye have made the commandment of God of none effect by your tradition." (*a*) I will not combat our modern legislators with my own words; I will grant them the victory, if they can vindicate themselves from this accusation of Christ. But how can they vindicate themselves, while they esteem it infinitely more criminal, to have omitted auricular confession at a stated time of the year, than to have lived a most iniquitous life for a whole year together; to have infected the tongue with the least taste of animal food on a Friday, than to have polluted the whole body by committing fornication every day; to have put a hand to any honest labour on a day consecrated to any pretended saint, than to have continually employed all the members in the most flagitious actions; for a priest to be connected in one lawful marriage, than to be defiled with a thousand adulteries; to have failed of performing one vow of pilgrimage, than to violate every other promise; not to have lavished any thing on the enormous, superfluous, and useless magnificence of Churches, than to have failed of relieving the most pressing necessities of the poor; to have passed by an idol

---

(*y*) Col. ii. 8.　(*z*) Gal. v. 1.　(*a*) Matt. xv. 6.

without some token of honour, than to have insulted all the men in the world; not to have muttered over, at certain seasons, a multitude of words without any meaning, than to have never offered a genuine prayer from the heart? What is it for men to make the commandment of God of none effect by their traditions, if this be not? When coldly and carelessly recommending the observance of the commandments of God, they insist on an exact obedience to their own, with as much zeal and anxiety as if the whole essence of piety consisted in them; when avenging the violation of the Divine law with slight penalties of satisfactions, they punish the smallest transgression of one of their decrees with nothing less than imprisonment, banishment, fire, or sword; when less severe and inexorable against the despisers of God, they persecute the despisers of themselves with implacable hatred even to death; and when they instruct all those whom they hold in the chains of ignorance in such a manner, that they would feel less concern at seeing the subversion of the whole law of God, than the violation of the smallest tittle of the commands of the Church? In the first place, here is a grievous error, that on account of things of no importance in themselves, and left free by God, one man despises, condemns, and rejects another. Now, as if this were not bad enough, "the beggarly elements of the world," (*b*) as Paul calls them, are esteemed of more force than the celestial oracles of God. He who is absolved in adultery, is condemned in meat; he who is allowed a harlot, is interdicted from a wife. This is the fruit of that prevaricating obedience, which recedes from God in proportion as it inclines to men.

XI. There are also two other faults, far from small ones, which we charge on these Constitutions. The first is, that they prescribe for the most part useless, and sometimes even foolish observances. The second is, that pious consciences are oppressed with the immense number of them, and being carried back to a species of Judaism, are so occupied with shadows as to be prevented from coming to Christ. When I call these observances useless and foolish, I know this will not be admitted by the wisdom of the flesh, which is so pleased with them, as to consider the Church alto-

(*b*) Gal. iv. 9. Col. ii. 8.

gether deformed where they are abolished. But these are the things which Paul describes as "having a show of wisdom in will-worship, and humility, and neglecting of the body; not in any honour to the satisfying of the flesh." (*c*) This is certainly a most salutary admonition, which ought never to be forgotten by us. Human traditions, he says, deceive under a show of wisdom. Is it inquired whence they have this appearance? I reply, that being contrived by man, the human mind recognizes them as its own, and recognizing them, embraces them with greater pleasure than it would any thing of the greatest excellence, but less agreeable to its vanity. A further recommendation of them is, that as they keep the minds of men depressed to the ground under their yoke, they appear well adapted to promote humility. Lastly, they are regarded as the expedients of prudence, from their supposed tendency to restrain corporeal indulgence, and to subdue sensuality by the rigour of abstinence. But what does Paul say to these things? Does he strip off such disguises, that the simple may not be deluded by false pretences? Satisfied that he had said enough to refute them, when he had called them "the commandments and doctrines of men," (*d*) he passes over all these things as undeserving of any particular refutation. And knowing that all services of human invention are condemned in the Church, and ought to excite the suspicion of believers in proportion to the pleasure they afford to the minds of men; knowing that false appearance of external humility to be at such an immense distance from true humility, that it might be easily distinguished from it; knowing that discipline to be entitled to no other consideration than as a mere exercise of the body,—he intended these very things, by which the traditions of men are recommended to the ignorant, to serve as their refutation with believers.

XII. So, at the present day, not only the unlearned vulgar, but those who are most inflated with worldly wisdom, are universally and wonderfully captivated with the pomp of ceremonies. Hypocrites and silly women think it impossible to imagine any thing more beautiful or excellent. But those who examine more minutely, and judge with more accuracy, according to the rule of

(*c*) Col. ii. 23. (*d*) Col. ii. 22.

piety, respecting the real value of those numerous ceremonies, perceive, in the first place, that they are frivolous, because they have no utility; and in the next place that they are delusive, because they deceive the eyes of the spectators with empty pomp. I speak of those ceremonies under which, the Roman doctors contend, are concealed great mysteries, but which, on examination, we find to be mere mockeries. And it is not to be wondered at, that the authors and advocates of them have fallen into such folly as to delude both themselves and others with contemptible absurdities; because they have taken their model in some things from the reveries of the heathen, and in others, without any judgment, have imitated the ancient rites of the Mosaic law, which were no more applicable to us than the sacrifices of animals and other similar ceremonies. Indeed, if there were no argument besides, yet no man in his senses would expect any thing good from such a heterogeneous compound. And the fact itself plainly demonstrates, that numerous ceremonies have no other use than to stupefy the people, instead of instructing them. So hypocrites attach great importance to those novel canons, which overturn discipline rather than preserve it; for on a more accurate investigation, they will be found a mere shadow of discipline, without any reality.

XIII. Now, to proceed to the other fault which I have mentioned, who does not see that traditions, by the continual accumulation of one upon another, have grown to such an immense number, that they are altogether intolerable to the Christian Church? Hence it is, that the ceremonies discover a kind of Judaism, and other observances inflict grievous tortures on pious souls. Augustine complained that, in his time, the commands of God were neglected, and every thing was so full of presumption, that a person was more severely censured for having touched the ground with his bare feet within eight days of his baptism, than for having drowned his senses in intoxication. He complained that the Church, which the mercy of God intended to place in a state of liberty, was so grievously oppressed, that the condition of the Jews was more tolerable. If that holy man had lived in our day, with what lamentations would he have deplored the present state of bondage? For the number of ordinances is ten times greater, and every tittle is enforced with a hundred times more rigour, than in his time. Such is the general consequence, when these corrupt legislators have seized the dominion, they make no end of commands and prohibitions, till they arrive at such an extreme that obedience is scarcely if at all practicable. This is finely expressed by Paul, when he says, "If ye be dead from the rudiments of the world, why, as though living in the world, are ye subject to ordinances? Eat not, taste not, handle not." (*e*) The word ἅψῃ, signifying both to *eat* and to *handle*, requires here to be understood in the former sense, to avoid an unnecessary repetition. Here, then, he most beautifully describes the progress of the false apostles. They begin with superstition, forbidding to eat not only a large quantity, but even a little; when they have carried this point, they next forbid to taste; and after this is submitted to them, they pronounce it unlawful even to touch with a finger.

XIV. In the present age, we justly censure this tyranny in human constitutions, which astonishingly torments miserable consciences with innumerable edicts, and the extreme rigour with which they are enforced. The canons relating to discipline have been already considered. What shall I say of the ceremonies, which have half buried Christ, and caused us to return to Jewish figures? "Christ our Lord," says Augustine, "has connected together the society of the new people with sacraments, very few in number, most excellent in signification, and very easy to observe." The immense distance of this simplicity from the multitude and variety of rites in which we see the Church now involved, can hardly be stated in terms sufficiently strong. I know with what artifice some ingenious men apologize for this corruption. They say, that there are great numbers among us as ignorant as there were among the Israelites; that for their sakes such discipline was instituted, which those who are stronger, though they do not find it necessary, ought not to neglect, when they perceive it to be useful to their weak brethren. I reply, that we are not ignorant of what is due from every Christian to the infirmity of his brethren; but, on the other hand, we reply, that this is not

(*e*) Col. ii. 20, 21.

the way to benefit the weak, by oppressing them with heavy loads of ceremonies. It was not without cause that the Lord has made this difference between his ancient people and us; that he chose to instruct them, like children, with emblems and figures, but has been pleased to teach us in a more simple manner, without such a large external apparatus. As "a child," says Paul, "is under tutors and governors until the time appointed of the father," (*f*) so the Jews were under the instruction and government of the law. But we resemble adults, who, having left a state of tuition and guardianship, have no need of puerile discipline. Surely the Lord foresaw what sort of common people there would be in his Church, and in what manner they would require to be governed. Yet he made the difference we have mentioned between us and the Jews. It is a foolish way, therefore, to pretend to benefit the ignorant by reviving Judaism, which has been abrogated by Christ. This diversity, between the people under the old dispensation and the new, was signified by Christ, when he said to the woman of Samaria, "The hour cometh, and now is, when the true worshippers shall worship the Father in spirit and in truth." (*g*) This, indeed, had always been the case; but the new worshippers differ from the ancient in this respect, that under Moses the spiritual adoration of God was concealed, and in some degree embarrassed with many ceremonies, which being now abolished, he is worshipped with greater simplicity. Wherefore those who confound this difference, subvert the order instituted and established by Christ. Shall no ceremonies, then, it will be asked, be given to the ignorant, to assist their weakness? I say no such thing; for I think some assistance of this kind very useful to them. I only contend that such means should be employed as would tend to make known Christ, not to conceal him. God has, therefore, given us few ceremonies, and those by no means laborious, to exhibit Christ to us as present; the Jews had a greater number, to represent him as absent. He was then absent, I say, not as to his power, but with respect to the manner of representing him. Therefore, to observe proper bounds, it is necessary to retain that paucity in number, that facility in observance, that

---

(*f*) Gal. iv. 1, 2. (*g*) John iv. 23.

dignity in signification, which consists in simplicity. That this has not been done, it is scarcely necessary to mention. The fact is visible to all.

XV. Here I forbear to remark the pernicious opinions with which the minds of men are impressed, that these ceremonies of human invention are sacrifices by which God is justly appeased, by which sins are expiated, by which righteousness and salvation are procured. It will be denied that things intrinsically good are corrupted by such adventitious errors, since equal guilt of this kind may be incurred in the performance of works commanded by God. But it is more intolerable to attribute so much honour to works presumptuously devised by the will of men, as to believe them to be meritorious of eternal life. For works commanded by God obtain a reward, because the Legislator himself accepts them as acts of obedience. They derive their value, therefore, not from their own dignity or intrinsic merit, but from God's estimation of our obedience to him. I speak here of that perfection of works which God commands, but which men never attain. For the works of the law which we perform, are only accepted through the gratuitous goodness of God, our obedience in them being weak and imperfect. But as we are not here discussing the value of works independent of Christ, let us drop this question. With regard to the present argument, I again repeat, that whatever value is attributed to works, they derive from the consideration of the obedience, which is alone regarded by God, as he declares by the prophet: "I commanded not concerning burnt-offerings of sacrifices, but this thing I commanded, saying, Obey my voice." (*h*) Of works of human device, he speaks in another place. "Wherefore do ye spend money for that which is not bread?" (*i*) Again: "In vain do they worship me by the precepts of men." (*k*) Our adversaries, therefore, can never excuse themselves for suffering the unhappy people to seek in those external fooleries a righteousness to present before God, and to support them at the heavenly tribunal. Besides, is it not a fault deserving of severe reprehension, that they exhibit ceremonies not understood, like the scenery of a stage or a magical incantation? For

---

(*h*) Jer. vii. 22, 23. (*i*) Isaiah lv. 2. (*k*) Isaiah xxix. 13. Matt. xv. 7—9.

it is certain that all ceremonies are corrupt and pernicious, unless they direct men to Christ. Now, the ceremonies practised in the Papacy have no connection with doctrine: they confine men to mere signs, destitute of all signification. Lastly, so ingenious is cupidity, it is evident that many of them have been invented by avaricious priests, merely as contrivances for the extortion of money. But whatever be their origin, they are all so prostituted to the acquisition of gain, that it is necessary to abolish the principal part of them, if we wish to prevent a profane and sacrilegious traffic from being carried on in the Church.

XVI. Though I may be considered as not delivering a doctrine of perpetual application respecting human constitutions, because the preceding observations have been wholly directed to the present age, yet nothing has been advanced which would not be useful in all ages. For wherever this superstition intrudes, that men are determined to worship God with their own inventions, all the laws made for this purpose presently degenerate into such gross abuses as we have described. It is a curse which God denounces, not against any particular age, but against all ages, that he will strike with blindness and stupidity all those who worship him with the doctrines of men. (*l*) The invariable effect of this blindness is, that no absurdity is too great to be embraced by persons who, in contempt of so many warnings from God, wilfully entangle themselves in such fatal snares. But if, irrespective of peculiar circumstances, any one wish to have a simple statement, what are the human traditions of all ages, which ought to be rejected and reprobated by the Church and all pious persons, the direction we have already given is clear and certain—that they are all laws made by men without the word of God, for the purpose, either of prescribing any method for the worship of God, or of laying the conscience under a religious obligation, as if they enjoined things necessary to salvation. If either or both of these be accompanied with other faults, such as, that the ceremonies, by their multitude, obscure the simplicity of the gospel; that they tend to no edification, but are useless and ridiculous occupations rather than real exercises of piety; that they are

---

(*l*) Isaiah xxix. 13, 14.

employed for the sordid purposes of dishonest gain; that they are too difficult to be observed; that they are polluted with impious superstitions;—these things will further assist us in discovering the vast evil which they contain.

XVII. I hear the answer which they make—that their traditions are not from themselves, but from God; for that the Church is directed by the Holy Spirit, so that it cannot err; and that they are in possession of his authority. When this point is gained, it immediately follows, that their traditions are the revelations of the Holy Spirit, which cannot be despised without impiety and contempt of God. That they may not appear to attempt any thing without high authorities, they wish it to be believed that the greatest part of their observances have descended from the apostles; and they contend that one example sufficiently shows what was the conduct of the apostles in other cases; when, being assembled together in a council, they determined and announced to all Gentiles, that they should "abstain from meats offered to idols, and from blood, and from things strangled." (*m*) We have already exposed the falsehood of their pretensions in arrogating to themselves the title of the Church. With regard to the present argument, if, stripping off all false disguises, we confine our attention to what ought to be our chief concern, and involves our highest interests, namely, what kind of a Church Christ requires, in order that we may conform ourselves to its standard,—it will be sufficiently evident to us, that the name of the Church does not belong to those who overleap all the limits of the word of God, and exercise an unbounded license of enacting new laws. For does not that law, which was once given to the Church, remain forever in force? "What thing soever I command you, observe to do it: thou shalt not add thereto, nor diminish from it." (*n*) And again: "Add not thou unto his words, lest he reprove thee, and thou be found a liar." (*o*) Since they cannot deny these things to have been spoken to the Church, do they not declare the rebellion of the Church, when they pretend that, notwithstanding such prohibitions, it has dared to mingle additions of its own with the doctrine of God? Far be it from us, however, to countenance their

(*m*) Acts xv. 28, 29. (*n*) Deut. xii. 32. (*o*) Prov. xxx.

falsehoods, by which they do so great an injury to the Church; let us know that the assumption of the name of the Church is a false pretence in all who are so carried away by the violence of human presumption, as to disregard all the restraints of the word of God, and to introduce a torrent of their own inventions. There is nothing involved, nothing intricate, nothing ambiguous in these words, by which the whole Church is forbidden to add any thing to the word, or to diminish any thing from it, in any question relating to the worship of God and his salutary precepts. But it will be alleged, that this was spoken exclusively of the law, which has been succeeded by the prophecies and the whole dispensation of the gospel. This I certainly admit, and at the same time assert, that these were accomplishments of the law, rather than additions to it, or retrenchments of it. But if the Lord suffered no enlargement or diminution of the ministry of Moses, notwithstanding it was enveloped in such great obscurity, till he dispensed a clearer doctrine by his servants the prophets, and finally by his beloved Son,—why do not we consider ourselves far more severely prohibited from making any addition to the law, the prophets, the psalms, and the gospel? No change has taken place in the Lord, who long ago declared that nothing was so highly offensive to him, as to attempt to worship him with the inventions of men. Hence those striking declarations in the prophets, which ought to be continually sounding in our ears: "I spake not unto your fathers, nor commanded them in the day that I brought them out of the land of Egypt, concerning burnt-offerings or sacrifices; but this thing commanded I them, saying, Obey my voice, and I will be your God, and ye shall be my people: and walk ye in all the ways that I have commanded you." (*p*) Again: "I earnestly protested unto your fathers, saying, Obey my voice." (*q*) There are many other similar passages, but the most remarkable of all is the following: "Hath the Lord," says Samuel, "as great delight in burnt-offerings and sacrifices, as in obeying the voice of the Lord? Behold, to obey is better than sacrifice, and to hearken than the fat of rams. For rebellion is as the sin of witchcraft, and stubbornness is as iniquity and idolatry." (*r*) There-

(*p*) Jer. vii. 22, 23. (*q*) Jer. xi. 7. (*r*) 1 Sam. xv. 22, 23.

fore, whatever human inventions relating to the worship of God, may be defended by the authority of the Church, since it is impossible to vindicate them from impiety, it is easy to infer that the imputation of them to the Church has no foundation in truth.

XVIII. For this reason we freely censure that tyranny of human traditions, which is imposed upon the world under the name of the Church. Nor do we hold the Church in contempt, as our adversaries, in order to render us obnoxious, falsely assert. We allow it the praise of obedience, than which no higher praise can be given. On the contrary, they are themselves the most outrageous violators of the Church, which they represent as guilty of rebellion against the Lord, when they pretend that it has gone beyond what was permitted by the word of God; to say nothing of the combination of impudence and wickedness discovered in their incessant vociferations respecting the authority of the Church, while they take no notice of the command of the Lord, or of the obedience due from the Church to that command. But if we desire, as we ought, to agree with the Church, it will be best for us to observe and remember what commands are given by the Lord, equally to us and to the whole Church, that we may all obey him with one consent. For there is no doubt that we shall fully agree with the Church, if we show ourselves in all things obedient to the Lord. Now, to attribute to the apostles the origin of the traditions which have hitherto oppressed the Church, is a mere imposture; for the whole tendency of the doctrine of the apostles was, that men's consciences should not be burdened with new observances, or the worship of God contaminated with human inventions. Besides, if there be any credit due to ancient histories and records, the apostles not only never knew, but never even heard of that which is ascribed to them. Nor let it be pretended, that the greatest part of their Constitutions were received in use and commonly practised, which were never committed to writing; namely, those things which, during the life of Christ, they were not able to understand, but which after his ascension, they learned from the revelation of the Holy Spirit. The meaning of that passage we have already examined. With respect to the present subject, we may observe, they make themselves truly ridiculous by maintaining that those great mysteries, which were so long unknown to the apostles, consisted partly of Jewish or heathen ceremonies, of which the former had long before been promulgated among the Jews, and the latter among the heathen, and partly of foolish gesticulations and unmeaning rites, which stupid priests, who scarcely know how to walk or speak, perform with the greatest exactness, and which even infants and fools counterfeit so well, that it might be thought there were no more suitable ministers of such solemnities. If there were no histories, yet men of sound judgment would conclude from the thing itself, that such a vast multitude of rites and observances did not break into the Church all on a sudden, but that they must have been introduced by degrees. For when those holy bishops, who were the immediate successors of the apostles, had made some appointments relating to order and discipline, they were followed by a series of others, who had too little consideration, and too much curiosity and cupidity, of whom every one in succession vied with his predecessors, from a foolish emulation to excel them in the invention of new observances. And because there was danger that their inventions, by which they desired to obtain the praises of posterity, might in a short time be disused, they were the more rigid in enforcing the observance of them. This foolish and perverse imitation has been the source of most of those rites which the Romanists urge upon us as apostolic. And this is also attested by various histories.

XIX. To avoid too much prolixity in composing a catalogue of them all, we shall content ourselves with one example. In the administration of the Lord's supper, the apostles used great simplicity. Their immediate successors, to adorn the dignity of the mystery, added some forms which were not to be altogether condemned. Afterwards followed those foolish imitators, who, by adding various fragments from time to time, at length formed those vestments of the priests, those ornaments of the altar, those gesticulations, and all that apparatus of useless things, which we see in the mass. But they object that it was an ancient opinion, that whatever was done with the common consent of the universal Church, had originated from the apostles. In proof of this, they cite the testimony of Augustine. I shall give them no other answer than in the words of Augustine himself. "Those things which are observed throughout the world," says he, "we may understand to have been ordained, either by the apostles themselves, or by general councils, whose authority is very useful in the Church; as that the sufferings, resurrection, and ascension of our Lord, and the descent of the Holy Spirit, are celebrated by solemn anniversaries; and if there be any thing else of a similar kind observed by the universal Church wherever it has extended itself." When he enumerates so few examples, who does not see that he intended to attribute to authors worthy of credit and reverence the observances which were then in use, and none but those simple, rare, and sober ones, which are useful in preserving the order of the Church? But how distant is this passage from the conclusion the Roman doctors would extort from it, that there is not the most insignificant ceremony among them which ought not to be considered as resting on the authority of the apostles!

XX. Not to be too tedious, I will produce only one example. If any one inquire whence they have their holy water, they immediately answer, From the apostles. As if the histories did not attribute this invention to a bishop of Rome, who, if he had taken counsel of the apostles, would certainly never have contaminated baptism by a strange and unseasonable symbol. Though it does not appear to me probable that the origin of that consecration was so ancient as those histories state. For the observation of Augustine, that some Churches in his time rejected the custom of washing the feet as a solemn imitation of Christ, lest that ceremony might be supposed to have any reference to baptism, implies that there was no other kind of washing then practised which bore any resemblance to baptism. Be this as it may, I shall never admit it to have been a dictate of the spirit of the apostles, that baptism should be recalled to the memory by a daily ablution, which would be little else than a repetition of it. It is of no consequence that Augustine elsewhere ascribes other things also to the apostles; for as he has nothing but conjectures, no conclusion ought to be drawn from them on such an important subject. Lastly, though we should even grant, that those things which he mentions had been transmitted from the time of the apostles, yet there is a wide difference between instituting some pious exercise which believers may use with a free conscience, or if they find not profitable, may abstain from the use of it, and making laws to entangle their consciences with bondage. But whoever was their author, since we see that they have fallen into so great an abuse, nothing prevents our abolishing them without any disrespect to him; because they were never instituted in order to be perpetual and unalterable.

XXI. Nor does the cause of our adversaries derive much advantage from their attempt to excuse their own tyranny, by alleging the example of the apostles. The apostles, they say, and elders of the primitive Church, passed a decree without the command of Christ, enjoining all the Gentiles to "abstain from meats offered to idols, and from blood, and from things strangled." (*s*) If this was lawful for them, why may it not be lawful for their successors, whenever circumstances require, to imitate their conduct? I sincerely wish they would imitate them in other things as well as in this. For I deny that the apostles, on that occasion, instituted or decreed any thing new, as it is easy to prove by a sufficient reason. For when Peter had declared in that assembly, that to "put a yoke upon the neck of the disciples" would be to "tempt God," (*t*) he would have contradicted his own opinion, if he had afterwards consented to the imposition of any yoke. Yet there was a yoke imposed, if the apostles decreed, from their own authority, that the Gentiles should be prohibited "from meats offered to idols, and from blood, and from things strangled." There still remains some difficulty, that nevertheless they seem to prohibit them. But this will be easily solved, if we more closely examine the meaning of the decree itself; of which the first point in order and principal in importance is, that the Gentiles were to be left in possession of their liberty, and not to be disturbed or troubled about the observance of the law. So far it is completely in our favour. The exception which immediately follows is not a new law made by the apostles, but the Divine and eternal command for the preservation of charity inviolate; nor does it diminish a tittle of that liberty: it only admonishes the Gentiles how they ought to accommodate themselves to their brethren, to avoid offending them by an abuse of their liberty. The second point, therefore, is, that the Gentiles were to use a harmless liberty, and

---

(*s*) Acts xv. 29. (*t*) Acts xv. 10.

without offence to their brethren. If it be still objected, that they prescribe a certain direction, I reply, that as far as was expedient for that period, they point out and specify the things in which the Gentiles were liable to give offence to their brethren, that they might refrain from them; yet they add nothing new of their own to the eternal law of God, by which offences against our brethren are prohibited.

XXII. As if any faithful pastors, who preside over churches not yet well regulated, were to recommend all their people not to eat meat openly on Fridays, or to labour publicly on festivals, or the like, till their weaker neighbours should be more established. For though, setting aside superstition, these things are in themselves indifferent, yet when they are attended with offences to brethren, they cannot be performed without sin; and the times are such that believers could not do these things in the presence of their weak brethren, without most grievously wounding their consciences. Who but a caviller would say that in this instance they made a new law, whereas it would evidently appear that their sole object was to guard against offences which are most expressly forbidden by the Lord? No more can it be said of the apostles, who had no other design in removing the occasion of offences, than to urge the Divine law respecting the avoidance of offence; as though they had said, It is the command of the Lord that you hurt not your weak brother; you cannot eat meats offered to idols, or blood, or things strangled, without your weak brethren being offended; therefore, we command you by the word of the Lord not to eat with offence. And that such was the intention of the apostles, Paul himself is an unexceptionable witness, who, certainly in consistence with their sentence, writes in the following manner: "As concerning the eating of those things that are offered in sacrifice unto idols, we know that an idol is nothing. Howbeit, there is not in every man that knowledge; for some with conscience of the idol, eat it as a thing offered unto an idol; and their conscience, being weak, is defiled. Take heed lest by any means this liberty of yours become a stumbling-block to them that are weak." (*v*) He who shall have duly considered

(*v*) 1 Cor. viii. 4, 7, 9.

these things, will not afterwards be deceived by the fallacy of those who attempt to justify their tyranny by the example of the apostles, as if they had begun to infringe the liberty of the Church by their decree. But that they may not be able to avoid confirming this solution by their own confession, let them tell me by what right they have dared to abrogate that decree. They can only reply, Because there was no more danger from those offences and dissensions which the apostles intended to guard against, and they knew that a law was to be judged of by the end for which it was made. As this law, therefore, is admitted to have been made from a consideration of charity, there is nothing prescribed in it any further than charity is concerned. When they confess that the transgression of this law is no other than a violation of charity, do they not thereby acknowledge that it is not a novel addition to the law of God, but a genuine and simple application of it to the times and manners for which it was designed?

XXIII. But it is contended, that though the ecclesiastical laws should in a hundred instances be unjust and injurious to us, yet they ought all to be obeyed without any exception; for that the point here is not that we should consent to errors, but that we, who are subjects, should fulfil even the severe commands of our governors, which we are not at liberty to reject. But here likewise the Lord most happily interposes with the truth of his word, delivers us from such bondage, and establishes us in the liberty which he has procured for us by his sacred blood, the benefit of which he has repeatedly confirmed by his word. For the question here is not, as they fallaciously pretend, merely whether we shall endure some grievous oppression in our bodies; but whether our consciences shall be deprived of their liberty, that is, of the benefit of the blood of Christ, and shall be tormented with a wretched bondage. Let us, however, pass over this also, as if it were matter of little importance. But do we think it a matter of little importance to deprive the Lord of his kingdom, which he claims to himself, in such a peremptory manner? And it is taken away from him whenever he is worshipped with laws of human invention, whereas he requires himself to be honored as the sole legislator of his own worship. And that no one may suppose it to be a thing of trivial importance, let us hear in what estimation it is held by the Lord. "Forasmuch," he says, "as this people draw near me with their mouth, but their fear toward me is taught by the precept of men; therefore, behold, I will proceed to do a marvellous work among this people, even a marvellous work and a wonder; for the wisdom of their wise men shall perish, and the understanding of their prudent men shall be hid." (*w*) Again: "In vain do they worship me, teaching for doctrines the commandments of men." (*x*) When the children of Israel polluted themselves by various idolatries, the cause of all the evil is attributed to the impure mixture which they made by devising new modes of worship in violation of the commands of God. Therefore, the sacred history relates that the strangers who had been transplanted by the king of Assyria from Babylon to inhabit Samaria, were torn in pieces and devoured by wild beasts, "because they knew not the statutes or ordinances of the God of the land." Though they had committed no fault in the ceremonies, yet vain pomp would not have been approved by God; but he did not fail to punish the violation of his worship, when men introduced new inventions inconsistent with his word. Hence it is afterwards stated, that being terrified with that punishment, they adopted rites prescribed in the law; yet because they did not yet worship the true God aright, it is twice repeated that "they feared the Lord," and, at the same time, that "they feared not the Lord." (*y*) Whence we conclude, that part of the reverence which is paid to him consists in our worshipping him in a simple adherence to his commands, without the admixture of any inventions of our own. Hence the frequent commendations of pious kings, that they "walked in all his commandments, and turned not aside to the right hand or to the left." (*z*) I go still further: though in some services of human invention there appears no manifest impiety, yet as soon as ever men have departed from the command of God, it is severely condemned by the Holy Spirit. The altar of Ahaz, the model of which was brought from Damascus, might seem to be an addition to the ornaments of the temple, because his design was to offer sacrifices upon it to God alone, with a view to perform these services in a more splendid manner than upon the

(*w*) Isaiah xxix. 13, 14. (*x*) Matt. xv. 9.
(*y*) 2 Kings xvii. 24—34. (*z*) 2 Kings xxii. 2. 2 Chron. xvii. 4, et alibi.

ancient and original altar; yet we see how the Holy Spirit detests such audacity, for no other reason than because all the inventions of men in the worship of God are impure corruptions. (*a*) And the more clearly the will of God is revealed to us, the more inexcusable is our presumption in making any such attempt. Wherefore the guilt of Manasseh is justly aggravated by the circumstance of his having "built" new "altars in the house of the Lord, of which the Lord said, In Jerusalem will I put my name;" (*b*) because such conduct was like an avowed rejection of the authority of God.

XXIV. Many persons wonder why the Lord so severely threatens that he would "do a marvellous work among the people," whose "fear toward him" was "taught by the precepts of men," and pronounces that he is "worshipped in vain" by "the commandments of men." But if such persons would consider what it is to follow the word of God alone in matters of religion, that is, of heavenly wisdom, they would immediately perceive it to be for no trivial reason that the Lord abominates such corrupt services, which are rendered to him according to the caprice of the human mind. For, though persons who obey such laws for the worship of God, have a certain appearance of humility in this their obedience, yet they are very far from being humble before God, to whom they prescribe the same laws which they observe themselves. This is the reason why Paul requires us to be so particularly cautious against being deceived by the traditions of men, and will-worship, that is, voluntary worship, invented by men, without the word of God. (*c*) And so indeed it is, that our own wisdom, and that of all other men, must become folly in our esteem, that we may allow God alone to be truly wise. This is very far from being the case with those who study to render themselves acceptable to him by petty observances of human contrivance, and obtrude upon him, in opposition to his commands, a hypocritical obedience, which in reality is rendered to men. This was the conduct of men in former ages; the same has happened within our own remembrance, and still happens in those places where the authority of the creature is more regarded than

(*a*) 2 Kings xvi. 10, &c. (*b*) 2 Kings xxi. 4. (*c*) Col. ii. 4, 8, 18, 23.

that of the Creator; where religion, if religion it deserves to be called, is polluted with more numerous and senseless superstitions than ever disgraced the worship of paganism. For what could proceed from the minds of men but things carnal, foolish, and truly expressive of their authors?

XXV. When the advocates of superstition allege, that Samuel sacrified in Ramah, that there this was done without the direction of the law, yet it was acceptable to God, (*d*) the answer is easy—that this was not the erection of a second altar, in opposition to one already erected, and appointed by the Divine command to supersede every other; but as there had yet been no fixed place assigned for the ark of the covenant, he appointed the town which he inhabited for the oblation of sacrifices, as the most convenient place. It certainly was not the intention of the holy prophet to make any innovation in religious worship, in which God had so strictly forbidden any thing to be added or diminished. The example of Manoah I consider as an extraordinary and singular case. Though a private man, he offered a sacrifice to God, yet not without the Divine approbation; because he did it not from the hasty impulse of his own mind, but in consequence of the secret inspiration of Heaven. (*e*) But of the Lord's utter abomination of all the contrivances of mortals in his worship, we have a memorable example in another person, not inferior to Manoah—I mean Gideon, whose ephod produced fatal consequences, not only to himself and his family, but to all the people. (*f*) In short, every additional invention by which men pretend to serve God is nothing but a pollution of true holiness.

XXVI. Why, then, it is inquired, was it the will of Christ that men should submit to those intolerable burdens which were imposed upon them by the scribes and Pharisees? (*g*) I ask, on the other hand, Why did Christ, in another place, direct men to "beware of the leaven of the Pharisees and of the Sadducees?" (*h*) by *leaven*, according to the interpretation given us by the evangelist, intending every doctrine of their own that they mixed with the pure word of God. What can we wish for plainer, than when he commands us to avoid and beware of all

(*d*) 1 Sam. vii. 17. (*e*) Judges xiii. 19. (*f*) Judges viii. 27. (*g*) Matt. xxiii. 3. (*h*) Matt. xvi. 6.

their doctrine? Hence it is very evident to us, that in the other passage our Lord did not intend that the consciences of his disciples should be harassed with the traditions of the Pharisees; and the words themselves, if they are not perverted, convey no such meaning. For, being about to deliver a severe invective against the conduct of the Pharisees, our Lord only prefaced it by instructing his hearers, that though they would see nothing in their lives worthy of imitation, yet they should continue to practise those things which were taught by them in their discourses, when they were sitting in the chair of Moses, that is to say, when they were expounding the law. His only design, therefore, was to guard the people against being induced to despise the doctrine by the bad examples of those who taught it. But, as some persons are never affected by arguments, but always require authority, I will subjoin the words of Augustine, who gives exactly the same interpretation: "The Lord's fold has pastors, some faithful, some hirelings. Those who are faithful are true shepherds; yet hear how the hirelings also are necessary. For many in the Church, pursuing worldly advantages, preach Christ, and the voice of Christ is heard through them; and the sheep follow not the hireling, but the Shepherd by means of the hireling. Hear how the hirelings are pointed out by the Lord himself. He says, The scribes and Pharisees sit in Moses' chair; what they say, do; but what they do, imitate not. Is not this equivalent to saying, Hear the voice of the Shepherd through the hirelings; for, sitting in the chair of Moses, they teach the law of God; therefore, God teaches by them; but if they choose to teach any thing of their own, neither attend to it, nor practise it?"

XXVII. But, as many ignorant persons, when they hear that the consciences of men ought not to be bound by human traditions, and that it is in vain to worship God by such services immediately conclude the same rule to be applicable to all the laws which regulate the order of the Church, we must also refute their error. It is easy, indeed, to be deceived in this point, because it does not immediately appear, at the first glance, what a difference there is between the one and the other; but I will place the whole subject in such a clear light, in a few words, that no one may be misled by the resemblance. In the first place, let us consider that if, in every society of men, we see the necessity of some polity in order to preserve the common peace, and to maintain concord; if in the transaction of business there is always some order, which the interest of public virtue, and even of humanity itself, forbids to be rejected, the same ought particularly to be observed in Churches, which are best supported by a well-ordered regulation of all their affairs and which without concord are no Churches at all. Wherefore, if we would make a proper provision for the safety of the Church, we ought to pay the strictest attention to the injunction of Paul, that "all things be done decently and in order." (*i*) But as there is such great diversity in the manners of men, so great a variety in their minds, and so much contrariety in their judgments and inclinations, no polity will be sufficiently steady unless it be established by certain laws; nor can any order be preserved without some settled form. The laws, therefore, which promote this end, we are so far from condemning, that, we contend, their abolition would be followed by a disruption of the bands of union, and the total disorganization and dispersion of the Churches. For it is impossible to attain what Paul requires, that "all things be done decently and in order," unless order and decorum be supported by additional regulations. But in regard to such regulations, care must always be taken, that they be not considered necessary to salvation, and so imposing a religious obligation on the conscience, or applied to the worship of God, and so represented as essential to piety.

XXVIII. We have an excellent and most certain mark, therefore, which distinguishes those impious constitutions, by which it has been stated that true religion is obscured and men's consciences subverted, and the legitimate regulations of the Church, which are always directed to one of these two ends, or to both together; that, in the holy assembly of believers, all things may be conducted with suitable decorum and dignity, that the community may be kept in order by the firm bonds of courtesy and moderation. For when it is once understood that a law is made for the sake of public order, this removes the superstition em-

(*i*) 1 Cor. xiv. 40.

braced by them who place the worship of God in human inventions. Moreover, when it is known that it only refers to matters of common practice, this overturns all that false notion of obligation and necessity, which filled men's consciences with great terror, when traditions were thought necessary to salvation. For here nothing is required but the maintenance of charity among us by the common intercourse of friendly offices. But it is proper to describe more fully what is comprehended under the decorum and the order which Paul recommends. The end of *decorum* is, partly, that while ceremonies are employed to conciliate veneration to sacred things, we may be excited to piety by such aids; partly that the modesty and gravity, which ought to be discovered in all virtuous actions, may be most of all conspicuous in the Church. In *order*, the first point is, that those who preside should be acquainted with the rule and law of good government, and that the people who are governed should be accustomed to an obedience to God and to just discipline; the second is, that when the Church is in a well regulated state, care should be taken to preserve its peace and tranquillity.

XXIX. We shall not call that *decorum,* therefore, which is merely a frivolous spectacle, yielding an unprofitable gratification; such as we see exemplified in the theatrical apparatus employed by the Papists in their services, where nothing is to be seen but a useless appearance of elegance and splendour, without any advantage. But we shall esteem that as *decorum,* which shall be so adapted to inspire a reverence of holy mysteries as to be calculated for an exercise of piety; or which at least shall contribute an ornament corresponding to the act; and that not without some beneficial tendency, but that believers may be admonished with what modesty, fear, and reverence, they ought to engage in sacred services. Now, that ceremonies may be exercises of piety, it is necessary that they should lead us directly to Christ. In like manner, we do not place *order* in those nugatory pomps which have nothing but a vain appearance of splendour, but in that well regulated polity, which excludes all confusion, incivility, obstinacy, clamours, and dissensions. Of the first kind, examples are furnished by Paul; as that profane banquets should not be connected with the sacred supper of the Lord; that women should not appear in public without being veiled; (*k*) and many others in common use among us; such as, that we pray with bended knees and with our heads uncovered; that we administer the sacraments of the Lord, not in a slovenly manner, but with due decorum; that we observe some decent order in the burial of the dead; and other things of a similar nature. Of the second sort are the hours appointed for public prayers, sermons, and sacraments; quietness and silence under sermons; the singing of hymns; the places appointed for these services, and the days fixed for the celebration of the Lord's supper; (*l*) the prohibition of Paul, that women should not teach in the Church, and the like; but especially the regulations for the preservation of discipline, as catechizing, ecclesiastical censures, excommunication, fastings, and every thing else that can be referred to the same class. Thus all the constitutions of the Church which we receive as holy and useful, may be classed under two heads; some refer to rites and ceremonies, others to discipline and peace.

XXX. But, because there is danger here, on the one hand, that the false bishops may seize a pretext to excuse their impious and tyrannical laws, and, on the other, that there may be some persons who, from an excessive fear of falling into the evils we have mentioned, will reject all ecclesiastical laws, however holy and useful they may be,—it is necessary to protest, that I approve of no human constitutions, except such as are founded on the authority of God, and deduced from the Scripture, so that they may be considered as altogether Divine. Let us take, as an example, the kneeling practised during solemn prayers. The question is, whether it be a human tradition, which every one is at liberty to reject or neglect. I answer that it is at once both human and Divine. It is of God, as it forms a branch of that decorum which is recommended to our attention and observance by the apostle; it is of men, as it particularly designates that which had in general been rather hinted than clearly expressed. From this single example, it is easy to judge what opinion ought to be entertained of all the rest. Because the Lord, in his holy oracles, has faithfully comprehended and plainly declared to us

(*k*) 1 Cor. xi. 5; xiv. 34. (*l*) 1 Cor. xi. 20—22.

the whole nature of true righteousness, and all the parts of Divine worship, with whatever is necessary to salvation,—in these things he is to be regarded as our only Master. Because, in external discipline and ceremonies, he has not been pleased to give us minute directions what we ought to do in every particular case, foreseeing that this would depend on the different circumstances of different periods, and knowing that one form would not be adapted to all ages,—here we must have recourse to the general rules which he has given, that to them may be conformed all the regulations which shall be necessary to the decorum and order of the Church. Lastly, as he has delivered no express injunctions on this subject, because these things are not necessary to salvation, and ought to be applied to the edification of the Church, with a variety suitable to the manners of each age and nation, therefore, as the benefit of the Church shall require, it will be right to change and abolish former regulations, and to institute new ones. I grant, indeed, that we ought not to resort to innovation rashly or frequently, or for trivial causes. But charity will best decide what will injure or edify, and if we submit to the dictates of charity, all will be well.

XXXI. Now, such regulations as have been made upon this principle and for this end, it is the duty of Christian people to observe, with a free conscience, indeed, and without any superstition, yet with a pious and ready inclination; they must not treat them with contempt or carelessness, much less violate them, in an open manner, through pride and obstinacy. It will be asked, What kind of liberty of conscience can be retained amidst so much attention and caution? I reply, It will very well be supported, when we consider, that these are not fixed and perpetual laws by which we are bound, but external aids for human infirmity, which though we do not need, yet we all use, because we are under obligations to each other to cherish mutual charity between us. This may be observed in the examples already mentioned. What! does religion consist in a woman's veil, so that it would be criminal for her to walk out with her face uncovered? Is the solemn decree respecting her silence such as cannot be violated without a capital offence? Is there any mystery in kneeling, or in the interment of a dead body, which cannot be omitted without sin? Certainly not; for if a woman, in the assistance of a neighbour, finds a necessity for such haste as allows her no time to cover her head, she commits no offence in running to the place with her head uncovered. And it is sometimes as proper for her to speak, as at other times to be silent. And he who from disease is unable to kneel, is quite at liberty to pray standing. Lastly, it is better to bury a dead body in proper season, even without a shroud, than, for want of persons to carry it to burial, to suffer it to putrefy without interment. Nevertheless, in these things, the customs and laws of the country we inhabit, the dictates of modesty, and even humanity itself, will direct us what to do, and what to avoid; and if an error be incurred through inadvertence or forgetfulness, no crime is committed; but if through contempt, such perverseness deserves to be reprobated. So it is of little importance what days and hours are appointed, what is the form of the places, what psalms are sung on the respective days. But it is proper that there should be certain days and stated hours, and a place capable of receiving all the people, if any regard be paid to the preservation of peace. For what a source of contentions would be produced by the confusion of these things, if every man were permitted to change, at his pleasure, what relates to the general order, for it would never happen that the same thing would be agreeable to all, if things were undetermined and left to the choice of every individual. If any one object, and resolve to be wiser on this subject than is necessary, let him examine by what reason he can justify his obstinacy to the Lord. We ought, however, to be satisfied with the declaration of Paul, "If any man seem to be contentious, we have no such custom, nor the Churches of God." (*m*)

XXXII. Now, it is necessary to exert the greatest diligence to prevent the intrusion of any error which may corrupt or obscure this pure use of ecclesiastical regulations. This end will be secured, if all the forms, whatever they may be, carry the appearance of manifest utility, if very few are admitted, and principally if they are accompanied with the instructions of a faithful pastor, to shut the door against all corrupt opinions. The consequence of this knowledge is, that every person will retain his liberty in all

---

(*m*) 1 Cor. xi. 16.

these things, and yet will voluntarily impose some restraint upon his liberty, so far as the decorum we have mentioned, or the dictates of charity, shall require. In the next place, it will be necessary, that, without any superstition, we should attend to the observance of these things ourselves, and not too rigidly exact it from others; that we should not esteem the worship of God to be improved by the multitude of ceremonies; and that one Church should not despise another on account of a variety of external discipline. Lastly, establishing no perpetual law of this kind for ourselves, we ought to refer the use and end of all such observances to the edification of the Church, according to the exigence of which we should be content not only with the change of some particular observance, but with the abolition of any that have hitherto been in use among us. For that the abrogation of some ceremonies, not otherwise inconsistent with piety or decorum, may become expedient from the circumstances of particular periods, the present age exhibits an actual proof. For such has been the blindness and ignorance of former times, Churches have heretofore adhered to ceremonies with such corrupt sentiments and such obstinate zeal, that it is scarcely possible for them to be sufficiently purified from monstrous superstitions without the abolition of many ceremonies, for the original institution of which, perhaps, there was some cause, and which are not in themselves remarkable for any impiety.

CHAPTER XI

The Jurisdiction of the Church, and Its Abuse Under the Papacy

WE COME now to the third branch of the power of the Church, and that which is the principal one in a well regulated state, which we have said consists in jurisdiction. The whole jurisdiction of the Church relates to the discipline of manners, of which we are about to treat. For as no city or town can exist without a magistracy and civil polity, so the Church of God, as I have already stated, but am now obliged to repeat, stands in need of a certain spiritual polity; which, however, is entirely distinct from civil polity, and is so far from obstructing or weakening it, that, on the contrary, it highly conduces to its assistance and advancement. This power of jurisdiction, therefore, will, in short, be no other than an order instituted for the preservation of the spiritual polity. For this end, there were from the beginning judiciaries appointed in the Churches, to take cognizance of manners, to pass censures on vices, and to preside over the use of the keys in excommunication. This order Paul designates in his First Epistle to the Corinthians, when he mentions "governments;" (*n*) and to the Romans, when he says, "He that ruleth," let him do it "with diligence." (*o*) He is not speaking of magistrates or civil governors, for there were at this time no Christian magistrates, but of those who were associated with the pastor in the spiritual government of the Church.

(*n*) 1 Cor. xii. 28. (*o*) Rom. xii. 8.

In the First Epistle to Timothy, also, he mentions two kinds of presbyters or elders, some "who labour in the word and doctrine," others who have nothing to do with preaching the word, and yet "rule well." (*p*) By the latter class, there can be no doubt that he intends those who were appointed to the cognizance of manners, and to the whole exercise of the keys. For this power, of which we now speak, entirely depends on the keys, which Christ has conferred upon the Church in the eighteenth chapter of Matthew, where he commands that those who shall have despised private admonitions shall be severely admonished in the name of the whole Church; and that if they persist in their obstinacy, they are to be excluded from the society of believers. (*q*) Now, these admonitions and corrections cannot take place without an examination of the cause; hence the necessity of some judicature and order. Wherefore, unless we would nullify the promise of the keys, and entirely abolish excommunication, solemn admonitions, and every thing of a similar kind, it is necessary to allow the Church some jurisdiction. Let it be observed, that the passage to which we have referred, relates not to the general authority of the doctrine to be preached by the apostles, as in the sixteenth chapter of Matthew and the twentieth chapter of John; but that the power of the sanhedrim is for the future transferred to the Church of Christ. Till that time, the Jews had their own method of government, which, as far as regards the pure institution, Jesus Christ established in his Church, and that with a severe sanction. For this was absolutely necessary, because the judgment of an ignoble and despised Church might otherwise be treated with contempt by presumptuous and proud men. And that the readers may not be embarrassed by the circumstance of Christ having used the same words to express different things, it will be useful to solve this difficulty. There are two places which speak of *binding* and *loosing*. One is in the sixteenth chapter of Matthew, where Christ, after having promised Peter that he would "give" him "the keys of the kingdom of heaven," (*r*) immediately adds, "Whatsoever thou shalt bind on earth, shall be bound in heaven; and whatsoever thou shalt loose on earth, shall be loosed in heaven." In

(*p*) 1 Tim. v. 17. (*q*) Matt. xviii. 15—18. (*r*) Matt. xvi. 19.

these words he means precisely the same as he intends in other language recorded by John, when, being about to send forth his disciples to preach, after having "breathed on them," he said, "Whose soever sins ye remit, they are remitted unto them; and whose soever sins ye retain, they are retained." (*s*) I shall offer an interpretation of this passage, without any subtlety, violence, or perversion, but natural, suitable, and obvious. This command respecting the remission and retention of sins, and the promise made to Peter respecting binding and loosing, ought to be wholly referred to the ministry of the word, which when our Lord committed to the apostles, he at the same time invested them with the power of binding and loosing. For what is the sum of the gospel, but that, being all slaves of sin and death, we are loosed and delivered by the redemption which is in Christ Jesus, and that those who never receive or acknowledge Christ as their Deliverer and Redeemer, are condemned and sentenced to eternal chains? When the Lord delivered this embassy to his apostles, to be conveyed to all nations, in order to evince it to be his, and to have proceeded from him, he honoured it with this remarkable testimony, and that for the particular confirmation both of the apostles themselves, and of all those to whom it was to be announced. It was of importance, that the apostles should have a strong and constant assurance of their preaching; which they were not only to undertake and execute amidst immense labours, cares, troubles, and dangers, but were at length to seal with their blood. That they might know this ministry not to be vain or ineffectual, but full of power and energy, it was of importance for them, in circumstances of such great anxiety, difficulty, and danger, to be persuaded that they were employed in the work of God; amidst all the hostility and opposition of the whole world, to know that God was on their side; and though Christ, the Author of their doctrine, was not present to their view on earth, to be certain that he was in heaven to confirm the truth of the doctrine which he had delivered to them. On the other hand, also, it was necessary that the most unequivocal testimony should be given to their hearers, that the doctrine of the gospel was not the word of the apostles, but of

(*s*) John xx. 22, 23.

God himself; not a voice issuing from the earth, but descended from heaven. For these things, the remission of sins, the promise of eternal life, and the message of salvation, cannot be in the power of man. Therefore Christ has testified that, in the preaching of the gospel, nothing belonged to the apostles, except the ministration of it; that it was he himself who spoke and promised every thing by the instrumentality of their mouths; and, consequently, that the remission of sins which they preached was the true promise of God, and that the condemnation which they denounced was the certain judgment of God. Now, this testification has been given to all ages, and remains unaltered, to certify and assure us all, that the word of the gospel, by whomsoever it may happen to be preached, is the very sentence of God himself, promulgated from his heavenly tribunal, recorded in the book of life, ratified, confirmed, and fixed in heaven. Thus we see, that the power of the keys, in these passages, is no other than the preaching of the gospel, and that, considered with regard to men, it is not so much authoritative as ministerial; for, strictly speaking, Christ has not given this power to men, but to his word, of which he has appointed men to be the ministers.

II. The other passage, which we have mentioned, relative to the power of binding and loosing, is in the eighteenth chapter of Matthew, where Christ says, "If any brother neglect to hear the Church, let him be unto thee as a heathen man and a publican. Verily I say unto you, Whatsoever ye shall bind on earth, shall be bound in heaven; and whatsoever ye shall loose on earth, shall be loosed in heaven." (*t*) This passage is not altogether similar to the first, but is to be understood in a manner somewhat different; though I do not conceive the difference to be so great, but that there is a considerable affinity between them. In the first place, they are both alike in this respect, that each contains a general declaration, the same power of always binding and loosing,—that is, by the word of God,—the same command, the same promise. But they differ in this, that the former passage peculiarly relates to the preaching of the gospel, which is performed by the ministers of the word; the latter relates to the discipline, which

(*t*) Matt. xviii. 17, 18.

is committed to the Church. The Church binds him whom it excommunicates; not that it consigns him to perpetual ruin and despair, but because it condemns his life and manners, and already warns him of his final condemnation, unless he repent. The Church looses him whom it receives into its communion; because it makes him, as it were, a partaker of the unity which it has in Christ Jesus. That no man, therefore, may contemn the judgment of the Church, or consider it as of little consequence that he is condemned by the voice of believers, the Lord testifies that such judgment of believers is no other than the promulgation of his sentence, and that what they do on earth shall be ratified in heaven. For they have the word of God, by which they condemn the perverse; they have the same word, by which they receive penitents into favour; and they cannot err or dissent from the judgment of God, because they judge only by the Divine law, which is not an uncertain or earthly opinion, but the holy will and heavenly oracle of God. From these two passages, which I think I have familiarly and correctly, as well as concisely, explained, these unreasonable men, without any judgment, under the influence of misguided zeal, endeavour to establish, sometimes auricular confession, sometimes excommunication, sometimes jurisdiction, sometimes the right of legislation, and sometimes indulgences. The former passage they allege to support the primacy of the Roman see. They are so expert in fitting their keys to any locks and doors they please, that it should seem as if they had followed the business of locksmiths all their lifetime.

III. The opinion entertained by some persons, that these things were only temporary, while all civil magistrates were strangers to the profession of Christianity, is a mistake for want of considering the great distinction, and the nature of the difference, between the ecclesiastical and civil power. For the Church has no power of the sword to punish or to coerce, no authority to compel, no prisons, fines, or other punishments, like those inflicted by the civil magistrate. Besides, the object of this power is, not that he who has transgressed may be punished against his will but that he may profess his repentance by a voluntary submission to chastisement. The difference therefore is very great; because the Church does not assume to itself what belongs to the magistrate, nor can the magistrate execute that which is executed by the Church. This will be better understood by an example. Is any man intoxicated? In a well regulated city he will be punished by imprisonment. Has he committed fornication? He will receive the same or a severer punishment. With this, the laws, the magistrate, and the civil judgment, will all be satisfied; though it may happen that he will give no sign of repentance, but will rather murmur and repine against his punishment. Will the Church stop here? Such persons cannot be admitted to the sacred supper without doing an injury to Christ and to his holy institution. And reason requires, that he who has offended the Church with an evil example, should remove, by a solemn declaration of repentance, the offence which he has excited. The argument adduced by those who espouse a contrary opinion, is of no force. They say, that Christ assigned this office to the Church, when there was no magistrate to execute it. But it frequently happens that the magistrate is too negligent, and sometimes that he even deserves to be chastised himself; which was the case with the emperor Theodosius. Besides, the same argument might be extended to the whole ministry of the word. Now, then, according to them, pastors must no longer censure notorious crimes; they must cease to chide, to reprove, to rebuke; for there are Christian magistrates, whose duty it is to correct such offences by the civil sword. But as it is the duty of the magistrate, by punishment and corporeal coercion, to purge the Church from offences, so it behoves the minister of the word, on his part, to relieve the magistrate by preventing the multiplication of offenders. Their respective operations ought to be so connected as to be an assistance, and not an obstruction to each other.

IV. And, indeed, whoever will closely examine the words of Christ, will easily perceive that they describe the stated and perpetual order, and not any temporary regulation, of the Church. For it is unreasonable for us to bring an accusation before a magistrate, against those who refuse to submit to our admonitions; yet this would be necessary if the magistrate succeeded to this office of the Church. What shall we say of this promise, "Verily I say unto thee, whatsoever ye shall bind on earth, shall be bound in heaven?" Was it only for one, or for a few years?

Besides, Christ here instituted nothing new, but followed the custom always observed in the ancient Church of his own nation; thereby signifying, that the spiritual jurisdiction, which had been exercised from the beginning, was indispensable to the Church. And this has been confirmed by the consent of all ages. For when emperors and magistrates began to assume the profession of Christianity, the spiritual jurisdiction was not in consequence abolished, but only regulated in such a manner as neither to derogate from the civil power, nor to be confounded with it. And that justly; for a pious magistrate will not wish to exempt himself from the common subjection of the children of God, which in no small degree consists in submitting to the Church, when it judges by the word of God: so very far is it from being his duty to abolish such a judicature. "For what is more honourable," says Ambrose, "than for the emperor to be called the son of the Church? For a good emperor is within the Church, not above the Church." Wherefore those who, to exalt the magistrate, despoil the Church of this power, not only pervert the language of Christ by a false interpretation, but pass a most severe censure on all the holy bishops who have lived since the time of the apostles, for having usurped to themselves, under a false pretext, the honour and dignity which belonged to the magistrate.

V. But, on the other hand, it is also worth while to examine what was the true and ancient use of the jurisdiction of the Church, and what a great abuse of it has been introduced; that we may know what ought to be abrogated, and what ought to be restored from antiquity, if we would overturn the reign of Antichrist, and reëstablish the true kingdom of Christ. In the first place, the object to be secured is the prevention of offences, or the abolition of any that may have arisen. In the use of it, two things require to be considered; first, that this spiritual power be entirely separated from the power of the sword; secondly, that it be administered, not at the pleasure of one man, but by a legitimate assembly. Both these things were observed in the purer ages of the Church. For the holy bishops never exercised their authority by fines, imprisonments, or other civil punishments; but, as became them, employed nothing but the word of the Lord. For the severest vengeance, the ultimate punishment of the Church, is excommunication, which is never resorted to without absolute necessity. Now, excommunication requires no external force, but is content with the power of the word of God. In short, the jurisdiction of the primitive Church was no other than a practical exposition of the description which Paul gives of the spiritual authority of pastors. This power he represents as conferred for the purpose of "casting down imaginations, and every high thing that exalteth itself against the knowledge of God, and bringing into captivity every thought to the obedience of Christ; and having in readiness to revenge all disobedience." (*u*) As this is accomplished by the preaching of the doctrine of Christ, so to preserve that doctrine from falling into contempt, they who profess themselves of the household of faith ought to be judged by what that doctrine contains. That cannot be done, except the ministry be accompanied with the power to take cognizance of those who are to be privately admonished, or more severely censured, and also to exclude from the communion of the Supper those who cannot be admitted without a profanation of such a solemn sacrament. Wherefore when he denies, in another place, that we have any right "to judge them that are without," (*v*) he makes the children of the church subject to the censures by which their faults are chastised, and implies the existence at that time of judicatures from which none of the believers were exempt.

VI. This power, as we have stated, was not in the hands of one man, for him to act according to his own pleasure, but resided in the assembly of the elders, which was in the Church what a senate is in a city. Cyprian, when he mentions by whom it was exercised in his time, generally unites all the clergy with the bishop; but in other passages he also shows, that the clergy presided in such a manner, that the people were not excluded from this cognizance. For he expresses himself in these words: "From the commencement of my episcopate, I have determined to do nothing without the counsel of the clergy and the consent of the people." But the common and usual custom was for the jurisdiction of the Church to be exercised by the council of the presbyters; of whom, as I have observed, there were two classes; for

(*u*) 2 Cor. x. 5, 6. (*v*) 1 Cor. v. 12.

some were ordained to the office of teaching, others were only censors of manners. This institution gradually degenerated from its original establishment; so that, in the time of Ambrose, the judicial administration of the Church was wholly in the hands of the clergy; of which he complains in the following language: "The ancient synagogue, and afterwards the Church, had elders, without whose advice nothing was done. I know not by what negligence this practice has been discontinued, except from the indolence of the doctors, or rather from their pride, while they wish none but themselves, to be seen." We perceive how indignant was that holy man, that there had been some declension from a better state of things, though they still retained an order that was at least tolerable. What would he say now, if he were to see the present deformed ruins, which exhibit scarcely a vestige of the ancient edifice! What a complaint would he make! First, in opposition to law and justice, that which had been given to the Church, the bishop usurped entirely to himself. This resembles the conduct of a consul or president, expelling the senate, and seizing the sole administration of a government. But as the bishop is superior to other persons in honour, so the assembly or congregation possesses more authority than one individual. It was a gross outrage, therefore, for one man to transfer to himself all the power of the community, and thereby to open a door to licentious tyranny, to deprive the Church of its rights, and to suppress and abolish an assembly appointed by the Spirit of Christ.

VII. But as one evil always produces another, bishops, disdaining this charge as unworthy of their attention, have delegated it to others. Hence the creation of officials, to discharge that duty. I say nothing, at present, of the characters of the persons; I only assert, that they differ in no respect from civil judges; yet they still call it a spiritual jurisdiction, where all the contention is about secular affairs. Though there were no other evil, what effrontery must they have, to call a court full of litigation the judicature of the Church! But, it is alleged it employs admonitions, and pronounces excommunication. Is it thus that they trifle with God? Does a poor man owe a sum of money? He is cited. If he appear, he is condemned; after the condemnation, if he do not pay, he is admonished: after the second admonition, they proceed to excommunication. If he do not appear to the citation, he is admonished to be forthcoming: if he delay, he is admonished a second time, and soon after is excommunicated. I ask, What is there in this that bears any resemblance to the institution of Christ, the ancient usage, or the order of the Church? It is further alleged, that this court also corrects vices. I reply, that acts of fornication, lasciviousness, and drunkenness, and similar enormities, they not only tolerate, but sanction and encourage, by a kind of tacit approbation, and that not only in the people, but even in the clergy themselves. Among multitudes of offenders, they only summon a few, either to avoid too flagrant an appearance of connivance, or for the purpose of extorting money. I say nothing of the robbery, the rapine, the peculation, the sacrilege, connected with this office. I say nothing of the characters of most of the persons selected to discharge it. It is more than sufficient for us, that while the Romanists boast of their spiritual jurisdiction, it is easy to show that nothing is more contrary to the order appointed by Christ, and that it has no more resemblance to the ancient practice, than darkness has to light.

VIII. Though we have not said all that might be adduced for this purpose, and what we have said has been condensed within a small compass, yet I trust we have so refuted our adversaries, as to leave no room for any one to doubt that the spiritual power arrogated by the pope and all his hierarchy, is a tyrannical usurpation, chargeable with impious opposition to the word of God, and injustice to his people. Under the term *spiritual power*, I include their audacity in fabricating new doctrines, by which they have seduced the unhappy people from the native purity of the word of God, the iniquitous traditions by which they have insnared them, and the pretended ecclesiastical jurisdiction which they exercise by their suffragans, vicars, penitentiaries, and officials. For if we allow Christ any kingdom among us, all this kind of domination must immediately fall to the ground. The power of the sword, which they also claim, as that is not exercised over consciences, but operates on property, is irrelevant to our present subject; though in this also it is worth while to remark, that they are always consistent with themselves, and are at the greatest possible distance from the character they would be thought to sustain, as pastors of the Church. Here I am not censuring the particular vices of individuals, but the general wickedness and common pest of the whole order, which they would consider as degraded, if it were not distinguished by wealth and lofty titles. If we consult the authority of Christ on this subject, there is no doubt that he intended to exclude the ministers of his word from civil dominion and secular sovereignty, when he said, "The kings of the Gentiles exercise dominion over them; but it shall not be so among you." (*w*) For by these words he signifies, not only that the office of a pastor is distinct from the office of a prince, but that they are so different, that they can never be properly united in one man. For though Moses held both these offices at once, it may be observed, first, that this was the result of a special miracle; secondly, that it was only a temporary arrangement, till things should be better regulated. But, as soon as God prescribed a certain form of government, Moses was left in possession of the civil administration, and was commanded to resign the priesthood to his brother; and that for a very sufficient reason; for it is beyond the ability of nature for one man to be capable of sustaining the burden of both. And this has been carefully observed in the Church in all ages. For as long as any real appearance of a Church remained, not one of the bishops ever thought of usurping the power of the sword; so that it was a common proverb in the time of Ambrose, "That emperors rather coveted the priesthood, than priests the empire;" for as he afterwards observes, it was the firm and universal opinion, "That palaces belonged to emperors, and churches to priests."

IX. But since a method has been contrived for bishops to retain the title, honour, and emoluments of their office without any burden or solicitude, that they might not be left entirely without occupation, the power of the sword has been given to them, or rather they have usurped it to themselves. With what plea will they defend such impudence? Was it for bishops to perplex themselves with judicial proceedings, to assume the government of cities and provinces, and to undertake various other occupations so incompatible with their office, which alone would furnish them

(*w*) Matt. xx. 25, 26. Luke xxii. 25, 26.

so much labour and employment, that even if they were entirely and assiduously devoted to it, without the least distraction of other avocations, they would scarcely be able to discharge its functions? But they have the hardihood to boast, that this causes the Church of Christ to flourish with a glory suitable to its dignity, and at the same time that they are not too much distracted from the duties of their vocation. With respect to the first point, if it be a becoming ornament of the sacred office, for those who sustain it to be elevated to a degree of power formidable to the greatest monarchs, they have reason to expostulate with Christ, by whom their honour has been so grievously wounded. For in their opinion, at least, what could have been said more disgraceful than the following language? "The kings of the Gentiles exercise dominion over them; but it shall not be so among you." (*x*) Nor has he prescribed a severer law to his servants than he first imposed upon himself. "Man," says he, "who made me a judge or a divider over you?" (*y*) We see he plainly refuses to act the part of a judge, which he would not have done, had it been a thing consistent with his office. Will not his servants allow themselves to be reduced to that rank, to which their Lord voluntarily submitted himself? With respect to the second point, I wish they could as easily prove it by experience as make the assertion. But since the apostles thought it not right for them "to leave the word of God, and serve tables," (*z*) this must confound those who are reluctant to admit, that it is not in the power of the same man to be at the same time a good bishop and a good prince. For if they, who by the extent of the gifts with which they were endued, were enabled to sustain far more numerous and weighty cares than any men who have lived since their time, after all confessed themselves incapable of attending to the word of God and the service of tables without fainting under the burden, how should it be possible for these men, who are by no means to be compared to the apostles, so vastly to surpass them in industry? The very attempt has betrayed the most consummate effrontery and presumptuous confidence. Yet we see it has been done; with what success, is obvious; the unavoidable consequence has been the desertion of

(*x*) Matt. xx. 25, 26. Luke xxii. 25, 26.
(*y*) Luke xii. 14. (*z*) Acts vi. 2.

their own functions, and intrusion into those which belonged to others.

X. It has, without doubt, been from small beginnings, that they have gradually risen to such eminence. For it was not possible for them to make so great an advance at one step. But sometimes by fraudulent and secret artifices, they exalted themselves in a clandestine manner, so that no one perceived the encroachment till it had been effected: sometimes, when opportunity offered, by terrifying and menacing princes, they extorted from them some augmentation of their power; sometimes, when they saw princes inclined to favour them, they abused their foolish and inconsiderate pliability. In early times, if any controversy arose, the believers, in order to avoid the necessity of litigation, used to refer it to the decision of their bishop, of whose integrity they were fully satisfied. The ancient bishops were frequently embarrassed with such arbitrations, which exceedingly displeased them, as Augustine somewhere declares; but to save the parties from lawsuits, they reluctantly undertook this troublesome business. From voluntary arbitrations, which were entirely different from the processes of civil courts, their successors have erected an ordinary jurisdiction. In a subsequent period, when cities and countries were oppressed with various distresses, they had recourse to the patronage of their bishops, that they might be protected by their influence; succeeding bishops, by wonderful artifice, of protectors have made themselves lords. Nor can it be denied, that the principal acquisitions they have made, have been effected by faction and violence. The princes, who voluntarily invested the bishops with jurisdiction, were actuated to this by various motives. But though their indulgence may have exhibited some appearance of piety, yet their preposterous liberality was by no means adapted to promote the benefit of the Church, the ancient and genuine discipline of which they thereby corrupted, or rather, to say the truth, utterly annihilated. But those bishops who have abused such kindness of princes to their own profit, have sufficiently evinced, by this one specimen, that they were in reality no bishops at all. For if they had possessed a particle of the apostolic spirit, they would unquestionably have answered, in the language of Paul, that "the weapons of our warfare are not carnal, but" (*a*) spiritual. Instead of this, hurried away with a blind cupidity, they have ruined themselves, and their successors, and the Church.

XI. At length the Roman pontiff, not content with small provinces, first laid his hand upon kingdoms, and then seized upon the empire. And to assign some plausible pretext for retaining a possession acquired by mere robbery, he sometimes boasts that he holds it by Divine right, sometimes pretends the donation from Constantine, and sometimes pleads some other title. In the first place, I answer with Bernard, that supposing he could vindicate his claim by any other reason, yet he cannot establish it by any apostolic right. "For Peter could not give what he never possessed; but he left his successors, what he did possess, the care of the churches. But as the Lord and Master said of himself, that he was not constituted a judge between two persons, the servant and disciple ought not to think it any disgrace not to be judge of all men." Bernard is speaking here of civil judgments, for he adds, addressing the pope, "Therefore your power is over sins, and not over possessions, since it is for the former, and not for the latter, that you have received the keys of the kingdom of heaven. For which appears to you the superior dignity, to remit sins, or to divide lands? There is no comparison. These low and earthly things are subject to the judgment of kings and princes of the earth. Why do you invade the province of others?" Again; "You are made a superior. For what purpose? Not to exercise dominion, I apprehend. However highly we think of ourselves, therefore, let us remember that we are appointed to a ministry not invested with a sovereignty. Learn that you want no sceptre, but a pruning-knife, to cultivate the Lord's vineyard." Again: "It is plain that sovereignty is forbidden to the apostles. Go then, if you dare, and sustaining the office of a temporal sovereign, usurp the name of an apostle, or filling an apostolical office, usurp a temporal sovereignty." And immediately after: "This is the apostolic form: they are forbidden to exercise any dominion; they are commanded to minister and serve." Though all these observations

(*a*) 2 Cor. x. 4.

of Bernard are evidently consistent with the truth, and even though the true state of the case must be obvious to all without any thing being said, yet the Roman pontiff was not ashamed, at the Council of Arles, to decree, that the supreme power of both swords belonged to him by Divine right.

XII. With respect to the donation of Constantine, persons who have only a moderate acquaintance with the histories of those times, need no information how fabulous, and even ridiculous, this is. But to leave the histories, Gregory, who lived above four hundred years after, is alone a competent and very sufficient witness of this fact. For, wherever he speaks of the emperor, he gives him the title of Most Serene Lord, and calls himself his unworthy servant. In one place he says, "Let not our lord, from his earthly power, be too ready to treat priests with disdain; but with excellent consideration, for the sake of him whose servants they are, let him rule over them in such a manner, as at the same time to pay them due reverence." We see how, in the common subjection, he wished to be considered as one of the people; for he is there pleading, not another person's cause, but his own. In another place he says, "I trust in Almighty God, that he will grant a long life to our pious lords, and will govern us under your hand according to his mercy." I have not quoted these passages with any design to discuss at large this question of the donation of Constantine, but merely to show my readers, by the way, what a puerile falsehood it is of the Romanists, to attempt to claim a temporal sovereignty for their pontiff. And so much the more contemptible is the impudence of Augustine Steuchus, the pope's librarian, who has had the effrontery to prostitute his labours to serve his master in such a desperate cause. Laurentius Valla had amply refuted that fable, which was no difficulty to a man of learning and an acute reasoner; yet, like a man little conversant in ecclesiastical affairs, he had not said all that would have corroborated the argument. Steuchus sallies forth, and scatters the most disgusting trash to obscure the clear light. But, in fact, he pleads the cause of his master with no more force than if some facetious wit, ironically professing the same object, were in reality supporting the opposite side of the question. But this cause is well worthy of such advocates as the pope hires to defend it; and equally worthy are those mercenary scribblers of being disappointed in their hopes of gain, as was the case with Eugubinus.

XIII. But if any one inquire the time when this fictitious empire began to arise, there have not yet elapsed five hundred years since the pontiffs were still in subjection to the emperors, and no pontiff was created without the authority of the emperor. The first occasion of innovation in this order was given to Gregory VII. by the emperor Henry, the fourth of that name, a man of rash and unsteady disposition, of no judgment, great audacity, and dissolute life. For when he had all the bishoprics of Germany in his court, either exposed to sale, or to be distributed as a booty, Hildebrand, who had been offended with him, seized a plausible pretext to avenge himself. Because he appeared to advocate a good and pious cause, he was assisted by the favour of many; and Henry, on the other hand, had rendered himself odious to the generality of princes, by the insolence of his government. At length Hildebrand, who assumed the name of Gregory VII., being a man of no piety or integrity, betrayed the wickedness of his heart; in consequence of which many, who had concurred with him. afterwards deserted him. He so far succeeded, however, as to enable his successors not only to cast off the imperial yoke with impunity, but even to oblige the emperors to submit to them. After that time there were many emperors, more like Henry than like Julius Cæsar, whom there was no difficulty in overcoming while they were sitting at home in indolence and unconcern, when there was the greatest necessity for every vigorous and legitimate exertion to repress the cupidity of the pontiffs. Thus we see with what plausibility they have represented this admirable donation of Constantine, by which the pope pretends himself to have been invested with the sovereignty of the Western empire.

XIV. From that period the pontiffs have never ceased encroaching on the jurisdictions, and seizing on the territories, of others, sometimes employing fraud, sometimes treachery, and sometimes open war; even the city of Rome itself, which till then was free, about a hundred and thirty years ago was compelled to submit to their dominion; in short, they proceeded to make continual advances, till they attained the power which they at present possess, and for the retention or augmentation of which, they have now, for the space of two hundred years, (for they had begun before they usurped the government of the city,) so disturbed and distracted the Christian world, that they have brought it to the brink of ruin. In the time of Gregory the First, when the guardians of the ecclesiastical property seized for themselves the lands which belonged to the Church, and, according to the custom of princes, set up their titles and armorial bearings on them in token of their claim, Gregory assembled a provincial council of bishops, in which he severely inveighed against that profane custom, and asked whether they would not excommunicate any ecclesiastic who should attempt the seizure of property by the inscription of a title, or even any bishop who should direct such a thing to be done, or if done without his direction, should not punish it. They all pronounced that every such offender should be excommunicated. But if claiming a field by the inscription of a title, be a crime deserving of excommunication in a priest,—when for two whole centuries the pontiffs have been meditating nothing but wars, effusion of blood, slaughter of armies, storming and pillaging cities, the destruction of nations, the devastation of kingdoms, for the sole purpose of seizing the dominions of others,—what excommunications can be sufficient for the punishment of such examples? It is clear beyond all doubt, that the glory of Christ is the object furthest from their pursuit. For if they voluntarily resign all the secular power which they possess, no danger will result to the glory of God, to sound doctrine, or to the safety of the Church; but they are infatuated, and stimulated by the mere lust of dominion; and consider nothing as safe, unless, as the prophet says, "they rule with force and with cruelty." (*b*)

XV. With jurisdiction is connected the immunity which the Roman ecclesiastics arrogate to themselves. For they consider it a degradation for them to appear before a civil judge in personal causes, and they imagine the liberty and dignity of the Church to consist in their exemption from the common judicature and laws. But the ancient bishops, who in other respects were the most rigid assertors of the rights of the Church, esteemed it no injury to

(*b*) Ezek. xxxiv. 4.

themselves, or to their order, to be subject to lay judges in civil causes. The pious emperors also, without any opposition, always summoned the clergy before their tribunals, whenever necessity required it. For this is the language of Constantine, in his epistle to the bishops of Nicomedia: "If any bishop excite any disturbance by his indiscretion, his presumption shall be restrained by the authority of the minister of God, that is, by mine." And Valentinian says, "Good bishops never traduce the power of the emperor, but sincerely observe the commands of God, the sovereign King, and obey our laws." At that time this principle was universally admitted, without any controversy. Ecclesiastical causes were referred to the judgment of the bishop. As for example if any ecclesiastic had committed no crime against the laws, but was only charged with offending against the canons, he was not summoned to the common tribunal, but was judged by the bishop. In like manner, if a question was agitated respecting an article of faith, or any other subject properly belonging to the Church, to the Church the cognizance of it was committed. In this sense is to be understood what Ambrose writes to the emperor Valentinian: "Your father, of august memory, not only answered verbally, but also ordained by edicts, that, in a cause relating to faith, he ought to judge, who is not disqualified by office or dignity." Again: "If we regard the Scriptures or ancient examples, who will deny that in a cause of faith,—I say, in a cause of faith,—it is customary for bishops to judge of Christian emperors, and not emperors of bishops?" Again: "I would have come to your consistory, sire, if either the bishops or the people would have suffered me to go; but they say, that a cause of faith ought to be discussed in the Church, in the presence of the people." He contended that a spiritual cause—that is, a cause affecting religion—ought not to be carried into a civil court, where secular controversies are agitated; and his constancy in this respect has been universally and justly applauded. Yet, notwithstanding the goodness of his cause, he went no further than to declare, that if the emperor proceeded to employ force, he would submit. He says, "I will not voluntarily desert the station committed to me: in case of compulsion, I know not how to resist, for our arms are prayers and tears." Let us observe the singular combination of moderation and prudence with magnanimity and confidence in this holy man. Justina, the mother of the emperor, because she could not induce him to join the Arians, endeavoured to deprive him of his bishopric. And she would have succeeded in her attempts, if, in compliance with the summons, he had gone to the palace of the emperor to plead his cause. Therefore he denied the emperor to be a competent judge of so important a controversy; and this was necessary both from the circumstances of that time, and from the invariable nature of the subject itself. For he was of opinion, that it was his duty to suffer death rather than, by his consent, to permit such an example to be transmitted to posterity; and yet in case of violence being employed, he cherished not a thought of resistance. For he denied it to be compatible with the character of a bishop to defend the faith and privileges of the Church by arms; but in other cases he showed himself ready to do whatever the emperor would command. "If he demands tribute," says he, "we do not refuse it; the lands of the Church pay tribute. If he demands the lands, he has power to take them; none of us will oppose him." Gregory also speaks in a similar manner. "I am not ignorant," he says, "of the mind of our most serene lord, that he is not in the habit of interfering in sacerdotal causes, lest he should in any respect be burdened with our sins." He does not entirely exclude the emperor from judging priests, but observes that there are certain causes which he ought to leave to the decision of the Church.

XVI. And even in this exception, the sole object of these holy men was to prevent the tyrannical violence and caprice of princes less favourable to religion from obstructing the Church in the discharge of its duty. For they did not disapprove of the occasional interposition of princes in ecclesiastical affairs, provided they would exert their authority for the preservation of the order of the Church, and not for the disturbance of it; for the establishment of discipline, and not for its relaxation. For as the Church neither possesses, nor ought to desire, the power to constrain,—I speak of civil coercion,—it is the part of pious kings and princes to support religion by laws, edicts, and judicial sentences. For this reason, when the emperor Mauritius commanded certain bishops to receive their neighbouring colleagues, who had been expelled from their sees by the barbarians, Gregory confirmed this command, and exhorted them to obey it. And when he himself was admonished by the same emperor to be reconciled to John, the bishop of Constantinople, he did, indeed, assign a reason why he ought not to be blamed, yet he boasted no immunity exempting him from the imperial authority, but on the contrary promised compliance as far as should be consistent with a good conscience; and at the same time acknowledged that Mauritius acted in a manner becoming a religious prince in giving such commands to the bishops.

CHAPTER XII

The Discipline of the Church; Its Principal Use in Censures and Excommunication

THE discipline of the Church, the discussion of which I have deferred to this place, must be despatched in a few words, that we may proceed to the remaining subjects. Now, the discipline depends chiefly on the power of the keys, and the spiritual jurisdiction. To make this more easily understood, let us divide the Church into two principal orders—the clergy and the people. I use the word *clergy* as the common, though improper, appellation of those who execute the public ministry in the Church. We shall, first, speak of the common discipline to which all ought to be subject; and in the next place we shall proceed to the clergy, who, beside this common discipline, have a discipline peculiar to themselves. But as some have such a hatred of discipline, as to abhor the very name, they should attend to the following consideration: That if no society, and even no house, though containing only a small family, can be preserved in a proper state without discipline, this is far more necessary in the Church, the state of which ought to be the most orderly of all. As the saving doctrine of Christ is the soul of the Church, so discipline forms the ligaments which connect the members together, and keep each in its proper place. Whoever, therefore, either desire the abolition of all discipline, or obstruct its restoration, whether they act from design or inadvertency, they certainly promote the entire dissolution of the Church. For what will be the consequence, if every man be at liberty to follow his own inclinations? But such would be the case, unless the preaching of the doctrine were accompanied with private admonitions, reproofs, and other means to enforce the doctrine, and prevent it from being altogether ineffectual. Discipline, therefore, serves as a bridle to curb and restrain the refractory, who resist the doctrine of Christ; or as a spur to stimulate the inactive; and sometimes as a father's rod, with which those who have grievously fallen may be chastised in mercy, and with the gentleness of the Spirit of Christ. Now, when we see the approach of certain beginnings of a dreadful desolation in the Church, since there is no solicitude or means to keep the people in obedience to our Lord, necessity itself proclaims the want of a remedy; and this is the only remedy which has been commanded by Christ, or which has ever been adopted among believers.

II. The first foundation of discipline consists in the use of private admonitions; that is to say, that if any one be guilty of a voluntary omission of duty, or conduct himself in an insolent manner, or discover a want of virtue in his life, or commit any act deserving of reprehension, he should suffer himself to be admonished; and that every one should study to admonish his brother, whenever occasion shall require; but that pastors and presbyters, beyond all others, should be vigilant in the discharge of this duty, being called by their office, not only to preach to the congregation, but also to admonish and exhort in private houses, if in any instances their public instructions may not have been sufficiently efficacious; as Paul inculcates, when he says, that he "taught publicly and from house to house," and protests himself to be "pure from the blood of all men," having "ceased not to warn every one night and day with tears." (*c*) For the doctrine then obtains its full authority, and produces its due effect, when the minister not only declares to all the people together what is their duty to Christ, but has the right and means of enforcing it upon them whom he observes to be inattentive, or not obedient

(*c*) Acts xx. 20, 26, 31.

to the doctrine. If any one either obstinately reject such admonitions, or manifest his contempt of them by persisting in his misconduct; after he shall have been admonished a second time in the presence of witnesses, Christ directs him to be summoned before the tribunal of the Church, that is, the assembly of the elders, and there to be more severely admonished by the public authority, that if he reverence the Church, he may submit and obey; but if this do not overcome him, and he still persevere in his iniquity, our Lord then commands him, as a despiser of the Church, to be excluded from the society of believers. (*d*)

III. But as Jesus Christ in this passage is speaking only of private faults, it is necessary to make this distinction—that some sins are private, and others public or notorious. With respect to the former, Christ says to every private individual, "Tell him his fault between thee and him alone." (*e*) With respect to those which are notorious, Paul says to Timothy, "Them that sin rebuke before all, that others also may fear." (*f*) For Christ has before said, "If thy brother shall trespass against thee;" which no person who is not contentious can understand in any other sense, than if our Lord had said, "If any one sin against thee, and thou alone know it, without any other persons being acquainted with it." But the direction given by the apostle to Timothy, to rebuke publicly those whose transgressions were public, he himself exemplified in his conduct to Peter. For when Peter committed a public offence, he did not admonish him in private, but brought him forward before all the Church. (*g*) The legitimate course, then will be,—in correcting secret faults, to adopt the different steps directed by Christ; and in the case of those which are notorious, to proceed at once to the solemn correction of the Church, especially if they be attended with public offence.

IV. It is also necessary to make another distinction between different sins; some are smaller delinquencies, others are flagitious or enormous crimes. For the correction of atrocious crimes, it is not sufficient to employ admonition or reproof; recourse must be had to a severer remedy; as Paul shows, when he does not content himself with censuring the incestuous Corinthian, but

---

(*d*) Matt. xviii. 15—17.
(*e*) Matt. xviii. 15.
(*f*) 1 Tim. v. 20.
(*g*) Gal. ii. 11, 14.

pronounces sentence of excommunication immediately on being certified of his crime. Now, then, we begin to have a clearer perception how the spiritual jurisdiction of the Church, which corrects sins according to the word of the Lord, is a most excellent preservative of health, foundation of order, and bond of unity. Therefore when the Church excludes from its society all who are known to be guilty of adultery, fornication, theft, robbery, sedition, perjury, false witness, and other similar crimes, together with obstinate persons, who, after having been admonished even of smaller faults, contemn God and his judgment,—it usurps no unreasonable authority, but only exercises the jurisdiction which God has given it. And that no one may despise this judgment of the Church, or consider it as of little importance that he is condemned by the voice of the faithful, God has testified that it is no other than a declaration of his sentence, and that what they do on earth shall be ratified in heaven. For they have the word of the Lord, to condemn the perverse; they have the word, to receive the penitent into favour. Persons who believe that the Church could not subsist without this bond of discipline, are mistaken in their opinion, unless we could safely dispense with that remedy which the Lord foresaw would be necessary for us; and how very necessary it is, will be better discovered from its various use.

V. Now, there are three ends proposed by the Church in those corrections, and in excommunication. The first is, that those who lead scandalous and flagitious lives, may not, to the dishonour of God, be numbered among Christians; as if his holy Church were a conspiracy of wicked and abandoned men. For as the Church is the body of Christ, it cannot be contaminated with such foul and putrid members without some ignominy being reflected upon the Head. That nothing may exist in the Church, therefore, from which any disgrace may be thrown upon his venerable name, it is necessary to expel from his family all those from whose turpitude infamy would redound to the profession of Christianity. Here it is also necessary to have particular regard to the Lord's supper, that it may not be profaned by a promiscuous administration. For it is certain that he who is intrusted with the dispensation of it, if he knowingly and intentionally admit an unworthy person, whom he might justly reject, is as guilty of sacrilege as if he were to give the Lord's body to dogs. Wherefore, Chrysostom severely inveighs against priests, who, from a fear of the great and the powerful, did not dare to reject any persons who presented themselves. "Blood," says he, "shall be required at your hands. If you fear man, he will deride you; if you fear God, you will also be honoured among men. Let us not be afraid of sceptres, or diadems, or imperial robes; we have here a great power. As for myself, I will rather give up my body to death, and suffer my blood to be shed, than I will be partaker of this pollution." To guard this most sacred mystery, therefore, from being reproached, there is need of great discretion in the administration of it, and this requires the jurisdiction of the Church. The second end is, that the good may not be corrupted, as is often the case, by constant association with the wicked. For, such is our propensity to error, nothing is more easy than for evil examples to seduce us from rectitude of conduct. This use of discipline was remarked by the apostle, when he directed the Corinthians to expel from their society a person who had been guilty of incest. "A little leaven," says he, "leaveneth the whole lump." (*h*) And the apostle perceived such great danger from this quarter, that he even interdicted believers from all social intercourse with the wicked. "I have written unto you, not to keep company, if any man that is called a brother be a fornicator, or covetous, or an idolater, or a railer, or a drunkard, or an extortioner; with such a one, no, not to eat." (*i*) The third end is, that those who are censured or excommunicated, confounded with the shame of their turpitude, may be led to repentance. Thus it is even conducive to their own benefit for their iniquity to be punished, that the stroke of the rod may arouse to a confession of their guilt, those who would only be rendered more obstinate by indulgence. The apostle intends the same when he says, "If any man obey not our word, note that man, and have no company with him, that he may be ashamed." (*k*) Again, when he says of the incestuous Corinthian. "I have judged to deliver such a one unto Satan, that the spirit may be saved in the day of the Lord;" (*l*) that is, as I understand it, that he had consigned him to a temporal condemnation,

(*h*) 1 Cor. v. 6.
(*i*) 1 Cor. v. 11.
(*k*) 2 Thess. iii. 14.
(*l*) 1 Cor. v. 3, 5.

that the spirit might be eternally saved. He therefore calls it *delivering to Satan,* because the devil is *without* the Church, as Christ is *in* the Church. For the opinion of some persons, that it relates to a certain torment of the body in the present life, inflicted by the agency of Satan, appears to me extremely doubtful.

VI. Having stated these ends, it remains for us to examine how the Church exercises this branch of discipline, which consists in jurisdiction. In the first place, let us keep in view the distinction before mentioned, that some sins are public, and others private, or more concealed. Public sins are those which are not only known to one or two witnesses, but are committed openly, and to the scandal of the whole Church. By private sins, I mean, not such as are entirely unknown to men, like those of hypocrites,—for these never come under the cognizance of the Church,—but those of an intermediate class, which are not without the knowledge of some witnesses, and yet are not public. The first sort requires not the adoption of the gradual measures enumerated by Christ; but it is the duty of the Church, on the occurrence of any notorious scandal, immediately to summon the offender, and to punish him in proportion to his crime. Sins of the second class, according to the rule of Christ, are not to be brought before the Church, unless they are attended with contumacy, in rejecting private admonition. When they are submitted to the cognizance of the Church, then attention is to be paid to the other distinction, between smaller delinquencies and more atrocious crimes. For slighter offences require not the exertion of extreme severity; it is sufficient to administer verbal castigation, and that with paternal gentleness, not calculated to exasperate or confound the offender, but to bring him to himself, that his correction may be an occasion of joy rather than of sorrow. But it is proper that flagitious crimes should receive severer punishment; for it is not enough for him who has grievously offended the Church by the bad example of an atrocious crime, merely to receive verbal castigation; he ought to be deprived of the communion of the Lord's supper for a time, till he shall have given satisfactory evidence of repentance. For Paul not only employs verbal reproof against the Corinthian transgressor, but excludes him from the Church, and blames the Corinthians for having tolerated him so long. This order was retained in the ancient and purer Church, while any legitimate government continued. For if any one had perpetrated a crime which was productive of offence, he was commanded, in the first place, to abstain from the Lord's supper, and, in the next place, to humble himself before God, and to testify his repentance before the Church. There were, likewise, certain solemn rites which it was customary to enjoin upon those who had fallen, as signs of their repentance. When the sinner had performed these for the satisfaction of the Church, he was then, by imposition of hands, readmitted to the communion. This readmission is frequently called *peace* by Cyprian, who briefly describes the ceremony. "They do penance," he says, "for a sufficient time; then they come to confession, and by the imposition of the hands of the bishop and clergy, are restored to the privilege of communion." But though the bishop and clergy presided in the reconciliation of offenders, yet they required the consent of the people; as Cyprian elsewhere states.

VII. From this discipline none were exempted; so that princes and plebeians yielded the same submission to it; and that with the greatest propriety, since it is evidently the discipline of Christ, to whom it is reasonable that all the sceptres and diadems of kings should be subject. Thus Theodosius when Ambrose excluded him from the privilege of communion, on account of a massacre perpetrated at Thessalonica, laid aside the ensigns of royalty with which he was invested, publicly in the Church bewailed his sin, which the deceitful suggestions of others had tempted him to commit, and implored pardon with groans and tears. For great kings ought not to think it any dishonour to prostrate themselves as suppliants before Christ the King of kings, nor ought they to be displeased at being judged by the Church. As they hear scarcely any thing in their courts but mere flatteries, it is the more highly necessary for them to receive correction from the Lord by the mouth of his *ministers;* they ought even to wish not to be spared by the *pastors*, that they may be spared by the Lord. I forbear to mention here by whom this jurisdiction is to be exercised, having spoken of this in another place. I will only add, that the legitimate process in excommunicating an offender, which is pointed out by Paul, requires it to be done, not by the elders alone, but with the knowledge and approbation of the Church: in such a manner, however, that the multitude of the people may not direct the proceeding, but may watch over it as witnesses and guardians, that nothing may be done by a few persons from any improper motive. Beside the invocation of the name of God, the whole of the proceeding ought to be conducted with a gravity declarative of the presence of Christ, that there may be no doubt of his presiding over the sentence.

VIII. But it ought not to be forgotten, that the severity becoming the Church must be tempered with a spirit of gentleness. For there is constant need of the greatest caution, according to the injunction of Paul respecting a person who may have been censured, "lest perhaps such a one should be swallowed up with overmuch sorrow;" (*m*) for thus a remedy would become a poison. But the rule of moderation may be better deduced from the end intended to be accomplished; for as the design of excommunication is, that the sinner may be brought to repentance, and evil examples taken away, to prevent the name of Christ from being blasphemed and other persons being tempted to imitation,—if we keep these things in view, it will be easy to judge how far severity ought to proceed, and where it ought to stop. Therefore, when the sinner gives the Church a testimony of his repentance, and by this testimony, as far as in him lies, obliterates the offence, he is by no means to be pressed any further; and if he be pressed any further, the rigour is carried beyond its proper limits. In this respect, it is impossible to excuse the excessive austerity of the ancients, which was utterly at variance with the directions of the Lord, and led to the most dangerous consequences. For when they sentenced an offender to solemn repentance, and exclusion from the holy communion, sometimes for three, sometimes for four, sometimes for seven years, and sometimes for the remainder of life,—what other consequence could result from it, but neither great hypocrisy or extreme despair? In like manner, when any one had fallen a second time, the refusal to admit him to a second repentance, and his exclusion from the Church to the end of his life, was neither useful nor reasonable. Whoever con-

(*m*) 2 Cor. ii. 7.

siders the subject with sound judgment, therefore, will discover their want of prudence in this instance. But I would rather reprobate the general custom, than accuse all those who practised it; among whom it is certain that some were not satisfied, but they complied with it because it was not in their power to effect a reformation. Cyprian declares that it was not from his own choice that he was so rigorous. "Our patience," he says, "and kindness and tenderness, is ready for all who come. I wish all to return into the Church: I wish all our fellow-soldiers to be assembled in the camp of Christ, and all our brethren to be received into the house of God our Father. I forgive everything; I conceal much; from a zealous wish to collect all the brotherhood together, even the sins committed against God I examine not with rigid severity; and am scarcely free from fault myself, in forgiving faults more easily than I ought. With ready and entire affection I embrace those who return with penitence, confessing their sin with humble and sincere satisfaction." Chrysostom is rather more severe; yet he expresses himself thus: "If God is so kind, why is his priest determined to be so austere?" We know, likewise, what kindness Augustine exercised towards the Donatists, so that he hesitated not to receive into the bishoprics those who renounced their error; and that immediately after their repentance. But because a contrary system had prevailed, they were obliged to relinquish their own judgment, in order to follow the established custom.

IX. Now, as it is required of the whole body of the Church, in chastising any one who has fallen, to manifest such gentleness and clemency as not to proceed to the extremity of rigour, but rather, according to the injunction of Paul, to "confirm their love toward him," (*n*) so it is the duty of every individual to moderate himself to the like tenderness and clemency. Such as are expelled from the Church, therefore, it is not for us to expunge from the number of the elect, or to despair of them as already lost. It is proper to consider them as strangers to the Church, and consequently from Christ, but this only as long as they remain in a state of exclusion. And even then, if they exhibit more appearance of obstinacy than of humility, still let us leave them to

---

(*n*) 2 Cor. ii. 8.

the judgment of God, hoping better things of them for the future than we discover at present, and not ceasing to pray to God on their behalf. And to comprehend all in a word, let us not condemn to eternal death the person himself, who is in the hand and power of God alone, but let us content ourselves with judging of the nature of his works according to the law of the Lord. While we follow this rule, we rather adhere to the judgment of God than pronounce our own. Let us not arrogate to ourselves any greater latitude of judging, unless we would limit the power and prescribe laws to the mercy of God; for, whenever it seems good to him, the worst of men are changed into the best, strangers are introduced, and foreigners are admitted into the Church. And this the Lord does, to frustrate the opinion and repress the presumption of men, which would usurp the most unwarrantable liberty of judging, if it were left without any restraint.

X. When Christ promises that what his ministers bind on earth shall be bound in heaven, he limits the power of binding to the censure of the Church; by which those who are excommunicated are not cast into eternal ruin and condemnation, but, by hearing their life and conduct condemned, are also certified of their final condemnation, unless they repent. For excommunication differs from anathema; the latter, which ought to be very rarely or never resorted to, precluding all pardon, execrates a person, and devotes him to eternal perdition; whereas excommunication rather censures and punishes his conduct. And though it does, at the same time, punish the person, yet it is in such a manner, that, by warning him of his future condemnation, it recalls him to salvation. If he obey, the Church is ready to re-admit him to its friendship, and to restore him to its communion. Therefore, though the discipline of the Church admits not of our friendly association and familiar intercourse with excommunicated persons, yet we ought to exert all the means in our power to promote their reformation, and their return to the society and communion of the Church; as we are taught by the apostle, who says, "Yet count him not as an enemy, but admonish him as a brother." (*o*) Unless this tenderness be observed by the individual members, as

---

(*o*) 2 Thess. iii. 15.

well as by the Church collectively, our discipline will be in danger of speedily degenerating into cruelty.

XI. It is also particularly requisite to the moderation of discipline, as Augustine observes in disputing with the Donatists, that private persons, if they see faults corrected with too little diligence by the council of elders, should not on that account immediately withdraw from the Church; and that the pastors themselves, if they cannot succeed according to the wishes of their hearts in reforming every thing that needs correction, should not, in consequence of this, desert the ministry, or disturb the whole Church with unaccustomed asperity. For there is much truth in his observation, that "whoever either corrects what he can by reproof; or what he cannot correct, excludes, without breaking the bond of peace; or what he cannot exclude, without breaking the bond of peace, censures with moderation and bears with firmness; he is free from the curse, and chargeable with no blame." In another passage he assigns the reason; because "all the pious order and method of ecclesiastical discipline ought constantly to regard the unity of the Spirit in the bond of peace; which the apostle commands to be kept by mutual forbearance; and without the preservation of which, the medicine of chastisement is not only superfluous, but even becomes pernicious, and consequently is no longer a medicine." Again: "He who attentively considers these things neither neglects severity of discipline for the preservation of unity, nor breaks the bond of fellowship by an intemperance of correction." He acknowledges indeed that it is not only the duty of the pastors to endeavour to purify the Church from every fault, but that it is likewise incumbent on every individual to exert all his influence for the same purpose; and he fully admits, that a person who neglects to admonish, reprove, and correct the wicked, though he neither favours them nor unites in their sins, is nevertheless culpable in the sight of the Lord; but that he who sustains such an office as to have power to exclude them from a participation of the sacraments, and does it not, is chargeable, in that case, not with the guilt of another, but with a sin of his own; he only recommends it to be done with the prudence required by our Lord, "lest while" they "gather up the tares," they "root up also the wheat with them." (*p*) Hence he concludes with Cyprian, "Let a man, therefore, in mercy correct what he can; what he cannot, let him patiently bear and affectionately lament."

XII. These remarks of Augustine were made in consequence of the rigour of the Donatists, who, seeing vices in the Church, which the bishops condemned by verbal reproofs, but did not punish with excommunication, which they thought not adapted to produce any good effects, inveighed in a most outrageous manner against the bishops, as betrayers of discipline, and by an impious schism separated themselves from the flock of Christ. The same conduct is pursued in the present day by the Anabaptists, who, acknowledging no congregation to belong to Christ, unless it be, in all respects, conspicuous for angelic perfection, under the pretext of zeal, destroy all edification. "Such persons," says Augustine, "not actuated by hatred against the iniquity of others, but stimulated by fondness for their own disputes, desire either wholly to pervert, or at least to divide the weak multitude by insnaring them with their boastful pretensions; inflated with pride, infuriated with obstinacy, insidious with calumnies, turbulent with seditions, that their destitution of the light of truth may not be detected, they conceal themselves under the covert of a rigorous severity; and those things which the Scripture commands to be done for the correction of the faults of our brethren, without violating the sincerity of love, or disturbing the unity of peace, but with the moderation of a remedial process, they abuse, to an occasion of dissension and to the sacrilege of schism. Thus Satan transforms himself into an angel of light, when from just severity he takes occasion to persuade men to inhuman cruelty, with no other object than to corrupt and break the bond of peace and unity; by the preservation of which among Christians, all his power to injure them is weakened, his insidious snares are broken, and his schemes for their ruin come to nothing."

XIII. There is one thing which this father particularly recommends—that if the contagion of any sin has infected a whole people, there is a necessity for the severity and mercy which are

(*p*) Matt. xiii. 29.

combined in strict discipline. "For schemes of separation," he says, "are pernicious and sacrilegious, because they proceed from pride and impiety, and disturb the good who are weak, more than they correct the wicked who are bold." And what he here prescribes to others, he faithfully followed himself. For writing to Aurelius, bishop of Carthage, he complained that drunkenness, which is so severely condemned in the Scripture, prevailed with impunity in Africa, and persuaded him to endeavour to remedy it by calling a provincial council. He immediately adds, "I believe these things are suppressed not by harshness, severity, or imperiousness, but by teaching rather than commanding, by admonitions rather than by menaces. For this is the conduct to be pursued with a multitude of offenders; but severity is to be exercised against the sins of a few." Yet he does not mean that bishops should connive or be silent, because they cannot inflict severe punishments for public crimes, as he afterwards explains; but he means that the correction should be tempered with such moderation, as to be salutary rather than injurious to the body. And therefore he at length concludes in the following manner: "Wherefore, also that command of the apostle, to put away the wicked, (*q*) ought by no means to be neglected, when it can be done without danger of disturbing the peace; for in this case alone did he intend that it should be enforced; and we are also to observe his other injunction, to forbear one another in love, endeavouring to keep the unity of the Spirit in the bond of peace." (*r*)

XIV. The remaining part of discipline, which is not strictly included in the power of the keys, consists in this—that the pastors, according to the necessity of the times, should exhort the people either to fastings or solemn supplications, or to other exercises of humility, repentance, and faith, of which the word of God prescribes neither the time, the extent, nor the form, but leaves all this to the judgment of the Church. The observation of these things, also, which are highly useful, was always practised by the ancient Church from the days of the apostles; though the apostles themselves were not the first authors of them, but derived

---

(*q*) 1 Cor. v. 13. (*r*) Eph. iv. 2, 3.

the example from the law and the prophets. For there we find, that whenever any important business occurred, the people were assembled, supplications commanded, and fasting enjoined. The apostles, therefore, followed what was not new to the people of God, and what they foresaw would be useful. The same reasoning is applicable to other exercises by which the people may be excited to duty, or preserved in obedience. Examples abound in the sacred history, which it is unnecessary to enumerate. The conclusion to be deduced from the whole is, that whenever a controversy arises respecting religion, which requires to be decided by a council or ecclesiastical judgment; whenever a minister is to be chosen; in short, whenever any thing of difficulty or great importance is transacting; and also when any tokens of the Divine wrath are discovered, such as famine, pestilence, or war;—it is a pious custom, and beneficial in all ages, for the pastors to exhort the people to public fasts and extraordinary prayers. If the testimonies which may be adduced from the Old Testament be rejected, as inapplicable to the Christian church, it is evident that the apostles practised the same. Respecting prayers, however, I suppose scarcely a person will be found disposed to raise any dispute. Therefore let us say something of fasting; because many, for want of knowing its usefulness, undervalue its necessity, and some reject it as altogether superfluous; while, on the other hand, where the use of it is not well understood, it easily degenerates into superstition.

XV. Holy and legitimate fasting is directed to three ends. For we practise it, either as a restraint on the flesh, to preserve it from licentiousness, or as a preparation for prayers and pious meditations, or as a testimony of our humiliation in the presence of God, when we are desirous of confessing our guilt before him. The first is not often contemplated in public fasting, because all men have not the same constitution or health of body; therefore it is rather more applicable to private fasting. The second end is common to both, such preparation for prayer being necessary to the whole Church, as well as to every one of the faithful in particular. The same may be said of the third. For it will sometimes happen that God will afflict a whole nation with war, pestilence, or some other calamity; under such a common scourge, it behoves all the people to make a confession of their guilt. When the hand of the Lord chastises an individual, he ought to make a similar confession, either alone or with his family. It is true that this acknowledgment lies principally in the disposition of the heart; but when the heart is affected as it ought to be, it can scarcely avoid breaking out into the external expression, and most especially when it promotes the general edification; in order that all, by a public confession of their sin, may unitedly acknowledge the justice of God, and may mutually animate each other by the influence of example.

XVI. Wherefore fasting, as it is a sign of humiliation, is of more frequent use in public, than among individuals in private; though it is common to both, as we have already observed. With regard to the discipline, therefore, of which we are now treating, whenever supplications are to be presented to God on any important occasion it would be right to enjoin the union of fasting with prayer. Thus when the believers at Antioch "laid their hands on Paul and Barnabas," the better to recommend their very important ministry to God, they "fasted" as well as "prayed." (*s*) So also when Paul and Barnabas afterwards "ordained elders in every Church," they used to "pray with fasting." (*t*) In this kind of fasting, their only object was, that they might be more lively and unembarrassed in prayer. And we find by experience, that after a full meal, the mind does not aspire towards God so as to be able to enter on prayer, and to continue in it with seriousness and ardour of affection. So we are to understand what Luke says of Anna, that she "served God with fastings and prayers." (*u*) For he does not place the worship of God in fasting, but signifies that by such means that holy woman habituated herself to a constancy in prayer. Such was the fasting of Nehemiah, when he prayed to God with more than common fervour for the deliverance of his people. (*v*) For this cause Paul declares it to be expedient for believers to practise a temporary abstinence from lawful enjoyments, that they may be more at liberty to "give themselves to fasting and prayer." (*w*) For by connecting fasting with prayer as an assistance to it, he signifies that fasting is

(*s*) Acts xiii. 2, 3. (*t*) Acts xiv. 23. (*u*) Luke ii. 37. (*v*) Neh. i. 4. (*w*) 1 Cor. vii. 5.

of no importance in itself, any further than as it is directed to this end. Besides, from the direction which he gives in that place to husbands and wives, to "render to" each other "due benevolence," it is clear that he is not speaking of daily prayers, but of such as require peculiar earnestness of attention.

XVII. In like manner, when war, pestilence, or famine begins to rage, or when any other calamity appears to threaten a country and people, then also it is the duty of pastors to exhort the Church to fasting, that with humble supplications they may deprecate the wrath of the Lord; for when he causes danger to appear, he announces himself as prepared and armed for vengeance. Therefore, as it was anciently the custom for criminals to appear with long beards, dishevelled hair, and mourning apparel, in order to excite the pity of the judge; so when we stand as criminals before the tribunal of God, it is conducive to his glory and the general edification, as well as expedient and salutary for ourselves, to deprecate his severity by external demonstrations of sorrow. That this was customary among the people of Israel, it is easy to infer from the language of Joel; for when he commands to "blow the trumpet, sanctify a fast, and call a solemn assembly," (*x*) and proceeds to give other directions, he speaks as of things commonly practised. He had just before said that inquisition was made respecting the crimes of the people, had announced that the day of the Lord was at hand, and had cited them, as criminals, to appear and answer for themselves; afterwards, he warns them to have recourse to sackcloth and ashes, to weeping and fasting, that is, to prostrate themselves before the Lord with external demonstrations of humility. Sackcloth and ashes, perhaps, were more suitable to those times; but there is no doubt that assembling, and weeping, and fastings, and similar acts, are equally proper for us in the present age, whenever the state of our affairs requires them. For as it is a holy exercise, adapted both to humble men and to confess their humility, why should it be less used by us than by the ancients in similar necessities? We read that fasting in token of sorrow was not only practised by the Israelitish Church, which was formed and regulated by the word

(*x*) Joel ii. 15.

of God, but also by the inhabitants of Nineveh, who had no instruction except the preaching of Jonah. (*y*) What cause, then, is there, why we should not practise the same? But, it will be said, it is an external ceremony, which, with all the rest, terminated in Christ. I reply, that even at this day it is, as it always has been, a most excellent assistance and useful admonition to believers to stimulate them, and guard them against further provocations of God by their carelessness and inattention, when they are chastised by his scourges. Therefore, when Christ excuses his apostles for not fasting, he does not say that fasting is abolished, but appoints it for seasons of calamity, and connects it with sorrow. "The days will come," says he, "when the bridegroom shall be taken away from them." (*z*).

XVIII. That there may be no mistake respecting the term, let us define what fasting is. For we do not understand it to denote mere temperance and abstinence in eating and drinking, but something more. The life of believers, indeed, ought to be so regulated by frugality and sobriety, as to exhibit, as far as possible, the appearance of a perpetual fast. But beside this, there is another temporary fast, when we retrench any thing from our customary mode of living, either for a day or for any certain time, and prescribe to ourselves a more than commonly rigid and severe abstinence in food. This restriction consists in three things,—in time, in quality, and in quantity of food. By time, I mean that we should perform, while fasting, those exercises on account of which fasts are instituted. As, for example, if any one fast for solemn prayer, he should not break his fast till he has attended to it. The quality consists in an entire abstinence from dainties, and contentment with simpler and humbler fare, that our appetite may not be stimulated by delicacies. The rule of quantity is, that we eat more sparingly and slightly than usual, only for necessity, and not for pleasure.

XIX. But it is necessary for us, above all things, to be particularly on our guard against the approaches of superstition, which has heretofore been a source of great injury to the Church. For it were far better that fasting should be entirely disused, than

(*y*) Jonah iii. 5. (*z*) Matt. ix. 15. Luke v. 34, 35.

that the practice should be diligently observed, and at the same time corrupted with false and pernicious opinions, into which the world is continually falling, unless it be prevented by the greatest fidelity and prudence of the pastors. The first caution necessary, and which they should be constantly urging, is that suggested by Joel: "Rend your heart, and not your garments;" (*a*) that is, they should admonish the people, that God sets no value on fasting, unless it be accompanied with a correspondent disposition of heart, a real displeasure against sin, sincere self-abhorrence, true humiliation, and unfeigned grief arising from a fear of God; and that fasting is of no use on any other account than as an additional and subordinate assistance to these things. For nothing is more abominable to God, than when men attempt to impose upon him by the presentation of signs and external appearances instead of purity of heart. Therefore he severely reprobates this hypocrisy in the Jews, who imagined they had satisfied God merely by having fasted, while they cherished impious and impure thoughts in their hearts. "Is it such a fast, saith the Lord, that I have chosen?" (*b*) The fasting of hypocrites, therefore, is not only superfluous and useless fatigue, but the greatest abomination. Allied to this is another evil, which requires the most vigilant caution, lest it be considered as a meritorious act, or a species of divine service. For as it is a thing indifferent in itself, and possesses no other value than it derives from those ends to which it ought to be directed, it is most pernicious superstition to confound it with works commanded by God, and necessary in themselves, without reference to any ulterior object. Such was formerly the folly of the Manichæans, in the refutation of whom Augustine most clearly shows, that fasting is to be held in no other estimation than on account of those ends which I here mention, and that it receives no approbation from God, unless it be practised for their sake. The third error is not so impious, indeed, yet it is pregnant with danger, to enforce it with extreme rigour as one of the principal duties, and to extol it with extravagant encomiums, so that men imagine themselves to have performed a work of peculiar excellence when they have fasted. In this respect, I dare not wholly excuse the

(*a*) Joel ii. 13. (*b*) Isaiah lviii. 5.

ancient fathers from having sown some seeds of superstition, and given occasion to the tyranny which afterwards arose. Their writings contain some sound and judicious sentiments on the subject of fasting; but they also contain extravagant praises, which elevate it to a rank among the principal virtues.

XX. And the superstitious observant of Lent had at that time generally prevailed, because the common people considered themselves as performing an eminent act of obedience to God, and the pastors commended it as a holy imitation of Christ; whereas it is plain that Christ fasted, not to set an example to others, but in order that by such an introduction to the preaching of the gospel, he might prove the doctrine not to be a human invention, but a revelation from heaven. And it is surprising that men of acute discernment could ever entertain such a gross error, which is disproved by such numerous and satisfactory arguments. For Christ did not fast often, which it was necesary for him to do, if he intended to establish a law for anniversary fasts, but only once, while he was preparing to enter on the promulgation of the gospel. Nor did he fast in the manner of men, as it behoved him to do, if he intended to stimulate men to an imitation of him: on the contrary, he exhibited an example calculated to attract the admiration of all, rather than to excite them to a desire of emulating his example. In short, there was no other reason for his fasting than for that of Moses, when he received the law from the hand of the Lord. For as that miracle was exhibited in Moses, to establish the authority of the law, it was necessary that it should not be omitted in Christ, lest the gospel should seem to be inferior to the law. But from that time, it never entered into any man's mind to introduce such a form of fasting among the people of Israel, under the pretext of imitating Moses; nor was it followed by any of the holy prophets and fathers, notwithstanding their inclination and zeal for all pious exercises. For the account of Elijah, that he lived forty days without meat and drink, was only intended to teach the people that he was raised up to be the restorer of the law, from which almost all Israel had departed. It was nothing but a vain and superstitious affectation, therefore, to dignify the fasting of Lent with the title and pretext of an imitation of Christ. In the manner of fasting, however, there was at that time a great diversity as Cassiodorus relates from Socrates, in the ninth book of his history. "For the Romans," he says, "had no more than three weeks; but during these there was a continual fast, except on the Sunday and Saturday. The Illyrians and Greeks had six weeks, and others had seven; but they fasted at intervals. Nor did they differ less as to the nature of their food. Some made use of nothing but bread and water; others added vegetables to fish; some did not abstain from fowl; others made no distinction at all between any kinds of food." This diversity is also mentioned by Augustine, in his second epistle to Januarius.

XXI. The times which followed were still worse; to the preposterous zeal of the multitude was added the ignorance and stupidity of the bishops, with their lust of dominion and tyrannical rigour. Impious laws were enacted to bind men's consciences with fatal chains. The eating of animal food was interdicted, as though it would contaminate them. Sacrilegious opinions were added one after another, till they arrived at an ocean of errors. And that no corruption might be omitted, they have begun to trifle with God by the most ridiculous pretensions to abstinence. For in the midst of all the most exquisite delicacies, they seek the praise of fasting; no dainties are then sufficient; they never have food in greater plenty or variety, or deliciousness. Such splendid provision they call fasting, and imagine it to be the legitimate service of God. I say nothing of the base gluttony practised at that season, more than at any other time, by those who wish to pass for the greatest saints. In short they esteem it the highest worship of God to abstain from animal food, and with this exception, to indulge themselves in every kind of dainties. On the other hand, to taste the least morsel of bacon or salted meat and brown bread they deem an act of the vilest impiety, and deserving of worse than death. Jerome relates, that there were some persons, even in his time, who trifled with God by such fooleries; who, to avoid making use of oil, procured the most delicate kinds of food to be brought from every country; and who, to do violence to nature, abstained from drinking water, but procured delicious and costly liquors to be made for them, which they drank, not from a cup, but from a shell. What was then the vice of a few, is now become common among all wealthy persons; they fast for no other purpose than to feast with more than common sumptuousness and delicacy. But I have no inclination to waste many words on a thing so notorious. I only assert, that neither in their fastings, nor in any other parts of their discipline, have the Papists any thing so correct, sincere, or well regulated, as to have the least occasion to pride themselves upon any thing being left among them worthy of praise.

XXII. There remains the second part of the discipline of the Church, which particularly relates to the clergy. It is contained in the canons which the ancient bishops imposed on themselves and their order; such as these: That no ecclesiastic should employ his time in hunting, gambling, or feasting; that no one should engage in usury or commerce; that no one should be present at dissolute dances; and other similar injunctions. Penalties were likewise annexed, to confirm the authority of the canons, and to prevent their being violated with impunity. For this end, to every bishop was committed the government of his clergy, to rule them according to the canons, and to oblige them to do their duty. For this purpose were instituted annual visitations and synods, that if any one were negligent in his duty, he might be admonished, and that any one who committed a fault might be corrected according to his offence. The bishops also had their provincial councils, once every year, and anciently even twice a year, by which they were judged, if they had committed any breach of their duty. For if a bishop was too severe or violent against his clergy, there was a right of appeal to the provincial councils, even though there was only a single complainant. The severest punishment was the deposition of the offender from his office, and his exclusion for a time from the communion. And because this was a perpetual regulation, they never used to dissolve a provincial council without appointing a time and place for the next. For, to summon a universal council, was the exclusive prerogative of the emperor, as all the ancient records testify. As long as this severity continued, the clergy required nothing more from the people than they exemplified in their own conduct. Indeed, they were far more severe to themselves than to the laity; and it is reasonable that the people should be ruled with a milder and less rigid discipline; and that the clergy should inflict heavier censures, and exercise far less indulgence to themselves than to other persons. How all this has become obsolete, it is unnecessary to relate, when nothing can be imagined more licentious and dissolute than this order of men in the present day; and their profligacy has gone to such a length, that the whole world is exclaiming against them. That all antiquity may not appear to have been entirely forgotten by them, I confess, they deceive the eyes of the simple with certain shadows, but these bear no more resemblance to the ancient usages, than the mimicry of an ape to the rational and considerate conduct of men. There is a remarkable passage in Xenophon, where he states how shamefully the Persians had degenerated from the virtues of their ancestors, and, from an austere course of life, had sunk into delicacy and effeminacy, but that, to conceal their shame, they sedulously observed the ancient forms. For whereas in the time of Cyrus, sobriety and temperance were carried so far, that it was unnecessary, and was even considered as a disgrace for any one to blow his nose; their posterity continued scrupulously to refrain from this act; but to absorb the mucus, and retain the fetid humours produced by their gluttony, even till they almost putrefied, was held quite allowable. So, according to the ancient rule, it was unlawful to bring cups to the table; but they had no objection to drink wine till they were obliged to be carried away drunk. It had been an established custom to eat only one meal a day; these good successors had not abolished this custom, but they had continued their banquets from noon to midnight. Because their ancient law enjoined men to finish their day's journey fasting, it continued to be a permanent custom among them; but they were at liberty, and it was the general practice, for the sake of avoiding fatigue, to contract the journey to two hours. Whenever the Papists bring forward their degenerate rules, for the purpose of showing their resemblance to the holy fathers, this example will sufficiently expose their ridiculous imitation, of which no painter could draw a more striking likeness.

XXIII. In one instance, they are too rigorous and inflexible, that is, in not permitting priests to marry. With what impunity fornication rages among them, it is unnecessary to remark; imboldened by their polluted celibacy, they have become hardened to every crime. Yet this prohibition clearly shows how pestilent are all their traditions; since it has not only deprived the Church of upright and able pastors, but has formed a horrible gulf of enormities, and precipitated many souls into the abyss of despair. The interdiction of marriage to priests was certainly an act of impious tyranny, not only contrary to the word of God, but at variance with every principle of justice. In the first place, it was on no account lawful for men to prohibit that which the Lord had left free. Secondly, that God had expressly provided in his word that this liberty should not be infringed, is too clear to require much proof. I say nothing of the direction, repeatedly given by Paul, that a bishop should be "the husband of one wife;" (*d*) but what could be expressed with greater force, than where he announces a revelation from the Holy Spirit, "that in the latter times some shall depart from the faith, forbidding to marry," and represents these not only as impostors, but as disseminating "doctrines of devils." (*e*) This, therefore, was a prophecy, a sacred oracle of the Holy Spirit, by which he intended from the beginning to forearm the Church against dangers—that the prohibition of marriage is a doctrine of devils. But our adversaries imagine themselves to have admirably evaded this charge, when they misapply it to Montanus, the Tatianists, Encratites, and other ancient heretics. It refers, say they, to those who have condemned marriage altogether; we by no means condemn it; we merely prohibit it to the clergy, from an opinion that it is not proper for them. As if, though this prophecy had once been accomplished in those ancient heretics, it might not also be applicable to them; or as if this puerile cavil, that they do not prohibit marriage, because they do not prohibit it to all, were deserving of the least attention. This is just as if a tyrant should contend that there can be no injustice in a law, the injustice of which only oppresses one part of a nation.

XXIV. They object, that there ought to be some mark to distinguish the clergy from the laity. As though the Lord did not foresee what are the true ornaments in which priests ought to excel. By this plea, thev charge the apostle with disturbing the order and violating the decorum of the Church, who, in delineat-

(*d*) 1 Tim. iii. 2. Titus i. 6. (*e*) 1 Tim. iv. 1, 3.

ing the perfect model of a good bishop, among the other virtues which he required in him, dared to mention marriage. I know that they interpret this to mean, that no one is chosen a bishop who shall have had a second wife. And I grant that this interpretation is not new; but that it is erroneous, is evident from the context itself; because he immediately after prescribes what characters the wives of bishops and deacons ought to possess. Paul places marriage among the virtues of a bishop; these men teach that it is a vice not to be tolerated in the clergy; and not content with this general censure, they call it carnal pollution and impurity, which is the language of Syricius, one of the pontiffs, recited in their canons. Let every man reflect from what source these things can have proceeded. Christ has been pleased to put such honour upon marriage, as to make it an image of his sacred union with the Church. What could be said more, in commendation of the dignity of marriage? With what face can that be called impure and polluted, which exhibits a similitude of the spiritual grace of Christ?

XXV. Now, though their prohibition is so clearly repugnant to the word of God, yet they find something in the Scriptures to urge in its defence. The Levitical priests, whenever it came to their turn to minister at the altar, were required not to cohabit with their wives, that they might be pure and immaculate to perform the sacrifices; it would therefore be exceedingly unbecoming for our sacraments, which are far more excellent and of daily recurrence, to be administered by married men. As though the evangelical ministry and the Levitical priesthood were one and the same office. On the contrary, the Levitical priests were antitypes, representing Christ, who, as the Mediator between God and man, was to reconcile the Father to us by his perfect purity. Now, as it was impossible for sinners to exhibit in every respect a type of his sanctity, yet in order to display some faint shadows of it, they were commanded to purify themselves in a manner beyond what is common among men, whenever they approach the sanctuary; because on those occasions they properly represented Christ, in appearing at the tabernacle, which was a type of the heavenly tribunal, as mediators to reconcile the people to God. As the pastors of the Church now sustain no such office, the comparison is nothing to the purpose. Wherefore the apostle, without any exception, confidently pronounces, that "marriage is honourable in all; but whoremongers and adulterers God will judge." (*f*) And the apostles themselves have proved by their own example that marriage is not unbecoming the sanctity of any office, however excellent; for Paul testifies that they not only retained their wives, but took them about with them. (*g*)

XXVI. It has also betrayed egregious impudence, to insist on this appearance of chastity as a necessary thing, to the great disgrace of the ancient Church, which abounded with such peculiar Divine knowledge, but was still more eminent for sanctity. For if they pay no regard to the apostles, whom they often have the hardihood to treat with contempt, what will they say of all the ancient fathers, who, it is certain, not only tolerated marriage in bishops, but likewise approved of it? It would follow that they must have practised a foul profanation of sacred things, since, according to the notion we are opposing, they did not celebrate the mysteries of the Lord with the requisite purity. The injunction of celibacy was agitated in the council of Nice; for there are never wanting little minds, absorbed in superstition, who endeavour to make themselves admired by the invention of some novelty. But what was the decision? The council coincided in the opinion of Paphnutius, who pronounced that "a man's cohabitation with his own wife is chastity." Therefore marriage continued to be held sacred among them, nor was it esteemed any disgrace to them, or considered as casting any blemish on the ministry.

XXVII. Afterwards followed times distinguished by a too superstitious admiration of celibacy. Hence those frequent and extravagant encomiums on virginity, with which scarcely any other virtue was in general deemed worthy to be compared. And though marriage was not condemned as impure, yet its dignity was so diminished, and its sanctity obscured, that he who did not refrain from it was not considered as aspiring to perfection with sufficient fortitude of mind. Hence those canons, which prohibited the contraction of marriage by those who had already entered on the office of priests; and succeeding ones, which prohibited the ad-

---

(*f*) Heb. xiii. 4. (*g*) 1 Cor. ix. 5.

mission to that office of any but those who had never been married, or who had abjured all cohabitation with their wives. Because these things seemed to add respectability to the priesthood, they were received, I confess, even in early times, with great applause. But our adversaries object antiquity against us. I answer, In the first place, in the days of the apostles, and for several ages after, the bishops were at liberty to marry; and the apostles themselves, as well as other pastors of the highest reputation who succeeded them, made use of this liberty without any difficulty. The example of the primitive Church we ought to hold in higher estimation than to deem that unlawful or unbecoming which was then received and practised with approbation. Secondly; even that age, which, from a superstitious attachment to virginity, began to be more unfavourable to marriage, did not impose the law of celibacy upon the priests as if it were absolutely necessary, but because they preferred celibacy to marriage. Lastly; this law did not require the compulsion of continence in those who were not able to keep it; for while the severest punishments were denounced on priests who were guilty of fornication, those who married were merely dismissed from their office.

XXVIII. Therefore, whenever the advocates of this modern tyranny attempt to defend their celibacy with the pretext of antiquity, we shall not fail to reply, that they ought to restore the ancient chastity in their priests, to remove all adulterers and fornicators, not to suffer those, whom they forbid the virtuous and chaste society of a wife, to abandon themselves with impunity to every kind of debauchery, to revive the obsolete discipline by which all indecencies may be repressed, to deliver the Church from this flagitious turpitude, by which it has been so long deformed. When they shall have granted this, it will still be necessary to admonish them not to impose that as necessary, which, being free in itself, depends on the convenience of the Church. Yet I have not made these observations from an opinion that we ought on any condition to admit those canons which impose the obligation of celibacy on the clergy, but to enable the more judicious to perceive the effrontery of our adversaries in alleging the authority of antiquity to bring disgrace on holy marriage in priests. With respect to the fathers, whose writings are extant, with the exception of Jerome, they have not so malignantly detracted from the virtue of marriage, when they have been expressing their own sentiments. We shall content ourselves with one testimony of Chrysostom, because he, who was a principal admirer of virginity, cannot be supposed to have been more lavish than others in commendation of marriage. He says, "The first degree of chastity is pure virginity; the second is faithful marriage. Therefore the second species of virginity is the chaste love of matrimony."

CHAPTER XIII

Vows: the Misery of Rashly Making Them

It is a thing truly to be deplored, that the Church, after its liberty had been purchased by the inestimable price of the blood of Christ, should have been so oppressed with a cruel tyranny, and almost overwhelmed with an immense mass of traditions; but the general frenzy of individuals shows that it has not been without the justest cause, that God has permitted so much to be done by Satan and his ministers. For it was not sufficient for them to neglect the command of Christ, and to endure every burden imposed on them by false teachers, unless they respectively added some of their own, and so sunk themselves deeper in pits of their own digging. This was the consequence of their rivalling each other in the contrivance of vows to add a stronger and stricter obligation to the common bonds. As we have shown that the service of God was corrupted by the audacity of those who domineered over the Church under the title of pastors, insnaring unhappy consciences with their unjust laws; it will not be irrelevant here to expose a kindred evil, in order to show that men, in the depravity of their hearts, have opposed every possible obstacle to those means by which they ought to have been conducted to God. Now, to make it more evident that vows have been productive of the most serious mischiefs, it is necessary to remind the readers of the principles already stated. In the first place, we have shown that every thing necessary to the regulation of a pious and holy life is comprehended in the law. We have also shown, that the Lord, in order to call us off more effectually from the contrivance of new works, has included all the praise of righteousness in simple obedience to his will. If these things be true, the conclusion is obvious, that all the services which we invent for the purpose of gaining the favour of God, are not at all acceptable to him, whatever pleasure they may afford to ourselves; and, in fact, the Lord himself, in various places, not only openly rejects them, but declares them to be objects of his utter abomination. Hence arises a doubt respecting vows which are made without the authority of the express word of God in what light they are to be considered; whether they may be rightly made by Christian men, and how far they are obligatory upon them. For what is styled a *promise* among men, in reference to God is called a *vow*. Now, we promise to men either such things as we think will be agreeable to them, or such as we owe them on the ground of duty. There is need, therefore, of far greater care respecting vows, which are addressed to God himself, towards whom we ought to act with the utmost seriousness. But here superstition has prevailed, in all ages, to a wonderful degree, so that, without judgment or discretion, men have precipitately vowed to God whatever was uppermost in their minds, or even on their lips. Hence those fooleries, and even monstrous absurdities of vows, by which the heathen insolently trifled with their gods. And I sincerely wish that Christians had not imitated them in such audacity. This ought never to have been the case; but we see, that for several ages nothing has been more common than this presumption; amidst the general contempt of the law of God, people have been all inflamed with a mad passion for vowing whatever had delighted them in their dreams. I have no wish to proceed to an odious exaggeration, or a particular enumeration of the enormity and varieties of this offence; but I have thought it proper to make these remarks by the way, to show that we are not instituting an unnecessary discussion, when we treat of vows.

II. If we would avoid any error in judging what vows are legitimate, and what are preposterous, it is necessary to consider three things—first, to whom vows are to be addressed; secondly, who we are that make vows; lastly, with what intention vows are made. The first consideration calls us to reflect, that we have to do with God; who takes such pleasure in our obedience, that he pronounces a curse on all acts of will-worship, however specious and splendid they may be in the eyes of men. If God abominates all voluntary services invented by us without his command, it follows, that nothing can be acceptable to him, except what is approved by his word. Let us not, therefore, assume to ourselves such a great liberty, as to presume to vow to God any thing that has no testimony of his approbation. For the maxim of Paul, that "whatsoever is not of faith is sin," (*a*) while it extends to every action, is without doubt principally applicable when a man addresses his thoughts directly to God. Paul is there arguing respecting the difference of meats; and if we err and fall even in things of the least moment, where we are not enlightened by the certainty of faith, how much greater modesty is requisite when we are undertaking a business of the greatest importance! For nothing ought to be of greater importance to us than the duties of religion. Let this, then, be our first rule in regard to vows—never to attempt vowing any thing without a previous conviction of conscience, that we are attempting nothing rashly. And our conscience will be secure from all danger of rashness, when it shall have God for its guide, dictating, as it were, by his word, what it is proper or useless to do.

III. The second consideration which we have mentioned, calls us to measure our strength, to contemplate our calling, and not to neglect the liberty which God has conferred on us. For he who vows what is not in his power, or is repugnant to his calling, is chargeable with rashness; and he who despises the favour of God, by which he is constituted lord of all things, is guilty of ingratitude. By this remark, I do not intend that we have any thing in our power, so as to enable us to promise it to God in a reliance on our own strength. For, with the strictest regard to truth, it was decreed in the council of Arausium, that nothing is rightly vowed to God but what we have received from his hand, seeing that all the things which are presented to him are merely gifts which he has imparted. But as some things are given to us

(*a*) Rom. xiv. 23.

by the goodness of God, and other things are denied to us by his justice, let every man follow the admonition of Paul, and consider the measure of grace which he has received. (*b*) My only meaning here, therefore, is, that vows ought to be regulated by that measure which the Lord prescribes to us, by what he has given us; lest, by attempting more than he permits, we precipitate ourselves into danger, by arrogating too much to ourselves. Luke gives us an example in those assassins who vowed "that they would neither eat nor drink till they had killed Paul:" (*c*) even though the design itself had not been criminal, yet it would have betrayed intolerable rashness, to make a man's life and death subject to their power. So Jephthah suffered the punishment of his folly, when, in the fervour of precipitation, he made an inconsiderate vow. (*d*) In vows of this class, distinguished by mad presumption, that of celibacy holds the preëminence. Priests, monks, and nuns, forgetting their infirmity, think themselves capable of celibacy. But by what revelation have they been taught that they shall preserve their chastity all their life-time, to the end of which their vow reaches? They hear the declaration of God concerning the universal condition of man; "It is not good for man to be alone." (*e*) They understand, and I wish they did not feel, that sin remaining in us is attended with the most powerful stimulants. With what confidence can they dare to reject that general calling for their whole life-time, whereas the gift of continence is frequently bestowed for a certain time, as opportunity requires? In such obstinacy let them not expect God to assist them, but rather let them remember what is written: "Thou shalt not tempt the Lord thy God." (*f*) Now, it is tempting God, to strive against the nature which he has implanted in us, and to despise the gifts which he presents, as though they were not at all suitable for us. And they not only do this, but even marriage itself, which God has deemed it no degradation of his majesty to institute, which he has pronounced to be "honourable in all," which our Lord Jesus Christ sanctified with his presence, which he deigned to dignify with his first miracle, they are not ashamed to stigmatize as pollution, for the mere purpose of extolling celibacy,

---

(*b*) Rom. xii. 3. 1 Cor. xii. 11. (*c*) Acts xxiii. 12.
(*d*) Judges xi. 30—40. (*e*) Gen. ii. 18. (*f*) Deut. vi. 16. Matt. iv. 7.

however it may be spent, with the most extravagant encomiums. As though they did not exhibit a striking proof in their own lives, that celibacy is one thing, and that virginity is another; and yet they have the consummate impudence to call such a life angelic. This is certainly doing a great injury to the angels of God, to whom they compare persons guilty of fornication, adultery, and other crimes far more atrocious and impure. And there is not the least need of arguments, when they are clearly convicted by the fact itself. For it is very evident what dreadful punishments the Lord generally inflicts on such arrogance, self-confidence, and contempt of his gifts. Modesty forbids me to animadvert on those things which are more secret, of which too much is already known. That we are not at liberty to vow any thing which may hinder us from serving God in our vocation, is beyond all controversy; as if a father of a family should vow that he will desert his wife and children, to undertake some other charge; or as if a person qualified to fill the office of magistrate, on being chosen to it, should vow that he would remain in a private station. But the observation we have made, that our liberty ought not to be despised, has some difficulty, which requires a further explication. Now, the meaning may be briefly explained in the following manner: As God has constituted us lords of all things, and has placed them in subjection to us, in order that we might use them all for our accommodation, we have no reason to hope that we should perform a service acceptable to God, by making ourselves slaves to external things, which ought to be subservient to our assistance. I say this, because some persons consider themselves entitled to the praise of humility, if they entangle themselves with many observances, from which the Lord, for the best of reasons, intended we should be exempt. Therefore, if we would escape this danger, let us always remember, that we are never to depart from that economy which the Lord has instituted in the Christian Church.

IV. I proceed now to the third consideration which I mentioned; that it is of great importance with what intention a vow is made, if we wish it to be approved by God. For as the Lord regards the heart, and not the external appearance, it happens that the same action, performed with different designs, is sometimes acceptable to him, and sometimes highly displeasing. If any one vow abstinence from wine as if there were any holiness in such abstinence, he is chargeable with superstition; if this be done for any other end which is not improper, no one can disapprove of it. Now, as far as I am able to judge, there are four ends to which our vows may be rightly directed. For the sake of further elucidation, I refer two of them to the time past, and the other two to the future. To the time past belong those vows by which we either testify our gratitude to God for benefits received, or, in order to deprecate his wrath, inflict punishment on ourselves for sins that we have committed. The former may be called vows of thanksgiving; the latter, vows of penitence. Of the former we have an example in Jacob, who vowed to give to God the tenth of all he should acquire, if the Lord would bring him again from his exile to his father's house in peace. (*g*) We have other examples of the same kind in the ancient peace-offerings, which used to be vowed by pious kings and generals, entering on just wars, to be offered in case they should obtain the victory; or by persons labouring under more than common difficulty, in case the Lord would deliver them. Thus we are to understand all those places in the Psalms which speak of vows. (*h*) Vows of this kind may also be now used among us, whenever God delivers us from any great calamity, from a severe disease, or from any other danger. For on such occasions, it is not inconsistent with the duty of a pious man to consecrate to God some oblation that he has vowed, merely as a solemn token of grateful acknowledgment, that he may not appear unthankful for his goodness. The nature of the second species of vows will sufficiently appear from only one familiar example. If a person has fallen into any crime through the vice of intemperance, nothing prevents him from correcting that vice by a temporary renunciation of all delicacies, and enforcing this abstinence by a vow, to lay himself under the stronger obligation. Yet I impose no perpetual law on those who have been guilty of such an offence; I only point out what they are at liberty to do, if they think that such a vow would be useful to them. I consider a vow of this kind, therefore, as lawful, but,

---

(*g*) Gen. xxviii. 20—22.

(*h*) Psalm xxii. 25; lvi. 12; cxvi. 14, 18.

at the same time, as left to the free choice of every individual.

V. Vows which regard the future as I have observed, have for their object, partly to render us more cautious of danger, partly to stimulate us to the performance of duty. For example; a person perceives himself to be so prone to a certain vice, that, in something not otherwise evil, he cannot restrain himself from falling into sin; he will commit no absurdity, if he should deny himself the use of that thing for a season by a vow. If any one be convinced that this or the other ornament of dress is dangerous to him, and yet feel excessive desire for it, he cannot do better than restrain himself by imposing a necessity of abstinence, in order to free himself from all hesitation. So, if any one be forgetful or negligent of the necessary duties of piety, why may he not arouse his memory, and shake off his negligence by the imposition of a vow? In both cases, I confess, there is an appearance of pupilage; but, considered as helps of infirmity, such vows may be used with advantage by the inexperienced and imperfect. Vows, therefore, which respect one of these ends, especially those relating to external things, we shall affirm to be lawful, if they be supported by the approbation of God, if they be suitable to our calling, and if they be limited by the ability of grace which God has given us.

VI. It will not now be difficult to conclude what ideas ought to be entertained of vows universally. There is one vow common to all believers, which is made in baptism, and confirmed and established by us in the profession of our faith in the Catechism, and in the reception of the Lord's supper. For the sacraments resemble covenants, or instruments of agreement, by which God conveys his mercy to us, and in it eternal life; and we, on the other hand, promise him obedience. Now, the form, or at least the sum of the vow is, that, renouncing Satan, we devote ourselves to the service of God, to obey his holy commands and not to follow the corrupt inclinations of the flesh. This vow being sanctioned by the Scripture, and even required of all the children of God, it ought not to be doubted that it is holy and useful. It is no objection to this, that no man in the present life performs the perfect obedience which God requires of us; for as this stipulation is included in the covenant of grace, which contains both remission of sins and the spirit of sanctification, the promise which we then make is connected with, and presupposes our supplication for mercy, and our solicitation for assistance. In judging of particular vows, it is necessary to remember the three rules which we have given, which will enable us to form a correct estimate of the nature of every vow. Yet I would not be thought to carry my recommendation, even of those vows which I maintain to be holy, so far as to wish their daily use. For though I venture to determine nothing respecting the number or time, yet, if any person would follow my advice, he will make none but such as are sober, and of short duration. For if any one often recur to the making of many vows, all religion will be injured by their frequency, and there will be great danger of falling into superstition. If any one bind himself by a perpetual vow, he will not discharge it without great trouble and difficulty; or, wearied by its long continuance, he will at length violate it altogether.

VII. Now, it is evident what great superstition has for some ages prevailed in the world on this subject. One person vowed that he would drink no wine; as though abstinence from wine were a service in itself acceptable to God. Another obliged himself to fast; another to abstain from meat on certain days, which he had falsely imagined to possess some peculiar sanctity beyond others. There were some vows far more puerile, though not made by children. For it was esteemed great wisdom to vow pilgrimages to places of more than common holiness, and to perform the journey either on foot, or with the body half naked, that the merit might be augmented by the fatigue. These, and similar vows, with an incredible rage for which the world has long been inflamed, examined according to the rules which we have laid down, will not only be found to be vain and nugatory, but replete with manifest impiety. For whatever may be the judgment of the flesh, God holds nothing in greater abomination than services of human invention. The following pernicious and execrable opinions are also entertained; hypocrites, when they have performed these fooleries, suppose themselves to have attained a high degree of righteousness; they place the whole substance of piety in external observances; and they despise all who discover less concern about these things than themselves.

VIII. To enumerate all the particular kinds of vows, would

answer no good purpose. But, because monastic vows are held in very high veneration, as they seemed to be sanctioned by the public authority of the Church, it is proper to make a few brief remarks respecting them. In the first place, that no one may defend monachism, as it exists in the present day, under the pretence of ancient and long-continued prescription, it must be observed, that the mode of life in monasteries, in ancient times, was very different from what it is now. They were the retreats of those who wished to habituate themselves to the greatest austerity and patience; for the discipline attributed to the Lacedæmonians, under the laws of Lycurgus, was equalled, and even considerably exceeded in rigour, by that which was then practised among the monks. They slept on the ground without any beds or couches; they drank nothing but water; their food consisted entirely of bread, herbs, and roots; their principal dainties were oil, pease, and beans. They abstained from all delicacy of victuals and ornaments of the body. These things might be thought incredible, if they were not attested by persons who saw and experienced them, Gregory of Nazianzum, Basil, and Chrysostom. But it was by such probationary discipline that they prepared themselves for higher offices. For that the monastic colleges were at that time the seminaries, from which the Church was furnished with ministers, is sufficiently evident from the examples of those whom we have mentioned, who were all educated in monasteries, and from that situation were called to the episcopal office, as well as of many other great and excellent men of their age. And Augustine shows that the same custom of supplying ministers for the Church from the monasteries continued in his time; for the monks of the Island of Capraria are addressed by him in the following manner: "We exhort you in the Lord, brethren, that you keep your purpose, and persevere to the end; and that, if at any time your mother the Church shall have need of your labour, you neither undertake the charge with eager pride, nor refuse it with flattering idolence; but that you obey God with gentleness of heart; not preferring your leisure to the necessities of the Church, whom, if no good men had been disposed to assist in the production of her children, you cannot discover how you could yourselves have been born." He here speaks of the ministry, which is the means of the regeneration of believers. Again, in an epistle to Aurelius, he says: "It causes an occasion of falling to themselves, and a most injurious indignity to the ecclesiastical order, if the deserters of monasteries are chosen to clerical offices; while of those who remain in the monastery, we are accustomed to promote to such offices only the best and most approved. Unless, perhaps, as the common people say, A bad dancer is a good musician, so it should be jocularly said of us, a bad monk will be a good minister. It is too much to be lamented, if we stimulate monks to such ruinous pride, and think the clergy deserving of such heavy disgrace; whereas, sometimes even a good monk will hardly make a good priest, if he has sufficient continence, and yet is deficient in necessary learning." From these passages it appears that pious men were accustomed to prepare themselves, by monastic discipline, for the government of the Church, that they might be the better qualified to undertake such an important office. Not that all monks attained this end; or even aimed at it; for they were in general illiterate men, but those who were qualified were selected.

IX. But Augustine has given us a portraiture of the ancient monachism, principally in two places; in his treatise On the Manners of the Catholic Church, in which he defends the sanctity of that profession against the calumnies of the Manichæans; and in another book, On the Labour of Monks, in which he inveighs against some degenerate monks, who had begun to corrupt that order. The different things which he states, I shall here collect in a brief summary, using, as far as possible, his own words. "Despising the allurements of this world, united in a common life of the strictest chastity and holiness, they spend their time together, living in prayers, in readings, and in conferences, neither inflated with pride, nor turbulent with obstinacy, nor pale with envy. No one possesses any thing of his own; no one is burdensome to another. By the labour of their hands, they procure those things which are sufficient to support the body, without hindering the mind from devotion to God. Their work they deliver to those who are called Deans. These Deans dispose of every thing with great care, and render an account to one, whom they call Father. Most holy in their manners, preëminent in divine learning, and excelling in every virtue, these Fathers, without any pride, consult the welfare of those whom they call children, commanding them with great authority, and obeyed by them with great cheerfulness. At the close of the day, while yet fasting, every one comes forth from his cell, and they all assemble to hear the Father; and each of these Fathers is surrounded by at least three thousand men," (he is speaking chiefly of Egypt and the East;) "there they take some bodily refreshment, as much as is sufficient for life and health; every one restraining his appetite that he may make but a sparing use even of the provisions placed before him, which are in small quantities, and of the plainest description. That they not only abstain from animal food and from wine, in order to repress libidinous desires, but from such things as stimulate the appetite with greater power, in proportion to the opinion entertained by some persons of their purity; under which pretence a vile longing after exquisite meats, with the exception of animal food, is wont to be ridiculously and shamefully defended. Whatever remains beyond their necessary food, (and the surplus is considerable, both from the diligence of their hands, and from the abstemiousness of their meals,) is distributed to the poor, with greater care than if it had been earned by those who distribute it. For they are not anxious to have an abundance of these things, but all their concern is, that none of their abundance may remain with them." Afterwards, having mentioned their austerity, of which he had seen examples at Milan and other places, he says, "In these circumstances, no one is urged to austerities which he is unable to bear; there is no imposition on any one, of that which he refuses; nor is he condemned by the rest, because he confesses himself too weak to imitate them; for they remember the high commendations given of charity; they remember that to the pure, all things are pure. (*i*) Therefore all their industry is exerted, not in rejecting certain kinds of food as polluted, but in subduing concupiscence and preserving the love of the brethren. They remember that it is said, Meats for the belly, and the belly for meats; but God shall destroy both it and them. (*k*) Yet many strong persons abstain on account of the weak. Many have a different reason for doing it; they are fond of living on meaner and less sumptuous food.

(*i*) Titus i. 15. (*k*) 1 Cor. vi. 13.

These persons, therefore, who are abstemious when in perfect health, if a state of indisposition requires, partake, without any fear, when they are sick. Many drink no wine; but this is not from an apprehension of being defiled with it; for they most humanely cause it to be given to those who are languid, and cannot obtain health of body without it; and some, who foolishly refuse it, they admonish, with brotherly affection, to beware lest their vain superstition debilitate them rather than promote their holiness. Thus they diligently exercise themselves in piety: but they know that the exercise of the body extends only to a short time. Charity is principally observed; to charity the food, the conversation, the apparel, the countenance, are subservient. They all assemble and combine into one charity; to violate this, is accounted unlawful, and a sin against God; if any one resist charity, he is expelled and shunned; if any one offend against it, he is not suffered to remain a single day." As Augustine appears, in these passages, to have exhibited a portraiture of the true character of ancient monachism, I have thought proper, notwithstanding their length, to insert them here; for I saw that, however I might study brevity, yet I should go into still greater length, if I were to collect the same things from different authors.

X. My design here is not to pursue the whole argument, but merely to point out, by the way, the characters of the monks who belonged to the ancient Church, and the nature of the monastic profession at that period, that the judicious readers may be able, from a comparison, to judge of the effrontery of those who plead antiquity in support of the monachism of the present day. When Augustine gives us a description of holy and legitimate monachism, he excludes from it all rigid exaction or imposition of those things which the Lord in his word has left free. But there is nothing at the present day more severely enforced. For they consider it a crime, never to be expiated, for any one to deviate in the minutest particular from the rules prescribed in the colour or shape of their apparel, the kind of food, or other frivolous and uninteresting ceremonies. Augustine strenuously contends, that it is not lawful for monks to live in idleness at the expense of others. He denies that there was such an example to be found in his time in any well regulated monastery. The present monks place the principal part of their sanctity in idleness. For if they were divested of idleness, what would become of that contemplative life, in which they boast of excelling other men, and of making near approaches to the life of angels? In fine, Augustine requires a monachism which would be no other than an exercise and assistance in the duties of piety, which are enjoined on all Christians. What! when he represents charity as the principal and almost only rule of it, can we suppose him to be commending a conspiracy, by which a few men are closely united to each other, and separated from the whole body of the Church? On the contrary, he would have them to enlighten others by their example, in order to the preservation of the unity of the Church. In both these respects, the nature of modern monachism, is so different, that it is scarely possible to find any thing more dissimilar or opposite. For, not content with that piety, to the study of which Jesus Christ commands his servants constantly to devote themselves, our present monks imagine I know not what new kind of piety, in the mediation of which they are become more perfect than all others.

XI. If they deny this, I would wish them to inform me why they dignify their order alone with the title of *perfection*, and deny this character to all the callings appointed by God. I am not unacquainted with their sophistical solution, that it is so called, not as containing perfection in it, but because it is the best calculated of all callings for the attainment of perfection. When they wish to elevate themselves in the estimation of the people, to entrap inexperienced and ignorant youths, to assert their privileges, to extol their own dignity to the degradation of others, they boast of being in a state of perfection. When they are so closely pressed, that they cannot defend such empty arrogance, they have recourse to this subterfuge—that they have not yet attained perfection, but that they are in a condition more favourable than any others for aspiring towards it. In the mean time they retain the admiration of the people, as though the monastic life, and that alone, were angelic, perfect, and purified from every blemish. Under this pretext they carry on a most lucrative traffic; but their moderation lies buried in a few books. Who does not see that this is an intolerable mockery? But let us argue the case as if they really attributed no higher honour to their profession, than to call it a state adapted to the attainment of perfection. Still, by giving it this designation, they distinguished it, as by a peculiar mark, from all other modes of life. And who can bear that such honour should be transferred to an institution, which has never received from God even a single syllable of approbation, and that such indignity should be cast on all the other callings of God, which have not only been enjoined, but adorned with signal commendations by his most holy word? And what an outrageous insult is offered to God, when a mere human invention is preferred beyond all the kinds of life which he has appointed and celebrated by his own testimony!

XII. Now, let them charge me with a calumny in what I have already alleged, that they are not content with the rule which God has prescribed to his servants. Though I were silent on the subject, they furnish more than sufficient ground for their own accusation; for they openly teach that they take upon themselves a greater burden than Christ laid upon his disciples, because they promise to keep the evangelical counsels, which inculcate the love of our enemies, and prohibit the desire of revenge and profane swearing, and which, they say, are not binding on Christians at large. What antiquity will they plead here? This notion never entered into the mind of one of the ancients. They all, with one consent, declare that there was not a syllable uttered by Christ which we are not bound to obey; and without any hesitation they uniformly and expressly represent the passages in question as commands, which these sagacious interpreters pretend to have been delivered by Christ merely as counsels. But as we have already shown that this is a most pestilent error, it may suffice to have briefly remarked here, that the monachism which exists at present, is founded on the opinion, which justly deserves to be execrated by all believers, that some rule of life may be imagined more perfect than the common one given by God to all the Church. Whatever superstructure is raised on this foundation, cannot but be abominable.

XIII. But they adduce another argument in proof of their perfection, which they consider as most conclusive; our Lord said to the young man who inquired what was the perfection of righteousness, "If thou wilt be perfect, go and sell that thou hast, and give to the poor." (*l*) Whether they do this, I shall not now dispute; let us at present put the case that they do. They boast, therefore, that they have been made perfect by forsaking all that they have. If the whole of perfection consist in this, what does Paul mean, when he says, "Though I bestow all my goods to feed the poor, and have not charity, I am nothing?" (*m*) What kind of perfection is that which is reduced to nothing by the absence of charity? Here they will be obliged to answer, that though this is the principal, yet it is not the only work of perfection. But here also they are contradicted by Paul, who hesitates not to make "charity," without any such renunciation, "the bond of perfection." (*n*) If it is certain, that there is no discordance between the Master and the disciple,—and Paul explicitly denies the perfection of a man to consist in the renunciation of his property, and, on the other hand, asserts that it may exist without that relinquishment,—it is necessary to examine in what sense we are to understand the declaration of Christ, "If thou wilt be perfect, go and sell that thou hast." Now, there will be no obscurity in the sense, if we consider, what ought always to be considered in all the discourses of Christ, to whom the words are addressed. A young man inquires, "What good thing shall I do, that I may inherit eternal life?" (*o*) As the question related to works, Christ refers him to the law; and that justly; for, considered in itself, it is the way of eternal life and is no otherwise insufficient to conduct us to salvation, than in consequence of our depravity. By this answer Christ declared, that he taught no other system of life than that which had anciently been delivered in the law of God. Thus he at the same time gave a testimony to the divine law as the doctrine of perfect righteousness, and precluded all calumnies, that he might not appear, by inculcating a new rule of life, to incite the people to a departure from the law. The young man, not indeed from badness of heart, but infected with vain confidence, replies respecting the precepts of the law, "All these things have I kept from my youth up." (*p*) It is certain beyond all doubt, that he was at an immense distance from that which he boasted of having attained; and had his boast been true, he would have

(*l*) Matt. xix. 21. (*m*) 1 Cor. xiii. 3. (*n*) Col. iii. 14.
(*o*) Matt. xix. 16. (*p*) Matt. xix. 20.

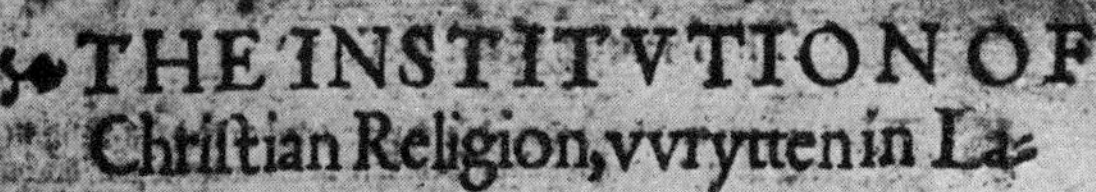

THE INSTITVTION OF Christian Religion, vvrytten in Latine by maister Ihon Caluin, and translated into Englysh according to the authors last edition.

Seen and allowed according to the order appointed in the Quenes maiesties iniunctions.

Imprinted at London by
Reinolde Vvolfe & Richarde Harison.
Anno. 1561.

Cum priuilegio ad imprimendum solum.

Title-Page of First English Translation, London, 1561
From the Library of the Department of History.

wanted nothing necessary to complete perfection. For it has been already proved that the law contains in itself a perfect righteousness; and it appears from this passage that the observance of it is called *the entrance* into eternal life. To teach him how little proficiency he had made in that righteousness, which he too confidently replied that he had fulfilled, it was necessary to investigate and expose a vice which lay concealed in his heart. He abounded in riches, and his heart was fixed on them. Because he was not sensible of this secret wound, therefore, Christ probes it. "Go," says he, "sell all that thou hast." If he had been so good an observer of the law as he imagined, he would not have gone away sorrowful on hearing this answer. For he who loves God with all his heart, not only esteems as worthless whatever is inconsistent with his love, but also abominates it as pernicious. Therefore, when Christ commands a rich and avaricious man to relinquish all his wealth, it is just the same as if he commanded an ambitious man to renounce all his honours, a voluptuous man to abandon all his delicacies, and an unchaste man to forsake all the instruments of temptation. Thus consciences, which receive no impression from general admonitions, require to be recalled to a particular sense of their own guilt. It is in vain, therefore, to extend this particular argument to a general maxim, as though Christ placed all the perfection of man in the renunciation of his possessions, whereas he only meant by this direction to drive this young man, who betrayed such excessive self-complacency, into a sense of his malady, that he might perceive himself to be still very far from the perfect obedience of the law, to which he arrogantly and falsely pretended. I confess that this passage was misunderstood by some of the fathers, and that their misconstruction gave rise to an affectation of voluntary poverty; so that they were supposed to be the only happy persons, who renounced all earthly things, and devoted themselves entirely to Christ. But I trust that the explication which I have given will be satisfactory to all good and peaceable persons, so as to leave them in no doubt of the true meaning of Christ.

XIV. Nothing, however, was further from the intention of the fathers, than to establish such a perfection as has since been fabricated by these hooded sophisters, which goes to set up two kinds of Christianity. For no one had then given birth to that sacrilegious dogma, which compares the monastic profession to baptism, and even openly asserts it to be a species of second baptism. Who can doubt that the fathers would have sincerely abhorred such blasphemy? As to the concluding observation of Augustine, respecting the ancient monks, that they devoted themselves wholly to charity, what need is there for a word to be said to demonstrate it to be altogether inapplicable to this modern profession? The fact itself declares, that all who retire into monasteries separate themselves from the Church. For do they not separate themselves from the legitimate society of believers, by taking to themselves a peculiar ministry and a private administration of the sacraments? What is a disruption of the communion of the Church, if this be not? And to pursue the comparison which I have commenced, and to conclude it at once, what resemblance have they in this respect to the monks of ancient times? Though they lived in a state of seclusion from other men, they had no separate Church; they received the sacraments with others; they attended the solemn assemblies to hear preaching, and to unite in prayers with the company of believers; and there they formed a part of the people. In erecting a private altar for themselves, what have the present monks done, but broken the bond of unity? For they have excommunicated themselves from the general body of the Church, and have shown contempt of the ordinary ministry, by which it has pleased God that peace and charity should be preserved among his servants. All the present monasteries, therefore, I maintain to be so many conventicles of schismatics, who disturb the order of the Church, and have been cut off from the legitimate society of believers. And to place this division beyond all doubt, they have assumed various names of sects; and have not been ashamed to glory in that which Paul execrates beyond all possibility of exaggeration. Unless we suppose that Christ was divided by the Corinthians, when every one boasted of his particular teacher; (*q*) and that it is now no derogation from the honour of Christ, when, instead of the name of Christians, some are called Benedictines, others Franciscans,

---

(*q*) 1 Cor. i. 12, 13; iii. 4.

others Dominicans; and when they haughtily assume these titles to themselves as the badges of their religious profession, from an affectation of being distinguished from the general body of Christians.

XV. The differences which I have stated, between the ancient monks and those of the present age, relate not to manners, but to the profession itself. Let it, therefore, be remembered by the readers, that I have spoken of monachism rather than of monks, and have censured those faults which are not merely chargeable on the lives of a few, but which are inseparable from the life itself. The great dissimilarity of their manners can hardly require a particular representation. It is obvious, that there is no order of men more polluted with all the turpitude of vice; none more disgraced by factions, animosities, cabals, and intrigues. In some few convents, indeed, they live in chastity; if chastity it must be called, where concupiscence is so far restrained as not to be publicly infamous; but it is scarcely possible to find one convent in ten which is not rather a brothel than a sanctuary of chastity. What frugality is there in their food? They are exactly like so many swine fattening in a sty. But lest they should complain that I handle them too roughly, I proceed no further; though in the few particulars upon which I have touched, whoever knows the matter of fact will acknowledge that I have confined my self to the simple truth. Augustine, at a time when, according to his own testimony, monks were so eminent for the strictest chastity, yet complains that there were many vagabonds among them, who, by wicked arts and impostures, extorted money from the unwary, who exercised a scandalous traffic by carrying about the relics of martyrs, and even sold the bones of any dead men as the bones of martyrs, and who brought disgrace on the order by a great number of similar crimes. As he declares that he had seen no better men than those who had been improved in monasteries, so he complains that he had seen no worse men than those who had been corrupted in monasteries. What would he say, at the present day, to see almost all monasteries, not only filled, but overflowing, with so many and such desperate vices? I say nothing but what is notorious to every person; though this censure is not applicable to all without any exception. For as the rule and discipline of holy living has never been so well established in monasteries, but that there were always some drones very different from the rest, so I do not say that the monks of the present day have so far degenerated from that holy antiquity, that there are not still some good men among their body; but they are few, dispersed and concealed among a vast multitude of the wicked and abandoned; and they are not only held in contempt, but insulted and molested, and sometimes even treated with cruelty by the rest; who, according to a proverb of the Milesians, think that no good man ought to be suffered to remain among them.

XVI. By this comparison of ancient and modern monachism I trust I have succeeded in my design of evincing the fallacy of the plea, which the present men of the hood allege in defence of their profession, from the example of the primitive Church; as they differ from the early monks just as apes do from men. At the same time, I admit that even in the ancient system which Augustine commends, there is something which I cannot altogether approve. I grant, they discovered no superstition in the external exercises of a too rigid discipline; but I maintain that they were not free from excessive affectation and misguided zeal. It seemed a good thing to forsake their property in order to exempt themselves from all earthly solicitude; but God sets a higher value on pious exertions for the government of a family, when a holy father of a family, free from all avarice, ambition, and other corrupt passions, devotes himself to this object, that he may serve God in a particular calling. It is a beautiful thing to live the life of a philosopher in retirement, at a distance from the society of men; but it is not the part of Christian charity for a man to act as if he hated all mankind, withdrawing to the solitude of a desert, and abandoning the principal duties which the Lord has commanded. Though we should grant that there was no other evil in this profession, yet certainly this was not a small one, that it introduced a useless and pernicious example into the Church.

XVII. Let us now examine the nature of the vows by which monks in the present day are initiated into this celebrated order. In the first place, their design is to institute a new service, in order to merit the favour of God; therefore I conclude, from the principles already established, that whatever they vow is an abomination in the sight of God. Secondly, without any regard to the calling of God, and without any approbation from him, they invent for themselves a new mode of life, in conformity with their own inclinations; therefore I maintain it to be a rash and unlawful attempt, because their consciences have nothing to rest upon before God, and "whatsoever is not of faith, is sin." (*r*) Thirdly, they bind themselves to many corrupt and impious services, comprehended in the monachism of the present day; therefore I contend, that they are not consecrated to God, but to the devil. For why was it lawful for the prophet to say of the Israelites, that "they sacrificed unto devils, not to God," (*s*) only because they had corrupted the true worship of God with profane ceremonies; and why shall it not be lawful for us to say the same of the monks, whose assumption of the hood is accompanied with the yoke of a thousand impious superstitions? Now, what is the nature of their vows? They promise to God to maintain perpetual virginity, as if they had previously stipulated with him that he should exempt them from the necessity of marriage. They have no room to plead, that they make this vow merely in a reliance on the grace of God; for as he declares that it is not given to all men, (*t*) we have no right to entertain a confidence that we shall receive the special gift. Let those who possess it use it: if they experience disquietude from the stimulations of passion, let them have recourse to his aid by whom alone they can be strengthened to resist. If they are unsuccessful, let them not despise the remedy which is offered to them. For those who are denied the gift of continence, are undoubtedly called to marriage by the voice of God. By continence I mean, not a mere abstinence of the body from fornication, but an unpolluted chastity of mind. For Paul enjoins the avoidance not only of external impurity, but also of the internal burning of libidinous desire. (*v*) It has been a custom, they say, from time immemorial, for persons who intended to devote themselves entirely to the Lord, to bind themselves by a vow of continence. I confess that this custom was practised in the early ages; but I cannot admit those ages to have been so free from every fault, that whatever was done then

(*r*) Rom. xiv. 23.
(*s*) Deut. xxxii. 17.
(*t*) Matt. xix. 11.
(*v*) 1 Cor. vii. 9.

must be received as a rule. And it was only by degrees that in process of time things were carried to such an extreme of rigour that no one, after having made the vow, was permitted to recall it. This is evident from Cyprian. "If virgins have faithfully dedicated themselves to God, let them persevere in modesty and chastity without any disguise. Thus, being firm and constant, they may expect the reward of virginity. But if they will not, or cannot persevere, it is better for them to be married, than with their pleasure to fall into the fire." With what reproaches would they now hesitate to stigmatize a person who would wish to introduce such a reasonable limitation of the vow of continence? They have widely departed, therefore, from the ancient custom, in refusing to admit the least moderation or relaxation, if any one be found incapable of performing the vow; and not only so, but they are not ashamed to pronounce that he commits a greater sin, if he remedies his intemperance by taking a wife, than if he contaminates his body and soul with fornication.

XVIII. But they still pursue the argument, and endeavour to show that vows of this kind were in use in the times of the apostles; because Paul says that widows who, after having been received into the public service of the church, married, had "cast off their first faith." (*w*) I do not deny that widows who dedicated themselves and their services to the Church, thereby entered into a tacit obligation never to marry again; not because they placed any religion in such abstinence, as began to be the case afterwards; but because they could not discharge that office without being at their own disposal, free from the restraint of marriage. But if, after having pledged their faith, they contemplated a second marriage, what was this but renouncing the calling of God? It is no wonder, therefore, if he says that with such desires "they wax wanton against Christ." Afterwards, by way of amplification, he subjoins, that they failed of performing what they had promised to the Church, so that they even violated and annulled their first faith pledged in baptism; which includes an engagement from every one to fulfil the duties of his calling. Unless it be thought better to understand the meaning to be, that having, as

(*w*) 1 Tim. v. 12.

it were, lost all shame, they would thenceforward have no longer any regard for virtue, but would abandon themselves to every kind of profligacy, and in a licentious and dissolute life exhibit the greatest contrariety to the character of Christian women—an interpretation which I much approve. We reply, therefore, that those widows, who were then received into the service of the Church, imposed on themselves the condition of perpetual widowhood; if they afterwards married, we easily understand their situation to have been as Paul states, that, casting off shame, they betrayed an insolence unbecoming Christian women; and that thus they not only sinned in breaking their faith pledged to the Church, but in departing from the common obligations of pious females. But first, I deny that they engaged to remain in a state of widowhood for any other reason than because marriage would be altogether incompatible with the office which they undertook; or that they bound themselves to widowhood at all, except as far as the necessity of their vocation should require. Secondly, I do not admit that their profession was so binding, but that even then it was better for them to marry than to be inflamed with concupiscence, or to be guilty of any impurity of conduct. Thirdly, I observe that Paul prescribes that age which is generally beyond all danger, forbidding any to be received under threescore years old; and especially when he directs that the choice shall be limited to those who have been content with one marriage, and have thus already given proof of their continence. And we condemn the vow of celibacy for no other reason, but because it is unjustly considered as a service acceptable to God, and is rashly made by those who have not the power to keep it.

XIX. But how was it possible to apply this passage of Paul to nuns? For widows were appointed deaconesses, not to charm God by songs or unintelligible murmurs, and to spend the rest of their time in idleness; but to serve the poor on behalf of the whole Church, and to employ themselves with all attention, earnestness, and diligence, in the duties of charity. They made a vow of widowhood, not with a view of performing any service to God in abstaining from marriage, but merely that they might be more at liberty for the discharge of their office. Lastly, they made this vow, not in their youth, nor in the flower of their age, to learn afterwards, by late experience, over what a precipice they had thrown themselves; but, when they appeared to have passed all danger, they made a vow equally consistent with safety and with piety. But, not to urge the two former considerations, it is sufficient to observe, that it was not allowable for women to be admitted to make vows of continence before the age of sixty years; since the apostle says, "Let not a widow be taken into the number under threescore years old." "I will that the younger women marry and bear children." (*x*) The subsequent admission of this vow at the age of forty-eight years, then forty years, and then thirty, can by no means be excused; and it is still more intolerable that unhappy girls, before they are old enough to be capable of knowing or having any experience of themselves, should be inveigled by fraud and compelled by threats to entangle themselves in those execrable snares. I shall not stay to oppose the other two vows, made by monks and nuns, of poverty and obedience. I will only observe, that beside the many superstitions with which, under existing circumstances, they are interwoven, they appear to be framed for the purpose of mocking both God and men. But that we may not seem too severe in agitating every particular point, we shall content ourselves with the general repetition already given.

XX. The nature of those vows which are legitimate and acceptable to God, I think, has been sufficiently declared. Yet as timid and inexperienced consciences, even after they are dissatisfied with a vow, and convinced of its impropriety, nevertheless fell doubts respecting the obligation, and are grievously distressed, on the one hand, from a dread of violating their promise to God, and, on the other, from a fear of incurring greater guilt by observing it, it is necessary here to offer them some assistance to enable them to extricate themselves from this difficulty. Now, to remove every scruple at once, I remark, that all vows, not legitimate or rightly made, as they are of no value with God, so they ought to have no force with us. For if in human contracts no promises are obligatory upon us, but those to which the party with whom we contract wishes to bind us, it is absurd to consider

(*x*) 1 Tim. v. 9, 14.

ourselves constrained to the performance of those things which God never requires of us; especially as our works cannot be good unless they please God, and are accompanied with the testimony of our conscience that he accepts them. For this remains a fixed principle, that "whatsoever is not of faith, is sin;" (*y*) by which Paul intends, that whatever work is undertaken with doubts, is consequently sinful, because all good works spring from faith, by which we are assured of their acceptance with God. Therefore, if it be not lawful for a Christian man to attempt any thing without this assurance, and if any one through ignorance has made a rash vow, and afterwards discovered his error, why should he not desist from the performance of it? since vows inconsiderately made, not only are not binding, but ought of necessity to be cancelled; and, also, as they are not only of no value in the sight of God, but are an abomination to him, as we have already demonstrated. It is useless to argue any longer on a subject which does not require it. This one argument appears to me sufficient to tranquillize pious consciences, and to liberate them from every scruple—That all works not proceeding from a pure source, and directed to a legitimate end, are rejected by God, and rejected in such a manner that he forbids our continuance, as much as our commencement, of them. Hence we may conclude, that vows which have originated in error and superstition, are of no value with God, and ought to be relinquished by us.

XXI. This solution will furnish an answer to the calumnies of the wicked, in defence of those who leave monachism for some honourable way of life. They are heavily accused of breach of faith and perjury; having broken, as it is commonly supposed, the indissoluble bond which held them to God and the Church. But I maintain that there is no bond, where that which man confirms is abrogated by God. Besides, though we should grant that they were bound while they were involved in error and ignorance of God,—now, since they have been enlightened with the knowledge of the truth, I maintain that the grace of Christ has delivered them from the obligation. For if the cross of Christ possesses such efficacy as to deliver us from the curse, under which we were held

(*y*) Rom. xiv. 23.

by the law of God, how much more, then, shall it extricate us from other bonds, which are nothing but delusive snares of Satan! Whomsoever, therefore, Christ illuminates with the light of his gospel, there is no doubt that he liberates them from all the snares in which they had entangled themselves by superstition. Though they are not at a loss for another defence, if they are not qualified to live in celibacy. For if an impossible vow be the ruin of souls, which it is the will of the Lord to save and not to destroy,—it follows that it is not right to persevere in it. But the impossibility of an observance of the vow of continence by those who are not endued with a special gift, we have already shown, and without my saying a word, experience itself declares; for it is notorious what extreme impurity prevails in almost all monasteries; and if any of them appear more virtuous and modest than the rest, it does not follow that they are really more chaste, because they conceal the vice of unchastity. Thus God inflicts awful punishments on the audacity of men, when, forgetting their weakness, they covet, in opposition to nature, that which is denied them, and, despising the remedies which God had put into their hands, indulge a contumacious and obstinate presumption that they are able to overcome the vice of incontinence. For what shall we call it but contumacy, when any one who is admonished that he stands in need of marriage, and that it has been given to him by the Lord as a remedy, not only contemns it, but binds himself by an oath to persevere in that contempt?

CHAPTER XIV

The Sacraments

CONNECTED with the preaching of the gospel, another assistance and support for our faith is presented to us in the sacraments; on the subject of which it is highly important to lay down some certain doctrine, that we may learn for what end they were instituted, and how they ought to be used. In the first place, it is necessary to consider what a sacrament is. Now, I think it will be a simple and appropriate definition, if we say that it is an outward sign, by which the Lord seals in our consciences the promises of his good-will towards us, to support the weakness of our faith; and we on our part testify our piety towards him, in his presence and that of angels, as well as before men. It may, however, be more briefly defined, in other words, by calling it a testimony of the grace of God towards us, confirmed by an outward sign, with a reciprocal attestation of our piety towards him. Whichever of these definitions be chosen, it conveys exactly the same meaning as that of Augustine, which states a sacrament to be "a visible sign of a sacred thing," or "a visible form of invisible grace;" but it expresses the thing itself with more clearness and precision; for as his conciseness leaves some obscurity, by which many inexperienced persons may be misled, I have endeavoured to render the subject plainer by more words, that no room might be left for any doubt.

II. The reason why the ancient fathers used this word in such a sense is very evident. For whenever the author of the old common version of the New Testament wanted to render the Greek word μυστηριον, *mystery*, into Latin, especially where it related to Divine things, he used the word *sacramentum*, "sacrament." Thus, in the Epistle to the Ephesians, "Having made known unto us the *mystery* of his will." (*a*) Again: "If ye have heard of the dispensation of the grace of God which is given me to you-ward; how that by revelation he made known unto me the *mystery*." (*b*) In the Epistle to the Colossians: "The *mystery* which hath been hid from ages and from generations, but now is made manifest to his saints; to whom God would make known what is the riches of the glory of this *mystery*." (*c*) Again, to Timothy: "Great is the *mystery* of godliness; God was manifest in the flesh." (*d*) In all these places, where the word *mystery* is used, the author of that version has rendered it *sacrament*. He would not say *arcanum*, or *secret*, lest he should appear to degrade the majesty of the subject. Therefore he has used the word *sacrament* for a sacred or Divine secret. In this signification it frequently occurs in the writings of the fathers. And it is well known, that baptism and the Lord's supper, which the Latins denominate *sacraments*, are called *mysteries* by the Greeks; a synonymous use of the terms, which removes every doubt. And hence the word *sacrament* came to be applied to those signs which contained a representation of sublime and spiritual things; which is also remarked by Augustine, who says, "It would be tedious to dispute respecting the diversity of signs, which, when they pertain to Divine things, are called *sacraments*."

III. Now, from the definition which we have established, we see that there is never any sacrament without an antecedent promise of God, to which it is subjoined as an appendix, in order to confirm and seal the promise itself, and to certify and ratify it to us; which means God foresees to be necessary, in the first place on account of our ignorance and dulness, and in the next place on account of our weakness; and yet, strictly speaking, not so much for the confirmation of his sacred word, as for our establishment in the faith of it. For the truth of God is sufficiently solid and certain in itself, and can receive no better confirmation from

---

(*a*) Eph. i. 9.
(*b*) Eph. iii. 2, 3.
(*c*) Col. i. 26, 27.
(*d*) 1 Tim. iii. 16.

any other quarter than from itself; but our faith being slender and weak, unless it be supported on every side, and sustained by every assistance, immediately shakes, fluctuates, totters, and falls. And as we are corporeal, always creeping on the ground, cleaving to terrestrial and carnal objects, and incapable of understanding or conceiving of any thing of a spiritual nature, our merciful Lord, in his infinite indulgence, accommodates himself to our capacity, condescending to lead us to himself even by these earthly elements, and in the flesh itself to present to us a mirror of spiritual blessings. "For if we were incorporeal," as Chrysostom says, "he would have given us these things pure and incorporeal. Now because we have souls enclosed in bodies, he gives us spiritual things under visible emblems; not because there are such qualities in the nature of the things presented to us in the sacraments, but because they have been designated by God to this signification."

IV. This is what is commonly said, that a sacrament consists of the word and the outward sign. For we ought to understand the *word*, not of a murmur uttered without any meaning or faith, a mere whisper like a magical incantation, supposed to possess the power of consecrating the elements, but of the gospel preached, which instructs us in the signification of the visible sign. That which is commonly practised under the tyranny of the pope, therefore, involves a gross profanation of the mysteries; for they have thought it sufficient for the priest to mutter over the form of consecration, while the people are gazing in ignorance. Indeed, they have taken effectual care that it should be all unintelligible to the people; for they have pronounced the consecration in Latin, before illiterate men; and have at length carried superstition to such a pitch as to consider it not rightly performed, unless it be done in a hoarse murmur, which few could hear. But Augustine speaks in a very different manner of the sacramental word. "Let the word," says he, "be added to the element, and it will become a sacrament. For whence does the water derive such great virtue, as at once to touch the body and purify the heart, except from the word? not because it is spoken, but because it is believed. For in the word itself the transient sound is one thing, the permanent virtue is another. 'This is the word of faith which we preach,' (*e*) says the apostle. Whence it is said of the Gentiles, in the Acts of the Apostles, that 'God purifies their hearts by faith.' (*f*) And the apostle Peter says, 'Baptism doth also now save us, (not the putting away of the filth of the flesh, but the answer of a good conscience towards God.)' (*g*) 'This is the word of faith which we preach,' by which baptism is consecrated to endue it with a purifying virtue." We see how he makes the preaching of the word necessary to the production of faith. And we need not labour much to prove this, because it is very plain what Christ did, what he commanded us to do, what the apostles followed, and what the purer Church observed. Even from the beginning of the world, whenever God gave the holy fathers any sign, it is well known to have been inseparably connected with some doctrine, without which our senses would only be astonished with the mere view of it. Therefore, when we hear mention made of the sacramental word, let us understand it of the promise, which, being audibly and intelligibly preached by the minister, instructs the people in the meaning and tendency of the sign.

V. Nor ought any attention to be paid to some, who endeavour to oppose this by a dilemma which discovers more subtlety than solidity. They say, Either we know that the word of God which precedes the sacrament is the true will of God, or we do not know it. If we know it, then we learn nothing new from the sacrament which follows. If we do not know it, neither shall we learn it from the sacrament, the virtue of which lies entirely in the word. Let it be concisely replied, that the seals appended to charters, patents, and other public instruments, are nothing, taken by themselves; because they would be appended to no purpose, if the parchment had nothing written upon it; and yet they nevertheless confirm and authenticate what is written on the instruments to which they are annexed. Nor can it be objected that this similitude has been recently invented by us; for it has been used by Paul himself, who calls circumcision a *seal,* (*h*) σφραγιδα, in a passage where he is professedly contending that circumcision did not constitute the righteousness of Abraham, but was a seal of that covenant, in the faith of which he had already been justified.

(*e*) Rom. x. 8. (*f*) Acts xv. 9.
(*g*) 1 Peter iii. 21. (*h*) Rom. iv. 11.

And what is there that ought to give any man much offence, if we teach that the promise is sealed by the sacraments, while it is evident that among the promises themselves one is confirmed by another? For in proportion to its superior clearness, it is the better calculated for the support of faith. Now, the sacraments bring us the clearest promises, and have this peculiarity beyond the word, that they give us a lively representation of them, as in a picture. Nor ought we to regard the objection, frequently urged, from the distinction between sacraments and seals of civil instruments, that while they both consist of the carnal elements of this world, the former cannot be fit to seal the promises of God, which are spiritual and eternal, as the latter are accustomed to be appended to seal the edicts of princes relative to frail and transitory things. For the believer, when the sacraments are placed before his eyes, does not confine himself to that carnal spectacle; but by those steps of analogy which I have indicated, rises in pious contemplation to the sublime mysteries which are concealed under the sacramental symbols.

VI. And since the Lord calls his promises *covenants,* and the sacraments *seals of covenants,* we may draw a similitude from the covenants of men. The ancients, in confirmation of their engagements, were accustomed to kill a sow. But what would have been the slaughter of a sow, if it had not been accompanied, and even preceded, by some words? For sows were often slaughtered without any latent or sublime mystery. What is the contact of one man's right hand with that of another, since hands are not unfrequently joined in hostility? But when words of friendship and compact have preceded, the obligations of covenants are confirmed by such signs, notwithstanding they have been previously conceived, proposed, and determined in words. Sacraments, therefore, are exercises, which increase and strengthen our faith in the word of God; and because we are corporeal, they are exhibited under corporeal symbols, to instruct us according to our dull capacities, and to lead us by the hand as so many young children. For this reason Augustine calls a sacrament "a visible word;" because it represents the promises of God portrayed as in a picture, and places before our eyes an image of them, in which every lineament is strikingly expressed. Other similitudes may also be adduced for the better elucidation of the nature of sacraments; as if we call them *pillars of our faith;* for as an edifice rests on its foundation, and yet, from the addition of pillars placed under it, receives an increase of stability, so faith rests on the word of God as its foundation; but when the sacraments are added to it as pillars, they bring with them an accession of strength. Or if we call them *mirrors,* in which we may contemplate the riches of grace which God imparts to us; for in the sacraments, as we have already observed, he manifests himself to us as far as our dulness is capable of knowing him, and testifies his benevolence and love towards us more expressly than he does by his word.

VII. Nor is there any force in their reasoning, when they contend that the sacraments are not testimonies of the grace of God, because they are often administered to the wicked, who yet do not, in consequence of this, experience God to be more propitious to them, but rather procure to themselves more grievous condemnation. For, by the same argument, neither would the gospel be a testimony of the grace of God, because it is heard by many who despise it, nor even Christ himself, who was seen and known by multitudes, of whom very few received him. A similar observation may be applied to royal edicts; for great numbers of people despise and deride that seal of authentication, notwithstanding they know that it proceeded from the monarch to confirm his will; some utterly disregard it, as a thing not relating to them; others even hold it in execration; so that a survey of the correspondence of the two cases ought to produce greater approbation of the similitude which I have before used. Therefore it is certain that the Lord offers us his mercy, and a pledge of his grace, both in his holy word and in the sacraments; but it is not apprehended except by those who receive the word and sacraments with a certain faith; as the Father has offered and presented Christ to all for salvation, but he is not known and received by all. Augustine, intending to express this sentiment, somewhere says, that the efficacy of the word is displayed in the sacrament, "not because it is spoken, but because it is believed." Therefore Paul, when he is addressing believers, speaks of the sacraments so as to include in them the communion of Christ; as when he says, "As many of you have been baptized into Christ, have put on Christ." (*i*) Again: "By one Spirit are we all baptized into one body." (*k*) But when he speaks of the improper use of the sacraments, he attributes no more to them than to vain and useless figures; by which he signifies that, however impious persons and hypocrites, by their perversion of the sacraments, may destroy or obscure the effect of Divine grace in them, yet that, notwithstanding this, whenever and wherever God pleases, they afford a true testimony of the communion of Christ, and the Spirit of God himself exhibits and performs the very thing which they promise. We conclude, therefore, that sacraments are truly called testimonies of the grace of God, and are, as it were, seals of the benevolence he bears to us, which, by confirming it to our minds, sustain, cherish, strengthen, and increase our faith. The reasons which some are in the habit of objecting against this sentiment are exceedingly weak and frivolous. They allege, that if our faith be good, it cannot be made better; for that there is no real faith except that which rests on the mercy of God, without any wavering, instability, or distraction. It would have been better for such persons to pray, with the apostles, that the Lord would increase their faith, (*l*) than confidently to boast of such a perfection of faith, as no one of the sons of men ever yet attained, or ever will attain, in this life. Let them answer what kind of faith they suppose him to have possessed, who said, "Lord, I believe; help thou mine unbelief." (*m*) For even that, though yet only in its commencement, was a good faith, and capable of being improved by the removal of unbelief. But there is no argument which more fully refutes them than their own conscience; for if they confess themselves sinners, which, whatever they may wish, they cannot deny, they must be obliged to impute it to the imperfection of their faith.

VIII. But they say, Philip answered the eunuch, that he might be baptized "if" he "believed with all" his "heart." (*n*) And what room, they ask, is there here for the confirmation of baptism, where faith fills the whole heart? On the other hand, I ask them, whether they do not feel a large part of their heart destitute of faith, and whether they do not daily know some fresh increase

(*i*) Gal. iii. 27. (*k*) 1 Cor. xii. 13. (*l*) Luke xvii. 5.
(*m*) Mark ix. 24. (*n*) Acts viii. 37.

of it. A heathen gloried that he grew old in learning. We Christians are miserable indeed if we grow old in making no improvement, whose faith ought to be advancing from one stage to another till its attainment of perfect manhood. "To believe with all the heart," therefore, in this passage, is not to believe Christ in a perfect manner, but only signifies embracing him with sincerity of soul and firmness of mind; not to be filled with him, but to hunger, thirst, and sigh after him with ardent affection. It is the custom of the Scriptures to say that any thing is done with the whole heart which is done with sincerity of mind, as in these and other passages: "With my whole heart have I sought thee;" "I will praise the Lord with my whole heart." (*o*) On the contrary, when it rebukes the fraudulent and deceitful, it reproaches them with "a double heart." (*p*) Our adversaries further allege, that if faith be increased by the sacraments, the Holy Spirit must have been given in vain, whose work and influence it is to commence, to confirm, and to consummate faith. I confess that faith is the peculiar and entire work of the Holy Spirit, by whose illumination we know God and the treasures of his goodness, and without whose light our mind is too blind to be capable of any sight, and too stupid to be capable of the least relish of spiritual things. But instead of one favour of God, which they mention, we acknowledge three. For, first, the Lord teaches and instructs us by his word; secondly, he confirms us by his sacraments; lastly, he illuminates our minds by the light of his Holy Spirit, and opens an entrance into our hearts for the word and sacraments; which otherwise would only strike the ears and present themselves to the eyes, without producing the least effect upon the mind.

IX. With respect to the confirmation and increase of faith, therefore, I wish the reader to be apprized, and I conceive I have already expressed, in language too plain to be misunderstood, that I assign this office to the sacraments; not from an opinion of their possessing a perpetual inherent virtue, efficacious of itself to the advancement or confirmation of faith; but because they have been instituted by the Lord for the express purpose of pro-

---

(*o*) Psalm cxix. 10; cxi. 1; cxxxviii. 1. (*p*) Psalm xii. 2.

moting its establishment and augmentation. But they only perform their office aright when they are accompanied by the Spirit, that internal Teacher, by whose energy alone our hearts are penetrated, our affections are moved, and an entrance is opened for the sacraments into our souls. If he be absent, the sacraments can produce no more effect upon our minds than the splendour of the sun on blind eyes, or the sound of a voice on deaf ears. I make such a distinction and distribution, therefore, between the Spirit and the sacraments, that I consider all the energy of operation as belonging to the Spirit, and the sacraments as mere instruments, which, without his agency, are vain and useless, but which, when he acts and exerts his power in the heart, are fraught with surprising efficacy. Now, it is evident how, according to this opinion, the faith of a pious mind is confirmed by the sacraments; namely, as the eyes see by the light of the sun, and the ears hear by the sound of a voice: the light would have no effect upon the eyes, unless they had a natural faculty capable of being enlightened; and it would be in vain for the ears to be struck with any sound, if they had not been naturally formed for hearing. But if it be true, as we ought at once to conclude, that what the visive faculty is in our eyes towards our beholding the light, and the faculty of hearing is in our ears towards our perception of sound, such is the work of the Holy Spirit in our hearts for the formation, support, preservation, and establishment of our faith; then these two consequences immediately follow—that the sacraments are attended with no benefit without the influence of the Holy Spirit; and that, in hearts already instructed by that Teacher, they still subserve the confirmation and increase of faith. There is only this difference that our eyes and ears are naturally endued with the faculties of seeing and hearing, but Christ accomplishes this in our hearts by special and preternatural grace.

X. This reasoning will also serve for a solution of the objections with which some persons are greatly disturbed; that if we attribute to creatures either the increase or confirmation of faith, we derogate from the Spirit of God, whom we ought to acknowledge as its sole Author. For we do not, at the same time, deny him the praise of its confirmation and increase; but we assert that the way in which he increases and confirms our faith is by preparing our minds, by his inward illumination, to receive that confirmation which is proposed in the sacraments. If the way in which this has been expressed be too obscure, it shall be elucidated by the following similitude. If you intend to persuade a person to do a certain act, you will consider all the reasons calculated to draw him over to your opinion, and to constrain him to submit to your advice. But you will make no impression upon him, unless he possess a perspicuous and acute judgment, to be able to determine what force there is in your reasons; unless his mind also be docile, and prepared to listen to instruction; and lastly, unless he have conceived such an opinion of your fidelity and prudence as may prepossess him in favour of your sentiments. For there are many obstinate spirits, never to be moved by any reasons; and where a person's fidelity is suspected, and his authority despised, little effect will be produced, even with those who are disposed to learn. On the contrary, let all these things be present, and they will insure the acquiescence of the person advised, in those counsels which he would otherwise have derided. This work also the Spirit effects within us. Lest the word should assail our ears in vain,—lest the sacraments should in vain strike our eyes,—he shows us that it is God who addresses us in them; he softens the hardness of our hearts, and forms them to that obedience which is due to the word of the Lord; in fine, he conveys those external words and sacraments from the ears into the soul. Our faith is confirmed, therefore, both by the word and by the sacraments, when they place before our eyes the good-will of our heavenly Father towards us, in the knowledge of which all the firmness of our faith consists, and by which its strength is augmented; the Spirit confirms it, when he makes this confirmation effectual by engraving it on our minds. In the mean time. the Father of lights cannot be prohibited from illuminating our minds by means of the lustre of the sacraments, as he enlightens our bodily eyes with the rays of the sun.

XI. That there is this property in the external word, our Lord has shown in a parable, by calling it "seed." (*q*) For as seed, if it fall on a desert and neglected spot of ground, will die without

(*q*) Matt. xiii. 3—23. Luke viii. 5—15

producing any crop, but if it be cast upon a well manured and cultivated field, it brings forth its fruit with an abundant increase,—so the word of God, if it fall upon some stiff neck, will be as unproductive as seed dropped upon the sea-shore; but if it light upon a soul cultivated by the agency of the heavenly Spirit, it will be abundantly fruitful. Now, if the word be justly compared to seed,—as we say that from seed, corn grows, increases, and comes to maturity,—why may we not say that faith derives its commencement, increase, and perfection, from the word of God? Paul, in different places, excellently expresses both these things. For, with a view to recall to the recollection of the Corinthians with what efficacy God had attended his labours, he glories in having the ministry of the Spirit, as if there were an indissoluble connection between his preaching and the power of the Holy Spirit operating to the illumination of their minds, and the excitement of their hearts. (*r*) But in another place, with a view to apprize them how far the power of the word of God extends, merely as preached by man, he compares ministers to husbandmen; who, when they have employed their labour and industry in cultivating the ground, have nothing more that they can do. But what would ploughing, and sowing, and watering, avail, unless heavenly goodness caused the seed to vegetate? Therefore he concludes, "Neither is he that planteth any thing, neither he that watereth; but God, that giveth the increase." (*s*) The apostles, then, in their preaching, exerted the power of the Spirit, as far as God made use of the instruments appointed by himself for the exhibition of his spiritual grace. But we must always keep in view this distinction, that we may remember how far the power of man extends, and what is exclusively the work of God.

XII. Now, it is so true that the sacraments are confirmations of our faith, that sometimes, when the Lord intends to take away the confidence of those things which had been promised in the sacraments, he removes the sacraments themselves. When he deprived Adam of the gift of immortality, he expelled him from the garden of Eden, saying, "Lest he put forth his hand, and take also of the tree of life, and eat, and live for ever." (*t*) What can

---

(*r*) 1 Cor. ii. 4. 2 Cor. iii. 6, 8. (*s*) 1 Cor. iii. 7. (*t*) Gen. iii. 22.

be the meaning of this language? Could the fruit restore to Adam the incorruption from which he had now fallen? Certainly not. But it was the same as if the Lord had said, Lest he should cherish a vain confidence, if he retain the symbol of my promise, let him be deprived of that which might give him some hope of immortality. For the same reason, when the apostle exhorts the Ephesians to "remember that" they "were without Christ, being aliens from the commonwealth of Israel, and strangers from the covenant of promise, having no hope, and without God in the world," he states that they were not partakers of circumcision; (*v*) thereby signifying that not having received the sign of the promise, they were excluded from the promise itself. To the other objection which they make, that the glory of God is transferred to creatures to whom so much power is attributed, and thereby sustains a proportionate diminution, it is easy to answer, that we place no power in creatures; we only maintain that God uses such means and instruments as he sees will be suitable, in order that all things may be subservient to his glory, as he is the Lord and Ruler of all. Therefore, as by bread and other aliments he feeds our bodies, as by the sun he enlightens the world, as by fire he produces warmth,—yet bread, the sun, and fire are nothing but instruments by which he dispenses his blessings to us,—so he nourishes our faith in a spiritual manner by the sacraments, which are instituted for the purpose of placing his promises before our eyes for our contemplation, and of serving us as pledges of them. And as we ought not to place any confidence in the other creatures, which, by the liberality and beneficence of God, have been destined to our uses, and by whose instrumentality he communicates to us the bounties of his goodness, nor to admire and celebrate them as the causes of our enjoyments,—so neither ought our confidence to rest in the sacraments, or the glory of God to be transferred to them; but, forsaking all other things, both our faith and confession ought to rise to him, the Author of the sacraments and of every other blessing.

XIII. The argument which some persons adduce from the very name of *sacrament* is destitute of any force;—though the word

---

(*v*) Eph. ii. 11, 12.

sacrament has various significations in authors of the first authority, yet it has but one which has any agreement or connection with *signs* or *standards,* (signa;) that is, when it denotes the solemn oath taken by a soldier to his commander when he enters on a military life. For as by the military oath new soldiers bind themselves to their commander, and assume the military profession, so by our signs we profess Christ to be our Leader, and declare that we fight under his banners. They add similitudes for the further elucidation of their opinion. As the dress of the Romans, who wore gowns, distinguished them from the Greeks, who wore cloaks; as the different orders among the Romans were distinguished from each other by their respective badges, the senatorial order from the equestrian by purple habits and round shoes, and the equestrian from the plebeian by a ring; as French and English ships of war are known by flags of different colours, the French flags being white and the English red; so we have our signs or badges to distinguish us from unbelievers. But from the observations already made, it is evident that the ancient fathers, who gave our signs the name of sacraments, were not at all guided by the previous use of this word in Latin writers; but that they gave it a new sense for their own convenience, simply denoting sacred signs. And if we wish to carry our researches any further, it may be found that they transferred this name to the signification now given, on the same principle of analogy which induced them to transfer the word *faith* to the sense in which it is now used. For as faith properly signifies truth in the fulfilment of promises, yet they have applied it to the assurance or certain persuasion which a person has of the truth itself; so, as a sacrament is an oath by which a soldier binds himself to his leader, they have applied it to the sign by which the leader receives soldiers into his army. For by the sacraments the Lord promises that he will be our God, and that we shall be his people. But we pass over such subtleties, as I think I have proved by sufficient arguments that the ancients had no other view, in their application of the word *sacrament,* than to signify that the ceremonies to which they applied it were signs of holy and spiritual things. We admit the comparison deduced from external badges, but we cannot bear that the last and least use of the sacraments should be represented as their principal and even sole object. The first object of them is, to assist our faith towards God; the second, to testify our confession before men. The similitudes which have been mentioned are applicable to this secondary design, but the primary one ought never to be forgotten; for otherwise, as we have seen, these mysteries would cease to interest us, unless they were aids of our faith, and appendices of doctrine, destined to the same use and end.

XIV. On the other hand, we require to be apprized, that as these persons weaken the force of the sacraments, and entirely subvert their use, so there are others of a contrary party, who attribute to the sacraments I know not what latent virtues, which are nowhere represented as communicated to them by the word of God. By this error the simple and inexperienced are dangerously deceived, being taught to seek the gifts of God where they can never be found, and being gradually drawn away from God to embrace mere vanity instead of his truth. For the sophistical schools have maintained, with one consent, that the sacraments of the new law, or those now used in the Christian Church, justify and confer grace, provided we do not obstruct their operation by any mortal sin. It is impossible to express the pestilent and fatal nature of this opinion, and especially as it has prevailed over a large part of the world, to the great detriment of the Church, for many ages past. Indeed, it is evidently diabolical; for by promising justification without faith, it precipitates souls into destruction: in the next place, by representing the sacraments as the cause of justification, it envelops the minds of men, naturally too much inclined to the earth, in gross superstition, leading them to rest in the exhibition of a corporeal object rather than in God himself. Of these two evils I wish we had not had such ample experience as to supersede the necessity of much proof. What is a sacrament, taken without faith, but the most certain ruin of the Church? For as nothing is to be expected from it, but in consequence of the promise, which denotes God's wrath against unbelievers as much as it offers his grace to believers,—the person who supposes that the sacraments confer any more upon him than that which is offered by the word of God, and which he receives by a true faith, is greatly deceived. Hence also it may be concluded, that confidence of salvation does not depend on the participation of the sacraments, as though that constituted our justification, which we know to be placed in Christ alone, and to be communicated to us no less by the preaching of the gospel than by the sealing of the sacraments, and that it may be completely enjoyed without this participation. So true is the observation, which has also been made by Augustine, that invisible sanctification may exist without the visible sign, and, on the contrary, that the visible sign may be used without real sanctification. For, as he also writes in another place, "Men put on Christ, sometimes by the reception of a sacrament, sometimes by sanctification of life." The first case may be common to the good and the bad; the second is peculiar to believers.

XV. Hence that distinction, if it be well understood, which is frequently stated by Augustine, between a sacrament and the matter of a sacrament. For his meaning is, not only that a sacrament contains a figure, and some truth signified by that figure, but that their connection is not such as to render them inseparable from each other; and even when they are united, the thing signified ought always to be distinguished from the sign, that what belongs to the one may not be transferred to the other. He speaks of their separation, when he observes, that "the sacraments produce the effect which they represent, in the elect alone." Again, when he is speaking of the Jews: "Though the sacraments were common to all, the grace which is the power of the sacrament was not common; so now, also, the washing of regeneration is common to all; but the grace itself, by which the members of Christ are regenerated with their Head, is not common to all." Again, in another place, speaking of the Lord's supper: "We also in the present day receive visible meat; but the sacrament is one thing, and the power of the sacrament is another. How is it that many receive of the altar and die, and die in consequence of receiving? For the morsel of bread given by the Lord to Judas was poison; not because Judas received an evil thing, but because, being a wicked man, he received a good thing in a sinful manner." A little after: "The sacrament of this thing, that is, of the unity of the body and blood of Christ, is prepared on the table of the Lord, in some places daily, in other places on appointed days, at stated intervals of time; and is thence received, by some to life, by others to destruction. But the thing signified by this sacrament is received, not to destruction, but to life, by every one who partakes of it." He had just before said, "He shall not die, who eats; I refer not to the visible sacrament, but to the power of the sacrament; who eats internally, not externally; he who eats in his heart, not he who presses with his teeth." In all these passages we find it maintained, that a sacrament is separated from the truth signified in it, by the unworthiness of a person who receives it amiss, so that there is nothing left in it but a vain and useless figure. In order to enjoy the thing signified together with the sign, and not a mere sign destitute of the truth it was intended to convey, it is necessary to apprehend by faith the word which is contained in it. Thus, in proportion to the communion we have with Christ by means of the sacraments, will be the advantage which we shall derive from them.

XVI. If this be obscure in consequence of its brevity, I will explain it more at large. I affirm that Christ is the matter, or substance, of all the sacraments; since they have all their solidity in him, and promise nothing out of him. So much more intolerable is the error of Peter Lombard, who expressly makes them causes of righteousness and salvation, of which they are parts. Leaving all causes, therefore, of human invention, we ought to adhere to this one cause. As far as we are assisted by their instrumentality, to nourish, confirm, and increase our faith in Christ, to obtain a more perfect possession of him and an enjoyment of his riches, so far they are efficacious to us; and this is the case when we receive by true faith that which is offered in them. Do the impious, then, it will be said, by their ingratitude, frustrate the ordinance of God, and cause it to come to nothing? I reply, that what I have said is not to be understood as implying, that the virtue and truth of a sacrament depends on the condition or choice of him who receives it. For what God has instituted continues unshaken, and retains its nature, however men may vary; but as it is one thing to offer, and another to receive, there is no incongruity in maintaining, that a symbol, consecrated by the word of the Lord, is in reality what it is declared to be, and preserves its virtue, and yet that it confers no benefit on a wicked and impious person.

But Augustine happily solves this question in a few words: he says, "If thou receive it carnally, still it ceases not to be spiritual; but it is not so to thee." And, as in the passages already cited, this father shows that the symbol used in a sacrament is of no value, if it be separated from the truth signified by it, so, on the other hand, he states that it is necessary to distinguish them, even where they are united, lest our attention be confined too much to the external sign. "As to follow the letter," says he, "and to take the signs instead of the things signified, betrays servile weakness, so it is the part of unsteadiness and error to interpret the signs in such a manner as to derive no advantage from them." He mentions two faults, against which it is necessary to guard. One is, when we take the signs as if they were given in vain, and disparaging or diminishing their secret significations by our perverse misconstruction, exclude ourselves from the advantage which we ought to derive from them. The other is, when, not elevating our minds beyond the visible sign, we transfer to the sacraments the praise of those benefits, which are only conferred upon us by Christ alone, and that by the agency of the Holy Spirit, who makes us partakers of Christ himself, by the instrumentality of the external signs which invite us to Christ, but which cannot be perverted to any other use, without a shameful subversion of all their utility.

XVII. Wherefore let us abide by this conclusion, that the office of the sacraments is precisely the same as that of the word of God; which is to offer and present Christ to us, and in him the treasures of his heavenly grace; but they confer no advantage or profit without being received by faith; just as wine, or oil, or any other liquor, though it be poured plentifully on a vessel, yet will it overflow and be lost, unless the mouth of the vessel be open; and the vessel itself, though wet on the outside, will remain dry and empty within. It is also necessary to guard against being drawn into an error allied to this, from reading the extravagant language used by the fathers with a view to exalt the dignity of the sacraments; lest we should suppose there is some secret power annexed and attached to the sacraments, so that they communicate the grace of the Holy Spirit, just as wine is given in the cup; whereas the only office assigned to them by God, is to testify and confirm his benevolence towards us; nor do they impart any benefit, unless they are accompanied by the Holy Spirit to open our minds and hearts, and render us capable of receiving this testimony: and here, also, several distinct favours of God are eminently displayed. For the sacraments, as we have before hinted, fulfil to us, on the part of God, the same office as messengers of joyful intelligence, or earnests for the confirmation of covenants on the part of men; they communicate no grace from themselves, but announce and show, and, as earnests and pledges, ratify, the things which are given to us by the goodness of God. The Holy Spirit, whom the sacraments do not promiscuously impart to all but whom God, by a peculiar privilege, confers upon his servants, is he who brings with him the graces of God, who gives the sacraments admission into our hearts, and causes them to bring forth fruit in us. Now, though we do not deny that God himself accompanies his institution by the very present power of his Spirit, that the administration of the sacraments which he has ordained may not be vain and unfruitful, yet we assert the necessity of a separate consideration and contemplation of the internal grace of the Spirit, as it is distinguished from the external ministry. Whatever God promises and adumbrates in signs, therefore, he really performs; and the signs are not without their effect, to prove the veracity and fidelity of their Author. The only question here is, whether God works by a proper and intrinsic power, as it is expressed, or resigns the office to external symbols. Now, we contend, that whatever instruments he employs, this derogates nothing from his supreme operation. When this doctrine is maintained respecting the sacraments, their dignity is sufficiently announced, their use plainly signified, their utility abundantly declared, and a proper moderation is preserved in all these particulars, so that nothing is attributed, which ought not to be attributed to them, and nothing that belongs to them is denied; while there is no admission of that figment, which places the cause of justification and the power of the Spirit in the sacramental elements, as in so many vehicles; and that peculiar power which has been omitted by others is clearly expressed. Here, also, it must be remarked, that God accomplishes within, that which the minister represents and testifies by the external act; that we may not attribute to a moral man what God challenges exclusively to himself. Augustine has judiciously suggested the same sentiment. "How," says he, "do Moses and God both sanctify? Not Moses instead of God. Moses does it with visible signs, by his ministry. God does it with invisible grace, by his Holy Spirit. Here also lies all the efficacy of visible sacraments. For what avail those visible sacraments without that sanctification of invisible grace?"

XVIII. The term *sacrament*, as we have hitherto treated of its nature, comprehends generally all the signs which God has ever given to men, to certify and assure them of the truth of his promises. These he has been pleased to place in natural things, and sometimes to exhibit in miracles. Examples of the former kind are such as these: when he gave Adam and Eve the tree of life, as a pledge of immortality, which they might assure themselves of enjoying as long as they should eat of the fruit of that tree; (*w*) and when he "set" his "bow in the cloud," as a token to Noah and his posterity, that there should "no more be a flood to destroy the earth." (*x*) These Adam and Noah had as sacraments. Not that the tree would actually communicate immortality to them, which it could not give to itself; or that the rainbow, which is merely a refraction of the rays of the sun on the opposite clouds, would have any efficacy in restraining the waters; but because they had a mark impressed upon them by the word of God, constituting them signs and seals of his covenants. The tree and the rainbow both existed before, but when they were inscribed with the word of God, they were endued with a new form; so that they began to be something that they were not before. And that no one may suppose this to be spoken in vain, the bow itself continues to be a witness to us in the present age, of that covenant which God made with Noah: whenever we behold it, we read this promise to God in it, that he would never more destroy the earth with a flood. Therefore, if any smatterer in philosophy, with a view to ridicule the simplicity of our faith, contend that such a variety of colours is the natural result of the refraction of the solar rays on an opposite cloud, we must immediately acknowledge it, but we may smile at his stupidity in not acknowl-

(*w*) Gen. ii. 9, 16, 17. (*x*) Gen. ix. 12—17.

edging God as the Lord and Governor of nature, who uses all the elements according to his will for the promotion of his own glory. And if he had impressed similar characters on the sun, on the stars, on the earth, and on stones, they would all have been sacraments to us. Why is not silver of as much value before it is coined, as it is after, since the metal is the very same? The reason is, that it has nothing added to its natural state; stamped with a public impression, it becomes money, and receives a new valuation. And shall not God be able to mark his creatures with his word, that they may become sacraments, though before they were mere elements? Examples of the second kind were exhibited, when God showed Abraham "a smoking furnace and a burning lamp;" (*y*) when he watered the fleece with dew while the earth remained dry, and afterwards bedewed the earth without wetting the fleece, to promise victory to Gideon; (*z*) when "he brought the shadow ten degrees backward in the dial," (*a*) to promise recovery to Hezekiah. As these things were done to support and establish the weakness of their faith, they also were sacraments.

XIX. But our present design is to treat particularly of those sacraments which the Lord has appointed to be ordinarily used in his Church, to keep his worshippers and servants in one faith and in the confession of the same. "For," to use the language of Augustine, "men cannot be united in any profession of religion, whether true or false, unless they are connected by some communion of visible signs or sacraments." Our most merciful Father, therefore, foreseeing this necessity, did, from the beginning, institute for his servants certain exercises of piety, which Satan afterwards depraved and corrupted in a variety of ways, transferring them to impious and idolatrous worship. Hence those initiations of the heathen into their mysteries, and the rest of their degenerate rites, which, though fraught with error and superstition, at the same time furnish an evidence that such external signs are indispensable to a profession of religion. But as they were neither founded on the word of God, nor referred to that truth which ought to be the object of all religious emblems, they are unworthy of notice, where mention is made of the sacred sym-

---

(*y*) Gen. xv. 17. (*z*) Judges vi. 37—40. (*a*) 2 Kings xx. 11.

bols which have been instituted by God, and which have never been perverted from their original principle, which constitutes them aids of true piety. Now, they consist not of mere signs, like the rainbow and the tree of life, but in ceremonies; or, rather, the signs which are here given are ceremonies. And, as we have before observed, as they are testimonies of grace and salvation on the part of the Lord, so on our part they are badges of our profession, by which we publicly devote ourselves to God, and swear obedience and fidelity to him. Chrysostom, therefore, somewhere properly calls them *compacts*, by which God covenants with us, and we bind ourselves to purity and sanctity of life; because a mutual stipulation is made in them between God and us. For as the Lord promises to obliterate and efface all the guilt and punishment that we have incurred by sin, and reconciles us to himself in his only begotten Son, so we, on our parts, by this profession, bind ourselves to him, to serve him in piety and innocence of life; so that such sacraments may justly be described as ceremonies by which God is pleased to exercise his people, in the first place, to nourish, excite, and confirm faith in their hearts; and in the next place, to testify their religion before men.

XX. And even the sacraments have been different according to the varieties of different periods, and corresponding to the dispensation by which it has pleased the Lord to manifest himself in different ways to mankind. For to Abraham and his posterity circumcision was commanded; to which the law of Moses afterwards added ablutions, sacrifices, and other rites. These were the sacraments of the Jews till the coming of Christ; which was followed by the abrogation of these, and the institution of two others, which are now used in the Christian Church; namely, baptism and the supper of the Lord. I speak of those which were instituted for the use of the whole Church; for as to the imposition of hands, by which the ministers of the Church are introduced into their office, while I make no objection to its being called a sacrament, I do not class it among the ordinary sacraments. What opinion ought to be entertained respecting those which are commonly reputed the five other sacraments, we shall see in a subsequent chapter. Those ancient sacrifices, however, referred to the same object towards which ours are now directed, their design being to point and lead to Christ, or rather, as images, to represent and make him known. For as we have already shown that they are seals to confirm the promises of God, and it is very certain that no promise of God was ever offered to man except in Christ,—in order to teach us any thing respecting the promises of God, they must of necessity make a discovery of Christ. This was the design of that heavenly pattern of the tabernacle and model of the legal worship, which was exhibited to Moses in the mount. There is only one difference between those sacraments and ours: they prefigured Christ as promised and still expected; ours represent him as already come and manifested.

XXI. All these things will be considerably elucidated by a particular detail. In the first place, circumcision was a sign to the Jews to teach them that whatever is produced from human seed —that is, the whole nature of man—is corrupt, and requires to be pruned: it was likewise a testification and memorial to confirm them in the promise given to Abraham respecting the blessed seed, in whom all the nations of the earth were to be blessed, and from whom their own blessing was also to be expected. (*b*) Now, that blessed seed, as Paul informs us, was Christ, on whom alone they relied for recovering that which they had lost in Adam. Wherefore circumcision was the same to them as Paul declares it to have been to Abraham, even "a seal of the righteousness of faith;" (*c*) that is, a seal for the further assurance that their faith, with which they expected that seed, would be imputed by God to them for righteousness. But the comparison between circumcision and baptism we shall have more suitable occasion for pursuing in another place. Ablutions and purifications placed before their eyes their uncleanness and pollution, by which they were naturally contaminated, and promised another ablution, by which they would be purified from all their defilement; and this ablution was Christ, washed in whose blood we bring his purity into the presence of God to cover all our impurities. (*f*) Their sacrifices accused and convicted them of their iniquity, and, at the same time, taught the necessity of some satisfaction to be made to the Divine justice, and that, therefore, there would come

(*b*) Gen. xii. 3; xxii. 18. Gal. iii. 16. (*c*) Rom. iv. 11.
(*f*) Heb. ix. 10—14. 1 John i. 7. Rev. i. 5.

a great High Priest, a Mediator between God and men, who was to satisfy the justice of God by the effusion of blood and the oblation of a sacrifice, which would be sufficient to obtain the remission of sins. This great High Priest was Christ; he shed his own blood, and was himself the victim; was obedient to his Father even unto death, and by his obedience obliterated the disobedience of man, which had provoked the indignation of God. (*g*)

XXII. Our two sacraments present us with a clearer exhibition of Christ, in proportion to the nearer view of him which men have enjoyed since he was really manifested by the Father in the manner in which he had been promised. For baptism testifies to us our purgation and ablution; the eucharistic supper testifies our redemption. Water is a figure of ablution, and blood of satisfaction. These things are both found in Christ, who, as John says, "came by water and blood;" (*h*) that is, to purify and redeem. Of this the Spirit of God is a witness; or, rather, "there are three that bear witness, the Spirit, the Water, and the Blood." (*i*) In the water and the blood we have a testimony of purgation and redemption; and the Spirit, as the principal witness, confirms and secures our reception and belief of this testimony. This sublime mystery was strikingly exhibited on the cross, when blood and water issued from Christ's sacred side; which, on this account, Augustine has justly called "the fountain of our sacraments;" of which we are yet to treat more at large. And there is no doubt, if we compare one time with another, but that the more abundant grace of the Spirit is also here displayed. For that belongs to the glory of the kingdom of Christ; as we gather from various places, and especially from the seventh chapter of John. In this sense we must understand that passage where Paul, speaking of the legal institutions, says, "which are a shadow of things to come, but the body is of Christ." (*k*) His design in this declaration is, not to deny the efficacy of those testimonies of grace, in which God was formerly pleased to attest his veracity to the fathers, as he does to us now in baptism and the sacred supper, but to represent the comparative superiority of what has

---

(*g*) Heb. iv. 14; ix. 11; x. 1—4. Phil. ii. 8. Rom. v. 19.
(*h*) 1 John v. 8. (*i*) 1 John v. 8. (*k*) Col. ii. 17.

been given to us, that no one might wonder at the ceremonies of the law having been abolished at the advent of Christ.

XXIII. I will just observe by the way, that the doctrine of the schools, which asserts such a wide difference between the sacraments of the old and new law, as though the former merely prefigured the grace of God, and the latter actually communicated it, ought to be altogether exploded. For the apostle speaks in a manner equally as honourable of the former as of the latter, when he states that the fathers, in the time of Moses, "did all eat the same spiritual meat" (*l*) with us, and explains that meat to be Christ. Who will dare to call that an empty sign, which exhibited to the Jews the real communion of Christ? And the state of the case, which the apostle is there discussing, is clearly in favour of our argument. For, that no man might dare to despise the judgment of God, in a reliance on a speculative knowledge of Christ, and the mere name of Christianity, with its external signs, he exhibits the examples of Divine severity displayed among the Jews, to teach us that the same punishments which they suffered await us, if we indulge in the same sins. Now, that the comparison might be pertinent, it was necessary to show that there was no inequality between us and them in those privileges of which he forbids us to indulge unfounded boasts. First, therefore, he shows them to have been equal to us in the sacraments, and leaves not a particle of superiority capable of exciting in our minds the least hope of impunity. Nor is it right to attribute to our baptism any thing more than he attributes to circumcision, when he calls it "a seal of the righteousness of faith." (*m*) Whatever is presented to us in the present day in our sacraments, was anciently received by the Jews in theirs—even Christ and his spiritual riches. Whatever power our sacraments have, they also experienced the same in theirs: they were seals of the Divine benevolence to them, confirming their hope of eternal salvation. If the advocates of the opinion which we are opposing had been skilful interpreters of the Epistle to the Hebrews, they would not have been so deceived; but when they read there that sins were not expiated by the legal ceremonies, and that the ancient shadows

(*l*) 1 Cor. x. 3. (*m*) Rom. iv. 11.

had no power to confer righteousness,—neglecting the comparison intended to be drawn, and confining their attention to this single consideration, that the law in itself was unprofitable to its observers, they have simply concluded that the figures were destitute of any truth. But the design of the apostle was to represent the ceremonial law as of no value till it was referred to Christ, on whom alone depended all its efficacy.

XXIV. But they will allege what Paul says of the "circumcision in the letter," (*n*) that it is in no estimation with God; that it confers no advantage; that it is in vain; for such a representation they conceive to degrade it far below baptism. But this is not true; for all that he says of circumcision might justly be affirmed of baptism. And it is actually asserted; first by Paul himself, where he shows that God regards not the external ablution by which we enter on the profession of religion, unless the heart be purified within, and persevere in piety to the end; and, secondly, by Peter, when he declares the truth of baptism to consist, not in "the putting away of the filth of the flesh, but the answer of a good conscience." (*o*) It will be objected, that Paul seems in another place utterly to despise "the circumcision made with hands," when he compares it with "the circumcision of Christ." (*p*) I reply, that that passage derogates nothing from its dignity. Paul is there disputing against those who required it as still necessary, after it had been abrogated. He therefore admonishes believers to leave the ancient shadows, and adhere to the truth. These teachers, he says, urge you to be circumcised in your bodies. But you have been spiritually circumcised both in body and soul: you have the substance itself, therefore, which is better than the shadow. Some one might object to this, that the figure was not to be despised in consequence of their having the substance; for that the fathers under the Old Testament had experienced the circumcision of the heart, and the putting off of the old man, of which the apostle was speaking, and yet that external circumcision had not been unnecessary or useless to them. He anticipates and supersedes this objection, by immediately adding, that the Colossians had been "buried with Christ in baptism;" by which he signifies

(*n*) Rom. ii. 25—29. 1 Cor. vii. 19. Gal. vi. 15.
(*o*) 1 Pet. iii. 21. (*p*) Col. ii. 11.

that baptism is to Christians what circumcision was to the ancient believers, and consequently that circumcision cannot be imposed upon Christians without injury to baptism.

XXV. But our objectors proceed to allege, that a still stronger argument in their favour arises from what follows, which I have lately quoted,—that all the Jewish ceremonies were "a shadow of things to come, but the body is of Christ;" (*q*) and that the strongest argument of all is what is contained in the Epistle to the Hebrews, that the blood of beasts did not reach the conscience, that "the law" had "a shadow of good things to come, and not the very image of the things, and that the worshippers could never attain perfection from the Mosaic ceremonies." (*r*) I repeat what I have already suggested, that Paul called the ceremonies *shadows*, not as if they had nothing solid in them, but because their accomplishment had been deferred till the manifestation of Christ. In the next place, I remark that this is to be understood, not of the efficacy of the ceremonies, but rather of the mode of representation. For till Christ was manifested in the flesh, all the signs prefigured him as absent; however, he displayed his power, and consequently himself, as present in the hearts of believers. But the principal thing to be observed is, that in all these places Paul is not speaking of the subject, considered simply in itself, but with reference to those against whom he is contending. As he was combating the false apostles, who maintained piety to consist in the ceremonies alone, without any regard to Christ,—nothing more was necessary for their confutation, than to discuss what value ceremonies possess of themselves. This also was the object pursued by the author of the Epistle to the Hebrews. Let us remember, therefore, that the question here does not respect ceremonies, taken in their true and natural signification, but as distorted by a false and perverse interpretation; the controversy is not about the legitimate use, but the superstitious abuse of them. What wonder, then, is it, if ceremonies, separated from Christ, are divested of all their virtue? For all signs are reduced to nothing, when the thing signified is taken away. So when Christ was addressing those who supposed the manna to have been mere

(*q*) Col. ii. 17

(*r*) Heb. ix. 9; x. 1, 2.

food for the body, he accommodated his discourse to their gross notion, and said that he would give them better food, to nourish their souls with the hope of immortality. (*s*) If a clearer solution be required, all that has been said may be comprised in these three observations: first, that all the ceremonies of the law of Moses, unless they were directed to Christ, were vain and useless; secondly, that they had reference to Christ, so that when he was manifested in the flesh, they received their accomplishment; lastly, that it was necessary for them to be abolished at his advent, as a shadow vanishes in the clear light of the sun. But as I defer the more extended discussion of this subject to the chapter in which I intend to compare baptism with circumcision, I touch the more briefly upon it here.

XXVI. It is possible that these miserable sophists have been led into this error by the extravagant encomiums on the sacraments which are found in the writings of the fathers; as when Augustine says, that "the sacraments of the old law only promised the Saviour, but ours give salvation." Not observing that these and other similar forms of expression were hyperbolical, they, also, on their part, have promulgated their hyperbolical dogmas, but in a sense altogether foreign from the writings of the fathers. For the meaning of Augustine in that passage was the same as in another where he says, "The sacraments of the Mosaic law announced Christ as afterwards to come; ours announce him as already come." Again: "They were promises of things to be fulfilled; these are signs of things accomplished;" as if he had said, that the old sacraments prefigured Christ while he was yet expected, but that ours exhibit him as present, since he has already come. Besides, he speaks of the mode of representation, as he also shows in another place, where he says, "The law and the prophets had sacraments announcing something future; but what they celebrated as about to come, the sacraments of our time announce as already come." His sentiments respecting their truth and efficacy he declares in several places; as when he says, "The sacraments of the Jews were different from ours in the signs; in the thing signified, they were equal; different in visible form, equal in

---

(*s*) John vi. 27.

spiritual efficacy." Again: "In different signs, the same faith; in different signs, just as in different words; because words change their sounds in different times, and words are no other than signs. The fathers drank the same spiritual drink as we; though their corporeal drink was different. See, then, the signs have been varied without any change in the faith. To them the Rock was Christ; to us, that which is placed on the altar is Christ. And as a great sacrament, they drank the water flowing from the Rock; what we drink, believers know. If we consider the visible form, there was a difference; if we regard the intelligible signification, they drank the same spiritual drink." In another place: "In the mystery their meat and drink were the same as ours; but the same in signification, not in form; because the very same Christ was prefigured to them in the Rock, and has been manifested to us in the flesh." Yet in this respect, also, we admit that there is some difference between their sacraments and ours. For both testify that the paternal benevolence of God is offered to us in Christ, together with the graces of the Holy Spirit; but ours testify it in a more clear and evident manner. In both there is an exhibition of Christ, but the exhibition of him in ours is richer and fuller, corresponding to the difference between the Old Testament and the New, of which we have already treated. And this is what was intended by Augustine, whom I quote more frequently than any other, as the best and most faithful writer of antiquity, when he states, that after the revelation of Christ, sacraments were instituted, "fewer in number, more noble in signification, and more excellent in efficacy." It is right, also, just to apprize the readers, that all the jargon of the sophists respecting the *work wrought* (*opus operatum*) is not only false, but repugnant to the nature of the sacraments; which God has instituted, in order that believers, being poor and destitute of every good, may come to them simply confessing their wants, and imploring him to supply them. Consequently, in receiving the sacraments, they perform nothing at all meritorious, and the action itself being, as far as they are concerned, merely passive, no *work* can be attributed to them in it.

CHAPTER XV

Baptism

BAPTISM is a sign of initiation, by which we are admitted into the society of the Church, in order that, being incorporated into Christ, we may be numbered among the children of God. Now, it has been given to us by God for these ends, which I have shown to be common to all sacraments: first, to promote our faith towards him; secondly, to testify our confession before men. We shall treat of both these ends of its institution in order. To begin with the first: from baptism our faith derives three advantages, which require to be distinctly considered. The first is, that it is proposed to us by the Lord, as a symbol and token of our purification; or, to express my meaning more fully, it resembles a legal instrument properly attested, by which he assures us that all our sins are cancelled, effaced, and obliterated, so that they will never appear in his sight, or come into his remembrance, or be imputed to us. For he commands all who believe to be baptized for the remission of their sins. Therefore those who have imagined that baptism is nothing more than a mark or sign by which we profess our religion before men, as soldiers wear the insignia of their sovereign as a mark of their profession, have not considered that which was the principal thing in baptism; which is, that we ought to receive it with this promise, "He that believeth and is baptized shall be saved." (*t*)

II. In this sense we are to understand what is said by Paul,

(*t*) Mark xvi. 16.

that Christ sanctifies and cleanses the Church "with the washing of water by the word;" (*u*) and in another place, that "according to his mercy he saved us, by the washing of regeneration, and renewing of the Holy Ghost;" (*v*) and by Peter, that "baptism doth save us." (*w*) For it was not the intention of Paul to signify that our ablution and salvation are completed by the water, or that water contains in itself the virtue to purify, regenerate, and renew; nor did Peter mean that it was the cause of salvation, but only that the knowledge and assurance of it is received in this sacrament; which is sufficiently evident from the words they have used. For Paul connects together the "word of life" and "the baptism of water;" as if he had said that our ablution and sanctification are announced to us by the gospel, and by baptism this message is confirmed. And Peter, after having said that "baptism doth save us," immediately adds that it is "not the putting away of the filth of the flesh, but the answer of a good conscience towards God," which proceeds from faith. But, on the contrary, baptism promises us no other purification than by the sprinkling of the blood of Christ; which is emblematically represented by water, on account of its resemblance to washing and cleansing. Who, then, can pretend that we are cleansed by that water, which clearly testifies the blood of Christ to be our true and only ablution? So that, to refute the error of those who refer all to the virtue of the water, no better argument could be found, than in the signification of baptism itself, which abstracts us, as well from that visible element which is placed before our eyes, as from all other means of salvation, that it may fix our minds on Christ alone.

III. Nor must it be supposed that baptism is administered only for the time past, so that for sins into which we fall after baptism it would be necessary to seek other new remedies of expiation in I know not what other sacraments, as if the virtue of baptism were become obsolete. In consequence of this error, it happened, in former ages, that some persons would not be baptized except at the close of their life, and almost in the moment of their death, that so they might obtain pardon for their whole life—a

---

(*u*) Eph. v. 26. (*v*) Titus iii. 5. (*w*) 1 Peter iii. 21.

preposterous caution, which is frequently censured in the writings of the ancient bishops. But we ought to conclude, that at whatever time we are baptized, we are washed and purified for the whole of life. Whenever we have fallen, therefore, we must recur to the remembrance of baptism, and arm our minds with the consideration of it, that we may be always certified and assured of the remission of our sins. For though, when it has been once administered, it appears to be past, yet it is not abolished by subsequent sins. For the purity of Christ is offered to us in it; and that always retains its virtue is never overcome by any blemishes, but purifies and obliterates all our defilements. Now, from this doctrine we ought not to take a license for the commission of future sins; for it is very far from inculcating such presumption; it is only delivered to those who, when they have sinned, groan under the fatigue and oppression of their transgressions; in order to afford them some relief and consolation, and to preserve them from sinking into confusion and despair. Thus Paul says, that Christ was "set forth to be a propitiation for the remission of sins that are past." (*x*) He does not deny that we have a constant and perpetual remission of sins in Christ, but signifies that he has been given by the Father only to miserable sinners, who sigh for the physician to heal the wounds of a guilty conscience. To such the mercy of God is offered; while those who, from a remission of punishment, seek to derive an occasion and license for sinning, do nothing but draw down upon themselves the wrath and vengeance of God.

IV. I know the common opinion is, that remission of sins, which at our first regeneration we receive by baptism alone, is afterwards obtained by repentance and the benefit of the keys. But the advocates of this opinion have fallen into an error, for want of considering that the power of the keys, of which they speak, is so dependent on baptism that it cannot by any means be separated from it. It is true, that the sinner receives remission by the ministry of the Church; but not without the preaching of the gospel. Now, what is the nature of that preaching? That we are cleansed from our sins by the blood of Christ. What sign and

(*x*) Rom. iii. 25.

testimony of that ablution is there, except baptism? We see, then, how this absolution is referred to baptism. This error has produced the imaginary sacrament of penance; on which I have touched a little already, and shall finish what remains in its proper place. Now, it is no wonder if men, whose groveling minds were inordinately attached to external things, have betrayed that corrupt propensity, by a discontent with the pure instituion of God, and an introduction of new expedients invented by themselves; as if baptism itself were not a sacrament of repentance; but if repentance be enjoined upon us as long as we live, the virtue of baptism ought to be extended to the same period. Wherefore it is evident that the pious, whenever, in any part of their lives, they are distressed with a consciousness of their sins, may justly have recourse to the remembrance of baptism, in order to confirm themselves in the confidence of their interest in that one perpetual ablution which is enjoyed in the blood of Christ.

V. Baptism is also attended with another advantage: it shows us our mortification in Christ, and our new life in him. For, as the apostle says, "So many of us as were baptized into Jesus Christ, were baptized into his death: therefore we are buried with him by baptism into death, that we should walk in newness of life." (*y*) In this passage he does not merely exhort us to an imitation of Christ, as if he had said, that we are admonished by baptism, that after the example of his death we should die to sin, and that after the example of his resurrection we should rise to righteousness; but he goes considerably further, and teaches us, that by baptism Christ has made us partakers of his death, in order that we may be ingrafted into it. And as the scion derives substance and nourishment from the root on which it is ingrafted, so they, who receive baptism with the faith with which they ought to receive it, truly experience the efficacy of Christ's death in the mortification of the flesh, and also the energy of his resurrection in the vivification of the spirit. Hence he deduces matter of exhortation, that, if we are Christians, we ought to be "dead unto sin, but alive unto God." (*z*) He uses the same argument in another place; that we "are circumcised, putting off the body of the

(*y*) Rom. vi. 3, 4. (*z*) Rom. vi. 11.

sins of the flesh," after we have been "buried with" Christ "in baptism." (*a*) And in this sense, in the passage already quoted, he calls it "the washing of regeneration and renewing." (*b*) Thus we are promised, first, the gratuitous remission of sins, and imputation of righteousness; and, secondly, the grace of the Holy Spirit to reform us to newness of life.

VI. The last advantage which our faith receives from baptism, is the certain testimony it affords us, that we are not only ingrafted into the life and death of Christ, but are so united as to be partakers of all his benefits. For this reason he dedicated and sanctified baptism in his own body, that he might have it in common with us, as a most firm bond of the union and society which he has condescended to form with us; so that Paul proves from it, that we are the children of God, because we have put on Christ in baptism. (*c*) Thus we see that the accomplishment of baptism is in Christ; whom, on this account, we call the proper object of baptism. Therefore it is no wonder if the apostles baptized in his name, (*d*) though they had also been commanded to baptize in the name of the Father and of the Spirit. (*e*) For all the gifts of God, which are presented in baptism, are found in Christ alone. Yet it cannot be but that he who baptizes into Christ, equally invokes the name of the Father and of the Spirit. For we have purification in his blood, because our merciful Father, in his incomparable goodness, being pleased to receive us to his mercy, has appointed this Mediator between us, to conciliate his favour to us. But we receive regeneration from his death and resurrection, when we are endued with a new and spiritual nature by the sanctification of the Spirit. Of our purification and regeneration, therefore, we obtain, and distinctly perceive, the cause in the Father, the matter in the Son, and the efficacy in the Spirit. Thus John first and the apostles afterwards, baptized "with the baptism of repentance for the remission of sins;" (*f*) by *repentance*, intending regeneration, and by *remission of sins*, ablution.

VII. Hence also it is very certain that the ministry of John was precisely the same as that which was afterwards committed

---

(*a*) Col. ii. 11, 12. (*b*) Titus iii. 6. (*c*) Gal. iii. 26, 27.
(*d*) Acts viii. 16. (*e*) Matt. xxviii. 19.
(*f*) Matt. iii. 6, 11. Luke iii. 3. John iii. 23; iv. 1. Acts ii. 38, 41.

to the apostles. For their baptism was not different, though it was administered by different hands; but the sameness of their doctrine shows their baptism to have been the same. John and the apostles agreed in the same doctrine; both baptized to repentance, both to remission of sins; both baptized in the name of Christ, from whom repentance and remission of sins proceed. John said of Christ, "Behold the Lamb of God, which taketh away the sin of the world;" (*g*) thus acknowledging and declaring him to be the sacrifice acceptable to the Father, the procurer of righteousness, and the author of salvation. What could the apostles add to this confession? Wherefore let no one be disturbed by the attempts of the ancient writers to distinguish and separate one baptism from the other; for their authority ought not to have weight enough to shake our confidence in the Scripture. For who will attend to Chrysostom, who denies that remission of sins was included in the baptism of John, rather than to Luke, who, on the contrary, affirms that "John came preaching the baptism of repentance, for the remission of sins?" (*h*) Nor must we admit that subtlety of Augustine, "that in the baptism of John sins were remitted in hope, but in the baptism of Christ they were remitted in fact." For as the evangelist clearly testifies that John, in his baptism, promised the remission of sins, why should we diminish this commendation, when no necessity constrains us to it? But if any difference be sought for in the word of God, the only difference that will be found is, that John baptized in the name of him who was to come, the apostles in the name of him who had already manifested himself.

VIII. The more abundant effusion of the graces of the Spirit, after the resurrection of Christ, contributes nothing to establish a diversity of baptisms. For the baptism administered by the apostles, during his life on earth, was called his; yet it was attended with no greater abundance of the Spirit than the baptism of John. And even after his ascension, the Samaritans, even though they had been baptized in the name of Jesus, received no other gifts of the Spirit than those which were common to all believers, till Peter and John were sent to lay their hands upon

(*g*) John i. 29. (*h*) Luke iii. 3.

them. (*i*) I suppose that the fathers were misled into an opinion, that the baptism of John was merely a preparation for that of Christ, (*k*) entirely from an apprehension that some persons, who had previously received the baptism of John, were baptized again by Paul. But that they were mistaken in this point, shall be very clearly shown in the proper place. What is the meaning, then, of the declaration of John, that he "baptized with water," but that Christ would come to "baptize with the Holy Ghost and with fire?" (*l*) This may be explained in few words; for he did not mean to distinguish between one baptism and the other, but was comparing himself with the person of Christ; that he was a minister of water, but that Christ was the giver of the Holy Spirit, and would display this power by a visible miracle, on that day when he would send down the Holy Spirit upon the apostles in the form of fiery tongues. (*m*) What could the apostles boast beyond this? What more can they pretend to, who baptize in the present day? For they are merely ministers of the outward sign, and Christ is the author of the inward grace; as the same ancient writers invariably teach, and especially Augustine, whose principal argument against the Donatists is, that whatever be the character of the person who administers baptism, yet Christ alone presides in it.

IX. These things, which we have stated respecting mortification and ablution, were adumbrated in the people of Israel, whom, on this account, the apostle declares to have been "baptized in the cloud and in the sea." (*n*) Mortification was figuratively represented, when the Lord, delivering them from the power and cruel servitude of Pharaoh, made a way for them through the Red Sea, and drowned Pharaoh himself, and the Egyptians, their enemies, who pursued, and almost overtook them. For in this manner, in baptism, he promises, and gives us a sign to assure us, that we are extricated and delivered by his power from the captivity of Egypt, that is, from the servitude of sin; that our Pharaoh, that is, the devil, is drowned, though still he ceases not to harass and fatigue us. But as the Egyptians did not remain sunk to the bottom of the sea, but, being cast upon the shore, still

(*i*) Acts viii. 14—17. (*k*) Acts xix. 3—5. (*l*) Matt. iii. 11.
(*m*) Acts ii. 3. (*n*) 1 Cor. x. 2.

terrified the Israelites with the dreadful sight, though they were not able to injure them, so this enemy of ours still threatens, displays his arms, and makes himself felt, but cannot overcome. In the cloud there was an emblem of ablution. For as the Lord there covered them with a cloud, affording them refreshment, that they might not faint and be consumed by the overpowering heat of the sun, so, in baptism, we acknowledge ourselves to be covered and protected by the blood of Christ, that the severity of God, which is indeed an intolerable flame, may not fall upon us. Though this mystery was then obscured, and known only to few persons, yet, as there is no other way of obtaining salvation but by those two blessings of grace, the Lord, having adopted the ancient fathers as his heirs, was pleased to bestow upon them tokens of both.

X. Now, we may clearly perceive the falsehood of the notion which some have long ago disseminated, and which others persist in maintaining,—that by baptism we are delivered and exempted from original sin, and from the corruption which has descended from Adam to all his posterity, and are restored to the same righteousness and purity of nature which Adam would have obtained if he had continued in the integrity in which he was first created. For teachers of this kind have never understood the nature of original sin, or original righteousness, or the grace of baptism. Now, we have already proved that original sin is the pravity and corruption of our nature, which first renders us obnoxious to the wrath of God, and then produces in us those works which the Scripture calls "works of the flesh." (*o*) Therefore these two things are to be distinctly observed: first, that our nature being so entirely depraved and vitiated, we are, on account of this very corruption, considered as convicted and justly condemned in the sight of God, to whom nothing is acceptable but righteousness, innocence, and purity. And therefore even infants themselves bring their own condemnation into the world with them, who, though they have not yet produced the fruits of their iniquity, yet have the seed of it within them; even their whole nature is, as it were, a seed of sin, and therefore cannot but be odious and abominable to God. By baptism, believers are

(*o*) Gal. v. 19.

certified that this condemnation is removed from them; since, as we said, the Lord promises us by this sign, that a full and entire remission is granted both of the guilt which is to be imputed to us, and of the punishment to be inflicted on account of that guilt; they also receive righteousness, such as the people of God may obtain in this life; that is, only by imputation, because the Lord, in his mercy, accepts them as righteous and innocent.

XI. The other thing to be remarked is, that this depravity never ceases in us, but is perpetually producing new fruits—those works of the flesh which we have already described, like the emission of flame and sparks from a heated furnace, or like the streams of water from an unfailing spring. For concupiscence never dies, nor is altogether extinguished in men, till by death they are delivered from the body of death, and entirely divested of themselves. Baptism, indeed, promises us the submersion of our Pharaoh, and the mortification of sin; yet not so that it no longer exists, or gives us no further trouble; but only that it may never overcome us. For as long as we live immured in this prison of the body, the relics of sin will dwell in us; but if we hold fast by faith the promise which God has given us in baptism, they shall not domineer or reign over us. But let no one deceive himself, let no one flatter himself in his guilt, when he hears that sin always dwells in us. These things are not said in order that those who are already too prone to do evil may securely sleep in their sins, but only that those who are tempted by their corrupt propensities may not faint and sink into despondency; but that they may rather reflect that they are yet in the way, and may consider themselves as having made some progress, when they experience their corruptions diminishing from day to day, till they shall attain the mark at which they are aiming, even the final destruction of their depravity, which will be accomplished at the close of this mortal life. In the mean time, let them not cease to fight manfully, to animate themselves to constant advances, and to press forward to complete victory. For it ought to give additional impulse to their exertions, to see that, after they have been striving so long, so much still remains for them to do. We conclude, therefore, that we are baptized into the mortification of the flesh, which commences in us at baptism, which we pursue from day to day, and which will be perfected when we shall pass out of this life to the Lord.

XII. Here we say nothing different from what is most clearly stated by Paul in the sixth and seventh chapters of the Epistle to the Romans. For after he had argued respecting gratuitous righteousness,—because some impious men concluded from that doctrine that they might live according to their own corrupt inclinations, as we are not accepted by God for the merit of our works, he adds, that all who are clothed with the righteousness of Christ are also regenerated by his Spirit, and that of this regeneration we have an earnest in baptism. Hence he exhorts believers not to suffer sin to reign in their members. Because he knew that there always remains some infirmity in them, that they might not be dejected on account of it, he adds for their consolation, that they are not under the law. On the other hand, as it might seem to encourage licentiousness in Christians, to say that they were not under the yoke of the law, he discusses the nature of that abrogation, and shows what is the use of the law—a question which he had already determined. The sum of all that he says is, that we are delivered from the rigour of the law to adhere to Christ; and that the office of the law is to convince us of our depravity, and lead us to a confession of our impotence and misery. Now, because the depravity of our nature is not so easily discovered in a profane man who indulges his corrupt passions without any fear of God, he gives an example in a regenerate man, that is, in himself. He says, therefore, that he has a perpetual conflict with the relics of his corruption, and that he is bound with a miserable servitude, which prevents his entire consecration of himself to an obedience of the Divine law; so that he is constrained to exclaim, "O wretched man that I am! Who shall deliver me from the body of this death?" If the children of God are captives detained in prison as long as they live, they cannot but feel great anxiety from reflection on their danger, unless there be something to obviate this fear. For this purpose, therefore, he has added a consolation, that "there is now no condemnation to them which are in Christ Jesus;" (*p*) by which he teaches, that those whom the

(*p*) Rom. viii. 1.

Lord has once received into his favour, incorporated into the communion of his Christ, and introduced by baptism into the society of his Church, notwithstanding they are surrounded and assaulted with sin, and even carry sin about within them, yet while they persevere in the faith of Christ, are absolved from guilt and condemnation. If this be the simple and genuine meaning of Paul, there is no reason why we should be considered as promulgating a new or strange doctrine.

XIII. Baptism also serves for our confession before men. For it is a mark by which we openly profess our desire to be numbered among the people of God, by which we testify our agreement with all Christians in the worship of one God, and in one religion, and by which we make a public declaration of our faith; that the praises of God may not only be breathed in the secret aspirations of our hearts, but may also be loudly proclaimed by our tongues, and by all the members of our body, in the different modes in which they are capable of expressing them. For thus all that we have is devoted, as it ought to be, to the glory of God, to which every thing ought to be subservient, and by our example others are incited to the same pursuit. It was with this view that Paul inquired of the Corinthians, whether they had not been baptized in the name of Christ; signifying that, in having been baptized in his name, they had dedicated themselves to him, had avowed him as their Lord and Master, and had bound themselves by a solemn obligation before men; so that they could never again confess any other except him, unless they intended to renounce the confession which they had made at their baptism.

XIV. Now, as we have stated what was the design of our Lord in the institution of baptism, it is easy to judge in what manner we ought to use and receive it. For as it is given for the support, consolation, and confirmation of our faith, it requires to be received as from the hand of the Author himself: we ought to consider it as beyond all doubt, that it is he who speaks to us by this sign; that it is he who purifies and cleanses us, and obliterates the remembrance of our sins; that it is he who makes us partakers of his death, who demolishes the kingdom of Satan, who weakens the power of our corrupt propensities, who even makes us one with himself, that, being clothed with him, we may be reckoned children of God; and that he as truly and certainly performs these things internally on our souls, as we see that our bodies are externally washed, immersed, and enclosed in water. For this analogy or similitude is a most certain rule of sacraments; that in corporeal things we contemplate spiritual things, just as if they were placed before our eyes, as it has pleased God to represent them to us by such figures: not that such blessings are bound or enclosed in the sacrament, or that it has the power to impart them to us; but only because it is a sign by which the Lord testifies his will, that he is determined to give us all these things: nor does it merely feed our eyes with a bare prospect of the symbols, but conducts us at the same time to the thing signified, and efficaciously accomplishes that which it represents.

XV. We may see this exemplified in Cornelius the centurion, who, after having received the remission of his sins and the visible graces of the Holy Spirit, was baptized; not with a view to obtain by baptism a more ample remission of sins, but a stronger exercise of faith, and an increase of confidence from that pledge. (*q*) Perhaps it may be objected, "Why, then, did Ananias say to Paul, 'Arise, and be baptized, and wash away thy sins' (*r*) if sins are not washed away by the efficacy of baptism itself?" I answer, We are said to receive or obtain that which our faith apprehends, as presented to us by the Lord, whether at the time that he first declares it to us, or when, by any subsequent testimony, he affords us a more certain confirmation of it. Ananias, therefore, only intended to say to Paul, "That thou mayest be assured that thy sins are forgiven, be baptized. For in baptism the Lord promises remission of sins; receive this and be secure." It is not my design, however, to diminish the efficacy of baptism; but the substance and truth accompanies the sign, as God works by external means. Nevertheless, from this sacrament, as from all others, we obtain nothing except what we receive by faith. If faith be wanting, it will be a testimony of our ingratitude, to render us guilty before God, because we have not believed the promise given in the sacrament; but as baptism is a sign of our confession, we ought to testify by it, that our confidence is in the mercy of God, and our

---

(*q*) Acts x. 44—48.

(*r*) Acts xxii. 16.

purity in the remission of sins, which is obtained for us by Jesus Christ; and that we enter into the Church of God in order to live in the same harmony of faith and charity, of one mind with all the faithful. This is what Paul meant when he said, that "by one Spirit we are all baptized into one body." (*s*)

XVI. Now, if it be true, as we have stated, that a sacrament is to be considered as received, not so much from the hand of him by whom it is administered, as from the hand of God himself, from whom, without doubt, it proceeded, we may conclude that it is not capable of any addition or diminution from the dignity of the person by whose hand it is delivered. And as, among men, if a letter be sent, provided the hand and seal of the writer be known, it is of very little importance who and what the carrier of it may be, so it ought to be sufficient for us to know the hand and seal of our Lord in his sacraments, by whatever messenger they may be conveyed. This fully refutes the error of the Donatists, who measured the virtue and value of the sacrament by the worthiness of the minister. Such, in the present day, are our Anabaptists, who positively deny that we are rightly baptized, because we were baptized by impious and idolatrous ministers in the kingdom of the pope, and therefore violently urge us to be baptized again; against whose follies we shall be fortified with an argument of sufficient strength, if we consider that we are baptized not in the name of any man, but in the name of the Father, and of the Son, and of the Holy Spirit, and consequently that it is not the baptism of man, but of God, by whomsoever it is administered. Though those who baptized us were chargeable with the grossest ignorance or contempt of God and of all religion, yet they did not baptize us into the fellowship of their own ignorance or sacrilege, but into the faith of Jesus Christ; because they invoked, not their own name, but the name of God, and baptized in no other name but his. Now, if it was the baptism of God, it certainly contained the promise of remission of sins, mortification of the flesh, spiritual vivification, and participation of Christ. Thus it was no injury to the Jews to have been circumcised by impure and apostate priests; nor was the sign on that

(*s*) 1 Cor. xii. 13.

account useless, so as to render it necessary to be repeated, but it was sufficient to recur to the genuine original. They object, that baptism ought to be celebrated in the congregation of the godly; but this does not prove that it loses all its value in consequence of being partially wrong. For when we teach what ought to be done to preserve baptism pure and free from every blemish, we do not abolish the institution of God, however idolaters corrupt it. For when circumcision was anciently corrupted with many superstitions, yet it ceased not to be considered as a sign of grace; nor, when Hezekiah and Josiah assembled together out of all Israel those who had revolted from God, did they call any of them to a second circumcision.

XVII. When they ask us what faith we had for many years after our baptism, in order to show that our baptism was vain, since baptism is not sanctified to us except by the word of promise received in faith,—to this inquiry we answer, that being blind and unbelieving for a long time, we did not embrace the promise which had been given us in baptism, yet that the promise itself, as it was from God, always remained steady, firm, and true. Though all men were false and perfidious, yet God ceases not to be true; though all men were lost, yet Christ remains a Saviour. We confess, therefore, that during that time we received no advantage whatever from baptism, because we totally neglected the promise offered to us in it, without which baptism is nothing. Now, since, by the grace of God, we have begun to repent, we accuse our blindness and hardness of heart for our long ingratitude to his great goodness; yet we believe that the promise itself never expired, but, on the contrary, we reason in the following manner:—By baptism God promises remission of sins, and will certainly fulfil the promise to all believers: that promise was offered to us in baptism; let us, therefore, embrace it by faith: it was long dormant by reason of our unbelief; now, then, let us receive it by faith. Wherefore, when God exhorts the Jewish people to repentance, he does not command them, who had been circumcised, as we have remarked, by impious and sacrilegious hands, and who had lived for some time immersed in the same impiety, to be circumcised again: he only urges conversion of heart. For however the covenant had been violated by them, yet the symbol of the covenant, according to the institution of the Lord, always remained firm and inviolable. On the sole condition of repentance, therefore, they were restored to the covenant which God had once made with them in circumcision; even though they had received it by the hands of the unfaithful priests, and had themselves done all that was in their power to corrupt it and render it ineffectual.

XVIII. But they conceive themselves to be armed with an invincible argument, when they allege that Paul rebaptized some who had previously been baptized with the baptism of John. (*t*) For if, by our own confession, the baptism of John was in all respects the same as ours is now,—as these persons who had first been erroneously instructed, after having been taught the right faith, were rebaptized into it, so that baptism, which was unaccompanied with the true doctrine, should be considered as nothing, and we ought to be baptized afresh into the true religion, which we have now first imbibed. It is supposed by some, that they had received the first baptism from a pretended and corrupt imitator of John, who had rather baptized them into a vain superstition than into the truth. This conjecture they seem to derive from the confession of those persons that they were entirely ignorant of the Holy Spirit—an ignorance in which it is concluded John would not have suffered his disciples to remain. But it is not probable that Jews, even though they had never been baptized at all, would have been destitute of all knowledge of the Holy Spirit, who is celebrated in so many testimonies of Scripture. The answer, therefore, which they gave, "We have not so much as heard whether there be any Holy Ghost," is to be understood as equivalent to a declaration that they had never heard whether the graces of the Spirit, respecting which Paul inquired, were given to the disciples of Christ. For myself, I grant that the baptism they had received was the true baptism of John, and the very same with the baptism of Christ; but I deny that they were baptized again. What is the meaning of these words, "They were baptized in the name of the Lord Jesus?" Some explain it to be, that they were only instructed by Paul in the pure doctrine; but I

(*t*) Acts xix. 1—6.

prefer understanding it, in a more simple manner, of the baptism of the Holy Spirit; that is, of the visible graces of the Spirit given by imposition of hands. It is not uncommon in the Scripture to designate those graces by the appellation of *baptism;* as on the day of Pentecost, the apostles are said to have remembered the words of the Lord respecting the baptism of the Spirit and of fire. And Peter declared that he remembered the same, when he saw those graces poured out on Cornelius and his family and relatives. Nor is this interpretation inconsistent with what is stated afterwards, that "When Paul had laid his hands upon them, the Holy Ghost came on them." For Luke does not relate two different things, but follows a mode of narration familiar to the Hebrews, who first propose a subject generally, and then unfold it more in detail. This is obvious from the very connection of the words; for he says, "When they heard this, they were baptized in the name of the Lord Jesus. And when Paul had laid his hands on them, the Holy Ghost came on them." The latter clause describes the kind of baptism intended in the former. If ignorance vitiate a first baptism, so that it requires to be corrected by a second, the first persons who ought to have been rebaptized were the apostles themselves, who for three years after their baptism had scarcely any knowledge of the least particle of pure doctrine. And among us, what rivers would be sufficient for the repetition of ablutions as numerous as the errors which are daily corrected in us by the mercy of the Lord!

XIX. The virtue, dignity, utility, and end of this mystery, have now, if I mistake not, been sufficiently explained. With respect to the external symbol, I sincerely wish that the genuine institution of Christ had the influence it ought to have, to repress the audacity of man. For, as though it were a contemptible thing to be baptized in water, according to the precept of Christ, men have invented a benediction, or rather incantation, to pollute the true consecration of the water. They afterwards added a wax taper with chrism; exorcism seemed to open the gate to baptism. Now, though I am not ignorant of the ancient origin of this adventitious medley, yet it is lawful for me and for all believers to reject every thing that men have presumed to add to the institution of Christ. Now, Satan, seeing that from the very first introduction of the gospel, his impostures had been easily received by the foolish credulity of the world, proceeded to grosser illusions; hence spittle, salt, and other fooleries, which were publicly introduced with an unlimited license, to the reproach of baptism. From these experiments we may learn that there is nothing holier, or better, or safer, than to content ourselves with the authority of Christ alone. How much better was it, therefore, omitting all theatrical pomps which dazzle the eyes and stupefy the minds of the simple, whenever any one was to be baptized, that he should be presented to the congregation of believers, and be offered to God in the presence and with the prayers of the whole Church; that the confession of faith, in which the catechumen was to be instructed, should be recited; that the promises which are included in baptism should be declared; that the catechumen should be baptized in the name of the Father, of the Son, and of the Holy Ghost; and lastly, that he should be dismissed with prayers and thanksgivings! Thus nothing material would be omitted; and that one ceremony, which was instituted by God, would shine with the greatest lustre, unencumbered with any extraneous corruptions. But whether the person who is baptized be wholly immersed, and whether thrice or once, or whether water be only poured or sprinkled upon him, is of no importance; Churches ought to be left at liberty, in this respect, to act according to the difference of countries. The very word *baptize*, however, signifies to immerse; and it is certain that immersion was the practice of the ancient Church.

XX. It is also necessary to state, that it is not right for private persons to take upon themselves the administration of baptism; for this, as well as the administration of the Lord's supper, is a part of the public ministry of the Church. Christ never commanded women, or men in general, to baptize; he gave this charge to those whom he had appointed to be apostles. And when he enjoined his disciples, in the celebration of the supper, to do as they had seen done by him when he executed the office of a legitimate dispenser, he intended, without doubt, that they should imitate his example. The custom, which has been received and practised for many ages past, and almost from the primitive times of the Church, for baptism to be performed by laymen, in cases where death was apprehended, and no minister was present in time, it appears to me impossible to defend by any good reason. Indeed, the ancients themselves, who either observed or tolerated this custom, were not certain whether it was right or not. Augustine betrays this uncertainty, when he says, "And if a layman, compelled by necessity, has given baptism, I know not whether any one may piously affirm that it ought to be repeated. For if it be done without the constraint of necessity, it is a usurpation of an office which belongs to another; but if necessity obliges, it is either no offence, or a venial one." Respecting women, it was decreed without any exception, in the Council of Carthage, that they should not presume to baptize at all, on pain of excommunication. But it is alleged, there is danger, lest a child, who is sick and dies without baptism, should be deprived of the grace of regeneration. This I can by no means admit. God pronounces that he adopts our infants as his children, before they are born, when he promises that he will be a God to us, and to our seed after us. This promise includes their salvation. Nor will any dare to offer such an insult to God as to deny the sufficiency of his promise to insure its own accomplishment. The mischievous consequences of that ill-stated notion, that baptism is necessary to salvation, are overlooked by persons in general, and therefore they are less cautious; for the reception of an opinion, that all who happen to die without baptism are lost, makes our condition worse than that of the ancient people, as though the grace of God were more restricted now than it was under the law; it leads to the conclusion that Christ came not to fulfil the promises, but to abolish them; since the promise, which at that time was of itself sufficiently efficacious to insure salvation before the eighth day, would have no validity now without the assistance of the sign.

XXI. What was the custom of the Church before Augustine was born, may be collected from the ancient fathers. In the first place, Tertullian says, "That it is not permitted for a woman to speak in the Church, neither to teach, nor to baptize, nor to offer, that she may not claim to herself the functions of any office belonging to men, and especially to priests." The same thing is fully attested by Epiphanius, when he censures Marcion for having given women liberty to baptize. I am aware of the answer made to this by persons of opposite sentiments—that there is a great difference between a common usage, and an extraordinary remedy employed in cases of urgent necessity; but when Epiphanius pronounces it to be a mockery, without making any exception, to give women liberty to baptize, it is sufficiently evident that he condemns this corruption, and considers it inexcusable by any pretext whatever; nor does he add any limitation, in his third book, where he observes that this liberty was not granted even to the holy mother of Christ.

XXII. The example of Zipporah is alleged, but is not applicable to the case. Because the angel of God was appeased after she had taken a stone and circumcised her son, (*v*) it is unreasonable to infer that her action was approved by God. On the same principle it might be maintained, that God was pleased with the worship established by the nations who were transplanted from Assyria to Samaria. But there are other powerful reasons to prove the absurdity of setting up the conduct of that foolish woman as a pattern for imitation. If I should allege, that this was a single act, which ought not to be considered as a general example, and especially as we nowhere find any special command that the rite of circumcision was to be performed by the priests, the case of circumcision is different from that of baptism; and this would be sufficient to refute the advocates of its administration by women. For the words of Christ are plain: "Go ye, therefore, and teach all nations, baptizing them." (*w*) Since he constitutes the same persons preachers of the gospel and administrators of baptism, "and no man," according to the testimony of the apostle, "taketh this honour upon himself, but he that is called of God as was Aaron," (*x*) whoever baptizes without a legitimate call intrudes into another person's office. Even in the minutest things, as in meat and drink, whatever we do with a doubtful conscience, Paul expressly declares to be sin. (*y*) Female baptism, therefore, being an open violation of the rule delivered by Christ, is a still greater sin; for we know that it is impious to dissever things which God has united. But all this I pass over; and would only request my readers to consider that nothing was further from the design of

---

(*v*) Exod. iv. 25.
(*w*) Matt. xxviii. 19.
(*x*) Heb. v. 4.
(*y*) Rom. xiv. 23.

Zipporah, than to perform a service to God. For seeing her son to be in danger, she fretted and murmured, and indignantly cast the foreskin on the ground, reproaching her husband in such a manner as to betray anger against God. In short, it is plain that all this proceeded from violence of temper, because she was displeased with God and her husband that she was constrained to shed the blood of her son. Besides, if she had conducted herself with propriety in all other respects, yet it was an act of inexcusable presumption for her to circumcise her son in the presence of her husband, and that husband not a private man, but Moses, the principal prophet of God, who was never succeeded by a greater in Israel, which was no more lawful for her to do, than it is for women now to baptize in the presence of a bishop. But this controversy will easily be decided by the establishment of this principle—that infants are not excluded from the kingdom of heaven, who happen to die before they have had the privilege of baptism. But we have seen that it is no small injustice to the covenant of God, if we do not rely upon it as sufficient of itself, since its fulfilment depends not on baptism, or on any thing adventitious. The sacrament is afterwards added as a seal, not to give efficacy to the promise of God, as if it wanted validity in itself, but only to confirm it to us. Whence it follows, that the children of believers are not baptized, that they may thereby be made the children of God, as if they had before been strangers to the Church; but, on the contrary, they are received into the Church by a solemn sign, because they already belonged to the body of Christ by virtue of the promise. If the omission of the sign, therefore, be not occasioned by indolence, or contempt, or negligence, we are safe from all danger. It is far more consistent with piety to show this reverence to the institution of God, not to receive the sacraments from any other hands than those to which the Lord has committed them. When it is impossible to receive them from the Church, the grace of God is not so attached to them, but that we may obtain it by faith from the word of the Lord.

CHAPTER XVI

Pœdobaptism Perfectly Consistent with the Institution of Christ and the Nature of the Sign

As some turbulent spirits in the present age have raised fierce disputes, which still continue to agitate the Church, on the subject of infant baptism, I cannot refrain from adding some observations with a view to repress their violence. If any one should think this chapter extended to an immoderate length, I would request him to consider, that purity of doctrine in a capital point, and the peace of the Church, ought to be of too much importance in our estimation for us to feel any thing tedious which may conduce to the restoration of both. I shall also study to make this discussion of as much use as possible to a further elucidation of the mystery of baptism. They attack infant baptism with an argument which carries with it an appearance of great plausibility, asserting that it is not founded on any institution of Christ, but was first introduced by the presumption and corrupt curiosity of man, and afterwards received with foolish and inconsiderate facility. For a sacrament rests on no authority, unless it stands on the certain foundation of the word of God. But what if, on a full examination of the subject, it shall appear that this is a false and groundless calumny on the holy ordinance of the Lord? Let us, therefore, inquire into its first origin. And if it shall be found to have been a mere invention of human presumption, we ought to renounce it, and regulate the true observance of baptism solely by the will of God. But if it shall be proved to be sanctioned by his undoubted authority, it behoves us to beware lest, by opposing the holy institutions of God, we offer an insult to their Author himself.

II. In the first place, it is a principle sufficiently known, and acknowledged by all believers, that the right consideration of sacramental signs consists not merely in the external ceremonies, but that it chiefly depends on the promise and the spiritual mysteries which the Lord has appointed those ceremonies to represent. Whoever, therefore, wishes to be fully informed of the meaning of baptism, and what baptism is, must not fix his attention on the element and the outward spectacle, but must rather elevate his thoughts to the promises of God which are offered to us in it, and to those internal and spiritual things which it represents to us. He who discovers these things, has attained the solid truth and all the substance of baptism, and thence he will also learn the reason and use of the external sprinkling. On the other hand, he who contemptuously disregards these things, and confines his attention entirely to the visible ceremony, will understand neither the force nor propriety of baptism, nor even the meaning or use of the water. This sentiment is established by testimonies of Scripture too numerous and clear to leave the least necessity for pursuing it any further at present. It remains, therefore, that from the promises given in baptism, we endeavour to deduce its nature and meaning. The Scripture shows, that the first thing represented in it, is the remission and purgation of sins, which we obtain in the blood of Christ; and the second the mortification of the flesh, which consists in the participation of his death, by which believers are regenerated to newness of life, and so into communion with him. This is the sum to which we may refer every thing delivered in the Scriptures concerning baptism, except that it is also a sign by which we testify our religion before men.

III. As the people of God, before the institution of baptism, had circumcision instead of it, let us examine the similarity and difference between these two signs, in order to discover how far we may argue from one to the other. When the Lord gave Abraham the command of circumcision, he prefaced it by saying, "I will be a God unto thee, and to thy seed after thee;" at the same time declaring himself to be "Almighty," having an abundance of all things at his disposal, that Abraham might expect to find his hand the source of every blessing. (*z*) These words contain the promise of eternal life, according to the interpretation of Christ, who deduces from this declaration an argument to evince the immortality and resurrection of believers. "For God," says he, "is not the God of the dead, but of the living." (*a*) Wherefore also Paul, in showing the Ephesians from what misery the Lord had delivered them, concludes, from their not having been admitted to the covenant of circumcision, that "at that time" they "were without Christ, strangers from the covenants of promise, having no hope and without God;" (*b*) all these things being comprehended in that covenant. But the first access to God, the first entrance into immortal life, is the remission of sins. Whence it follows that this promise corresponds with the promise of baptism respecting our purgation. The Lord afterwards stipulated with Abraham, that he should walk before him in sincerity and purity of heart: this belongs to mortification, or regeneration. And to preclude any doubt that circumcision is a sign of mortification, Moses more expressly declares it in another place, when he exhorts the Israelites to circumcise their hearts, because the Lord had chosen them for himself above all the nations of the earth. As God, when he adopts the posterity of Abraham to be his people, commands them to be circumcised, so Moses pronounces it to be necessary to circumcise the heart, thereby declaring the true signification of that carnal circumcision. (*c*) Then, that no one might attempt this in his own strength, he teaches that it is the work of Divine grace. (*d*) All these things are so often inculcated by the prophets, that there is no need to collect here the numerous testimonies which every where present themselves. We have ascertained, therefore, that a spiritual promise, the very same which is given to us in baptism, was given to the fathers in circumcision; which represented to them the remission of sins and the mortification of the flesh. Moreover, as we have shown

(*z*) Gen. xvii. 1—14. (*a*) Matt. xxii. 32. Luke xx. 37, 38.
(*b*) Ephes. ii. 12. (*c*) Deut. x. 16. (*d*) Deut. xxx. 6.

that Christ, in whom both these things are obtained, is the foundation of baptism, the same must be evident of circumcision. For he was promised to Abraham, and in him the blessing of all nations; and the sign of circumcision was added in confirmation of this grace.

IV. There is now no difficulty in discovering what similarity or what difference there is between these two signs. The promise, in which we have stated the virtue of the signs to consist, is the same in both; including the paternal favour of God, remission of sins, and eternal life. In the next place, the thing signified also is one and the same, namely, regeneration. The foundation, on which the accomplishment of these things rests, is the same in both. Wherefore there is no difference in the internal mystery, by which all the force and peculiar nature of sacraments must be determined. All the difference lies in the external ceremony, which is the smallest portion of it; whereas the principal part depends on the promise and the thing signified. We may conclude, therefore, that whatever belongs to circumcision, except the difference of the visible ceremony, belongs also to baptism. To this inference and comparison we are led by the apostle's rule, which directs us to examine every interpretation of Scripture by the proportion of faith. (*e*) And, indeed, the truth on this subject is obvious to the slightest observation. For as circumcision was a pledge to the Jews, by which they were assured of their adoption as the people and family of God, and on their parts professed their entire subjection to him, and therefore was their first entrance into the Church, so now we are initiated into the Church of God by baptism, are numbered among his people, and profess to devote ourselves to his service. Hence it is evident, beyond all controversy, that baptism has succeeded in the place of circumcision.

V. Now, if it be inquired, whether baptism may rightly be administered to infants, shall we not pronounce it an excess of folly, and even madness, in any one who resolves to dwell entirely on the element of water and the external observance, and cannot bear to direct his thoughts to the spiritual mystery; a due consideration of which will prove, beyond all doubt, that baptism

---

(*e*) Rom. xii. 3, 6

is justly administered to infants, as that to which they are fully entitled? For the Lord, in former ages, did not favour them with circumcision without making them partakers of all those things which were then signified by circumcision. Otherwise, he must have deluded his people with mere impostures, if he deceived them by fallacious symbols; which it is dreadful even to hear. For he expressly pronounces that the circumcision of a little infant should serve as a seal for the confirmation of the covenant. But if the covenant remains firm and unmoved, it belongs to the children of Christians now, as much as it did to the infants of the Jews under the Old Testament. But if they are partakers of the thing signified, why shall they be excluded from the sign? If they obtain the truth, why shall they be debarred from the figure? Though the external sign in the sacrament is so connected with the word, as not to be separated from it, yet if it be distinguished, which shall we esteem of the greater importance? Certainly, when we see that the sign is subservient to the word, we shall pronounce it to be inferior to it, and assign it the subordinate place. While the word of baptism, then, is directed to infants, why shall the sign, which is an appendix to the word, be prohibited to them? This one reason, if there were no others, would be abundantly sufficient for the refutation of all opposers. The objection that there was a particular day fixed for circumcision, is a mere evasion. We admit that we are not now bound to certain days, like the Jews; but when the Lord, though he prescribes no particular day, yet declares it to be his pleasure that infants shall be received into his covenant by a solemn rite, what do we want more?

VI. The Scripture, however, still affords a more certain knowledge of the truth. For it is most evident that the covenant which the Lord once made with Abraham continues as much in force with Christians in the present day, as it did formerly with the Jews; and consequently that that word is no less applicable to Christians than it was to the Jews. Unless we suppose that Christ by his advent diminished or curtailed the grace of the Father; which is execrable blasphemy. Wherefore the children of the Jews, because they were made heirs of that covenant, and distinguished from the children of the impious, were called a holy seed; and for the same reason, the children of Christians, even when only one of the parents is pious, are accounted holy, and according to the testimony of the apostle, differ from the impure seed of idolaters. Now, as the Lord, immediately after having made the covenant with Abraham, commanded it to be sealed in infants by an external sacrament, what cause will Christians assign why they should not also at this day testify and seal the same in their children? Nor let it be objected, that the Lord commanded not his covenant to be confirmed by any other symbol than that of circumcision, which has long ago been abolished. For it is easy to reply, that during the time of the Old Testament he appointed circumcision for the confirmation of his covenant; but that since the abrogation of circumcision, there always remains the same reason for confirming it, which we have in common with the Jews. It is necessary, therefore, to be careful in observing what we have in common with them, and what they had different from us. The covenant is common, the reason for confirming it is common. Only the mode of confirmation is different; for to them it was confirmed by circumcision, which among us has been succeeded by baptism. Otherwise, if the testimony by which the Jews were assured of the salvation of their seed be taken away from us, the effect of the advent of Christ has been to render the grace of God more obscure and less attested to us than it was to the Jews. If this cannot be affirmed without great dishonour to Christ, by whom the infinite goodness of God has been diffused over the earth, and manifested to men in a more conspicuous and liberal manner than at any former period, we must be obliged to confess, that at least it ought not to be more concealed or less attested than under the obscure shadows of the law.

VII. Wherefore the Lord Jesus, to exhibit a specimen from which the world might understand that he was come to extend rather than to limit the mercy of the Father, kindly received the infants that were presented to him, and embraced them in his arms, chiding his disciples who endeavoured to forbid their approach to him, because they would keep those, of whom was the kingdom of heaven, at a distance from him who is the only way of entrance into it. But some will object, What resemblance does this embrace of Christ bear to baptism? for he is not said to have baptized them, but to have received them, taken them in his arms, and blessed them; therefore, if we desire to imitate his example, let us assist infants with our prayers, but let us not baptize them. But it is necessary to consider the conduct of Christ with more attention than it receives from persons of this class. For it is not to be passed over as a thing of little importance, that Christ commanded infants to be brought to him, and added, as a reason for this command, "For of such is the kingdom of heaven;" and afterwards gave a practical testimony of his will, when, embracing them in his arms, he commended them to his Father by his prayers and benedictions. If it be reasonable for infants to be brought to Christ, why is it not allowable to admit them to baptism, the symbol of our communion and fellowship with Christ? If of them is the kingdom of heaven, why shall they be denied the sign, which opens, as it were, an entrance into the Church, that, being received into it, they may be enrolled among the heirs of the heavenly kingdom? How unjust shall we be, if we drive away from Christ those whom he invites to him; if we deprive them of the gifts with which he adorns them; if we exclude those whom he freely admits! But if we examine how far what Christ did on that occasion differs from baptism, how much greater importance shall we attach to baptism, by which we testify that infants are included in the covenant of God, than to the reception, the embrace, the imposition of hands, and the prayers by which Jesus Christ himself acknowledged them as his, and declared them to be sanctified by him! The other cavils by which our opponents endeavour to elude the force of this passage, only betray their ignorance. For they argue that as Christ said, "Suffer little children to *come*," they must have been grown to such an age and stature as to be capable of walking. But they are called by the evangelists Βρεφη and παιδια, two words used by the Greeks to signify little infants hanging on the breast. The word "*come*," therefore, is merely used to denote "*access*." To such evasions are persons obliged to have recourse, who resist the truth. Nor is there any more solidity in the objection, that the kingdom of heaven is not said to belong to infants, but to those who resemble them, because the expression is, not of *them*, but "of *such* is the kingdom of heaven." For if this be admitted, what kind of reason would it be that Christ assigns, with a view to show that infants in age ought not to be prevented from approaching him, when he says, "Suffer little children to come unto me?" Nothing can be plainer than that he intends those who are in a state of real infancy. And to prevent this from being thought unreasonable, he adds, "Of such is the kingdom of heaven." And if infants be necessarily comprehended, it is beyond all doubt that the word "*such*" designates both infants themselves and those who resemble them. (*e*)

VIII. Now, every one must perceive, that the baptism of infants, which is so strongly supported by the authority of Scripture, is very far from being an invention of men. Nor is there much plausibility in the objection, that it is nowhere stated that even a single infant was baptized by the hands of the apostles. For though no such circumstance is expressly mentioned by the evangelists, yet, on the other hand, as they are never excluded when mention happens to be made of the baptism of any family, who can rationally conclude from this, that they were not baptized? If there were any force in such arguments, women might as well be interdicted from the Lord's supper, because we have no account of their having been admitted to it in the days of the apostles. But in this we are content with the rule of faith. For when we consider the design of the institution of the Lord's supper, the conclusion is easy respecting the persons who ought to be admitted to a participation of it. We observe the same rule also in the case of baptism. For when we consider the end of its institution, we evidently perceive that it belongs to infants as well as to adults. Therefore they cannot be deprived of it without a manifest evasion of the will of the Divine Author. What they circulate among the uninformed multitude, that after the resurrection of Christ, a long series of years passed, in which infant baptism was unknown, is shamefully contrary to truth, for there is no ancient writer who does not refer its origin, as a matter of certainty, to the age of the apostles.

IX. It remains for us briefly to show what advantage results from this ceremony, both to believers who present their children to the Church to be baptized, and to the infants themselves who

---

(*e*) Matt. xix. 13—15. Mark x. 13—16. Luke xviii. 15—17.

are washed in the holy water; to guard it from being despised as useless or unimportant. But if any man takes it into his head to ridicule infant baptism on this pretext, he holds the command of circumcision, which was given by the Lord, in equal contempt. For what will they allege to impugn the baptism of infants, which may not be retorted against circumcision? Thus the Lord avenges the arrogance of those, who forthwith condemn what their carnal sense does not comprehend. But God furnishes us with other weapons to repel their folly; nor does this sacred ordinance of his appointment, which we experience to be a source of peculiar support and consolation to our faith, deserve to be called unnecessary. For this sign of God, communicated to a child, like the impress of a seal, ratifies and confirms the promise given to the pious parent, declaring that the Lord will be a God, not only to him, but also to his seed, and that he is determined to exercise his goodness and grace, not only towards him, but towards his posterity even to a thousand generations. The manifestation here given of the mercy of God, in the first place, furnishes the most abundant matter for the celebration of his glory; and in the second place, fills pious breasts with more than common joy, by which they are excited to a more ardent return of affection to such an indulgent Father, in whom they discover such care of their posterity on their account. Nor shall I regard an objection, if it should be urged, that the mere promise of God ought to be sufficient to assure us of the salvation of our children; since God, who knows our weakness, and has been pleased in this instance to indulge it, has decided otherwise. Let those, therefore, who embrace the promise of God that he will perpetuate his mercy to their offspring, consider it their duty to present them to the Church to be signed with the symbol of mercy, and thereby to animate their minds to stronger confidence, when they actually see the covenant of the Lord engraven on the bodies of their children. The children also receive some advantage from their baptism, their ingrafting into the body of the Church being a more peculiar recommendation of them to the other members; and afterwards, when they grow to years of maturity, it operates upon them as a powerful stimulus to a serious attention to the worship of God, by whom they were accepted as his children by the solemn symbol of adoption, before they were capable of knowing him as their Father. Finally, we ought to be alarmed by the vengeance which God threatens to inflict, if any one disdains to mark his son with the symbol of the covenant; for the contempt of that symbol involves the rejection and abjuration of the grace which it presents.

X. Let us now discuss the arguments with which some violent disputants continue to impugn this holy institution of God. In the first place, finding themselves very hardly pressed and exceedingly embarrassed by the similarity of baptism and circumcision, they labour to establish a considerable difference between these two signs, that one may appear to have nothing in common with the other. For they affirm, first, that different things are signified; secondly, that the covenant is entirely different; and thirdly, that the children are mentioned in a different manner. But when they endeavour to prove the first point, they allege that circumcision was a figure of mortification, and not of baptism; which we most readily grant, for it is an excellent argument in our favour. We urge no other proof of our sentiment, than that baptism and circumcision are equally signs of mortification. Hence we conclude, that baptism was introduced in the place of circumcision, and represents to us the very same thing which that formerly did to the Jews. In asserting a difference of the covenant, with what presumption and absurdity do they corrupt the Scripture, and that not in a single passage, but without leaving any part of it secure from their perversions. For they represent the carnality of the Jews to be such, as to give them a greater resemblance to brutes than to rational beings; contending that the covenant made with them was limited to a temporary life, and that the promises given to them were all confined to present and corporeal enjoyments. If this notion be admitted, what remains but to consider the Jewish people as pampered for a season by the Divine bounty, (like a herd of swine, fattened in a sty,) to perish at length in eternal ruin? For whenever we adduce circumcision and the promises annexed to it, they reply, that circumcision was a literal sign, and that the promises connected with it were all carnal.

XI. Certainly, if circumcision was a literal sign, the same opinion must be formed of baptism; for the apostle makes one no more spiritual than the other. He says to the Colossians, "In Christ ye are circumcised with the circumcision made without hands, in putting off the body of the sins of the flesh;" and this he calls "the circumcision of Christ." In explication of this sentiment, he adds, that they were "buried with Christ in baptism." (*f*) What is the meaning of this language, but that the accomplishment and truth of baptism is the same with the accomplishment and truth of circumcision, since they both represent the same thing? For his design is to show that baptism was to Christians the same that circumcision had before been to the Jews. But as we have now clearly evinced that the promises of these two signs, and the mysteries represented by them, are precisely the same, we shall insist no longer on this point at present. I will only recommend believers to consider, whether that sign ought to be accounted earthly and literal, which contains nothing but what is spiritual and heavenly. But to guard the simple against their fallacies, we shall briefly reply by the way to one objection, by which they endeavour to support this shameful misrepresentation. It is very certain that the principal promises of the covenant, which God made with the Israelites under the Old Testament, were spiritual, and had reference to eternal life; and that they were also understood by the fathers, as they ought to be, in a spiritual sense, and inspired them with confident hopes of the life to come, towards which they aspired with all the powers of their souls. At the same time, we are far from denying that he testified his benevolence to them by terrestrial and carnal advantages, by which we also maintain that their hopes of spiritual promises were confirmed. Thus, when he promised eternal blessedness to his servant Abraham, he added, in order to set a manifest token of his favour before his eyes, another promise respecting the possession of the land of Canaan. In this manner we ought to understand all the terrestrial promises which were given to the Jewish nation; so that the spiritual promise may always be considered as a source and foundation, to which the others may be referred. But having treated these points more at large in discussing the difference of the Old and New Testaments, I touch the more slightly upon them here.

(*f*) Col. ii. 11, 12.

XII. In the mention of the children they find this variety, that under the Old Testament, those were called the children of Abraham, who derived their natural descent from him; but that now this appellation is given to those who imitate his faith; and that, therefore, that carnal infancy, which was ingrafted into the fellowship of the Church by circumcision, prefigured those spiritual infants of the New Testament, who by the word of God are regenerated to an immortal life. In this language we discover, indeed, a small spark of truth; but it is a great error of these persons, that while they lay hold of whatever first comes to their hands, when they ought to pursue it much further, and to compare many things together, they pertinaciously insist on a single word; hence it necessarily happens that they are often deceived, because they acquire no solid knowledge of any thing. We confess that the natural seed of Abraham did for a time hold the place of those spiritual children which are incorporated with him by faith. For we are called his children, notwithstanding there is no natural relationship between him and us. But if they understand, as they certainly do, that no spiritual blessing was ever promised by God to the carnal seed of Abraham, they are greatly deceived. It behoves us to aim at a more correct sentiment, to which we are directed by the certain guidance of the Scripture. The Lord, therefore, promised to Abraham, that he should have a Seed, in whom all the nations of the earth were to be blessed, and accompanied this promise with an assurance that he would be a God to him, and to his seed. All those, who by faith received Christ, the Author of the blessing, are heirs of this promise, and are therefore denominated "children of Abraham."

XIII. Though, after the resurrection of Christ, the boundaries of the kingdom of God began to be extended far and wide into all nations, without any distinction, that, according to the declaration of Christ, believers might be collected "from the east, and from the west, and from the north, and from the south," to "sit down with Abraham, and Isaac, and Jacob," (*g*) in the glory of heaven, yet he had embraced the Jews with this great mercy for many ages before; and because he had passed by all others, and

(*g*) Matt. viii. 11. Luke xiii. 29.

selected this one nation, to be for a season the exclusive objects of his grace, he called them his "peculiar treasure" and "special people." (*h*) In attestation of this beneficence, the Lord gave them circumcision, which was a sign to teach the Jews that he would be their defence and salvation; and the knowledge of this inspired their hearts with the hope of eternal life. For what can be wanting to them whom God has taken into his charge? Wherefore the apostle, with a view to prove that the Gentiles are children of Abraham as well as the Jews, expresses himself in the following manner: "Faith was reckoned to Abraham for righteousness in uncircumcision. And he received the sign of circumcision, a seal of the righteousness of the faith which he had yet being uncircumcised; that he might be the father of all them that believe, though they be not circumcised; that righteousness might be imputed unto them also; and the father of circumcision to them who are not of the circumcision only, but who also walk in the steps of that faith of our father Abraham, which he had being yet uncircumcised." (*i*) Do not we see that equal dignity is attributed to Jews and Gentiles? For during the time fixed by the degree of God, Abraham was the father of circumcision. When the "middle wall of partition between" them was "broken down," (*k*) as the apostle says in another place, to give the Gentiles an entrance into the kingdom of God, he became also their father, and that without the sign of circumcision; for instead of circumcision, they have baptism. The express intimation, that Abraham was not a father to them who were of the circumcision only, was introduced by the apostle, to repress the vain confidence of some who neglected all concern about piety, and prided themselves in mere ceremonies. In the same manner, we may now refute the vanity of those who in baptism never carry their thoughts beyond the water.

XIV. But in objection to this, another passage is adduced from the same apostle, in which he states, "that they which are the children of the flesh" are not "the children of Abraham," but that only "the children of the promise are counted for the seed." (*l*) For this passage seems to imply, that carnal descent from Abraham is nothing, though we attribute some importance to it. But it

(*h*) Exod. xix. 5. Deut. vii. 6. (*i*) Rom. iv. 9—12.
(*k*) Eph. ii. 14. (*l*) Rom. ix. 7, 8.

is requisite to pay more particular attention to the subject which the apostle is here discussing. For in order to show to the Jews, that the goodness of God was not confined to the seed of Abraham, and even that carnal descent from him was of no value in itself he alleges, in proof of it, the cases of Ishmael and Esau, who, notwithstanding they were the true offspring of Abraham according to the flesh, were rejected as if they had been strangers, and the blessing remained with Isaac and Jacob. Hence follows what he afterwards affirms—that salvation depends on the mercy of God, which he imparts to whom he pleases; but that the Jews have no reason for satisfaction, or glorying in the name of the covenant, unless they observe the law of the covenant; that is, obey the Divine word. Yet, after having demolished their vain confidence in their descent, knowing, on the other hand, that the covenant which God had once made with the posterity of Abraham could by no means be invalidated, he argues, that the natural descendants are not to be deprived of their dignity; by virtue of which he shows that the Jews were the first and natural heirs of the gospel, only that they had been rejected as unworthy, on account of their ingratitude, yet that the heavenly benediction had not entirely departed from their nation. For which reason, though they were rebels and violators of the covenant, yet he calls them holy; such high honours does he give to the holy generation, which God honoured with his sacred covenant; but he considers us, in comparison with them, as the posthumous, and even abortive children of Abraham, and that not by nature, but by adoption; as if a branch broken off from its native tree were ingrafted on another stock. That they might not be defrauded of their prerogative, therefore, it was necessary for the gospel to be first announced to them; for they are, as it were, the first-born in the family of God. Wherefore this honour was to be given to them, till they rejected the offer of it, and by their ingratitude caused it to be transferred to the Gentiles. Nor, whatever be the obstinacy with which they persist in opposing the gospel, ought they, on that account, to be despised by us, if we consider that, for the sake of the promise, the blessing of God still remains among them; as the apostle clearly testifies that it will never entirely depart from them; "for the gifts and calling of God are without repentance." (*m*)

XV. See, now, the importance and the estimate to be formed of the promise given to the posterity of Abraham. Therefore, though we have no doubt that the distinction of the heirs of the kingdom from those who have no share in it, is the free act of the sovereign election of God, yet, at the same time, we perceive that he has been pleased to display his mercy in a peculiar manner on the seed of Abraham, and to testify and seal it by circumcision. The same reason is applicable to the Christian Church. For as Paul, in that passage, argues that the children of the Jews were sanctified by their parents, so, in another place, (*n*) he teaches that the children of Christians derive the same sanctification from their parents; whence it is inferred, that they who, on the contrary, are condemned as impure, are deservedly separated from others. Now, who can doubt the falsehood of the consequence attempted to be established, that the infants who were circumcised in former ages, only prefigured those who are infants in a spiritual sense, being regenerated by the word of God? Paul does not reason in this manner, when he says, "that Jesus Christ was a minister of the circumcision for the truth of God, to confirm the promises made unto the fathers;" (*o*) as if he had said, Since the covenant made with Abraham relates to his seed, Jesus Christ, in order to execute and discharge the promise once pledged by the Father, came to save the people of the Jews. We see how, even after the resurrection of Christ, Paul understands that the promise of the covenant is to be fulfilled, not only in an allegorical sense, but, according to the literal import of the words, to the natural seed of Abraham. To the same effect is the declaration of Peter to the Jews, "The promise is unto you and to your children," (*p*) and the appellation under which he addresses them, "Ye are the children of the covenant," (*q*) and if children, then heirs. A similar sentiment is conveyed in another passage of the apostle, which we have already quoted, where he represents the circumcision performed on infants as a testimony of the communion which they have with Christ. (*r*) And, on the contrary principle, what will

(*m*) Rom. xi. 29. (*n*) 1 Cor. vii. 14. (*o*) Rom. xv. 8.
(*p*) Acts ii. 39. (*q*) Acts iii. 25. (*r*) Eph. i. 11, 12.

become of that promise, by which the Lord, in the second precept of his law, declares to his servants, that he will be merciful to their seed, even to a thousand generations? (*s*) Shall we here have recourse to allegories? That would be a frivolous evasion. Shall we say that this promise is cancelled? That would be subversive of the law, which, on the contrary, Christ came to establish, as a rule, for a holy life. It ought to be admitted, therefore, beyond all controversy, that God is so kind and liberal to his servants, as, for their sakes, to appoint even the children who shall descend from them to be enrolled among his people.

XVI. The other differences which they endeavour to establish between baptism and circumcision, are not only ridiculous, and destitute of every appearance of reason, but are even repugnant to each other. For after they have affirmed that baptism belongs to the first day of the spiritual conflict, but circumcision to the eighth, when the mortification is already completed,—immediately forgetting this, they change their story, and call circumcision a sign of the mortification of the flesh, and baptism a symbol of a burial, to which none are to be consigned but those who are already dead. Where can we find another instance of such levity of self-contradiction? For, according to the first proposition, baptism ought to precede circumcision; according to the second, it ought to follow it. Yet it is not a new thing for the minds of men to run into such inconsistencies, when they prefer their own dreams to the unerring word of God. We say, therefore, that the first of these differences is a mere dream. If they wished to allegorize on the eighth day, yet there was no propriety in this manner of doing it. It would have been much better to follow the ancients, and refer the number of the day either to the resurrection of Christ, which took place on the eighth day, and on which we know that newness of life depends; or to the whole course of the present life, which ought to be a course of progressive mortification, till, at the termination of life, the mortification also should be completed. It is probable, however, that God deferred circumcision to the eighth day on account of the tenderness of young infants, whose lives might be endangered by the

(*s*) Exod. xx. 6.

performance of that rite immediately on their birth. Nor is there much more solidity in the second position, that, after being dead, we are buried by baptism; since the Scripture expressly teaches, that "we are buried by baptism into death," (*t*) in order to our entrance on a course of mortification, and continuance in it from that time forward! Nor is there any more propriety in the objection, that, if it be necessary to conform baptism to circumcision, women ought not to be baptized. For if it be evident, that the sign of circumcision testified with sanctification of the seed of Israel, there can be no doubt that it was given equally for the sanctification of males and females. And though only the males were circumcised, they alone being capable of it, the females were in a certain sense partakers of their circumcision. Dismissing such follies, therefore, let us never forget the similarity of baptism and circumcision, between which we discover a complete agreement in the internal mystery, the promises, the use, and the efficacy.

XVII. They consider themselves as advancing a most powerful argument for excluding infants from baptism, when they allege, that by reason of their age they are not yet capable of understanding the mystery signified in it; that is, spiritual regeneration, which cannot take place in early infancy. Therefore they conclude, they are to be considered in no other view than as children of Adam, till they have attained an age which admits of a second birth. But all these things are uniformly contradicted by the truth of God. For if they must be left among the children of Adam, they are left in death; for in Adam we can only die. On the contrary, Christ commands them to be brought to him. Why? Because he is life. To give them life, therefore, he makes them partakers of himself, while these men, by driving them away from him, adjudge them to death. For if they pretend that infants do not perish, even though they are considered as children of Adam, their error is abundantly refuted by the testimony of Scripture. For when it pronounces that "in Adam all die," (*v*) it follows that there remains no hope of life but in Christ. In order to become heirs of life, therefore, it is necessary for us to be partakers of

(*t*) Rom. vi. 4. (*v*) 1 Cor. xv. 22.

him. So, when it is said, in other places, that we are "by nature the children of wrath," (*w*) and "conceived in sin," (*x*) with which condemnation is always connected, it follows, that we must depart from our own nature, to have any admission to the kingdom of God. And what can be more explicit than this declaration, "that flesh and blood cannot inherit the kingdom of God?" (*y*) Let every thing of our own, therefore, be destroyed, which will not be effected without regeneration, and then we shall see this possession of the kingdom. Lastly, if Christ speaks the truth, when he declares himself to be "life," (*z*) it is necessary for us to be ingrafted into him, that we may be rescued from the bondage of death. But how, it is inquired, are infants regenerated, who have no knowledge either of good or evil? We reply, that the work of God is not yet without existence, because it is not observed or understood by us. Now, it is certain that some infants are saved; and that they are previously regenerated by the Lord, is beyond all doubt. For if they are born in a state of corruption, it is necessary for them to be purified before they are admitted into the kingdom of God, into which "there shall in no wise enter any thing that defileth." (*a*) If they are born sinners, as both David and Paul affirm, either they must remain unacceptable and hateful to God, or it is necessary for them to be justified. And what do we require more, when the Judge himself declares that there is no entrance into the heavenly life, except for those who are born again? (*b*) And, to silence all objectors, by sanctifying John the Baptist in his mother's womb, he exhibited an example of what he was able to do for others. Nor can they gain any advantage by their frivolous evasion, that this was only a single case, which does not justify the conclusion that the Lord generally acts in this manner with infants. For we use no such argument. We only mean to show, that they unjustly confine the power of God within those narrow limits to which it does not suffer itself to be restricted. Their other subterfuge is equally weak. They allege that, according to the usage of the Scripture, the phrase *from the womb* denotes *from childhood.* But it is easy to see that, in the declaration of the angel to Zacharias, it was used in a different sense, and that

(*w*) Eph. ii. 3. (*x*) Psalm li. 5. (*y*) 1 Cor. xv. 50.
(*z*) John xi. 25; xiv. 6. (*a*) Rev. xxi. 27. (*b*) John iii. 3, 5.

John was to be filled with the Holy Spirit, even before he was born. (*c*) Let us not attempt, therefore, to impose laws upon God, whose power has sustained no diminution, but who is able to sanctify whom he pleases, as he sanctified this child.

XVIII. And for this reason, Christ was sanctified from his earliest infancy, that he might sanctify in himself all his elect, of every age, without any difference. For as, in order to obliterate the guilt of the transgression which had been perpetrated in our flesh, he assumed to himself that very flesh, that he might perform a perfect obedience in it, on our account, and in our stead, so he was conceived of the Holy Spirit, that, having the whole body which he assumed, fully endued with the sanctity of the Spirit, he might communicate the same to us. If Christ exhibits a perfect exemplar of all the graces which God bestows upon his children, he will also furnish us with a proof, that the age of infancy is not altogether incompatible with sanctification. But, however this may be, we consider it as clear, beyond all controversy, that not one of the elect is called out of the present life, without having been previously regenerated and sanctified by the Spirit of God. Their objection, that the Holy Spirit, in the Scriptures, acknowledges no regeneration, except from "the incorruptible seed," that is, "the word of God," (*d*) is a misinterpretation of that passage of Peter, which merely comprehends believers who had been taught by the preaching of the gospel. To such persons, indeed, we grant that the word of the Lord is the only seed of spiritual regeneration; but we deny that it ought to be concluded from this, that infants cannot be regenerated by the power of God, which is as easy to him as it is wonderful and mysterious to us. Besides, it would not be safe to affirm, that the Lord cannot reveal himself in any way so as to make himself known to them.

XIX. But our opponents say, "Faith cometh by hearing," (*e*) of which they have not yet acquired the use, and they cannot be capable of knowing God; for Moses declares them to "have no knowledge between good and evil." (*f*) But they do not consider, that when the apostle makes hearing the source of faith, he only

(*c*) Luke i. 15.
(*d*) 1 Peter i. 23.
(*e*) Rom. x. 17.
(*f*) Deut. i. 39.

describes the ordinary economy and dispensation of the Lord, which he generally observes in the calling of his people; but does not prescribe a perpetual rule for him, precluding his employment of any other method; which he has certainly employed in the calling of many, to whom he has given the true knowledge of himself in an internal manner, by the illumination of his Spirit, without the intervention of any preaching. But as they think it would be such a great absurdity for any knowledge of God to be given to infants, to whom Moses denies the knowledge of good and evil, I would beg them to inform me, what danger can result from our affirming that they already receive some portion of that grace, of which they will ere long enjoy the full abundance. For if the plenitude of life consists in the perfect knowledge of God,—when some of them, whom death removes from the present state in their earliest infancy, pass into eternal life, they are certainly admitted to the immediate contemplation of the presence of God. As the Lord, therefore, will illuminate them with the full splendour of his countenance in heaven, why may he not also, if such be his pleasure, irradiate them with some faint rays of it in the present life; especially if he does not deliver them from all ignorance before he liberates them from the prison of the body? Not that I would hastily affirm them to be endued with the same faith which we experience in ourselves, or at all to possess a similar knowledge of faith, which I would prefer leaving in suspense; my design is only to check their foolish arrogance, who presumptuously assert or deny whatever they please.

XX. To strengthen their cause still further, our opponents proceed to allege, that baptism is a sacrament of repentance and faith; and that, therefore, as neither of these can be exercised in infancy, infants ought not to be admitted to a participation of baptism, the signification of which would thereby be rendered vain. But these arguments are directed against God, more than against us. For it is very evident, from many testimonies of Scripture, that circumcision also was a sign of repentance, and Paul calls it "a seal of the righteousness of faith." (*g*) Let the

---

(*g*) Jer. iv. 4. Rom. iv. 11.

reason, then, be demanded of God himself, why he commanded it to be impressed on the bodies of infants. For, as baptism and circumcision both stand on the same ground, they can attribute nothing to the latter which they must not also grant to the former. If they recur to their favourite subterfuge, that the age of infancy then prefigured spiritual infants, it has been already answered. We say, therefore, that since God formerly communicated to infants the rite of circumcision, which was a sacrament of repentance and faith, it appears to be no absurdity for them now to be admitted to a participation of baptism; unless these men wish to offer a direct insult to the institution of God. But in this, as well as in all the proceedings of God, his wisdom and righteousness are sufficiently conspicuous to repress the opposition and detraction of the impious. For though infants, at the time of their circumcision, did not understand the meaning of that sign, they were nevertheless truly circumcised into the mortification of their corrupt and polluted nature, which they were to pursue in mature years. In short, this objection may be answered without any difficulty, by saying that they are baptized into future repentance and faith; for though these graces have not yet been formed in them, the seeds of both are nevertheless implanted in their hearts by the secret operation of the Spirit. This answer at once overturns every argument they urge against us, derived from the signification of baptism; as when they allege the designation given it by Paul, where he calls it "the washing of regeneration and renewing;" (*h*) whence they argue that it ought to be given only to such as are capable of being regenerated and renewed. But we may reply, on the other hand, neither was circumcision, which was a sign of regeneration, to be given to any but such as were already regenerated; and this, in their apprehension, will be to condemn the ordinance of God. Therefore, as we have suggested several times before, whatever arguments tend equally to invalidate circumcision, can have no force in the controversy against baptism. Nor can they escape from any difficulty, by saying, that whatever clearly rests on the authority of God, we ought to consider as fixed and

(*h*) Titus iii. 5.

determined, though we can discover no reason for it; but that this reverence is not due to infant baptism, or to other similar things, which are not enjoined upon us by the express word of God; for they will always be held fast by this dilemma. Either the command of God, respecting the circumcision of infants, was legitimate and liable to no objections, or it was deserving of censure. If there was no absurdity in that command, neither can any absurdity be detected in the practice of infant baptism.

XXI. The charge of absurdity, with which they endeavour to stigmatize it, we thus refute: If any of those who are the objects of divine election, after having received the sign of regeneration, depart out of this life before they have attained years of discretion, the Lord renovates them by the power of his Spirit, incomprehensible to us, in such a manner as he alone foresees will be necessary. If they happen to live to an age at which they are capable of being instructed in the true signification of baptism, they will hence be the more inflamed to the pursuit of that renovation, with the token of which they find themselves to have been favoured in their earliest infancy, that it might be the object of their constant attention all their lifetime. In the same sense must be understood what Paul states in two places, that we are "buried with Christ by baptism." (*i*) For he does not mean that he who is to be baptized, must previously be buried with Christ, but simply declares the doctrine which is contained in baptism, and that to persons already baptized; so that it would be unreasonable to argue from those passages, that such burial with Christ must precede baptism. In this manner Moses and the prophets reminded the people what was the meaning of circumcision, though they had received that rite when they were infants. To the same effect is what Paul writes to the Galatians, that "as many as have been baptized into Christ, have put on Christ." (*k*) For what purpose? Why, that they might thenceforward live to Christ, who had never lived to him before. And though in adults a knowledge of the mystery ought to precede the reception of the sign, yet a different rule is to be applied to infants, as we shall presently show. Nor can any other conclusion be drawn from that passage of Peter,

(*i*) Rom. vi. 4. Col. ii. 12. (*k*) Gal. iii. 27.

which they consider as decisive in their favour—that baptism is "not the putting away of the filth of the flesh, but the answer of a good conscience toward God, by the resurrection of Jesus Christ." (*l*) They contend that this passage leaves not the least room for the baptism of infants, who are not capable of that in which the truth of baptism is here stated to consist. But they frequently fall into this error, of maintaining that the thing signified should always precede the sign. For the truth of circumcision also consisted in the same answer of a good conscience; but if it ought of necessity to precede it, infants would never have been circumcised by the command of God. But by showing us that the answer of a good conscience is comprehended in the truth of circumcision, and at the same time commanding infants to be circumcised, he sufficiently indicates that it is administered with a view to something future. Wherefore, all the present efficacy to be required in the baptism of infants, is to ratify and confirm the covenant made with them by the Lord. The remaining signification of this sacrament will follow afterwards, at the time foreseen and appointed by the Lord.

XXII. It must now, I think, be evident to every person, that all arguments of this kind are mere perversions of Scripture. Those which remain, and are nearly allied to these, we shall run over in a cursory manner. They object, that baptism is given for the remission of sins: this we admit, and it is completely in favour of our opinion. For being born sinners, we need pardon and remission even from our birth. Now, as the Lord does not exclude infants from the hope of mercy, but rather assures them of it, why shall we refuse them the sign, which is so far inferior to the thing signified? Wherefore, the argument which they urge against us, we retort upon themselves; infants are favoured with remission of sins,—therefore they ought not to be deprived of the sign. They also adduce that passage where the Lord is said to "cleanse the Church with the washing of water by the word." (*m*) But no text could be quoted more conclusive against their error; it furnishes an obvious confirmation of our sentiment. If it be the will of Christ that the ablution, with which

---

(*l*) 1 Peter iii. 21.   (*m*) Ephes. v. 26.

he cleanses his Church, be testified by baptism, it appears unreasonable that its testimony should be wanting in infants, who are justly considered as part of the Church, since they are called heirs of the kingdom of heaven. For Paul speaks of the whole Church, when he describes it as cleansed with the washing of water. And, on the same principle, from that passage where he says that we are all baptized into the body of Christ, (*n*) we conclude that infants, whom he numbers among his members, ought to be baptized, that they may not be separated from his body. See with what violence, and with what variety of weapons, they attack the bulwarks of our faith!

XXIII. They proceed, in the next place, to the practice of the apostolic age, in which no one is found to have been admitted to baptism without a previous profession of faith and repentance. For in answer to those who "were pricked in their heart, and said, What shall we do? Peter said unto them," first, "repent," and then "be baptized for the remission of sins." (*o*) In like manner Philip, when the eunuch requested to be baptized, replied, "If thou believest with all thine heart, thou mayest." (*p*) Hence they think themselves justified in concluding, that baptism ought never to be administered to any person without being preceded by faith and repentance. But if we adopt this reasoning, the first of these passages, which makes no mention of faith, will evince the sufficiency of repentance alone: the second, where repentance is not required, will prove that faith alone is sufficient. I suppose they will reply that one passage is elucidated by the other, and that therefore they ought to be connected together. I also contend that other places ought to be consulted, which may contribute to the solution of this difficulty. For there are many passages of Scripture, the sense of which depends on the circumstances connected with them. This is exemplified in the cases now under consideration. For the persons addressed by Peter and Philip were of an age capable of exercising repentance and faith. We strenuously deny that such persons ought to be baptized, without a knowledge of their repentance and faith, as far, at least, as they are capable of being ascertained by the judgment of men. But that

(*n*) 1 Cor. xii. 13. (*o*) Acts ii. 37, 38. (*p*) Acts viii. 37.

infants ought to be ranked in a different class, is sufficiently evident; for, under the former dispensation, if any person connected himself with the Israelites in religious communion, it was necessary for him to be taught the covenant of the Lord, and instructed in the law, before he received circumcision, because he was an alien by birth, not one of the Israelitish people, with whom the covenant, which was confirmed by circumcision, had been made.

XXIV. So the Lord himself, when he adopts Abraham, does not begin with circumcision, concealing for a time what was intended by that sign; but he first announces the covenant which he designs to make with him, and then, after he has received that promise in faith, makes him a partaker of that sacrament. Why does the sacrament follow faith in the case of Abraham, and in Isaac, his son, precede all exercise of understanding? Because it is reasonable that a person, who at an adult age is admitted to the fellowship of a covenant, to which he had hitherto been a stranger, should first learn the conditions of it; but this is not necessary in the case of an infant, who, by hereditary right, according to the form of the promise, is already included in the covenant from its very birth. Or, to express it with greater clearness and brevity, if the children of believers, without the aid of understanding, are partakers of the covenant, there is no reason why they should be excluded from the sign because they are not capable of expressing their consent to the stipulation of the covenant. This is evidently the reason why God sometimes declares the children descended from the Israelites to be born to himself; (*q*) for he undoubtedly considers as his children, the children of those to whose seed he has promised to be a Father. But he who is an unbeliever, descended from impious parents, is accounted an alien from the communion of the covenant, till he be united to God by faith. It is no wonder, therefore, if he be not a partaker of the sign, the signification of which in him would be delusive and vain. In this sense Paul tells the Ephesians, that as long as they were immersed in idolatry, they were "strangers from the covenant." (*r*) The whole of the subject, if

(*q*) Ezek. xvi. 20; xxiii. 37. (*r*) Eph. ii. 12.

I mistake not, may be clearly and summarily stated in the following position; that persons of adult age, who embrace the Christian religion, having been hitherto aliens from the covenant, are not to receive the sign of baptism without the intervention of faith and repentance, which alone can give them an admission to the fellowship of the covenant; but that the infant children of Christian parents, being admitted by God to the inheritance of the covenant as soon as they are born, are also to be admitted to baptism. To this must be referred what is related by the evangelists, that the people "were baptized of John, confessing their sins" (*s*)—an example which we think ought to be followed in the present day. For if a Turk or heathen were to offer himself to baptism, we would not hastily admit him to that sacrament, without his having first made a confession to the satisfaction of the Church.

XXV. Moreover, they adduce the language of Christ, which is recorded by John, and which they suppose to represent a present regeneration as requisite to baptism; "Except a man be born of water and the Spirit, he cannot enter into the kingdom of God." (*t*) See, they say, how baptism is called *regeneration* by the mouth of the Lord. When it is evident, then, that infants are utterly incapable of regeneration, on what pretence do we admit them to baptism, to which regeneration is indispensably necessary? In the first place, they are deceived in supposing that this passage refers to baptism, because it mentions water. For, after Christ had declared to Nicodemus the corruption of nature, and shown him the necessity of being born again,—because Nicodemus was dreaming of a second corporeal birth, he here indicates the manner in which God regenerates us, namely, by water and by the Spirit; as if he had said, by the Spirit who, in the ablution and purification of the souls of believers, performs the office of water. I therefore understand by "water and the Spirit," simply, the Spirit who is water. Nor is this a novel mode of expression; for it perfectly corresponds with that declaration of John the Baptist, "He that cometh after me shall baptize with the Holy Ghost and with fire." (*v*) As *to baptize with the Holy Spirit and*

(*s*) Matt. iii. 6. (*t*) John iii. 5. (*v*) Matt. iii. 11.

with fire, therefore, is to confer the Holy Spirit, who, in regeneration, has the office and nature of fire, so *to be born of water and of the Spirit* is no other than to receive that influence of the Spirit, which does in the soul what water does on the body. I know that others give a different interpretation, but I have no doubt that this is the genuine sense; because the intention of Christ is simply to teach that all must be divested of their own nature, who aspire to the kingdom of heaven. However, if we were desirous of imitating their cavils, it would be easy for us, granting what they require, to retort upon them, that baptism is prior to faith and repentance, because in the words of Christ, water is mentioned before the Spirit. It is certain that this phrase denotes spiritual gifts; and, if these follow baptism, I have established what I wish. But, leaving all subterfuges, let us adhere to the simple interpretation which I have proposed—that no one, till he is renewed by living water, that is, by the Spirit, can enter into the kingdom of God.

XXVI. It is further evident that their notion ought to be exploded, because it adjudges all unbaptized persons to eternal death. Let us suppose their tenet to be admitted, and baptism to be administered to adults alone; what will they say will become of a youth who is rightly instructed in the first principles of piety, if he desires to be baptized, but, contrary to the expectation of all around, happens to be snatched away by sudden death? The Lord's promise is clear: "Whosoever believeth on the Son, shall not come into condemnation;" but "is passed from death unto life." (*w*) We are nowhere informed of his having condemned one who had yet not been baptized. By this I would not be understood as implying that baptism may be despised with impunity; for, so far from attempting to excuse such contempt, I affirm it to be a violation of the covenant of the Lord; I only mean to evince that it is not so necessary, as that a person, who is deprived of the opportunity of embracing it, must immediately be considered as lost. But if we assent to their notion, we shall condemn all, without exception, whom any circumstance whatever prevents from being baptized, whatever faith they may otherwise

(*w*) John iii. 18; v. 24.

have, even that faith by which Christ himself is enjoyed. Moreover, they sentence all infants to eternal death, by denying them baptism, which, according to their own confession, is necessary to salvation. Let them see, now, how well they agree with the language of Christ, which adjudges the kingdom of heaven to little children. But though we should grant them every thing they contend for relative to the sense of this passage, still they will gain no advantage from it, unless they first overturn the doctrine which we have already established respecting the regeneration of infants.

XXVII. But the strongest argument of all in favour of their opinion, they boast, is contained in the original institution of baptism, which they quote from the last chapter of Matthew, where Christ, sending forth his disciples to all nations, gave them a commission, first to teach, and then to baptize. "Go ye therefore and teach all nations, baptizing them in the name of the Father, and of the Son, and of the Holy Ghost; teaching them to observe all things whatsoever I have commanded you." (*x*) Then, from the last chapter of Mark, they add, "He that believeth and is baptized shall be saved." (*y*) What more do we require, say they, when the language of our Lord clearly expresses that teaching ought to precede baptism, and represents baptism as subsequent to faith? Of this order, an example was furnished even by the Lord Jesus himself, who was not baptized till he was "about thirty years of age." (*z*) In what various ways do they embarrass themselves, and betray their ignorance! For it is a mistake, worse than childish, to consider that commission as the original institution of baptism, which Christ had commanded his apostles to administer from the commencement of his preaching. They have no reason to contend, therefore, that the law and rule of baptism ought to be derived from those two passages, as if they contained the first institution of it. Though we should indulge them by admitting this error, yet what force is there in their reasoning? Indeed, if we wanted to evade the force of their arguments, we need not have recourse to any little subterfuge; a most ample field presents itself before us. For while they so violently insist on the order of the words, as to argue,

(*x*) Matt. xxviii. 19, 20. (*y*) Mark xvi. 16. (*z*) Luke iii. 23.

that, when it is said, "Go teach and baptize," and "he that believeth and is baptized" the meaning is, that preaching ought to precede baptism, and that faith ought to precede the reception of baptism,—why may not we, on the other hand, reply, that baptizing ought to precede teaching the observance of those things which Christ has commanded, because it is said, "Baptize, teaching them to observe all things whatsoever I have commanded you." We have remarked the same thing on the declaration of Christ, which has just been quoted, respecting the regeneration of water and of the Spirit; for if it be understood according to their interpretation, it will appear from that passage that baptism is prior to regeneration, because it is mentioned first: Christ teaches that we must be born again, not of the Spirit and of water, but of water and of the Spirit.

XXVIII. Their invincible bulwark, in which they place such great confidence, seems already somewhat shaken; but as the truth may be sufficiently defended by simplicity, I have no inclination to escape with such sophistical and trivial arguments; they shall therefore have a solid reply. The principal command which Christ here gives to his apostles, is to preach the gospel, to which he subjoins the administration of baptism as an appendage. Besides, he says nothing of baptism, any otherwise than as its administration is subordinate to the office of teaching. For Christ sends his apostles to promulgate the gospel of all the nations of the world, that by the doctrine of salvation they may collect, from every land, men who before were lost, and introduce them into his kingdom. But what men, or men of what description? It is certain that there is no mention of any, but those who are capable of receiving instruction. He afterwards adds, that such persons, when they have been instructed, are to be baptized, and subjoins a promise: "He that believeth and is baptized shall be saved." Is there even a single syllable in the whole discourse respecting infants? What kind of argumentation, then, is that with which they assail us? Persons of *adult* age are to be instructed, in order that they may believe before they are to be baptized; *therefore* it is unlawful to administer baptism to *infants*. It will be impossible for them, with all their ingenuity, to prove any thing from this passage, except that the gospel is first to be preached to those who are capable of hearing it, before they are baptized; for it relates to no others. Let them raise an obstacle from this, if they can, to exclude infants from baptism.

XXIX. But to render their fallacies still more palpable, I will show the absurdity of them by a very plain similitude. The apostle says, "that if any would not work, neither should he eat." (*a*) Now, if any man should pretend to infer from this, that infants ought to be deprived of food, would he not deserve universal contempt? Why so? Because it would be a perverse application to all men, indiscriminately, of what was spoken of men of a certain class and a certain age. Nor is there any greater propriety in their reasoning in the present case. For what every one sees to belong exclusively to persons of adult age, they apply to infants, in order to make them subject to a rule, which was only prescribed for persons of riper years. The example of Christ is far from affording any support to their cause. He was not baptized till he was "about thirty years of age." That is true indeed; but the reason is obvious; because he then intended to lay a solid foundation for baptism by his preaching, or rather to establish that which had a little before been laid by John. Intending, therefore, to institute baptism in his doctrine, in order to conciliate the greater authority to his institution, he sanctified it in his own body, and that at the point of time which he knew to be most proper, namely, when he was about to commence his ministry. In short, they can prove nothing else from this circumstance, except that baptism derived its origin and commencement from the preaching of the gospel. If they approve of fixing the thirtieth year, why do they not observe it, but admit every one to baptism as soon as he is, in their judgment, sufficiently qualified for it? And even Servetus, one of their leaders, though he pertinaciously insisted on this age, yet began to boast of being a prophet himself when he had only attained his twenty-first year. As though it ought to be tolerated for a man to arrogate the office of a teacher in the Church before he is a member of it.

XXX. At length they object, that there is no more reason why infants should be admitted to baptism than to the Lord's supper,

---

(*a*) 2 Thess. iii. 10.

which, however, is not administered to them. As though the Scriptures did not make a considerable difference between the two cases in every respect. Infant communion was practised, indeed, in the ancient Church, as appears from Cyprian and Augustine; but the custom has very properly been discontinued. For if we consider the nature and property of baptism, we find it to be an entrance or initiation into the Church, by which we are enrolled among the people of God—a sign of our spiritual regeneration, by which we are born again as the children of God; whereas, on the contrary, the supper is appointed for those of riper years, who, having passed the tender state of infancy, are capable of bearing solid meat. This difference is very evidently marked in the Scripture; in which, as far as relates to baptism, the Lord makes no distinction of age, whereas he does not present the supper to the participation of all alike, but only to those who are capable of discerning the body and blood of the Lord, of examining their own consciences, of showing forth the Lord's death, and considering the power of it. Do we wish for any thing plainer than what the apostle inculcates in the following exhortation? "Let a man examine himself, and so let him eat of that bread, and drink of that cup." (*b*) It must, therefore, be preceded by examination, which would in vain be expected from infants. Again: "He that eateth and drinketh unworthily, eateth and drinketh damnation to himself, not discerning the Lord's body." (*c*) If no persons can be worthy partakers of it, except those who can truly distinguish the holiness of the body of Christ, why should we give to our tender infants poison instead of salutary food? What is that precept of the Lord, "This do in remembrance of me?" (*d*) What is the inference which the apostle deduces from it? "As often as ye eat this bread, and drink this cup, ye do show the Lord's death till he come." (*e*) What remembrance, I ask, shall we require from infants of that event, of which they have never attained any knowledge? What preaching of the cross of Christ, the virtue and benefit of which their minds are not yet capable of comprehending? Not one of these things is prescribed in baptism. Between these two signs, therefore, there is a con-

(*b*) 1 Cor. xi. 28.
(*c*) 1 Cor. xi. 29.
(*d*) 1 Cor. xi. 24, 25.
(*e*) 1 Cor. xi. 26.

siderable difference; such as we observe, also, between similar signs under the Old Testament. Circumcision, which is known to correspond to our baptism, was destined for infants. The passover, which has now been succeeded by the sacred supper, did not admit guests of all descriptions promiscuously, but was rightly eaten only by those who were of sufficient age to be able to inquire into its signification. If our opponents had a grain of sound sense, would they shut their eyes against a thing so clear and obvious?

XXXI. Though I am sorry to burden my readers with such an accumulation of reveries, yet it will be worth while to refute the specious arguments adduced in this controversy by Servetus, one of the most eminent of the Anabaptists, and even the chief glory of that sect. 1. He pretends that the symbols appointed by Christ, as they are perfect, require also those who receive them to be perfect, or persons capable of perfection. But the answer is easy—that the perfection of baptism reaches even unto death, and cannot with propriety be restricted to one instant of time. I observe, also, that it is foolish to expect a man on the first day to attain perfection, towards which baptism invites us to proceed, by continual advances, as long as we live. 2. He objects, that the symbols of Christ were instituted as memorials, that every one may remember that he has been buried with Christ. I answer, that what he has framed from his own head requires no refutation; and that he applies to baptism what the language of Paul shows to be peculiar to the sacred supper, namely, that every one should examine himself; but that nothing like this is any where said of baptism; from which we conclude, that though, by reason of their age, infants are not capable of examination, it is nevertheless right to baptize them. 3. He adduces the declaration of Christ, that "he that believeth not the Son shall not see life, but the wrath of God abideth on him;" (*g*) and concludes that infants, who are incapable of believing, remain in their condemnation. I answer, that in this passage Christ is not speaking of the general guilt in which all the descendants of Adam are involved, but only threatening the despisers of the gospel, who

(*g*) John iii. 36.

proudly and obstinately reject the grace which is offered to them; and this has nothing to do with infants. I likewise oppose a contrary argument; all those whom Christ blesses are exempted from the curse of Adam and the wrath of God; and as it is known that infants were blessed by him, it follows that they are exempted from death. He falsely alleges, as a passage of Scripture, that "whosoever is born of the Spirit heareth the voice of the Spirit;" which, though we were to admit as a genuine text, yet he could infer nothing more from it, than that believers are formed to obedience as the Spirit operates within them. But that which is affirmed of a certain number, it is wrong to apply equally to all. 4. He objects, that because "that is first which is natural," (*h*) we ought to wait the proper time for baptism, which is spiritual. Now, though I grant that all the descendants of Adam, being carnal, bring their condemnation into the world with them, yet I deny that this is any impediment to the communication of a remedy, as soon as ever God is pleased to impart it. For Servetus can show no Divine appointment, that many years shall elapse before the newness of spiritual life can begin; for according to the testimony of Paul, though the infant children of believers are in a ruined condition by nature, yet they are sanctified by supernatural grace. (*i*) 5. He next produces an allegory, that when David went up to the fortress of Zion, he took with him neither the blind nor the lame, but hardy soldiers. (*k*) And what if I oppose him with a parable, in which God invites the blind and the lame to the celestial feast? (*l*) how will he extricate himself from this difficulty? I ask, also, whether the blind and the lame had not previously served as soldiers with David. But it is useless to insist longer on this argument, which the readers will discover from the sacred history to be founded on mere falsehood. 6. Then follows another allegory, that the apostles were "fishers of men," (*m*) not of infants. I ask, what is the meaning of that declaration of Christ, that "the kingdom of heaven is like unto a net, that was cast into the sea, and gathered of every kind?" (*n*) But as I am not fond of allegorical trifling, I answer, that when the apostles were appointed to the office of teaching, they were not

(*h*) 1 Cor. xv. 46. (*i*) 1 Cor. vii. 14. (*k*) 2 Sam. v. 6—8.
(*l*) Luke xiv. 21. (*m*) Matt. iv. 19. (*n*) Matt. xiii. 47.

forbidden to baptize infants. I would further wish to be informed, since the evangelist uses the word ανθρωπους, (a word which comprehends all the human race, without any exception,) why infants should be denied to be ανθρωπους, (human beings.) 7. He pretends, that as spiritual things belong to spiritual persons, (*o*) infants who are not spiritual are not fit subjects of baptism. But here it is evident that he is guilty of a gross perversion of that passage of Paul, the subject of which relates to doctrine. When the Corinthians discovered too much complacency in a vain subtlety, the apostle reproved their stupidity, because they still required to be taught the first principles of Christian doctrine. Who can infer from this, that baptism ought to be denied to infants, whom, though they are born of the flesh, yet God consecrates to himself by gratuitous adoption? 8. He objects, that if they are new men, they ought to be fed with spiritual food. The answer is easy—that they are admitted into the flock of Christ by baptism, and that the symbol of that adoption is sufficient for them, till they grow to an age capable of bearing solid food; and that it is therefore necessary to wait for the time of that examination, which God expressly requires in the sacred supper. 9. He next objects, that Christ invites all his people to the sacred supper. I answer, it is sufficiently clear that he admits none but such as are already prepared to celebrate the remembrance of his death. Whence it follows, that infants, whom he condescended to take into his arms, remain in a distinct and peculiar class, till they grow to riper years, and yet that they are not strangers to the Church. To this he objects, that it is a monstrous thing for a person that is born, not to eat. I reply, that the external participation of the supper is not the only way in which souls are fed; and therefore that Christ is food to infants, notwithstanding they abstain from the sign; but that the case of baptism is different, by which alone they are admitted into the Church. He further objects, that "a faithful and wise servant, whom his lord hath made ruler over his household, giveth them meat in due season." (*p*) This I readily grant; but by what authority will he determine the time of baptism for us, so as to prove that it is not administered to

(*o*) 1 Cor. ii. 13. (*p*) Matt. xxiv. 45.

infants at a proper time? 10. He likewise adduces the command of Christ to his apostles, to hasten to the harvest, while the fields are whitening. (*q*) The sole design of Christ on that occasion was to stimulate the apostles, that, seeing the present fruit of their labours, they might exert themselves in their ministry with the greater cheerfulness. Who can infer from this that the time of harvest is the only time proper for baptism? 11. His next argument is, that in the primitive Church Christians and disciples were the same persons. (*r*) But here we see that he injudiciously reasons from a part to the whole. The appellation of disciples was given to persons of adult age, who had been already instructed, and had made a profession of Christianity; just as the Jews under the law were the disciples of Moses; yet no one can justly infer from this, that infants were strangers, God having declared them to be part of his family. 12. Moreover he alleges, that all Christians are brethren, but that we treat infants as not of that number, as long as we exclude them from the Lord's supper. But I return to that principle, that none are heirs of the kingdom of heaven, except those who are members of Christ; and that the embrace with which he honoured infants was a true pledge of the adoption, by which they are united with adults, and that their temporary abstinence from the supper does not prevent them from belonging to the body of the Church. The thief who was converted on the cross was a brother of believers, though he never partook of the Lord's supper at all. 13. He proceeds to assert, that no person becomes our brother but by the spirit of adoption communicated "by the hearing of faith." (*s*) I reply, that he is constantly reverting to the same false reasoning, by a preposterous application to infants of that which is spoken exclusively of adults. Paul is there showing that the ordinary method which God uses in calling his elect, and bringing them to the faith, is to raise them up faithful teachers, by whose labours and instructions he extends his assistance to them. But who will dare to impose a law to prevent his ingrafting infants into Christ by some other secret method? 14. He objects, that Cornelius was baptized after he had received the Holy Ghost. (*t*) But the absurdity of attempting to extract a

(*q*) John iv. 35—38.
(*r*) Acts xi. 26.
(*s*) Gal. iii. 2.
(*t*) Acts x. 44—48.

general rule from this one example, is evident from the cases of the eunuch and the Samaritans, (*v*) in whom the Lord observed a different order, for their baptism preceded their reception of the gifts of the Spirit. 15. His next argument is worse than absurd; he says, that by regeneration we are made gods; (*x*) but that they are gods to whom the word of God comes,. (*y*) which is not applicable to infants. The ascription of deity to believers is one of his reveries, which it is irrelevant to our present subject to discuss; but to pervert that quotation from the Psalms to a sense so remote from its genuine meaning, betrays the most monstrous impudence. Christ says that the appellation of *gods* is given by the prophet to kings and magistrates, because they sustain an office of Divine appointment. But that which is directed to certain individuals respecting the particular charge of governors, this dexterous interpreter applies to the doctrine of the gospel, in order to exclude infants from the Church. 16. He objects, again, that infants cannot be accounted new creatures, because they are not begotten by the word. I must again repeat, what I have so often remarked, that the doctrine of the gospel is the incorruptible seed, to regenerate those who are capable of understanding it; but that where, by reason of age, there is not yet any capacity of learning, God has his different degrees of regenerating those whom he has adopted. 17. Then he returns to his allegories, and alleges that sheep and goats were not offered in sacrifice immediately after they were brought forth. (*z*) If I approved of the application of figures to this subject, I might easily retort, that all the first born immediately on their birth are consecrated to the Lord, (*a*) and that a lamb was to be sacrificed in its first year; whence it should follow, that it is not at all necessary to wait for many years, but that our children ought to be dedicated to God in their earliest infancy. 18. He further contends, that none can come to Christ but those who have been prepared by John; as though the office of John had not been a temporary one. But to pass over this; the children whom Christ took up in his arms and blessed, had certainly no such preparation. Wherefore let him depart with his

(*v*) Acts viii. 16, 17, 26, &c. (*x*) 2 Peter i. 4.
(*y*) John x. 35. Psalm lxxxii. 6. (*z*) Exod. xii. 5.
(*a*) Exod. xiii. 12. Numb. viii. 17.

false principle. 19. At length he calls in the assistance of Trismegistus and the Sibyls, to show that sacred ablutions are not suitable to any but adults. See what honourable sentiments he entertains respecting the baptism of Christ, which he would conform to the profane rites of the heathen, that its administration might be regulated by the pleasure of Trismegistus. But we have more reverence for the authority of God, who has been pleased to consecrate infants to himself, and to initiate them by a sacred sign, the meaning of which they were too young to be able to understand. Nor do we esteem it lawful to borrow from the ablutions of the heathen any thing that may introduce into our baptism the least change of that eternal and inviolable law which God has established respecting circumcision. 20. In the last place, he argues, that if it be lawful to baptize infants without understanding, baptism may be, in mimicry and jest, administered by boys in play. But he must contest this subject with God, by whose command circumcision was performed upon infants, before they had attained any understanding. Was it a ludicrous ceremony, then, or a fit subject for the sports of children, that they could overturn the sacred institution of God? But it is no wonder that these reprobate spirits, as if transported with frenzy, bring forward the most enormous absurdities in defence of their errors; for such delusion is the just judgment of God upon their pride and obstinacy. And I trust I have clearly shown the futility of all the arguments with which Servetus has endeavoured to assist the cause of his Anabaptist brethren.

XXXII. No doubt, I conceive, can now remain in the mind of any sober man, that those who raise controversies and contentions on the subject of infant baptism are presumptuous disturbers of the Church of Christ. But it is worth while to notice the object which Satan aims at promoting by so much subtlety; which is, to deprive us of the peculiar benefit of confidence and spiritual joy, which is to be derived from this source, and in the same degree also to diminish the glory of the Divine goodness. For how delightful is it to pious minds, not only to have verbal assurances, but even ocular proof, of their standing so high in the favour of their heavenly Father, that their posterity are also the objects of his care! For here we see how he sustains the character of a most provident Father to us, since he discontinues not his solicitude for us even after our death, but regards and provides for our children. Ought we not, then, after the example of David, to exult in praise and thanksgiving to God with our whole heart, that his name may be glorified by such an expression of his goodness? This is evidently the reason why Satan makes such great exertions in opposition to infant baptism; that the removal of this testimony of the grace of God may cause the promise which it exhibits before our eyes gradually to disappear, and at length to be forgotten. The consequence of this would be, an impious ingratitude to the mercy of God, and negligence of the instruction of our children in the principles of piety. For it is no small stimulus to our education of them in the serious fear of God, and the observance of his law, to reflect, that they are considered and acknowledged by him as his children as soon as they are born. Wherefore, unless we are obstinately determined to obscure the goodness of God, let us present to him our children, to whom he assigns a place in his family, that is, among the members of his Church.

CHAPTER XVII

The Lord's Supper and Its Advantages

AFTER God has once received us into his family, and not only so as to admit us among his servants, but to number us with his children,—in order to fulfil the part of a most excellent father, solicitous for his offspring, he also undertakes to sustain and nourish us as long as we live; and not content with this, he has been pleased to give us a pledge, as a further assurance of this never-ceasing liberality. For this purpose, therefore, by the hand of his only begotten Son, he has favoured his Church with another sacrament, a spiritual banquet, in which Christ testifies himself to be the bread of life, to feed our souls for a true and blessed immortality. Now, as the knowledge of so great a mystery is highly necessary, and on account of its importance, requires an accurate explication; and, on the other hand, as Satan, in order to deprive the Church of this inestimable treasure, long ago endeavoured, first by mists, and afterwards by thicker shades, to obscure its lustre, and then raised disputes and contentions to alienate the minds of the simple from a relish for this sacred food, and in our time also has attempted the same artifice; after having exhibited a summary of what relates to the subject, adapted to the capacity of the unlearned, I will disentangle it from those sophistries with which Satan has been labouring to deceive the world. In the first place, the signs are bread and wine, which represent to us the invisible nourishment which we receive from the body and blood of Christ. For as in baptism God regenerates us, incorporates us into the society of his Church, and makes us his children by adoption, so we have said, that he acts towards us the part of a provident father of a family, in constantly supplying us with food, to sustain and preserve us in that life to which he has begotten us by his word. Now, the only food of our souls is Christ; and to him, therefore, our heavenly Father invites us, that being refreshed by a participation of him, we may gain fresh vigour from day to day, till we arrive at the heavenly immortality. And because this mystery of the secret union of Christ with believers is incomprehensible by nature, he exhibits a figure and image of it in visible signs, peculiarly adapted to our feeble capacity; and, as it were, by giving tokens and pledges, renders it equally as certain to us as if we beheld it with our eyes; for the dullest minds understand this very familiar similitude, that our souls are nourished by Christ, just as the life of the body is supported by bread and wine. We see, then, for what end this mystical benediction is designed; namely, to assure us that the body of the Lord was once offered as a sacrifice for us, so that we may now feed upon it, and, feeding on it, may experience within us the efficacy of that one sacrifice; and that his blood was once shed for us, so that it is our perpetual drink. And this is the import of the words of the promise annexed to it: "Take, eat; this is my body, which is given for you." The body, therefore, which was once offered for our salvation, we are commanded to take and eat; that seeing ourselves made partakers of it, we may certainly conclude, that the virtue of that life-giving death will be efficacious within us. Hence, also, he calls the cup "the new testament," or rather *covenant*, in his blood. (*d*) For the covenant which he once ratified with his blood, he in some measure renews, or rather continues, as far as relates to the confirmation of our faith, whenever he presents us that sacred blood to drink.

II. From this sacrament pious souls may derive the benefit of considerable satisfaction and confidence; because it affords us a testimony that we are incorporated into one body with Christ, so that whatever is his, we are at liberty to call ours. The consequence of this is, that we venture to assure ourselves of our interest in eternal life, of which he is the heir, and that the kingdom of

(*d*) Matt. xxvi. 26, 28. Mark xiv. 22, 24. Luke xxii. 19, 20. 1 Cor. xi. 24, 25.

heaven, into which he has already entered, can no more be lost by us than by him; and, on the other hand, that we cannot be condemned by our sins, from the guilt of which he absolved us, when he wished them to be imputed to himself, as if they were his own. This is the wonderful exchange which, in his infinite goodness, he has made with us. Submitting to our poverty, he has transferred to us his riches; assuming our weakness, he has strengthened us by his power; accepting our mortality, he has conferred on us his immortality; taking on himself the load of iniquity with which we were oppressed, he has clothed us with his righteousness; descending to the earth, he has prepared a way for our ascending to heaven; becoming with us the Son of man, he has made us, with himself, the sons of God.

III. Of all these things we have such a complete attestation in this sacrament, that we may confidently consider them as truly exhibited to us, as if Christ himself were presented to our eyes, and touched by our hands. For there can be no falsehood or illusion in this word, "Take, eat, drink; this is my body which is given for you; this is my blood which is shed for the remission of sins." By commanding us to take, he signifies that he is ours; by commanding us to eat and drink, he signifies that he is become one substance with us. In saying that his body is given for us, and his blood shed for us, he shows that both are not so much his as ours, because he assumed and laid down both, not for his own advantage, but for our salvation. And it ought to be carefully observed, that the principal and almost entire energy of the sacrament lies in these words, "which is given for you;" "which is shed for you;" for otherwise it would avail us but little, that the body and blood of the Lord are distributed to us now, if they had not been once delivered for our redemption and salvation. Therefore they are represented to us by bread and wine, to teach us that they are not only ours, but are destined for the support of our spiritual life. This is what we have already suggested—that by the corporeal objects which are presented in the sacrament, we are conducted, by a kind of analogy, to those which are spiritual. So, when bread is given to us as a symbol of the body of Christ, we ought immediately to conceive of this comparison, that, as bread nourishes, sustains, and preserves the life of the body, so the body of Christ is the only food to animate and support the life of the soul. When we see wine presented as a symbol of his blood, we ought to think of the uses of wine to the human body, that we may contemplate the same advantages conferred upon us in a spiritual manner by the blood of Christ; which are these—that it nourishes, refreshes, strengthens, and exhilarates. For if we duly consider the benefits resulting to us from the oblation of his sacred body, and the effusion of his blood, we shall clearly perceive that these properties of bread and wine, according to this analogy, are most justly attributed to those symbols, as administered to us in the Lord's supper.

IV. The principal object of the sacrament, therefore, is not to present us the body of Christ, simply, and without any ulterior consideration, but rather to seal and confirm that promise, where he declares that his "flesh is meat indeed, and" his "blood drink indeed," by which we are nourished to eternal life; where he affirms that he is "the bread of life," and that "he that eateth of this bread shall live for ever;" (*e*) to seal and confirm that promise, I say; and, in order to do this, it sends us to the cross of Christ, where the promise has been fully verified, and entirely accomplished. For we never rightly and advantageously feed on Christ, except as crucified, and when we have a lively apprehension of the efficacy of his death. And, indeed, when Christ called himself "the bread of life," he did not use that appellation on account of the sacrament, as some persons erroneously imagine, but because he had been given to us as such by the Father, and showed himself to be such, when, becoming a partaker of our human mortality, he made us partakers of his Divine immortality; when, offering himself a sacrifice, he sustained our curse, to fill us with his blessing; when, by his death, he destroyed and swallowed up death; when, in his resurrection, this corruptible flesh of ours, which he had assumed, was raised up by him, in a state of incorruption and glory.

V. It remains for all this to be applied to us; which is done in the first place by the gospel, but in a more illustrious manner by the sacred supper, in which Christ offers himself to us with all his

---

(*e*) John vi. 35, 55—58.

benefits, and we receive him by faith. The sacrament, therefore, does not first constitute Christ the bread of life; but, by recalling to our remembrance that he has been made the bread of life, upon which we may constantly feed, and by giving us a taste and relish for that bread, it causes us to experience the support which it is adapted to afford. For it assures us, in the first place, that whatever Christ has done or suffered, was for the purpose of giving life to us; and, in the next place, that this life will never end. For as Christ would never have been the bread of life to us, if he had not been born, and died, and risen again for us, so now he would by no means continue so, if the efficacy and benefit of his nativity, death, and resurrection, were not permanent and immortal. All this Christ has beautifully expressed in these words: "The bread that I will give is my flesh, which I will give for the life of the world;" (*f*) in which he clearly signifies, that his body would be as bread to us, for the spiritual life of the soul, because it was to be exposed to death for our salvation; and that it is given to us to feed upon it, when he makes us partakers of it by faith. He gave it once, therefore, to be made bread, when he surrendered it to be crucified for the redemption of the world; he gives it daily, when, by the word of the gospel, he presents it to us, that we may partake of it as crucified; when he confirms that presentation by the sacred mystery of the supper; when he accomplishes within that which he signifies without. Here it behoves us to guard against two errors; that, on the one hand, we may not, by undervaluing the signs, disjoin them from the mysteries with which they are connected; nor, on the other hand, by extolling them beyond measure, obscure the glory of the mysteries themselves. That Christ is the bread of life, by which believers are nourished to eternal salvation, there is no man, not entirely destitute of religion, who hesitates to acknowledge; but all are not equally agreed respecting the manner of partaking of him. For there are some who define in a word, that to eat the flesh of Christ, and to drink his blood, is no other than to believe in Christ himself. But I conceive that, in that remarkable discourse, in which Christ recommends us to feed upon his body, he intended to teach

(*f*) John vi. 51.

us something more striking and sublime; namely, that we are quickened by a real participation of him, which he designates by the terms of *eating* and *drinking*, that no person might suppose the life which we receive from him to consist in simple knowledge. For as it is not *seeing*, but *eating* bread, that administers nourishment to the body, so it is necessary for the soul to have a true and complete participation of Christ, that by his power it may be quickened to spiritual life. At the same time, we confess that there is no other eating than by faith, as it is impossible to imagine any other; but the difference between me and the persons whose sentiment I am opposing, is this; they consider eating to be the very same as believing; I say, that in believing we eat the flesh of Christ, because he is actually made ours by faith, and that this eating is the fruit and effect of faith; or, to express it more plainly, they consider the eating to be faith itself; but I apprehend it to be rather a consequence of faith. The difference is small in words, but in the thing itself it is considerable. For though the apostle teaches that "Christ dwelleth in our hearts by faith," (*g*) yet no one will explain this inhabitation to be faith itself. Every one must perceive that the apostle intended to express a peculiar advantage arising from faith, of which the residence of Christ in the hearts of believers is one of the effects. In the same manner, when the Lord called himself "the bread of life," (*h*) he intended not only to teach that salvation is laid up for us in the faith of his death and resurrection, but also that, by our real participation of him, his life is transferred to us, and becomes ours; just as bread, when it is taken for food, communicates vigour to the body.

VI. When Augustine, whom they bring forward as their advocate, said that we eat the body of Christ by believing in him, it was with no other meaning than to show that this eating is not of a corporeal nature, but solely by faith. This I admit; but at the same time I add, that we embrace Christ by faith, not as appearing at a distance, but as uniting himself with us, to become our head, and to make us his members. I do not altogether disapprove, however, such a mode of expression, but if they mean to define what it is to eat the flesh of Christ, I deny this to be a complete

---

(*g*) Eph. iii. 17. (*h*) John vi. 35.

explanation. Otherwise, I see that Augustine has frequently used this phrase; as when he says, "Except ye eat the flesh of the Son of man, ye have no life in you; (*i*) this is a figure which enjoins a participation of the sufferings of our Lord, and a sweet and useful recollection in the memory, that his flesh was wounded and crucified for us:" and again, when he says, "That the three thousand, who were converted by the preaching of Peter, (*k*) drank the blood of Christ by believing in him, which they had shed in persecuting him." But in many other passages he highly celebrates that beneficial consequence of faith, and states our souls to be as much refreshed by the communion of the body of Christ, as our bodies are by the bread which we eat. And the very same idea is conveyed by Chrysostom, when he says, "That Christ makes us his body, not only by faith, but also in reality." For he does not mean that this benefit is obtained any otherwise than by faith; he only intends to preclude a supposition from being entertained by any one, that this faith is nothing more than a speculative apprehension. I say nothing at present of those who maintain the Lord's supper to be a mere mark of external profession, because I think I have sufficiently refuted their error, when treating of the sacraments in general. Only let it be observed, that when Christ says, "This cup is the new testament, or covenant, in my blood," (*l*) this is the expression of a promise calculated for the confirmation of faith; whence it follows, that unless we direct our views to God, and embrace what he offers us, we never properly celebrate the sacred supper.

VII. Nor am I satisfied with those persons, who, after having acknowledged that we have some communion with Christ, when they mean to describe it, represent us merely as partakers of his Spirit, but make no mention of his flesh and blood; as though there were no meaning in these and other similar expressions: "That his flesh is meat indeed; that his blood is drink indeed; that except we eat his flesh, and drink his blood, we have no life in us." Wherefore, if it be evident that the full communion of Christ goes beyond their too confined description of it, I will endeavour to state, in few words, how far it extends, before I

(*i*) John vi. 53. (*k*) Acts ii. 41. (*l*) Luke xxii. 20.

speak of the contrary error of carrying it to excess. For I shall have a longer controversy with the hyperbolical doctors, who, while in their folly they imagine an absurd and extravagant way of eating the flesh of Christ, and drinking his blood, deprive him of his real body, and metamorphose him into a mere phantom; if, however, it be possible, in any words, to unfold so great a mystery, which I find myself incapable of properly comprehending, even in my mind; and this I am ready to acknowledge, that no person may measure the sublimity of the subject by my inadequate representation of it. On the contrary, I exhort my readers not to confine their thoughts within such narrow and insufficient limits, but to endeavour to rise much higher than I am able to conduct them; for as to myself, whenever I handle this subject, after having endeavoured to say every thing, I am conscious of having said but very little, in comparison of its excellence. And though the conceptions of the mind can far exceed the expressions of the tongue, yet, with the magnitude of the subject, the mind itself is oppressed and overwhelmed. Nothing remains for me, therefore, but to break forth in admiration of that mystery, which the mind is unable clearly to understand, or the tongue to express. I will nevertheless state the substance of my opinion, which, as I have no doubt of its truth, I trust will also be received with approbation by godly minds.

VIII. In the first place, we learn from the Scriptures, that Christ was from the beginning that life-giving Word of the Father, the fountain and origin of life, from which all things have ever derived their existence. Therefore John in one place calls him "The Word of life," and in another says, that "in him was life;" (*m*) signifying, that even then he diffused his energy over all the creatures, and endued them with life and breath. Yet the same apostle immediately adds, that "the life was manifested" then, and not before, when the Son of God, by assuming our flesh, rendered himself visible to the eyes, and palpable to the hands of men. For though he diffused his influence over all the creatures before that period, yet, because man was alienated from God by sin, had lost the participation of life, and saw nothing on

(*m*) 1 John 1—4.

every side but impending death, it was necessary to his recovery of any hope of immortality, that he should be received into the communion of that word. For what slender hopes shall we form, if we hear that the Word of God contains in himself all the plenitude of life, while we are at an infinite distance from him, and, withersoever we turn our eyes, see nothing but death presenting itself on every side? But since he who is the fountain of life has taken up his residence in our flesh, he remains no longer concealed at a distance from us, but openly exhibits himself to our participation. He also makes the very flesh in which he resides the means of giving life to us, that, by a participation of it, we may be nourished to immortality. "I am the living bread," says he, "which came down from heaven. And the bread that I will give is my flesh, which I will give for the life of the world." (*n*) In these words, he shows, not only that he is life, as he is the eternal Word who descended from heaven to us, but that in descending he imparted that power to the flesh which he assumed, in order that it might communicate life to us. Hence follow these declarations: "That his flesh is meat indeed, and that his blood is drink indeed;" (*o*) meat and drink by which believers are nourished to eternal life. Here, then, we enjoy peculiar consolation, that we find life in our own flesh. For in this manner we not only have an easy access to it, but it freely discovers and offers itself to our acceptance; we have only to open our hearts to its reception, and we shall obtain it.

IX. Now, though the power of giving life to us is not an essential attribute of the body of Christ, which, in its original condition, was subject to mortality, and now lives by an immortality not its own, yet it is justly represented as the source of life, because it is endued with a plenitude of life to communicate to us. In this I agree with Cyril, in understanding that declaration of Christ, "As the Father hath life in himself, so hath he given to the Son to have life in himself." (*p*) For in this passage, he is not speaking of the attributes which he possessed with the Father from the beginning, but of the gifts with which he was adorned in the flesh in which he appeared; therefore he showed that the fulness

(*n*) John vi. 51. (*o*) John vi. 55. (*p*) John v. 26.

of life dwelt in his humanity, that whoever partook of his flesh and blood might, at the same time, enjoy a participation of life. For, as the water of a fountain is sometimes drunk, sometimes drawn, and sometimes conveyed in furrows for the irrigation of lands, yet the fountain does not derive such an abundance for so many uses from itself, but from the spring which is perpetually flowing to furnish it with fresh supplies, so the flesh of Christ is like a rich and inexhaustible fountain, which receives the life flowing from the Divinity, and conveys it to us. Now, who does not see that a participation of the body and blood of Christ is necessary to all who aspire to heavenly life? This is implied in those passages of the apostle, that the Church is the body of Christ, and his fulness; (*q*) that he is "the head, from whom the whole body, joined together and compacted by that which every joint supplieth, maketh increase of the body;" (*r*) that our bodies are "the members of Christ;" (*s*) things which we know can no otherwise be effected than by his entire union both of body and spirit with us. But that most intimate fellowship, by which we are united with his flesh, the apostle has illustrated in a still more striking representation, when he says, "We are members of his body, of his flesh, and of his bones." (*t*) At length, to declare the subject to be above all description, he concludes his discourse by exclaiming, "This is a great mystery." (*u*) It would be extreme stupidity, therefore, to acknowledge no communion of believers with the body and blood of the Lord, which the apostle declares to be so great, that he would rather admire than express it.

X. We conclude, that our souls are fed by the flesh and blood of Christ, just as our corporeal life is preserved and sustained by bread and wine. For otherwise there would be no suitableness in the analogy of the sign, if our souls did not find their food in Christ; which cannot be the case unless Christ truly becomes one with us, and refreshes us by the eating of his flesh and the drinking of his blood. Though it appears incredible for the flesh of Christ, from such an immense local distance, to reach us, so as to become our food, we should remember how much the secret power of the Holy Spirit transcends all our senses, and what folly it is

(*q*) Eph. i. 23. (*r*) Eph. iv. 15, 16. (*s*) 1 Cor. vi. 15.
(*t*) Eph. v. 30. (*u*) Eph. v. 32.

to apply any measure of ours to his immensity. Let our faith receive, therefore, what our understanding is not able to comprehend, that the Spirit really unites things which are separated by local distance. Now, that holy participation of his flesh and blood, by which Christ communicates his life to us, just as if he actually penetrated every part of our frame, in the sacred supper he also testifies and seals; and that not by the exhibition of a vain or ineffectual sign, but by the exertion of the energy of his Spirit, by which he accomplishes that which he promises. And the thing signified he exhibits and offers to all who come to that spiritual banquet; though it is advantageously enjoyed by believers alone, who receive such great goodness with true faith and gratitude of mind. For which reason the apostle said, "The cup of blessing which we bless, is it not the communion of the blood of Christ? The bread which we break, is it not the communion of the body of Christ?" (*v*) Nor is there any cause to object, that it is a figurative expression, by which the name of the thing signified is given to the sign. I grant, indeed, that the breaking of the bread is symbolical, and not the substance itself: yet, this being admitted, from the exhibition of the symbol we may justly infer the exhibition of the substance; for, unless any one would call God a deceiver, he can never presume to affirm that he sets before us an empty sign. Therefore, if, by the breaking of the bread, the Lord truly represents the participation of his body, it ought not to be doubted that he truly presents and communicates it. And it must always be a rule with believers, whenever they see the signs instituted by the Lord, to assure and persuade themselves that they are also accompanied with the truth of the thing signified. For to what end would the Lord deliver into our hands the symbol of his body, except to assure us of a real participation of it? If it be true that the visible sign is given to us to seal the donation of the invisible substance, we ought to entertain a confident assurance, that in receiving the symbol of his body, we at the same time truly receive the body itself.

XI. In harmony, therefore, with the doctrine which has always been received in the Church, and which is maintained in the pres-

(*v*) 1 Cor. x. 16.

ent day by all who hold right sentiments, I say, that the sacred mystery of the supper consists of two parts: the corporeal signs, which, being placed before our eyes, represent to us invisible things in a manner adapted to the weakness of our capacities; and the spiritual truth, which is at the same time typified and exhibited by those symbols. When I intend to give a familiar view of this truth, I am accustomed to state three particulars which it includes: the signification; the matter, or substance, which depends on the signification; and the virtue, or effect, which follows from both. The signification consists in the promises which are interwoven with the sign. What I call the matter or substance, is Christ, with his death and resurrection. By the effect, I mean redemption, righteousness, sanctification, eternal life, and all the other benefits which Christ confers upon us. Now, though all these things are connected with faith, yet I leave no room for this cavil; as though, when I say that Christ is received by faith, I intended that he is received merely in the understanding and imagination; for the promises present him to us, not that we may rest in mere contemplation and simple knowledge, but that we may enjoy a real participation of him. And, in fact, I see not how any man can attain a solid confidence that he has redemption and righteousness in the cross of Christ, and life in his death, unless he first has a real communion with Christ himself; for those blessings would never be imparted to us, if Christ did not first make himself ours. I say, therefore, that in the mystery of the supper, under the symbols of bread and wine, Christ is truly exhibited to us, even his body and blood, in which he has fulfilled all obedience to procure our justification. And the design of this exhibition is, first, that we may be united into one body with him, and, secondly, that being made partakers of his substance, we may experience his power in the communication of all blessings.

XII. I now proceed to the hyperbolical additions which superstitution has made to this sacrament. For here Satan has exerted amazing subtlety to withdraw the minds of men from heaven, and involve them in a preposterous error, by persuading them that Christ is attached to the element of bread. In the first place, we must be careful not to dream of such a presence of Christ in the sacrament as the ingenuity of the Romanists has invented; as if the body of Christ were exhibited, by a local presence, to be felt by the hand, bruised by the teeth, and swallowed by the throat. For this was the form of recantation which Pope Nicolas directed to Berengarius as a declaration of his repentance; the language of which is so monstrous, that the scholiast exclaims, that there is danger, unless the readers be very prudent and cautious, of their imbibing from it a worse heresy than that of Berengarius; and Peter Lombard, though he takes great pains to defend it from the charge of absurdity, yet rather inclines to a different opinion. For, as we have not the least doubt that Christ's body is finite, according to the invariable condition of a human body, and is contained in heaven, where it was once received, till it shall return to judgment, so we esteem it utterly unlawful to bring it back under these corruptible elements, or to imagine it to be present every where. Nor is there any need of this, in order to our enjoying the participation of it; since the Lord by his Spirit gives us the privilege of being united with himself in body, soul, and spirit. The bond of this union, therefore, is the Spirit of Christ, by whom we are conjoined, and who is, as it were, the channel by which all that Christ himself is and has is conveyed to us. For, if we behold the sun darting his rays and transmitting his substance, as it were, in them, to generate, nourish, and mature the roots of the earth, why should the irradiation of the Spirit of Christ be less effectual to convey to us the communication of his body and blood? Wherefore, the Scripture, when it speaks of our participation of Christ, attributes all the power of it to the Spirit. One passage shall suffice instead of many. In the eighth chapter of the Epistle to the Romans, Paul represents Christ as dwelling in us no otherwise than by his Spirit. (*w*) By this representation, the apostle does not destroy that communion of the body and blood of Christ of which we are now treating, but teaches that it is solely owing to the agency of the Spirit that we possess Christ with all his benefits, and have him dwelling within us.

XIII. Deterred by a horror of such barbarous impiety, the schoolmen have expressed themselves in more modest language, yet they only trifle with equal fallacy and greater subtlety. They

---

(*w*) Rom. viii. 9, 11.

admit that Christ is not contained in the bread and wine in a local or corporeal manner; but they afterwards invent a manner which they neither understand themselves nor can explain to others; which, however, amounts to this, that Christ is to be sought, as they express it, in the form of bread. When they say that the substance of bread is transmuted into Christ, do they not attach his substance to the whiteness, which they pretend is all that remains of the bread? But, they say, he is contained in the sacrament, that he remains in heaven, and we maintain no other presence than that of *habitude*. But whatever words they employ to gloss over their notions, they all terminate in this, that, by the consecration, that which was before bread becomes Christ, so that the substance of Christ is concealed under the colour of bread. This they are not ashamed to express in plain terms; for Lombard says, "That the body of Christ, which is visible in itself, is hidden and concealed, after the consecration, under the form of bread." Thus the figure of the bread is nothing but a veil, which prevents the flesh from being seen. Nor is there any need of many conjectures, to discover what snares they intended to lay in these words, which the thing itself plainly evinces. For it is evident in what profound superstition not only the people in general, but even the principal men, have now for several ages been involved, and are involved, at the present day, in the Papal churches. True faith, which is the sole medium of our union and communion with Christ, being an object of little solicitude to them, provided they have that carnal presence which they have fabricated without any authority from the Divine word, they consider him as sufficiently present with them. The consequence of this ingenious subtlety, therefore, we find to be this, that bread has been taken for God.

XIV. Hence proceeded that pretended transubstantiation, for which they now contend with more earnestness than for all the other articles of their faith. For the first inventors of the local presence were unable to explain how the body of Christ could be mixed with the substance of the bread, without being immediately embarrassed by many absurdities. Therefore they found it necessary to have recourse to this fiction, that the bread is transmuted into the body of Christ; not that his body is properly made of the bread, but that Christ annihilates the substance of the bread, and conceals himself under its form. It is astonishing that they could fall into such ignorance, and even stupidity, as to promulgate such a monstrous notion, in direct opposition to the Scripture and to the doctrine of the primitive Church. I confess, indeed, that some of the ancient writers sometimes used the word *conversion*, not with a view to destroy the substance of the external signs, but to signify that the bread dedicated to that sacrament is unlike common bread, and different from what it was before. But they all constantly and expressly declare, that the sacred supper consists of two parts, earthly and heavenly; and the earthly part they explain, without the least hesitation, to be bread and wine. Whatever the Romanists may pretend, it is very clear that the authority of the ancients, which they frequently presume to oppose to the plain word of God, affords them no assistance in the support of this dogma; and, indeed, it is comparatively but of recent invention, for it was not only unknown to those better times, when the doctrine of religion still flourished in its purity, but even when that purity had already been much corrupted. There is not one of the ancient writers who does not acknowledge in express terms that the consecrated symbols of the supper are bread and wine; though, as we have observed, they sometimes distinguish them with various titles, to celebrate the dignity of the mystery. For when they say, that a secret *conversion* takes place in the consecration, so that they are something different from bread and wine, I have already stated their meaning to be, not that the bread and wine are annihilated, but that they are to be considered in a different light from common aliments, which are merely designed for the nourishment of the body; because, in those elements, we are presented with the spiritual meat and drink of the soul. In this we also coincide. But, say our opponents, if there be a conversion, one thing must be changed into another. If they mean that something is made what it was not before, I agree with them. If they wish to apply this to their absurd notion, let them tell me what change they think takes place in baptism. For in that also the fathers state a wonderful conversion, when they say, that from the corruptible element proceeds a spiritual ablution of the soul, yet not one of them denies that it retains the substance of water. But there is no such declaration, they say, respecting baptism as there is respecting the supper: "This is my body." As though the question related to those words, which have a meaning obvious enough, and not rather to the conversion or change spoken of, which ought to signify no more in the supper than in baptism. Let them cease their verbal subtleties, therefore, which only betray their own absurdity. Indeed, there would be no consistency in the signification, if the external sign were not a living image of the truth which is represented in it. By the external sign, Christ intended to declare that his flesh is meat. If he were to set before us a mere spectre of bread, and not real bread, where would be the analogy or similitude, which ought to lead us from the visible emblem to the invisible substance? For, to preserve the correspondence complete, the signification would extend no further than that we should be fed with an appearance of the flesh of Christ. As in baptism, if there were nothing but an appearance of water to deceive our eyes, we should have no certain pledge of our ablution; and such an illusive representation we should find a source of painful uncertainty. The nature of the sacrament, therefore, is subverted, unless the earthly sign correspond in its signification to the heavenly substance; and, consequently, we lose the truth of this mystery, unless the true body of Christ be represented by real bread. I repeat it again; since the sacred supper is nothing but a visible attestation of the promise, that Christ is "the bread of life which cometh down from heaven," (*x*) it requires the use of visible and material bread to represent that which is spiritual; unless we are determined that the means which God kindly affords to support our weakness shall be altogether unavailing to us. With what reason could Paul conclude that "we, being many, are one bread, for we are all partakers of that one bread," (*y*) if there were nothing but a mere phantom of bread, and not the true and real substance of it?

XV. They would never have been so shamefully deluded by the fallacies of Satan, if they had not been previously fascinated with this error—that the body of Christ contained in the bread was received in a corporeal manner into the mouth, and actually swallowed. The cause of such a stupid notion was, that they considered

(*x*) John vi. 35, 50. (*y*) 1 Cor. x. 17.

the consecration as a kind of magical incantation. But they were unacquainted with this principle, that the bread is a sacrament only to those to whom the word is addressed; as the water of baptism is not changed in itself, but on the annexation of the promise, begins to be to us that which it was not before. This will be further elucidated by the example of a similar sacrament. The water which flowed from the rock in the wilderness, was to the fathers a token and sign of the same thing which is represented to us by the wine in the sacred supper; for Paul says, "They did drink the same spiritual drink." (*z*) But the same water served also for their flocks and herds. Hence it is easily inferred, that when earthly elements are applied to a spiritual use, no other change takes place in them than with regard to *men,* to whom they become seals of the promises. Besides, since the design of God is, as I have often repeated, by suitable vehicles to elevate us to himself, this object is impiously frustrated by the obstinacy of those who invite us to Christ indeed, but invisibly concealed under the form of bread. It is not possible for the human mind to overcome the immensity of local distance, and to penetrate to Christ the highest heavens. What nature denied them, they attempted to correct by a remedy yet more pernicious, that while remaining on the earth, they might attain a proximity to Christ without any need of ascending to heaven. This is all the necessity which constrained them to metamorphose the body of Christ. In the time of Bernard, though a harsh mode of expression had been adopted, still transubstantiation was yet unknown; and in all preceding ages it was a common similitude, in the mouths of all, that in this sacrament the body and blood of Christ were spiritually united with the bread and wine. They argue respecting the terms, in their own apprehension, with great acuteness, but without adducing any thing applicable to the present subject. The rod of Moses, they say, though it took the form of a serpent, still retained its original name, and was called a rod. (*a*) So they think it equally probable, that though the bread be changed into another substance, yet it may by a catachresis, without any violation of propriety, be denominated according to its visible appearance. But

(*z*) 1 Cor. x. 4. (*a*) Exod. iv. 2—4; vii. 10, 12.

what similitude or connection can they discover between that illustrious miracle and their fictitious illusion, which no eye on earth witnesses? The magicians had practised their sorceries, so that the Egyptians believed them to possess a Divine power to effect changes in the creatures above the order of nature. Moses confronted them, and defeating all their enchantments, showed the invincible power of God to be on his side; because his one rod swallowed up all the rest. But that being a transmutation visible to the eye, makes nothing to the present argument, as we have already observed; and the rod soon after visibly returned to its original form. Moreover, it is not known whether that was in reality a temporary transmutation of substance or not. The allusion to the rods of the magicians deserves also to be observed; for Moses says, that "Aaron's rod swallowed up their *rods:*" he would not call them serpents, lest he might appear to imply a transmutation which did not exist; for those impostors had done nothing but dazzle the eyes of the spectators. What resemblance has this to the following and other similar expressions: "The bread which we break;" (*b*) "As often as ye eat this bread;" (*c*) "They continued in breaking of bread?" (*d*) It is certain that their eyes were only deceived by the incantations of the magicians. There is greater uncertainty with respect to Moses, by whose hand it was no more difficult for God to make a rod into a serpent, and afterwards to make the serpent into a rod again, than to invest angels with material bodies, and soon after to disembody them again. If the nature of this sacrament were the same, or bore any affinity to the case we have mentioned, our opponents would have some colour for their solution. We must, therefore, consider it as a fixed principle, that the flesh of Christ is not truly promised to us for food in the sacred supper, unless the true substance of the external symbol corresponds to it. And as one error gives birth to another, a passage of Jeremiah is so stupidly perverted, in order to prove transubstantiation, that I am ashamed to recite it. The prophet complains that wood was put into his bread; (*e*) signifying that his enemies by their cruelty had taken away all the relish of his food; as David in a similar figure utters the fol-

(*b*) 1 Cor. x. 16. (*c*) 1 Cor. xi. 26. (*d*) Acts ii. 42.
(*e*) Jer. xi. 19, (according to the Vulgate and Septuagint.)

lowing complaint: "They gave me also gall for my meat, and in my thirst they gave me vinegar to drink." (*f*) These disputants explain it as an allegory, that the body of Christ was affixed to the wood of the cross; and this, they say, was the opinion of some of the fathers. I reply, we ought rather to pardon their ignorance, and bury their disgrace in oblivion, than to add the effrontery of constraining them continually to combat the genuine meaning of the prophet.

XVI. Others, who perceive it to be impossible to destroy the analogy of the sign and the thing signified, without subverting the truth of the mystery, acknowledge that the bread in the sacred supper is the true substance of that earthly and corruptible element, and undergoes no change in itself; but they maintain that it has the body of Christ included under it. If they explain their meaning to be, that when the bread is presented in the sacrament, it is attended with an exhibition of the body of Christ, because the truth represented is inseparable from its sign, I should make little objection; but as, by placing the body itself in the bread, they attribute ubiquity to it, which is incompatible with its nature, and by stating it to be *under the bread*, represent it as lying concealed in it; it is necessary to unmask such subtleties: not that it is my intention to enter on a professed examination of the whole of this subject at present; I shall only lay the foundations of the discussion, which will follow in its proper place. They maintain the body of Christ, therefore, to be invisible and infinite, that it may be concealed under the bread; because they suppose it to be impossible for them to partake of him, any otherwise than by his descending into the bread; but they know nothing of that descent of which we have spoken, by which he elevates us to himself. They bring forward every plausible pretext that they can; but when they have said all, it is evident that they are contending for a local presence of Christ. And what is the reason of it? It is because they cannot conceive of any other participation of his flesh and blood, except what would consist in local conjunction and contact, or in some gross enclosure.

XVII. And to defend with obstinacy the error which they have

(*f*) Psalm lxix. 21.

once embraced, some of them hesitate not to affirm that the body of Christ never had any other dimensions than the whole extent of heaven and earth. His birth as an infant, his growth to maturity, his extension on the cross, his incarceration in the sepulchre,—all this, they say, took place in consequence of a kind of dispensation, that he might as a man accomplish every thing necessary to our salvation. His appearance in the same corporeal form after his resurrection, his ascension to heaven, his subsequent appearances to Stephen and to Paul,—all this also resulted from a similar dispensation, that he might manifest himself to the view of man as appointed King in heaven. Now, what is this but to raise Marcion from the dead? For if such were the condition of Christ's body, every one must perceive it to have been a mere phantom or visionary form, without any real substance. Some plead, with a little more subtlety, that the body of Christ, which is given in the sacrament, is glorious and immortal, and that therefore it involves no absurdity, if it be contained under the sacrament in various places, or in no place, or without any form. But I ask what kind of body did Jesus Christ give to his disciples, the night before he suffered? Do not the words imply, that he gave them the same mortal body which was just about to be betrayed? They reply, that he had already manifested his glory in the eyes of three of his disciples, on the mount. That is true; but his design was, in that splendour, to give them a transient glimpse of his immortality. They will not find there a twofold body, but the very same which Christ was accustomed to carry about with him, adorned with unusual glory, from which it speedily returned to its natural condition. When he distributed his body at the institution of the sacred supper, the hour was approaching, in which, "stricken and smitten of God," he was to lie down like a leper "without form or comeliness:" (*g*) he was then far from intending to display the glory of his resurrection. What a door does this open to the error of Marcion, if the body of Christ appeared in one place mortal and mean, and in another was received as immortal and glorious? On their principle, however, this happens every day; for they are constrained to confess that the body of

---

(*g*) Isaiah liii. 2, 4.

Christ is visible in itself, while at the same time they say that it is invisibly concealed under the symbol of bread. And yet the promulgators of such monstrous absurdities are so far from being ashamed of their disgrace, that they stigmatize us with unprovoked and enormous calumnies, because we refuse to subscribe to them.

XVIII. If they are determined to fasten the body and blood of the Lord to the bread and wine, one must of necessity be severed from the other. For as the bread is presented separately from the cup, the body, being united to the bread, must consequently be divided from the blood contained in the cup. For when they affirm that the body is in the bread, and the blood in the cup, while the bread and the wine are at some distance from each other, no sophistry will enable them to evade this conclusion—that the body is separated from the blood. Their usual pretence, that the blood is in the body, and the body in the blood, by what they call *concomitance*, is perfectly frivolous, while the symbols in which they are contained are so divided. But if we elevate our views and thoughts towards heaven, to seek Christ there in the glory of his kingdom, as the symbols invite us to him entire, under the symbol of bread we shall eat his body, under the symbol of wine we shall distinctly drink his blood, so that we shall thus enjoy him entire. For though he has removed his flesh from us, and in his body is ascended to heaven, yet he sits at the Father's right hand, that is, he reigns in the power, and majesty, and glory of the Father. This kingdom is neither limited to any local space, nor circumscribed by any dimensions; Christ exerts his power wherever he pleases in heaven and earth, exhibits himself present in his energetic influence, is constantly with his people, inspiring his life into them, lives in them, sustains them, strengthens and invigorates them, just as if he were corporeally present; in short, he feeds them with his own body, of which he gives them a participation by the influence of his Spirit. This is the way in which the body and blood of Christ are exhibited to us in the sacrament.

XIX. It is necessary for us to establish such a presence of Christ in the sacred supper, as neither, on the one hand, to fasten him to the element of bread, or to enclose him in it, or in any way to circumscribe him, which would derogate from his celestial glory; nor, on the other hand, to deprive him of his corporeal dimensions, or to represent his body as in different places at once, or to assign it an immensity diffused through heaven and earth, which would be clearly inconsistent with the reality of his human nature. Let us never suffer ourselves to be driven from these two exceptions; that nothing be maintained derogatory to Christ's celestial glory; which is the case when he is represented as brought under the corruptible elements of this world, or fastened to any earthly objects; and that nothing be attributed to his body incompatible with the human nature; which is the case when it is represented as infinite, or is said to be in more places than one at the same time. These absurdities being disclaimed, I readily admit whatever may serve to express the true and substantial communication of the body and blood of the Lord, which is given to believers under the sacred symbols of the supper; and to express it in a manner implying not a mere reception of it in the imagination or apprehension of their mind, but a real enjoyment of it as the food of eternal life. Nor can any cause be assigned, why this opinion is so odious to the world, and the minds of multitudes are so unjustly prejudiced against any defence of it, but that they have been awfully infatuated with the delusions of Satan. It is certain that the doctrine we advance is in all respects in perfect harmony with the Scriptures; it contains nothing absurd, ambiguous, or obscure; it is not at all inimical to true piety, or solid edification; in short, it includes nothing that can offend, except that for several ages, while the ignorance and barbarism of the sophists prevailed over the Church, this very clear light and obvious truth was shamefully suppressed. Yet, as, in the present age also, Satan is making the most powerful exertions to oppose it, and is employing turbulent spirits to endeavour to blacken it by every possible calumny and reproach, it is necessary to be the more diligent in asserting and defending it.

XX. Now, before we proceed any further, it is requisite to discuss the institution itself; because the most plausible objection of our adversaries is, that we depart from the words of Christ. To exonerate ourselves from the false charge which they bring against us, it is highly proper, therefore, to begin with an exposition of the words. The account given by three of the evangelists, and by Paul, informs us, that "Jesus took bread, and gave thanks, and blessed it, and brake it, and gave it to the disciples, and said, Take, eat; this is my body, which is given or broken for you. And he took the cup, and said, This cup is my blood of the new testament, or the new testament in my blood, which is shed for you, and for many, for the remission of sins." (*h*) The advocates of transubstantiation contend that the pronoun *this* denotes the appearance of the bread, because the consecration is made by the whole of the sentence, and there is no visible substance, according to them, which can be indicated by it. But if they are guided by a scrupulous attention to the words, because Christ declared that which he gave into the hands of his disciples to be his body, nothing can be more at variance with a just interpretation of them, than the notion that what before was bread had now become the body of Christ. For it was that which Christ took into his hands to deliver to his disciples, that he asserts to be his body; but he took "*bread.*" Who does not perceive, then, that that to which this pronoun referred was bread still? and therefore nothing would be more absurd than to transfer to a mere appearance or visionary form that which was spoken of real bread. Others, when they explain the word *is* to denote transubstantiation, have recourse to an interpretation still more violently perverted and unnatural. They have not the least colour, therefore, for a pretence that they are influenced by a scrupulous reverence for the words of Christ. For to use the word *is* to signify a transmutation into another substance, is a thing never heard of, in any country or in any language. Those who acknowledge the continuance of bread in the supper, and affirm that it is accompanied with the real body of Christ, differ considerably among themselves. Those of them who express themselves more modestly, though they strenuously insist on the literal meaning of these words, "*This is my body,*" yet afterwards depart from their literal precision, and explain them to import that the body of Christ is with the bread, in the bread, and under the bread. Of the opinion maintained by them, we have already spoken, and shall soon have occasion to take further notice; at present I am only arguing respecting the words, by which they consider themselves bound, so that they

(*h*) Matt. xxvi. 26—28. Mark xiv. 22—24. Luke xxii. 19, 20. 1 Cor. xi. 23—25.

cannot admit the bread to be called *his body,* because it is a sign of it. But if they object to every trope, and insist on taking the words in a sense strictly literal, why do they forsake the language of Christ, and adopt a phraseology of their own so very dissimilar? For there is a wide difference between these two assertions, that "the bread is the body," and that "the body is with the bread." But because they perceived the impossibility of supporting this simple proposition, "that the bread is the body," they have endeavoured to escape from their embarrassment by those evasions. Others, more daring, hesitate not to assert, that, in strict propriety of speech, the bread *is* the body; and thereby prove themselves to be advocates for a truly literal interpretation. If it be objected, that then the bread is Christ, and Christ is God, they will deny this, because it is not expressed in the words of Christ. But they will gain nothing by their denial of it, for it is universally admitted that the whole person of Christ is offered to us in the sacrament. Now, it would be intolerable blasphemy to affirm of a frail and corruptible element, without any figure, that it is Christ. I ask them whether these two propositions are equivalent to each other—*Christ is the Son of God,* and *Bread is the body of Christ.* If they confess them to be different,—a confession which, if they hesitated, it would be easy to extort from them,—let them say wherein the difference consists. I suppose they will adduce no other point of difference, than that the bread is called *the body* in a sacramental sense. Whence it follows, that the words of Christ are not subject to any common rule, and ought not to be examined on the principles of grammar. I would likewise inquire of the inflexible champions of a literal interpretation, whether the words attributed to Christ, by Luke and Paul, "This cup *is* the new testament in my blood," do not express the same idea as the former clause, in which the bread is called his body. Surely the same reverence ought to be shown to one part of the sacrament as to the other; and because brevity is obscure, the sense is elucidated by a fuller statement. Whenever, therefore, they shall argue, from that one word, that the bread is the body of Christ, I shall adduce the interpretation furnished by the fuller account, that it is the *testament* in his body. For shall we seek for an expositor of greater fidelity or accuracy than Paul and Luke?

Nor is it my design to diminish in the smallest degree that participation of the body of Christ, which I have acknowledged is enjoyed; my only object is, to silence that foolish obstinacy which displays itself in violent contentions about words. From the authority of Paul and Luke, I understand the bread to be the body of Christ, because it is the covenant in his body. If they resist this, their contention is not with me, but with the Spirit of God. Notwithstanding they profess to be influenced by such reverence for the words of Christ, that they dare not understand an explicit declaration of his in a figurative sense, yet this pretext is not sufficient to justify their pertinacious rejection of all the reasons which we alleged to the contrary. At the same time, as I have already suggested, it is necessary to understand what is meant by "the testament in the body and blood of Christ;" because we should derive no benefit from the covenant ratified by the sacrifice of his death, if it were not followed by that secret communication by which we become one with him.

XXI. It remains for us, therefore, to acknowledge that, on account of the affinity which the things signified have with their symbols, the name of the substance has been given to the sign, in a figurative sense indeed, but by a most apt analogy. I forbear to introduce any thing of allegories and parables, lest any one should accuse me of having recourse to subterfuges, and travelling out of the present subject. I observe that this is a metonymical form of expression, which is commonly used in the Scripture in reference to sacraments. For in no other sense is it possible to understand such passages as these; when of circumcision it is said, "This is my covenant;" (*i*) of the paschal lamb, "It is the Lord's passover;" (*k*) of the legal sacrifices, that they were expiations, or atonements; (*l*) of the rock, from which the water issued in the desert, "That Rock was Christ." (*m*) And not only is the name of something superior transferred to that which is inferior, but, on the contrary, the name of the visible sign is likewise given to the thing signified; as when God is said to have appeared to Moses in the bush, (*n*) when the ark of the covenant is

---

(*i*) Gen. xvii. 10.
(*k*) Exod. xii. 11.
(*l*) Exod. et Lev. passim.
(*m*) 1 Cor. x. 4.
(*n*) Exod. iii. 2.

called God, (*o*) and the Holy Spirit, a dove. (*p*) For, though there is an essential difference between the symbol and the thing signified, the former being corporeal, terrestrial, and visible, and the latter spiritual, celestial, and invisible, yet, as the symbol is not a vain and useless memorial, a mere adumbration of the thing which it has been consecrated to represent, but also a true and real exhibition of it, why may not the name of that which it signifies be justly applied to it? If symbols invented by man, which are rather emblems of things absent, than tokens of things present, of which also they very frequently give a delusive representation, are, nevertheless, sometimes distinguished by the names of the things which they signify, there is far greater reason why the symbols instituted by God should borrow the names of those things of which they always exhibit a correct and faithful representation, and by the truth of which they are always accompanied. So great, therefore, is the similitude and affinity of the one to the other, that there is nothing at all unnatural in such a mutual interchange of appellations. Let our adversaries cease, then, to assail us with their ridiculous wit, by calling us Tropologists, because we explain the sacramental phraseology according to the common usage of the Scripture. For as there is a great similarity in many respects between the various sacraments, so this metonymical transfer of names is common to them all. As the apostle, therefore, states, that "the Rock" from which flowed "spiritual drink" for the Israelites, "was Christ," (*q*) because it was a visible symbol, under which "that spiritual drink" was received, though not in a manner discernible by the corporeal eye, so bread is now called the body of Christ, because it is the symbol under which the Lord truly offers us his body to eat. And that no one may despise this as a novel sentiment, we shall show that the same was entertained by Augustine. He says, "If the sacraments had not some similitude to those things of which they are sacraments, they would be no sacraments at all. On account of this similitude, they frequently take the names even of the things which they represent. Therefore, as the sacrament of the body of Christ is in some sense that body itself, and the sacrament of the

---

(*o*) Psalm lxxxiv. 7; xlii. 2. (*p*) Matt. iii. 16. (*q*) 1 Cor. x. 4.

blood of Christ, is that blood itself, so the sacrament of faith is called faith." His works contain many similar passages, which it would be useless to collect, as this one is sufficient; only the reader ought to be apprized that this holy father repeats and confirms the same observation in an epistle to Euodius. It is a frivolous subterfuge to plead, that when Augustine speaks of metonymical expressions, as frequently and commonly used respecting the sacraments, he makes no mention of the Lord's supper; for, if this were admitted, we could no longer reason from the genus to the species, or from the whole to a part; it would not be a good argument to say, that every animal is endued with the power of motion, therefore oxen and horses are endued with the power of motion. All further dispute on this point, however, is precluded by the language of the same writer on another occasion—"that Christ did not hesitate to call it his body, when he gave it as the sign of his body." Again: "It was wonderful patience in Christ, to admit Judas to the feast, in which he instituted and gave to his disciples the emblem of his body and of his blood."

XXII. But if some obstinate man, shutting his eyes against every other consideration, should insist on this single expression, "*This is* my body," as though it made a distinction between the supper and all other sacraments, the answer is easy. They allege that the verb substantive is too emphatical to admit of any figure. If we grant this, the verb substantive is also used by Paul, where he says, "The bread which we break, *is* it not the *communion* of the body of Christ?" (*r*) But the communion of the body is something different from the body itself. In almost all cases of sacraments, we find the same word used—"This *is* my covenant." "It *is* the Lord's passover." (*s*) And to mention no more, when Paul says, "That Rock *was* Christ," (*t*) why do they consider the verb substantive less emphatical in that passage than in the speech of Christ? Let them also explain the force of the verb substantive in that place where John says, "The Holy Ghost *was* not yet, because that Jesus was not yet glorified." (*u*) For if they obstinately adhere to their rule, they will destroy the eternal existence of the Spirit, as if it commenced at the ascension of Christ. Let them

(*r*) 1 Cor. x. 16. (*s*) Gen. xvii. 10. Exod. xii. 11.
(*t*) 1 Cor. x. 4. (*u*) John vii. 39.

answer, in the last place, what is the meaning of Paul, when he calls baptism "the washing of regeneration, and renewing," (*v*) though it is evidently useless to many. But nothing is more conclusive against them than that passage where Paul says, that the Church is Christ. For having drawn a similitude from the human body, he adds, "So also is Christ;" (*w*) by which he means not the only begotten Son of God, in himself, but in his members. I think I have so far succeeded, that all men of sense and integrity must be disgusted with the foul calumnies of our adversaries, when they charge us with giving no credit to the words of Christ, which we receive with as much submission as themselves, and consider with greater reverence. Indeed, their supine negligence is a proof that it is a subject of little concern to them, what was the will or meaning of Christ, provided they can use him as a shield to defend their obstinacy; as our diligence in inquiring into Christ's true meaning is a sufficient proof of our high regard to his authority. They maliciously represent, that human reason prevents us from believing what Christ himself has declared with his sacred mouth; but how unjustly they stigmatize us with this reproach, I have explained, in a great measure, already, and shall presently make still more evident. Nothing prevents us, therefore, from believing Christ when he speaks, and immediately acquiescing in every word he utters. The only question is, whether it be criminal to inquire into his genuine meaning.

XXIII. To show themselves men of letters, these good doctors prohibit even the least departure from the literal signification. I reply, When the Scripture calls God "a man of war," because this language would be too harsh, unless it be explained in a figurative sense, I hesitate not to consider it as a comparison borrowed from men. And indeed it was upon no other pretext that the ancient Anthropomorphites molested the orthodox fathers, than by laying hold of such expressions as these: "The eyes of the Lord behold; It entereth into the ears of the Lord; His hand is stretched out; The earth is his footstool;" and accusing them of depriving God of his body, which the Scripture ascribes to him. If this canon of interpretation be admitted, all the light of faith

(*v*) Titus iii. 2. (*w*) 1 Cor. xii. 12.

will be overwhelmed in the crudest barbarism. For what monstrous absurdities will not fanatics be able to elicit from the Scripture, if they are permitted to allege every detached and ill-understood word and syllable in confirmation of their notions? The objection which they urge, from the improbability that Christ, when he was preparing peculiar consolation for his disciples in seasons of adversity, should express himself in enigmatical or obscure language, is completely in our favour. For if it had not been understood by the apostles, that the bread was called his body in a figurative sense, because it was a symbol of his body, they would undoubtedly have been disturbed about so monstrous a declaration. Almost at the same moment, John states that they were embarrassed and perplexed with every minute difficulty. They who debated among themselves how Christ was to go to the Father, and were at a loss to know how he would depart from this world; who could understand nothing that was said of a heavenly Father, because they had not seen him; how could they have been so ready to believe any thing so entirely repugnant to every dictate of reason, as that Christ was sitting at the table before their eyes, and yet was invisibly enclosed in the bread? By eating the bread without any hesitation, they testified their consent, and hence it appears that they understood the words of Christ in the same sense that we do, considering that it is common in all sacraments for the name of the sign to be transferred to the thing signified. To the disciples, therefore, it was, as it is to us, a certain and clear consolation, involved in no enigma; nor is there any other cause to be assigned why some reject our interpretation, except that the devil has blinded them by his delusions, in consequence of which they imagine enigmatical obscurities, where a beautiful figure furnishes such an obvious and natural meaning. Besides, if we rigidly adhere to the letter, what Christ said of the bread would be inconsistent with what he said of the cup. He calls the bread *his body*, he calls the wine *his blood:* either this must be a vain repetition, or a distinction which separates the body from the blood. It might be said of the cup, This is my body, as truly as of the bread; and the converse of this proposition would be equally correct, that the bread is his blood. If they reply, that we ought to consider for what end or use the symbols were instituted,

—this I acknowledge; but it is impossible to free their error from this absurd consequence, that the bread is the blood, and the wine the body. Now I am at a loss how to understand them, when they admit the bread and the body to be different things, and yet assert that the bread is properly and without any figure called the body; as if any one should say that a garment is different from a man, and yet that it is properly called a man. At the same time, as if their victory consisted in obstinacy and calumny, they charge us with accusing Christ of falsehood, if we inquire into the true meaning of his words. Now, it will be easy for the readers to judge how unjustly we are treated by these syllable-hunters, when they persuade the simple to believe that we derogate from the authority due to the words of Christ, which we have proved to be outrageously perverted and confounded by them, but to be faithfully and accurately explained by us.

XXIV. But the infamy of this falsehood cannot be entirely effaced, without repelling another calumny; for they accuse us of being so devoted to human reason, as to limit the power of God by the order of nature, and to allow him no more than our own understanding teaches us to ascribe to him. Against such iniquitous aspersions I appeal to the doctrine which I have maintained; which will sufficiently evince that I am far from measuring this mystery by the capacity of human reason, or subjecting it to the laws of nature. Is it from natural philosophy that we have learned that Christ feeds our souls with his flesh from heaven, just as our bodies are nourished with bread and wine? Whence is it that flesh has the power of giving life to our souls? Every one will pronounce it not to be from nature. No more will it accord with human reason that the flesh of Christ descends to us to become nourishment to us. In short, whoever shall understand our doctrine, will be enraptured with admiration of the secret power of God. But these good zealots contrive a miracle, without which God himself, with all his power, disappears from their view. I would again request of my readers a diligent consideration of the nature and tendency of our doctrine, whether it depends on human reason, or on the wings of faith rises above the world and ascends to heaven. We say that Christ descends to us both by the external symbol and by his Spirit, that he may truly vivify our souls with the substance of his flesh and blood. He who perceives not that many miracles are comprehended in these few words, is more than stupid; for there is nothing more preternatural than for souls to derive spiritual and heavenly life from the flesh, which had its origin from the earth, and was subject to death; nothing is more incredible than for things separated from each other by all the distance of heaven and earth, notwithstanding that immense local distance, to be not only connected, but united, so that our souls receive nourishment from the flesh of Christ. Let these fanatics, then, no longer attempt to render us odious by such a foul calumny, as though we, in any respect, limited the infinite power of God; which is either a most stupid mistake, or an impudent falsehood. For the question here respects not what God could do, but what he has chosen to do. We affirm that what pleased him, came to pass. It pleased him for Christ to become in all respects like his brethren, sin excepted. (*x*) What is the nature of our body? Has it not its proper and certain dimensions? is it not contained in some particular place, and capable of being felt and seen? And why, say they, may not God cause the same flesh to occupy many different places, to be contained in no particular place, and to have no form or dimensions? But how can they be so senseless as to require the power of God to cause a body to be a body, and not to be a body, at the same time? It is like demanding of him to cause light to be at once both light and darkness. But he wills light to be light, darkness to be darkness, and flesh to be flesh. Whenever it shall be his pleasure, indeed, he will turn darkness into light, and light into darkness; but to require that light and darkness shall no longer be different, is to aim at perverting the order of Divine wisdom. Therefore body must be body, spirit must be spirit, every thing must be subject to that law, and retain that condition, which was fixed by God at its creation. And the condition of a body is such, that it must occupy one particular place, and have its proper form and dimensions. In this condition did Christ assume a body, to which, as Augustine observes, "he gave incorruption and glory, but without depriving it of its nature and reality." The testimony of the Scrip-

(*x*) Heb. ii. 14; iv. 15.

ture is clear—that he ascended to heaven, whence he will come again, in like manner as he was seen to ascend. (*y*)

XXV. They reply, that they have the word in which the will of God is clearly revealed; that is, if they be allowed to banish from the Church the gift of interpretation which elucidates the word. I confess that they have the word and quote the letter of Scripture; but just as did the Anthropomorphites in past ages, who represented God to be corporeal; just as did Marcion and the Manichæans, who attributed to Christ a celestial or visionary body. For they quoted these texts: "The first man is of the earth, earthy; the second man is the Lord from heaven." (*z*) "Christ made himself of no reputation, and took upon him the form of a servant, and was made in the likeness of man." (*a*) These groveling souls imagine that God can have no power, unless the whole order of nature be reversed by the monster which they have fabricated in their own brains; but this is an attempt to circumscribe God, and to measure his power by the fancies of men. For from what word have they learned that the body of Christ is visible in heaven, and yet is on earth, concealed in an invisible manner under innumerable pieces of bread? They will say that necessity requires this, in order to the body of Christ being given in the supper. The truth is, that when they had determined to conclude, from the language of Christ, that his body was eaten in a carnal manner, carried away with this prejudice, they found it necessary to invent that subtlety, which the whole tenor of the Scripture contradicts. That we derogate any thing from the power of God, is so far from being true, that our doctrine peculiarly tends to magnify it. But as they never cease to accuse us of defrauding God of his due honour, by a rejection of every thing which natural reason finds it difficult to believe, though promised by the mouth of Christ himself, I repeat the answer which I have lately given, that we consult not natural reason respecting the mysteries of faith, but that, with the placid docility and gentleness of spirit recommended by James, (*b*) we receive the doctrine which comes down from heaven. Yet, in a point in which they run into a pernicious error, I admit that we pursue a useful moderation. On hear-

(*y*) Acts i. 11.
(*z*) 1 Cor. xv. 47.
(*a*) Phil. ii. 7.
(*b*) James i. 21.

ing the words of Christ, "This is my body," they imagine a miracle the most distant from his intention. This notion gives birth to prodigious absurdities; but, having already embarrassed themselves by their foolish precipitation, they plung themselves into the abyss of the Divine omnipotence, in order to extinguish the light of truth. Hence the haughty presumption, with which they profess to have no wish to know how Christ is concealed under the bread, being content with that declaration, "This is my body." We, on the contrary, with equal obedience and care, endeavour to ascertain the true meaning of this passage, as we do of all others; nor do we, with preposterous eagerness, temerity, and indiscretion, seize the first thought which presents itself to our minds, but after diligent meditation we embrace that sense which the Spirit of God suggests; established in which, we look down with contempt on every opposition made to it by the wisdom of this world; we even impose restraints on our own minds, that they may not dare to utter a word of cavil, and keep them humble to prevent their murmuring against the authority of God. Hence has proceeded that exposition of the words of Christ, which all, who are but moderately versed in the Scripture, know to be agreeable to its invariable usage respecting sacraments. Nor do we esteem it unlawful, in a difficult case, after the example of the holy virgin, to inquire how it can be. (*c*)

XXVI. But as nothing will be more effectual to confirm the faith of true believers, than a knowledge that the doctrine which we have advanced is drawn from the pure word of God, and rests upon its authority, I will demonstrate this with all possible brevity. It is not from Aristotle, but from the Holy Spirit, that we have learned that the body of Christ, since its resurrection, is limited, and received into heaven till the last day. I am fully aware that our adversaries contemptuously elude the passages which are adduced for this purpose. (*d*) Whenever Christ speaks of his approaching departure from the world, they reply that this departure was nothing more than a change of his mortal state. But if this were correct, Christ would not substitute the Holy Spirit to supply the defect of his absence, as they express it, since

---

(*c*) Luke i. 34. (*d*) John xiv. 2, 3, 28.

the Spirit does not succeed to his place, nor does Christ himself descend again from the glory of heaven to assume the condition of this mortal life. The advent of the Spirit, and the ascension of Christ, are clearly opposed to each other; and, therefore, it is impossible for Christ to dwell with us, according to his flesh, in the same manner in which he sends his Spirit. Besides, he expressly declares that he shall not always be with his disciples in the world. (*e*) This declaration also they think they have completely explained away, by saying that Christ merely intended that he should not always be poor and mean, and exposed to the necessities of this transitory life. But they are evidently contradicted by the context, which relates, not to his poverty, or indigence, or any of the miseries of this life, but to his reception of respect and honour. The unction performed by the woman displeased the disciples, because they thought it an unnecessary and useless expense, bordering on luxury; and, therefore, they wished that the value of the ointment, which they considered as improperly lavished, had been distributed to the poor. Christ said, that he should not always be present to receive such honour. Augustine has given the same explanation of this passage, in the following explicit language:—"When Christ said, Me ye have not always with you, he spoke of the presence of his body. For according to his majesty, his providence, and his ineffable and invisible grace, is accomplished what he said on another occasion—Lo, I am with you always, even to the end of the world; but, with respect to the body, which the Word assumed, which was born of the virgin, which was apprehended by the Jews, which was affixed to the tree, which was taken down from the cross, which was wrapped in linen clothes, which was laid in the sepulchre, which was manifested at the resurrection, this declaration is fulfilled—Me ye have not always with you. Why? Because in his corporeal presence he conversed with his disciples for forty days, and while they were attending him, seen, but not followed by them, he ascended to heaven. He is not here; for he sits at the right hand of the Father: and yet he is here; for he has not withdrawn the presence of his majesty: otherwise, according to the presence of

(*e*) Matt. xxvi. 11.

his majesty, we have Christ always with us; but, with respect to his corporeal presence, he said with truth, Me ye have not always with you. For the Church had his bodily presence for a few days; now it retains him by faith, but does not behold him with corporeal eyes." Here let us briefly remark, this father represents Christ as present with us in three respects—in his majesty, his providence, and his ineffable grace; under the last of which I comprehend the wonderful communion of his body and blood; only we must understand this to be effected by the power of the Holy Spirit, and not by a fictitious enclosure of his body under the bread. For our Lord has declared that he has flesh and bones, capable of being felt and seen; and *to go away* and *to ascend* import not a mere appearance of ascent and departure, but an actual performance of that which the words express. Shall we, then, it will be said by some, assign to Christ a particular district of heaven? I reply, with Augustine, that this question is too curious, and altogether unnecessary; provided we believe that he is in heaven, that is enough.

XXVII. Does not the term *ascension,* which is so frequently repeated, signify a removal from one place to another? This they deny, because they consider his exaltation as only denoting the majesty of his empire. But I ask, What was the manner of his ascent? Was he not carried up on high in the view of his disciples? Do not the evangelists expressly state that he was received up into heaven? (*f*) These acute sophists reply that he was concealed from their sight by an interposing cloud, to teach believers that thenceforward he would not be visible in the world. As though, to produce a belief of his invisible presence, he ought not rather to have vanished in a moment, or to have been enveloped in the cloud without moving from where he stood. But as he was carried up into the air, and, by the interposition of a cloud between him and his disciples, showed that he was no longer to be sought for on earth, we confidently conclude that his residence is now in heaven. This also is affirmed by Paul, who teaches us to expect him from thence. (*g*) For this reason the angels admonished the disciples—"Why stand ye gazing up into

(*f*) Mark xvi. 19. Luke xxiv. 51. Acts i. 9.

(*g*) Phil. iii. 20.

heaven? This same Jesus, which is taken up from you into heaven, shall so come in like manner as ye have seen him go into heaven." (*h*) Here also the adversaries of sound doctrine have recourse to what they think an ingenious evasion—that he will then become visible who has never departed from the word, but remained invisible with his people. As though the angels, in that address, insinuated a twofold presence, and did not simply make the disciples ocular witnesses of his ascension, with a view to preclude every doubt; just as if they had said, Received up into heaven in your sight, he has taken possession of the celestial empire; it remains for you to wait with patience till he shall come again as the judge of the world; for he is now entered into heaven, not to occupy it alone, but to assemble you and all the godly to enjoy it with him.

XXVIII. As the advocates of this spurious doctrine are not ashamed to defend it by the suffrages of the fathers, and particularly of Augustine, I will briefly expose the disingenuousness of this attempt. Their testimonies having been collected by learned and pious writers, I have no inclination to go over the same ground; any one who wishes may consult their writings. Nor even from Augustine shall I adduce every passage which would serve the argument; but shall content myself with showing, by a few extracts, that he is, beyond all doubt, perfectly in harmony with us. In order to deprive us of him, our adversaries allege that, in various parts of his works, he states the flesh and blood of Christ, even the victim once offered on the cross, to be dispensed in the sacred supper; but this is altogether frivolous; since he also calls the consecrated symbols either "the eucharist," or "the sacrament of Christ's body and blood." But in what sense he uses the words *flesh* and *blood*, it is unnecessary to make any long or circuitous inquiry; for he explains himself by saying, "that sacraments take their names from the similitude of those things which they signify, and, therefore, in some sense, the sacrament of the body is *the body*." With this corresponds another well known passage: "The Lord hesitated not to say, This is my body, when he delivered the sign of it." They object again, that Augustine expressly says, that

(*h*) Acts i. 11.

the body of Christ falls to the earth, and enters into the mouth. I reply, that he says this in the same sense in which he affirms it to be consumed; because he connects both these things together. Nor does any objection arise from his saying, that when the mystery is finished, the bread is consumed; because he had just before said, "As these things are known to man, being done by man, they may have honour as holy things, but not as miracles." And to the same effect is another expression, which our adversaries, without sufficient consideration, represent as in their favour; that, "when Christ presented the mystical bread to his disciples, he, in a certain sense, held himself in his own hands." For, by introducing this qualifying phrase *in a certain sense,* he sufficiently declares that the body of Christ was not truly or really enclosed in the bread. Nor ought this to be thought strange, for in another place he expressly maintains, "That if bodies be deprived of their local spaces, they will be nowhere, and consequently will cease to have any existence." It is a poor cavil, to say that this passage does not relate to the sacred supper, in which God exerts a special power; because the question had been agitated respecting the body of Christ, and this holy father, professedly answering it, says, "Christ has given immortality to his body, but has not deprived it of its nature. In a corporeal form, therefore, he is not to be considered as universally diffused; for we must beware of asserting his Divinity in such a way as to destroy the truth of his body. It does not follow, that, because God is every where, all that is in him is every where also." The reason is immediately added—"For one person is God and man, and both constitute one Christ; as God, he is every where; as man, he is in heaven." What stupidity would it have betrayed not to except the mystery of the supper, a thing so serious and important, if it contained any thing inconsistent with the doctrine he was maintaining! Yet, if any one will attentively read what follows, he will find, that under that general doctrine, the Lord's supper is also comprehended. He says, that Christ, who is, in one person, the only begotten Son of God and the Son of man, is every where present as God; that as God, he resides in the temple of God that is, in the Church; and yet that he occupies some particular place in heaven, according to the dimensions of a real body. To unite Christ with his Church, we see he does not bring down his body from heaven; which he certainly would have done, if that body could not become our food without being enclosed under bread. In another place, describing how Christ is now possessed by believers, he says, "You have him by the sign of the cross, by the sacrament of baptism, by the food and drink of the altar." Whether he is correct in placing a superstitious ceremony among the symbols of Christ's presence, I am not now discussing; but in comparing the presence of the flesh to the sign of the cross, he sufficiently shows that he does not imagine Christ to have two bodies, one visibly seated in heaven, and the other invisibly concealed under the bread. If any further explication be necessary, it is soon after added, "That we always have Christ, according to the presence of his majesty; but that, according to the presence of his flesh, it is rightly said, Me ye have not always." Our adversaries reply, that it is also observed, at the same time, "That according to his ineffable and invisible grace, his declaration is fulfilled—Lo, I am with you always, even to the end of the world." But this is nothing in their favour, because, after all, it is restricted to that majesty which is always opposed to the body, and his flesh is expressly distinguished from his power and grace. In another passage of this author, we find the same antithesis, or contrast, "that Christ left his disciples in his corporeal presence, that he might be with them by his spiritual presence;" which clearly distinguishes the substance of the flesh from the power of the Spirit, which conjoins us with Christ, notwithstanding we are widely separated from him by local distance. He frequently uses the same mode of expression, as when he says, "Christ will come again, in his corporeal presence, to judge the living and the dead, according to the rule of faith and sound doctrine. For in his spiritual presence, he was to come to his disciples, and to be with his whole Church on earth, to the end of time. This discourse, therefore, was addressed to the believers, whom he had already begun to keep with his corporeal presence, and whom he was about to leave by his corporeal absence, that with the Father he might keep them by his spiritual presence." To explain *corporeal* to mean *visible*, is mere trifling; for he opposes the body of Christ to his Divine power; and by adding, "that *with the Father he might keep them*," clearly expresses that the Saviour communicates his grace to us from heaven by the Holy Spirit.

XXIX. As they place so much confidence in this subterfuge of an invisible presence, let us see how far it serves their cause. In the first place, they cannot produce a single syllable from the Scriptures to prove that Christ is invisible; but they take for granted, what no man of sound judgment will concede to them, that the body of Christ cannot be given in the supper, without being concealed under the form of bread. Now, so far is this from being an admitted axiom, that it is the very point in dispute between them and us. And while they talk in this way, they are constrained to attribute to Christ a double body, because, upon their principle, he is visible in heaven, and at the same time, by a special dispensation, is invisible in the sacred supper. Whether this is correct or not, it is easy to judge from various passages of Scripture, and particularly from the testimony of Peter; who says of Christ, that "the heavens must receive him, until the times of restitution of all things." (*i*) These men maintain that he is in all places, but without any form. They object that it is unreasonable to subject the nature of a glorified body to the laws of common nature. But this objection leads to the extravagant notion of Servetus, which justly deserves the detestation of all believers, that the body of Christ, after his ascension, was absorbed in his Divinity. I will not assert, that they hold this opinion; but if it be considered as one of the attributes of the glorified body, to fill all places in an invisible manner, it is evident that the corporeal substance must be destroyed, and no difference will be left between the Divinity and the humanity. Besides, if the body of Christ be multiform and variable, so as to appear in one place, and to be invisible in another, what becomes of the nature of a body which consists in having its proper dimensions? and where is its unity? With far greater propriety Tertullian argues, that the body of Christ was a true and natural body, because the emblem of it is presented to us in the mystery of the supper, as a pledge and assurance of spiritual life. And, indeed, it was of his glorified body, that Christ said, "Handle me, and see; for a spirit

(*i*) Acts iii. 21.

hath not flesh and bones, as ye see me have." (*k*) We see how the truth of his body is proved by the lips of Christ himself, because it can be felt and seen; deprive it of these qualities, and it will cease to be a body. They are always recurring to their subterfuge of the dispensation which they have invented. But it is our duty to receive what Christ absolutely declares, in such a manner, as to admit, without any exception, whatever he is pleased to affirm. He proved that he was not a phantom, because he was visible in his flesh. If that be taken away which he asserts to belong to the nature of his body, will it not be necessary to frame a new definition of a body? Now, with all their sophistry, they can extract nothing to support their imaginary *dispensation* from that passage of Paul, where he says, that "From heaven we look for the Saviour, who shall change our vile body, that it may be fashioned like unto his glorious body." (*l*) For we cannot hope for a conformity to Christ in those qualities which they attribute to him, which would make all our bodies invisible and infinite; nor will they find a man foolish enough to be persuaded to believe so great an absurdity. Let them, then, no longer ascribe to the glorified body of Christ the property of being in many places at once, or of being contained within no particular space. In short, let them either deny the resurrection of the flesh, or admit that Christ, though clothed with celestial glory, has not divested himself of his flesh; for he will make us, in our flesh, partakers of the same glory, as we shall enjoy a resurrection similar to his. For what is there more clearly stated in any part of the Scripture, than that as Christ really assumed our flesh when he was born of the virgin, and suffered in our flesh to atone for our sins, so he resumed the same flesh, at his resurrection, and carried it up into heaven? For all the hope that we have of our resurrection and ascension to heaven, is founded on the resurrection and ascension of Christ; who, as Tertullian says, "has taken the pledge of our resurrection into heaven with him." Now, how weak and faint would this hope be, if the real flesh of Christ had not truly risen from the dead, and entered into the kingdom of heaven! But it is essential to a real body, to have its particular form and dimensions, and to

(*k*) Luke xxiv. 39. (*l*) Phil. iii. 20, 21.

be contained within some certain space. Let us hear no more, then, of this ridiculous notion, which fastens the minds of men, and Christ himself, to the bread. For what is the use of this invisible presence concealed under the bread, but to lead those who desire to be united to Christ, to confine their attention to that symbol? But the Lord intended to withdraw, not only our eyes, but all our senses, from the earth, when he forbade the woman to touch him, because he was not yet ascended to his Father. (*m*) When he saw Mary, with pious affection and reverence, hastening to kiss his feet, there was no reason for his disapprobation and prohibition of such an act, before his ascension to heaven, except that heaven was the only place where he chose to be sought. It is objected, that he was afterwards seen by Stephen; (*n*) but the answer is easy; for, in order to this, no change of place was necessary for Christ, who could impart to the eyes of his servant a supernatural perspicacity, capable of penetrating into heaven. The same observation is applicable to his appearance to Paul. (*o*) They allege that Christ came out of the sepulchre, while the sepulchre remained closed, and entered into the room where his disciples were assembled, while the doors continued shut; but this contributes no support to their error. For as the water was like a solid pavement, forming a road for Christ when he walked on the lake, so it is no wonder if the hardness of the stone gave way, to make him a passage; though it is more probable that the stone removed at his command, and after his departure returned to its place. And to enter while the doors remained shut, does not imply his penetrating through the solid matter, but his opening an entrance for himself by his Divine power, so that, in a miraculous manner, he instantaneously stood in the midst of his disciples, though the doors were shut. What they adduce from Luke, that "he vanished out of the sight" of his two disciples, with whom he had walked to Emmaus, (*p*) is of no service to their cause, but is in favour of ours; for, according to the testimony of the same evangelist, when he joined these disciples, he assumed no new appearance in order to conceal himself; but "their eyes were holden, that they should not know him." (*q*) Our adversaries, however, not only transform

(*m*) John xx. 17. (*n*) Acts vii. 55. (*o*) Acts xxii. 18. 1 Cor. xv. 8.
(*p*) Luke xxiv. 31. (*q*) Luke xxiv. 16.

Christ, to keep him in the world, but they represent him as unlike himself, and altogether different on earth from what he is in heaven. By such extravagances, in short, they turn the body of Christ into a spirit, though not by positive assertion yet by direct implication; and not content with this, they attribute to it qualities utterly incompatible with each other, whence it follows, of necessity, that he must have two bodies.

XXX. Though we should grant them what they contend for, respecting its invisible presence, still this would be no proof of its infinity, without which it will be a vain attempt to enclose Christ under the bread. Unless the body of Christ be capable of being every where at once, without any limitation of place, it will not be credible that it is concealed under the bread in the sacred supper. It was this necessity which caused them to introduce their monstrous notion of its ubiquity. But it has been shown, by clear and strong testimonies of Scripture, that the body of Christ was, like other human bodies, circumscribed by certain dimensions; and its ascension to heaven made it evident that it was not in all places, but that it left one place, when it removed to another. Nor is the promise, "I am with you always, even unto the end of the world," (*r*) to be applied, as they suppose it should be, to his body. In the first place, on this supposition, there will be no such perpetual connection, unless Christ dwells in us in a corporeal manner, without the use of the sacramental supper; and therefore they have no sufficient cause for contending so fiercely respecting the words of Christ, in order to enclose Christ under the bread. In the next place, the context evinces, that Christ there has not the most distant reference to his flesh, but promises his disciples invincible aid to sustain and defend them against all the assaults of Satan and the world. For having assigned them a difficult province, to encourage them to undertake it without hesitation, and to discharge it with undaunted resolution, he supports them with the assurance of his presence; as though he had said, they should never want his aid, which nothing could overcome. Unless these men wished to involve every thing in confusion, ought they not to distinguish the nature of this presence? It is evident that some

(*r*) Matt. xxviii. 20.

persons would rather incur the greatest disgrace by betraying their ignorance, than relinquish even the least particle of their error. I speak not of the Romanists, whose doctine is more tolerable, or at least more modest; but some are so carried away with the heat of contention, as to affirm that, on account of the union of the two natures in Christ, wherever his Divinity is, his flesh, which cannot be separated from it, is there also; as if that union had mingled the two natures so as to form some intermediate kind of being, which is neither God nor man. This notion was maintained by Eutyches, and since his time by Servetus. But it is clearly ascertained from the Scriptures, that in the one person of Christ the two natures are united in such a manner, that each retains its peculiar properties undiminished. That Eutyches was justly condemned as a heretic, our adversaries will not deny; it is surprising that they overlook the cause of his condemnation, which was, that by taking away the difference between the two natures, and insisting on the unity of the person, he made the Divinity human, and deified the humanity. What absurdity, therefore, is it to mingle heaven and earth together, rather than not to draw the body down from the celestial sanctuary! They endeavour to justify themselves by adducing these texts: "No man hath ascended up to heaven, but he that came down from heaven, even the Son of man, which is in heaven;" and, "The only begotten Son, which is in the bosom of the Father, he hath declared him." (*s*) But it argues the same stupidity to disregard the communication of properties, a term which was with good reason adopted by the holy fathers in the early ages. When Paul says that "The Lord of glory" was "crucified," (*t*) he certainly does not intend that Christ suffered any thing in his Divinity, but that the same person, who suffered as an abject and despised man, was also, as God, the Lord of glory. In the same sense, the Son of man was in heaven; because the same Christ, who, according to the flesh, dwelt on earth as the Son of man, as God, was always in heaven. For this reason, in the same passage he represents himself as having descended from heaven, according to his Divinity; not that his Divinity quitted heaven to confine itself in the prison of the body; but because,

---

(*s*) John iii. 13; i. 18. (*t*) 1 Cor. ii. 8.

though it filled all space, yet it dwelt corporeally, or naturally, and in a certain ineffable manner, in the humanity. It is a distinction common in the schools, and which I am not ashamed to repeat, that though Christ is every where entire, yet all that is in him is not every where. And I sincerely wish that the schoolmen themselves had duly considered the meaning of this observation; for then we should never have heard of their stupid notion of the corporeal presence of Christ in the sacrament. Therefore, our Mediator, as he is every where entire, is always near to his people; and in the sacred supper exhibits himself present in a peculiar manner, yet not with all that belongs to him; because, as we have stated, his body has been received into heaven, and remains there till he shall come to judgment.

XXXI. They are exceedingly deceived, who cannot conceive of any presence of the flesh of Christ in the supper, except it be attached to the bread. For on this principle they leave nothing to the secret operation of the Spirit, which unites us to Christ. They suppose Christ not to be present, unless he descends to us; as though we cannot equally enjoy his presence, if he elevates us to himself. The only question between us, therefore, respects the manner of this presence; because they place Christ in the bread, and we think it unlawful for us to bring him down from heaven. Let the readers judge on which side the truth lies. Only let us hear no more of that calumny, that Christ is excluded from the sacrament, unless he be concealed under the bread. For as this is a heavenly mystery, there is no necessity to bring Christ down to the earth, in order to be united to us.

XXXII. If any one inquire of me respecting the manner, I shall not be ashamed to acknowledge, that it is a mystery too sublime for me to be able to express, or even to comprehend; and, to be still more explicit, I rather experience it, than understand it. Here, therefore, without any controversy, I embrace the truth of God, on which I can safely rely. He pronounces his flesh to be the food and his blood the drink, of my soul. I offer him my soul, to be nourished with such aliment. In his sacred supper, he commands me, under the symbols of bread and wine, to take, and eat, and drink, his body and blood. I doubt not that he truly presents, and that I receive them. Only I reject the absurdities which appear to be either degrading to his majesty, or inconsistent with the reality of his human nature, and are at the same time repugnant to the word of God, which informs us that Christ has been received into the glory of the celestial kingdom, where he is exalted above every condition of the world, and which is equally careful to attribute to his human nature the properties of real humanity. Nor ought this to seem incredible or unreasonable, because, as the kingdom of Christ is wholly spiritual, so his communications with his Church are not at all to be regulated by the order of the present world; or, to use the words of Augustine, "This mystery, as well as others, is celebrated by man, but in a Divine manner; it is administered on earth, but in a heavenly manner." The presence of Christ's body, I say, is such as the nature of the sacrament requires; where we affirm that it appears with so much virtue and efficacy, as not only to afford our minds an undoubted confidence of eternal life, but also to give us an assurance of the resurrection and immortality of our bodies. For they are vivified by his immortal flesh, and in some degree participate his immortality. Those who go beyond this in their hyperbolical representations, merely obscure the simple and obvious truth by such intricacies. If any person be not yet satisfied, I would request him to consider, that we are now treating of a sacrament, every part of which ought to be referred to faith. Now, we feed our faith by this participation of the body of Christ which we have mentioned, as fully as they do, who bring him down from heaven. At the same time, I candidly confess, that I reject that mixture of the flesh of Christ with our souls, or that transfusion of it into us, which they teach; because it is sufficient for us that Christ inspires life into our souls from the substance of his flesh, and even infuses his own life into us, though his flesh never actually enters into us. I may also remark, that the analogy of faith, to which Paul directs us to conform every interpretation of the Scripture, is in this case, beyond all doubt, eminently in our favour. Let the adversaries of so clear a truth examine by what rule of faith they regulate themselves. "He that confesseth not that Jesus Christ is come in the flesh, is not of God." (*v*) Such

---

(*v*) 1 John iv. 3.

persons, though they may conceal it, or may not observe it, do, in effect, deny the reality of his flesh.

XXXIII. The same judgment is to be formed of our participation, which they suppose not to be enjoyed at all, unless the flesh of Christ be swallowed in the bread. But we do no small injury to the Holy Spirit, unless we believe that our communion with the flesh and blood of Christ is the effect of his incomprehensible influence. Even if the virtue of this mystery, such as we have represented it, and as it was understood by the ancient Church, had received the consideration justly due to it, for four hundred years past, there would have been quite enough to satisfy us, and the door would have been shut against many pernicious errors, which have kindled dreadful dissensions, by which the Church has been miserably agitated in the present, as well as past ages. But sophistical men insist on a hyperbolical kind of presence, which is never taught in the Scripture; and they contend as eagerly for this foolish and absurd imagination, as if the whole of religion consisted in the enclosure of Christ in the bread. It principally concerns us to know how the body of Christ, which was once delivered for us, is made ours, and how we are made partakers of his blood which was shed; for the entire possession of Christ crucified consists in an enjoyment of all his benefits. Now, leaving these things, which are of such great importance, and even neglecting and forgetting them, these sophists take no pleasure but in this thorny question; how the body of Christ is concealed under the bread, or under the form of the bread. They falsely pretend that all that we teach respecting a spiritual participation, is contrary to what they call the true and real participation; because we regard nothing but the manner, which in their opinion, is corporeal, as they enclose Christ in the bread, but in ours is spiritual, because the secret influence of the Spirit is the bond which unites us to Christ. Nor is there any more truth in their other objection, that we attend to nothing but the fruit or effect which believers experience from feeding on the flesh of Christ. For we have already said, that Christ himself is the matter or substance of the sacred supper, and that it is in consequence of this, that we are absolved from our sins by the sacrifice of his death, are washed in his blood, and by his resurrection are raised to the hope of the heavenly life. But the foolish imagination, of which Lombard was the author, has perverted their minds, while they have supposed the sacrament to consist in eating the flesh of Christ. For these are his words: "The sacrament, without the thing, consists in the forms of bread and wine; the sacrament and the thing are the flesh and blood of Christ; the thing, without the sacrament, is his mystical flesh." Again, a little after: "The thing signified and contained is the proper flesh of Christ; the thing signified and not contained, is his mystical body." With his distinction between the flesh of Christ, and the power which it has to nourish, I fully agree; but his notion, of what is a sacrament, and as contained under the bread, is an error not to be endured. Hence proceeded a false idea of sacramental eating, because they supposed the body of Christ to be eaten by impious and profane persons, notwithstanding they were strangers to him. But the flesh of Christ itself, in the mystery of the supper, is as much a spiritual thing, as our eternal salvation. Whence we conclude, that persons who are destitute of the Spirit of Christ, can no more eat the flesh of Christ, than drink wine which has no taste. It is certainly offering an insult, and doing violence to Christ, to attribute to him a body all feeble and dead, which is promiscuously distributed to unbelievers; and it is expressly contradicted by his own words: "He that eateth my flesh, and drinketh my blood, dwelleth in me, and I in him." (*x*) They reply, that the discourse from which this text is quoted does not treat of sacramental eating; and this I concede to them; only let them not be perpetually striking on the same rock, that the flesh of Christ may be eaten without any benefit. But I would wish them to inform me how long they retain it after they have eaten it. Here I believe they will find it impossible to escape. But they object, that the truth of the promises of God can sustain no diminution or failure from the ingratitude of men. This I admit; and I also maintain, that the virtue of this mystery remains unimpaired, notwithstanding wicked men exert their utmost efforts to destroy it. It is one thing, however, for the body of Christ to be offered, and another for it to be received. Christ presents this spiritual meat and

(*x*) John vi. 56.

spiritual drink to all; some receive them with avidity, others fastidiously reject them; shall their rejection cause the meat and drink to lose their nature? They will plead, that their sentiment is supported by this similitude—that the flesh of Christ, though it be not relished by unbelievers, nevertheless still continues to be flesh. But I deny that it can ever be eaten without the taste of faith; or, if the language of Augustine be preferred, I deny that men carry away from the sacrament any more than they collect in the vessel of faith. Thus, nothing is taken from the sacrament, but its truth and efficacy remain unimpaired, notwithstanding the wicked depart empty from its external participation. If our adversaries object again, that it derogates from these words, "This is my body," if the wicked receive corruptible bread, and nothing more, the answer is easy—That God will have his veracity discovered, not in the reception itself, but in the constancy of his goodness, since he is ready to impart to the unworthy, and even liberally offers to them, that which they reject. And this is the perfection of the sacrament, which the whole world cannot violate, that the flesh and blood of Christ are as truly given to the unworthy, as to the elect and faithful people of God; but it is likewise true, that as rain, falling upon a hard rock, runs off from it without penetrating into the stone, thus the wicked, by their obduracy repel the grace of God so that it does not enter into their hearts. Besides, a reception of Christ, without faith, is as great an absurdity, as for seed to germinate in the fire. Their inquiry, how Christ came for condemnation to some, unless they receive him unworthily, is a groundless cavil; for we nowhere read that the perdition of man is owing to an unworthy reception of Christ, but rather to a rejection of him. Nor can they derive any assistance from the parable in which Christ speaks of some seed springing up among thorns, and being afterwards choked and destroyed; for he is there showing what value belongs to that temporary faith, which our adversaries suppose to be unnecessary to a participation of the flesh and blood of Christ, placing Judas, in this respect, on an equality with Peter. Their error is rather refuted by another part of the same parable, in which Christ speaks of some seed as having fallen by the way-side, and some on stony ground, neither of which took any root. (*y*) Whence it follows, that the obduracy of unbelievers is such an obstacle, that Christ does not reach them. Whoever desires our salvation to be promoted by this mystery, will find nothing more proper than that believers, conducted to the fountain should derive life from the Son of God. But the dignity of it is sufficiently magnified, when we remember, that it is a medium by which we are incorporated into Christ; or by which, after our incorporation into him, the connection is more and more strengthened, till he perfectly unites us with himself, in the heavenly life. They object that Paul ought not to have made unbelievers "guilty of the body and blood of the Lord," (*z*) unless they had been partakers of them. But I answer, that they are not condemned for having eaten and drunk his body and blood, but only for having profaned the mystery, by trampling under foot the pledge of our holy union with God, which ought to have been received by them with reverence.

XXXIV. Now, because Augustine is the principal among the ancient fathers who has asserted this point of doctrine, that the sacraments sustain no diminution, and that the grace which they represent is not frustrated by the unbelief or wickedness of men, it will be useful to adduce his own words, which will clearly prove that those who expose the body of Christ to be eaten by dogs, (*a*) are chargeable with an injudicious and culpable perversion of his meaning, in applying it to the present argument. Sacramental eating, according to them, is that by which the wicked receive the body and blood of Christ without any influence of his Spirit, or any effect of his grace. Augustine, on the contrary, carefully examining these words, "Whoso eateth my flesh and drinketh my blood hath eternal life," (*b*) says, "This is the virtue of the sacrament, not the mere visible sacrament; and that internally, not externally; he who eats with his heart, and not with his teeth;" from which he concludes that the sacrament of the union which we have with the body and blood of Christ, is presented in the sacred supper, to some to life, to others to perdition; but that the thing signified by the sacrament is only given to life to all who partake of it, and in no case to perdition.

(*y*) Matt. xiii. 4—7.
(*z*) 1 Cor. xi. 27.
(*a*) Matt. vii. 6.
(*b*) John vi. 54.

To preclude any cavil here, that the thing signified is not the body, but the grace of the Spirit, which may be separated from the body, he obviates such misrepresentations by the use of the contrasted epithets of *visible* and *invisible;* for the body of Christ cannot be comprehended under the former. Hence it follows, that unbelievers receive nothing but the visible symbol. And, for the more complete removal of every doubt, after having said that this bread requires the hunger of the inner man, he adds, "Moses, and Aaron, and Phinehas, and many others who ate the manna, were acceptable to God. Why? Because they spiritually understood the visible food, they spiritually hungered, they spiritually ate, that they might be spiritually satisfied. For we also, in the present day, have received visible food; but the sacrament is one thing, and the virtue of the sacrament is another." A little after he says, "Therefore he who abides not in Christ, and in whom Christ does not abide, spiritually neither eats his flesh nor drinks his blood, though he may carnally and visibly press the sign of the body and blood with his teeth." Here, again, we find the visible sign opposed to the spiritual eating; which contradicts that error, that the invisible body of Christ is really eaten sacramentally, though it be not eaten spiritually. We are informed also that nothing is granted to the profane and impure, beyond the visible reception of the sign. Hence that well known observation of his, that the other disciples ate *the bread which was the Lord,* but that Judas merely ate *the Lord's bread;* by which he clearly excludes unbelievers from the participation of the body and blood. And to the same purpose is what he says in another place: "Why do you wonder if the bread of Christ was given to Judas to enslave him to the devil, when you see, on the other hand, that the messenger of Satan was given to Paul to make him perfect in Christ?" (*b*) He says, indeed, in another place, "That the sacramental bread was the body of Christ to those to whom Paul said, He that eateth and drinketh unworthily, eateth and drinketh judgment to himself; (*c*) and that they could not, therefore, be affirmed to have received nothing, because they had received amiss." But his meaning is more fully explained in another passage. For professedly

---

(*b*) 2 Cor. xii. 7. (*c*) 1 Cor. xi. 29.

undertaking to describe how the body of Christ is eaten by the wicked and profligate, who confess the Christian faith with their lips while they deny it in their actions, and that in opposition to the opinion of some who suppose them to eat not only the sacramental symbol, but the substance itself, he says, "They must not be considered as eating the body of Christ, because they are not to be numbered among the members of Christ. For, to mention nothing else, they cannot, at the same time, be the members of Christ and the members of a harlot. And where the Lord himself says, He that eateth my flesh, and drinketh my blood, dwelleth in me, and I in him; (*d*) he shows what it is to eat his body, not merely in a sacramental way, but in truth; for this is to dwell in Christ, that Christ may dwell in us. This is the same as if he had said, "Whoever dwelleth not in me, and in whom I dwell not, let him not say or think he eateth my body or drinketh my blood." Let the readers consider the opposition here stated between eating *merely in a sacramental way*, and *in truth*, and there will remain no doubt respecting his meaning. He confirms the same with equal perspicuity in the following passage: "Prepare not your jaws, but your heart; it is for this that the supper is enjoined. Behold, we believe in Christ when we receive him by faith; in receiving him, we know what we think; we take a bit of bread, and our hearts are satisfied. We are fed, therefore, not by what we see, but by what we believe." Here, also, what the wicked partake of he restricts to the visible sign, and pronounces that Christ is only received by faith. So, in another place, he expressly remarks that the good and the wicked partake of the elements in common, and excludes the latter from the true participation of the body of Christ. For, if they had enjoyed the substance itself, he would not have been entirely silent on that which would have strengthened his argument. In another place also, treating of the eating, and the benefit of it, he concludes thus: "Then will the body and blood of Christ be life to every one, if that which is visibly received in the sacrament, be, in the truth which is signified, spiritually eaten and spiritually drunk." Let those, therefore, who, in order to agree with Augustine, make unbelievers partakers of

(*d*) John vi. 56.

the flesh and blood of Christ, exhibit to us the body of Christ in a visible manner, since he pronounces the whole truth of the sacrament to be spiritual. And the evident conclusion from his language is, that the sacramental eating is nothing more than eating the visible and external sign, when unbelief precludes the entrance of the substance. If the body of Christ could be eaten truly, without being eaten spiritually, what could be the meaning of Augustine, when he said, "You are not to eat this body which you see, and to drink the blood which will be shed by those who shall crucify me. I have appointed a sacrament for you; spiritually understood, it shall vivify you." He certainly did not mean to deny that the same body which Christ offered in sacrifice is exhibited in the supper; but he designates the mode of participating in it—that though it has been received into celestial glory, it inspires us with life by the secret influence of the Holy Spirit. I acknowledge that he frequently speaks of the body of Christ as eaten by unbelievers, but he explains his meaning by adding that it is done sacramentally; and, in another place, he describes the spiritual eating as not consisting in a corporeal swallowing of the grace of God. And that my adversaries may not charge me with a wish to overwhelm them by an accumulation of passages, I would request them to inform me how they can evade that one declaration of his, where he says, "that the sacraments realize what they represent in the elect alone." Surely they will not dare to deny that the bread represents the body of Christ. Hence it follows, that the reprobate are excluded from the participation of it. The following passage of Cyril also shows him to have been of the same opinion: "As when any one pours melted wax upon other wax, the whole will be mingled together into one mass, so it is necessary to any person's reception of the body and blood of Christ, for him to be united with Christ, so that Christ may be found in him, and he in Christ." These words, I think, sufficiently prove that those who eat the body of Christ merely in a sacramental way are deprived of the true and real participation of it, as the body itself cannot be separated from its efficacious power; and yet that this is no impeachment of the truth of the promises of God, who still continues to send us rain from heaven, though rocks and stones imbibe none of the moisture.

XXXV. This knowledge will also easily dissuade us from the carnal adoration which has been introduced into the sacrament by the perverse temerity of some, who reasoned in this manner: If the body be there, consequently the soul and the Divinity are there together with the body, for they cannot be separated from it; therefore Christ ought to be adored there. In the first place, what will they do, if we refuse to admit what they call *concomitance?* For, however they may urge the absurdity of separating the soul and the Divinity from the body, what man in his senses can be persuaded that the body of Christ is Christ? They consider it, indeed, as fully demonstrated by their arguments. But as Christ speaks distinctly of his body and blood, without specifying the nature of the presence, how can they establish what they wish by that which is itself doubtful? What then? If their consciences happen to be exercised with any peculiar affliction, will they not, with all their syllogisms, be confounded and overwhelmed; when they shall perceive themselves to be destitute of the certain word of God, which furnishes the only support for our souls when they are called to give an account, and without which they sink in a moment; when they shall reflect that the doctrine and examples of the apostles are against them, and that they are themselves the sole authors of their error? To such reflections will be added other sentiments of compunction, and those by no means inconsiderable. What! was it a thing of no consequence to adore God in this form, without any such thing being enjoined upon us? In a case where the true worship of God was concerned, ought that to have been so lightly undertaken, which not a word in the Scripture could be found to sanction? But if, with becoming humility, they had kept all their thoughts in subjection to the word of God, they would certainly have listened to what Christ said, "Take, eat, drink," and would have obeyed this command, which enjoins the sacrament to be taken, not to be adored. Those who, as the Lord has commanded, receive it without adoration, are assured that they do not deviate from the Divine command; and such an assurance is the best satisfaction we can have in any thing in which we engage. They have the example of the apostles, of whom we read, not that they prostrated themselves in adoration, but that, as they were sitting at the table, they took, and did eat.

They have the practice of the apostolic Church, in which Luke states that the communion of believers consisted, not in adoration, but in "the breaking of bread." (*e*) They have the apostolic doctrine with which Paul instructed the Church of the Corinthians, accompanying it with this declaration: "I have received of the Lord that which also I delivered unto you." (*f*)

XXXVI. All these things lead the pious reader to consider how unsafe it is, in matters of such importance, to leave the pure word of God for the reveries of our own brains. The remarks which have already been made, ought to relieve our minds from every difficulty on this subject. For, in order to a due reception of Christ in the sacrament, it is necessary for pious souls to be elevated to heaven. If it be the design of the sacrament to assist the mind of man, which is otherwise weak, that it may be enabled to rise to discover the sublimity of spiritual mysteries,—those who confine themselves to the external sign, wander from the right way seeking Christ. What, then, shall we deny it to be a superstitious worship, when men prostrate themselves before a piece of bread to adore Christ in it? There is no doubt that the Council of Nice intended to guard against this evil, when it prohibited Christians from having their attention humbly fixed on the visible signs. And this was the only reason for that custom in the ancient Church, that, before the consecration, one of the deacons should, with an audible voice, admonish the people to have their *hearts above.* The Scripture itself, also, in addition to the particular account which it gives us of the ascension of Christ, by which he removed his corporeal presence from the view and society of men, in order to divest us of every carnal idea respecting him, whenever it mentions him, calls us to lift our minds upwards, and to seek for him seated "at the right hand of God." (*g*) According to this rule, it was our duty to adore him spiritually in the glory of heaven, rather than to invent such a dangerous kind of adoration, involving such gross and carnal conceptions of God. Wherefore, those who have invented the adoration of the sacrament, have not only dreamed it of themselves, without the sanction of the Scripture, in which not the least mention of it can be found, though, if it had been agreeable to God, it would not

(*e*) Acts ii. 42. (*f*) 1 Cor. xi. 23. (*g*) Col. iii. i.

have been omitted; but even in direct opposition to the Scripture, forsaking the living God, they have fabricated a new deity, according to their own wayward inclinations. For what is idolatry, if it be not to worship the gifts instead of the giver himself? In which they have fallen into a double sin; for the honour has been taken away from God to be transferred to the creature; and God himself has also been dishonoured by the pollution and profanation of his gift, when his holy sacrament has been made an execrable idol. Let us, on the contrary, lest we fall into the same danger, fix our ears, our eyes, our minds, and our tongues, entirely on the sacred doctrine of God. For that is the school of the Holy Spirit, the best of all teachers; whose instructions require nothing to be added from any other quarter, and omit nothing of which we ought not to be willing to remain in ignorance.

XXXVII. Now, as superstition, when it has once gone beyond the proper limits, proceeds in sinning without end, they have wandered still further; they have invented ceremonies altogether incompatible with the institution of the sacred supper, for the sole purpose of giving divine honours to the sign. When we remonstrate with them, they reply, that they pay this veneration to Christ. In the first place, if this were done in the supper, I would still say that that is the only legitimate adoration, which terminates not in the sign, but is directed to Christ enthroned in heaven. Now, what pretence have they for alleging that they worship Christ in the bread, when they have no promise of such a thing? They consecrate their *host,* as they call it, to carry it about in procession, to display it in pomp, and to exhibit it in a box, to be seen, adored, and invoked by the people. I inquire how they consider it to be rightly consecrated. They immediately adduce these words: "This is my body." I object, that it was said at the same time, "Take and eat." And I have sufficient reason for this; for when a promise is annexed to a precept, it is so included in the precept, that, separated from it, it ceases to be a promise at all. This shall be further elucidated by a similar example. The Lord gave a command, when he said, "Call upon me;" he added a promise, "I will deliver thee." (*h*) If any one should invoke Peter or Paul, and boast of this promise, will not his conduct be

(*h*) Psalm l. 15.

universally condemned? And wherein would this differ from the conduct of those who suppress the command to eat, and lay hold of the mutilated promise, "This is my body," in order to misapply it to ceremonies foreign from the institution of Christ? Let us remember, then, that this promise is given to those who observe the commandment connected with it, but that they are entirely unsupported by the word of God, who transfer the sacrament to any other usage. We have already shown how the mystery of the supper promotes our faith before God. But as God here not only recalls to our remembrance the vast exuberance of his goodness, but delivers it, as it were, into our hands, as we have already declared, and excites us to acknowledge it, so he also admonishes us not to be ungrateful for such a profusion of beneficence, but, on the contrary, to magnify it with the praises it deserves, and to celebrate it with thanksgivings. Therefore, when he gave the institution of this sacrament to the apostles, he said to them, "This do in remembrance of me;" (*i*) which Paul explains to be "showing the Lord's death;" (*k*) that is, publicly, and all together, as with one mouth, to confess that all our confidence of life and salvation rests on the death of the Lord; that we may glorify him by our confession, and by our example may exhort others to give him the same glory. Here, again, we see the object to which the sacrament tends, which is, to exercise us in a remembrance of the death of Christ. For the command which we have received, to "show the Lord's death till he come" to judgment, is no other than to declare, by the confession of our lips, what our faith has acknowledged in the sacrament, that the death of Christ is our life. This is the second use of the sacrament, which relates to external confession.

XXXVIII. In the third place, the Lord intended it to serve us as an exhortation, and no other could be better adapted to animate and influence us in the most powerful manner to purity and sanctity of life, as well as to charity, peace, and concord. For there the Lord communicates his body to us in such a manner that he becomes completely one with us, and we become one with him. Now, as he has only one body, of which he makes us all partakers, it follows, of necessity, that, by such participation, we

(*i*) Luke xxii. 10. (*k*) 1 Cor. xi. 26.

also are all made one body; and this union is represented by the bread which is exhibited in the sacrament. For as it is composed of many grains, mixed together in such a manner that one cannot be separated or distinguished from another,—in the same manner we ought, likewise, to be connected and united together, by such an agreement of minds, as to admit of no dissension or division between us. This I prefer expressing in the language of Paul: "The cup of blessing which we bless, is it not the communion of the blood of Christ? The bread which we break, is it not the communion of the body of Christ? For we, being many, are one bread and one body; for we are all partakers of that one bread." (*l*) We have derived considerable benefit from the sacrament, if this thought be impressed and engraven upon our minds, that it is impossible for us to wound, despise, reject, injure, or in any way to offend one of our brethren, but we, at the same time, wound, despise, reject, injure, and offend Christ in him; that we have no discord with our brethren without being, at the same time, at variance with Christ; that we cannot love Christ without loving him in our brethren; that such care as we take of our own body, we ought to exercise the same care of our brethren, who are members of our body; that as no part of our body can be in any pain without every other part feeling correspondent sensations, so we ought not to suffer our brother to be afflicted with any calamity without our sympathizing in the same. Wherefore, it is not without reason that Augustine so frequently calls this sacrament "the bond of charity." For what more powerful stimulus could be employed to excite mutual charity among us, than when Christ, giving himself to us, not only invites us by his example mutually to devote ourselves to the promotion of one another's welfare, but also, by making himself common to all makes us all to be one with himself?

XXXIX. This furnishes the best confirmation of what I have stated before, that there is no true administration of the sacrament without the word. For whatever advantage accrues to us from the sacred supper requires the word; whether we are to be confirmed in faith, exercised in confession, or excited to duty, there is need of preaching. Nothing more preposterous, therefore,

(*l*) 1 Cor. x. 16, 17.

can be done with respect to the supper, than to convert it into a mute action, as we have seen done under the tyranny of the pope. For they have maintained that all the validity of the consecration depends on the intention of the priests, as if it had nothing to do with the people, to whom the mystery ought principally to be explained. They fell into this error, for want of observing that those promises on which the consecration rests, are not directed to the elements themselves, but to the persons who receive them. Christ does not address the bread, to command it to become his body; but enjoins his disciples to eat, and promises them the communication of his body and blood. Nor does Paul teach any other order than that the promises should be offered to believers, together with the bread and the cup. And this is the truth. We are not to imagine any magical incantation, or think it sufficient to have muttered over the words, as if they were heard by the elements, but we are to understand those words, by which the elements are consecrated, to be a lively preaching, which edifies the hearers, which penetrates their minds, which is deeply impressed upon their hearts, which exerts its efficacy in the accomplishment of that which it promises. These considerations clearly show that the reservation of the sacrament, insisted upon by many persons, for the purpose of extraordinary distribution to the sick, is perfectly useless. For either they will receive it without any recital of the institution of Christ, or the minister will accompany the sign with a true explication of the mystery. If nothing be said, it is an abuse and corruption. If the promises are repeated and the mystery declared, that those who are about to receive it may communicate with advantage, we have no reason to doubt that this is the true consecration. What end will be answered, then, by the former consecration, which, having been pronounced when the sick persons were not present, is of no avail to them? But it will be alleged, that those who adopt this practice have the example of the ancient Church in their favour. This I confess; but in a matter of such great importance, and in which any error must be highly dangerous, there is nothing so safe as to follow the truth itself.

XL. Now, as we perceive this sacred bread of the Lord's supper to be spiritual food, grateful and delicious as well as salutary to the sincere worshippers of God, who, in the participation of it, experience Christ to be their life, whom it stimulates to thanksgiving, whom it exhorts to mutual charity among themselves; so, on the contrary, it is changed into a most noxious poison to all whose faith it does not nourish and confirm, and whom it does not excite to thanksgiving and charity. For as corporeal food, when it offends a diseased stomach, becoming itself corrupted, is found rather noxious than nutritious, so this spiritual food, when it meets with a soul polluted by iniquity, only precipitates it into a more dreadful ruin; not, indeed, from any fault in the food, but because "unto them that are defiled and unbelieving nothing is pure," (*l*) however it may be otherwise sanctified by the blessing of the Lord. For, as Paul says, "He that eateth and drinketh unworthily is guilty of the body and blood of the Lord, and eateth and drinketh judgment to himself, not discerning the Lord's body." (*m*) Persons of this description, who, without one particle of faith, or the least feeling of charity, intrude themselves, like so many swine, to seize the supper of the Lord, have no discernment of the Lord's body. For, as they do not believe that body to be their life, they treat it with the utmost dishonour they are capable of casting upon it, robbing it of its dignity, and receiving it in such a manner as to pollute and profane it. And as, amidst their dissension and alienation from their brethren, they presume to mingle the sacred symbol of Christ's body with their discords, it is not owing to them that the body of Christ is not divided, and every member severed from the rest. Therefore they are justly represented as guilty of the body and blood of the Lord, which they so shamefully pollute with their sacrilegious impiety. By this unworthy eating they receive their own condemnation. For though they have no faith fixed on Christ, yet in their reception of the sacrament they profess that there is no salvation for them any where except in him, and renounce every other dependence. Wherefore they are their own accusers; they give testimony against themselves; they seal their own condemnation. Moreover, while divided and distracted from their brethren, that is, from

(*l*) Titus i. 15.

(*m*) 1 Cor. xi. 27, 29.

the members of Christ, they have no part in Christ, yet they testify that the only way of salvation is to participate of Christ, and to be united to him. For this reason, Paul gave the following injunction: "Let a man examine himself, and so let him eat of that bread, and drink of that cup;" (*n*) by which, I apprehend, he meant that every man should retire into himself, and consider whether, with sincere confidence of heart, he relies on the salvation procured by Christ; whether he acknowledges it by the confession of his mouth; whether he aspires after an imitation of Christ in the pursuit of integrity and holiness; whether, after the example of Christ, he is ready to devote himself to his brethren, and to communicate himself to them with whom he has a common interest in Christ; whether, as he himself is acknowledged by Christ, he in like manner considers all his brethren as members of his body; whether he desires to cherish, preserve, and assist them as his own members. Not that these duties of faith and charity can now be perfect in us; but because this is the point which we ought to feel the most ardent desires and exert the most strenuous efforts to attain, that our faith may be more and more increased, and our charity strengthened from day to day.

XLI. In general, when they have intended to prepare persons for this worthy participation of the sacrament, they have dreadfully harassed and tortured miserable consciences, and yet have not mentioned a single thing which the case required. They have said that those "eat worthily," who are in a state of grace. To be in a state of grace, they have explained to consist in being pure and cleansed from all sin—a doctrine which would exclude all the men who now live, or ever have lived upon earth, from the benefit of this sacrament. For if it be necessary for us to derive our worthiness from ourselves, we are undone; nothing awaits us but ruin, confusion, and despair. Though we strive with all our powers, we shall gain nothing, at last, but a discovery that we are most unworthy, after having laboured to the utmost to find some worthiness. To heal this wound, they have contrived a method of attaining worthiness; which is, that having, as far as

---

(*n*) 1 Cor. xi. 28.

we can, examined our consciences, and required from ourselves an account of all our actions, we should purge ourselves from our unworthiness by contrition, confession, and satisfaction; but what kind of purgation this is, we have already stated in a place more suitable to the discussion of it. As far as relates to the present subject, I observe that these consolations are too poor and unsubstantial for consciences disturbed, distressed, dejected, and overwhelmed with a sense of their sins. For if the Lord, by his express interdiction, admits none to a participation of the supper, but those who are righteous and innocent, it requires no little care in any individual to attain an assurance of his possession of that righteousness, which he finds to be required by God. Now, what ground of assurance have we, that God is satisfied with persons who have done what they could? And even if this were the case, when shall any man be found who can venture to declare that he has done all that he could? Thus, while no certain assurance of our worthiness can be obtained, the entrance to the sacrament will always remain closed by that dreadful interdiction, which denounces that "he that eateth and drinketh unworthily, eateth and drinketh judgment to himself."

XLII. Now, it is easy to judge what kind of doctrine this is which prevails in the Papacy, and from what author it has proceeded; which by its extreme austerity deprives and robs miserable sinners, who are already afflicted with trepidation and sorrow, of the consolation of this sacrament, in which all the comforts of the gospel were set before them. It was certainly impossible for the devil to take a more compendious method of ruining men, than by infatuating them in such a manner as to deprive them of all taste and relish for such food which their heavenly and most merciful Father had intended for their nourishment. That we may not precipitate ourselves into this abyss, therefore, let us remember that this sacred banquet is medicine to the sick, comfort to the sinner, alms to the poor; but that it would confer no advantage on the healthy, the righteous, and the rich, if any such could be found. For as Christ is given to us in it for food, we understand, that without him we pine, starve, and faint, as the body loses its vigour from want of sustenance. Moreover, as he is given to us for life, we understand that without him we are utterly dead in ourselves. Wherefore the best and only worthiness that we can present to God, is to offer him our vileness and unworthiness, that he may make us worthy of his mercy; to despair in ourselves, that we may find consolation in him; to humble ourselves, that we may be exalted by him; to accuse ourselves, that we may be justified by him; likewise to aspire to that unity which he enjoins upon us in his supper; and as he makes us all to be one in himself, so it should be our desire that we may all have one mind, one heart, and one tongue. If we have these things well considered and digested in our minds, though we may be disturbed, we shall never be subverted by such reflections as this: Needy and destitute of every good, defiled with the pollution of sin, and half dead, how could we worthily eat the Lord's body? We shall rather consider, that we come as paupers to the liberal Benefactor, as patients to the Physician, as sinners to the Author of righteousness, as persons dead to the fountain of life; that the worthiness which is required by God consists principally in faith, which attributes every thing to Christ, and places no dependence on ourselves, and, secondly, in charity, even that charity which it is enough for us to present to God in an imperfect state, that he may increase and improve it; for we cannot produce it in a state of perfection. Others, who have agreed with us that the worthiness which is enjoined consists in faith and charity, have nevertheless fallen into a considerable error respecting the degree of that worthiness, requiring a perfection of faith to which nothing can ever approach, and a charity equal to that which Christ has manifested toward us. But by this requisition they exclude all men from access to this sacred supper, as much as the persons to whom we adverted before. For if their opinion were admitted, no person could receive it, but unworthily; since all, without a single exception, would be convinced of their imperfection. And surely it must betray extreme ignorance, not to say stupidity, to require in the reception of the sacrament, that perfection which would render the sacrament unnecessary and useless; for it was not instituted for the perfect, but for the imperfect and feeble, to awaken, excite, stimulate, and exercise their graces of faith and charity, and to correct the defects of both.

XLIII. With respect to the external ceremonial, whether believers take the bread in their hands or not; whether they divide it between them, or every individual eat that which is given to him; whether they return the cup into the hand of the deacon, or deliver it to the person who is next; whether the bread be leavened or unleavened; whether the wine be red or white; is not of the least importance. These things are indifferent, and left to the liberty of the Church. It is certain, however, that the custom of the ancient Church was, that every one should take the bread into his hand. And Christ said, "Divide it among yourselves." (*o*) History informs us, that leavened and common bread was used before the time of Alexander, bishop of Rome, who was the first advocate for unleavened bread; but for what reason I know not, unless it was to dazzle the eyes of the people with admiration of a new spectacle, rather than to instruct their minds in pure religion. I appeal to all who feel the least concern for piety, whether they do not clearly perceive, how much more conspicuously the glory of God appears in this use of the sacrament, and how much greater abundance of spiritual consolation and delight believers enjoy in it, than in those insignificant and theatrical fooleries which only tend to deceive the minds of the gazing multitude. This they call keeping the people in religion, when they lead them into any thing they please, under the stupefaction and infatuation of superstition. If any one be inclined to defend such inventions by the plea of antiquity, I am equally aware how early chrism and exorcism were used in baptism, and how soon after the age of the apostles, corruptions were introduced into the Lord's supper; but this is the confidence of human presumption, which can never restrain itself from trifling with the mysteries of God. But let us remember, that God holds the obedience of his word in such high estimation, that it is the standard by which he appoints us to judge even his angels and the whole world. Now, leaving all this mass of ceremonies, let us remark, that the Lord's supper might be most properly administered, if it were set before the Church very frequently, and at least once in every week in the following manner: The

(*o*) Luke xxii. 17.

service should commence with public prayer; in the next place, a sermon should be delivered; then, the bread and wine being placed upon the table, the minister should recite the institution of the supper, should declare the promises which are left to us in it, and, at the same time, should excommunicate all those who are excluded from it by the prohibition of the Lord; after this, prayer should be offered, that with the same benignity with which our Lord has given us this sacred food, he would also teach and enable us to receive it in faith and gratitude of heart, and that, as of ourselves we are not worthy, he would, in his mercy, make us worthy of such a feast. Then either some psalms should be sung, or a portion of Scripture should be read, and believers, in a becoming order, should participate of the sacred banquet, the ministers breaking the bread and distributing it, and presenting the cup, to the people; after the conclusion of the supper, an exhortation should be given to sincere faith, and a confession of the same; to charity, and a deportment worthy of Christians. Finally, thanksgivings should be rendered, and praises sung, to God; and to close the whole, the Church should be dismissed in peace.

XLIV. The observations which we have already made respecting the sacrament, abundantly show that it was not instituted for the purpose of being received once in a year, and that in a careless and formal manner, as is now the general practice; but in order to be frequently celebrated by all Christians, that they might often call to mind the sufferings of Christ; the recollection of which would sustain and strengthen their faith, would incite them to sing praises to God, and to confess and celebrate his goodness, and would also cherish in their hearts, and promote the mutual exercise of that charity, the bond of which they would see in the unity of the body of Christ. For whenever we communicate in the symbol of the Lord's body, it is like the interchange of a mutual pledge, by which we reciprocally bind ourselves to all the duties of charity, that no one among us will do any thing by which he may injure his brother, or will omit any thing by which he can assist him, when necessity requires and opportunity admits. That such was the practice of the apostolic Church, is mentioned by Luke, when he says that believers "continued steadfastly in the apostles' doctrine and fellowship, and in breaking of bread, and in prayers." (*p*) The invariable custom, therefore, was, that no assembly of the Church should be held without the word being preached, prayers being offered, the Lord's supper administered, and alms given. That this was the order established among the Corinthians, may be fairly concluded from the Epistles of Paul; and it is well known to have been followed for many ages after. For hence those ancient canons which are attributed to Anacletus and Calixtus, "that, after the consecration is finished, all shall communicate, on pain of expulsion from the Church." And the ancient canons which are ascribed to the apostles, say, "that those who continue not to the end, and receive not the sacrament, ought to be corrected as disturbers of the Church." In the Council of Antioch, also, it was decreed, that those who enter into the Church, hear the sermon, and retire from the communion, be excluded from the Church till they shall have corrected this fault. And though in the first Council of Toledo, this decree was either mitigated, or at least enacted in a milder form, yet there also it was ordained, that those who shall be found never to communicate after having heard the sermon, be admonished; and that, if they obey not the first admonition, they be excommunicated.

XLV. These decrees were evidently passed by the holy fathers with a view to retain and perpetuate the frequent celebration of the communion, which had been transmitted by the apostles themselves, and which they perceived to be highly beneficial to believers, but by negligence to be gradually falling into general disuse. Augustine testifies respecting the age in which he lived, when he says, "The sacrament of this thing, that is, of the unity of the body of our Lord, is prepared on the table of the Lord, in some places daily, in other places on appointed days, at stated intervals of time; and is thence received by some to life, by others to destruction." And in his first epistle to Januarius: "Some receive the body and blood of the Lord every day, and others receive them on certain days; in some Churches, not a day passes without the administration of the sacrament; in others, it is

(*p*) Acts ii. 42.

administered only on Saturday and Sunday; and in others only on Sunday." But the people in general, being, as we have observed, sometimes too remiss, the holy fathers stimulated them with severe reproofs, that they might not appear to connive at such negligence. Of this we have an example in a homily of Chrysostom, on the Epistle to the Ephesians: "To him who dishonoured the feast, it is not said, Wherefore didst thou sit down? but, How camest thou in hither? (*q*) Whoever is present here, and is not a partaker of the mysteries, is wicked and impudent. I appeal to you, if any one be invited to a feast, and come, wash his hands, sit down, and apparently make every preparation for partaking of it, and after all taste nothing,—will he not offer an insult both to the feast and to him who has provided it? So you, who appear among them who, by prayer prepare themselves to receive the sacred food, who by the very circumstance of not departing, confess yourself to be one of their number, and after all do not participate with them, would it not have been better for you not to have made your appearance among them? You will tell me you are unworthy. Neither then were you worthy of the communion of prayer, which is a preparation for the reception of the holy mystery."

XLVI. Augustine and Ambrose unite in condemning the practice which in their time had already been adopted in the Eastern Churches, for the people to attend as spectators of the celebration of the sacrament, and not to partake of it. And that custom, which enjoins believers to communicate only once a year, is unquestionably an invention of the devil, whoever were the persons by whom it was introduced. It is said that Zepherinus, bishop of Rome, was the author of that decree; which there is not the least reason for believing to have been such as is now represented. It is probable that the regulation which he made was not ill calculated for the interest of the Church under the circumstances of those times. For there is no doubt that the sacred supper was then set before the faithful whenever they assembled for worship; nor is there any more doubt that the principal part of them used to communicate; but as it would scarcely ever

(*q*) Matt. xxii. 12.

happen that all could communicate together, and it was necessary that those who were mixed with unbelievers and idolaters, should testify their faith by some external sign,—that holy man, for the sake of order and discipline, appointed that day for all the Christians at Rome to make a public confession of their faith by a participation of the Lord's supper. The regulation of Zepherinus was good in itself, but was grossly perverted by his successors, when they made a certain law that there should be one communion in a year; the consequence of which has been, that almost all men, when they have communicated once, resign themselves to lethargic repose, as if they had fairly excused themselves for all the rest of the year. A very different practice ought to have been pursued. At least once in every week the table of the Lord ought to have been spread before each congregation of Christians, and the promises to have been declared for their spiritual nourishment; no person ought to have been compelled to partake, but all ought to have been exhorted and stimulated, and those who were negligent, to have been reproved. Then all, like persons famished, would have assembled in crowds to such a banquet. I have sufficient reason for complaining that it was the artifice of the devil that introduced this custom, which, by prescribing one day in a year, renders men slothful and careless all the rest of the time. We see that this abuse had already begun to prevail in the time of Chrysostom, but we see at the same time how greatly it displeased him. For in the place which I have just quoted, he severely complains of a great inequality in this matter, that oftentimes people would not come to the sacrament all the rest of the year, notwithstanding they were prepared, but that they would come at Easter even without preparation. Then he exclaims, "O custom! O presumption! In vain, then, is the daily oblation; in vain do we stand at the altar. There is no one to partake with us." So far is such a practice from being sanctioned by the authority of Chrysostom.

XLVII. From the same source proceeded another regulation, which has robbed or deprived the principal part of the people of God of one half of the sacred supper; I mean the symbol of the blood, which has been interdicted to the laity and the profane,—for by these titles they distinguish the Lord's heritage,—

and has become the peculiar privilege of the few who have received ecclesiastical unction and tonsure. The ordinance of the eternal God is, "Drink ye all of it;" which man has repealed and abrogated by a new and contrary law, ordaining that all shall not drink of it. And these legislators, that they may not appear to resist their God without reason, plead the dangers which might result if this sacred cup were indiscriminately presented to all; as though those dangers had not been foreseen and considered by the eternal wisdom of God. In the next place, they argue with great subtlety, that one is sufficient for both. For, if it be the body, they say, it is the whole of Christ, who cannot now be separated from his body. The body, therefore, contains the blood. See how human reason is at variance with God, when it has once been left to its own vagaries. Exhibiting the bread, our Lord says, "This is my body;" exhibiting the cup, he says, "This is my blood." The audacity of human reason contradicts this, and affirms that the bread is the blood, and that the wine is the body; as if the Lord had distinguished his body from his blood, both by words and by signs, without any cause, and as if it had ever been heard that the body or blood of Christ was called God and man. Certainly, if he had intended to designate his whole person, he might have said, "It is I," as the Scripture tells us he did on other occasions; and not, "This is my body; this is my blood." But, with a view to aid the weakness of our faith, he exhibits the bread and the cup separately, to teach us that he is sufficient for drink as well as for food. Now, let one of these parts be taken away, and we shall find only half of our nourishment in him. Though it were true, then, as they pretend, that the blood is in the bread, and the body in the cup, yet they defraud the souls of believers of that confirmation which Christ has delivered as necessary for them. Therefore, leaving their subtleties, let us hold fast the benefit which arises from the double pledge which Christ has ordained.

XLVIII. I am aware of the cavils advanced on this subject by the ministers of Satan, who are accustomed to treat the Scripture with contempt. In the first place, they plead, that a simple act affords no sufficient ground from which to deduce a rule of perpetual obligation on the observance of the Church. But it is false to call it a simple act; for Christ not only gave the cup to his apostles, but also commanded them to do the same in time to come. For it is the language of command, "Drink ye all of it." And Paul mentions its having been practised in such a way as fully implies its being a positive ordinance. The second subterfuge is, that Christ admitted none but the apostles to a participation of this supper, whom he had already chosen and admitted into the order of sacrificing priests. But I would wish them to give me answers to five questions from which they will not be able to escape, but their misrepresentations will be easily refuted. First; By what oracle have they obtained this solution, so inconsistent with the word of God? The Scripture mentions twelve who sat down with Jesus; but it does not obscure the dignity of Christ so as to call them sacrificing priests—a name which I shall notice in the proper place. Though he then gave the sacrament to the twelve, yet he commanded that they should do the same; that is, that they should distribute it among them in a similar manner. Secondly; why, in that purer period, for almost a thousand years after the apostles, were all, without exception, admitted to the participation of both symbols? Was the ancient Church ignorant what guests Christ had admitted to his supper? Any hesitation or evasion would betray the most consummate impudence. Ecclesiastical histories and works of the fathers are still extant, which furnish clear testimonies of this fact. Tertullian says, "The flesh is fed with the body and blood of Christ, that the soul may be nourished by God." Ambrose said to Theodosius, "With such hands how will you receive the sacred body of the Lord? With what audacity will you drink his sacred blood?" Jerome says, "The priests consecrate the eucharist and distribute the Lord's blood to the people." Chrysostom says, "It is not as it was under the ancient law, when the priest ate one part, and the people another; but to all is presented one body and one cup. Every thing in the eucharist is common to the priest and to the people." And the same is attested in various places by Augustine.

XLIX. But why do I dispute about a thing that is so evident? Let any one read all the Greek and Latin fathers, and he will find them abound with such testimonies. Nor did this custom fall into disuse while a particle of purity remained in the Church. Gregory, who may be justly called the last bishop of Rome, shows that it was observed in his time. He says, "You have now learned what the blood of the Lamb is, not by hearing, but by drinking. His blood is drunk by the faithful." And it even continued for four hundred years after his death, notwithstanding the universal degeneracy which had taken place. Nor was it considered merely as a custom, but as an inviolable law. For the Divine institution was then reverenced, and no doubt was entertained of the criminality of separating things which the Lord had united. For Gelasius, bishop of Rome, speaks in the following manner: "We have understood that some, only receiving the Lord's body, abstain from the cup; who, as they appear to be enslaved by an unaccountable superstition, should, without doubt, either receive the sacrament entire, or entirely abstain from it. For no division of this mystery can be made without great sacrilege." Attention was paid to those reasons of Cyprian, which surely ought to be sufficient to influence a Christian mind. He says, "How do we teach or stimulate them to shed their blood in the confession of Christ, if we refuse his blood to them who are about to engage in the conflict? Or how do we prepare them for the cup of martyrdom, if we do not first admit them, by the right of communion, to drink the cup of the Lord in the Church?" The canonists restrict the decree of Gelasius to the priests, but this is too puerile a cavil to need any refutation.

L. Thirdly; Why did Christ, when he presented the bread, simply say, "Take, eat;" but when he presented the cup, "Drink ye *all* of it;" as if he expressly intended to guard against the subtlety of Satan? Fourthly; If, as our adversaries pretend, our Lord admitted to his supper none but sacrificing priests, what man can be found so presumptuous as to invite to a participation of it strangers whom the Lord has excluded? and to participation of that gift, over which they could have no power, without any command from him who alone could give it? And with what confidence do they now take upon them to distribute to the people the symbol of the body of Christ, if they have neither the command nor example of the Lord? Fifthly; Did Paul affirm what was false, when he said to the Corinthians, "I have received of the Lord that which also I delivered to you?" (*r*) For he afterwards declares what he had delivered, which was, that all, without any distinction, should communicate in both symbols. If Paul had "received of the Lord," that all were to be admitted without any distinction, let them consider from whom they have received, who exclude almost all the people of God; for they cannot now pretend their doctrine to have originated from God, with whom is "not yea and nay." (*s*) And yet they dare to shelter such abominations under the name of the Church, and to defend them under that pretext; as if the Church could consist of those antichrists, who so easily trample under foot, mutilate, and abolish the doctrine and institutions of Christ; or as if the apostolic Church, in which true religion displayed all its influence, were not the true Church.

(*r*) 1 Cor. xi. 23. (*s*) 2 Cor. i. 18.

CHAPTER XVIII

The Papal Mass Not Only a Sacrilegious Profanation of the Lord's Supper, but a Total Annihilation of It

With these, and similar inventions, Satan has endeavoured to obscure, corrupt, and adulterate the sacred supper of Christist, that, at least, its purity might not be preserved in the Church. But the perfection of the dreadful abomination was his establishment of a sign, by which it might be not only obscured and perverted, but altogether obliterated and abolished, so as to disappear from the view, and to depart from the remembrance of men. I refer to that most pestilent error with which he has blinded almost the whole world, persuading it to believe that the mass is a sacrifice and oblation to procure the remission of sins. How this dogma was at first understood by the sounder schoolmen, who did not fall into all the absurdities of their successors, I shall not stay to inquire, but shall take leave of them and their thorny subtleties; which, however they may be defended by subterfuges and cavils, ought to be rejected by all good men, because they merely serve to obscure the lustre of the sacred supper. Leaving them, therefore, I wish the readers to understand that I am now combating that opinion with which the Roman antichrist and his agents have infected the whole world; namely, that the mass is an act by which the priest who offers Christ, and others who participate in the oblation, merit the favour of God; or that it is an expiatory victim by which they reconcile God to them. Nor has this been merely an opinion generally received by the multitude; but the act itself is so ordered, as to be a kind of expiation, to make satisfaction to God for the sins of the living and the dead. This is fully expressed also in the words which they use; nor can any thing else be concluded from its daily observance. I know how deeply this pest has stricken its roots, what a plausible appearance of goodness it assumes, how it shelters itself under the name of Christ, and how multitudes believe the whole substance of faith to be comprehended under the single word *mass*. But when it shall have been most clearly demonstrated by the word of God, that this mass, however it may be varnished and adorned, offers the greatest insult to Christ, suppresses and conceals his cross, consigns his death to oblivion, deprives us of the benefit resulting from it, and invalidates and destroys the sacrament which was left as a memorial of that death,—will there be any roots too deep for this most powerful axe—I mean the word of God—to cut in pieces and eradicate? Will there be any varnish too specious for this light to detect the evil which lurks behind it?

II. Let us proceed, therefore, to establish what we have asserted; in the first place, that the mass offers an intolerable blasphemy and insult to Christ. For he was constituted by his Father a priest and a high-priest, not for a limited time, like those who are recorded to have been consecrated priests under the Old Testament, who, having a mortal life, could not have an immortal priesthood; wherefore, there was need of successors, from time to time, to fill the places of those who died; but Christ, who is immortal, requires no vicar to be substituted in his place. Therefore he was designated by the Father as "a priest for ever, after the order of Melchisedec;" that he might for ever execute a permanent priesthood. This mystery had long before been prefigured in Melchisedec, whom the Scripture has introduced once as "the priest of the Most High God," but never mentions him afterwards, as if there had been no end to his life. From this resemblance Christ is called a priest after his order. (*t*) Now, those who sacrifice every day must necessarily appoint priests to conduct the oblations, and those priests must be

(*t*) Gen. xiv. 18. Psalm cx. 4. Heb. v. 5, 6, 10; vii. 17, 21, 23, 24; ix. 11; x. 21.

substituted in the room of Christ, as his successors and vicars. By this substitution they not only despoil Christ of his due honour, and rob him of the prerogative of an eternal priesthood, but endeavour to degrade him from the right hand of the Father, where he cannot sit in the enjoyment of immortality, unless he also remain an eternal priest. Nor let them plead that their sacrificing priests are not substituted in the place of Christ, as though he were dead, but are merely assistants in his eternal priesthood, which does not, on this account, cease to remain; for the language of the apostle is too precise for them to avail themselves of such an evasion; when he says that "they truly were many priests, because they were not suffered to continue by reason of death." (*u*) Christ, therefore, whose continuance is not prevented by death, is only one, and needs no companions. Yet they have the effrontery to arm themselves with the example of Melchisedec in defence of their impiety. For, because he is said to have "brought forth bread and wine," they conclude this to have been a prefiguration of their mass, as though the resemblance between him and Christ consisted in the oblation of bread and wine; which is too unsubstantial and frivolous to need any refutation. Melchisedec gave bread and wine to Abraham and his companions, to refresh them when they were fatigued on their return from battle. What has this to do with a sacrifice? Moses praises the humanity and liberality of the pious king; these men presumptuously fabricate a mystery, of which the Scripture makes no mention. Yet they varnish their error with another pretext, because the historian immediately afterwards says, "And he was the priest of the Most High God." I answer, that they misapply to the bread and wine what the apostle refers to the benediction, "For this Melchisedec, priest of the Most High God, met Abraham and blessed him;" from which the same apostle, than whom it is unnecessary to seek for a better expositor, argues his superior dignity; "for without all contradiction, the less is blessed of the better." (*x*) But, if the offering of Melchisedec had been a figure of the sacrifice of the mass, is it credible that the apostle, who discusses all the minutest circumstances, would

(*u*) Heb. vii. 23. (*x*) Heb. vii. 1, 7.

have forgotten a thing of such high importance? It will be in vain for them, with all their sophistry, to attempt to overturn the argument which the apostle himself adduces, that the right and dignity of priesthood ceases among mortal men, because Christ, who is immortal, is the alone and perpetual priest.

III. A second property of the mass we have stated to be, that it suppresses and conceals the cross and passion of Christ. It is beyond all contradiction, that the cross of Christ is subverted as soon as ever an altar is erected; for if Christ offered up himself a sacrifice on the cross, to sanctify us for ever, and to obtain eternal redemption for us, the virtue and efficacy of that sacrifice must certainly continue without any end. (*y*) Otherwise, we should have no more honourable ideas of Christ, than of the animal victims which were sacrificed under the law, the oblations of which are proved to have been weak and inefficacious, by the circumstance of their frequent repetition. Wherefore, it must be acknowledged, either that the sacrifice which Christ accomplished on the cross wanted the virtue of eternal purification, or that Christ has offered up one perfect sacrifice, once for all ages. This is what the apostle says, that this great high-priest, even Christ, "now once, in the end of the world, hath appeared to put away sin by the sacrifice of himself." Again: "By the will of God we are sanctified, through the offering of the body of Jesus Christ, once for all." Again: "That by one offering Christ hath perfected for ever them that are sanctified." To which he subjoins this remarkable observation: "That where remission of iniquities is, there is no more offering for sin." (*z*) This was likewise signified by the last words of Christ, when, with his expiring breath, he said, "It is finished." (*a*) We are accustomed to consider the last words of dying persons as oracular. Christ, at the moment of his death, declared that by his own sacrifice every thing necessary to our salvation had been accomplished and finished. To such a sacrifice, the perfection of which he so explicitly declares, shall it be lawful for us to make innumerable additions every day, as though it were imperfect? While God's most holy word not only affirms, but proclaims and protests,

(*y*) Heb. vii. 27; x. 10, 14; ix. 12. (*z*) Heb. ix. 26; x. 10; xiv. 18.
(*a*) John xix. 30.

that this sacrifice was once perfect, and that its virtue is eternal,—do not they who require another sacrifice charge this with imperfection and inefficacy? But what is the tendency of the mass, which admits of a hundred thousand sacrifices being offered every day, except it be to obscure and suppress the passion of Christ, by which he offered himself as the alone sacrifice to the Father? Who, that is not blind, does not see that such an opposition to the clear and manifest truth must have arisen from the audacity of Satan? I am aware of the fallacies with which that father of falsehood is accustomed to varnish over this fraud; as, that these are not various or different sacrifices, but only a repetition of that one sacrifice. But such illusions are easily dissipated. For, through the whole argument, the apostle is contending, not only that there are no other sacrifices, but that that one sacrifice was offered once, and is never to be repeated. The more artful sophisters have recourse to a deeper subterfuge; that the mass is not a repetition of that sacrifice, but an application of it. This sophistry also may be confuted, without any more difficulty than the former. For Christ once offered up himself, not that his sacrifice might be daily ratified by new oblations, but that the benefit of it might be communicated to us by the preaching of the gospel, and the administration of the sacred supper. Thus Paul says that "Christ our passover is sacrificed for us," and commands us to feast on him. (*b*) This, I say, is the way in which the sacrifice of the cross of our Lord Jesus Christ is rightly applied to us, when it is communicated to us for our enjoyment, and we receive it with true faith.

IV. But it is worth while to hear on what other foundation they rest the sacrifice of the mass. They apply to this purpose the prophecy of Malachi, in which the Lord promises, that "from the rising of the sun even unto the going down of the same, incense shall be offered unto" his "name, and a pure offering." (*c*) As though it were a new or unusual thing for the prophets, when they speak of the calling of the Gentiles, to designate the spiritual worship of God, to which they exhort them, by the external ceremonies of the law; in order to show, in a more familiar manner,

(*b*) 1 Cor. v. 7, 8. (*c*) Mal. i. 11.

to the men of their own times, that the Gentiles were to be introduced to a participation of the true religion; as it is their invariable practice, on all occasions, to describe the realities which have been exhibited in the gospel, under the types and figures of the dispensation under which they lived. Thus, conversion to the Lord they express by going up to Jerusalem; adoration of God, by oblations of various gifts; the more extensive knowledge to be bestowed on believers, in the kingdom of Christ, by dreams and visions. (*d*) The prophecy which they adduce, therefore, is similar to another prediction of Isaiah, where he foretells the erection of three altars, in Assyria, Egypt, and Judea. (*e*) I ask the Romanists, first, whether they do not admit this prediction to have been accomplished in the kingdom of Christ; secondly, where are these altars, or when were they ever erected; thirdly, whether they think that those two kingdoms were destined to have their respective temples, like that at Jerusalem. A due consideration of these things, I think, will induce them to acknowledge, that the prophet, under types adapted to his own time, was predicting the spiritual worship of God, which was to be propagated all over the world. This is our solution of the passage which they adduce from Malachi; but as examples of this mode of expression are of such frequent occurrence, I shall not employ myself in a further enumeration of them. Here, also, they are miserably deceived, in acknowledging no sacrifice but that of the mass; whereas, believers do in reality now sacrifice to the Lord, and offer a pure oblation, of which we shall presently treat.

V. I now proceed to the third view of the mass, under which I am to show how it obliterates and expunges from the memory of mankind the true and alone death of Jesus Christ. For as among men the confirmation of a testament depends on the death of the testator, so also our Lord, by his death, has confirmed the testament in which he has given us remission of sins, and everlasting righteousness. Those who dare to attempt any variation or innovation in this testament, thereby deny his death, and represent it as of no value. Now, what is the mass, but a new and totally different testament? For does not every separate

---

(*d*) Isaiah xix. 23. Joel ii. 28.

(*e*) Isaiah xix. 19, 23, 24.

mass promise a new remission of sins, and a new acquisition of righteousness; so that there are now as many testaments as masses? Let Christ, therefore, come again, and by another death ratify this new testament, or rather, by innumerable deaths, confirm these innumerable testaments of masses. Have I not truly said, then, at the beginning, that the true and alone death of Christ is obliterated and consigned to oblivion by the masses? And is not the direct tendency of the mass, to cause Christ, if it were possible, to be put to death again? "For where a testament is," says the apostle, "there must also, of necessity, be the death of the testator." (*f*) The mass pretends to exhibit a new testament of Christ; therefore it requires his death. Moreover the victim which is offered must, of necessity, be slain and immolated. If Christ be sacrificed in every mass, he must be cruelly murdered in a thousand separate places at once. This is not *my* argument; it is the reasoning of the apostle: "It was not necessary that he should offer himself often; for then must he often have suffered since the foundation of the world." (*g*) In reply to this, I confess, they are ready to charge us with calumny; alleging that we impute to them sentiments which they never have held, nor ever can hold. We know, indeed, that the life and death of Christ are not in their power; and whether they intend to murder him, we do not inquire; we only mean to show the absurdities which follow from their impious and abominable doctrine, and this we have proved from the mouth of the apostle. They may reply a hundred times, if they please, that this sacrifice is without blood; but I shall deny that sacrifices can change their nature, at the caprice of men; for thus the sacred and inviolable institution of God would fall to the ground. Hence it follows, that this principle of the apostle can never be shaken, that "without shedding of blood is no remission." (*h*)

VI. We are now to treat of the fourth property of the mass, which is, to prevent us from perceiving and reflecting on the death of Christ, and thereby to deprive us of the benefit resulting from it. For who can consider himself as redeemed by the death of Christ, when he sees a new redemption in the mass? Who

---

(*f*) Heb. ix. 16. (*g*) Heb. ix. 23, 25, 26. (*h*) Heb. ix. 22.

can be assured that his sins are remitted, when he sees another remission? It is not a sufficient answer, to say, that we obtain remission of sins in the mass, only because it has been already procured by the death of Christ. For this is no other than pretending that Christ has redeemed us in order that we may redeem ourselves. For this is the doctrine which has been disseminated by the ministers of Satan, and which they now defend by clamours, and fire, and sword; that when we offer up Christ to his Father, in the sacrifice of the mass, we, by that act of oblation, obtain remission of sins, and become partakers of the passion of Christ. What remains, then, to the passion of Christ, but to be an example of redemption, by which we may learn to be our own redeemers? Christ himself, when he seals the assurance of pardon in the sacred supper, does not command his disciples to rest in this act, but refers them to the sacrifice of his death; signifying that the supper is a monument, or memorial, appointed to teach us that the expiatory victim by which God was to be appeased ought to be offered but once. Nor is it sufficient to know that Christ is the sole victim, unless we also know that there is only one oblation, so that our faith may be fixed upon his cross.

VII. I come now to the concluding observation; that the sacred supper, in which our Lord had left us the memorial of his passion impressed and engraven, has, by the erection of the mass, been removed, abolished, and destroyed. For the supper itself is a gift of God, which ought to be received with thanksgiving. The sacrifice of the mass is pretended to be a price given to God, and received by him as a satisfaction. As far as *giving* differs from *receiving*, so far does the sacrifice of the mass differ from the sacrament of the supper. And this is the most miserable ingratitude of man, that where the profusion of the Divine goodness ought to have been acknowledged with thanksgivings, there he makes God his debtor. The sacrament promised, that by the death of Christ we are not only restored to life, but are perpetually vivified, because every part of our salvation was then accomplished. The sacrifice of the mass proclaims a very different doctrine; that it is necessary for Christ to be sacrificed every day, in order to be of any advantage to us. The supper ought to be distributed in the public congregation of the Church, to instruct us in the communion by which we are all connected together in Christ Jesus. The sacrifice of the mass dissolves and destroys this communion. For the reception of this error rendered it necessary that there should be priests to sacrifice for the people; and the supper, as if it had been resigned to them, ceased to be administered to the Church of believers, according to the commandment of the Lord. A way was opened for the admission of private masses, which represented a kind of excommunication, rather than that communion which had been instituted by our Lord, when the mass-priest separates himself from the whole congregation of believers, to devour his sacrifice alone. That no person may be deceived, I call it a private mass, wherever there is no participation of the Lord's supper among believers, whatever number of persons may be present as spectators of it.

VIII. With respect to the word *mass* itself, I have never been able certainly to determine whence it originated; only I think it may probably have been derived from the oblations which used to be made at the sacrament. Hence the ancient fathers generally use it in the plural number. But to forbear all controversy respecting the term, I say that private masses are diametrically repugnant to the institution of Christ, and are consequently an impious profanation of the sacred supper. For what has the Lord commanded us? Is it not to take and divide it among us? (*k*) What observance of the command does Paul inculcate? Is it not the breaking of the bread, which is the communion of the body of Christ? (*l*) When one man takes it, therefore, without any distribution, what resemblance does this bear to the command? But it is alleged, that this one man does it in the name of the whole Church. I ask, by what authority? Is not this an open mockery of God, when one person does separately, by himself, that which ought not to have been done but among many? The words of Christ, and of Paul, are sufficiently clear to authorize the conclusion, that wherever there is no breaking of the bread for common distribution among believers, there is not the supper of the Lord, but a false and preposterous imitation of it. But a false imitation is a corruption; and the corruption of so great

(*k*) Luke xxii. 17. (*l*) 1 Cor. x. 16.

a mystery cannot take place without impiety. Private masses, therefore, are an impious abuse. And as one abuse in religion soon produces another, after the introduction of this custom of offering without communicating, they began by degrees to have innumerable masses in all the corners of the temples, and thus to divide the people from each other, who ought to have united in one assembly, to celebrate the mystery of their union. Now, let the Romanists deny, if they can, that they are guilty of idolatry in exhibiting bread in their masses, to be worshipped instead of Christ. In vain do they boast of those promises of the presence of Christ; for however they may be understood, they certainly were not given in order that impure and profane men, whenever they please, and for whatever improper use, may transmute bread into the body of Christ; but in order that believers, religiously observing the command of Christ, in celebrating the supper, may enjoy a true participation of him in it.

IX. In the purer times of the Church, this corruption was unknown. For, however the more impudent of our adversaries endeavour to misrepresent this matter, yet it is beyond all doubt that all antiquity is against them, as we have already evinced in other points, and may be more fully determined by a diligent perusal of the ancient fathers. But before I conclude this subject, I will ask our advocates for masses, since they know that "the Lord hath" not "as great delight in sacrifices, as in obeying the voice of the Lord," and that "to obey is better than sacrifice," (*m*) how they can believe this kind of sacrificing to be acceptable to God, for which they have no command, and which they do not find to be sanctioned by a single syllable of the Scripture. Moreover, since they hear the apostle say, that "no man taketh" the name and "honour" of the priesthood "unto himself, but he that is called of God, as was Aaron," and that even "Christ glorified not himself to be made a high-priest," but obeyed the call of his Father; (*n*) either they must prove God to be the author and institutor of their priesthood, or they must confess the honour not to be of God, into which they have presumptuously and wickedly obtruded themselves, without any call. But they cannot

(*m*) 1 Sam. xv. 22.

(*n*) Heb. v. 4, 5.

produce a tittle which affords the least support to their priesthood. What, then, will become of their sacrifices, since no sacrifices can be offered without a priest?

X. If any one should bring forward mutilated passages, extracted from different parts of the writings of the fathers, and contend, on their authority, that the sacrifice which is offered in the supper ought to be understood in a different manner from the representation we have given of it, he shall receive the following brief reply: If the question relate to an approbation of this notion of a sacrifice which the Papists have invented in the mass, the ancient fathers are very far from countenancing such a sacrilege. They do, indeed, use the word *sacrifice*, but they at the same time fully declare, that they mean nothing more than the commemoration of that true and only sacrifice which Christ, whom they invariably speak of as our only Priest, completed on the cross. Augustine says, "The Hebrews, in the animal victims which they offered to God, celebrate the prophecy of the future victim which Christ has since offered; Christians, by the holy oblation and participation of the body of Christ, celebrate the remembrance of the sacrifice which is already completed." Here he evidently inculcates the same sentiment that is expressed more at large in the Treatise, on Faith, which has been attributed to him, though it is doubtful who was the author, addressed to Peter the Deacon; in which we find the following passage: "Hold this most firmly, and admit not the least doubt, that the only begotten Son of God himself, being made flesh for us, hath offered himself for us an offering and a sacrifice to God for a sweet-smelling savour; to whom, with the Father and the Holy Spirit, animals were sacrificed in the time of the Old Testament; and to whom now, with the Father and the Holy Spirit, (with whom he has one and the same Divinity,) the holy Church, throughout the world, ceases not to offer the sacrifice of bread and wine. For in those carnal victims there was a prefiguration of the flesh of Christ, which he himself was to offer for our sins, and of his blood, which he was to shed for the remission of our sins. But in the present sacrifice, there is a thanksgiving and commemoration of the flesh of Christ, which he has offered, and of his blood, which he has shed for us." Hence Augustine himself, in various passages, explains it to be nothing more than a sacrifice of praise. And it is a remark often found in his writings, that the Lord's supper is called a sacrifice, for no other reason than because it is a memorial, image, and attestation, of that singular, true, and only sacrifice, by which Christ has redeemed us. There is also a remarkable passage in his Treatise on the Trinity, where, after having treated of the only sacrifice, he thus concludes: "In a sacrifice, four things are to be considered—to whom it is offered, by whom it is offered, what is offered, and for whom it is offered. The alone and true Mediator, by a sacrifice of peace, reconciling us to God, remains one with him to whom he has offered it; makes them for whom he has offered it one in himself; is the one who alone has offered it; and is himself the oblation which he has offered." Chrysostom also speaks to the same purpose. And they ascribe the honour of the priesthood so exclusively to Christ, that Augustine declares, that if any one should set up a bishop as an intercessor between God and man, it would be the language of Antichrist.

XI. Yet we do not deny that the oblation of Christ is there exhibited to us in such a manner, that the view of his cross is almost placed before our eyes; as the apostle says, that by the preaching of the cross to the Galatians, "Christ had been evidently set forth before their eyes, crucified among them." (*o*) But as I perceive that those ancient fathers misapplied this memorial to a purpose inconsistent with the institution of the Lord, because the supper, as celebrated by them, represented I know not what appearance of a reiterated, or at least renewed oblation, the safest way for pious minds will be to acquiesce in the pure and simple ordinance of the Lord, whose supper this sacrament is called, because it ought to be regulated by his sole authority. Finding them to have retained orthodox and pious sentiments of this whole mystery, and not detecting them of having intended the least derogation from the one and alone sacrifice of Christ, I dare not condemn them for impiety; yet I think it impossible to exculpate them from having committed some error in the external form. For they imitated the Jewish

(*o*) Gal. iii. 1.

mode of sacrificing, more than Christ had commanded, or the nature of the gospel admitted. The censure which they have deserved, therefore, is for this preposterous conformity to the Old Testament; that, not content with the simple and genuine institution of Christ, they have symbolized too much with the shadows of the law.

XII. If any person will attentively examine, he will observe this distinction clearly marked by the word of the Lord, between the Mosaic sacrifices and our eucharist; that though those sacrifices represented to the Jewish people the same efficacy of the death of Christ which is now exhibited to us in the Lord's supper, yet the mode of representation was different. For the Jewish priests were commanded to prefigure the sacrifice which was to be accomplished by Christ; a victim was presented in the place of Christ himself; there was an altar on which it was to be immolated; in short, every thing was conducted in such a manner as to set before the eyes of the people a representation of the sacrifice which was to be offered to God as an atonement for sins. But since that sacrifice has been accomplished, the Lord has prescribed to us a different method, in order to communicate to believers the benefit of the sacrifice which has been offered to him by his Son. Therefore he has given us a table at which we are to feast, not an altar upon which any victim is to be offered: he has not consecrated priests to offer sacrifices, but ministers to distribute the sacred banquet. In proportion to the superior sublimity and sanctity of the mystery, with the greater care and reverence it ought to be treated. The safest course, therefore, is to relinquish all the presumption of human reason, and to adhere strictly to what the Scripture enjoins. And surely, if we consider that it is the supper of the Lord, and not of men, there is no cause why we should suffer ourselves to be moved a hair's breadth from the scriptural rule by any authority of men or prescription of years. Therefore, when the apostle was desirous of purifying it from all the faults which had already crept into the Church at Corinth, he adopted the best and readiest method, by recalling it to the one original institution, which he shows ought to be regarded as its perpetual rule.

XIII. That no wrangler may take occasion to oppose us from

the terms *sacrifice* and *priest,* I will briefly state what I have meant by these terms all through this argument. Some extend the word *sacrifice* to all religious ceremonies and actions; but for this I see no reason. We know that, by the constant usage of the Scripture, the word *sacrifice* is applied to what the Greeks call sometimes θυσια, sometimes προσφορα, and sometimes τελετη, which, taken generally, comprehends whatever is offered to God. Wherefore it is necessary for us to make a distinction, but such a distinction as may be consistent with the sacrifices of the Mosaic law; under the shadows of which the Lord designed to represent to his people all the truth of spiritual sacrifices. Though there were various kinds of them, yet they may all be referred to two classes. For either they were oblations made for sin in a way of satisfaction, by which guilt was expiated before God, or they were symbols of Divine worship and attestations of devotion. This second class comprehended three kinds of sacrifices: some were offered in a way of supplication, to implore the favour of God; some in a way of thanksgiving, to testify the gratitude of the mind for benefits received; and some as simple expressions of piety, to renew the confirmation of the covenant: to this class belonged burnt-offerings and drink-offerings, first-fruits and peace-offerings. Therefore let *us* also divide sacrifices into two kinds, and for the sake of distinction call one the *sacrifice of worship* and *piety,* because it consists in the veneration and service of God, which he demands and receives from believers; or it may be called, if you prefer it, the *sacrifice of thanksgiving;* for it is presented to God by none but persons who, loaded with his immense benefits, devote themselves and all their actions to him in return. The other may be called the *sacrifice of propitiation* or *expiation.* A sacrifice of expiation is that which is offered to appease the wrath of God, to satisfy his justice, and thereby to purify and cleanse from sins, that the sinner, delivered from the defilement of iniquity, and restored to the purity of righteousness, may be re-admitted to the favour of God. This was the designation, under the law, of those victims which were offered for the expiation of sins; not that they were sufficient to effect the restoration of the favour of God, or the obliteration of iniquity, but because they prefigured that true sacrifice which at length was actually accomplished by Christ alone; by him alone, because it could be made by no other; and once for all, because the virtue and efficacy of that one sacrifice is eternal; as Christ himself declared, when he said, "It is finished;" (*p*) that is to say, whatever was necessary to reconcile us to the Father, and to obtain remission of sins, righteousness, and salvation, was all effected and completed by that one oblation of himself, which was so perfect as to leave no room for any other sacrifice afterwards.

XIV. Wherefore, I conclude, that it is a most criminal insult, and intolerable blasphemy, both against Christ himself, and against the sacrifice which he completed on our behalf by his death upon the cross, for any man to repeat any oblation with a view to procure the pardon of sins, propitiate God, and obtain righteousness. But what is the object of the mass, except it be that by the merit of a new oblation we may be made partakers of the passion of Christ? And that there might be no limits to their folly, they have not been satisfied with affirming it to be a common sacrifice offered equally for the whole Church, without adding, that it was in their power to make a peculiar application of it to any individual they chose, or rather to every one who was willing to purchase such a commodity with ready money. Though they could not reach the price of Judas, yet, to exemplify some characteristic of their author, they have retained the resemblance of number. Judas sold Jesus for thirty pieces of silver; these men, as far as in them lies, sell him, in French money, for thirty pieces of copper; Judas sold him but once; they sell him as often as they meet with a purchaser. In this sense, we deny that they are priests; that they can intercede with God on behalf of the people by such an oblation; that they can appease the wrath of God, or obtain the remission of sins. For Christ is the sole Priest and High-Priest of the New Testament, to whom all the ancient priesthoods have been transferred, and in whom they are all terminated and closed. And even if the Scripture had made no mention of the eternal priesthood of Christ, yet as God, since the abrogation of the former priesthoods, has instituted no other, the argument of the apostle is irrefragable,

(*p*) John xix. 30.

that "no man taketh this honour unto himself, but he that is called of God." (*q*) With what effrontery, then, do these sacrilegious mortals, who boast of being the executioners of Christ, dare to call themselves priests of the living God!

XV. There is a beautiful passage in Plato, in which he treats of the ancient expiations among the heathen, and ridicules the foolish confidence of wicked and profligate men, who thought that such disguises would conceal their crimes from the view of their gods, and, as if they had made a compromise with their gods, indulged themselves in their vices with the greater security. This passage almost seems as if it had been written with a view to the missal expiation as it is now practised in the world. To defraud and circumvent another person, every one knows to be unlawful. To injure widows, to plunder orphans, to harass the poor, to obtain the property of others by wicked arts, to seize any one's fortune by perjuries and frauds, to oppress a neighbour with violence and tyrannical terror, are universally acknowledged to be enormous crimes. How, then, do so many persons dare to commit all these sins, as if they might perpetrate them with impunity? If we duly consider, we shall find that they derive fresh encouragement from no other cause than the confidence which they feel that they shall be able to satisfy God by the sacrifice of the mass, as a complete discharge of all their obligations to him, or at least that it affords them an easy mode of compromising with him. Plato afterwards goes on to ridicule the gross stupidity of those who expect by such expiations to be delivered from the punishments which they would otherwise have to suffer in hell. And what is the design of the obits, or anniversary obsequies, and the greater part of the masses, but that those who all their lifetime have been the most cruel of tyrants, the most rapacious of robbers, or abandoned to every enormity, as if redeemed with this price, may escape the fire of purgatory?

XVI. Under the other kind of sacrifices, which we have called *the sacrifice of thanksgiving*, are included all the offices of charity, which when we perform to our brethren, we honour the Lord himself in his members; and likewise all our prayers, praises,

---

(*q*) Heb. v. 4.

thanksgivings, and every thing that we do in the service of God; all which are dependent on a greater sacrifice, by which we are consecrated in soul and body as holy temples to the Lord. It is not enough for our external actions to be employed in his service: it is necessary that first ourselves, and then all our works, be consecrated and dedicated to him; that whatever belongs to us may conduce to his glory, and discover a zeal for its advancement. This kind of sacrifice has no tendency to appease the wrath of God, to procure remission of sins, or to obtain righteousness: its sole object is to magnify and exalt the glory of God. For it cannot be acceptable and pleasing to God, except from the hands of those whom he has already favoured with the remission of their sins, reconciled to himself, and absolved from guilt; and it is so necessary to the Church as to be altogether indispensable. Therefore it will continue to be offered for ever, as long as the people of God shall exist; as we have already seen from the prophet. For so far are we from wishing to abolish it, that in that sense we are pleased to understand the following prediction: "From the rising of the sun, even unto the going down of the same, my name shall be great among the Gentiles; and in every place incense shall be offered unto my name, and a pure offering; for my name shall be great among the heathen, saith the Lord of hosts." (*r*) So Paul enjoins us to "present" our "bodies, a living sacrifice, holy, acceptable unto God," which is our "reasonable service." (*s*) He has expressed himself with the strictest propriety, by adding that this is our reasonable service; for he intended a spiritual kind of Divine worship, which he tacitly opposed to the carnal sacrifices of the Mosaic law. So "to do good, and to communicate," are called "sacrifices with which God is well pleased." (*t*) So the liberality of the Philippians in supplying the wants of Paul was "an odour of a sweet smell, a sacrifice acceptable and well pleasing to God." (*v*) So all the good works of believers are spiritual sacrifices.

XVII. Why do I multiply quotations? This form of expression is perpetually occurring in the Scriptures. And even while the people were kept under the external discipline of the law, it was

(*r*) Mal. i. 11. (*s*) Rom. xii. 1.
(*t*) Heb. xiii. 16. (*v*) Phil. iv. 18.

sufficiently declared by the prophets that those carnal sacrifices contained a reality and truth which is common to the Christian Church, as well as to the nation of the Jews. For this reason David prayed, "Let my prayer be set forth before thee as incense; and the lifting up of my hands as the evening sacrifice." (*w*) And Hosea called thanksgiving "the calves of our lips," (*x*) which David calls "offering thanksgiving" and "offering praise." (*y*) In imitation of the Psalmist, the apostle himself says, "Let us offer the sacrifice of praise to God continually;" and by way of explanation adds, "that is, the fruit of our lips," confessing or giving "thanks to his name." (*z*) This kind of sacrifice is indispensable in the supper of the Lord, in which, while we commemorate and declare his death, and give thanks, we do no other than offer the sacrifice of praise. From this sacrificial employment, all Christians are called "a royal priesthood;" (*a*) because, as the apostle says, "By Christ we offer the sacrifice of praise to God, that is, the fruit of our lips, giving thanks to his name." For we do not appear in the presence of God with our oblations without an intercessor; Christ is the Mediator, by whom we offer ourselves and all that we have to the Father. He is our High Priest, who, having entered into the celestial sanctuary, opens the way of access for us. He is our altar, upon which we place our oblations, that whatever we venture to do, we may attempt in him. In a word, it is he that "hath made us kings and priests unto God." (*b*)

XVIII. What remains, then, but for the blind to see, the deaf to hear, and even children to understand, this abomination of the mass? which, being presented in a vessel of gold, has so inebriated and stupefied all the kings and people of the earth, from the highest to the lowest, that, more senseless than the brutes themselves, they have placed the whole of their salvation in this fatal gulf. Surely Satan never employed a more powerful engine to assail and conquer the kingdom of Christ. This is the Helen, for which the enemies of the truth in the present day contend with cruelty, rage, and fury; a Helen, indeed, with which they so pollute themselves with spiritual fornication, which is the most

(*w*) Psalm cxli. 2. (*x*) Hosea xiv. 2. (*y*) Psalm l. 14, 23.
(*z*) Heb. xiii. 15. (*a*) 1 Peter ii. 9. (*b*) Rev. i. 6.

execrable of all. Here I touch not, even with my little finger, the gross abuses which they might pretend to be profanations of the purity of their holy mass; what a scandalous traffic they carry on, what sordid gains they make by their masses, with what enormous rapacity they gratify their avarice. I only point out, and that in few and plain words, the true nature of the most sanctimonious sanctity of the mass, on account of which it has attracted so much admiration and veneration for so many ages. For an illustration of such great mysteries proportioned to their dignity, would require a larger treatise; and I am unwilling to introduce those disgusting corruptions which are universally notorious; that all men may understand that the mass, considered in its choicest and most estimable purity, without any of its appendages, from the beginning to the end, is full of every species of impiety, blasphemy, idolatry, and sacrilege.

XIX. The readers may now see, collected into a brief summary, almost every thing that I have thought important to be known respecting these two sacraments; the use of which has been enjoined on the Christian Church from the commencement of the New Testament until the end of time; that is to say, baptism, to be a kind of entrance into the Church, and an initiatory profession of faith; and the Lord's supper, to be a continual nourishment, with which Christ spiritually feeds his family of believers. Wherefore, as there is but "one God, one Christ, one faith," one Church, the body of Christ, so there is only "one baptism" and that is never repeated; but the supper is frequently distributed, that those who have once been admitted into the Church, may understand that they are continually nourished by Christ. Beside these two, as no other sacrament has been instituted by God, so no other ought to be acknowledged by the Church of believers. For that it is not left to the will of man to institute new sacraments, will be easily understood if we remember what has already been very plainly stated—that sacraments are appointed by God for the purpose of instructing us respecting some promise of his, and assuring us of his good-will towards us; and if we also consider, that no one has been the counsellor of God, capable of affording us any certainty respecting his will, (*c*) or furnish-

(*c*) Isaiah xl. 14. Rom. xi. 34.

ing us any assurance of his disposition towards us, what he chooses to give or to deny us. Hence it follows, that no one can institute a sign to be a testimony respecting any determination or promise of his; he alone can furnish us a testimony respecting himself by giving a sign. I will express myself in terms more concise, and perhaps more homely, but more explicit—that there can be no sacrament unaccompanied with a promise of salvation. All mankind, collected in one assembly, can promise us nothing respecting our salvation. Therefore they can never institute or establish a sacrament.

XX. Let the Christian Church, therefore, be content with these two, and not only neither admit nor acknowledge any other at present, but neither desire nor expect any other to the end of the world. For as the Jews, beside the ordinary sacraments given to them, had also several others, differing according to the varying circumstances of different periods, such as the manna, the water issuing from the rock, the brazen serpent, and the like, they were admonished by this variation not to rest in such figures, which were of short duration, but to expect from God something better, which should undergo no change and come to no end. But our case is very different: to us Christ has been revealed, "in whom are hid all the treasures of wisdom and knowledge," (*c*) in such abundance and profusion, that to hope or desire any new accession to these treasures would really be to displease God, and provoke his wrath against us. We must hunger after Christ, we must seek, contemplate, and learn him alone, till the dawning of that great day, when our Lord will fully manifest the glory of his kingdom, and reveal himself to us, so that "we shall see him as he is." (*d*) And for this reason, the dispensation under which we live is designated in the Scriptures as "the last time," "these last times," "the last days," (*e*) that no one may deceive himself with a vain expectation of any new doctrine or revelation. For "God, who at sundry times and in divers manners spake in time past unto the fathers by the prophets, hath, in these last days, spoken unto us by his Son," (*f*) who alone is able to "reveal the

---

(*c*) Col. ii. 3. (*d*) 1 John iii. 2.
(*e*) 1 John ii. 18. 1 Peter i. 20. Acts ii. 17. (*f*) Heb. i. 1, 2.

Father," (*g*) and who, indeed, "hath declared him" (*h*) fully, as far as is necessary for our happiness, while "now we see" him "through a glass darkly." (*i*) As men are not left at liberty to institute new sacraments in the Church of God, so it were to be wished that as little as possible of human invention should be mixed with those which have been instituted by God. For as wine is diluted and lost by an infusion of water, and as a whole mass of meal contracts acidity from a sprinkling of leaven, so the purity of Divine mysteries is only polluted when man makes any addition of his own. And yet we see, as the sacraments are observed in the present day, how very far they have degenerated from their original purity. There is every where an excess of pageantries, ceremonies, and gesticulations; but no consideration or mention of the word of God, without which even the sacraments themselves cease to be sacraments. And the very ceremonies which have been instituted by God are not to be discerned among such a multitude of others, by which they are overwhelmed. In baptism, how little is seen of that which ought to be the only conspicuous object—I mean baptism itself? And the Lord's supper has been completely buried since it has been transformed into the mass; except that it is exhibited once a year, but in a partial and mutilated form.

(*g*) Luke x. 22. (*h*) John i. 18. (*i*) 1 Cor. xiii. 12.

CHAPTER XIX

The Five Other Ceremonies, Falsely Called Sacraments, Proved Not to Be Sacraments; Their Nature Explained

The preceding discussion respecting the sacraments might satisfy persons of docile and sober minds, that they ought not to carry their curiosity any further, or without the sanction of the word of God, to receive any other sacraments beside those two which they know to have been instituted by the Lord. But as the opinion of seven sacraments has been so generally admitted in the common conversation of mankind, and pervaded the controversies of the schools, and the sermons of the pulpit,—as it has gathered strength from its antiquity, and still keeps its hold on the minds of men,—I have thought I should perform a useful service by entering into a closer and distinct examination of the five ceremonies, which are commonly numbered among the true and genuine sacraments of the Lord, by clearing away every fallacy, and exhibiting to the view of plain Christians the real nature of those ceremonies, and how falsely they have hitherto been considered as sacraments. Here, in the first place, I wish to declare to all believers, that I am not induced to enter on this controversy respecting the term, by the least desire of contention, but that I am urged by important reasons to resist the abuse of it. I am aware that Christians have power over names as well as things, and may therefore apply words to things at their own pleasure, provided they retain a pious meaning, even though there be some impropriety of expression. All this I admit, though it would be better for words to be subject to things, than for things to be subject to words. The case of the term *sacrament*, however, is different. For those who maintain seven sacraments, give them all the same definition—that they are visible forms of invisible grace; they make them all alike vessels of the Holy Spirit, instruments of communicating righteousness, causes of obtaining grace. And the Master of the Sentences, Lombard, denies that the sacraments of the Mosaic law are properly designated by this appellation; because they did not communicate that which they prefigured. Is it to be endured, that those symbols, which the Lord consecrated with his own mouth, and which he adorned with excellent promises, should not be acknowledged as sacraments; and, at the same time, that this honour should be transferred to those rites which are merely inventions of men, or, at least, are observed without any express command of God? Either, therefore, let them change their definition, or abstain from this abuse of the term, which afterwards generates false and absurd opinions. Extreme unction, they say, is a figure and cause of invisible grace, because it is a sacrament. If we ought by no means to admit their inference from the term, it certainly behoves us to lose no time in resisting their application of the term itself, that we may not be chargeable with giving any occasion to such an error. Again: to prove that ceremony to be a sacrament, they allege this reason—that it consists of the external sign and the word of God. If we find neither command nor promise respecting it, can we do otherwise than oppose it?

II. Now, it appears that we are not debating about the word, but raising a necessary and useful controversy respecting the thing itself. We must strenuously maintain, therefore, what we have already established by irrefragable argument that the power to institute sacraments belongs to God alone; for a sacrament ought to exhibit the certain promise of God, for the assurance and consolation of the consciences of believers; which could never receive such assurance and consolation from man. A sacrament ought to be a testimony to us of the good-will of God towards us—a testimony which no man or angel can ever give, as none has been "his counsellor." It is he alone, therefore, who, with legitimate authority, testifies to us concerning himself by means of his word. A sacrament is a seal by which the testament or promise of God is sealed. But it could not be sealed by corporeal things and the elements of this world, unless they were marked out and appointed for this purpose by the power of God. Therefore man cannot institute a sacrament; because it is not in human power to cause such great and Divine mysteries to be concealed under such mean symbols. "The word of God must precede," as is excellently remarked by Augustine, "in order to make a sacrament to be a sacrament." Moreover, if we would avoid falling into many absurdities, it is requisite to preserve some distinction between a sacrament and other ceremonies. The apostles prayed on bended knees; shall we, therefore, never kneel without making it a sacrament? The early Christians are said to have turned their faces towards the east when they prayed; shall looking towards the east, then, be regarded as a sacrament? Paul says, "I will that men pray every where, lifting up holy hands," (*k*) and the prayers of the saints appear to have been often made with uplifted hands; shall elevation of hands also be made a sacrament? On this principle all the gestures of the saints would become sacraments. I would not insist on these things, however, if they were not connected with those greater inconveniences.

III. If they wish to press us with the authority of the ancient Church, I assert that this is a groundless pretence. For the number of seven sacraments can nowhere be found in the ecclesiastical writers, nor is it clear when it was introduced. I grant, indeed, that the fathers sometimes make too free a use of the word sacrament; but they use it indifferently to signify all ceremonies and external rites, and all exercises of piety. But, when they speak of those signs which we ought to regard as testimonies of the grace of God, they are content with these two, baptism and the eucharist. That this may not be supposed to be a false allegation, I shall here cite a few testimonies from Augustine. To Januarius he says,

---

(*k*) 1 Tim. ii. 8.

"First, I wish you to know what is the principal point of this controversy—that our Lord Jesus Christ, as he says in the gospel, has laid upon us an easy yoke and a light burden. And, therefore, he has linked together the society of the Christian Church by sacraments, very few in number, most easy to observe, and excellent in signification. Such are baptism, consecrated in the name of the Trinity, and the communion of the body and blood of the Lord, and if there be any other enjoined in the canonical Scriptures." Again, in his treatise On the Christian Doctrine: "Since the resurrection of our Lord, our Lord himself, and the practice of his apostles, instead of many signs, have given us few, and those most easy in performance, most excellent in signification, and most pure in observance; such are baptism, and the celebration of the body and blood of the Lord." Why does he make no mention here of the sacred or septenary number? Is it probable that he would have omitted it, if it had then been instituted in the Church; especially as, in other cases, he was more curious in the observation of numbers than was at all necessary? And, when he names baptism and the Lord's supper, and is silent respecting any others, does he not sufficiently indicate, that these two mysteries possess superior and peculiar dignity, and that all other ceremonies occupy an inferior station? Wherefore I affirm that these advocates for seven sacraments are not only unsupported by the word of the Lord, but also by the consent of the ancient Church, however they may boast of such consent. Let us now proceed to the particular ceremonies.

CONFIRMATION

IV. It was an ancient custom in the Church for the children of Christians, after they were come to years of discretion, to be presented to the bishop in order to fulfil that duty which was required of adults who offered themselves to baptism. For such persons were placed among the catechumens, till, being duly instructed in the mysteries of Christianity, they were enabled to make a confession of their faith before the bishop and all the people. Therefore those who had been baptized in their infancy, because they had not then made such a confession of faith before the Church, at the close of childhood, or the commencement of adolescence, were again presented by their parents, and were examined by the bishop according to the form of the catechism which was then in common use. That this exercise, which deserved to be regarded as sacred and solemn, might have the greater dignity and reverence, they also practised the ceremony of imposition of hands. Thus the youth, after having given satisfaction respecting his faith, was dismissed with a solemn benediction. This custom is frequently mentioned by the ancient writers. Leo, the pope, says, "If any one be converted from heresy, let him not be baptized again; but let the influence of the Spirit, which he wanted among the heretics, be communicated to him by the imposition of the hands of the bishop." Here our adversaries will exclaim that any ceremony, by which the Holy Spirit is conferred, is properly denominated a sacrament. But the meaning of Leo in these words is sufficiently unfolded by himself in another place: "Whoever is baptized among heretics, let him not be rebaptized; but let him be confirmed by imposition of hands with invocation of the Holy Spirit; because he has received the mere form of baptism, without the sanctification." It is also mentioned by Jerome against the Luciferians. And though I confess that Jerome is not altogether correct in stating it to have been a custom of the apostles, yet he is very far from the absurdities now maintained by the Romanists; and he even corrects that very statement by adding, that this benediction was committed wholly to the bishops, "rather in honour of the priesthood than from necessity imposed by any law." Such imposition of hands, therefore, as is simply connected with benediction, I highly approve, and wish it were now restored to its primitive use, uncorrupted by superstition.

V. Succeeding times have almost obliterated that ancient practice, and introduced I know not what counterfeit confirmation as a sacrament of God. They have pretended that the virtue of confirmation is to give the Holy Spirit for the augmentation of grace, who in baptism is given for innocence; to strengthen for warfare those who in baptism had been regenerated to life. This confirmation is performed by unction and the following form of words: "I sign thee with the sign of the cross, and confirm thee with the chrism of salvation, in the name of the Father, and of the Son, and of the Holy Spirit." All this sounds very beautifully and pleasantly. But where is the word of God which promises the presence of the Holy Spirit in this ceremony? They cannot allege a single iota. How, then, will they assure us that their chrism is the vessel of the Holy Spirit? We see oil, a thick and viscid liquid, and we see nothing besides. Augustine says, "Let the word be added to the element, and it will become a sacrament." Let the Romanists produce this word, if they wish us to contemplate in the oil any thing beyond the oil itself. If they acknowledged themselves ministers of the sacraments, as they ought to do, there would be no need of any further contention. The first law of a minister is to undertake nothing without a command. Now, let them produce any command for this service, and I will not add another word on the subject. If they have no command, they can have no excuse for such sacrilegious audacity. On the same principle, our Lord interrogated the Pharisees: "The baptism of John, whence was it? from heaven or of men?" (*k*) If they had answered, From men, he would have extorted a confession that it was vain and frivolous; if, From heaven, they would be constrained to admit the doctrine of John. To avoid too great an injury to John, therefore, they did not dare to confess it was from men. So, if confirmation be "of men," it is evinced to be vain and frivolous; if they wish to persuade us that it is from heaven, let them prove it.

VI. They defend themselves, indeed, by the example of the apostles, whom they consider as having done nothing without sufficient reason. This consideration is correct; nor would they receive any reprehension from us, if they showed themselves imitators of the apostles. But what was the practice of the apostles? Luke relates, that "when the apostles, which were at Jerusalem, heard that Samaria had received the word of God, they sent unto them Peter and John; who, when they were come down, prayed for them, that they might receive the Holy Ghost; for as yet he was fallen upon none of them; only they were baptized in the name of the Lord Jesus. Then laid they their hands on them, and they received the Holy Ghost." (*l*) And this imposition of hands is men-

(*k*) Matt. xxi. 25. (*l*) Acts viii. 14—17.

tioned by the sacred historian on several occasions. I perceive what the apostles did—that they faithfully executed their ministry. It was the Lord's will, that those visible and wonderful graces of the Holy Spirit, which he then poured out upon his people, should be administered and distributed by his apostles with imposition of hands. Now, I do not conceive that the imposition of hands concealed any higher mystery, but am of opinion that this ceremony was employed by them as an external expression of their commending, and, as it were, presenting to God, the person upon whom they laid their hands. If the ministry which was then executed by the apostles were still continued in the Church, imposition of hands ought also to be still observed; but since such grace is no longer conferred, of what use is the imposition of hands? It is true that the people of God still enjoy the presence of the Holy Spirit, whose guidance and direction are indispensable to the existence of the Church. For we have the eternal promise, which can never fail, and in which Christ has said, "If any man thirst, let him come unto me, and drink living water." (*m*) But those miraculous powers and manifest operations, which were distributed by imposition of hands, have ceased; and it was right that they should continue but for a time. For it was necessary that the first preaching of the gospel, and the kingdom of Christ, at its commencement, should be illustrated and magnified by miracles never seen or heard before; the subsequent cessation of which does not argue the Lord's desertion of his Church, but is equivalent to a declaration from him that the magnificence of his reign and the dignity of his word had been sufficiently manifested. In what respect, then, will these impostors affirm that they imitate the apostles? They should have effected, by imposition of hands, that the evident power of the Spirit might immediately show itself. This they do not practise. Why, then, do they boast that they are countenanced by the imposition of hands, which we find was used by the apostles, but for a totally different purpose.

VII. This is just as reasonable as it would be for any one to affirm the afflation, with which the Lord breathed upon his dis-

(*m*) John vii. 37, 38.

ciples, to be a sacrament by which the Holy Spirit is conferred. (*n*) But though the Lord did this once, he has never directed it to be done by us. In the same manner, the apostles practised imposition of hands during that period in which the Lord was pleased to dispense the visible graces of the Holy Spirit in compliance with their prayers; not in order that persons in succeeding times might counterfeit a vain and useless sign, as a mere piece of mimicry destitute of any reality. Besides, even if they could prove themselves to imitate the apostles in the imposition of hands, in which they have nothing similar to the apostles, except this preposterous mimicry, whence do they derive their oil, which they call the oil of salvation? Who has taught them to seek salvation in oil? Who has taught them to attribute to it the property of imparting spiritual strength? Is it Paul, who calls us off from the elements of this world, and severely condemns an attachment to such observances? (*o*) On the contrary, I fearlessly pronounce, not of myself, but from the Lord, that those who call oil the oil of salvation, abjure the salvation which is in Christ, reject Christ, and have no part in the kingdom of God. For oil is for the belly, and the belly for oil; the Lord shall destroy both; all these weak elements "which perish with the using," (*p*) have no connection with the kingdom of God, which is spiritual, and shall never perish. What, then, it will be said, do you apply the same rule to the water with which we are baptized, and to the bread and wine used in the Lord's supper? I answer, that in sacraments of Divine appointment, two things are to be regarded—the substance of the corporeal symbol which is proposed to us, and the character impressed upon it by the word of God, in which consists all its virtue. Therefore, as the bread, and wine, and water, which are presented to our view in the sacraments, retain their natural substance, that observation of Paul is always applicable: "Meats for the belly, and the belly for meats; but God shall destroy both it and them;" (*q*) for they pass and vanish away with the fashion of this world. But as they are sanctified by the word of God to be sacraments, they do not confine us to the flesh, but impart to us true and spiritual instruction.

(*n*) John xx. 22. (*o*) Gal. iv. 9. Col. ii. 20.
(*p*) Col. ii. 22. (*q*) 1 Cor. vi. 13.

VIII. Let us examine still more narrowly how many monsters are fostered by this oil. The dispensers of it say, that the Holy Spirit is given, in baptism for innocence, in confirmation for an augmentation of grace; that in baptism we are regenerated to life, and that by confirmation, we are armed for warfare; and they have so far lost all shame, as to deny that baptism can be rightly performed without confirmation. What corruption! Are we not, then, "in baptism buried with Christ, planted together in the likeness of his death," that we may be "also in the likeness of his resurrection?" Now this fellowship with the death and life of Christ, Paul explains to consist in the mortification of the flesh, and the vivification of the Spirit; "that our old man is crucified with him, that we should walk in newness of life." (*r*) What is it to be armed for the spiritual warfare, if this be not? If they deemed it of no importance to trample under foot the word of God, why did they not at least reverence the Church, to which they wish to appear so uniformly obsequious? But what can be produced more severe against this doctrine of theirs, than the following decree of the Council of Milevum? "Whoever asserts that baptism is only given for the remission of sins, and not for assistance of future grace, let him be accursed." When Luke, in a passage which we have already cited, speaks of some as having been "baptized in the name of the Lord Jesus," (*s*) who had not received the Holy Ghost, he does not absolutely deny that any gift of the Spirit had been imparted to those persons who had believed in Christ with the heart, and had confessed him with the mouth; he intends that gift of the Spirit which communicated his manifest powers and visible graces. So the apostles are said to have received the Holy Spirit on the day of Pentecost; though Christ had long before declared to them, "It is not ye that speak, but the Spirit of your Father, which speaketh in you." (*t*) Let all who are of God, here observe the malicious and pestilent artifice of Satan. That which was truly given in baptism, he falsely asserts to be given in his confirmation, with the crafty design of seducing us unawares from baptism. Who can doubt, now, that this is the doctrine of Satan, which severs from baptism the promises which be-

(*r*) Rom. vi. 4—6. (*s*) Acts viii. 16; xix. 5.
(*t*) Acts ii. 4, &c. Matt. x. 20.

long to that sacrament, and transfers them to something else? It is now discovered on what kind of a foundation this famous unction rests. The word of God is, that "as many as have been baptized into Christ, have put on Christ," (*u*) with his gifts. The word of these anointers is, That we have received no promise in baptism to arm us for the spiritual warfare. The word of God is the voice of truth; consequently the word of the anointers must be the voice of falsehood. I can, therefore, give a more correct definition of this confirmation than they have yet given of it; namely, that it is a manifest insult against baptism, obscuring and even abolishing its use; that it is a deceitful promise of the devil, seducing us from the truth of God; or, if the following be preferred, that it is oil polluted with the falsehood of the devil, to darken and deceive the minds of the simple.

IX. They further assert that all believers after baptism ought to receive the Holy Spirit by imposition of hands, that they may be found complete Christians; for that no one can be altogether a Christian who is never anointed with episcopal confirmation. These are their own words. But I thought that all things relating to Christianity had been comprehended and declared in the Scriptures. Now, it seems, the true form of religion is to be sought and learned from some other quarter. The wisdom of God, therefore, celestial truth, all the doctrine of Christ, only *begins* to make Christians; oil *completes* them. Such a sentiment condemns all the apostles, and a number of martyrs who, it is certain, had never received this unction. For the holy chrism, the perfusion of which would complete their Christianity, or rather make them Christians from being no Christians at all, had not then been manufactured. But these chrismatics abundantly confute themselves, without my saying a word. For how small a part of their people do they anoint after baptism? Why, then, do they suffer such semi-Christians in their own community, from an imperfection which they might easily remedy? Why do they, with such supine negligence, suffer them to omit that which cannot be omitted without great criminality? Why do they not more rigidly insist upon a thing so necessary and indispensable to salvation, unless any one

(*u*) Gal. iii. 27.

be prevented by sudden death? Surely while they suffer it to be so easily despised, they tacitly confess it not to be of so much importance as they pretend it to be.

X. In the last place, they determine that this sacred unction ought to be held in greater reverence than baptism; because it is only dispensed by the hands of the greatest prelates, whereas baptism is commonly administered by all priests. Must they not be considered as evidently mad, who discover such fondness for their own inventions, that, in comparison with them, they presume to undervalue the sacred institutions of God? Sacrilegious mouth, dost thou dare to place an unction, which is only defiled with thy fetid breath, and enchanted by the muttering of a few words, on a level with the sacrament of Christ, and to compare it with water sanctified by the word of God? But this would not satisfy thy presumption; thou hast even given it the preference! These are the responses of the Holy See; they are the oracles of the apostolic tripod. But some of them have begun to moderate this infatuation, which even in their opinion was carried beyond all due limits. Confirmation is to be regarded, they say, with greater reverence than baptism; not, perhaps, for the greater virtue and advantage that it confers, but because it is dispensed by persons of superior dignity, and is applied to the nobler part of the body, that is, the forehead; or because it contributes a greater augmentation of virtues, though baptism is more available to remission. But in the first reason, do they not betray themselves to be Donatists, who estimate the virtue of the sacrament by the dignity or worthiness of the minister? I will grant, however, that confirmation be considered as more excellent from the dignity of episcopal hands. But if any one inquire of them how such a prerogative has been conferred on bishops, what reason will they assign but their own pleasure? They allege that the apostles alone exercised that right, being the sole dispensers of the Holy Spirit. Are bishops the only apostles; or are they apostles at all? Let us, however, grant that also; why do they not on the same principle contend that none but bishops ought to touch the sacrament of the blood in the Lord's supper; which they refuse to the laity, because the Lord, as they say, only gave it to the apostles? If our Lord gave it to the apostles alone, why do they not infer, Therefore it ought now to be given to bishops alone? But in this case they make the apostles simple presbyters; now, they are hurried away with an extravagant notion suddenly to create them bishops. Lastly, Ananias was not an apostle; yet to him Paul was sent, that he might receive his sight, be baptized, and be filled with the Holy Ghost. (*x*) I will add one question more: If this was the peculiar office of bishops by a Divine right, why have they dared to transfer it to common presbyters, as we read in one of the epistles of Gregory?

XI. How frivolous and foolish is the second reason, That they call their confirmation more excellent than the baptism instituted by God, because in confirmation the forehead is anointed with oil, and in baptism the crown of the head; as though baptism were performed with oil, and not with water! I appeal to all believers, whether these deceivers do not direct all their efforts to this one object; to corrupt the purity of the sacraments by the leaven of their false doctrine. I have already remarked, in another part of this book, that in the sacraments it is scarcely possible to discern that which is of Divine institution among the multiplicity of human inventions. If any one did not give credit to that observation of mine, let him now at least believe his own masters. By their passing over the water without the least notice, it appears that the only thing to which they attribute much importance in baptism, is their own oil. We, therefore, on the contrary, affirm, that in baptism the forehead also is laved with water. In comparison with this, we esteem all their oil perfectly worthless, whether in baptism or in confirmation. If any one allege that it is sold for more, this accession of price would only corrupt the good, if it contained any; an imposture of the foulest kind can never be legalized by robbery. In the third reason, they expose their impiety, when they pretend that a greater augmentation of virtues is conferred in confirmation than in baptism. The apostles, by imposition of hands, dispensed the visible graces of the Spirit. In what respect does their unction appear to be productive of any advantage? Let us leave these moderators therefore, who cover one sacrilege with a number of others. It is a

(*x*) Acts ix. 17, 18.

Gordian knot, which it is better to cut asunder than to spend much labour to untie.

XII. Now, when they find themselves stripped of the word of God, and of every probable argument, they resort to their usual pretext, that it is a very ancient usage, and confirmed by the consent of many ages. Though this allegation were true, it would not at all serve their cause. A sacrament is not from earth, but from heaven; not of men, but of God alone. If they wish their confirmation to be regarded as a sacrament, they must prove God to be the Author of it. But why do they allege antiquity, seeing that the ancient fathers, whenever they mean to express themselves with strict propriety, nowhere enumerate more than two sacraments? If it were necessary to fortify our faith by the authority of men, we have an impregnable fortress, that those ceremonies, which our adversaries falsely pretend to be sacraments, were never acknowledged as sacraments by the ancients. The fathers speak of imposition of hands; but do they call it a sacrament? Augustine explicitly affirms that it is no other than prayer. Here let them not oppose me with their foolish distinctions, that Augustine applied this remark to imposition of hands, not as practised in confirmation, but as used for the purpose of healing, or of reconciliation. The book is extant, and is in many hands. If I pervert the passage to any meaning different from that of Augustine himself, I am content to submit to their severest censure and contempt. For he is speaking of schismatics, who returned to the unity of the Church; and denies that they have any need of the reiteration of baptism, for that imposition of hands was sufficient, in order that, by the bond of peace, the Lord might give them his Holy Spirit. And as it might appear unreasonable to repeat imposition of hands rather than baptism, he shows the difference. "For what," he says, "is imposition of hands, but prayer over a man?" And that this was his meaning, is evident from another passage, where he says, "We lay hands upon reclaimed heretics, for the union of charity, which is the principal gift of the Holy Spirit, and without which whatever else may be holy in man is unavailing to salvation."

XIII. I sincerely wish that we retained the custom, which I have stated was practised among the ancients before this abortive image of a sacrament made its appearance. For it was not such a confirmation as the Romanists pretend, which cannot be mentioned without injury to baptism; but a catechetical exercise, in which children or youth used to deliver an account of their faith in the presence of the Church. Now, it would be the best mode of catechetical instruction, if a formulary were written for this purpose, containing and stating, in a familiar manner, all the articles of our religion, in which the universal Church of believers ought to agree, without any controversy: a boy of ten years of age might present himself to make a confession of his faith; he might be questioned on all the articles, and might give suitable answers: if he were ignorant of any, or did not fully understand them, he should be taught. Thus the Church would witness his profession of the only true and pure faith, in which all the community of believers unanimously worship the one God. If this discipline were observed in the present day, it would certainly sharpen the inactivity of some parents, who carelessly neglect the instruction of their children as a thing in which they have no concern, but which, in that case, they could not omit without public disgrace; there would be more harmony of faith among Christian people, nor would many betray such great ignorance and want of information; some would not be so easily carried away with novel and strange tenets; in short, all would have a regular acquaintance with Christian doctrine.

PENANCE

XIV. In the next place, they add penance; of which they treat in such a confused and disorderly manner, that the consciences of men can deduce no certain or solid conclusion respecting their doctrine. In another part of this treatise, we have stated at large what we learn from the Scriptures respecting repentance, and likewise what is inculcated on that subject by the Romanists. Our present business is only to inquire briefly into the reasons of those persons who promulgated the opinion which has prevailed for a long period in the churches and in the schools, that penance is a sacrament. In the first place, I will make a few remarks on the practice of the ancient Church, the pretence of which they have abused for the introduction and establishment of their foolish invention. The order observed by the ancients in public penitence was, that persons who had completed the satisfactions enjoined upon them, were reconciled to the Church by solemn imposition of hands. This was a sign of absolution, to encourage the sinner himself with an assurance of pardon before God, and to admonish the Church that they ought to obliterate the memory of his offence, and kindly to receive him into favour. This Cyprian often calls "giving peace." To increase the importance of this act, and give it a greater recommendation among the people, it was ordained that it should always be done by the authority of a bishop. Hence that decree of the second Council of Carthage: "Let no presbyter be permitted to reconcile a penitent publicly at the mass." And another decree of the Council of Arausium: "Let those who, during the period of their penitence, depart out of this life, be admitted to the communion without the reconciliatory imposition of hands. If they recover from their illness, let them complete the period of their penitence, and then let them receive from the bishop the reconciliatory imposition of hands." Also the decree of the third Council of Carthage: "Let not a presbyter reconcile a penitent without the authority of the bishop." The design of all these decrees was, to prevent the severity which they wished to preserve in this matter from falling into disuse. Therefore they committed it to the cognizance of the bishop, who was likely to be more circumspect in conducting the examination. But Cyprian states that it was not the bishop alone who laid hands on the penitent, but that all the clergy also united in this act. These are his words: "They do penance for a proper time, and then they come to the communion, and are restored to the right of communion by the imposition of the hands of the bishop and clergy." Afterwards, in process of time, the custom was corrupted, so that they used this ceremony in private absolutions, without any public expression of penitence. Hence that distinction in Gratian, between public and private reconciliation. I consider that ancient custom, which is mentioned by Cyprian, to have been holy and useful to the Church, and could wish it were revived in the present day. This more recent one, though I venture not to condemn or censure it with severity, yet I consider less necessary. We see, however, that imposition of hands on repentance is a ceremony of human, not of Divine institution, and is to be placed among indifferent things and external exercises, such as are not to be despised, but ought to hold a station far below the sacraments, which are enjoined upon us by the word of God.

XV. Now, the Romish theologians and schoolmen, who are in the habit of corrupting every thing by misinterpretation, take very great pains here to discover a sacrament, but to no purpose. Nor ought this to be wondered at, for they seek it where it is not to be found. When they have done their best, they leave the subject perplexed, doubtful, uncertain, and confounded with a variety of opinions. They say, then, that external penitence is a sacrament, and if it be so, that it ought to be considered as a sign of internal penitence, that is, of contrition of heart, which is the substance of the sacrament; or that both together constitute the sacrament, not two sacraments, but one complete one; but that external penitence is merely the sacrament; while that which is internal is both the sacrament and the substance of the sacrament; and remission of sins is the substance only, and not the sacrament. Let those who bear in mind the definition of a sacrament which we have already given, apply it to the examination of this pretended sacrament, and they will find that it is not an external ceremony instituted by God for the confirmation of our faith. If they plead that my definition is not a law which they are bound to obey, let them hear Augustine, whom they profess to regard with the greatest reverence. He says, "Visible sacraments are instituted for carnal persons, that by the steps of the sacraments they may be led from those things which are visible to the eye, to those which are intelligible to the mind." What resemblance to this do they themselves see, or are they able to point out to others, in that which they call the sacrament of penance? The same writer says in another place, "It is therefore called a sacrament, because one thing is seen, another is understood in it. That which is seen has corporeal form; that which is understood has spiritual fruit." These things are not at all applicable to the sacrament of penance, which they have invented, in which there is no corporeal form to represent any spiritual fruit.

XVI. And to vanquish these champions on their own ground,

if any sacrament be sought for here, would it not be far more plausible to say that the sacrament consists in the absolution of the priest, rather than in penitence, either internal or external? For it would be easy to say, that this is a ceremony appointed for the confirmation of our faith in the remission of sins, and has what they call the promise of the keys: "Whatsoever ye shall bind on earth, shall be bound in heaven; and whatsoever ye shall loose on earth, shall be loosed in heaven." (*y*) But some would have objected, that many who are absolved by priests, derive no such benefits from their absolution; whereas, upon their principle, the sacraments of the new law actually accomplish that which they represent. To this it might be replied, that, as in the eucharist there is a twofold eating,—sacramental, which is equally common to the good and the wicked; and spiritual, which is peculiar to the good—why might they not also imagine the reception of a twofold absolution? Yet I have never yet been able to comprehend what they intended by that principle of theirs, respecting the efficacious virtue of the sacraments of the new law; which we have proved to be altogether at variance with the truth of God, when we professedly discussed that subject. Here I only mean to show that this difficulty is no objection to their calling sacerdotal absolution a sacrament. For they might answer, in the language of Augustine, "That sanctification is sometimes without the visible sacrament, and that the visible sacrament is sometimes unaccompanied by internal sanctification." Again: "That the sacraments effect that which they represent in the elect alone." Again: "That some persons put on Christ as far as the reception of the sacrament, and others even to sanctification;" that the former is equally the case with the good and evil; and the latter with none but the good. Surely they have betrayed more than the weakness of children, and shown themselves blind to the broad day, who, in the midst of such difficulty and perplexity, have not discovered a thing so plain and obvious to every one.

XVII. Yet let them not flatter themselves, for in whatever part they place their sacrament, I deny that it ought to be considered as a sacrament at all; first, because it is not accompanied with

---

(*y*) Matt. xviii. 18.

any special promise of God, which is the only foundation of a sacrament; secondly, because all the ceremony exhibited here is the mere invention of men; whereas it has been already ascertained that sacramental ceremonies cannot be instituted, except by God himself. All that they have fabricated, therefore, respecting the sacrament of penance, is nothing but falsehood and imposture. This counterfeit sacrament they have adorned with a suitable title, calling it "a second plank after a shipwreck;" for that, if any one by sin has soiled the garment of innocence received in baptism, he may purify it by penance. But this, they say, is the language of Jerome. Whose language soever it may be, it cannot be exculpated from manifest impiety, if it be explained according to their notion of it. As if baptism were effaced by sin, and ought not rather to be recalled to the memory of the sinner whenever he thinks of remission of sins, that it may serve to comfort his mind, inspire him with courage, and confirm his confidence of obtaining the remission of sins, which was promised to him in baptism. But that which Jerome has expressed with some degree of harshness and impropriety, that baptism, from which those who deserve to be excommunicated from the Church have fallen away, is repaired by penitence, these admirable expositors apply to their impiety. We shall speak with the greatest propriety, therefore, if we call baptism the sacrament of penitence; since it is given for a confirmation of grace, and seal of confidence, to those who meditate repentance. And this must not be considered as an invention of ours, for, beside its conformity to the language of Scripture, it appears to have been generally received in the ancient Church as an indubitable axiom. For in the treatise on Faith addressed to Peter, which is attributed to Augustine, it is called "the sacrament of faith and repentance." And why do we resort to uncertain testimonies? Nothing can be required more explicit than what is recited by the evangelists, that "John did preach the baptism of repentance for the remission of sins." (*z*)

(*z*) Matt. iii. 1—6. Luke iii. 3.

EXTREME UNCTION

XVIII. The third counterfeit sacrament is extreme unction; which is never performed but by a priest, and that in the last moments of life, with oil consecrated by a bishop, and the following form of words: "By this holy unction, and by his most tender mercy, may God pardon thee whatever sin thou hast committed by sight, by hearing, by smell, by taste, and by touch." They pretend that it has two virtues—remission of sins, and relief from bodily disease, if that be expedient, or otherwise the salvation of the soul. They say that the institution of it is established by James, who says, "Is any sick among you? let him call for the elders of the Church; and let them pray over him, anointing him with oil in the name of the Lord; and the prayer of faith shall save the sick, and the Lord shall raise him up; and if he have committed sins, they shall be forgiven him." (*a*) This unction of theirs is of the same kind as we have already proved their imposition of hands to be: it is a mere hypocritical farce, by which, without any reason, and without any advantage, they affect to mimic the apostles. It is related by Mark, that the apostles, at their first mission, according to the command which they had received from the Lord, raised the dead, ejected demons, cleansed lepers, healed the sick, and that in the cure of the sick they made use of oil. "They anointed with oil," he says, "many that were sick, and healed them." (*b*) James had this in view when he directed the elders of the Church to be sent for to anoint the sick. That such ceremonies concealed no higher mystery, will easily be concluded by any attentive observers of the great liberty used by our Lord and his apostles in external things. When our Lord was about to restore sight to a blind man, he made clay of dust and spittle; some he healed with a touch, others with a word. In the same manner, the apostles cured some maladies with a mere word, others with a touch, others with unction. But it may be alleged that it is probable that this unction, like the other methods, was not employed without reason. This I confess; not, however, that

(*a*) James v. 14, 15. (*b*) Mark vi. 13.

they used it as an instrument of cure, but merely as a sign, to instruct the ignorance of the simple whence such virtue proceeded, that they might not ascribe the praise of it to the apostles. Now, it is very common in the Scriptures for the Holy Spirit and his gifts to be signified by oil. But that grace of healing has disappeared, like all the other miraculous powers, which the Lord was pleased to exhibit for a time, that he might render the preaching of the gospel, which was then new, the object of admiration for ever. Even though we should fully grant, therefore, that unction was a sacrament of the powers which were administered by the instrumentality of the apostles, it has nothing to do with us, to whom the administration of those powers has not been committed.

XIX. And what greater reason have they to make a sacrament of this unction than of all the other signs or symbols which are mentioned in the Scriptures? Why do not they appoint some pool of Siloam, in which the sick may bathe themselves at certain seasons? (*c*) That, they say, would be a vain attempt. Surely not more in vain than unction. Why do they not "fall upon and embrace" the dead, because Paul resuscitated a deceased young man by such means? (*d*) Why is not clay, composed of spittle and dust, converted into a sacrament? All the others, they say, were single examples, but the use of unction is commanded by James. I reply, that James was speaking in reference to that period in which this benediction of God was still enjoyed by the Church. They affirm, indeed, that there is even now the same virtue in their unction; but we find it to be otherwise by experience. Let no one now wonder how they have so confidently deluded souls, whom they know to be stupid and blind when deprived of the word of God, which is their life and light, since they are not at all ashamed to attempt to deceive the living and observing senses of the body. They make themselves ridiculous, therefore, when they boast that they are endued with the gift of healing. The Lord is undoubtedly present with his people to assist them in all ages; and, whenever it is necessary, he heals their diseases as much as he did in ancient times; but he does not display those visible powers, or dispense miracles by the hands of apostles; because

(*c*) John ix. 7. (*d*) Acts xx. 10.

that gift was only of temporary duration, and was soon lost, in some measure, by the ingratitude of men.

XX. As the apostles, therefore, had sufficient cause for using the symbol of oil as an evident testimony that the gift of healing, which had been committed to them, was not a power of their own, but of the Holy Spirit, so, on the other hand, they do a great injury to the Holy Spirit who represent a fetid oil, destitute of all efficacy, as his power. This is just as if any one were to affirm, that all oil is the power of the Holy Spirit, because it is called by that name in the Scripture; or that every dove is the Holy Spirit, because he appeared under that form. But let them look to these things. For us, it is sufficient, at present, that we see beyond all doubt that their unction is not a sacrament, being a ceremony which is neither of God's institution, nor accompanied with any promise from him. For when we require these two things in a sacrament, that it be a ceremony instituted by God, and that it have some promise of God, we at the same time require that the ceremony be enjoined upon us, and that the promise have reference to us. For no one contends that circumcision is now a sacrament of the Christian Church, notwithstanding it was instituted by God, and had a promise annexed to it; because it is not enjoined upon us, nor is the promise which was subjoined to it given to us on that condition. That the promise which they presumptuously boast of in their unction is not given to us, we have clearly proved, and they themselves declare by experience. The ceremony ought not to have been used, except by those who were endued with the gift of healing; and not by these butchers, who are more capable of killing and murdering than of healing.

XXI. Even if they had established, what they are very far from having established, that the injunction of James respecting unction is applicable to the present age, still they would have made but little progress in defending their unction with which they have hitherto besmeared us. James directs that all sick persons be anointed; these men bedaub with their unguent not sick persons, but half-dead corpses, when their souls are at the point of departing from them. If in their sacrament they have a present medicine, by which they can either alleviate the anguish of disease, or at least communicate some consolation to the soul, they are cruel never to apply the remedy in time. James directs, that the sick person be anointed by the elders of the Church; these men admit no anointer but a priest. Their explanation that the term *elders* denotes priests, and the plural number is used for the sake of dignity, is frivolous in the extreme; as though the Churches in that age abounded with priests, to be able to march in a long procession, carrying their box of consecrated oil. When James simply commands that sick persons be anointed, he appears to me to intend no other unction than of common oil; nor is any other mentioned in the narrative of Mark. These men deign to use no oil which has not been consecrated by the bishop; that is, warmed with his breath, enchanted by his muttering, and nine times saluted by him on bended knees; three times, *Hail, holy oil;* three times, *Hail, holy chrism;* three times, *Hail, holy balm.* From whom have they derived such incantations? James says, that when the elders shall have prayed over the sick person, anointing him with oil, if he have committed sins they shall be forgiven him; that, being absolved from guilt, he may obtain relief from pain; not meaning that sins are effaced by unction, but that the prayers of the believers, by which the afflicted brother shall have been commended to God, shall not be in vain. These men impiously pretend, that sins are remitted by their holy, or, to speak more properly, abominable unction. See what lengths they will go, when they shall be allowed to abuse that passage of James by their absurd interpretation. And we need not labour any longer in the proof; even their own histories relieve us from this difficulty. For they relate, that Pope Innocent, who presided over the Church of Rome in the time of Augustine, decreed that not only elders, but also all Christians, should use oil, in case of illness, for the purpose of anointing themselves or their friends.

ECCLESIASTICAL ORDERS

XXII. The fourth place in their catalogue is occupied by the sacrament of orders; but this is so fertile that it is the parent of seven little sacraments which arise out of it. Now, it is truly ridiculous for them to affirm, that there are *seven* sacraments, and when they proceed to specify them, to enumerate *thirteen.* Nor can they plead, that the seven sacraments of orders are only one sacrament, because they all belong to one priesthood, and form, as it were, so many steps to it. For, as it appears that in all of them there are different ceremonies, and they themselves say that there are different graces, no person can doubt that, if their principles be admitted, they ought to be called seven sacraments. And why do we controvert it as a doubtful thing, when they themselves plainly and distinctly declare that there are seven? In the first place, we will briefly suggest by the way what numerous and great absurdities they obtrude upon us, when they wish us to receive their orders as sacraments; and then we will inquire, whether the ceremony which the churches use in ordaining ministers ought to be called a sacrament at all. They mention seven ecclesiastical orders or degrees, which they dignify with the name of sacrament. They are—beadles, readers, exorcists, acolothists, subdeacons, deacons, priests. And they are seven, it is said, on account of the sevenfold grace of the Holy Spirit, with which those who are promoted to them ought to be endued; but it is increased, and more abundantly communicated to them, in their promotion. Now, the number itself is consecrated by a perverse interpretation of the Scripture; because they think they have read in Isaiah of seven virtues of the Holy Spirit; though, in truth, that prophet mentions only six, and had no intention of enumerating them all in that passage; for in other passages of Scripture, he is called "the Spirit of life, of holiness, and of adoption," as he is there called "the Spirit of wisdom and understanding, the Spirit of counsel and might, the Spirit of knowledge, and of the fear of the Lord." (*f*) Other persons of greater subtlety limit not the orders to seven, but extend them to nine, in resemblance, they say, of the church triumphant. And they are not agreed among themselves; for some represent the clerical tonsure to be the first order of all, and the episcopate the last: others exclude the tonsure, and place the archiepiscopal office among the orders. Isidore distinguishes them in a different way; for he makes psalmists and readers two separate orders, appointing the former to the chantings, and the latter to the reading of the Scriptures, for the in-

---

(*f*) Ezek. i. 20. Rom. i. 4; viii. 15. Isaiah xi. 2, 3.

struction of the people. And this distinction is observed in the canons. In such a diversity, what do they wish us to pursue or to avoid? Shall we say that there are seven orders? So teaches the master of the sentences, Lombard; but the most illuminated doctors determine otherwise; and these doctors differ among themselves. Moreover, the most sacred canons call us another way. This is the harmony exhibited by men, when they discuss Divine subjects without the word of God.

XXIII. But this surpasses all folly, that in every one of their orders they make Christ a colleague with them. First, they say, he executed the office of beadle, when he made a whip of small cords, and drove all the buyers and sellers out of the temple. He showed himself to be a beadle, when he said, "I am the door." He assumed the place of a reader, when he read a passage of Isaiah in the synagogue. He discharged the function of an exorcist, when, applying spittle to the ears and tongue of a man who was deaf and dumb, he restored his hearing and speech. He declared himself to be an acolothist in these words: "He that followeth me shall not walk in darkness." He discharged the duty of a subdeacon, when he girded himself with a towel, and washed the feet of his disciples. He sustained the character of a deacon, when he distributed his body and blood in the supper. He acted the part of a priest, when he offered himself on the cross a sacrifice to the Father. It is impossible to hear these things without laughing, so that I wonder they were written without laughing; at least, if those who wrote them were men. But the most remarkable of all is, the subtlety with which they reason on the word *acolothist,* which they call *ceroferarius,* a taper-bearer; a term of magic, I suppose, certainly unknown in any nation or language; whereas the Greek word ακολουθος, *acolothist,* simply signifies a *follower* or *attendant.* But I should justly incur ridicule myself, if I were to dwell on a serious refutation of such things, they are so frivolous and ludicrous.

XXIV. To prevent them, however, from continuing their impositions on silly women, it is necessary, as we proceed, to expose their vanity. They create with great pomp and solemnity their readers, psalmists, beadles, acolothists, to discharge those offices in which they employ either boys, or at least those whom they call laymen. For who, in most cases, lights the wax tapers, who pours wine and water out of the flagon, but a boy, or some mean layman, who gets his livelihood by it? Do not the same persons chant? Do they not open and shut the doors of the churches? For who ever saw in their temples an acolothist or beadle performing his office? On the contrary, he who, when a boy, discharged the duty of an acolothist, as soon as he is admitted into that order, ceases to be what he begins to be called; so that it should seem to be their deliberate intention to discard the office when they assume the title. We see what need they have to be consecrated by sacraments, and to receive the Holy Spirit; it is, that they may do nothing. If they allege, that this arises from the perverseness of the present age, that men desert and neglect their official duties, let them at the same time confess, that their holy orders, which they so wonderfully extol, are of no use or benefit to the Church in the present day, and that their whole Church is filled with a curse, since it permits boys and laymen to handle the tapers and flagons, which none are worthy of touching except those who have been consecrated as acolothists; and since it leaves boys to chant those services, which ought never to be heard but from a consecrated mouth. But for what purpose do they consecrate their exorcists? I know that the Jews had their exorcists; but I find that they derived their name from the exorcisms which they practised. Respecting these counterfeit exorcists, who ever heard of their exhibiting one specimen of their profession? It is pretended that they are invested with power to lay hands upon maniacs, demoniacs, and catechumens; but they cannot persuade the demons that they are endued with such power; not only because the demons do not submit to their commands, but because they even exercise dominion over them. For scarcely one in ten can be found among them who is not influenced by an evil spirit. Whatever ridiculous pretensions they may set up respecting their contemptible orders, are the mere compositions of ignorance and falsehood. Of the ancient acolothists, beadles, and readers, we have spoken already, when we discussed the order of the Church. Our present design is only to combat that novel invention of a sevenfold sacrament in ecclesiastical orders; on which not a syllable is any where to be found, except among those sapient theologues, the Sorbonists and Canonists.

XXV. Let us now examine the ceremonies which they employ. In the first place, all whom they enrol in their army they initiate into the rank of clergy by a common sign. They shave them on the crown of the head, that the crown may denote regal dignity; because ecclesiastics ought to be kings, to rule themselves and others, according to the language in which Peter addresses them: "Ye are a chosen generation, a royal priesthood, a holy nation, a peculiar people." But it was sacrilege for them to arrogate exclusively to themselves that which is attributed to the whole Church, and proudly to glory in the title which they had stolen from the believers. Peter addresses the whole Church; they misapply his words to a few shavelings, as if they were the only holy persons, as if they alone had been redeemed by the blood of Christ, as if they alone had been made by him kings and priests unto God. They proceed to assign other reasons; that the top of their head is laid bare, to show that their mind is free to the Lord, and can with open face contemplate the glory of God; or to indicate that the faults of their mouth and eyes ought to be cut off. Or the tonsure of the crown signifies the relinquishment and renunciation of temporal things; and the hair left round the crown denotes the relics of property which are reserved for their sustenance. Every thing is symbolical; because, with respect to them, the veil of the temple has not yet been rent asunder. Therefore, having persuaded themselves that they have completely discharged their duties, when they have represented such things by their shaven crown, they, in reality, fulfil none of them. How long will they impose upon us with such deceptions and falsehoods? Ecclesiastics, by shaving off a few hairs, signify that they have relinquished an abundance of temporal possessions, to be at liberty to contemplate the glory of God, and that they have mortified the inordinate propensities of their ears and eyes; but there is no class of men more rapacious, ignorant, or libidinous. Why do they not make an actual exhibition of sanctity, rather than counterfeit the appearance of it by false and delusive symbols?

XXVI. When they say that their clerical tonsure derives its

origin and reason from the Nazarites, what is this but declaring that their mysteries have sprung from Jewish ceremonies, or, rather, are mere Judaism? But when they add, that Priscilla, Aquila, and Paul himself, after having made a vow, shaved their heads in order to purify themselves, they betray their gross ignorance. For this is nowhere said of Priscilla; and there is some uncertainty even respecting Aquila; for that tonsure may as well be referred to Paul as to Aquila. (*g*) But not to leave them what they require, that they have an example of this tonsure in Paul, it ought to be observed by the plain reader, that Paul never shaved his head with a view to any sanctity, but merely to accommodate himself to the weakness of his brethren. I am accustomed to call vows of this kind vows of charity, and not of piety; that is to say, they were not made for any purpose of religion, or as acts of service to God, but in order to bear the ignorance of weak brethren; as the apostle himself says: "Unto the Jews I became as a Jew, that I might gain the Jews." (*h*) Therefore he did this act, and that once, and for a short period, that he might accommodate himself to the Jews. When these men desire, without any cause, to imitate the purifications of the Nazarites, what is this but raising up a new Judaism by a culpable affectation of emulating that which is abolished? The same superstition dictated that decretal epistle which prohibits ecclesiastics, according to the apostle, to let their hair grow, but enjoins them to shave in a circular form; as though the apostle, when he mentioned what is becoming to all men, were concerned about the circular tonsure of the clergy. Hence the readers may form some opinion of the importance and dignity of other succeeding mysteries, to which there is such an introduction.

XXVII. The true origin of the clerical tonsure is very evident from the testimony of Augustine. As, in that age, no persons suffered their hair to grow long, but such as were effeminate, and affected an elegance and delicacy not sufficiently manly, it was thought that it would be a bad example to permit this custom in the clergy. They were, therefore, commanded to shave their heads, that they might exhibit no appearance of effeminate ornament.

(*g*) Acts xviii. 18. (*h*) 1 Cor. ix. 20.

The tonsure then became so common, that some monks, to display their superior sanctity by something remarkable and distinguished from others, left their hair to grow very long. Afterwards, when the custom of wearing long hair was revived, and several nations were converted to Christianity, who had always been accustomed to wear their hair, as France, Germany, and England, it is probable that ecclesiastics every where shaved their heads, that they might not appear to be fond of the ornament of hair. At length, in a more corrupt age, when all the ancient institutions were either perverted or degenerated into superstition, because they saw no reason in the clerical tonsure (for they had retained nothing but a foolish imitation of their predecessors,) they had recourse to a mystery, which they now superstitiously obtrude upon us as a proof of their sacrament. Beadles, at their consecration, receive the keys of the Church, as a sign that the custody of it is committed to them. Readers are presented with the Holy Bible. To exorcists are given the forms of exorcisms to be used over catechumens and maniacs. Acolothists receive their tapers and flagons. These are the ceremonies which, if we believe them, contain such secret virtue as to be, not only signs and tokens, but even causes, of an invisible grace. For, according to their definition, all this is assumed when they insist on their being numbered among the sacraments. But, to conclude in a few words, I maintain it to be absurd for canonists and scholastic theologues to give the title of sacraments to these, which they themselves call *lesser orders;* since, even according to their own confession, they were unknown to the primitive Church, and were invented many years after. But, as sacraments contain some promises of God, they cannot be instituted by men or angels, but by God alone, whose prerogative it is to give the promise.

XXVIII. There remain three orders, which they call *greater orders;* of which sub-deaconry, they say, was transferred to this class after the number of the lessor orders began to increase. As they think that they have a testimony for these from the word of God, they peculiarly denominate them, for the sake of honour, *holy orders.* But we must now examine how perversely they abuse the Divine appointments of God in their own vindication. We will begin with the order of presbyters, or priests. For by these two names they signify one thing; and these are the appellations which they apply to those whose office, they say, it is, to offer the sacrifice of the body and blood of Christ upon the altar, to say prayers and to pronounce benedictions on the gifts of God. Therefore, at their ordination, they receive a chalice, with the patine and host, as symbols of the power committed to them to offer expiatory sacrifices to God; and their hands are anointed with oil, as a symbol to show that they are invested with power to consecrate. The ceremonies we shall notice hereafter. Of the thing itself, I affirm, that it is so far from having a syllable of the Divine word to support it, that it was impossible for them to have introduced a viler corruption of the order instituted by God. In the first place, it ought to be taken for granted, as we have shown in the preceding chapter, on the Papal Mass, that great injury is done to Christ by all those who call themselves priests to offer sacrifices of expiation. He was constituted and consecrated by the Father, with an oath, a priest after the order of Melchisedec, without end, and without a successor. He once offered a sacrifice of eternal expiation and reconciliation; and now, having entered into the sanctuary of heaven, intercedes for us. In him we are all priests; but it is only to offer to God praises and thanksgivings, in short, ourselves and all that belongs to us. It was his province alone, by his oblation, to appease God and expiate sins. When these men usurp that office to themselves, what follows, but that their priesthood is chargeable with impiety and sacrilege? They certainly betray the greatest effrontery when they dare to dignify it with the title of a sacrament. The imposition of hands, which is used at the introduction of the true presbyters and ministers of the Church into their office, I have no objection to consider as a sacrament; for, in the first place, that ceremony is taken from the Scripture, and, in the next place, it is declared by Paul to be not unnecessary or useless, but a faithful symbol of spiritual grace. (*i*) I have not enumerated it as the third among the sacraments, because it is not ordinary or common to all believers, but a special rite for a particular office. The ascription of this honour to the Christian ministry, however, furnishes no rea-

(*i*) 1 Tim. iv. 14.

son for the pride of Romish priests; for Christ has commanded the ordination of ministers to dispense his gospel and his mysteries, not the inauguration of priests to offer sacrifices. He has commissioned them to preach the gospel and to feed his flock, and not to immolate victims. He has promised them the grace of the Holy Spirit, not in order to effect an expiation for sins, but rightly to sustain and conduct the government of the Church.

XXIX. There is an excellent correspondence between the ceremonies and the thing itself. Our Lord, when he sent forth his disciples to preach the gospel, "breathed upon them;" (*k*) by that symbol representing the power of the Holy Spirit which he imparted to them. These sapient theologues retain the *breathing*, and, as if they disgorged the Holy Spirit from their throats, they mutter over the priests whom they ordain, *Receive ye the Holy Ghost.* Thus they leave nothing that they do not preposterously counterfeit, I do not say like comedians, whose gesticulations are not without art and meaning, but like apes, who imitate every thing without any taste or design. We observe, they say, the example of our Lord. But our Lord did many things which he never intended to be examples to us. He said to his disciples, "Receive ye the Holy Ghost." He said to Lazarus, "Larzarus, Come forth." (*l*) He said to the paralytic, "Arise and walk." (*m*) Why do not they say the same to all deceased persons and paralytics? When he breathed upon his apostles, and filled them with the grace of the Holy Spirit, he exhibited a specimen of his Divine power. If they attempt to do the same, they emulate God, and, as it were, challenge him to contend with them; but they are very far from producing a similar effect, and the foolish mimicry is a mere mockery of Christ. They have the effrontery, indeed, to dare to assert, that they confer the Holy Ghost; but how far this is true is shown by experience, which proves, that those who are consecrated priests, from being horses become asses, and are changed from fools to madmen. Nor do I contend with them on this account; I only condemn the ceremony itself, which ought not to be made a precedent, since it was used by Christ as a special sign of

(*k*) John xx. 22. (*l*) John xi. 43.
(*m*) Matt. ix. 5. John v. 8.

a particular miracle; so far is their pretence of imitating him from justifying their conduct.

XXX. But from whom have they received the unction? Their answer is, that they have received it from the sons of Aaron, from whom also their order derived its origin. Thus they always prefer defending themselves by improper examples, to confessing that which they practise without just reason to be their own invention; but at the same time, they do not consider that, in professing themselves successors of the sons of Aaron, they do an injury to the priesthood of Christ; which was the only thing adumbrated and prefigured by all the ancient priesthoods. In him, therefore, they were all accomplished and concluded; in him they ceased, as we have more than once already stated, and the Epistle to the Hebrews declares without the help of any comment. But, if they are so highly delighted with the Mosaic ceremonies, why do they not take oxen, and calves, and lambs, and offer them as sacrifices? They have, indeed, a great part of the ancient tabernacle, and of all the Jewish worship; but their religion is still deficient in that they do not sacrifice animal victims. Who does not see that this custom of anointing is far more pernicious than circumcision; especially when it is attended with superstition and a pharisaical opinion of the merit of the act? The Jews placed a confidence of righteousness in circumcision; in unction these men place spiritual graces. Therefore, while they desire to be imitators of the Levites, they become apostates from Christ, and renounce the office of pastors.

XXXI. This is their consecrated oil, which, it is pretended, impresses a character never to be effaced; as though oil could not be cleansed away with dust and salt, or, if it be more adhesive, with soap. But this character, they say, is spiritual. What connection has oil with the soul? Have they forgotten an observation, which they often quote to us from Augustine—That, if the word be separated from the water, it will be nothing but water, and that it is the word which makes it a sacrament? What word will they show in their unction? Will they produce the command which was given to Moses to anoint the sons of Aaron? But in that case there was also a command given respecting the coat, the ephod, the mitre, the holy crown, with which Aaron was to be adorned; and respecting the coats, girdles, and mitres, with which his sons were to be invested. It was commanded to kill a bullock, to burn his fat, to cut one ram asunder and burn it, to sanctify their ears and garments with the blood of another ram; and numerous other observances, which I wonder how it is that they have entirely omitted, and taken only the anointing oil. But if they are fond of being sprinkled, why are they sprinkled with oil rather than with blood? They attempt, indeed, a most ingenious thing; to frame one religion out of a number of fragments collected together from Christianity, Judaism, and Paganism. Their unction, therefore, is quite fetid, for want of the salt, the word of God. There remains imposition of hands, which I confess to be a sacrament in true and legitimate ordinations, but I deny that it has any place in this farce, in which they neither obey the command of Christ, nor regard the end to which the promise ought to lead us. If they wish the sign not to be refused to them, they must apply it to the very object to which it was dedicated.

XXXII. Respecting the order of deacons, also, I should have no controversy with them, if that office were restored to its primitive purity, as it existed under the apostles, and in the purer times of the Church. But what resemblance to it is to be found among those whom the Romanists pretend to be deacons? I speak not of the persons, lest they should complain that it is unjust to estimate their doctrine by the faults of individuals; but I contend that, taking their deacons exactly as their doctrine describes them to us, it is absurd to fetch any testimony in their favour from the examples of those who were appointed deacons by the apostolic Church. They say that it belongs to their deacons to assist the priests, to minister in every thing that is done in the sacraments, as in baptism, in chrism, to pour the wine into the chalice, to place the bread in the patine; to lay and dispose the oblations upon the altar, to prepare and cover the table of the Lord, to bear the cross, to read and chant the gospel and epistle to the people. Is there in all this a single word of the true duty of deacons? Now, let us hear how they are inaugurated. On the deacon who is ordained the bishop alone lays his hand; on his left shoulder he places a stole, to teach him that he has taken upon him the light yoke of the Lord, to subject to the fear of God every thing belonging to the left side. He gives him the text of the gospel, that he may know himself to be a herald of it. And what have these things to do with deacons? It is no better than if any one pretended to ordain apostles while he only appointed them to burn incense, to adorn the images, to trim the lamps, to sweep the Churches, to catch mice, and to drive out dogs. Who could suffer such persons to be called apostles, and to be compared with the apostles of Christ? Let them never again falsely represent those as deacons, whom they merely appoint to act a part in their farcical exhibitions. The very name which they bear sufficiently declares the nature of their office. For they call them Levites, and wish to deduce their origin from the sons of Levi. This I have no objection to their doing, provided they drop their pretensions to Christianity.

XXXIII. Of what use is it to say any thing respecting subdeacons? In ancient times they actually had the care of the poor. The Romanists attribute to them I know not what nugatory functions; as to bring the chalice and patine, the flagon with water, and the towel to the altar, to pour out water for washing the hands of the priests, and similar services. When they speak of the subdeacons receiving and bringing oblations, they mean those which they devour as consecrated to their use. With this office the ceremony of their initiation perfectly corresponds: they receive from the bishop the patine and chalice, from the archdeacon the flagon with water, the manual, and similar trumpery. They require us to confess the Holy Ghost to be contained in these fooleries. What pious person can bear to admit this? But to come to an end, we may draw the same conclusion respecting them as respecting the rest; nor is it necessary to repeat any more of what we have already stated. This will be sufficient for persons of modest and docile minds, to whom this book is addressed; that there is no sacrament of God, which does not exhibit a ceremony annexed to a promise, or rather which does not present a promise in a ceremony. In this case not a syllable is to be found of any certain promise; and, therefore, it is in vain to seek for a ceremony to confirm the promise. And of all the ceremonies which they use, not one appears to have been instituted by God; therefore there can be no sacrament.

MATRIMONY

XXXIV. The last of their sacraments is matrimony, which all confess to have been instituted by God, but which no one, till the time of Gregory, ever discovered to have been enjoined as a sacrament. And what man, in his sober senses, would ever have taken it into his head? It is alleged to be a good and holy ordinance of God; and so agriculture, architecture, shoemaking, and many other things, are legitimate ordinances of God, and yet they are not sacraments. For it is required in a sacrament, not only that it be a work of God, but that it be an external ceremony appointed by God for the confirmation of a promise. That there is nothing of this kind in matrimony even children can judge. But, they say, it is a sign of a sacred thing, that is, of the spiritual union of Christ with the Church. If by the word *sign*, they mean a symbol presented to us by God to support our faith, they are very far from the truth. If by a sign they merely understand that which is adduced as a similitude, I will show how acutely they reason. Paul says, "One star differeth from another star in glory: so also is the resurrection of the dead. (*n*) Here is one sacrament. Christ says, "The kingdom of heaven is like to a grain of mustard seed." Here is another. Again: "The kingdom of heaven is like unto leaven." (*o*) Here is a third. Isaiah says, "Behold, the Lord shall feed his flock like a shepherd." (*p*) Here is a fourth. Again: "The Lord shall go forth as a mighty man." (*q*) Here is a fifth. And what end will there be? Upon this principle, every thing will be a sacrament; as many parables and similitudes as there are in the Scripture, there will be so many sacraments. Even theft will be a sacrament; because it is written, "The day of the Lord cometh as a thief." (*r*) Who can bear the foolish babblings of these sophists? I confess indeed, that, whenever we see a vine, it is very desirable to recall to remembrance the language of

(*n*) 1 Cor. xv. 41, 42. (*o*) Matt. xiii. 31, 33. (*p*) Isaiah xl. 10, 11. (*q*) Isaiah xlii. 13. (*r*) 1 Thess. v. 2.

Christ: "I am the vine, ye are the branches, and my Father is the husbandman." (*s*) Whenever we meet a shepherd with his flock, it is good for us to remember another declaration of our Lord: "I am the good shepherd: the good shepherd giveth his life for the sheep." (*t*) But if any one should class such similitudes among the sacraments, it would argue a want of mental sanity.

XXXV. They obtrude upon us the language of Paul, in which, they say, he expressly calls matrimony a sacrament. "He that loveth his wife, loveth himself. For no man ever yet hated his own flesh; but nourisheth and cherisheth it, even as the Lord the Church; for we are members of his body, of his flesh, and his bones; for this cause shall a man leave his father and mother, and shall be joined unto his wife, and they two shall be one flesh. This is a great mystery (or *sacrament,* as the word is rendered in the Vulgate;) but I speak concerning Christ and the Church." (*u*) But to treat the Scriptures in this manner, is to confound heaven and earth together. To show to husbands what peculiar affection they ought to bear to their wives, Paul proposes Christ to them as an example. For as he has poured forth all the treasures of his kindness upon the Church, which he had espoused to himself, so the apostle would have every man to evince a similar affection towards his wife. It follows, "He that loveth his wife, loveth himself; even as the Lord the Church." Now, to declare how Christ has loved the Church, even as himself, and how he has made himself one with the Church his spouse, Paul applies to him what Moses relates Adam to have spoken of himself. For when Eve was brought into his presence, knowing her to have been formed out of his side, he said, "This is bone of my bones, and flesh of my flesh." (*w*) Paul testifies that all this has been spiritually fulfilled in Christ and us, when he says, "We are members of his body, of his flesh, and of his bones," and consequently "one flesh" with him. At length he concludes with an exclamation, "This is a great mystery;" and, that no one might be deceived by an ambiguity of language, he expressly states, that he intends not the conjugal union of man and woman, but the spiritual marriage of Christ and his Church: "I speak concerning Christ and the

---

(*s*) John xv. 1, 5.
(*t*) John x. 11.
(*u*) Ephes. v. 28—32.
(*w*) Gen. ii. 23.

Church." And, indeed, it is a great mystery that Christ has suffered a rib to be taken from him, of which we might be formed: that is to say, though he was strong, he voluntarily became weak, that we might be strengthend with his might; so that now we "live, yet not" we, "but Christ liveth in" us. (*x*)

XXXVI. They have been deceived by the word *sacrament* in the Vulgate version. But was it reasonable that the whole Church should suffer the punishment of their ignorance? Paul has used the word μυστηριον, *mystery*—a word which the translator might have retained, *mysterium* being not unfamiliar to Latin ears, or he might have rendered it *arcanum*, secret; he preferred, however, to use the word *sacramentum*, sacrament, but in the same sense in which Paul has used the Greek word μυστηριον, *mystery*. Now, let them go and clamorously rail against the critical knowledge of languages, through ignorance of which they have so long been most shamefully deceived in a thing so easy and obvious to every one. But why do they so strenuously insist on the word *sacrament* in this one passage, and pass it over in so many others without the least notice? For that translator has used it twice in the First Epistle to Timothy, (*y*) and in another place in this Epistle to the Ephesians, (*z*) and in every other case where the word *mystery* occurs. Let this oversight, however, be forgiven them; liars ought, at least, to have good memories. For, after having dignified matrimony with the title of a sacrament, what brainless versatility is it for them to stigmatize it with the characters of impurity, pollution, and carnal defilement! What an absurdity is it to exclude priests from a sacrament! If they deny that they are interdicted from the sacrament, but only from the conjugal intercourse, I shall not be satisfied with this evasion. For they inculcate that the conjugal intercourse itself is part of the sacrament, and that it represents the union which we have with Christ in conformity of nature; because it is by that intercourse that a husband and wife become one flesh. Here some of them have found two sacraments; one, of God and the soul, in the man and woman when betrothed; the other, of Christ and the Church, in the husband and wife. The conjugal intercourse, upon their principles, however, is a sacrament, from which no Christian ought to be

(*x*) Gal. ii. 20. (*y*) 1 Tim. iii. 9, 16. (*z*) Ephes. iii. 9.

prohibited; unless the sacraments of Christians are so incompatible, that they cannot consist together. There is also another absurdity in their doctrine. They affirm that the grace of the Holy Spirit is conferred in every sacrament; they acknowledge that the conjugal intercourse is a sacrament; yet they deny that the Holy Spirit is ever present in that intercourse.

XXXVII. And, not to deceive the Church in one thing only, what a long series of errors, falsehoods, frauds, and iniquities, have they joined to that false principle! It may truly be affirmed that, when they made matrimony into a sacrament, they only sought a den of all abominations. For, when they had once established this notion, they assumed to themselves the cognizance of matrimonial causes; for matrimony was a spiritual thing, and not to be meddled with before lay judges. Then they made laws for the confirmation of their tyranny; and some of them manifestly impious towards God, and others most unjust towards men. Such as, that marriages contracted between young persons subject to the authority of parents, without the consent of their parents, remain valid and permanent; that no marriages be lawful between persons related, even to the seventh degree; and that, if any such be contracted, they be dissolved, (and the degrees themselves they state in opposition to the laws of all nations, and to the institution of Moses, so that what they call the fourth degree is, in reality, the seventh;) that it be unlawful for a man, who has repudiated his wife for adultery, to marry another; that spiritual relatives be not united in marriage; that no marriages be celebrated from Septuagesima, or the third Sunday before Lent, to the octaves of Easter, or eight days after that festival; for three weeks before the nativity of John the Baptist, or Midsummer-day, instead of which three weeks they now substitute the Whitsun week, and the two weeks which precede it; or from Advent to the Epiphany; and innumerable other regulations, which it would be tedious to enumerate. We must now quit their corruptions, in which we have been detained longer than I could wish: but I think I have gained some advantage by stripping these asses, in some measure, of the lion's skin, and so far unmasking their principles, and exposing them to the world in their true colors.

CHAPTER XX

On Civil Government

HAVING already stated that man is the subject of two kinds of government, and having sufficiently discussed that which is situated in the soul, or the inner man, and relates to eternal life,—we are, in this chapter, to say something of the other kind, which relates to civil justice, and the regulation of the external conduct. For, though the nature of this argument seems to have no connection with the spiritual doctrine of faith which I have undertaken to discuss, the sequel will show that I have sufficient reason for connecting them together, and, indeed, that necessity obliges me to it; especially since, on the one hand, infatuated and barbarous men madly endeavour to subvert this ordinance established by God; and, on the other hand, the flatterers of princes, extolling their power beyond all just bounds, hesitate not to oppose it to the authority of God himself. Unless both these errors be resisted, the purity of the faith will be destroyed. Besides, it is of no small importance for us to know what benevolent provision God has made for mankind in this instance, that we may be stimulated by a greater degree of pious zeal to testify our gratitude. In the first place, before we enter on the subject itself, it is necessary for us to recur to the distinction which we have already established, lest we fall into an error very common in the world, and injudiciously confound together these two things, the nature of which is altogether different. For some men, when they hear that the gospel promises a liberty which acknowledges no king or magistrate among men, but submits to Christ alone, think they can enjoy no advantage of their liberty, while they see any power exalted above them. They imagine, therefore, that nothing will prosper, unless the whole world be modelled in a new form, without any tribunals, or laws, or magistrates, or any thing of a similar kind, which they consider injurious to their liberty. But he who knows how to distinguish between the body and the soul, between this present transitory life and the future eternal one, will find no difficulty in understanding, that the spiritual kingdom of Christ and civil government are things very different and remote from each other. Since it is a Jewish folly, therefore, to seek and include the kingdom of Christ under the elements of this world, let us, on the contrary, considering what the Scripture clearly inculcates, that the benefit which is received from the grace of Christ is spiritual; let us, I say, remember to confine within its proper limits all this liberty which is promised and offered to us in him. For why is it that the same apostle, who, in one place, exhorts to "stand fast in the liberty wherewith Christ hath made us free, and be not entangled again with the yoke of bondage," (*a*) in another, enjoins servants to "care not for" their servile condition; (*b*) except that spiritual liberty may very well consist with civil servitude? In this sense we are likewise to understand him in these passages: "There is neither Jew nor Greek, there is neither bond nor free, there is neither male nor female." (*c*) Again: "There is neither Greek nor Jew, circumcision nor uncircumcision, Barbarian, Scythian, bond nor free: but Christ is all, and in all;" (*d*) in which he signifies, that it is of no importance, what is our condition among men, or under the laws of what nation we live, as the kingdom of Christ consists not in these things.

II. Yet this distinction does not lead us to consider the whole system of civil government as a polluted thing, which has nothing to do with Christian men. Some fanatics, who are pleased with nothing but liberty, or rather licentiousness without any restraint, do indeed boast and vociferate, That since we are dead with Christ to the elements of this world, and, being translated into the kingdom of God, sit among the celestials, it is a degradation to us,

(*a*) Gal. v. 1. (*b*) 1 Cor. vii. 21.
(*c*) Gal. iii. 28. (*d*) Col. iii. 11.

and far beneath our dignity, to be occupied with those secular and impure cares which relate to things altogether uninteresting to a Christian man. Of what use, they ask, are laws without judgments and tribunals? But what have judgments to do with a Christian man? And if it be unlawful to kill, of what use are laws and judgments to us? But as we have just suggested that this kind of government is distinct from that spiritual and internal reign of Christ, so it ought to be known that they are in no respect at variance with each other. For that spiritual reign, even now upon earth, commences within us some preludes of the heavenly kingdom, and in this mortal and transitory life affords us some prelibations of immortal and incorruptible blessedness; but this civil government is designed, as long as we live in this world, to cherish and support the external worship of God, to preserve the pure doctrine of religion, to defend the constitution of the Church, to regulate our lives in a manner requisite for the society of men, to form our manners to civil justice, to promote our concord with each other, and to establish general peace and tranquillity; all which I confess to be superfluous, if the kingdom of God, as it now exists in us, extinguishes the present life. But if it is the will of God, that while we are aspiring towards our true country, we be pilgrims on the earth, and if such aids are necessary to our pilgrimage, they who take them from man deprive him of his human nature. They plead that there should be so much perfection in the Church of God, that its order would suffice to supply the place of all laws; but they foolishly imagine a perfection which can never be found in any community of men. For since the insolence of the wicked is so great, and their iniquity so obstinate that it can scarcely be restrained by all the severity of the laws, what may we expect they would do, if they found themselves at liberty to perpetrate crimes with impunity, whose outrages even the arm of power cannot altogether prevent?

III. But for speaking of the exercise of civil polity, there will be another place more suitable. At present we only wish it to be understood, that to entertain a thought of its extermination, is inhuman barbarism; it is equally as necessary to mankind as bread and water, light and air, and far more excellent. For it not only tends to secure the accommodations arising from all these things, that men may breathe, eat, drink, and be sustained in life, though it comprehends all these things while it causes them to live together, yet, I say, this is not its only tendency; its objects also are, that idolatry, sacrileges against the name of God, blasphemies against his truth, and other offences against religion, may not openly appear and be disseminated among the people; that the public tranquillity may not be disturbed; that every person may enjoy his property without molestation; that men may transact their business together without fraud or injustice; that integrity and modesty may be cultivated among them; in short, that there may be a public form of religion among Christians, and that humanity may be maintained among men. Nor let any one think it strange that I now refer to human polity the charge of the due maintenance of religion, which I may appear to have placed beyond the jurisdiction of men. For I do not allow men to make laws respecting religion and the worship of God now, any more than I did before; though I approve of civil government, which provides that the true religion which is contained in the law of God, be not violated, and polluted by public blasphemies, with impunity. But the perspicuity of order will assist the readers to attain a clearer understanding of what sentiments ought to be entertained respecting the whole system of civil administration, if we enter on a discussion of each branch of it. These are three: The magistrate, who is the guardian and conservator of the laws: The laws, according to which he governs: The people, who are governed by the laws, and obey the magistrate. Let us, therefore, examine, first, the function of a magistrate, whether it be a legitimate calling and approved by God, the nature of the duty, and the extent of the power; secondly, by what laws Christian government ought to be regulated; and lastly, what advantage the people derive from the laws, and what obedience they owe to the magistrate.

IV. The Lord has not only testified that the function of magistrates has his approbation and acceptance, but has eminently commended it to us, by dignifying it with the most honourable titles. We will mention a few of them. When all who sustain the magistracy are called "gods," (*e*) it ought not to be considered as an

(*e*) Psalm lxxxii. 1, 6.

appellation of trivial importance; for it implies, that they have their command from God, that they are invested with his authority, and are altogether his representatives, and act as his vicegerents. This is not an invention of mine, but the interpretation of Christ, who says, "If he called them gods, unto whom the word of God came, and the Scripture cannot be broken." (*f*) What is the meaning of this, but that their commission has been given to them by God, to serve him in their office, and, as Moses and Jehoshaphat said to the judges whom they appointed, to "judge not for man, but for the Lord?" (*g*) To the same purpose is the declaration of the wisdom of God by the mouth of Solomon: "By me kings reign, and princes decree justice. By me princes rule, and nobles, even all the judges of the earth." (*h*) This is just as if it had been affirmed, that the authority possessed by kings and other governors over all things upon earth is not a consequence of the perverseness of men, but of the providence and holy ordinance of God, who has been pleased to regulate human affairs in this manner; forasmuch as he is present, and also presides among them, in making laws and in executing equitable judgments. This is clearly taught by Paul, when he enumerates governments (ὁ προϊσταμενος) (*i*) among the gifts of God, which being variously distributed according to the diversity of grace, ought to be employed by the servants of Christ to the edification of the Church. For though in that place he is properly speaking of the council of elders, who were appointed in the primitive Church to preside over the regulation of the public discipline, the same office which in writing to the Corinthians he calls κυβερνησεις, "governments," (*k*) yet, as we see that civil government tends to promote the same object, there is no doubt that he recommends to us every kind of just authority. But he does this in a manner much more explicit, where he enters on a full discussion of that subject. For he says, "There is no power but of God; the powers that be are ordained of God. Rulers are ministers of God, revengers to execute wrath upon him that doeth evil. Do that which is good, and thou shalt have praise of the same." (*l*) This

(*f*) John x. 35.
(*g*) Deut. i. 16, 17. 2 Chron. xix. 6.
(*h*) Prov. viii. 15, 16.
(*i*) Rom. xii. 8.
(*k*) 1 Cor. xii. 28.
(*l*) Rom. xiii. 1, 3, 4.

is corroborated by the examples of holy men; of whom some have been kings, as David, Josiah, Hezekiah; some have been viceroys, as Joseph and Daniel; some have held civil offices in a commonwealth, as Moses, Joshua, and the Judges; whose functions God declared to be approved by him. Wherefore no doubt ought now to be entertained by any person that civil magistracy is a calling not only holy and legitimate, but far the most sacred and honourable in human life.

V. Those who would wish to introduce anarchy, reply, that though, in ancient times, kings and judges presided over a rude people, that servile kind of government is now quite incompatible with the perfection which accompanies the gospel of Christ. Here they betray not only their ignorance, but their diabolical pride, in boasting of perfection, of which not the smallest particle can be discovered in them. But whatever their characters may be, they are easily refuted. For, when David exhorts kings and judges to kiss the Son of God, (*m*) he does not command them to abdicate their authority and retire to private life, but to submit to Christ the power with which they are invested, that he alone may have the preëminence over all. In like manner Isaiah, when he predicts that "kings shall be nursing-fathers and queens nursing-mothers" to the Church, (*n*) does not depose them from their thrones; but rather establishes them by an honourable title, as patrons and protectors of the pious worshippers of God; for that prophecy relates to the advent of Christ. I purposely omit numerous testimonies, which often occur, and especially in the Psalms, in which the rights of all governors are asserted. But the most remarkable of all is that passage where Paul, admonishing Timothy that in the public congregation, "supplications, prayers, intercessions, and giving of thanks, be made for kings and for all that are in authority," assigns as a reason, "that we may lead a quiet and peaceable life in all godliness and honesty;" (*o*) language in which he recommends the state of the Church to their patronage and defence.

VI. This consideration ought continually to occupy the magistrates themselves, since it is calculated to furnish them with a

---

(*m*) Psalm ii. 10—12. (*n*) Isaiah xlix. 23. (*o*) 1 Tim. ii. 1, 2.

powerful stimulus, by which they may be excited to their duty, and to afford them peculiar consolation, by which the difficulties of their office, which certainly are many and arduous, may be alleviated. For what an ardent pursuit of integrity, prudence, clemency, moderation, and innocence ought they to prescribe to themselves, who are conscious of having been constituted ministers of the Divine justice! With what confidence will they admit iniquity to their tribunal, which they understand to be the throne of the living God? With what audacity will they pronounce an unjust sentence with that mouth which they know to be the destined organ of Divine truth? With what conscience will they subscribe to impious decrees with that hand which they know to be appointed to register the edicts of God? In short, if they remember that they are the vicegerents of God, it behoves them to watch with all care, earnestness, and diligence, that in their administration they may exhibit to men an image, as it were, of the providence, care, goodness, benevolence, and justice of God. And they must constantly bear this in mind, that if in all cases "he be cursed that doeth the work of the Lord deceitfully," (*p*) a far heavier curse awaits those who act fraudulently in a righteous calling. Therefore, when Moses and Jehoshaphat wished to exhort their judges to the discharge of their duty, they had nothing to suggest more efficacious than the principle which we have already mentioned. Moses says, "Judge righteously between every man and his brother, and the stranger that is with him. For the judgment is God's." (*q*) Jehoshaphat says, "Take heed what ye do; for ye judge not for man, but for the Lord, who is with you in the judgment. Wherefore now let the fear of the Lord be upon you: take heed and do it; for there is no iniquity with the Lord our God." (*r*) And in another place it is said, "God standeth in the congregation of the mighty: he judgeth among the gods;" (*s*) that they may be animated to their duty, when they understand that they are delegated by God, to whom they must one day render an account of their administration. And this admonition is entitled to have considerable weight with them; for if they fail in their duty, they not only injure men by criminally distressing them, but even

(*p*) Jer. xlviii. 10.
(*q*) Deut. i. 16, 17.
(*r*) 2 Chron. xix. 6, 7.
(*s*) Psalm lxxxii. 1.

offend God by polluting his sacred judgments. On the other hand, it opens a source of peculiar consolation to them to reflect, that they are not employed in profane things, or occupations unsuitable to a servant of God, but in a most sacred function, inasmuch as they execute a Divine commission.

VII. Those who are not restrained by so many testimonies of Scripture, but still dare to stigmatize this sacred ministry as a thing incompatible with religion and Christian piety, do they not offer an insult to God himself, who cannot but be involved in the reproach cast upon his ministry? And in fact they do not reject magistrates, but they reject God, "that he should not reign over them." (*t*) For if this was truly asserted by the Lord respecting the people of Israel, because they refused the government of Samuel, why shall it not now be affirmed with equal truth of those who take the liberty to outrage all the authorities which God has instituted? But they object that our Lord said to his disciples, "The kings of the Gentiles exercise lordship over them, but ye shall not be so; but he that is greatest among you, let him be as the younger; and he that is chief, as he that doth serve:" (*v*) and they contend that these words prohibit the exercise of royalty, or any other authority, by any Christians. Admirable expositors! A contention had arisen among the disciples "which of them should be accounted the greatest." To repress this vain ambition, our Lord taught them that their ministry was not like temporal kingdoms, in which one person has the preëminence over all others. Now, what dishonour does this comparison cast upon regal dignity? What does it prove at all, except that the regal office is not the apostolic ministry? Moreover, though there are various forms of magistracy, yet there is no difference in this respect, but we ought to receive them all as ordinances of God. For Paul comprehends them all together, when he says, that "there is no power but of God;" and that which was furthest from giving general satisfaction, is recommended to us in a remarkable manner beyond all others; namely, the government of one man; which, as it is attended with the common servitude of all, except the single individual to whose will all others are subjected, has never been

(*t*) 1 Sam. viii. 7. (*v*) Luke xxii. 25, 26.

so highly approved by heroic and noble minds. But the Scripture, on the contrary, to correct these unjust sentiments, expressly affirms, that it is by the providence of Divine wisdom that kings reign, and particularly commands us to "honour the king." (*w*)

VIII. And for private men, who have no authority to deliberate on the regulation of any public affairs, it would surely be a vain occupation to dispute which would be the best form of government in the place where they live. Besides, this could not be simply determined, as an abstract question, without great impropriety, since the principle to guide the decision must depend on circumstances. And even if we compare the different forms together, without their circumstances, their advantages are so nearly equal, that it will not be easy to discover of which the utility preponderates. The forms of civil government are considered to be of three kinds: Monarchy, which is the dominion of one person, whether called a king, or a duke, or any other title; Aristocracy, or the dominion of the principal persons of a nation; and Democracy, or popular government, in which the power resides in the people at large. It is true that the transition is easy from monarchy to despotism; it is not much more difficult from aristocracy to oligarchy, or the faction of a few; but it is most easy of all from democracy to sedition. Indeed, if these three forms of government, which are stated by philosophers, be considered in themselves, I shall by no means deny, that either aristocracy, or a mixture of aristocracy and democracy, far excels all others; and that indeed not of itself, but because it very rarely happens that kings regulate themselves so that their will is never at variance with justice and rectitude; or, in the next place, that they are endued with such penetration and prudence, as in all cases to discover what is best. The vice or imperfection of men therefore renders it safer and more tolerable for the government to be in the hands of many, that they may afford each other mutual assistance and admonition, and that if any one arrogate to himself more than is right, the many may act as censors and masters to restrain his ambition. This has always been proved by experience, and the Lord confirmed it by his authority, when he established a government of this kind among the people of

(*w*) Rom. xiii. 1, &c. Prov. viii. 15. 1 Pet. ii. 13, 14, 17.

Israel, with a view to preserve them in the most desirable condition, till he exhibited in David a type of Christ. And as I readily acknowledge that no kind of government is more happy than this, where liberty is regulated with becoming moderation, and properly established on a durable basis, so also I consider those as the most happy people, who are permitted to enjoy such a condition; and if they exert their strenuous and constant efforts for its preservation and retention, I admit that they act in perfect consistence with their duty. And to this object the magistrates likewise ought to apply their greatest diligence, that they suffer not the liberty, of which they are constituted guardians, to be in any respect diminished, much less to be violated: if they are inactive and unconcerned about this, they are perfidious to their office, and traitors to their country. But if those, to whom the will of God has assigned another form of government, transfer this to themselves so as to be tempted to desire a revolution, the very thought will be not only foolish and useless, but altogether criminal. If we limit not our views to one city, but look round and take a comprehensive survey of the whole world, or at least extend our observations to distant lands, we shall certainly find it to be a wise arrangement of Divine Providence that various countries are governed by different forms of civil polity; for they are admirably held together with a certain inequality, as the elements are combined in very unequal proportions. All these remarks, however, will be unnecessary to those who are satisfied with the will of the Lord. For if it be his pleasure to appoint kings over kingdoms, and senators or other magistrates over free cities, it is our duty to be obedient to any governors whom God has established over the places in which we reside.

IX. Here it is necessary to state in a brief manner the nature of the office of magistracy, as described in the word of God, and wherein it consists. If the Scripture did not teach that this office extends to both tables of the law, we might learn it from heathen writers; for not one of them has treated of the office of magistrates, of legislation, and civil government, without beginning with religion and Divine worship. And thus they have all confessed that no government can be happily constituted, unless its first object be the promotion of piety and that all laws are preposterous which neglect the claims of God, and merely provide for the interests of men. Therefore, as religion holds the first place among all the philosophers, and as this has always been regarded by the universal consent of all nations, Christian princes and magistrates ought to be ashamed of their indolence, if they do not make it the object of their most serious care. We have already shown that this duty is particularly enjoined upon them by God; for it is reasonable that they should employ their utmost efforts in asserting and defending the honour of him, whose vicegerents they are, and by whose favour they govern. And the principal commendations given in the Scripture to the good kings are for having restored the worship of God when it had been corrupted or abolished, or for having devoted their attention to religion, that it might flourish in purity and safety under their reigns. On the contrary, the sacred history represents it as one of the evils arising from anarchy, or a want of good government, that when "there was no king in Israel, every man did that which was right in his own eyes." (*x*) These things evince the folly of those who would wish magistrates to neglect all thoughts of God, and to confine themselves entirely to the administration of justice among men; as though God appointed governors in his name to decide secular controversies, and disregarded that which is of far greater importance—the pure worship of himself according to the rule of his law. But a rage for universal innovation, and a desire to escape with impunity, instigate men of turbulent spirits to wish that all the avengers of violated piety were removed out of the world. With respect to the second table, Jeremiah admonishes kings in the following manner: "Execute ye judgment and righteousness, and deliver the spoiled out of the hand of the oppressor; and do no wrong, do no violence to the stranger, the fatherless, nor the widow, neither shed innocent blood." (*y*) To the same purpose is the exhortation in the eighty-second psalm: "Defend the poor and fatherless: do justice to the afflicted and needy: deliver the poor and needy: rid them out of the hand of the wicked." (*z*) And Moses "charged the judges" whom he appointed to supply his place, saying, "Hear the causes between

(*x*) Judges xxi. 25. (*y*) Jer. xxii. 3. (*z*) Psalm lxxxii. 3, 4.

your brethren, and judge righteously between every man and his brother, and the stranger that is with him: ye shall not respect persons in judgment; but ye shall hear the small as well as the great; ye shall not be afraid of the face of man; for the judgment is God's." (*a*) I forbear to remark the directions given by him in another place respecting their future kings: "He shall not multiply horses to himself; neither shall he greatly multiply to himself silver and gold; his heart shall not be lifted up above his brethren; he shall read in the law all the days of his life;" (*b*) also that judges show no partiality, nor take bribes, with similar injunctions, which abound in the Scriptures; because, in describing the office of magistrates in this treatise, my design is not so much to instruct magistrates themselves, as to show to others what magistrates are, and for what end God has appointed them. We see, therefore, that they are constituted the protectors and vindicators of the public innocence, modesty, probity, and tranquillity, whose sole object it ought to be to promote the common peace and security of all. Of these virtues, David declares that he will be an example, when he shall be exalted to the royal throne. "I will set no wicked thing before mine eyes. I will not know a wicked person. Whoso privily slandereth his neighbour, him will I cut off: him that hath a high look and a proud heart will I not suffer. Mine eyes shall be upon the faithful of the land, that they may dwell with me: he that walketh in a perfect way, he shall serve me." (*c*) But as they cannot do this, unless they defend good men from the injuries of the wicked, and aid the oppressed by their relief and protection, they are likewise armed with power for the suppression of crimes, and the severe punishment of malefactors, whose wickedness disturbs the public peace. For experience fully verifies the observation of Solon: "That all states are supported by reward and punishment; and that when these two things are removed, all the discipline of human societies is broken and destroyed." For the minds of many lose their regard for equity and justice, unless virtue be rewarded with due honour; nor can the violence of the wicked be restrained, unless crimes are followed by severe punishments. And these two

(*a*) Deut. i. 16, 17. (*b*) Deut. xvii. 16, 17, 19, 20. (*c*) Psalm ci. 3—6.

parts are included in the injunction of the prophet to kings and other governors, to "execute judgment and righteousness." (*d*) *Righteousness* means the care, patronage, defence, vindication, and liberation of the innocent: *judgment* imports the repression of the audacity, the coercion of the violence, and the punishment of the crimes, of the impious.

X. But here, it seems, arises an important and difficult question. If by the law of God all Christians are forbidden to kill, (*e*) and the prophet predicts respecting the Church, that "they shall not hurt nor destroy in all my holy mountain, saith the Lord," (*f*) how can it be compatible with piety for magistrates to shed blood? But if we understand, that in the infliction of punishments, the magistrate does not act at all from himself, but merely executes the judgments of God, we shall not be embarrassed with his scruple. The law of the Lord commands, "Thou shalt not kill;" but that homicide may not go unpunished, the legislator himself puts the sword into the hands of his ministers, to be used against all homicides. (*g*) *To hurt* and *to destroy* are incompatible with the character of the godly; but to avenge the afflictions of the righteous at the command of God, is neither *to hurt* nor *to destroy*. Therefore it is easy to conclude that in this respect magistrates are not subject to the common law; by which, though the Lord binds the hands of men, he does not bind his own justice, which he exercises by the hands of magistrates. So, when a prince forbids all his subjects to strike or wound any one, he does not prohibit his officers from executing that justice which is particularly committed to them. I sincerely wish that this consideration were constantly in our recollection, that nothing is done here by the temerity of men, but every thing by the authority of God, who commands it, and under whose guidance we never err from the right way. For we can find no valid objection to the infliction of public vengeance, unless the justice of God be restrained from the punishment of crimes. But if it be unlawful for us to impose restraints upon him, why do we calumniate his ministers? Paul says of the magistrate, that "He beareth not the sword in vain; for he is the minister of God, a revenger to execute

(*d*) Jer. xxii. 3. (*e*) Exod. xx. 13.
(*f*) Isaiah xi. 9; lxv. 25. (*g*) Gen. ix. 6. Exod. xxi. 12.

wrath upon him that doeth evil." (*h*) Therefore, if princes and other governors know that nothing will be more acceptable to God than their obedience, and if they desire to approve their piety, justice, and integrity before God, let them devote themselves to this duty. This motive influenced Moses, when, knowing himself to be destined to become the liberator of his people by the power of the Lord, "he slew the Egyptian;" (*i*) and when he punished the idolatry of the people by the slaughter of three thousand men in one day. (*k*) The same motive actuated David, when, at the close of his life, he commanded his son Solomon to put to death Joab and Shimei. (*l*) Hence, also, it is enumerated among the virtues of a king, to "destroy all the wicked of the land, that he may cut off all wicked doers from the city of the Lord." (*m*) The same topic furnishes the eulogium given to Solomon: "Thou lovest righteousness, and hatest wickedness." (*n*) How did the meek and placid disposition of Moses burn with such cruelty, that, after having his hands imbrued in the blood of his brethren, he continued to go through the camp till three thousand were slain? How did David, who discovered such humanity all his lifetime, in his last moments bequeath such a cruel injunction to his son respecting Joab? "Let not his hoar head go down to the grave in peace;" and respecting Shimei: "His hoar head bring down to the grave with blood." Both Moses and David, in executing the vengeance committed to them by God, by this severity sanctified their hands, which would have been defiled by lenity. Solomon says, "It is an abomination to kings to commit wickedness; for the throne is established by righteousness." (*o*) Again: "A king that sitteth in the throne of judgment, scattereth away all evil with his eyes." (*p*) Again: "A wise king scattereth the wicked, and bringeth the wheel over them." (*q*) Again: "Take away the dross from the silver, and there shall come forth a vessel for the finer. Take away the wicked from before the king, and his throne shall be established in righteousness." (*r*) Again: "He that justifieth the wicked, and

(*h*) Rom. xiii. 4. (*i*) Exod. ii. 12. (*k*) Exod. xxxii. 26—28.
(*l*) 1 Kings ii. 5—9. (*m*) Psalm ci. 8. (*n*) Psalm xlv. 7
(*o*) Prov. xvi. 12. (*p*) Prov. xx. 8.
(*q*) Prov. xx. 26. (*r*) Prov. xxv. 4, 5.

he that condemneth the just, even they both are an abomination to the Lord." (*s*) Again: "An evil man seeketh only rebellion; therefore a cruel messenger shall be sent against him." (*t*) Again: "He that saith unto the wicked, Thou art righteous; him shall the people curse, nations shall abhor him." (*u*) Now, if it be true justice for them to pursue the wicked with a drawn sword, let them sheathe the sword, and keep their hands from shedding blood, while the swords of desperadoes are drenched in murders; and they will be so far from acquiring the praise of goodness and justice by this forbearance, that they will involve themselves in the deepest impiety. There ought not, however, to be any excessive or unreasonable severity, nor ought any cause to be given for considering the tribunal as a gibbet prepared for all who are accused. For I am not an advocate for unnecessary cruelty, nor can I conceive the possibility of an equitable sentence being pronounced without mercy; of which Solomon affirms, that "mercy and truth preserve the king; and his throne is upholden by mercy." (*v*) Yet it behoves the magistrate to be on his guard against both these errors; that he do not, by excessive severity, wound rather than heal; or, through a superstitious affectation of clemency, fall into a mistaken humanity, which is the worst kind of cruelty, by indulging a weak and ill-judged lenity, to the detriment of multitudes. For it is a remark not without foundation, that was anciently applied to the government of Nerva, that it is bad to live under a prince who permits nothing, but much worse to live under one who permits every thing.

XI. Now, as it is sometimes necessary for kings and nations to take up arms for the infliction of such public vengeance, the same reason will lead us to infer the lawfulness of wars which are undertaken for this end. For if they have been intrusted with power to preserve the tranquillity of their own territories, to suppress the seditious tumults of disturbers, to succour the victims of oppression, and to punish crimes,—can they exert this power for a better purpose, than to repel the violence of him who disturbs both the private repose of individuals and the general tranquillity of the nation; who excites insurrections, and perpe-

(*s*) Prov. xvii. 15. (*t*) Prov. xvii. 11.
(*u*) Prov. xxiv. 24. (*v*) Prov. xx. 28.

trates acts of oppression, cruelty and every species of crime? If they ought to be the guardians and defenders of the laws, it is incumbent upon them to defeat the efforts of all by whose injustice the discipline of the laws is corrupted. And if they justly punish those robbers, whose injuries have only extended to a few persons, shall they suffer a whole district to be plundered and devastated with impunity? For there is no difference, whether he, who in a hostile manner invades, disturbs, and plunders the territory of another to which he has no right, be a king, or one of the meanest of mankind: all persons of this description are equally to be considered as robbers, and ought to be punished as such. It is the dictate both of natural equity, and of the nature of the office, therefore, that princes are armed, not only to restrain the crimes of private individuals by judicial punishments, but also to defend the territories committed to their charge by going to war against any hostile aggression; and the Holy Spirit, in many passages of Scripture, declares such wars to be lawful.

XII. If it be objected that the New Testament contains no precept or example, which proves war to be lawful to Christians, I answer, first, that the reason for waging war which existed in ancient times, is equally valid in the present age; and that, on the contrary, there is no cause to prevent princes from defending their subjects. Secondly, that no express declaration on this subject is to be expected in the writings of the apostles, whose design was, not to organize civil governments, but to describe the spiritual kingdom of Christ. Lastly, that in those very writings it is implied by the way, that no change has been made in this respect by the coming of Christ. "For," to use the words of Augustine, "if Christian discipline condemned all wars, the soldiers who inquired respecting their salvation ought rather to have been directed to cast away their arms, and entirely to renounce the military profession; whereas the advice given them was, 'Do violence to no man, neither accuse any falsely; and be content with your wages.' (*w*) An injunction to be content with their wages was certainly not a prohibition of the military life." But here all magistrates ought to be very cautious, that they

(*w*) Luke iii. 14.

follow not in any respect the impulse of their passions. On the contrary, if punishments are to be inflicted, they ought not to be precipitated with anger, exasperated with hatred, or inflamed with implacable severity: they ought, as Augustine says, "to commiserate our common nature even in him whom they punish for his crime." Or, if arms are to be resorted to against an enemy, that is, an armed robber, they ought not to seize a trivial occasion, nor even to take it when presented, unless they are driven to it by extreme necessity. For, if it be our duty to exceed what was required by that heathen writer who maintained that the evident object of war ought to be the restoration of peace, certainly we ought to make every other attempt before we have recourse to the decision of arms. In short, in both cases they must not suffer themselves to be carried away by any private motive, but be wholly guided by public spirit; otherwise they grossly abuse their power, which is given them, not for their own particular advantage, but for the benefit and service of others. Moreover, on this right of war depends the lawfulness of garrisons, alliances, and other civil munitions. By *garrisons,* I mean soldiers who are stationed in towns to defend the boundaries of a country. By *alliances,* I mean confederations which are made between neighbouring princes, that, if any disturbance arise in their territories, they will render each other mutual assistance, and will unite their forces together for the common resistance of the common enemies of mankind. By *civil munitions,* I mean all the provisions which are employed in the art of war.

XIII. In the last place, I think it necessary to add, that tributes and taxes are the legitimate revenues of princes; which, indeed, they ought principally to employ in sustaining the public expenses of their office, but which they may likewise use for the support of their domestic splendour, which is closely connected with the dignity of the government that they hold. Thus we see that David, Jehoshaphat, Hezekiah, Josiah, and other pious kings, and likewise Joseph and Daniel, without any violation of piety, on account of the office which they filled, lived at the public expense; and we read in Ezekiel of a very ample portion of land being assigned to the kings; (*x*) in which passage, though the prophet is describ-

(*x*) Ezek. xlviii. 21, 22.

ing the spiritual kingdom of Christ, yet he borrows the model of it from the legitimate kingdoms of men. On the other hand, princes themselves ought to remember, that their finances are not so much private incomes, as the revenues of the whole people, according to the testimony of Paul, (y) and therefore cannot be lavished or dilapidated without manifest injustice; or, rather, that they are to be considered as the blood of the people, not to spare which is the most inhuman cruelty; and their various imposts and tributes ought to be regarded merely as aids of the public necessity, to burden the people with which, without cause, would be tyrannical rapacity. These things give no encouragement to princes to indulge profusion and luxury; and certainly there is no need to add fuel to their passions, which of themselves are more than sufficiently inflamed; but, as it is of very great importance, that whatever they undertake they attempt it with a pure conscience before God, it is necessary, in order to their avoiding vain confidence and contempt of God, that they be taught how far their rights extend. Nor is this doctrine useless to private persons, who learn from it not to pronounce rash and insolent censures on the expenses of princes, notwithstanding they exceed the limits of common life.

XIV. From the magistracy, we next proceed to the laws, which are the strong nerves of civil polity, or, according to an appellation which Cicero has borrowed from Plato, the *souls of states*, without which magistracy cannot subsist, as, on the other hand, without magistrates laws are of no force. No observation, therefore, can be more correct than this, that the law is a silent magistrate, and a magistrate a speaking law. Though I have promised to show by what laws a Christian state ought to be regulated, it will not be reasonable for any person to expect a long discussion respecting the best kind of laws; which is a subject of immense extent, and foreign from our present object. I will briefly remark, however, by the way, what laws it may piously use before God, and be rightly governed by among men. And even this I would have preferred passing over in silence, if I did not know that it is a point on which many persons run into dangerous errors. For some deny that a state is well constituted,

(y) Rom. xiii. 6.

which neglects the polity of Moses, and is governed by the common laws of nations. The dangerous and seditious nature of this opinion I leave to the examination of others; it will be sufficient for me to have evinced it to be false and foolish. Now, it is necessary to observe that common distinction, which distributes all the laws of God promulgated by Moses into moral, ceremonial, and judicial; and these different kinds of laws are to be distinctly examined, that we may ascertain what belongs to us, and what does not. Nor let any one be embarrassed by this scruple, that even the ceremonial and judicial precepts are included in the moral. For the ancients, who first made this distinction, were not ignorant that these two kinds of precepts related to the conduct of moral agents; yet, as they might be changed and abrogated without affecting the morality of actions, therefore they did not call them moral precepts. They particularly applied this appellation to those precepts without which there can be no real purity of morals, nor any permanent rule of a holy life.

XV. The moral law, therefore, with which I shall begin, being comprised in two leading articles, of which one simply commands us to worship God with pure faith and piety, and the other enjoins us to embrace men with sincere love,—this law, I say, is the true and eternal rule of righteousness, prescribed to men of all ages and nations, who wish to conform their lives to the will of God. For this is his eternal and immutable will, that he himself be worshipped by us all, and that we mutually love one another. The ceremonial law was the pupilage of the Jews, with which it pleased the Lord to exercise that people during a state resembling childhood, till that "fulness of the time" should come, (*z*) when he would fully manifest his wisdom to the world, and would exhibit the reality of those things which were then adumbrated in figures. The judicial law, given to them as a political constitution, taught them certain rules of equity and justice, by which they might conduct themselves in a harmless and peaceable manner towards each other. And as that exercise of ceremonies properly related to the doctrine of piety, inasmuch

---

(*z*) Gal. iii. 24; iv. 4.

as it kept the Jewish Church in the worship and service of God, which is the first article of the moral law, and yet was distinct from piety itself, so these judicial regulations, though they had no other end than the preservation of that love, which is enjoined in the eternal law of God, yet had something which distinguished them from that precept itself. As the ceremonies, therefore, might be abrogated without any violation or injury of piety, so the precepts and duties of love remain of perpetual obligation, notwithstanding the abolition of all these judicial ordinances. If this be true, certainly all nations are left at liberty to enact such laws as they shall find to be respectively expedient for them; provided they be framed according to that perpetual rule of love, so that, though they vary in form, they may have the same end. For those barbarous and savage laws which rewarded theft and permitted promiscuous concubinage, with others still more vile, execrable, and absurd, I am very far from thinking ought to be considered as laws; since they are not only violations of all righteousness, but outrages against humanity itself.

XVI. What I have said will be more clearly understood, if in all laws we properly consider these two things—the constitution of the law and its equity, on the reason of which the constitution itself is founded and rests. Equity, being natural, is the same to all mankind; and consequently all laws, on every subject, ought to have the same equity for their end. Particular enactments and regulations, being connected with circumstances, and partly dependent upon them, may be different in different cases without any impropriety, provided they are all equally directed to the same object of equity. Now, as it is certain that the law of God, which we call the moral law, is no other than a declaration of natural law, and of that conscience which has been engraven by God on the minds of men, the whole rule of this equity, of which we now speak, is prescribed in it. This equity, therefore, must alone be the scope, and rule, and end, of all laws. Whatever laws shall be framed according to that rule, directed to that object, and limited to that end, there is no reason why we should censure them, however they may differ from the Jewish law or from each other. The law of God forbids theft. What punishment was enacted for thieves, among the Jews, may be seen in the book of Exodus. (*a*) The most ancient laws of other nations punished theft by requiring a compensation of double the value. Subsequent laws made a distinction between open and secret theft. Some proceeded to banishment, some to flagellation, and some to the punishment of death. False witness was punished, among the Jews, with the same punishment as such testimony would have caused to be inflicted on the person against whom it was given; (*b*) in some countries it was punished with infamy, in others with hanging, in others with crucifixion. All laws agree in punishing murder with death, though in several different forms. The punishments of adulterers in different countries have been attended with different degrees of severity. Yet we see how, amidst this diversity, they are all directed to the same end. For they all agree in denouncing punishment against those crimes which are condemned by the eternal law of God; such as murders, thefts, adulteries, false testimonies, though there is not a uniformity in the mode of punishment; and, indeed, this is neither necessary, nor even expedient. One country, if it did not inflict the most exemplary vengeance upon murderers, would soon be ruined by murders and robberies. One age requires the severity of punishments to be increased. If a country be disturbed by any civil commotion, the evils which generally arise from it must be corrected by new edicts. In time of war all humanity would be forgotten amidst the din of arms, if men were not awed by more than a common dread of punishment. During famine and pestilence, unless greater severity be employed, every thing will fall into ruin. One nation is more prone than others to some particular vice, unless it be most rigidly restrained. What malignity and envy against the public good will be betrayed by him who shall take offence at such diversity, which is best adapted to secure the observance of the law of God? For the objection made by some, that it is an insult to the law of God given by Moses, when it is abrogated, and other laws are preferred to it, is without any foundation; for neither are other laws preferred to it, when they are more approved, not on a simple comparison,

(*a*) Exod. xxii. 1, &c. (*b*) Deut. xix. 18, 19.

but on account of the circumstances of time, place, and nation; nor do we abrogate that which was never given to us. For the Lord gave not that law by the hand of Moses to be promulgated among all nations, and to be universally binding; but after having taken the Jewish nation into his special charge, patronage, and protection, he was pleased to become, in a peculiar manner, their legislator, and, as became a wise legislator, in all the laws which he gave them, he had a special regard to their peculiar circumstances.

XVII. It now remains for us, as we proposed, in the last place, to examine what advantage the common society of Christians derives from laws, judgments, and magistrates; with which is connected another question—what honour private persons ought to render to magistrates, and how far their obedience ought to extend. Many persons suppose the office of magistracy to be of no use among Christians, for that they cannot, consistently with piety, apply for their assistance, because they are forbidden to have recourse to revenge or litigation. But as Paul, on the contrary, clearly testifies that the magistrate is "the minister of God to us for good," (*c*) we understand from this that he is divinely appointed, in order that we may be defended by his power and protection against the malice and injuries of wicked men, and may lead peaceable and secure lives. But if it be in vain that he is given to us by the Lord for our protection, unless it be lawful for us to avail ourselves of such an advantage, it clearly follows that we may appeal to him, and apply for his aid, without any violation of piety. But here I have to do with two sorts of persons; for there are multitudes inflamed with such a rage for litigation, that they never have peace in themselves, unless they are in contention with others; and they commence their lawsuits with a mortal bitterness of animosities, and with an infuriated cupidity of revenge and injury, and pursue them with an implacable obstinacy, even to the ruin of their adversary. At the same time, that they may not be thought to do any thing wrong, they defend his perverseness under the pretext of seeking justice. But, though it is allowable for a man to endeavour to obtain justice from his

(*c*) Rom. xiii. 4.

neighbour by a judicial process, he is not therefore at liberty to hate him, or to cherish a desire to hurt him, or to persecute him without mercy.

XVIII. Let such persons, therefore, understand, that judicial processes are lawful to those who use them rightly; and that the right use, both for the plaintiff and for the defendant, is this: First, if the plaintiff, being injured either in his person or in his property, has recourse to the protection of the magistrate, states his complaint, makes a just and equitable claim, but without any desire of injury or revenge, without any asperity or hatred, without any ardour for contention, but rather prepared to waive his right, and to sustain some disadvantage, than to cherish enmity against his adversary. Secondly, if the defendant, being summoned, appears on the day appointed, and defends his cause by the best arguments in his power, without any bitterness, but with the simple desire of maintaining his just right. On the contrary, when their minds are filled with malevolence, corrupted with envy, incensed with wrath, stimulated with revenge, or inflamed with the fervour of contention, so as to diminish their charity, all the proceedings of the justest cause are inevitably wicked. For it ought to be an established maxim with all Christians, that however just a cause may be, no lawsuit can ever be carried on in a proper manner by any man, who does not feel as much benevolence and affection towards his adversary, as if the business in dispute had already been settled and terminated by an amicable adjustment. Some, perhaps, will object, that such moderation in lawsuits is far from being ever practised, and that if one instance of it were to be found, it would be regarded as a prodigy. I confess, indeed, that, in the corruption of these times, the example of an upright litigator is very rare; but the thing itself ceases not to be good and pure, if it be not defiled by an adventitious evil. But when we hear that the assistance of the magistrate is a holy gift of God, it behoves us to use the more assiduous caution that it be not contaminated by our guilt.

XIX. Those who positively condemn all controversies at law, ought to understand that they thereby reject a holy ordinance of God, and a gift of the number of those which may be "pure to the pure;" unless they mean to charge Paul with a crime, who repelled the calumnies of his accusers, exposing their subtlety and malice; who, before his judges, asserted his right to the privileges of a Roman citizen; and who, when he found it necessary, appealed from an unjust governor to the tribunal of Cæsar. It is no objection to this that all Christians are forbidden the desire of revenge, which we also wish to banish to the greatest distance from all Christian judicatures. For, in a civil cause, no man proceeds in the right way, who does not, with innocent simplicity, commit his cause to the judge as to a public guardian, without the least thought of a mutual retaliation of evil, which is the passion of revenge. And in any more important or criminal action we require the accuser to be one who goes into the court, influenced by no desire of revenge, affected by no resentment of private injury, and having no other motive than to resist the attempts of a mischievous man, that he may not injure the public. But if a vindictive spirit be excluded, no offence is committed against that precept by which revenge is forbidden to Christians. It may probably be objected, that they are not only forbidden to desire revenge, but are also commanded to wait for the hand of the Lord, who promises that he will assist and revenge the afflicted and oppressed, and therefore that those who seek the interference of the magistrate on behalf of themselves or others, anticipate all that vengeance of the celestial protector. But this is very far from the truth. For the vengeance of the magistrate is to be considered, not as the vengeance of man, but of God, which, according to the testimony of Paul, he exercises by the ministry of men for our good.

XX. Nor do we any more oppose the prohibition and injunction of Christ, "Resist not evil; but whosoever shall smite thee on thy right cheek, turn to him the other also; and if any man will sue thee at the law, and take away thy coat, let him have thy cloak also." (*d*) In this passage, indeed, he requires the minds of his servants to be so far from cherishing a desire of retaliation, as rather to suffer the repetition of an injury against themselves than to wish to revenge it; nor do we dissuade them from this patience. For it truly behoves Christians to be a people, as it

(*d*) Matt. v. 39, 40.

were, formed to bear injuries and reproaches, exposed to the iniquity, impostures, and ridicule of the worst of mankind; and not only so, but they ought to be patient under all these evils; that is to say, so calm and composed in their minds, that, after having suffered one affliction, they may prepare themselves for another, expecting nothing all their lifetime but to bear a perpetual cross. At the same time, they are required to bless and pray for them from whom they receive curses, to do good to them from whom they experience injuries, (*e*) and to aim at that which constitutes their only victory, to "overcome evil with good." (*f*) With this disposition they will not demand "an eye for an eye, and a tooth for a tooth," as the Pharisees taught their disciples to desire revenge; but, as we are instructed by Christ, they will suffer injuries in their persons and property in such a manner as to be ready to forgive them as soon as they are committed. (*g*) Yet this equanimity and moderation will be no obstacle, but that, without any breach of friendship towards their enemies, they may avail themselves of the assistance of the magistrate for the preservation of their property; or, from zeal for the public good, may bring a pestilent offender to justice, though they know he can only be punished with death. For it is very correctly explained by Augustine, that the end of all these precepts is, "that a just and pious man should be ready to bear with patience the wickedness of those whom he desires to become good; rather in order that the number of the good may increase, not that with similar wickedness he may himself join the number of the evil; and in the next place, that they relate to the internal affection of the heart more than to the external actions; in order that in the secrecy of our minds we may feel patience and benevolence, but in our outward conduct may do that which we see tends to the advantage of those to whom we ought to feel benevolent affections."

XXI. The objection which is frequently alleged, that lawsuits are universally condemned by Paul, has no foundation in truth. (*h*) It may be easily understood from his words, that in the Church of the Corinthians there was an immoderate rage for liti-

(*e*) Matt. v. 44.
(*f*) Rom. xii. 21.
(*g*) Matt. v. 38—40.
(*h*) 1 Cor. vi. 1—8.

gation, so that they exposed the gospel of Christ, and all the religion which they professed, to the cavils and reproaches of the impious. The first thing which Paul reprehended in them was, that the intemperance of their dissensions brought the gospel into discredit among unbelievers. And the next thing was, that they had such altercations among them, brethren with brethren; for they were so far from bearing an injury, that they coveted each other's property, and molested and injured one another without any provocation. It was against that rage for litigation, therefore, that he inveighed, and not absolutely against all controversies. But he pronounces it to be altogether a vice or a weakness, that they did not suffer the injury or loss of their property rather than to proceed to contentions for the preservation of it: when they were so disturbed or exasperated at every loss or injury, that they had recourse to lawsuits on the most trivial occasions, he argues that this proved their minds to be too irritable, and not sufficiently patient. It is certainly incumbent on Christians, in all cases, to prefer a concession of their right to an entrance on a lawsuit; from which they can scarcely come out without a mind exasperated and inflamed with enmity to their brother. But when one sees that, without any breach of charity, he may defend his property, the loss of which would be a serious injury to him; if he do it, he commits no offence against that sentence of Paul. In a word, as we have observed at the beginning, charity will give every one the best counsel; for, whatever litigations are undertaken without charity, or are carried to a degree inconsistent with it, we conclude them, beyond all controversy, to be unjust and wicked.

XXII. The first duty of subjects towards their magistrates is to entertain the most honourable sentiments of their function, which they know to be a jurisdiction delegated to them from God, and on that account to esteem and reverence them as God's ministers and vicegerents. For there are some persons to be found, who show themselves very obedient to their magistrates, and have not the least wish that there were no magistrates for them to obey, because they know them to be so necessary to the public good; but who, nevertheless, consider the magistrates themselves as no other than necessary evils. But something more than this is required of us by Peter, when he commands us to "honour the king;" (*i*) and by Solomon, when he says, "Fear thou the Lord and the king;" (*k*) for Peter, under the term *honour,* comprehends a sincere and candid esteem; and Solomon, by connecting the king with the Lord, attributes to him a kind of sacred veneration and dignity. It is also a remarkable commendation of magistrates which is given by Paul, when he says, that we "must needs be subject, not only for wrath, but also for conscience sake;" (*l*) by which he means, that subjects ought to be induced to submit to princes and governors, not merely from a dread of their power, as persons are accustomed to yield to an armed enemy, who they know will immediately take vengeance upon them if they resist; but because the obedience which is rendered to princes and magistrates is rendered to God, from whom they have received their authority. I am not speaking of the persons, as if the mask of dignity ought to palliate or excuse folly, ignorance, or cruelty, and conduct the most nefarious and flagitious, and so to acquire for vices the praise due to virtues; but I affirm that the station itself is worthy of honour and reverence; so that, whoever our governors are, they ought to possess our esteem and veneration on account of the office which they fill.

XXIII. Hence follows another duty, that, with minds disposed to honour and reverence magistrates, subjects approve their obedience to them, in submitting to their edicts, in paying taxes, in discharging public duties, and bearing burdens which relate to the common defence, and in fulfilling all their other commands. Paul says to the Romans, "Let every soul be subject unto the higher powers. Whosoever resisteth the power, resisteth the ordinance of God." (*m*) He writes to Titus, "Put them in mind to be subject to principalities and powers, to obey magistrates, to be ready to every good work." (*n*) Peter exhorts, "Submit yourselves to every ordinance of man for the Lord's sake; whether it be to the king, as supreme; or unto governors, as unto them that are sent by him for the punishment of evil-doers, and for the praise of them that do well." (*o*) Moreover, that subjects may testify that theirs is not a hypocritical but a sincere and cordial submission, Paul teaches, that they ought to pray to God for the safety and pros-

(*i*) 1 Peter ii. 17. (*k*) Prov. xxiv. 21. (*l*) Rom. xiii. 5.
(*m*) Rom. xiii. 1, 2. (*n*) Titus iii. 1. (*o*) 1 Peter ii. 13, 14.

perity of those under whose government they live. "I exhort," he says, "that supplications, prayers, intercessions, and giving of thanks, be made for all men; for kings, and for all that are in authority; that we may lead a quiet and peaceable life in all godliness and honesty." (*p*) Here let no man deceive himself. For as it is impossible to resist the magistrate without, at the same time, resisting God himself; though an unarmed magistrate may seem to be despised with impunity, yet God is armed to inflict exemplary vengeance on the contempt offered to himself. Under this obedience I also include the moderation which private persons ought to prescribe to themselves in relation to public affairs, that they do not, without being called upon, intermeddle with affairs of state, or rashly intrude themselves into the office of magistrates, or undertake any thing of a public nature. If there be any thing in the public administration which requires to be corrected, let them not raise any tumults, or take the business into their own hands, which ought to be all bound in this respect, but let them refer it to the cognizance of the magistrate, who is alone authorized to regulate the concerns of the public. I mean, that they ought to attempt nothing without being commanded; for when they have the command of a governor, then they also are invested with public authority. For, as we are accustomed to call the counsellors of a prince *his eyes and ears,* so they may not unaptly be called *his hands* whom he has commissioned to execute his commands.

XXIV. Now, as we have hitherto described a magistrate who truly answers to his title; who is the father of his country, and, as the poet calls him, the pastor of his people, the guardian of peace, the protector of justice, the avenger of innocence; he would justly be deemed insane who disapproved of such a government. But, as it has happened, in almost all ages, that some princes, regardless of every thing to which they ought to have directed their attention and provision, give themselves up to their pleasures in indolent exemption from every care; others, absorbed in their own interest, expose to sale all laws, privileges, rights, and judgments; others plunder the public of wealth, which they afterwards lavish in mad prodigality; others commit flagrant outrages, pillaging

(*p*) 1 Tim. ii. 1, 2.

houses, violating virgins and matrons, and murdering infants; many persons cannot be persuaded that such ought to be acknowledged as princes, whom, as far as possible, they ought to obey. For in such enormities, and actions so completely incompatible, not only with the office of a magistrate, but with the duty of every man, they discover no appearance of the image of God, which ought to be conspicuous in a magistrate; while they perceive no vestige of that minister of God who is "not a terror to good works, but to the evil," who is sent "for the punishment of evil-doers, and for the praise of them that do well;" nor recognize that governor, whose dignity and authority the Scripture recommends to us. And certainly the minds of men have always been naturally disposed to hate and execrate tyrants as much as to love and reverence legitimate kings.

XXV. But, if we direct our attention to the word of God, it will carry us much further; even to submit to the government, not only of those princes who discharge their duty to us with becoming integrity and fidelity, but of all who possess the sovereignty, even though they perform none of the duties of their function. For, though the Lord testifies that the magistrate is an eminent gift of his liberality to preserve the safety of men, and prescribes to magistrates themselves the extent of their duty, yet he at the same time declares, that whatever be their characters, they have their government only from him; that those who govern for the public good are true specimens and mirrors of his beneficence; and that those who rule in an unjust and tyrannical manner are raised up by him to punish the iniquity of the people; that all equally possess that sacred majesty with which he has invested legitimate authority. I will not proceed any further till I have subjoined a few testimonies in proof of this point. It is unnecessary, however, to labour much to evince an impious king to be a judgment of God's wrath upon the world, as I have no expectation that any one will deny it: and in this we say no more of a king than of any other robber who plunders our property; or adulterer who violates our bed; or assassin who attempts to murder us; since the Scripture enumerates all these calamities among the curses inflicted by God. But let us rather insist on the proof of that which the minds of men do not so easily admit; that a man of the worst character, and most undeserving of all honour, who holds the sovereign power, really possesses that eminent and Divine authority, which the Lord has given by his word to the ministers of his justice and judgment; and, therefore, that he ought to be regarded by his subjects, as far as pertains to public obedience, with the same reverence and esteem which they would show to the best of kings, if such a one were granted to them.

XXVI. In the first place, I request my readers to observe and consider with attention, what is so frequently and justly mentioned in the Scriptures,—the providence and peculiar dispensation of God in distributing kingdoms and appointing whom he pleases to be kings. Daniel says, "God changeth the times and the seasons: he removeth kings and setteth up kings." (*q*) Again: "That the living may know that the Most High ruleth in the kingdom of men, and giveth it to whomsoever he will." (*r*) Passages of this kind abound throughout the Scriptures, but particularly in this prophecy. Now, the character of Nebuchadnezzar, who conquered Jerusalem, is sufficiently known, that he was an invader and depopulator of the territories of others. Yet by the mouth of Ezekiel the Lord declares that he had given him the land of Egypt, as a reward for the service which he had performed in devastating Tyre. (*s*) And Daniel said to him, "Thou, O king, art a king of kings; for the God of heaven hath given thee a kingdom, power, and strength, and glory; and wheresoever the children of men dwell, the beasts of the field, and the fowls of the heaven, hath he given into thine hand, and hath made thee ruler over all." (*t*) Again: to his grandson Belshazzar Daniel said, "The most high God gave Nebuchadnezzar thy father a kingdom, and majesty, and glory, and honour; and for the majesty that he gave him, all people, nations, and languages, trembled and feared before him." (*v*) When we hear that Nebuchadnezzar was placed on the throne by God, let us, at the same time, call to mind the celestial edicts which command us to fear and honour the king; and we shall not hesitate to regard the most iniquitous tyrant with the honour due to the station in which the Lord has deigned to place him. When Samuel denounced to the children of Israel what

(*q*) Dan. ii. 21. (*r*) Dan. iv. 17. (*s*) Ezek. xxix. 18—20.
(*t*) Dan. ii. 37, 38. (*v*) Dan. v. 18, 19.

treatment they would receive from their kings, he said, "This will be the manner* of the king that shall reign over you; he will take your sons and appoint them for himself, for his chariots, and to be his horsemen, and to ear his ground, and to reap his harvest, and to make his instruments of war. And he will take your daughters to be confectionaries, and to be cooks, and to be bakers. And he will take your fields, and your vineyards, and your oliveyards, even the best of them, and give them to his servants. And he will take the tenth of your seed, and of your vineyards, and give to his officers and to his servants. And he will take your men-servants, and your maid-servants, and your goodliest young men, and your asses, and put them to his work. He will take the tenth of your sheep; and ye shall be his servants." (*w*) Certainly the kings would not do all this by "right," for they were excellently instructed by the law to observe all moderation; but it was called a "right" with respect to the people who were bound to obey, and were not at liberty to resist it. It was just as if Samuel had said, The cupidity of your kings will proceed to all these outrages, which it will not be your province to restrain; nothing will remain for you, but to receive their commands and to obey them.

XXVII. But the most remarkable and memorable passage of all is in the Prophecy of Jeremiah, which, though it is rather long, I shall readily quote, because it most clearly decides the whole question: "I have made the earth, the man and the beast that are upon the ground, by my great power and by my outstretched arm, and have given it unto whom it seemed meet unto me. And now I have given all these lands into the hand of Nebuchadnezzar, the king of Babylon, my servant. And all nations shall serve him, and his son, and his son's son, until the very time of his land come. And it shall come to pass, that the nation and kingdom which will not serve the same king of Babylon, that nation will I punish with the sword, and with the famine, and with the pestilence. Therefore serve the king of Babylon and live." (*x*) We see what great obedience and honour the Lord required to be rendered to that pestilent and cruel tyrant, for no other reason than because he possessed the kingdom; and it was by the heavenly decree that he was seated

---

* In the Latin translation, it is *jus*, right.

(*w*) 1 Sam. viii. 11—17.

(*x*) Jer. xxvii. 5—9, 12.

on the throne of the kingdom, and exalted to that regal majesty, which it was not lawful to violate. If we have this constantly present to our eyes and impressed upon our hearts, that the most iniquitous kings are placed on their thrones by the same decree by which the authority of all kings is established, those seditious thoughts will never enter our minds, that a king is to be treated according to his merits, and that it is not reasonable for us to be subject to a king who does not on his part perform towards us those duties which his office requires.

XXVIII. In vain will any one object that this was a special command given to the Israelites. For we must observe the reason upon which the Lord founds it. He says, "I have given these lands to Nebuchadnezzar; therefore serve him and live." To whomsoever, therefore, a kingdom shall evidently be given, we have no room to doubt that subjection is due to him. And as soon as he exalts any person to royal dignity, he gives us a declaration of his pleasure that he shall reign. The Scripture contains general testimonies on this subject. Solomon says, "For the transgression of a land, many are the princes thereof." (*y*) Job says, "He looseth the bonds of kings," or divests them of their power; "and girdeth their loins with a girdle," (*z*) or restores them to their former dignity. This being admitted, nothing remains for us but to serve and live. The prophet Jeremiah likewise records another command of the Lord to his people: "Seek the peace of the city whither I have caused you to be carried away captives, and pray unto the Lord for it; for in the peace of it ye shall have peace." (*a*) Here, we see, the Israelites, after having been stripped of all their property, torn from their habitations, driven into exile, and forced into a miserable servitude, were commanded to pray for the prosperity of their conqueror; not in the same manner in which we are all commanded to pray for our persecutors; but that his kingdom might be preserved in safety and tranquillity, and that they might live in prosperity under him. Thus David, after having been already designated as king by the ordination of God, and anointed with his holy oil, though he was unjustly persecuted by Saul, without having given him any cause of offence,

---

(*y*) Prov. xxviii. 2. (*z*) Job. xii. 18. (*a*) Jer. xxix. 7.

nevertheless accounted the person of his pursuer sacred, because the Lord had consecrated it by the royal dignity. "And he said, The Lord forbid that I should do this thing unto my master, the Lord's anointed, to stretch forth mine hand against him, seeing he is the anointed of the Lord." Again: "Mine eye spared thee; and I said, I will not put forth mine hand against my lord; for he is the Lord's anointed." (*b*) Again: "Who can stretch forth his hand against the Lord's anointed, and be guiltless? As the Lord liveth, the Lord shall smite him; or his day shall come to die, or he shall descend into battle, and perish. The Lord forbid that I should stretch forth mine hand against the Lord's anointed." (*c*)

XXIX. Finally, we owe these sentiments of affection and reverence to all our rulers, whatever their characters may be; which I the more frequently repeat, that we may learn not to scrutinize the persons themselves, but may be satisfied with knowing that they are invested by the will of the Lord with that function, upon which he has impressed an inviolable majesty. But it will be said, that rulers owe mutual duties to their subjects. That I have already confessed. But he who infers from this that obedience ought to be rendered to none but just rulers, is a very bad reasoner. For husbands owe mutual duties to their wives, and parents to their children. Now, if husbands and parents violate their obligations; if parents conduct themselves with discouraging severity and fastidious moroseness towards their children, whom they are forbidden to provoke to wrath; (*d*) if husbands despise and vex their wives, whom they are commanded to love and to spare as the weaker vessels; (*e*) does it follow that children should be less obedient to their parents, or wives to their husbands? They are still subject, even to those who are wicked and unkind. As it is incumbent on all, not to inquire into the duties of one another, but to confine their attention respectively to their own, this consideration ought particularly to be regarded by those who are subject to the authority of others. Wherefore, if we are inhumanly harassed by a cruel prince; if we are rapaciously plundered by an avaricious or luxurious one; if we are neglected by an indolent one; or if we are persecuted, on account of piety, by an impious

(*b*) 1 Sam. xxiv. 6, 11. (*c*) 1 Sam. xxvi. 9—11.
(*d*) Ephes. vi. 1. Col. iii. 21. (*e*) Ephes. v. 25. 1 Pet. iii. 7.

and sacrilegious one,—let us first call to mind our transgressions against God, which he undoubtedly chastises by these scourges. Thus our impatience will be restrained by humility. Let us, in the next place, consider that it is not our province to remedy these evils, and that nothing remains for us, but to implore the aid of the Lord, in whose hand are the hearts of kings and the revolutions of kingdoms. It is "God" who "standeth in the congregation of the mighty," and "judgeth among the gods;" (*f*) whose presence shall confound and crush all kings and judges of the earth who shall not have kissed his Son; (*g*) "that decree unrighteous decrees, to turn aside the needy from judgment, and to take away the right from the poor, that widows may be their prey, and that they may rob the fatherless." (*h*)

XXX. And here is displayed his wonderful goodness, and power, and providence; for sometimes he raises up some of his servants as public avengers, and arms them with his commission to punish unrighteous domination, and to deliver from their distressing calamities a people who have been unjustly oppressed: sometimes he accomplishes this end by the fury of men who meditate and attempt something altogether different. Thus he liberated the people of Israel from the tyranny of Pharaoh by Moses; from the oppression of Chusan by Othniel; and from other yokes by other kings and judges. Thus he subdued the pride of Tyre by the Egyptians; the insolence of the Egyptians by the Assyrians; the haughtiness of the Assyrians by the Chaldeans; the confidence of Babylon by the Medes and Persians, after Cyrus had subjugated the Medes. The ingratitude of the kings of Israel and Judah, and their impious rebellion, notwithstanding his numerous favours, he repressed and punished, sometimes by the Assyrians, sometimes by the Babylonians. These were all the executioners of his vengeance, but not all in the same manner. The former, when they were called forth to the performance of such acts by a legitimate commission from God, in taking arms against kings, were not chargeable with the least violation of that majesty with which kings are invested by the ordination of God; but, being armed with authority from Heaven, they punished an inferior power by a su-

(*f*) Psalm lxxxii. 1. (*g*) Psalm ii. 10—12. (*h*) Isaiah x. 1, 2.

perior one, as it is lawful for kings to punish their inferior officers. The latter, though they were guided by the hand of God in such directions as he pleased, and performed his work without being conscious of it, nevertheless contemplated in their hearts nothing but evil.

XXXI. But whatever opinion be formed of the acts of men, yet the Lord equally executed his work by them, when he broke the sanguinary sceptres of insolent kings, and overturned tyrannical governments. Let princes hear and fear. But, in the mean while, it behoves us to use the greatest caution, that we do not despise or violate that authority of magistrates, which is entitled to the greatest veneration, which God has established by the most solemn commands, even though it reside in those who are most unworthy of it, and who, as far as in them lies, pollute it by their iniquity. For though the correction of tyrannical domination is the vengeance of God, we are not, therefore, to conclude that it is committed to us, who have received no other command than to obey and suffer. This observation I always apply to private persons. For if there be, in the present day, any magistrates appointed for the protection of the people and the moderation of the power of kings, such as were, in ancient times, the Ephori, who were a check upon the kings among the Lacedæmonians, or the popular tribunes upon the consuls among the Romans, or the Demarchi upon the senate among the Athenians; or with power such as perhaps is now possessed by the three estates in every kingdom when they are assembled; I am so far from prohibiting them, in the discharge of their duty, to oppose the violence or cruelty of kings, that I affirm, that if they connive at kings in their oppression of their people, such forbearance involves the most nefarious perfidy, because they fraudulently betray the liberty of the people, of which they know that they have been appointed protectors by the ordination of God.

XXXII. But in the obedience which we have shown to be due to the authority of governors, it is always necessary to make one exception, and that is entitled to our first attention,—that it do not seduce us from obedience to him, to whose will the desires of all kings ought to be subject, to whose decrees all their commands ought to yield, to whose majesty all their sceptres ought to submit. And, indeed, how preposterous it would be for us, with a view to satisfy men, to incur the displeasure of him on whose account we yield obedience to men! The Lord, therefore, is the King of kings; who, when he has opened his sacred mouth, is to be heard alone, above all, for all, and before all; in the next place, we are subject to those men who preside over us; but no otherwise than in him. If they command any thing against him, it ought not to have the least attention; nor, in this case, ought we to pay any regard to all that dignity attached to magistrates; to which no injury is done when it is subjected to the unrivalled and supreme power of God. On this principle Daniel denied that he had committed any crime against the king in disobeying his impious decree; (*i*) because the king had exceeded the limits of his office, and had not only done an injury to men, but, by raising his arm against God, had degraded his own authority. On the other hand, the Israelites are condemned for having been too submissive to the impious edict of their king. For when Jeroboam had made his golden calves, in compliance with his will, they deserted the temple of God and revolted to new superstitions. Their posterity conformed to the decrees of their idolatrous kings with the same facility. The prophet severely condemns them for having "willingly walked after the commandment:" (*k*) so far is any praise from being due to the pretext of humility, with which courtly flatterers excuse themselves and deceive the unwary, when they deny that it is lawful for them to refuse compliance with any command of their kings; as if God had resigned his right to mortal men when he made them rulers of mankind; or as if earthly power were diminished by being subordinated to its author, before whom even the principalities of heaven tremble with awe. I know what great and present danger awaits this constancy, for kings cannot bear to be disregarded without the greatest indignation; and "the wrath of a king," says Solomon, "is as messengers of death." (*l*) But since this edict has been proclaimed by that celestial herald, Peter, "We ought to obey God rather than men," (*m*)—let us console ourselves with this thought, that we truly perform the obedience which God requires of us, when we suffer any thing rather

(*i*) Dan. vi. 22.
(*k*) Hos. v. 11.
(*l*) Prov. xvi. 14.
(*m*) Acts v. 29.

than deviate from piety. And that our hearts may not fail us, Paul stimulates us with another consideration—that Christ has redeemed us at the immense price which our redemption cost him, that we may not be submissive to the corrupt desires of men, much less be slaves to their impiety. (*n*)

(*n*) 1 Cor. vii. 23.

END OF THE INSTITUTES

INDEX

OF THE

PRINCIPAL MATTERS

The first number indicates the Book; the second, the Chapter

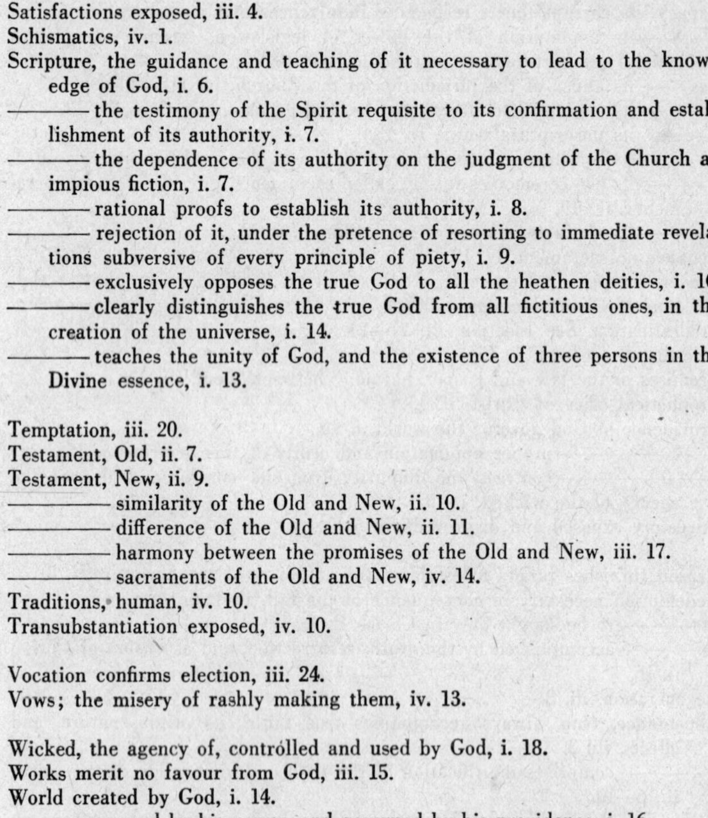

The quotations from different Authors, chiefly the fathers, which occur in this work are not in general referred to in the margin; such references having been considered of no use, except to persons who will probably be furnished with the original, in which they are all inserted.

THE END